ALSO BY JAMES F. SIMON

*Lincoln and Chief Justice Taney: Slavery, Secession,
and the President's War Powers*

*What Kind of Nation: Thomas Jefferson, John Marshall,
and the Epic Struggle to Create a United States*

*The Center Holds: The Power Struggle Inside
the Rehnquist Court*

*The Antagonists: Hugo Black, Felix Frankfurter,
and Civil Liberties in Modern America*

Independent Journey: The Life of William O. Douglas

The Judge

*In His Own Image: The Supreme Court in
Richard Nixon's America*

The President,
the Supreme Court,
and the
Epic Battle over the New Deal

Simon & Schuster ★ New York   London   Toronto   Sydney   New Delhi

FDR *and* Chief Justice Hughes

JAMES F. SIMON

Simon & Schuster
1230 Avenue of the Americas
New York, NY 10020

First Simon & Schuster hardcover edition February 2012

SIMON & SCHUSTER and colophon are registered trademarks of Simon & Schuster, Inc.

For information about special discounts for bulk purchases, please contact Simon & Schuster Special Sales at 1-866-506-1949 or business@simonandschuster.com.

The Simon & Schuster Speakers Bureau can bring authors to your live event. For more information or to book an event contact the Simon & Schuster Speakers Bureau at 1-866-248-3049 or visit our website at www.simonspeakers.com.

Designed by Jill Putorti

Manufactured in the United States of America

10 9 8 7 6 5 4 3 2 1

Library of Congress Cataloging-in-Publication Data

Simon, James F.
   FDR and Chief Justice Hughes : the president, the Supreme Court, and the epic battle over the New Deal / by James F. Simon.
       p.   cm.
   Includes bibliographical references and index.
   1. Roosevelt, Franklin D. (Franklin Delano), 1882–1945—Political and social views.   2. Roosevelt, Franklin D. (Franklin Delano), 1882–1945—Adversaries.   3. Hughes, Charles Evans, 1862–1948.   4. New Deal, 1933–1939.   5. Political questions and judicial power—United States—History—20th century.   6. Executive power—United States—History—20th century.   7. United States. Supreme Court—History—20th century.   8. United States—Politics and government—1933–1945.   I. Title.
   E806.S5527 2012
   973.917092—dc23   2011028825

ISBN 978-1-4165-7328-9
ISBN 978-1-4165-7889-5 (ebook)

To Marcia
and our grandchildren,
Ryan, Justin, Aaron, Audrey,
Lindsay, Natalie, and Ethan

Contents

FDR *and* Chief Justice Hughes

Prologue

On the gray, chilly morning of November 12, 1921, Charles Evans
Hughes, the fifty-nine-year-old U.S. Secretary of State, prepared to address delegates to the first international disarmament
conference in more than a decade. Hughes hoped that the venue for the
Washington Conference, Continental Hall, the quietly dignified building
dedicated to the heroes of the American Revolution, offered more than a
cosmetic contrast to the ornate French Foreign Ministry, the scene of the
Peace Conference held in Paris less than three years earlier. If the disarmament conference proceeded as Hughes planned, discussions would rise
above the stubborn, selfish negotiations of the Paris conference. He also
expected participants to move beyond the grand platitudes of earlier disarmament conferences. Having insisted that the United States host the
conference, he intended to pressure delegates representing the major naval
powers (Great Britain, Japan, and the United States) to produce positive,
tangible results that had eluded the world's best statesmen for two decades.

The distinguished Secretary of State, his full, white beard immacu-
lately groomed, sat in the center seat of a large U-shaped table. He was
flanked, on his right, by the U.S. delegation, which he had handpicked to
project bipartisanship. It included Republican Henry Cabot Lodge, chairman of the Senate's Foreign Relations Committee, and Oscar Underwood,

the Democratic leader of the Senate, as well as Elihu Root, the respected former U.S. senator and Secretary of State. On Hughes's left sat Arthur James Balfour, the chief of the British delegation. Prince Tokugawa, descendant of the first ruling Shogun, represented Japan's royal family, but Admiral Baron Tomosaburo Kato, the shrewd minister of the navy, was his country's chief negotiator. Premier Aristide Briand of France also sat at the table, as did government leaders from Italy, Belgium, the Netherlands, and Portugal.

The delegations were surrounded by three hundred journalists, including the veteran foreign correspondent Henry Nevinson of the *Manchester Guardian*, editors of *The Times* of London and the Shanghai *Shun Pao*, and the midwestern sage William Allen White of the *Emporia* [Kansas] *Gazette*. The author H. G. Wells carried press credentials, as did William Jennings Bryan, the three-time Democratic presidential candidate and former Secretary of State. The gallery was filled with dignitaries: Vice President Calvin Coolidge, Chief Justice William Howard Taft, Associate Justices Louis Brandeis and Oliver Wendell Holmes, Jr., Mrs. Warren G. Harding, the president's wife, and Alice Longworth, Theodore Roosevelt's daughter.

Balfour initiated the formal proceedings by making the motion, unanimously approved by the delegates, that Hughes serve as permanent chairman of the conference. The Secretary of State then rose, briefly acknowledged the applause, and began his speech. He recounted the disappointing history of earlier disarmament conferences, dating back to the 1898 conference convened by Tsar Nicholas II of Russia at The Hague. At the outset, Hughes's manner was stiff and impersonal, reminding reporters who had covered his losing campaign as the Republican Party's presidential candidate in 1916 of his tendency to be thorough and excruciatingly dull.

But when Hughes introduced his disarmament proposal, his voice suddenly rose to a dramatic, commanding pitch. "Competition—in armament—must stop," he said emphatically. Actions, not words, were needed to end the competition, he declared, and promised that the United States would take the lead. On behalf of the U.S. government, he said, he was authorized to scrap all American warships under construction, including six battle cruisers and seven battleships (costing more than $330 million), as well as fifteen existing battleships. The total number of capital ships to be eliminated comprised an aggregate weight of 845,740 tons. No nation had ever made such an offer to reduce its armaments. Hughes paused to let the delegates absorb his stunning statement.

When the excited whispering throughout the conference hall subsided, Hughes turned his attention to the British and Japanese delegations, demanding that their nations make comparable sacrifices. For Great Britain, he said, it meant halting construction on four enormous "Hoods," the Royal Navy's giant new warships, as well as the destruction of nineteen other battleships The British scrap heap, he added, must include HMS *King George V*, the battleship viewed most reverentially by His Majesty's Royal Navy. While Balfour scribbled notes on an envelope, an astonished Lord Beatty, Great Britain's First Sea Lord, hunched forward in his chair and cast a menacing look at the Secretary of State. Hughes had sunk more British warships than "all the admirals of the world had destroyed in a cycle of centuries," the *Guardian*'s Nevinson later wrote.

Hughes manhandled the Japanese fleet with equal fervor. Baron Kato, who had appeared supremely pleased when Hughes devastated the American and British naval arsenals, was chagrined to hear what the Secretary of State had in mind for his navy. Hughes insisted that plans for eight Japanese warships be abandoned, an additional seven battleships and cruisers under construction be scrapped, and that ten older ships be destroyed. The toll included the giant *Mutsu*, the pride of the Japanese Empire.

"With the acceptance of this plan," Hughes concluded, "the burden of meeting the demands of competition in naval armament will be lifted." As a result, "[e]normous sums will be released to aid the progress of civilization."

Hughes's idealism was tempered with a healthy dose of pragmatism. He well knew that his formula to reduce the world's most powerful navies would meet with stiff resistance from Great Britain and Japan. For the next two and half months, Hughes pressured and cajoled his British and Japanese counterparts in public meetings and behind closed doors. He did not win every argument. Japan refused to destroy the *Mutsu*, forcing Hughes to adjust the requirements for the United States and Great Britain to maintain a rough tonnage ratio among the three great powers. In early February 1922, Hughes announced the agreement between the three major naval superpowers to drastically reduce their fleets. The international accord was hailed as an historic achievement, and Hughes emerged as one of the world's leading statesmen.

*   *   *

While Hughes received accolades for his disarmament conference triumph, Franklin D. Roosevelt was being fitted with 14-pound braces that extended from his heels to above his waist. The braces were the latest and harshest acknowledgment that Roosevelt had infantile paralysis and might never walk again. Only a year earlier, Roosevelt seemed destined for high public office, perhaps the presidency. He was a descendant of one of the nation's most illustrious political families. His distant cousin, Theodore Roosevelt, had risen in the Republican Party to become president. Though Franklin's side of the family were Democrats, he had consciously patterned his political career on his cousin. Like Teddy, he had served as Assistant Secretary of the Navy and campaigned as his party's vice-presidential candidate. Though the Democrats' 1920 presidential ticket of Ohio governor James Cox and Roosevelt was trounced in the election, Franklin's political prospects remained bright. There was immediately talk that the handsome, athletic thirty-nine-year-old New Yorker might well head his party's national ticket in 1924 or 1928.

Roosevelt's high ambitions appeared to be irredeemably shattered on August 10, 1921. That was the day he went to bed with severe chills after a vigorous schedule of boating and swimming with his children near the family's summer estate on Campobello, a small island off the coast of Maine. He thought he had a bad cold, a diagnosis mistakenly confirmed by the local family doctor. Two days later, he had lost the ability to move his legs. Dr. Robert Lovett, a faculty member at the Harvard Medical School and the nation's leading expert on infantile paralysis, was summoned to Campobello. After Lovett examined Roosevelt, who was paralyzed from the waist down, he was certain that his patient had contracted poliomyelitis.

In September, Roosevelt was transported to New York by private railroad car. *The New York Times*'s front-page story informed the public, for the first time, that the Democratic Party's rising star had polio and was to be treated at New York's Presbyterian Hospital by Dr. George Draper, Dr. Lovett's protégé. At first, Draper assured reporters that Roosevelt would walk again. But when his patient made no significant progress in the hospital, Draper began to doubt his early prognosis. He worried, moreover, that the extent of Roosevelt's debilitating disease might destroy the patient's psychological health as well as his body.

Only Roosevelt himself possessed absolute confidence that he would fully recover. By October, when he was discharged from the hospital to return to the family's town house on East 65th Street, he could pull himself up by a strap and, with assistance, swing himself into a wheelchair. A trained physiotherapist, Mrs. Kathleen Lake, came to the house three days a week, laid Roosevelt out on a stiff board, and stretched his legs. Franklin demanded that she administer the painful exercises every day. Throughout his ordeal, Roosevelt maintained his usual ebullience, gaily greeting family member and friend alike, often cheering them up.

A raging battle, meanwhile, was being fought in the family town house. Franklin's mother, Sara, had written off any future political career for her son and made plans for him to retire to Hyde Park, where she could lovingly care for him, as she had done for her elderly husband, James, before his death. But the imperious Sara faced a formidable challenge from Franklin's wife, Eleanor, and his wily and indefatigable political adviser, Louis Howe, who had moved into the house to plot Roosevelt's political comeback. They aggressively challenged every subtle maneuver by Sara to bring Franklin permanently home to Hyde Park. Eleanor supervised Franklin's physical recovery, while Howe worked laboriously to preserve Roosevelt's political future, sending out a steady stream of press releases and maintaining close contact with Democratic leaders across the country. Though Roosevelt remained paralyzed from the waist down, Howe continued to believe that he would be elected president of the United States.

Charles Evans Hughes's ascent to the nation's highest judicial office was predictable, if not preordained. No one was better equipped by training and experience to be Chief Justice of the United States. He had been a brilliant lawyer, a fearless investigator of corruption in the utilities and insurance industries, a progressive Republican governor of New York, and a former associate justice of the Supreme Court. In his extraordinary career, he had succeeded in almost every challenge he faced. The one exception: he narrowly lost the presidency to Woodrow Wilson in 1916. After his successful four-year term as Secretary of State, highlighted by the Washington Disarmament Conference, he returned to his lucrative private law practice in New York City and was elected president of the American Bar Association. He also remained active in the Republican Party, campaigning vigorously for Herbert Hoover in 1928 in his successful presidential campaign. After Chief Justice Taft died in the winter of 1930, Hoover nominated Hughes to be the nation's eleventh Chief Justice.

Roosevelt's paralysis discouraged virtually any serious thought of future elective office outside of the family's home on East 65th Street. But by 1924, Roosevelt had mastered the use of his heavy braces and prepared to resume his political career. At the Democratic National Convention in Madison Square Garden, he moved slowly toward to the podium, leaning heavily on the arm of his strapping sixteen-year-old son James. At the podium, Roosevelt, though perspiring profusely from his exertion, beamed at the wildly applauding delegates, and delivered a rousing nominating speech for New York governor Al Smith. In confident, dulcet tones, he praised Smith as the " 'Happy Warrior' on the political battlefield." The delegates erupted in thunderous applause, a stirring tribute to Roosevelt as much as to the man he had nominated. Four years later, Roosevelt was elected governor of New York, and, in 1930, he was reelected by a landslide. Howe's political timetable called for Roosevelt to run for the presidency in 1936, after Hoover had completed what Howe presumed would be his second term. But Hoover's ineffectual response to the Great Depression destroyed his presidency and accelerated Howe's schedule. In November 1932, Roosevelt was elected president, beating Hoover in the electoral college, 472–59.

Shortly before his presidential inauguration on March 4, 1933, Roosevelt wrote a cordial note to Hughes, recalling their long friendship and expressing his admiration and respect for the Chief Justice. He asked if he might break tradition and recite the entire presidential oath. Hughes readily agreed and wrote that he "especially prized the opportunity of being associated with you in our great American enterprise."

In his inaugural address, Roosevelt promised "direct, vigorous action" to lift the nation out of the disastrous economic depression. Immediately upon taking office, he transformed his pledge of "a new deal for the American people" into a fusillade of legislative proposals to the Democratically controlled Congress. Congress responded by passing laws that shut down insolvent banks, regulated stock sales, imposed industrial codes, subsidized farmers, and put more than a quarter million unemployed young men to work in the Civilian Conservation Corps.

In official Washington, only the U.S. Supreme Court appeared immune to FDR's contagious spirit. The Hughes Court was anchored by four ideological conservatives intractably opposed to Roosevelt's New Deal.

The Court's liberal wing was led by Justice Louis Brandeis, supported by Associate Justices Benjamin Cardozo and Harlan Fiske Stone.

Chief Justice Hughes and his fellow Hoover appointee, Associate Justice Owen Roberts, held the balance of judicial power throughout the critical constitutional battles over New Deal legislation. By force of his commanding intellect and exemplary public service, Hughes was expected to lead the Court. But in which direction? He sometimes appeared to split the difference between the two warring factions, writing eloquent majority opinions protecting civil liberties but frequently joining the Court's conservatives in striking down New Deal statutes.

Roosevelt publicly derided the Court's anti–New Deal decisions as relics of a bygone "horse-and-buggy" era. His criticism did nothing to deter a Court majority that continued to declare one New Deal statute after another unconstitutional. Not even his triumphant landslide re-election appeared to influence the justices. Finally, in frustration and anger in early 1937, the president proposed a so-called reform plan that would allow him to appoint one new justice for every sitting justice seventy years of age or older. Because six justices were over seventy, including Hughes, the plan would have permitted FDR to stack the Court with new appointees favorable to the New Deal. His radical proposal raised two unsettling constitutional questions: Should a president be able to mold a Court to meet his political goals? And should ideologically driven justices be allowed to frustrate the public will? Both questions are as relevant in the twenty-first century as they were during the Great Depression.

Roosevelt's Court-packing plan created a dramatic confrontation between the President and Chief Justice. Roosevelt promoted his plan as an effort to bring new energy to an overworked and aging Court. But he did a poor job in disguising his true purpose: to undermine the power of life-tenured justices to thwart his popular mandate. Hughes proved more than a match for Roosevelt in defending the Court. He deftly rebutted the president's claim that the justices were incapable of keeping abreast of the Court calendar, and the proposal was resoundingly defeated. In grudging admiration of Hughes, Roosevelt later said that the Chief Justice was the best politician in the country. That was hardly the way Hughes would have chosen to be remembered, though there was much truth in the president's remark.

Shortly after the defeat of his Court-packing plan, Roosevelt made the first of five appointments to the Court in less than three years. All of the new justices, from former Senator Hugo Black to Roosevelt's Attorney General, Frank Murphy, were Democrats and loyal New Dealers. But with each new Roosevelt appointee, Chief Justice Hughes seemed more assured in leading the Court. Administration insiders expected the president's third appointee, Harvard Law professor Felix Frankfurter, a Roosevelt confidant and scathing critic of the Court's anti–New Deal decisions, to challenge Hughes for the Court's intellectual leadership. But Frankfurter quickly deferred to Hughes and became one of his most avid admirers, ranking him as one of the nation's great chief justices.

Roosevelt was slow to recover from the Court-packing debacle. Emboldened conservative Democrats and Republicans blocked the liberal president's legislative agenda. Midway through his second term, Roosevelt appeared to be a weak, lame-duck president. But he never lost his confidence and, like Hughes, never ceded leadership. He outmaneuvered isolationists senators, many of whom had opposed his Court-packing plan, to expedite essential aid to Great Britain as the Allies hovered on the brink of defeat at the start of the Second World War.

When Hughes announced his retirement from the Court in June 1941, Roosevelt issued a heartfelt letter of regret and invited the Chief Justice to lunch at the White House. They talked alone, sharing for the last time their common bond of national leadership at a critical point in American history.

"An Honest, Fearless, Square Man"

After reading Benjamin Franklin's *Autobiography*, David Charles Hughes, an impulsive and passionate young Welshman, decided that he must immigrate to America. He promptly settled his affairs in Wales, where he worked as a printer and licensed Wesleyan preacher, and bought a steamship ticket for New York. When he arrived in 1855 at the age of twenty-three, he had no friends or acquaintances and no job prospects. He was confident in his decision, nonetheless, because he had received a "providential call" to preach in the United States. He would become the father of the future Chief Justice of the United States, Charles Evans Hughes.

Armed only with a few letters of recommendation from his fellow Methodists in England and Wales, the Reverend Hughes was interviewed by the Presiding Elder of the New York Conference.

"I see you are from Hingland," the Elder said.

"No sir," replied Hughes, who took pride in speaking English without a trace of a Welsh accent. "I am from England."*

"You'll do," the Elder said.

Hughes was sent to a little parish at Vail's Gate, located on a slope

---

* Hughes was born in Tredegar, England, near the Welsh border, but grew up in Wales.

overlooking the Hudson River north of New York City. The Elder was so impressed with Hughes's work there that he approved the young minister's request a year later to be transferred to a private school in Maryland where he could study and teach. In 1858, Hughes was again assigned to a pulpit, this time in a Methodist church at Eddyville, New York, on Rondout Creek in the Lower Hudson Valley. After only a year at Eddyville he took a second leave of absence. With savings from his clerical income, supplemented by private tutoring, he enrolled at Wesleyan University in Middletown, Connecticut. In his year at Wesleyan, he studied mathematics (trigonometry, analytical geometry, and calculus), English literature and logic, the Greek tragedies, Plato's *Gorgias* and Homer's *Iliad*. His intense dedication to learning, both religious and secular, would continue throughout his life.

Before leaving Eddyville for Wesleyan, Hughes was introduced to his future wife, Mary Catherine Connelly, whose parents lived on the opposite side of Rondout Creek in New Salem. Compared to Hughes, who was the first in his family to live in the United States, Mary Catherine's American roots were buried deep. Her maternal ancestor, Jacob Burhans, immigrated to the United States from the Netherlands about 1660 and settled at Wiltwyck, near Kingston, New York. The Connellys, Mary Catherine's paternal ancestors, came to America from England and Northern Ireland. The family took particular pride in the military service of Michael Connelly, Mary Catherine's great-grandfather, who was an officer in the Revolutionary War serving as an aide to General George Clinton.

Both in temperament and physical appearance, the reserved, fair-haired Mary Catherine seemed ill-suited for David Charles Hughes, the emotional, swarthy Welsh minister. Certainly that was the strong opinion of her mother, Margaret Ann Connelly. "Who was this upstart, this dark-hued Welshman?" she asked indignantly. "Who knew but that he had left a wife in Wales?"

Undeterred, Mary Catherine, a young woman of gentle demeanor but strong will, was convinced that she had found her soul mate in the Reverend Hughes. She too loved to learn, and to teach. For a woman of her time, she possessed an unusually impressive academic résumé. She had studied American history, Cicero, and languages (French and German) at Fort Edward Institute, and later enrolled at the Hudson River Institute at Claverack, where she concentrated on the study of French. After completing her studies, she opened her own school for girls in Kingston.

Even more important than their shared intellectual ambitions, Mary Catherine and David were devotees of evangelical Christianity. In her religious fervor, she proved more zealous than her future husband. She had been brought up in the Baptist faith, and those who knew her were convinced that "she would have gone to the stake rather than be untrue to her religious convictions." During their courtship, she persuaded David to become a Baptist. They were married in Kingston in November 1860, only a few days before he was ordained and appointed pastor of the First Baptist Church in Glens Falls, New York, a village at the southeast corner of the Adirondack foothills.

Charles Evans Hughes, the only child of the Reverend and Mrs. Hughes, was born on April 11, 1862, in the couple's modest, one-story frame house on Maple Street in Glens Falls, a block away from David's church. From infancy, little Charlie, as he was called, was the focus of his parents' exuberant spiritual and intellectual energies. Mary Catherine taught her son to read at the age of three and a half. After she discovered that his eyes were weak, she gave him a large-type edition of the *New Testament and Psalms*. She also grilled him in "mental arithmetic," making Charlie toe a line marked on the floor while he computed sums without aid of pencil and paper. She soon introduced him to French, starting with Fasquelle's *Leçous*, and German, assisted by a German-language primer.

The Reverend Hughes was too busy delivering sermons on the word of God, as well as the justness of the Union cause,* to participate in his wife's daily intensive tutorials with their son. He nonetheless guided his son's early reading habits. When Charlie was five, his father gave him a copy of Miss Corner's *England and Wales*. On his sixth birthday, he received *Wonders of Science*, followed by Chambers's *Miscellany*, a compendium of information and selected literature. Proficient in Latin and Greek, David instructed his son in Greek, aided by a copy of the *Greek New Testament with Lexicon*. In his spare time, Charlie browsed through his father's large library and seized anything that looked interesting. He read *Pilgrim's Progress* several times as well as Bunyan's *Holy War*. He also discovered Byron

---

* One of Charlie's earliest memories was the day that his father came home with the tragic news that Lincoln had been assassinated. "Mary," cried the distraught pastor, "I could not feel worse if you had been killed."

and Shakespeare (his early favorites: *The Tempest, Twelfth Night,* and *The Merry Wives of Windsor*).

For the first six years of his life, Charlie received instruction exclusively from his parents. After the Hughes family moved in 1866 to Oswego, New York, on Lake Ontario, where the Reverend Hughes had been invited to lead a larger Baptist congregation, Charlie was sent to a school as an experiment in formal education. The experiment lasted only four weeks. Charlie reported that he was bored with his teacher's rote instruction. Taking matters into his own hands, he presented his parents with a carefully drafted document, entitled "Charles E. Hughes' Plan of Study." In separate columns he listed each subject he wished to study at home and the hour allotted to the lesson. His plan was accepted. During the severe winters in Oswego, before his parents awoke, Charlie sat next to the great coal-burning stove in their living room and methodically completed his lessons, as scheduled.

As an only child, Charlie was aware that he personified his parents' deepest ambitions. He thrived on their attention and did his part to discourage competition from a sibling. After he overheard his parents discussing the adoption of a child to provide him with a companion, he marched into their room to protest. With their meager financial resources, he argued, it was more important that they furnish him with a first-rate education rather than a brother or sister.

When he was sick—and the delicate Charlie was vulnerable to infection—his mother nursed him back to health, often with homeopathic remedies. Later, his father, concerned about his son's thin, fragile frame, erected a horizontal bar and two flying rings in their backyard to encourage healthy exercise.

Despite the constant attention from his parents, Charlie knew how to create both mental and physical space for himself. After his father accepted a pastorate in Newark, New Jersey, when Charlie was seven, the boy found refuge in his attic playroom. There he climbed on an enormous hobbyhorse given to him by one of his father's parishioners and prepared for fantastic adventures. Using trunk straps as reins and travel books propped up in front of him as inspiration, he traveled around the world. His imagination was often guided by Thomson's *Land and the Book,* which offered vivid descriptions of Palestine, supplemented by the boy's recollections of Bible stories.

Every summer he eagerly anticipated a trip to his Grandfather Connelly's farm on Rondout Creek. He left on the steamer *Mary Powell* from New York Harbor in the afternoon, reaching Rondout in the early evening. With his cousins, he picked apples in the orchard, then rode in his grandfather's horse and buggy to the dock where the fruit was loaded on a steamer destined for New York. For Charlie, nothing compared to the thrill of mounting Billy, the trusted family horse, and galloping along dusty country roads to the crest of a knoll commanding a spectacular view of the Hudson River. He loved to gaze at the broad sweep of the river and looming Catskill Mountains, which seemed to him to be full of mystery and legend. On warm summer days, he recalled, "I would sit and watch the river in a sort of enchantment."

"It was the fondest hope of my parents that I should enter the ministry and I was early 'dedicated,' " Hughes recalled. "Their chief concern was that as soon as possible I should apprehend religious truth as they understood it." Toward that end, his parents worked tirelessly to instill in him a rigorous religious discipline. At the age of two he had begun to attend church regularly, though, as a tot, he was allowed to sit on a little rocking chair that had been brought to the gallery for him while his mother sang in the choir. At home he read the Scriptures and was regularly warned by his mother of the necessity of subduing his evil inclinations. He was not only obliged to listen to his father's sermons but also was taken to hear other preachers, including the spellbinding abolitionists Henry Ward Beecher and Wendell Phillips. At the family table he absorbed the religious and moral teachings of his parents and "sat in silent appreciation of the words of wisdom of the visiting grown-ups, usually preachers." He was admitted at the age of nine to membership in the Baptist Church and soon organized a boys' club for his peers. He also attended his father's classes for Sunday School teachers and prepared references for his syllabi.

Despite his parents' relentless efforts, young Charlie drifted from the path they had chosen for him. Their religious indoctrination was too constant and rigorous, he later admitted—"For in the end, it largely defeated its own purpose by creating in me a distaste for religious formalities." What interested the precocious boy was "the dialectic rather than the premises." Ever the dutiful son, he continued to ask for their spiritual guidance. "I hope that you will pray earnestly for me," he wrote from Grandpa Connelly's farm in June 1875, that "if it be possible, I may regain some of the spiritual power I once possessed and more completely obey the sentiments expressed in Ephesians 6:1, 'Children, obey your parents in the Lord: for this is right.' "

But his spirit, he admitted, "had begun to flutter in its cage." He bristled at required church attendance and questioned his father about the problem of evil. He wanted to know "how what I observed in the ways of nature and of men could be reconciled with the goodness, the omniscience and the omnipotence of the Creator." His sense of despair deepened during the family's dinner-table conversations when he heard about his father's arguments with overbearing church elders and other mundane problems of the pastorate. Even before Charlie reached his teenage years, he had secretly concluded that he would not enter the ministry.

Hughes's rejection of the ministry at an early age demonstrated his independence from the parents he loved so dearly. But in every other way, he was very much his parents' son and the embodiment of their highest hopes. From childhood, they instilled in him an unwavering sense of duty. He must dedicate himself to worthy goals and work indefatigably to achieve those goals—sometimes, as it turned out, to the point of emotional and physical exhaustion.

Except for a few months of study at the Newark High School when he was eleven, Hughes received virtually no formal education until he entered New York City's Public School 35 in September 1874. By this time, the Reverend Hughes had left his Newark pastorate to serve as secretary to the American Bible Union, located on Great Jones Street in Manhattan. Charlie loved his commute by ferry from Brooklyn, where the family resided, to the dock in lower Manhattan, then the walk to his school at 13th Street and Sixth Avenue. Although P.S. 35 was the city's most famous public school for boys, young Hughes was not overawed. "I found that I was going over much that I had already studied," he wrote. Some of the faculty did not meet his high standards, including the French instructor, "whose teaching came to practically nothing," and a lecturer in chemistry "who was almost toothless and not easily understood."

Fortunately, he found an inspiring middle-aged teacher named Gates, "who delighted the class when he put aside his books and spoke of the great world outside and his philosophy of life." The Reverend Hughes nonetheless remained his son's most important male mentor. For an essay assignment, his father suggested that he write on "The Elements of Success." Charlie immediately warmed to the task, writing expansively on Knowledge, Industry, and Determination (he gave Ulysses S. Grant's example to "fight it out on this line if it took all summer"). In an essay on Happiness, he wrote that "an untroubled conscience" was a prerequisite and warned that "[W]henever we turn aside from following Duty's beckoning finger, that moment happiness ceases." His most provocative essay was on the subject of "Light Reading and Its Consequences," in which he condemned popular weeklies that "will not educate our moral sense, but will blind, pervert and weaken it." At the age of thirteen, Charlie graduated from P.S. 35, receiving a silver medal for composition and delivering the salutatory address on the subject of "Self Help."

The boy's compositions suggest that he was unusually serious, if somewhat priggish. But there was also a fun-loving, adventuresome side to his personality. When his family had sailed to Europe in the summer of 1873 (made possible by a loan to the Reverend Hughes from one of his best friends), Charlie devoured the guidebooks and planned many of the sightseeing excursions. One night on the return voyage, the ship experienced engine trouble, providing him with an unscheduled drama. He witnessed a slightly drunk, naked young woman (who had entered the wrong cabin, undressed, and grabbed the beard of the man sleeping in the top berth) running hysterically through the corridors. "I thought we might be going down," he recalled, "and I shall never forget that scene."

At times, he created his own adventures. In the months before he entered P.S. 35, he roamed the streets and explored some of the best, and worst, neighborhoods in New York City, from the Battery at the southern tip of the island to Central Park. "When I was tired of walking," he wrote, "I would jump on the tail-end of an empty truck and ride joyously with dangling legs."

When Charlie graduated from high school in 1875, he was too young to be admitted to college. He was forced to wait a year, then expected to enter New York University. A family acquaintance who was a sophomore at Madison (now Colgate) changed his mind, regaling the boy with delightful stories of college life on the upstate campus. But how was he to convince his parents that faraway Madison in Hamilton, New York, was the best choice? As usual, Charlie did his homework, studying the Madison catalogue for useful arguments to be deployed in the crucial discussion with his parents.

He assured them, at the outset, that he would remain at home for a year to prepare for the college's rigorous entrance exams. As a minister's son, he noted, he would receive a discount on his room and tuition. He also emphasized that Madison was a Baptist institution, with many students studying for the ministry. "Was not Hamilton a safe and wholesome place," he asked, "and did I not need the invigoration of life in the country, among the hills?" If only his parents would grant his wish, he would be so careful, so obedient! Despite such fervent advocacy, his mother remained skeptical. She worried that her frail son would not survive the harsh winters without her constant and tender care. But she was overruled by her husband, who fondly remembered his own stimulating college experience at Wesleyan.

In preparation for Madison's entrance exam, Charlie studied Latin and Greek grammar and prose composition, reading six books of the *Aeneid*, four Orations of Cicero, and three books of the *Anabasis* of Xenophon. Confident in his knowledge of English and math, he spent little time on those subjects. One day in late June 1876, after his father had dropped him off at the college campus, he passed the written exams without difficulty. To his surprise, a professor of Greek took the young man to his library for an oral examination. The professor handed him a copy of the *Anabasis*, pointed to various passages, and told him that he would return for the examination in a few minutes. Charlie passed that unexpected exam, too.

For the first time in his life, he was truly on his own, far away from his parents' domineering supervision—and he savored every moment. Thanks to his superbly honed study habits, Charlie breezed through the required courses. Latin and Greek hardly challenged him, and he was so far ahead in French that he volunteered for extra work. After making a perfect score on a written exam, he was permitted to skip the freshman course in geometry and calculus. As a result of his sterling academic performance, he had much leisure time to indulge his great interest in English literature. On Sundays, after an early dinner at three, Charlie would curl up next to the stove in his room to read Scott, Dickens, or Thackeray into the early morning hours.

Since his courses did not pose much challenge, Charlie chose to fill a considerable amount of his idle time by joining Delta Upsilon, one of two national fraternities on campus. Informing his parents, the young man received a prompt list of objections from his father. Fraternities encourage "party spirit, which leads to envy and jealousy," the Reverence Hughes wrote, and consume time that "ought to be devoted to private meditation or to thorough and systematic reading." Most important, he feared that Delta Upsilon would divert his son from "maintaining a strictly spiritual life."

Charlie gently rejected his father's advice and soon was taking his meals at his fraternity house. In a reassuring letter to his parents, he reported that "there is not even loud laughter but conversation in groups" at the dining table. And they should not worry about his spiritual welfare. "The Lord is abundantly blessing me with tokens of His love and mercy."

Before semester's end, Charlie was playing cards (usually whist) and smoking, both forbidden in the Hughes household. He also joined friends who drove to nearby Morrisville to march in a torchlight parade in support of the Republican presidential candidates, including the eventual winner, Rutherford B. Hayes. "Returning to Hamilton in the early morning hours," he recalled, "we rang the chapel bell and I felt that I was duly initiated into politics."

Meanwhile, his mother was writing her "darling boy" to express her myriad concerns. "Charlie, I fear you don't sleep enough," she wrote early in the semester. "You will never amount to anything in the world of letters, etc. if you overwork now." Three weeks later, she warned that unless he hung his wet clothes around the stove after washing, "the result might be rheumatism, or consumption, if not death in a short time." And later: "I am so apprehensive that you may be turned from the path of rectitude, by the indulgences of your worldly associates, that I feel that I was under the shadow of great sorrow. . . . In respect to song, treasure up hymns of praise to God, instead of foolish pointless college songs—worse than nothing, for it is like feeding on husks, causing one to be full of emptiness."

From his father, Charlie received advice on a wide range of topics, always tinged with a moral lesson. On debating: "NEVER for the sake of argument, take a wrong side." On living with a roommate: "Freedom to throw yourself on your knees frequently and whenever you were inclined to do so, would be out of the question." On character: "And pray tell me, my dear Charlie, what is the very essence, spirit, vital breath of character, if it be not *true piety?*" Never far from the Reverence Hughes's mind, and his wife's, was the question: Was Charlie being a good Christian?

"In regard to my inner life," he responded, "the Lord is caring for me and watching over me. I am weak & helpless but with his strength may overcome. Pray for me." His chief interests at Madison, however, were decidedly secular. He knew that his parents expected him to excel academically, and he did not disappoint them. "Studies are going swimmingly," he wrote them. At the commencement ceremonies of his freshman year, he was one of only four members of his class chosen to speak in an elocution contest. At the climax of his address, he gave a rousing Civil War cavalry charge, shouting: "Come on, old Kentucky, I am with you!" The judges were sufficiently stirred to award him second prize.

By the end of his sophomore year, Hughes had posted superb grades (5 was a perfect score): 4.97 in analytical geometry, 4.91 in rhetoric, 4.90 in calculus, 4.84 in French, 4.71 in Greek, and 3.92 in Latin. By then, he was sixteen years old and growing fast. He continued to enjoy life at Madison, but had become restless, hungry for greater opportunities at a larger college in an urban environment. He applied to Brown, also a Baptist institution, in Providence, Rhode Island. The university admitted Hughes into the sophomore class without examination, and awarded him a scholarship of $60 a year.

The curriculum at Brown was not significantly more challenging than Madison's had been. With the exception of an outstanding Latin teacher, he did not find the faculty especially stimulating. His academic performance nonetheless was stellar; he received fourteen excellent sets of marks in fifteen courses. After his junior year he was one of five members of his class elected to Phi Beta Kappa.

Although Hughes had received a scholarship and, as a minister's son, did not have to pay room rent, his financial resources were meager. To help pay for a pair of ice skates, he earned two dollars by writing an essay for a fellow student. He proudly informed his parents of the enterprise, noting that he had successfully emulated the other student's style and that the task had only taken ten hours to complete. When his parents objected, Charlie vigorously defended himself. He noted that skating was very healthy exercise and that "earning money is also a fine thing for the young." Writing the essay, he contended, was no different from helping a fellow student with a lesson. "Hack writing, or writing for money is a perfectly legitimate business," he concluded. His spirited advocacy did not convince his parents, and he conceded defeat. "Well, I might as well say out & out that I will pull in my horns," he wrote, "& you stand victor in the arena."

As he had anticipated, Brown and surrounding Providence offered more interesting diversions than had been available at Madison. For the first time, he attended the theater, relishing a performance of *Hamlet* with Edwin Booth in the title role. A committed young Republican, he helped organize a Garfield battalion on campus in support of the 1880 Republican presidential nominee, James Garfield. He and his colleagues marched for Garfield in Providence and Bristol, Rhode Island, and in Boston, wearing caps and capes, and holding banners and torches. They returned late at night after "a heavy dose of campaign oratory." Hughes also served as editor of the college newspaper, the *Brunonian*, generally confining his editorial opinions to campus issues. He ridiculed the school's prohibitions against playing cards, using profane language, going to the theater, and entering a tavern where liquor was served.

Hughes did not abandon formal religion, though he now charted his own course, not the one chosen by his parents. He quickly tired of the sermons at the First Baptist Meeting-House, but attended services at two other Providence churches where he found the preachers more stimulating. Occasionally, at his father's request, he prepared a synopsis for the Reverend Hughes's expository articles published in the *Homiletic Review*. "Despite my new experiences, my increasing liberality of thought, and my love of a good time," Hughes wrote, "I had by no means lost my religious feeling or my interest in religious subjects."

During his years at Brown, Hughes's letters home contained fewer references to religion and prayer than in previous years. Still, he acknowledged a profound and lasting debt to his parents for their moral guidance. "Whatever I do, wherever I go, when the question of right or wrong comes up, it is decided by what Pa or Ma will say if I did it," he wrote. At Brown, however, he expressed increasing confidence in his own opinions. In his senior year he informed his mother that he would not fulfill her dream of entering the priesthood. "I want to do just that which will enable me to do most for the world around me according to the divine will," he told her. "As yet, I feel no call to the ministry, & I know that such a sphere of life is not exactly suitable to my abilities."

In 1881, Hughes graduated third in his class and delivered the "classical oration" (on Sophocles) at commencement. He was also chosen to be the class prophet. A fellow student wanted to know Hughes's prophecy for himself. He would become a teacher, Hughes responded. "Of course, you'll be a lawyer," his friend insisted. "I've picked out law for myself, and if you are not a lawyer too, I'm no prophet." In fact, Hughes had already begun to give serious thought to a legal career. "The more I think of the future," he wrote, "the more I incline toward the legal profession, as the one for which I am most fitted & the one most favorable to a high ambition."

To earn money for law school tuition, Hughes applied for a teaching job at Delaware Academy in Delhi, New York. In an interview at the academy, the principal, James Griffin, duly acknowledged the recent Brown graduate's impressive academic credentials. But he feared that the callow nineteen-year-old would not be able to control a class of rambunctious teenage boys. Hughes was nearly six feet tall, but weighed less than 125 pounds and had not begun to shave. In an early example of his prowess as an advocate, Hughes convinced the principal that he could impose discipline in the classroom. He was hired at an annual salary of $200 to teach Latin, Greek, and mathematics (algebra and plane geometry).

Hughes taught his classes at Delaware Academy in the morning and worked in the afternoons at the law office of William Gleason, a former county judge and prominent lawyer in upstate New York. After a year of teaching, Hughes moved to New York City with the intention of enrolling in Columbia Law School's two-year program. In the summer of 1882, he was hired at the generous salary of $200 a month by the Gill Rapid Transit Company, which had been formed to provide cheap cab service in the city. The smooth-talking secretary of the company, one Edgar Gray, requested that he buy a small amount of stock in the company so that he might better identify with the enterprise. Hughes reluctantly asked his father to buy the stock. At the same time, he began an investigation of the company and the man who had hired him. Examining the books, he discovered that Gray was a swindler who signed various names to company letters, including that of Hughes himself. He also checked out Gray's prior history in newspaper clippings and found that he had been involved in a series of shady deals. Gray had absconded with $300,000 from a Wall Street banking firm and had been arrested in London and again in Paris. He was extradited to New York and subsequently convicted of embezzlement.

Before confronting Gray, Hughes contacted the founder of the transit company and informed him of his findings. Accompanied by the company's founder and his own father, Hughes met with Gray and demanded that he return his father's money. He was successful, but the sobering experience gave him "a new insight into the ways of men." It also provided a preview of Hughes's professional approach to investigating wrongdoing, replicated more than a decade later in a large, public forum. When Hughes was asked by New York's governor in 1905 to investigate mismanagement and corruption in the state utilities industry, he would demonstrate the same penchant for meticulous preparation and determination to wring the truth from his witnesses.

In the fall of 1882, Hughes entered Columbia Law School and eagerly absorbed the lessons of every law school class, particularly the brilliant lectures and legal commentaries of Professor Theodore Dwight. He joined several study groups, and to make his note-taking more thorough, took a shorthand course in the summer after his first year. That summer he also worked without pay at the prominent New York City law firm of Chamberlain, Carter & Hornblower.

Predictably, his hard work paid off. He graduated at the top of his class and was awarded the prize fellowship for the law school's outstanding graduate, which provided an annual stipend of $500 for three years to tutor Columbia law students. He also accepted a clerkship with the Chamberlain law firm. After graduation, Hughes scored the highest grade ever recorded on the state bar exam (99½).

Hughes's relentless work ethic produced superior grades but eroded his physical health. By the end of law school, he realized that his long nights of study had depleted his energy. He still weighed less than 125 pounds and, after he caught cold, a persistent cough developed. Hughes decided that he ought to postpone his clerkship. Fortunately, a wealthy classmate offered him an attractive alternative to immersing himself immediately in the rigors of law practice. Hughes was hired to prepare his classmate's brother-in-law at the family home on the Jersey shore for the bar exam. The tutoring only required two hours a day, so Hughes could spend the remainder of his time resting and enjoying a leisurely summer vacation. When Walter Carter, one of the partners in the Chamberlain law firm, sent Hughes a note gently nudging him to join them in early September, he was ready, his health fully restored.

On September 1, 1884, Hughes began the practice of law at Chamberlain, Carter & Hornblower, drawing a salary of $30 a month with increases of $5 every two months. In one of his first cases he successfully represented a man named Wellenkamp, who had sustained severe injuries while saving his two young children from a fire in the family home. While he was recuperating in the hospital, his wife had left him and refused to allow him to see their children. At trial, Hughes displayed devastating skills at cross-examination, puncturing the fabrications of Wellenkamp's wife and her brother who represented her. His client was awarded custody of the children.

Hughes's courtroom resolve was severely tested later when he represented the petitioner in a bankruptcy proceeding before a judge named Van Brunt, known as "Sitting Bull." The judge's intimidating manner was only part of the problem. Van Brunt, who was also a family friend of the lawyer representing the bankrupt defendant, tried to bully Hughes into abandoning several affidavits in support of his argument. "Who appears on the other side?" the judge yelled in Hughes's direction. "It's an imposition on the court to present such papers," he declared.

Hughes knew that if he caved in under the judge's pressure, his case was lost. Though he later admitted that he "suffered keenly" from the judge's attack, he nonetheless held his ground. He insisted on being heard and, between interruptions by the judge, cited affidavits in the record that undermined the defendant's claims. Hughes also made it clear to Van Brunt that if he ruled for the defendant, he would appeal. The judge did not act upon his threat and Hughes was eventually victorious.

Hughes's law practice increased in difficulty and responsibility as he gained courtroom experience, prepared complex pleadings, wrote briefs, drafted contracts, and held interviews with clients. In addition to working long hours at the law firm, Hughes tutored Columbia students under the terms of his fellowship and gave them quizzes four nights a week. To relieve the burdens of his professional life, he scheduled trips abroad during the summers, first to Scotland and Wales, and later to London, Paris, and Amsterdam.

In 1885, Hughes met the woman who would become the love of his life, Antoinette Carter, the youngest daughter of Walter Carter, the senior partner in his law firm. They had first exchanged knowing glances at a joke that no one else caught at a dinner at Delmonico's for one of Hughes's departing colleagues. Sensitive to the proprieties, Hughes did not want to rush into courtship of the boss's daughter. He waited more than two years, after he had become a partner in the firm, to seriously pursue the tall, demure, Wellesley-educated Antoinette. She was poised and sweet-tempered, athletic and intellectual, with refined tastes in literature, music, and art. In his opinion, he had found the perfect mate.

They were married in a simple ceremony at the Carter home in Brooklyn in December 1888. Eleven months later, the couple's first child, Charles Evans Hughes, Jr., was born. Hughes's joy in his family knew no bounds. With his partner's salary and savings, he purchased a four-story redbrick house for his family on the Upper West Side of Manhattan, near Riverside Drive. By this time, Hughes had grown a full beard and was the very picture of familial bliss and professional success.

Beneath the surface, however, all was not well. His health deteriorated as his accomplishments mounted. "I inherited a continuing ambition to excel in good work and to do my job as well as it could be done," he recalled. That meant that he left no task undone, exhausting himself in the pursuit of perfection. "In truth, despite a gratifying degree of professional success and an excellent outlook, I was nervously depressed." At the age of twenty-nine, Hughes's health was so precarious that he could not qualify for life insurance. Shortly after the family had moved into their new town house, Hughes received an offer to teach at Cornell Law School in Ithaca, New York. "Now I was tired, and the offer of an academic retreat, affording what I thought would be abundant time for study and reading, was so attractive," he wrote, "that I could not refuse it."

At Cornell, Hughes felt emancipated. He exulted in the fresh country air as he walked briskly up the hill overlooking the Cayuga River to his daily classes on campus. Within months, Hughes had begun to regain his physical vigor. Meanwhile, Antoinette gave loving attention to every detail of their domestic life, caring for Charlie Junior and their second child, Helen, who was born in Ithaca. In his second year at the university, Hughes purchased a house on campus with a fine library. "What a happy home ours is!" he wrote his parents. "And it is not rarely that I think of my great debt to you, for the quiet, wholesome training in childhood—the learning to live contentedly without luxury or extravagance—the fondness for books—for the really good things of life—above all for the constant incitements to probity and integrity, which your examples will ever furnish."

Though his spirits soared, Hughes's life at Cornell did not provide relief from the professional pressures that had plagued him in his law practice.

This was due, in part, to his heavy teaching schedule. But more important, he could not restrain his ambition to excel at every task. He taught fifteen hours of classes a week, with subjects ranging from elementary law and contracts to partnership, sales, and evidence. In preparation for his classes, he pored over legal textbooks and hundreds of cases, as well as casebooks written by experts in the fields that he had been assigned to teach. When he entered the classroom, he had mastered his subject, much as he did in the cases he had argued in Manhattan courtrooms. His photographic memory allowed him to lecture for three hours without a note, citing dozens of cases and quoting judicial decisions verbatim. In addition to teaching his classes, Hughes held moot courts and counseled graduate students. "Far from being an academic retreat," he admitted, "I found Cornell to be a hive of industry, and aside from the occasional and enjoyable evening I spent with my colleagues, my life was one of constant toil; in truth, I was about as busy with my courses as I had been with my practice in New York."

And he carried a financial burden in Ithaca that had been absent in Manhattan. He had left New York City without being able to sell the family's home there. After he bought the house in Ithaca, Hughes was paying off two mortgages on his annual academic income of $3,000—compared to the $13,500 he had earned in his last year in practice. Aware of the plight of their popular young law professor, Cornell's trustees voted to increase Hughes's salary to $4,000 a year. At the same time, Hughes's father-in-law pleaded with him to return to his prosperous law practice for the sake of his family.

Hughes learned of the trustees' action to increase his salary and was leaning toward a decision to remain at Cornell. But in his meeting with Dr. Jacob Schurman, the university's president, Schurman made the mistake of offering to renew Hughes's contract at his old $3,000 annual salary. Hughes was incensed by the president's failure to disclose the trustees' action, and decided to return to law practice in New York City.

For the next twelve years, Hughes practiced law with characteristic intensity, representing a wide range of corporate clients, from bondholders of a bankrupt Oregon railroad company to a New York manufacturer negotiating a contract with a Belgian chemical firm. One of his clients was the owner of a yacht that had been stranded in Cuban waters during the Spanish-American War. In that case, Hughes was successful in recovering damages from the *New York Sun*, which had leased the yacht for its reporters to cover the conflict. He also advised Joseph Pulitzer, the owner of the *New York World*, on contractual matters. Pulitzer was so impressed with Hughes's work that he made him a trustee of the parent company that owned the *World*.

Although he was an enormously successful lawyer, the practice did not give Hughes the professional enjoyment he had experienced in the classroom at Cornell. The financial problems imposed by his modest law professor's salary had evaporated, to be sure, though Hughes never collected the large legal fees that he could have commanded, nor did he and his family live lavishly. The anxiety that had afflicted Hughes as a young lawyer returned. He attempted to maintain his health by vigorous exercise, including hiking, biking, and golf. "But I needed more than exercise to overcome the fits of depression which often followed exertions in difficult cases," he admitted later. "A good deal of my professional work seemed to be unrequited drudgery."

Hughes escaped the drudgery of his practice by participating in a variety of civic activities. He served on a special committee of the state bar that recommended the revision of the Code of Civil Procedure, and joined the board of his alma mater, Brown University. He was also elected a trustee of the Fifth Avenue Baptist Church, joining John D. Rockefeller, who was president of the board.

In addition to his board business at the Fifth Avenue Baptist Church, Hughes taught a class on the Old Testament prophets. He had retained his early interest in the study of the Bible, but "that interest now lay more in the critical and literary study rather than in the rather narrow routine of the Sunday School." He created a minor furor at the church when he invited the African-American leader Booker T. Washington to speak. By this time, he had rejected the traditional orthodoxies of the church. "While I maintained my Baptist connection, I had long since ceased to attach importance to what many regard as the distinctive tenets of the denomination," he wrote. "Rather, I cherished the noble tradition of the Baptists as protagonist in the struggle for religious liberty."

When his mother scolded him for abandoning church dogma and ritual, particularly collective prayer, Hughes responded with a mixture of sadness and defiance: "I hold what religious convictions I have, as sacredly as you do yours. I am perplexed by many questions, but I believe my heart is open to the truth. I want to be honest with myself. I do not want to use the form of prayer when I am not praying. . . . When I really want to *pray* I want to be *alone*—and it is at those times when the reality of the unseen comes upon one irresistibly and the sense of one's own littleness and helplessness draws one, half-doubtfully—half-trustfully but altogether reverently to the Father of all."

Hughes's family continued to provide emotional ballast to his life. Antoinette was his "dear wife," who performed her maternal tasks flawlessly, it seemed, and served as her husband's loving mate and trusted confidante. She understood the high-strung Charles's need for periods of complete freedom, cheerfully encouraging him to take summer vacations abroad, often alone, to rejuvenate his spirits in Paris and Germany and on trails in the Swiss Alps. The couple frequently rode their bicycles as far as Long Island on weekends and regularly attended the theater. Hughes reserved Sunday afternoons for his children, taking them rowing on Central Park lake in warm weather and sledding in the winter. They visited the Museum of Natural History, the Zoo, and the Metropolitan Museum of Art. At home, Hughes delighted in reading to them aloud, often the humorist Finley Peter Dunne's "Mr. Dooley" stories in the narrator's Irish brogue. On their birthdays, he composed whimsical rhymes of congratulations.*

When Hughes reached early middle age shortly after the turn of the century, he was a respected corporate attorney, active private citizen, and devoted family man. But rarely did his name appear in the city's newspapers. That quiet state of affairs changed suddenly in 1905 after Hughes was appointed counsel to special state legislative committees investigating the utilities and life insurance industries.

In December 1904, the *New York World*'s headlines blared that New York City was paying exorbitant rates for lighting its streets. Civic and merchants' organizations demanded an investigation of the charges of rate-gouging by the city's gas and electric companies. The Board of Aldermen promised action, but Tammany Hall's boss, Charles Murphy, was not interested, and so advised Tammany's aldermen. Attention focused on the state legislature, but rumors swirled in Albany that the powerful utilities lobby was offering big money to legislators to vote no to an investigation.

---

* The Hughes's third child, Catherine, was born in 1898, joining Charles Junior, nine years old, and Helen, seven.

In the spring of 1905, however, Governor Francis Higgins bowed to public pressure and appointed a legislative committee to investigate the utilities industry, headed by Senator Frederick Stevens.

The legislative committee at first looked for an attorney to lead the investigation who was well known to the public and would give the investigation immediate credibility. The job was offered to several high-profile New York lawyers, including Henry Taft, brother of the Secretary of War, William Howard Taft. All turned down the committee. Hughes was then recommended by a former state judge, William Cohen, who as an attorney years earlier had opposed Hughes in several complicated creditors' lawsuits. Cohen's recommendation was seconded by Henry Taft, who, like the former judge, had faced Hughes in court and been impressed with his tenacity and command of complex corporate issues. "Take Hughes," advised Taft. "If any one can take you through the maze of technical testimony about the practical business as well as the stock manipulations, it is Hughes."

Hughes did not want the job. He had no confidence in the integrity of legislative investigations in general, and in this investigation in particular, since he feared that the influential utilities industry would in some way undermine the committee's work. Under those circumstances, Hughes thought the work of committee counsel was doomed to failure and would be subject to widespread public criticism. When he met with the committee chairman, Senator Stevens, Hughes raised his objections to accepting the appointment. But the more Hughes objected, the more Stevens became convinced that he was precisely the attorney the committee needed.

"Mr. Stevens, I belong to the same church as Mr. Rockefeller," Hughes said, confident that this choice piece of information would discourage his appointment to investigate an industry controlled by plutocrats. Stevens brushed aside that information and assured Hughes that he would have complete freedom to take the investigation wherever it might lead. Finally, Hughes accepted.

When Hughes met with reporters after Stevens had announced his appointment, the new committee counsel made sure that Stevens would not renege on his pledge of independence. "I told Senator Stevens that I would not become counsel to the committee unless I could be absolutely free from political dictation of any and every sort," he said. "When we get this investigation started we will follow the trail that leads us to the information we desire, no matter where that trail leads us."

The New York press remained skeptical. William Randolph Hearst's

New York American ran a three-column banner headline on the front page:
FRIEND OF ROCKEFELLER, LONG A FELLOW TRUSTEE OF HIS CHURCH, LEADER
IN HIS SON'S SUNDAY SCHOOL CLASS,* COUNSEL FOR GAS INVESTIGATORS.
Next to the headline, the newspaper published a political cartoon depicting
Rockefeller and Hughes holding a Bible while passing a collection plate.

Hughes's early, plodding approach to the investigation did not reassure
the press corps. "If Hughes gets out of a witness anything he does not wish
to reveal," wrote James Montague in the *New York Journal*, "it will be a
surprise to those who watched his initial operations." But slowly, methodically, he began to pile fact on top of incriminating fact. Hughes's primary
target was the gas trust, a gigantic conglomerate that controlled the manufacturing and sale of gas in the city. He showed that the trust, the Consolidated Gas Company, charged the city $80,000 for the same amount of
electricity that it supplied to large private consumers for only $25,000. The
rate-gouging also reached small private consumers. Hughes proved that the
New York Gas & Electric Light, Heat & Power Company, wholly owned
by the gas trust, produced and distributed electricity to the city's individual
consumers at a rate more than twice the cost to the company.

How did the gas trust avoid public disclosure of its outrageously high
profits? In his interrogation of the trust's officers, Hughes forced them to
admit to a sophisticated version of cooking the books. Two decades earlier,
the trust had absorbed six gas companies, at a cost of just under $21 mil-
lion; the new properties, however, were capitalized at almost $38 million
without tangible improvements to the acquired properties. Hughes challenged the company's right to grossly increase its valuation based on nothing more than the speculative assessment of goodwill and earning capacity.

Later in the hearing, the trust's counsel attempted to explain how the
company's bloated valuation had been built up, in part, by adding the cost
of every new unit and improvement to its plants—with only small allowances for depreciation. For years, he said, the trust had spent millions of
dollars to improve its plants, so it was only reasonable for those improvements to be reflected in the company's valuation.

"I once had an umbrella," Hughes responded. During the fifteen years
that he owned the umbrella, he had had it re-covered periodically. Over
the years, this may have cost him $50 or $60. "Would you say therefore
that the value of that umbrella might be $50 or $60?" he asked.

---

* One of Hughes's Sunday School students was Rockefeller's son, John D. Junior.

The trust's tricky bookkeeping practices amounted to nothing less than extortion, Hughes charged. "The company is entitled to a fair return upon its capital actually invested," he concluded, "but it is not entitled to capitalize its grip upon the public." In only three weeks of hearings, Hughes exposed gross manipulation of the trust's books to maximize profits to its shareholders at the same time that it squeezed every available penny out of consumers. He also showed that the trust had underreported the value of its assets to the State Board of Tax Commissioners to reduce its tax burden. And he demonstrated that the utilities companies had delivered an adulterated quality of gas that was both dangerous and highly profitable to the trust.

Suddenly, the committee's counsel, who had been described at the beginning of the hearings as cold, aloof, and ineffectual, was the darling of the press. He was strong, his shoulders square, "and his whiskers thick and somewhat aggressive." Hughes's final report card for the investigation, like his earlier academic grades, was superb. "The people wanted to know the facts," said the *World*, "and the facts have been brought out without cavil." The *Globe* pronounced the investigation "a model inquiry under able and adroit direction."

Hughes knew that his investigative triumph would mean nothing unless his findings could be translated into reform legislation in Albany. He carted his voluminous records to the Fifth Avenue Hotel, and, working day and night for a week, organized data to produce a scathing report on the utilities industry. He concluded that the industry could earn a reasonable profit and still cut gas rates by 25 percent and electricity rates that it charged to light the city's streets by one third. Most important, Hughes recommended that the legislature create a public service commission to supervise the utility companies serving the entire state to compel them to operate in the public interest.

After finishing his report, Hughes boarded the Empire State Express for Albany to fight for his reforms. When he arrived in the state capital, he delivered his report to the Stevens Committee and helped draft legislation to correct abuses in the utilities industry. All of the bills that Hughes helped draft were passed.* Savings in New York City's lighting bills alone, as a result of Hughes's recommendation, were later estimated at $780,000

---

* The legislature delayed passage of the bill on a revised gas rate for a year and in its final form slightly boosted the rate that Hughes had recommended.

a year. As Hughes requested, the legislature created a State Commission of Gas and Electricity to supervise the operations of the state's gas and lighting companies.

Having finished his investigative assignment, Hughes sailed to Europe in July to meet Antoinette and their children for an extended holiday. He joined his family in Nuremberg. From there, they journeyed to the mountainous regions of Germany, Austria, and northern Italy. At the end of a strenuous day trip to Austria's remote Gross-Glockner Glacier, the family's dinner was interrupted by a waiter who handed Hughes a telegram. It was from State Senator William Armstrong, chairman of the newly formed committee charged with investigating abuses in the life insurance industry. Armstrong urged Hughes to become the committee's counsel.

The next day Antoinette chided her preoccupied husband for ignoring the beautiful scenery. "My dear, you don't know what this investigation would mean," said Hughes. "It would be the most tremendous job in the United States." He quickly arranged for a return passage to New York in mid-August to prepare for public hearings in early September.

When Chairman Armstrong opened the insurance hearings in the aldermanic chambers of Manhattan's City Hall on September 6, 1905, Hughes, as the committee's chief counsel, faced a phalanx of reporters as well as a formidable array of high-priced attorneys representing officers of the nation's largest insurance companies. He was not intimidated. Perfectly composed, always polite, he asked the most probing questions "as unemotionally as a teacher finding a mild enthusiasm in leading a child to concede the irrefutable verities of mathematics."

Hughes's interrogation of Richard McCurdy, the supremely confident president of the Mutual Life Insurance Company, was typically low-key, and devastating. McCurdy removed his gold-rimmed pince-nez to request that the shades be lowered to cut the glare from the sunlight. Once he was comfortable, Hughes inquired about the salaries paid to McCurdy and other officers of the Mutual. An indignant McCurdy considered it his duty to educate Hughes about the public calling of the men who had always run Mutual. Those who organized Mutual did so "from a pure spirit of philanthropy," McCurdy said, on the theory that "it was a great beneficent missionary institution."

"Well," Hughes responded, "the question comes back to the salaries of the missionaries."

McCurdy was forced to admit that he and Mutual's vice president held sufficient proxies from policyholders to control the election of the company's trustees who set the officers' compensation. McCurdy's handpicked trustees had increased his annual salary from $30,000 to $150,000. Another Mutual "missionary," McCurdy's son, had been paid $530,788 over a sixteen-year period in addition to commissions on the company's foreign business worth $1,268,390 (a portion of which was shared with an associate). For a single year, McCurdy's son-in-law received $147,687 in commissions. By the time Hughes had finished his inquiry into executive compensation at Mutual, the *New York World* estimated the McCurdy family's compensation alone, including syndicate and trust company profits, at $15 million.

To determine what expertise McCurdy brought to his highly compensated position, Hughes asked him to explain how his company calculated its premiums.

"You are trying to prove me a fool," a flustered McCurdy replied, and he referred Hughes to the company's actuary.

"Without commenting on that, Mr. McCurdy," Hughes said, "I want to ask *you*."

McCurdy repeatedly refused to answer Hughes's questions testing his elementary knowledge of the insurance industry. By the end of the examination, no one in the room doubted that Mutual's president was incapable of passing counsel's test.

Hughes moved on to a mysterious entry in Mutual's books of $364,254 in 1904 listed as "legal expenses." Oddly, the amounts for legal expenses were paid by one Andrew Fields, listed as the head of the company's supply department. Before long, Hughes had discovered that Fields maintained a house for Mutual (and Equitable Life Insurance) in Albany in which some influential lawmakers lived and many more were lavishly entertained. Wages for the cook, the rent, and all supplies for the house were charged to the company's legal expenses. Prominent members of the Senate's Insurance Committee were paid as much as $3,000 a year out of the same account to serve as Mutual's "advisers on legislation." Not surprisingly, no effective oversight regulation of the industry was voted out of the Insurance Committee.

Mutual did not confine its largesse to Albany's lawmakers. The company made large gifts to the Republican Party's presidential campaign every four years and to the campaigns of Republican congressmen deemed important to protecting the industry's interests. It also secretly paid off corrupt reporters to write favorable stories on the company.

While Mutual's executives as well as pliable politicians and reporters were generously rewarded, policyholders did not fare so well. Dividends to them fell from $3,183,023 to $2,674,207 at the same time that the company's total income had quadrupled to $81,002,984. McCurdy dismissed the discrepancy. "Large rewards," he said, were justified by "large achievements."

When McCurdy's counsel, James Beck, accused Hughes of unfairly badgering his client, Hughes calmly responded: "The witness who gets himself into a false position has only himself to blame." He was defended by a surprising source, McCurdy himself, who said that Hughes had conducted the hearing with admirable restraint. McCurdy voluntarily cut his salary in half; several weeks before the end of the hearings, he resigned from the company, as did his son and son-in-law.

The strain of the hearings took its toll on Hughes. He remembered that "occasionally at night I would feel worn out and utterly depressed." He told his wife, "I can't see any end to this. It is too much. I simply can't go on." But after a night's rest, he would feel sufficiently refreshed to resume his interrogations.

The president of the New York Life Insurance Company, John McCall, initially treated Hughes's inquiry as an annoying diversion from the serious business of running one of the country's largest insurance companies. But, like Mutual's McCurdy, he soon learned that Hughes would not be diverted from *his* serious business.

McCall drew an annual salary of $100,000 and ran the company as if it were his personal fiefdom. Through his patient questioning, Hughes revealed just how completely McCall dominated his company's business. McCall alone could direct the drawing of checks in excess of $25,000.

McCall's confidence was soon shattered by Hughes's penetrating interrogation about a mysterious company payment of $235,000. Visibly uncomfortable, McCall offered evasive answers to Hughes's direct questions. He admitted authorizing the payment but said that he could not recall the purpose of the disbursement. After a break in the hearings, Hughes returned and informed McCall that he had examined the company's financial records and concluded that the $235,000 could not have been spent on legitimate insurance business.

McCall then admitted that he had secretly advanced the funds to Andrew Hamilton, a lobbyist on New York Life's payroll.* A tense colloquy between McCall and Hughes ensued:

> McCall: The money was used by Hamilton in connection with the purchase of a mortgage for the company.
>
> Hughes: That was not possible since he [Hughes] had examined the company's records and found that no purchase of a mortgage for $235,000 had been made.
>
> McCall: The money was spent by Hamilton to buy land in his capacity as purchasing agent for the company's "Home Office Annex."
>
> Hughes: That too was impossible since he had reviewed the company's accounts of every parcel of land purchased for the annex and found no such expenditure. Hamilton could not have spent the $235,000 for that purpose.

Finally, McCall confessed that the illicitly spent $235,000 belonged to the company and arranged to repay it by the end of the year.

The press hailed Hughes's performance as heroic, but Hughes's own appraisal of his work was more modest. "The sensational disclosures which came out in the testimony were generally as much of a surprise to me as to others," he said later. "I would plan for a day's work, but almost invariably something would soon be developed in the course of the examination of witnesses which would give a lead that had to be followed up at once, and in so doing new and important facts would be elicited."

Hughes's fact-driven investigation again produced newspaper headlines when he sought an explanation for an unaccountable payment for $48,702 on New York Life's books. He was told by one officer of New York Life that George Perkins, a company vice president and partner at J. P. Morgan & Company, could answer his questions. Once Perkins had taken the witness stand, he embarked on a meandering tribute to his own life and

---

* Hamilton was paid $1,312,197 by New York Life over a period of eleven years. He fled to Paris when the hearings began, claiming ill-health, and refused to return until the investigation was completed.

professional accomplishments. Hughes listened patiently and eventually brought Perkins around to the mysterious payment.

At a break in the hearings, Perkins asked to speak to Hughes privately. "Mr. Hughes," he said, "you're handling dynamite. That $48,000 was a contribution to President [Theodore] Roosevelt's campaign fund. You want to think very carefully before you put that into the evidence. You can't tell what may come of it."

"After lunch," Hughes replied, "I'm going to ask you what was done with that $48,000; and I expect a candid answer."

As promised, Hughes asked Perkins the question and, as Perkins anticipated, his answer sent reporters scrambling to the nearest telephones to call their editors.

"Hughes calls himself a Republican," one Republican boss grumbled, "but he's ripping the party wide open." Immediately, political pressure was put on the legislative committee to rein in Hughes or, at least, to give party leaders advance notice of his revelations. Hughes was so advised by the committee. Advance notice was not possible, Hughes responded, since he often did not know where his investigation would lead. He was the committee's counsel, he reminded them, and the committee was free to give him instructions on how to conduct the inquiry. He would either follow those instructions, he said, or resign and give his reasons publicly for his resignation. Key members of the committee backed Hughes. His authority to conduct the investigation as he saw fit was never again challenged.

If Hughes could not be controlled, New York City's Republican bosses decided, then he must be persuaded to leave his job. They made Hughes their consensus choice to be the Republican candidate for mayor of New York City. Without Hughes's consent, he was nominated. A committee of Republican chieftains then descended upon Hughes's apartment late one Friday evening to persuade him to accept the nomination. Over the weekend, Hughes pondered his dilemma: he could accept the nomination and resign as counsel to the committee or he could remain counsel and reject the mayoralty nomination. On Monday, he issued a statement declaring that "[i]n my judgment, I have no right to accept the nomination. A paramount public duty forbids it."

For the remainder of the four-month investigation, Hughes continued to uncover a trail of political corruption, corporate mismanagement, and excess profits in the life insurance industry. Political payoffs were routine. U.S. Senator Thomas Platt conceded that the big insurance companies wrote him checks for $10,000 annually, which he turned over to the Republican State Committee to elect legislators who would do the industry's bidding in Albany. Senator Chauncey Depew did even better, telling the committee that he was paid a $20,000 annual retainer from Equitable Life Assurance Society, where he was a director. Hughes showed that the nation's three largest insurance companies—Equitable, Mutual, and New York Life—divided the country politically into geographic regions so that each company was responsible, through bribes and lobbying, for preventing the passage of legislation in their assigned regions that would be unfriendly to the industry.

Conflicts of interest, such as Depew's with Equitable, were commonplace. While serving on Equitable's board, Jacob Schiff, a partner in the investment banking firm of Kuhn, Loeb & Company, sold securities to the insurance company valued at $49,704,408 during a five-and-a-half-year period. George Perkins, the New York Life vice president and partner at J. P. Morgan, represented both New York Life and Morgan in a $4 million bond deal.

Hughes's investigation revealed that all of the major insurance companies engaged in financial chicanery, moving vast sums on and off the books to hide illegal dealings and profits. New York Life, in order to conceal its ownership of stocks in Prussia in violation of that country's law, made fictitious loans for more than $3 million to a bond clerk and a messenger through an affiliated New York company. Equitable, during an eleven-month period in 1904, kept an average balance of more than $36 million on deposit in various trust companies and banks, drawing a modest annual interest of 2 to 3 percent. To conceal the size of the deposits in their annual reports, Equitable made pro forma loans for a few days to Kuhn, Loeb & Company (in 1904, the loan was $10,250,000).

During his six years in office, Francis Hendricks, the state superintendent of insurance charged with oversight of the industry, failed to detect any of the irregularities that Hughes had revealed in just four months of hearings. How, Hendricks was asked, could his office have accepted the "glaringly false returns" of the companies? He could not answer the question. "Most of the evils which have been disclosed by the investigation," Hughes concluded, "would have been impossible had there been a vigorous performance of the duties already laid upon the department." Shortly after giving his testimony, Hendricks retired.

As a result of Hughes's investigation, the president and two vice presidents of one of the insurance companies were indicted, as were two vice presidents of another. All of the presidents and most of the other high officials of the three big companies resigned or were forced out. Members of the finance committee of New York Life who had sanctioned contributions to political campaign committees paid back $148,000 to the company out of their own pockets.

Hughes's major aim was not to punish illegal behavior but to reform the insurance industry. He devoted six weeks to writing a comprehensive report on the hearings and recommending sweeping legislation. In Albany, he drafted a series of bills that were promptly enacted by the state legislature. The reforms prohibited insurance companies from making contributions to political campaigns; mandated registration of lobbyists with public disclosure of their services, expenses, and compensation; forbade executives from profiting in transactions with their companies; required new corporate elections with wider policyholder participation; and opened the courts to policyholder suits against the companies.

Joseph Pulitzer's *New York World* declared that the investigation "has given us Charles E. Hughes as another magnificent example of the man who is willing to serve the public, who has a service of the highest order to give to the public, and who can be neither intimidated nor betrayed." William Randolph Hearst's *New York American* echoed the praise: "Nobody in New York will question the excellence of the work done by the counsel for the people, Mr. Charles E. Hughes." Hughes's name began to circulate among Republican leaders as their choice for the party's gubernatorial nomination.

Shortly after completing his work for the insurance committee in Albany, Hughes, accompanied by Charles Junior, now a student at Brown, embarked on a holiday in Edinburgh. The companionship of his son in the bracing Scottish air provided a fitting antidote to the stress of the hearings. But he missed his beloved Antoinette and responding passionately to one of her letters: "To think of one at my age receiving such a love letter as I received this morning! Dearest, we must arrange in the future not to be separated in our holidays—life is too short and our love is too strong. Your letter was like a long draught from the old home well. And the sweet poem, darling, I shall always cherish."

Upon his return to New York, Hughes looked forward to resuming a normal family life and practicing law. He doubted that he had any political future for two reasons. He believed that he had permanently alienated the city's Republican leaders by refusing to accept the party's nomination for mayor. And he had exposed the failure of the Republican-controlled state insurance department to protect the interests of policyholders.

Still, his name continued to be raised as the most likely Republican candidate for governor. In a letter to his parents, Hughes disavowed any political ambitions, indeed, dreaded the prospect of running for governor. "It gives me a cold sweat to think of going through a campaign with the alternative of defeat or two years at Albany," he wrote. "I don't [know] which would be worse. I can be of more service and far happier in my cho- sen profession. So 'fling away' any political ambition you may have for your son—and take counsel of your philosophy—for of all vanities there is no vanity like that of politics."

But others, most notably President Theodore Roosevelt, would not hear of Hughes returning to private life when the party needed him. TR was not discouraged by Hughes's exposure of the insurance companies' co- vert financial support for Roosevelt's 1904 presidential campaign. In the spring of 1906, the president asked Hughes to lead an investigation of the coal industry. When Hughes met the president for the first time at the White House in May, Roosevelt confided that he had already cast his vote for Hughes as the party's gubernatorial nominee. By the fall, Hughes had accepted his party's nomination to run for governor against the Democratic candidate, the powerful newspaper publisher William Randolph Hearst.

Hughes campaigned as the reform candidate against Hearst, who had received the endorsement of Tammany Hall's boss, Charles Murphy. And he attacked the demagoguery of Hearst's newspapers, charging that they ignored reason and dispassionate discussion. No progress could be made, he said, when "[f]lame feeds flame." TR applauded from the sidelines: "My dear sir, I feel that you are fighting the battle of civilization," he wrote Hughes. "[Y]ou are an honest, fearless, square man. . . . If I were not Presi- dent I should be stumping New York from one end to the other for you."

Hughes was too stiff and high-minded to viscerally appeal to the or- dinary voter. But he was a vigorous campaigner, often making as many as twenty speeches a day, and his message of fighting the bosses resonated with New Yorkers. While never a charismatic speaker, he became more comfortable on the stump and even risked making fun of his public image as a humorless automaton. "I hope that, if an autopsy is ever performed upon me," he told one crowd, "you will find something besides sawdust and useful information."

With the endorsement of every major newspaper in the state except Hearst's, Hughes won the election by a comfortable margin: 749,002 votes to Hearst's 691,105.

In his inaugural address, Hughes promised to clean house of inept or corrupt state officials. Applying the same problem-solving method that he had employed so successfully in the gas and insurance investigations, he laboriously collected the facts and then recommended action. But the political barons in the state legislature posed obstacles for Hughes that did not exist in his celebrated investigations. Unlike the utility and insurance executives that Hughes had interrogated, the entrenched legislative leaders could not be intimidated or shamed into action by his factual analyses. They had seen reform governors come and go, and had no intention of relinquishing their levers of power.

One of Hughes's first efforts to fulfill his good government pledge was his attempt to have the honest but ineffectual superintendent of insurance, Otto Kelsey, removed from office. For Hughes, it was imperative that a superintendent be installed who could rid the office of the ineptitude and dishonesty that he had exposed in the insurance hearings. The new governor discovered that eight months after the legislature had enacted reforms to police the industry, Kelsey ran his office as if the new laws did not exist. Hughes privately offered to appoint Kelsey to another public office for which he was qualified, but he insisted that he could not remain as superintendent. Kelsey's fate, however, would ultimately be decided by the State Senate, which retained the power to remove him.

Kelsey, a former legislator with close ties to the Senate leadership, refused to resign. Hughes, acting under an old statute authorizing him to conduct hearings to determine the fitness of state officials, held a hearing and mercilessly interrogated Kelsey. He showed that Kelsey was incompetent and unwilling to fire those under him who had created the scandal in the department under the previous superintendent, Francis Hendricks. The governor won praise in the press for his skillful interrogation. But neither Kelsey nor his supporters in the Senate budged. In the end, the Senate refused to remove Kelsey, as Hughes had demanded.

Hughes was unbowed. "I'm not disheartened at all," he said. "I simply showed the people that I was trying to do all I could to reform the Insurance

Department. The conduct of the department is now the responsibility of the Senate." He may have appeared unperturbed in his public statements, but Hughes refused to allow Kelsey's recalcitrance to go unchallenged. He saw to it that formal charges were filed against him. And he appointed his assistant in the insurance investigation, Matthew Fleming, to review the work in the superintendent's office and file a report. The Senate ignored the report; Kelsey remained in office.

President Roosevelt attempted to help the frustrated governor in his fight against the bosses by removing a minor anti-Hughes appointee, Archie Sanders, Rochester's collector of customs. But even that gesture backfired, causing the initially warm relations between Hughes and TR to cool. The episode was precipitated by the Albany reporter for the *New York Evening Post*, Frank Simonds, who had openly boasted of his close relationship with Hughes. He reported that the governor had had no advance notice of TR's removal of the state appointee and, further, that Hughes disapproved of the president's action. Hughes made no effort to assure the president that Simond's report was inaccurate. Afterward, TR's support for Hughes's administration was notably less enthusiastic.

Despite this initial setback in his battle with the legislature, Hughes continued to insist on competence in government. The legislative leaders, just as determined, refused to cooperate. Flouting the governor's directives, they appointed old-line loyalists to key legislative committees. And they referred derisively to the reform governor as "Charles the Baptist."

Having failed to enlist the legislators (or the corporate lobbyists who supported them) in his cause, Hughes appealed directly to the voters. He made speeches across the state pillorying the Senate that had defied him in refusing to remove Kelsey. He must have the authority to remove ineffectual commissioners like Kelsey, he insisted, without the consent of the State Senate and its corporate sponsors. Feeling the pressure of public opinion, the Senate reluctantly gave Hughes the power he requested, as well as the authority to investigate the operations of all executive departments.

Hughes also fought the corporations that wanted easy access to the courts to challenge his new removal power. In his defense, Hughes made his most famous statement on judicial review. "We are under a Constitution," he said, "but the Constitution is what the judges say it is." He meant that judges should not be burdened with oversight of administrative agencies, but concentrate on serious constitutional questions. Though Hughes explained the meaning of his statement, it is persistently quoted out of context to represent an abjectly cynical view of constitutional interpretation.

Once he had moved past the Kelsey fiasco, Hughes backed his good government rhetoric with strong action. In one of his most important initiatives, he advocated the creation of two new public service commissions with broad mandates and enforcement powers to regulate railroads and utilities throughout the state. The commissions—one for New York City and adjacent counties and the other for the remainder of the state—were given the power to impose reasonable, non-discriminatory rates with the authority to examine the books and rates of utilities. Their orders were to be enforced through legal action brought by the commissions themselves and given preference in the courts. In its breadth and enforcement powers, the New York legislation served as a model for the nation, exceeding in scope progressive laws in other states, including Massachusetts, where the proposals of Louis Brandeis, another lawyer-reformer, had been enacted.

In his first year in office, Hughes vetoed 297 bills and various items in six appropriation measures that were, in his view, poorly drafted, discriminatory, or that catered to special interests. He also called the legislature into extraordinary session to enact a bill reapportioning seats in the state legislature that more accurately represented population shifts. With the aid of a young Democratic assemblyman named Alfred E. Smith, he induced the legislature to pass a "clean elections" bill that limited the amounts that candidates for major public offices could spend in their campaigns and required strict accountability for expenditures.* In his most dramatic fight with vested interests, Hughes successfully crusaded for an anti–race track gambling law. His objection, he declared in speeches throughout the state, was not to horse racing but to the illegal bookmaking that harmed the poor and ignorant.

Hughes requested and was granted new powers to investigate the organization and conduct of executive departments and the state militia. Turning to New York City, he purged the borough governments of incompetent leaders. After conducting hearings, he fired Manhattan and Bronx borough presidents for flagrant mismanagement. The Queens borough president resigned after being summoned to a hearing to be conducted by Hughes.

---

* In the 1906 gubernatorial campaign, Hearst spent $500,000 compared to Hughes's expenditures of $619.

*   *   *

As governor, Hughes kept to the same rigorous routine that he had maintained in his private practice. He rose early, dressed formally, ate breakfast with his family at precisely the same time every morning, and went to the office as soon as the day's mail (ranging from forty to four hundred letters) had been sorted. In a symbolic gesture, he demonstrated that he led an open government, holding daily morning conferences in the large, high-ceilinged executive chamber of the Capitol, seeing visitors on a first-come, first-serve basis. He usually worked at his desk through lunch (a sandwich, apple, and tea), listening to complaints or advice from visitors until six or seven in the evening. Invariably, he brought a sheaf of papers home for further study, finally retreating to bed in the early morning hours.

By the end of his first two-year term, Hughes had compiled an impressive progressive record, as he had promised. In addition to his early initiatives, he pushed through labor reforms, strengthening executive oversight of factory conditions and supporting legislation regulating child labor and providing additional safety protection for workers. He also lobbied for the preservation of natural resources. Speaking at a Conference of Governors convened by the president at the White House, Hughes urged reforms in his own state. He criticized New York for allowing 550,000 horsepower of energy worth $6,600,000 to run to waste each year because the state had failed to develop a comprehensive plan for its utilization. In the area of civil liberties, he advocated equal opportunity for African-Americans. "We cannot maintain our democratic ideals as to one set of our people," he said, "and ignore them as to others."

Inevitably, Hughes, now the progressive Republican governor of New York, was mentioned as a possible presidential candidate in 1908 to succeed Theodore Roosevelt, the former progressive Republican governor of the Empire State. But Hughes was not convinced that Roosevelt would retire. He also was undoubtedly aware that his relations with the president had cooled off, and that he would not be TR's choice as his successor. As expected, Roosevelt endorsed William Howard Taft, the Secretary of War, who received the Republican Party's nomination for president. Taft then asked Hughes to join the ticket as the party's candidate for vice president. Hughes declined but actively campaigned for Taft's election. His attacks on Taft's Democratic opponent, William Jennings Bryan, earned kudos from the White House. "In a fight like this," Roosevelt wrote Hughes, "people do not want a mealy-mouthed man, and your aggressive hard-hitting against Bryan and Bryanism has been of enormous consequence."

Hughes's expressed desire to return to private practice after one term as governor was motivated, in part, by financial considerations. On his annual gubernatorial salary of $10,000, he was supporting his wife and four children (his youngest child, Elizabeth, was born in Albany in 1907), as well as his parents. He was also exhausted by his battles with the old guard in the legislature, which promised to continue unabated if Hughes served a second term. Hughes's now familiar strategy of taking his reform agenda directly to the people rankled not only the ruling elite in the legislature but also his party's state executive committee. In their eyes, he was aloof and insufferably self-righteous, convinced that he alone represented the public interest.

But the two most important members of the Republican Party, Roosevelt and Taft, concluded that Hughes was their party's best hope to retain the governor's office and urged him to run for reelection. Hughes reluctantly acquiesced and was renominated at the party's convention at Saratoga. Conservative party regulars, particularly in rural upstate New York, offered tepid support for their gubernatorial candidate. Hughes nonetheless gamely campaigned throughout the state and won the election. But his margin of victory, 69,000 votes, over the Democratic candidate was far less than the plurality of 203,000 polled by the Republican presidential nominee, Taft, who enjoyed the enthusiastic backing of the state's Republican loyalists.

Hughes again made political reform the centerpiece of his agenda for his second term, proposing a direct election bill that would have taken local, state, and national nominations (except the presidency) out of the hands of the political bosses. It was a bold attempt to wrest control of state politics from the powerful party machinery in Albany. Even with the support of Roosevelt and Taft, his proposal was defeated. Hughes's efforts depleted whatever goodwill he had accumulated with the legislature in his first term. Still, he could point to significant accomplishments, including the expansion of the Public Service Commissions Act to cover the telegraph and telephone companies and securing the enactment of the first workmen's compensation law in the nation. Despite these achievements, he was despondent and longed to leave the executive mansion.

In March 1910, President Taft visited the beleaguered governor in Albany and told him that he had a public duty to run for a third term.

Hughes resisted. "I do not dare to run the chance of breaking down mentally," he said, repeating warnings that he had received from his doctor. "I must get out and make my family safe while I am able."

Two days after meeting with Hughes in Albany, Taft told his White House aide, Captain Archie Butt, "I don't know the man I admire more than Hughes," adding, "[i]f ever I have the chance I shall offer him the Chief Justiceship." A week later, Associate Justice David Brewer died. Taft decided that he could not wait to name Hughes Chief Justice of the United States, and offered him the seat on the Court left vacant by Brewer's death.

In his letter to Hughes, the president candidly presented the attractive options open to the governor, should he reject the judicial appointment. First, he described a tantalizing future in national politics for Hughes. "I believe as strongly as possible that you are likely to be nominated and elected President sometime in the future unless you go upon the Bench or make such associations at the Bar to prevent it," he wrote. He also conceded that Hughes could earn a handsome income if he chose to return to private practice in New York, far exceeding his judicial salary, even if, as Taft anticipated, Congress raised the associate justices' annual salary of $12,500 to $17,500.

Taft nonetheless urged Hughes to accept the appointment. Hughes would restore confidence in the Court, he said, adding much needed youth and intellectual vigor to the institution. He also intimated that he would probably promote Hughes to Chief Justice, should he have the opportunity during his presidential term. But with a lawyer's caution, Taft declined to make his wish a binding offer: "Don't misunderstand me as to the Chief Justiceship. I mean that if that office were now open, I should offer it to you and it is probable that if it were to become vacant during my term, I should promote you to it; but, of course, conditions change, so that it would not be right for me to say by way of promise what I would do in the future."

Hughes immediately accepted Taft's offer. "My training and professional interest have been such that I should undertake this work with a personal satisfaction which no other line of effort could command in the same degree," he wrote the president. As to the possibility that he might be elevated to Chief Justice, Hughes said he appreciated Taft's confidence in him, but that he, "in common with all our citizens," wanted the president to be free to exercise his best judgment in any future appointment. The U.S. Senate unanimously confirmed Hughes's judicial nomination on May 2, 1910. Afterward, Hughes announced in Albany that he would resign his office in October, in time for him to join his new judicial colleagues for the opening of the Supreme Court term.

In July, the ailing Chief Justice Melville Fuller died, leading to speculation that Hughes would be named Fuller's successor. Taft had not nominated a replacement for Fuller when Hughes met his judicial brethren on October 10 for the first time. His first days on the Court were particularly awkward since at least two of his new colleagues, Associate Justices John Marshall Harlan and Edward White, coveted the chief justiceship for themselves. To make matters worse, leading newspapers anticipated a Hughes appointment. HUGHES TO HEAD COURT, declared *The Washington Post*. Hughes's most illustrious judicial colleague, Justice Oliver Wendell Holmes, Jr., made the same prediction. "I should bet," Holmes wrote to his friend Sir Frederick Pollock, "that he [Taft] will appoint Hughes, who has given up a chance of being Republican nominee for the Presidency."

But Taft kept his own counsel and refused to be pressured into the appointment. On Sunday, December 11, Hughes received a telephone call from the White House, asking him to come to a meeting with the president. But thirty minutes later, while he was dressing for his meeting with Taft, he received a second call cancelling the appointment. The next day, Taft nominated Associate Justice White to succeed Fuller as Chief Justice.

Hughes accepted the news of White's appointment with equanimity. He later wrote that he never felt that Taft owed him the appointment, despite the president's intimations that Hughes would be his choice to succeed Fuller. "I felt, too, that it might well be thought that I was too young and inexperienced to deserve the appointment as Chief Justice and I fully appreciated the burden it would cast upon me," he noted.

Taft never explained why he chose White over Hughes. But the issues that Hughes himself raised probably influenced the president. He had never argued a case before the Court and, at forty-eight, he was nine years younger than any of his brethren. It might have proved difficult for Hughes to lead senior brethren, like Harlan and White, who had served on the Court for many years. Besides, White was sixty-six years old and in fragile health. Taft could yet have the opportunity to appoint Hughes to be Chief Justice.

When he arrived at the Supreme Court, Hughes was appalled by the accommodations. The justices met in a small, poorly ventilated courtroom in the old Senate chamber that had been their official home since the pre–Civil War days of the Taney Court. In another cramped room across the hall, the justices robed and took their lunch. One floor below, they crowded around a table in a cluttered conference room to discuss the cases that had been argued. Since members of the Court were not assigned individual offices in the Capitol, they were forced to rent or own residences large enough to provide working space for themselves and their secretaries.

In his first months on the Court, Hughes felt overwhelmed by the work. The cases arrived in clusters for argument. Once heard, the justices were expected to vote on their disposition later in the week. Hughes attacked his judicial assignments with characteristic thoroughness and zeal. He not only studied the lower court decisions and lawyers' briefs but also read widely outside the cases to enhance his understanding of the underlying judicial issues. It was not long before he had caught the rhythm of the Court's calendar and was in control of his workload. In preparation for the week's work, he came to the oral arguments and conferences with meticulously drafted notes on each case.

When he attended his first judicial conferences, Hughes was startled by the rancorous relations among three of the Court's most influential justices, White, Harlan, and Holmes. Before he was appointed Chief Justice, White had appeared discontent and distant, particularly so when the senior justice, Harlan, spoke. Harlan and White had disliked each other instantly at their first meeting, and their animosity remained intact for all of their sixteen years together on the Court. The voluble seventy-seven-year-old Harlan, who had been appointed by President Rutherford B. Hayes in 1877, thrived on dissent and sometimes seemed genuinely disappointed if anyone agreed with him.* That was rarely a problem for Harlan after he read the opinions of the venerable Justice Holmes. He complained of Holmes's "obscure phrases" and what he considered his colleague's unsound constitutional views. For his part, Holmes responded with studied bemusement to "my lion-hearted friend."

After his initial shock, Hughes adjusted to the charged atmosphere in conference and became good friends with all three men. Once Edward

---

* To his great credit, Harlan was the lone dissenter in *Plessy v. Ferguson*, the 1896 decision in which the majority ruled that separate railroad cars for whites and blacks was constitutional. In dissent, Harlan wrote: "Our Constitution is color-blind, and neither knows nor tolerates classes among citizens."

White was appointed Chief Justice, he relaxed and actively cultivated Hughes's friendship. Cordial relations between Hughes and Harlan were never a problem. The Kentuckian had sent a letter of congratulations to Hughes in Albany after his judicial appointment and withheld the verbal spears that he routinely directed at others around the conference table. And Hughes shared with Holmes, above all others on the Court, a common interest in intellectual combat at the highest level, leavened by humor and mutual respect and affection.

When Hughes had first taken his seat in the courtroom, the chair between Holmes and him was empty because Associate Justice William Moody, the assigned occupant, was ill. Holmes gestured to Hughes to move into the vacant seat, an invitation that he politely refused. "I knew enough of the traditions not to make such a *faux pas,* and I tremble to think what might have happened if I had been innocent enough to follow Justice Holmes's kindly but rather thoughtless suggestion," Hughes recalled. "The other Justices would have regarded me as a fresh and bumptious newcomer, and even the Chief Justices in their marble busts might have raised their eyebrows."

After that somewhat awkward beginning, Holmes and Hughes delighted in their professional camaraderie. Hughes had never met anyone with Holmes's rare combination of qualities—"his intellectual power and literary skill, his freshness of view and inimitable way of expressing it, his enthusiasms and cheerful skepticism, his abundant vitality and gaiety of spirit." Holmes's work habits were as fastidious as Hughes's. He made comprehensive notes on 10- by 8-inch sheets of paper during oral argument, writing down the most important points of the case and jotting his brief comments in the margin. Hughes cherished the insouciant comments that Holmes wrote on his draft opinions: "Clear as a bell and sound as a nut"; "So I expect to shut up" and "Wee—Mussoo—Ye crags & Peaks. I'm with you once again."

In his first major opinion, written for the Court in January 1911, Hughes established himself as a stalwart defender of civil rights. The case involved Lonzo Bailey, an African-American from Alabama who had agreed to work on a farm for a year at a wage of $12 a month. After thirty days he quit and did not return $15 that his employer had advanced to him. Under Alabama law, Bailey's failure to perform the work or refund the money advanced was considered prima facie evidence of his intent to defraud. He was convicted under the state peonage law and sentenced to 136 days of hard prison labor.

The question before the Court was whether Bailey could be punished for fraud for simply refusing to perform the work for which he had been advanced $15. In overturning the defendant's conviction, Hughes declared that Bailey's rights under the Thirteenth Amendment, which prohibited involuntary servitude, had been violated. Although the original purpose of the amendment was to abolish slavery, Hughes interpreted the language broadly to prohibit any state of bondage, which included the coercive effect of Alabama's statute. He wrote: "Without imputing any actual motive to oppress, we must consider the natural operation of the statute here in question, and it is apparent that it furnishes a convenient instrument for the coercion which the Constitution and the act of Congress [the Civil Rights Act of 1866] forbid; an instrument of compulsion peculiarly effective as against the poor and the ignorant, its most likely victims." The freedom to work would be meaningless, he added, if the statutory presumption of fraud could be held over the heads of laborers, like Bailey, merely for failing to repay a debt owed to an employer.

With Holmes, Hughes represented the liberal wing of the Court, often in dissent. Their defense of civil liberties was demonstrated in Hughes and Holmes's joint dissenting opinion declaring that Leo Frank, a young Jew from New York who had been convicted of murder in a Georgia courtroom, had not been given a fair trial. Frank's trial occurred in a pervasive atmosphere of anti-Semitism, and suspicion of outsiders like the New York defendant. Frank, the manager of a pencil factory, had been accused of murdering a girl who had worked in the factory. During the trial, a crowd palpably hostile to the defendant had filled the courtroom and spilled onto the street outside. The judge failed to restrain the angry onlookers as they clapped their hands and stamped their feet in support of the prosecution. After the jury retired for deliberations, Frank's lawyer was warned by the judge that he anticipated violence should there be an acquittal or a hung jury. Frank was kept out of the courtroom when the jury announced the guilty verdict. The crowd's boisterous approval of the verdict was so loud that the judge had difficulty polling the jurors.

On appeal, Frank's lawyer claimed that the "mob influence" of the crowd had prejudiced the jurors. The Georgia Supreme Court rejected the claim, and the federal district court refused to grant Frank's petition for a writ of habeas corpus. The U.S. Supreme Court majority affirmed the lower court ruling, but Holmes and Hughes insisted that the federal courts had a duty to inquire into the facts to decide, independent of the Georgia courts, if "the trial was dominated by a hostile mob and was nothing but an empty form." They wrote: "[W]e must look facts in the face . . . we think the presumption overwhelming that the jury responded to the passions of the mob . . . it is our duty . . . to declare lynch law as little valid when practised by a regularly drawn jury as when administered by one elected by a mob intent on death."

Hughes continued to build a strong civil liberties record with his majority opinion declaring that Arizona's anti-alien statute violated the equal protection clause of the Fourteenth Amendment. The state law requiring employers to hire a workforce of at least 80 percent U.S. citizens was challenged by a legal immigrant from Austria named Mike Raich who was fired from his job as a cook by the owner of a restaurant in Bisbee, Arizona. The right to work was the very essence of the personal freedom guaranteed by the Fourteenth Amendment, Hughes reasoned. "If this could be refused solely upon the ground of race or nationality," he wrote, the constitutional protection "would be a barren form of words."

In the first of two seminal opinions exploring the scope of the U.S. Congress's authority to regulate interstate commerce* (an issue that would become the focus of constitutional controversy during the New Deal), Hughes insisted that both the federal and state governments possessed the authority to regulate the exploitive rates charged by the nation's powerful railroad corporations. Pierce Butler, the lawyer for the railroads (and future judicial colleague of Hughes), had argued in a 900-page brief that neither Congress nor the state of Minnesota had the constitutional power to impose rates on the railroads. He also claimed that the rates set by the Minnesota Warehouse Commission were so unfair as to be confiscatory, depriving the railroads of their property without due process of law.

In the spring of 1912, Chief Justice White assigned the majority opinion in what would be known as the *Minnesota Rate Cases* to Hughes, whose extraordinary talent for sifting through masses of complex, and contradictory, commercial claims had been demonstrated in his gas and insurance

---

* Art. I, sect. 8 provides: "The Congress shall have Power . . . [t]o regulate Commerce . . . among the several States . . ."

investigations. Hughes worked on his opinion through the summer and following fall, finally delivering a 100-page unanimous opinion for the Court. One of Hughes's colleagues, Justice Joseph McKenna, only concurred in the result, since he decided that Hughes's opinion was too long to read.

Hughes's description of Congress's broad power to regulate commerce was reminiscent of the expansive nationalistic opinions of the great Chief Justice, John Marshall. The Framers had given Congress the supreme power to regulate interstate commerce, Hughes wrote, because of the failed experiment of the Articles of Confederation, which allowed states to discriminate against each other by erecting trade barriers. "In order to end these evils, the grant in the Constitution conferred upon Congress an authority at all times adequate to secure the freedom of interstate commercial intercourse from State control and provide effective regulation of that intercourse as the National interest may demand." At the same time, Hughes acknowledged that states could regulate commercial activity within their borders, and that Minnesota's regulation was constitutional. Finally, he shredded the railroads' claim that the Minnesota Warehouse Commission's rate was confiscatory. He pointed out in intricate detail that the railroads had inflated their valuations for the purpose of charging exorbitant rates, just as he had earlier destroyed the arguments of Consolidated Gas Company in his investigation of New York City's utility rates.

The opinion was "[a]dmirably well done," wrote a grateful Chief Justice White. "The country and Court owe you a debt they would have to go into bankruptcy if called upon to pay."

In his second major commerce clause opinion, Hughes dealt with the authority of the Interstate Commerce Commission (created by Congress) to prohibit railroad rates within the state of Texas that discriminated against interstate railroad traffic. The ICC had ordered railroads in Texas to stop setting rates for hauls within the state that were lower than rates for comparable distances between Texas and Louisiana. The railroads had challenged the ICC order as exceeding Congress's authority to regulate interstate commerce since it applied to rates within Texas borders.

Hughes rejected the railroads' claim that they were free to set intrastate rates as they pleased. Taking a pragmatic approach to the problem, Hughes wrote in Houston & Texas Ry v. U.S. [the Shreveport Rate Case] that the ICC's order was constitutional since the discriminatory Texas rates had a "close and substantial relation" to interstate commerce. He concluded:

"Whenever the interstate and intrastate transactions of carriers are so re-lated that the government of the one involves the control of the other, it is Congress, and not the State, that is entitled to prescribe the final and dominant rule, for otherwise Congress would be denied the exercise of its constitutional authority and the State, and not the Nation, would be su-preme within the national field."

After his move from Albany to Washington, Hughes expected to re-gain his health with the presumably more tranquil life of a Supreme Court justice. But, of course, his nervous energy and perfectionism prevented it. His daily regimen was as unforgiving as ever. His children joked that they had no need for a clock to meet their early morning schedules, but only had to wait for their father to sit down to breakfast at precisely the same minute every day. He worked from early morning until late at night. Al-though he and Antoinette were much in demand on the Washington party circuit, they invariably bid good-bye to their hosts at 10 p.m. so that the justice could return to his study for another three or four hours of work.

If Hughes could not control his workaholic ways, he decided that he could at least change his personal habits to build up his physical stamina. As a first step, he stopped smoking cigars. Instead of puffing contentedly after breakfast, he began to take half hour walks. He also dispensed with his nightly cocktail before going to sleep. To take him away from the everyday rigors of the Court, Antoinette bought an electric car so they could motor in the country on weekends. In the summers, the couple and their children headed to the lakes and mountains of upstate New York or Maine for a holiday, since the justice's salary did not allow them the luxury of European trips that they had so enjoyed when he was in private practice.*

On the Court, Hughes extended constitutional support to social wel-fare reforms that were similar to those he had advocated as governor. He upheld an Illinois child labor law, writing that "freedom of contract" could not be used as an excuse to take advantage of helpless children. In two other cases, Hughes found himself on the bench face-to-face with his fel-low social reformer and future judicial colleague, Louis Brandeis. In the first, Hughes sustained the conviction of a hotel proprietor for working a chambermaid nine hours a day, in violation of California's law imposing an

---

* The exception was his first summer on the Court, when President Taft pressured a reluctant Hughes to remain in Washington to serve on a commission to study and make recommendations for second-class postal rates.

eight-hour-day regulation for women. California was also free, he wrote in a second case argued by Brandeis, to apply its eight-hour regulation to some women and not to others who were less vulnerable, like graduate nurses.

A third case argued by Brandeis posed a similar constitutional challenge, but involved the regulation of women's wages, rather than maximum hours. In December 1914, the Court heard the case of Elmira Simpson, a young woman who worked in an Oregon paper box factory. The Oregon Industrial Welfare Commission had ordered Simpson's employer, Frank Stettler, to add 64 cents a week to her weekly wage to comply with the state's minimum wage law. In the state courts, Stettler's attorneys had argued that, unlike maximum hours legislation, Oregon's minimum wage law exceeded its regulatory authority, since wages had no direct effect on health or morals. Without that authority, they contended, the state had undercut Stettler's freedom of contract, depriving him of his property without due process of law. The Oregon Supreme Court had unanimously rejected Stettler's claim, and his attorneys appealed to the U.S. Supreme Court.

Addressing the justices, Brandeis insisted that there was no constitutional distinction between minimum wage and maximum hour legislation in protecting the morality of poor, factory-bound women. If young women, like Elmira Simpson, were not paid a living wage, they could not dress decently or eat enough to keep them away from a life of moral depravity. It was, in a constitutional sense, no different from forcing young women to work unconscionably long hours, leaving them similarly exposed to moral temptation.

A troubled Chief Justice White suggested to counsel that Oregon's minimum wage law could force employers out of business. But Justice Holmes reminded his colleagues and counsel that England's factory laws had deprived employers of their freedom of contract in order to curb the degeneracy of the working classes. Hughes then cut to the core of Stettler's argument, asking his counsel to explain the difference between hours and wages as a matter of "freedom of contract."

"Long hours break down women so that they become public charges; it is a condition growing *out* of employment," the lawyer replied. "The amount of wages has no relation to health and morals."

"But suppose it has," Hughes persisted. "Suppose this court finds that these evils are in consequence of wages paid in employment?"

At conference, Hughes and Holmes expressed the view that the Oregon law should be upheld, taking the position that Hughes had hypothesized to Stettler's counsel at oral argument. But other justices were not persuaded. With members of the Court obviously divided over the issue, Chief Justice White decided to postpone a formal vote. When the case was next brought up for decision in January 1916, the Court divided, 4–4, and reargument was set for the next Court term.*

Hughes would not hear the reargument. On June 10, 1916, he resigned from the Court to accept the nomination of the Republican Party to be president of the United States.

---

* The 4–4 vote was the result of the vacancy left by the death of Associate Justice Joseph Lamar. After the *Stettler* case was reargued, the Court again divided 4–4, thereby upholding the Oregon law. Brandeis, by this time, had been appointed to the Court to replace Lamar and recused himself from participating in the decision in the case he had previously argued.

2

"Rising Star"

F ranklin Delano Roosevelt traced his American lineage to Claes van Rosenvelt, who arrived in New Amsterdam in the 1650s from the Netherlands and farmed 48 acres of land on what is now New York City's Lower East Side. His only son, Nicholas, engaged in fur trading along the lower Hudson River before moving to Manhattan to operate a successful grain-grinding mill. In Roosevelt family history, Nicholas is best known for siring two sons, Johannes and Jacobus, the progenitors of two American presidents. Johannes established the Long Island branch of the Roosevelt family that produced Teddy Roosevelt, while Jacobus settled in the Hudson Valley where Franklin grew up.

The Hudson Valley Roosevelts prospered as landowners and businessmen but did not otherwise distinguish themselves in the history of the young country. The one exception was Isaac Roosevelt, FDR's great-great-grandfather, who was known to his contemporaries as Isaac the Patriot. Having established Manhattan's first large-scale sugar refinery, Isaac signed a letter in 1775 as a member of the Provincial Congress to the British government declaring that "the horrors of Civil War will never compel America to submit to taxation by Parliament." A year later he was a delegate to the convention that drew up the first state constitution in New York. With Alexander Hamilton and others, he founded the Bank of New York and became its second president. In 1788, he attended the state Constitutional Convention and voted to ratify the U.S. Constitution. Isaac was sufficiently prominent and wealthy to be the subject of a fine portrait attributed to Gilbert Stuart, which hangs in the Roosevelt home at Hyde Park.

James Roosevelt, FDR's father, was a more typical male member of the Hudson River clan than his great-grandfather Isaac. Born in 1828, James graduated from Union College in Schenectady, New York, and the Harvard Law School. After law school, he clerked in the prestigious Wall Street law firm of Benjamin Silliman, but found the practice of law tedious. Fortuitously, James's grandfather and namesake, who had made a small fortune in the sugar-refining business, died, leaving him the bulk of his estate, including a large house on the Hudson River north of Poughkeepsie, and a well-appointed New York brownstone. At the age of twenty-five James married Rebecca Howland, the daughter of his mother's first cousin and heiress to a shipping fortune. Soon he and his wife retreated to his inherited Hudson River estate, named Mount Hope, where their only child, James Roosevelt (known as "Rosy"), was born.

James devoted much of his time to managing and investing his inherited wealth. He was also a good citizen of Dutchess County, serving on the Poughkeepsie school board and nearby mental health hospital, but demonstrated no enthusiasm for public service. He was happiest on his estate, living the life of a country squire and socializing exclusively with other members of the landed gentry.

In late autumn every year, James and Rebecca traveled in his private railroad car to Manhattan to take up residence in their town house on Washington Square. While in New York City, James attended board meetings of the Delaware & Hudson Railroad and the Consolidated Coal Company, the nation's largest bituminous coal company, and lunched at one of his private clubs. Every summer, the Roosevelts sailed to Europe to spend three months on the continent. In the summer of 1865, while the Roosevelts were touring the Swiss Alps, Mount Hope burned down. Rather than immediately returning to their destroyed home, James and Rebecca spent another year on the continent, visiting St. Moritz, Paris, and London.

When James finally got back to Mount Hope, he sold the estate and, with the proceeds of the sale, bought another tract of land two miles north in Hyde Park. He named the 110-acre estate Springwood, supervised repairs of the slightly decrepit seventeen-room mansion, cultivated the land, and expanded his holdings, which he eventually increased to 900 acres. He also bought a herd of fine dairy cattle, but was proudest of his stable of trotting horses, which he bred with great care and success. Known throughout the Hyde Park community as "Mr. James," he served as vestryman and senior warden at the town's St. James Episcopal Church.

In the national recession of 1873, James's investments plummeted, and so did his standing in the corporate community. He was dismissed as a director of the Consolidated Coal Company and resigned as president of the Southern Railway Security Company, the nation's first holding company, which controlled railroads across the southern United States. But he had never invested so much of his holdings as to jeopardize his solvency, or his comfort. Roiled by his business setbacks, James did what came naturally, retreating to his beloved Springwood.

James's personal life was shattered in 1876 when his wife, Rebecca, died at the age of forty-five of a massive heart attack. After an appropriate mourning period, James, then fifty-two, visited his Long Island cousins with the intention of courting twenty-two-year-old Anna ("Bamie") Roosevelt, Theodore Roosevelt's older sister. Bamie politely rejected his overtures. Her mother, Mittie, felt badly for her cousin and soon invited him to a dinner party where he could meet the young woman she had in mind to become James's second wife. She was Sara Delano, only twenty-six years old, but a woman with worldly experience who was extremely interested in marriage. James was immediately captivated by the regal, self-assured Sara, the daughter of Warren Delano, a hugely successful sea merchant who had become rich trading in the Far East.

The Delanos more than matched the Roosevelts in their American genealogy. Philippe de la Noye,* Sara's paternal ancestor, arrived at Plymouth in 1621, unsuccessfully courted Priscilla Mullins (who became the wife of John Alden), then married Hester Dewsbury in 1634. The couple raised a large family, including a son, Jonathan, who fought in King Philip's War and was rewarded for his bravery with a grant of 800 acres near New Bedford, Massachusetts. The Delanos joined other enterprising New Bedfordites in the seafaring trade, with each successive generation accumulating greater wealth than the last.

---

* The family name was variously recorded in colonial documents as De Lane, Delanow, and Delannoy.

Sara's grandfather, the first Warren Delano, commanded a merchant ship in his twenties, then established a clipper-ship trade with the Orient before retiring to the whaling industry in New Bedford. His son, Warren Delano II, Sara's father, was even more successful. Born in 1809, Warren sailed to China at the age of twenty-four and was hired by Russell, Sturgis & Company (later Russell & Co.), the largest American firm in the China tea-exporting trade. At thirty-one, he was named a senior partner, heading the firm's operations in Macao, Canton, and Hong Kong. In 1843, he returned to the United States, met and courted Catherine Robbins Lyman, the eighteen-year-old daughter of Judge and Mrs. Joseph Lyman of Northampton, Massachusetts. They were married and sailed to China so that Warren could resume his executive duties. Three years later, Warren, now a millionaire, resigned his position with Russell & Company to return to the United States. The Delanos settled in New York City, where Warren poured his prodigious energy into new business ventures, buying New York Harbor property, anthracite coal mines in Pennsylvania, and copper mines in Tennessee and Maryland, as well as clipper ships and paddle-steamers.

The couple purchased a fashionable five-story town house on Lafayette Place (one of nine Greek Revival dwellings there known as "Colonnade Row"), but decided that they preferred life in the country. In 1851, Warren bought a 60-acre fruit farm with a modest brick and stucco house overlooking the Hudson River near Newburgh, New York. He named it Algonac and, like James Roosevelt, whose Springwood estate was located on the opposite bank of the Hudson, eagerly proceeded to enhance the appearance and value of his newly purchased property. He hired the nation's premier landscape architect, Andrew Jackson Downing, to remodel and expand Algonac. When Downing was finished, the house had been transformed into an elegant mansion, with forty rooms that were furnished opulently with carved rosewood furniture, teakwood screens, fine porcelains, and Buddhist temple bells, reflecting the great good fortune that Warren had enjoyed in the Orient.

On September 21, 1854, Sarah, the seventh (and fifth surviving) child of Warren and Catherine Delano, was born at Algonac. She was named for her father's unmarried aunt who lived with the family; to distinguish the baby from her namesake, the "h" was dropped. Growing up with her brothers and sisters on the family's Hudson River estate, Sara (nicknamed Sallie) enjoyed an idyllic existence. She rode in the family sleigh on frosty winter days, climbed apple trees in the spring, and swam with her siblings in the summer.

Sara's father ruled Algonac. He limited visitors to family and friends, and closely supervised all of the children's activities. When one of the children complained about a rainy day, their father interrupted. "Nonsense," he said. "All weather is good weather." That was the end of the discussion.

In the summer of 1857, Warren Delano's fortune was decimated by a stock market crash. Facing financial ruin, he sold his Manhattan house and put Algonac on the market, but failed to receive a reasonable sale price. In 1860, at the age of fifty, he left his family at Algonac and sailed to China, where he proceeded to earn a second fortune trading in opium.

In 1862, Delano chartered the 183-foot clipper ship *Surprise* to transport his family to China. It was the adventure of a lifetime for seven-year-old Sara. During the four-month journey, which took the family around the Cape of Good Hope, Sara memorized the crew's sea chanties and joined the captain to celebrate their birthdays (her eighth, his twenty-eighth) with a feast of roast goose and two birthday cakes. When the family arrived at Rose Hill, Warren's magnificent estate in Hong Kong, they were treated like foreign royalty, with scores of Chinese servants catering to their every wish. Two years later, Sara and three of her siblings returned to Algonac to resume their education. But in 1866 they were reunited with other family members in Paris, where Warren had rented a spacious apartment on the Right Bank in time for the Paris Exposition. From Paris, the Delanos moved to comfortable quarters in Dresden. Sara studied music and German at a local school and later at a finishing school at Celle, north of Hannover. In 1870, on the eve of the Franco-Prussian War, Sara and her siblings returned to Algonac, where their father again oversaw their education, entertainment, and introduction to New York society.

Two years later, the eighteen-year-old Sara, with her dark, penetrating eyes and aristocratic bearing, had grown to her full height of five feet ten inches, and was referred to in fashionable New York City circles as one of "the beautiful Delano sisters." She was a constant guest, and enthusiastic dancer, at winter debutante parties, but over the next three years only one suitor, Stanford White, truly interested her. White was a passionate, talented, struggling twenty-three-year-old draftsman in the Boston firm of the famed architect Henry Hobson Richardson. He assiduously courted Sara, but to no avail. Her father dismissed White as "that red-headed trial," and sent his dutiful daughter to Europe for an extended tour.

In 1880, Sara was introduced to James Roosevelt, who, in age, heritage, and temperament, presented a stark contrast to White. Sara did not return James's romantic ardor, but nonetheless agreed to become his wife. He was kind, a member of a respectable family, and wealthy enough. Besides, she had watched her younger sisters marry and did not know how many more chances she would have to make a suitable match.

James and Sara were married at Algonac on October 7, 1880, in a modest ceremony attended by family and close friends. Afterward, the bride and groom were driven in the Delano carriage to approximately midway between Algonac and Springwood, where they transferred to the Roosevelt coach. With James at the reins, the couple completed their journey to Hyde Park.

After a life-threatening labor of twenty-six hours, Sara Delano Roosevelt gave birth to a ten-pound baby boy at Springwood on January 30, 1882. For almost two months after the birth, Sara and James Roosevelt engaged in a genteel tug-of-war over the baby's name. James wanted to name him Isaac, restoring the Roosevelt family tradition of naming the first male son after his paternal grandfather.* Sara, who rarely challenged her husband's authority, insisted that their son be named Warren, after her father. But in deference to the wishes of her brother, whose infant son named after their father had just died, Sara settled on the name of her favorite uncle, Franklin. And so, on March 20, 1883, at St. James' Episcopal Church in Hyde Park, Sara and James's son was christened Franklin Delano Roosevelt.

Sara was determined that her son would be sheltered from the harsh outside world, as she had been growing up at Algonac. Franklin was coddled by nursemaids and eagerly attended by the Roosevelts' large staff of servants. But primary responsibility for raising the boy would be hers. "Every mother ought to learn to care for her own baby," she said, "whether she can afford to delegate the task to someone or not." She breast-fed him for almost a year and recorded his daily triumphs in her diary ("Baby Franklin . . . crows and laughs all the time"). At her direction, his blond curls grew to shoulder length, and he wore dresses until he was five years old. She bathed him for the first eight years of his life and strictly super-

---

* In his first marriage, he had flouted family tradition by naming his son James.

vised his early education, hiring his tutors and summarily firing those who did not please her.

Franklin traveled widely as a boy, always in the company of his parents. The family regularly sailed to Europe on one of the White Star's premier ocean liners, usually the *Germania*. When Franklin was three, a violent storm almost caused the ship to capsize. Sara instinctively wrapped her son in her fur coat. "If he must go down he is going down warm," she said. For their summer European tours, the Roosevelts always traveled first class, staying in the finest London and Paris hotels and socializing with wealthy family, friends, and titled Europeans.

They also made frequent trips to Washington, D.C., where James pursued his business and political interests. A generous contributor to the Democratic Party, he and his family received invitations to visit President Grover Cleveland at the White House. On one visit, when Franklin was five, the beleaguered president expressed an unusual wish for his young visitor: "My little man, I am making a strange wish for you. It is that you may never be president of the United States."

Franklin's education for the first fourteen years of his life was managed by Sara and confined to private tutors at Springwood.* Sara also read to him every night, first from elaborately illustrated European children's books and later chapters from *Robinson Crusoe* and *The Swiss Family Robinson*. Her supervision did not mean that she gave her son a gentlemanly pass to skimp on his lessons. His tutors drilled him in arithmetic, history, and English literature, as well as Latin, French, and German. At the age of six, he wrote his mother a two-sentence letter in German script, promising that "I shall try always to improve it [his German], so that you will be really pleased." As this letter indicates, Sara's approval was important to Franklin throughout his childhood; indeed, for the remainder of her life.

Though he was an obedient son, Franklin found mischievous ways to evade his mother's lofty intentions. He regularly developed headaches on Saturdays in anticipation of Sunday church services. Incapacitating, mysterious pains in his hands often preceded his scheduled piano and drawing lessons.

Franklin became a voracious reader, taking in paragraphs at a glance, particularly naval histories and fictional thrillers about land and sea bat-

---

* With one exception: when he was nine, he was enrolled in a six-week summer class to improve his German at a Bad Nauheim public school.

tles, including Kipling's *Plain Tales from the Hills*. But his extensive reading did not make him an especially reflective or philosophical young man. He learned primarily by doing. After he inherited Sara's large stamp collection, he spent hundreds of hours filling albums with stamps from around the world, absorbing wide-ranging lessons of geography, history, and politics. In his walks around Springwood with his father, he became an avid student of the surrounding trees and, in time, could name every variety on the family estate. When Franklin was ten, James gave him a gun for hunting birds. Before long, he had acquired an impressive knowledge of ornithology and had stuffed and mounted a collection of birds that eventually included every species spotted at Springwood. After his family bought a four-acre lot and built a summer house on the tiny island of Campobello, off the coast of Maine, he became a passionate and expert sailor. First, he sailed on his father's 51-foot sailing yacht, the *Half Moon*. Later, he was given his own smaller knockabout, the *New Moon*, on which he spent countless hours navigating through the dangerous coastal waters.

Though he enjoyed every privilege, Franklin appeared outwardly unaffected by his pampered existence. He was shy as a small boy, often hiding behind his mother's skirts in company, even among the family's servants. His playmates were confined to wealthy neighbors and his cousins. He nonetheless enjoyed the small pleasures that transcended class: playing "London Brige," going to "Barnoms Circus," sailing (and sinking) a makeshift wooden raft on the Hudson. In his one public school experience at Bad Nauheim, he was not only a good student but also popular with his classmates.

Despite his extensive travels, Roosevelt always considered Springwood to be the center of his childhood universe. His doting parents deprived him of no pleasure that their considerable wealth could provide. More important, their unstinting love instilled in him a confidence and optimism about life's opportunities that would sustain him in his extraordinary career of public service. Although Sara imposed a strict daily regimen on her son, Franklin never seriously resisted her attention or demands. There was no need to rebel. As long as he attended to his lessons and other family obligations, he was free to pursue his own broad interests. All the while, he returned his parents' love and demonstrated his affection by making every effort to please them.

*   *   *

Franklin's gilded life came to an abrupt end in September 1896 when his parents took the boy in their private railroad car to deposit him at the redbrick dormitory on the campus of Groton, an Episcopal prep school located thirty-five miles northwest of Boston. The school was the inspiration of the Reverend Endicott Peabody, the thirty-nine-year-old rector, who had imported firm ideas of a proper education for wealthy, well-connected American teenage boys from his own experiences at an English public school, Cheltenham, and Cambridge, while his father served as a J. P. Morgan partner in London. Peabody believed, above all else, in building a young man's character, and he did so by imposing Spartan living conditions, twice-daily worship services, compulsory athletics, and a strict classical education.* For the 110 Groton students, Peabody served as an awesome authority figure—a powerfully built man, who stood over six feet tall, with broad shoulders, square jaw, and booming voice.

Like every other Grotonian, Roosevelt lived in a six- by ten-foot cubicle, furnished with a bed, plain bureau, chair, and a curtain (but no door). At six forty-five every weekday morning, Franklin and his classmates stumbled down the hall to the communal bathroom for a cold shower. Breakfast was served at 7:30 a.m., then chapel, morning classes, lunch, more classes, three hours of athletics, another cold shower, dinner (stiff collar and black pumps required), evening study, and prayer. At bedtime, each boy was bid goodnight with a handshake from the Reverend Peabody and his wife. The exhausting daily regimen reflected Peabody's philosophy: "The best thing for a boy is to work hard . . . to play hard . . . and then, when the end of the day has come, to be so tired that he wants to go to bed and go to sleep. That is the healthy and good way for a boy to live."

Since he entered Groton two years after the other boys his age, Franklin was immediately viewed by his peers as an outsider. It did not help that Taddy ("Rosy" Roosevelt's son) was a grade ahead of him and was generally considered an oddball (a curse among cliquish Grotonians). Inevitably, he was known as "Uncle Frank." His response was to try very hard to please those around him. He demonstrated an awkward agility in his first year when he was cornered by a group of upperclassmen who insisted that he dance for them—and prodded him with swipes of their hockey sticks at

---

* Peabody also preached the ideal of public service, a sermon that was largely ignored by Grotonian graduates who overwhelmingly migrated to the world of finance, business, and the professions.

his ankles. Franklin performed an impromptu dance, complete with wild pirouettes, affecting a manner of forced gaiety. His contrived grace under pressure apparently impressed his tormentors; they never picked on him again. Indeed, for the next four years, Franklin managed to avoid the two worst punishments meted out by older boys: "bootboxing" (cramming a underclassman into his locker and shutting the door) and "pumping" (a prep school form of waterboarding in which water was poured down the student's throat for about ten seconds, effecting the sensation of drowning).

Franklin also managed to avoid trouble in the classroom. If a boy accumulated too many black marks, he was called to the rector's office, a meeting dreaded by even the toughest senior. Roosevelt did not receive his first black mark until the spring of his freshman year (for talking in class) and was relieved. "I have served off my first black mark today, and I am very glad I got it, as I was thought to have no school-spirit before." He received a sufficient number of black marks to assure his classmates that he was a regular fellow but never so many that he risked punishment.

At five feet three inches and 105 pounds, Franklin failed dismally on the athletic fields. Every boy was assigned to football and baseball teams; his football team was ranked sixth out of eight and his baseball team, the "Bum Baseball Boys," was the worst at the school. He distinguished himself in only one contest, a peculiar high jump competition in which a saucer was hung from the gymnasium ceiling and each boy was asked to leap toward the saucer, feet first. Franklin won with a jump of 7 feet 3½ inches, landing so hard on his neck that he was sore for weeks.

Throughout his early, difficult days and for the next four years at Groton, Franklin maintained a relentlessly cheerful tone in his twice-a-week letters to his parents. "I am getting on finely, both mentally and physically," he wrote in his first letter. The upbeat reports never wavered. He vowed to win the punctuality prize, which he did three of his four years at the school. He also was awarded the Latin prize in his senior year (a forty-volume set of Shakespeare). His grades were very good, but not superb (fourth in his first-year class of seventeen and always in the top fifth). Peabody later described Roosevelt as "a quiet, satisfactory boy of more than ordinary intelligence." FDR could never be compared to his future adversary, Chief Justice Charles Evans Hughes, in sheer intellectual brilliance. But he had an extraordinary capacity to absorb vast amounts of information and an enthusiasm for testing himself in new circumstances.

If Groton was not the cushy world of Roosevelt's childhood, or even one that took full advantage of his talents, he nonetheless adjusted and made the most of the experience. He joined the choir and the debating team (arguing for an increased navy and against the annexation of Hawaii). He was thrilled when his cousin, Teddy, then the Assistant Secretary of the Navy, regaled his classmates with "killing stories about policemen and their doings" when he had served as president of the Board of Police Commissioners in New York City. And he volunteered to be the manager of the baseball team, hardly a prestigious position, but one that underscored his school spirit. When the Groton football team beat arch rival St. Mark's by a lopsided score, Franklin wrote his parents: "I am hoarse, deaf, and ready to stand on my coconut!"

Franklin's absence from Springwood left a terrible void in Sara's and James's lives. If one of his letters did not arrive on the appointed day, they called the school to assure themselves that he had not been injured or fallen ill. Each parceled out advice to their son. James applauded Franklin's debating efforts and suggested sources to support his positions. Sara's reassuring letters were more general in their encouragement, with a constantly expressed concern for his health. Like Mary Catherine Hughes, she was forever alert to any danger to her son. When Franklin contracted a case of scarlet fever in his senior year and developed inflamed kidneys, Sara and James immediately returned from Europe. When Sara arrived on campus, she was told that visitors were not allowed in the infirmary. Undaunted, she climbed a stepladder and sat outside Franklin's second-story window, reading to him daily during his convalescence.

In his senior year, Franklin became a dormitory prefect, mentoring underclassmen, a role that he embraced enthusiastically. He strolled confidently with his young charges across campus, offering advice and encouragement. He also joined the Groton Missionary Society, performing good works off campus, including trudging through winter snowdrifts to make certain that an elderly black woman who lived nearby had enough food and coal for her stove.

Although Roosevelt's four years at Groton were not outstanding in terms of academic or extracurricular achievement, he always looked back fondly on the experience. Eleanor Roosevelt later speculated that her husband's happy memories of prep school may have improved with hindsight. Whatever the accuracy of FDR's reminiscences, nothing detracted from his enduring view that Endicott Peabody was a model educator and moral leader. "More than forty years ago," he wrote Peabody in 1940, "you said, in a sermon in the Old Chapel, something about not losing boyhood ideals in later life. Those were Groton ideals—taught by you—and I try not to forget—and your words are still with me and with hundreds of others of 'us boys.' "

The words of another speaker at Groton may also have been filed away in his mind for future inspiration. "If a man has courage, goodness and brains," Theodore Roosevelt told Franklin's graduating class in 1900, "no limit can be placed to the greatness of the work he may accomplish—he is the man needed today in politics."

In many ways, Roosevelt's freshman year at Harvard was an extension of his years at Groton. He and his roommate, Lathrop Brown, adorned their suite of three rooms on Westmorly Court in the neighborhood known as the "Gold Coast" with Groton pennants, certificates, and photographs. They ate breakfast, lunch, and dinner with other Grotonians at a Cambridge eating house that, according to Roosevelt, was "great fun & most informal." And they spent many weekday evenings at Sanborn's billiard parlor on Massachusetts Avenue with other wealthy Groton, St. Mark's, and St. Paul's graduates.

Roosevelt attempted to improve upon his dismal athletic record at Groton, suiting up for Harvard's freshman football team and crew, but with only limited success. He was quickly relegated to one of the scrub football teams and to intramural crew. But he proudly reported to his parents that he had been elected captain of his football team and crew, as well as secretary of the freshman glee club, the first indication that he was not just one of the boys, but potentially a leader of men. With sixty-seven other freshmen, he competed for a position on the school newspaper, the *Harvard Crimson*, but failed in his first effort to make the staff. He vowed to try again in the spring. His membership in Harvard's Republican Club was a matter of family loyalty as well as political judgment since his distant cousin, Theodore, was running for vice president on the national party ticket with the presidential incumbent, William McKinley. A week before the November election, Franklin and his fellow Harvard Republicans donned red caps and gowns to march for the McKinley-Roosevelt ticket in a torchlight parade through the streets of downtown Boston. A few days later, the Republicans won a decisive electoral victory.

At times, it appeared that Roosevelt's classes were almost incidental to his Harvard experience. Like other Grotonians, he had completed the required university curriculum in his senior year at prep school, allowing him to choose among the broad range of electives that President Charles Eliot insisted was the core of a Harvard education. Franklin maintained a gentleman's C average; in his first semester, his grades ranged from a B in history to a D⁺ in Latin. He appeared singularly uninspired by the university's illustrious humanities faculty, which included William James, Josiah Royce, and George Santayana in the philosophy department, George Lyman Kittredge, the noted Shakespeare scholar, and A. Lawrence Lowell, the future university president, who taught a course on "The Science of Government." Franklin simply did not respond to abstract theory, no matter how brilliantly conceived and articulated. He compared courses in theory to an electric lamp that, for him, was not plugged into a socket. "You need the lamp for light," he wrote, "but it's useless if you can't switch it on."

In the fall of Roosevelt's freshman year, 1900, his father's chronic heart condition seriously deteriorated. After James suffered a mild heart attack in October, Sara wrote Franklin that she had made plans to rent a cottage in South Carolina for his recuperation. It did not help James's condition that the New York tabloids gleefully reported that Taddy Roosevelt, his grandson by his first marriage, had secretly married a dance hall habituée of dubious reputation, Sadie Meisinger (known as "Dutch Sadie"). Franklin, when told of the scandal, advised his parents that "[I]t will be well for him [Taddy] to go to parts unknown . . . and begin life anew." A month later, James suffered a second heart attack, and, on December 8, he died at the age of seventy-two.

Sara was devastated by James's death. "I wonder how I lived when he left me," she later wrote. Naturally, she sought the solace and companionship of her son. Following James's funeral at St. James' Church, Franklin stayed with his mother at Hyde Park until the new year. At his suggestion, they planned a summer cruise together along the Norwegian coast. After he returned to Harvard, he wrote his mother regular, chatty letters that rarely mentioned his father's death. And he resumed his frenetic schedule on campus, focusing his greatest energy (six hours a day) on being elected to the staff of the Crimson.

In late April 1901, he scored a journalistic coup, thanks to Cousin Teddy. Aware that TR was scheduled to visit Harvard, Franklin asked if he might meet with him. The vice president responded that he would be happy to meet after his lecture to Professor Lowell's government class.

Franklin immediately informed his *Crimson* editor of the vice president's unannounced lecture. In the next issue, the school newspaper ran a four-column headline announcing the time and location of the lecture. When TR arrived at the lecture hall, 2,000 students were milling outside, hoping to secure seats in the 500-seat auditorium. Professor Lowell was furious at the *Crimson*'s exclusive. But, of course, Franklin was elated.* He was rewarded in June when the newspaper announced that he was one of five students elected to its staff.

On their summer cruise, Franklin and Sara's ship anchored in a fjord next to Kaiser Wilhelm II's yacht. The Roosevelts were among a select group of vacationers invited aboard while the emperor was ashore, and Franklin later claimed that he had pilfered a lead pencil from the Kaiser's desk. After the cruise, they visited Dresden, Geneva, and Paris. At their hotel in Paris, they learned that President McKinley had been shot by a deranged anarchist, but newspapers reported that the president would recover. When they docked in New York in mid-September, however, McKinley had died. Cousin Teddy was now the president of the United States.

In his sophomore year at Harvard, Franklin took particular pride in his work on the *Crimson* and continued to put in long hours at the newspaper's office. He was chosen to represent the *Crimson* at the Yale bicentennial celebration and sat on the platform with President Roosevelt and another future commander in chief, Princeton's president Woodrow Wilson. Though he expressed little enthusiasm for his courses, he maintained a heavy academic schedule† and rarely skipped a class.

He was outraged by reported British atrocities against imprisoned Boer women and children in South Africa, and, with two classmates, established a Boer Relief Fund. After he was incorrectly identified by one

---

* FDR later circulated the story of another of his scoops for the *Crimson*. During the fall freshman competition, according to Roosevelt, he had knocked on the front door of President Eliot's house; after he was invited in, he asked Eliot whom he supported in the presidential election. Eliot, somewhat taken aback, nonetheless told the cub reporter that he intended to vote for McKinley and Roosevelt. The next day, the *Crimson* broke the news. The story was true except for one salient detail: the scoop was the work of another Harvard student, Albert De Roode, not FDR, a fact that Roosevelt only admitted in 1931 after a reporter pressed him for a copy of the interview with Eliot.

† He took courses in economics, early American history, U.S. constitutional and political history, English parliamentary history, paleontology, English composition, and public speaking.

Boston newspaper as TR's nephew, Franklin was hailed for sharing "many of the qualities that have put his uncle at the front. He is a hard worker, thoroughly democratic," which, the article concluded, assured the fund's success. Franklin cabled $336 that he had collected to victims in South Africa.

Franklin's letters to his mother rarely mentioned TR's actions, but he did criticize the president when he intervened to stop the strike of anthracite coal miners. "In spite of his success in settling the trouble, I think that the President made a serious mistake in interfering—politically, at least," he wrote. His concern that Cousin Teddy was overstepping his constitutional authority would later appear acutely ironic, given his own sweeping actions as president three decades afterward. "His [TR's] tendency to make the executive power stronger than the Houses of Congress is bound to be a bad thing," he wrote, "especially when a man of weaker personality succeeds him in office."

In January 1902, Franklin attended the most important social event of the year: the debut of Alice Roosevelt, the president's daughter. The party in the East Room of the White House, he reported, was "most glorious fun." He stayed for the weekend, attending a reception given by the Austrian ambassador and tea at the White House before returning to Cambridge.

Early in the spring semester, Franklin waited anxiously for an invitation to one of Harvard's "final" clubs. He wanted desperately to be invited to join Porcellian, the most prestigious club, whose alumni included both his father and Theodore Roosevelt. He failed to receive that coveted invitation, which he considered to be his greatest disappointment during his four years in Cambridge. All was not lost, however, since he was invited to join another final club, Alpha Delta Phi (the Fly Club), as well as the Hasty Pudding Club.

Franklin became the librarian for both the Fly Club and Hasty Pudding and could be seen browsing in secondhand bookshops on their behalf. As a result of his keen eye for quality, he built fine collections for his clubs as well as adding to his personal library. He particularly indulged his passion for naval history, selecting valuable books, manuscripts, and rare prints in the field.

Meanwhile, Sara, still handsome and physically vigorous at the age of forty-six, attempted to fill the void left by James's death. She supervised the multitude of daily tasks required on the Springwood estate, emulating her late husband in her attention to detail. But Franklin was never far from her mind. She dusted off his ornithology collection and eagerly awaited his next letter. Finally, in the winter of his sophomore year, she rented an apartment on Commonwealth Avenue in Boston to be "near enough to the University to be on hand should he want me and far enough removed not to interfere with his college life."

Outwardly, Franklin appeared delighted to have his mother nearby. He dined with her frequently and arranged to have parties for his friends in her apartment. But he kept his personal affairs to himself, including his amorous interests. As a teenager, he had not dated much and seemed satisfied to have his mother arrange his social calendar. Sara had made recommendations for his escorts to dances, often cousins or neighbors of her acquaintance. But his attitude toward girls, and his mother's arrangements on his behalf, changed during his years at Harvard. He was now a handsome young man of six feet one, with considerable charm—and he was related to the president. Though Franklin was circumspect in his diary, we know that he dated several young women. His first serious girlfriend was Alice Sohier, a beautiful seventeen-year-old Boston debutante. By the summer of 1902, Franklin was an avid suitor and may have proposed marriage. In October, Alice's concerned parents sent her to Europe for a long vacation.

Within months of Alice's departure, Franklin had begun to court his fifth cousin, nineteen-year-old Anna Eleanor Roosevelt, President Theodore Roosevelt's favorite niece. She was not a natural beauty like Alice, but she was an attractive, shapely young woman, with clear blue eyes and soft, thick brown hair. Though Franklin and Eleanor shared a family name and grew up in material comfort, their backgrounds were otherwise very different. He had been raised in isolated splendor, the object of his parents' constant affections. Hers had been a sad childhood. Her adored father, Elliott, was absent for long periods, suffering from alcoholism that led to inconsolable despair. Her mother, Anna Hall Roosevelt, was a beautiful, intensely religious woman who was strict and disapproving of Eleanor. Both of Eleanor's parents died when she was a child.

At the age of nine, the orphaned Eleanor was sent to live with her maternal Grandmother Hall at Tivoli, New York, on the Hudson River north of Hyde Park. Eleanor's grandmother proved to be even stricter than her mother. And like her mother, her grandmother made Eleanor feel unattractive and not especially loved. Only when she was sent abroad at the age of fifteen to Allenswood, a girls' boarding school outside London, did Eleanor begin to feel that she was special. That message was sent to her daily by the headmistress, Mademoiselle Marie Souvestre, a stout, white-haired Frenchwoman who read poetry and the tragedies of Racine to the girls. She also taught them to challenge conventional ideas, proudly defending her atheism and expounding on her liberal political views (she supported the Boers against the British). Eleanor quickly became Mlle Souvestre's favorite student, excelling in her classes, sitting next to her at dinner, and accompanying her on trips to the continent. After three years at Mlle Souvestre's school, Eleanor returned to the United States a young woman of quiet charm and broad, cultivated interests.

Franklin found her to be shy, serious, intellectually alert, and a good listener—all qualities that were attractive to him. He was accustomed to socializing with relatives, and Eleanor presented a particularly compelling case for choosing a mate within the family. Her late father, Eliott, had been Franklin's godfather, and, of course, her Uncle Teddy was Franklin's idol and role model.

Though Eleanor and Franklin had met occasionally at family gatherings, Franklin's serious interest in Eleanor began in the spring of 1902, after he had joined her on a train headed up the Hudson. He became her frequent escort to parties in Boston, New York, and Hyde Park; in September 1903, he invited Eleanor, accompanied by her maid as chaperone, for a five-day visit to Campobello. She sailed with him on the family yacht, the *Half Moon*, which Franklin expertly piloted around the island. They went on picnics, read aloud to each other, and attended Sunday church services. Later that fall, Franklin proposed marriage, and Eleanor accepted. All that remained was to inform his mother, who was completely unaware of the seriousness of the relationship.

Sara was not pleased. Responding to his mother's cool reception to his surprising news, Franklin wrote her a delicately phrased letter, expressing his love for her—and his resolve to marry Eleanor: "Dearest Mama—I know what pain I must have caused you and you know I wouldn't do it if I really could help it! . . . I know my own mind, have known it for a long time, and know that I could never think otherwise: Result: I am the happiest man just now in the world; likewise the luckiest—And for you, dear Mummy, you know that nothing can ever change what we have always been & always will be to each other—only now you have two children to love & to love you. . . ."

Sara pleaded with Franklin to postpone the formal announcement of his engagement, reminding him that he was only twenty-two years old, more than a decade younger than her father when he had proposed marriage. And when Warren Delano had asked for Catherine Lyman's hand—Sara pointed out—he was "a man who had made a name and place for himself, who had something to offer a woman." Reluctantly, Franklin acquiesced and agreed to join his mother and his roommate, Lathrop Brown, on a six-week Caribbean cruise that winter. He climbed San Juan Hill in Cuba, the scene of his Cousin Teddy's military exploits six years earlier, and heard Enrico Caruso sing *Pagliacci* in Caracas. But when he returned to the United States, his love for Eleanor was as strong as ever. By the spring of 1904, Sara had accepted the inevitable, and Franklin and Eleanor made plans to announce their engagement in the fall.

Although he had satisfied the requirements for his undergraduate degree in three years, Franklin chose to return to Harvard for his senior year so that he could serve as president of the *Crimson*. His election to the top editorial position was the culmination of three years of hard work, and he intended to make the most of it. He had taken a thick batch of past *Crimson* editorials to study on a European cruise during the summer of 1903.

Once in charge, however, Roosevelt's editorials were not noticeably different in subject matter or style from his predecessor. His primary concern appeared to be the sagging fortunes of the football team. He also scolded Harvard students for their lackluster performance in cheering the team and even tried to teach by example, exhorting the crowd in the Brown-Harvard game, though he "felt like a D . . . F . . . waiving [sic] my arms & legs before several thousand amused spectators!" He urged his readers "to be always active," taking advantage of all that Harvard had to offer, whether athletics, campus publications, religious or philanthropic work. One activity he conspicuously omitted from his list: classes. At the *Crimson*, Franklin demonstrated impressive qualities of leadership, managing the staff with "frictionless" efficiency, according to one colleague, and working well with notoriously crusty printers to meet deadlines.

During his senior year, Franklin enrolled in a master's program and signed up for courses in economics and history. But he admitted that he was "quite indifferent" about earning the degree and was satisfied to post mediocre grades. He was not disturbed when he missed six weeks of classes while he, his mother, and Lathrop Brown cruised in the Caribbean. Besides his work for the *Crimson*, his greatest energy was expended on being elected to a class office. He failed to win the nomination for class marshal but was chosen to be permanent chairman of his class committee. The election entitled him to sit on stage during the class day exercises with his two greatest admirers, Eleanor and Sara, in the audience.

Overall, Franklin could point to an impressive array of extracurricular activities at Harvard and considerable achievement, especially his rise through the editorial ranks of the *Crimson*. But his focus was essentially campus-bound and provincial. He later admitted that his Harvard years did not mold his political philosophy or prepare him for his public career. His extraordinary political talents remained largely untapped.

Franklin chose to enroll at Columbia Law School, rather than Harvard, in the fall of 1904, so that he could be near Eleanor. But he demonstrated no greater interest in his law school courses than in the undergraduate curriculum at Harvard. The lectures, like many of his Harvard classes, were highly theoretical and, to Franklin, uninspiring. Most of his grades ranged from B to D, but he flunked courses in contracts and civil procedure and was forced to retake the exams, which he passed.

He was hardly dismayed by his poor law school performance. His enthusiasm for life outside the classroom continued at its usual buoyant level. He had drinks and dinner with friends and relatives in the city, spent weekends at Hyde Park, and, most of all, enjoyed the company and love of Eleanor. He cast his first vote in a presidential election for Eleanor's Uncle Ted in November 1904. After TR's victory, Eleanor and Franklin were treated as honored guests in the nation's capital. At the inauguration, the couple sat on the Capitol steps, immediately behind the president and his family. Afterward, they had lunch at the White House, watched the parade with other VIPs, and danced together at the inaugural ball.

To accommodate the president's schedule, Franklin and Eleanor set the date of March 17, 1905, for their marriage. After TR reviewed the city's St. Patrick's Day Parade, he went directly to the adjoining homes of Eleanor's cousin, Susie Parish, and her mother, on East 76th Street for the ceremony. At Franklin's request, the Reverend Endicott Peabody presided, and Lathrop Brown stood beside the groom as his best man. Eleanor, wearing an elegant long white satin gown, was escorted down the stairs from the second floor by her Uncle Theodore. When the Reverend Peabody asked: "Who giveth this woman to be married to this man?" the president of the United States replied emphatically: "I do."

After the wedding, Franklin and Eleanor spent a relaxing week at Hyde Park, postponing their official honeymoon until the summer. In June, after Franklin had completed his first year's exams at Columbia, the couple sailed on the *Oceanic* to England. Franklin rejoiced in the fresh sea air while Eleanor, chronically prone to seasickness, did her best not to spoil the experience for her new husband. Once their ship had docked, the couple embarked on a three-month grand tour of the continent, staying in the finest hotels, eating sumptuous meals, touring museums and cathedrals, and enjoying breathtaking visits to the Austrian and Italian Alps. And they shopped and shopped. At an old printshop in Paris, they purchased a few Rembrandt engravings "and a cunning little original sketch by Claude Lorraine." In Venice, Franklin rummaged through an old bookstore "and got covered with dust and germs and secured one or two bargains." They also bought themselves clothes for every occasion, including a long sable coat for Eleanor and a silver fox overcoat for Franklin.

Occasionally, Franklin indulged his insatiable appetite for a good time or adventure alone. One evening at their hotel in Travoi, Franklin "danced with Mme. Menardi [the proprietress] and talked to the cook and smoked with a porter and had the time of my life." In Cortina, he arose "at the UnChristian hour of 7," so that he could join a young woman named Kitty Gandy for a day of mountain climbing in the Dolomites. Many years later, Eleanor, who did not share her husband's love of trekking, admitted that she was intensely jealous of Miss Gandy and relieved when she and Franklin left the hotel.

Both of them wrote collaborative letters to Sara during their honeymoon. Eleanor's correspondence revealed her eagerness to please her new mother-in-law. In thanking Sara for the treats she had sent to their cabin on the *Oceanic*, Eleanor gushed, "You are always just the sweetest, dearest Mama to your children and I shall look forward to our next long evening together, when I shall want to be kissed all the time!" For his part, Franklin often engaged in good-natured teasing of his mother, gleefully boasting of extravagant purchases of clothes and champagne. Their letters to Sara foreshadowed the complicated triangulated relationship that would soon undermine the marriage.

Upon their return to New York, Sara refused to leave the couple alone. She rented the newlyweds' first apartment three blocks from her own, furnished and redecorated it, and hired their servants. Two years later, she bought land on East 65th Street for the construction of two adjoining five-story residences, with sliding doors on each level that would allow Sara to drop in on the couple at her pleasure. Franklin and Sara supervised the plans; Eleanor was left out of the discussions. She finally protested. "When my bewildered young husband asked me what on earth was the matter with me," she recalled, "I said I did not like to live in a house which was not in any way mine, one that I had done nothing about and which did not represent the way I wanted to live." By then it was too late. Franklin told her to pull herself together, and he moved on. His reaction presaged his attitude of good-humored indifference to Eleanor's struggle to maintain her independence from Sara. The pattern continued after Eleanor gave birth to the first of six children,* Anna Eleanor, in May 1906. At first, Sara hired the children's nurses; and even after Eleanor took over, Sara subverted her authority by giving them expensive gifts in defiance of their mother's wishes.

Meanwhile, Franklin forged ahead, rather unenthusiastically, toward a career in the law. He passed the bar without completing his law studies. Many years later, Columbia's president, Nicholas Murray Butler, chided FDR for failing to earn his law degree. "You will never be able to call yourself an intellectual until you come back to Columbia and pass your law exams," Butler told him. Roosevelt replied in a similar jocular vein, "That just shows how unimportant the law really is."

For three years, beginning in 1907, Roosevelt practiced law with the Wall Street law firm of Carter, Ledyard, & Milburn, whose clients included some of the nation's most powerful corporations (e.g., Standard Oil, American Tobacco). If he was concerned that his firm was often engaged in defending its clients against TR's trust-busting policies, it was not recorded. As a lowly clerk, his work was far removed from his firm's prolonged antitrust battles with the federal government. His responsibilities were usually limited to keeping a docket of the firm's cases, filing court papers, and answering calendar calls. The day-to-day practice, though very different

---

* A second child, James, was born in 1907, and two years later, Franklin Junior, who died at the age of eight months from complications of influenza. Later, Eleanor gave birth to Elliott, the second Franklin Junior, and John Roosevelt.

from the theory taught in his law school classes, did not prove much more stimulating.

Franklin knew then that he would not make a career of the law, according to one of his fellow clerks, Grenville Clark. He intended to run for political office at the first opportunity, he told Clark and other young clerks, and thought that he had "a real chance to be President." He described his road to the White House, as it turned out, with uncanny accuracy. He would first be elected to the state legislature, then serve as Assistant Secretary of the Navy, governor of New York and, finally, president. Not surprisingly, his proposed political trajectory closely approximated that of President Theodore Roosevelt. "I do not recall that even then, in 1907, any of us deprecated his ambition or even smiled at it as we might perhaps have done," Clark said. "It seemed proper and sincere; and moreover, as he put it, entirely reasonable."

At his law firm, Franklin became the managing clerk in charge of municipal cases, defending clients such as the American Express Company against minor claims. For the first time, he matched wits with other, sometimes unscrupulous lawyers and relished the challenge. And he learned firsthand some of the problems of those less fortunate than himself. But his astonishing rapport with the lower and middle classes would develop later, beginning in 1910, after he seized his first opportunity to run for statewide political office.

John Mack, the district attorney of Dutchess County, came to Franklin's Wall Street law office in the fall of 1910 ostensibly to obtain the young lawyer's signature on some legal papers for the Roosevelt family. Once the formalities were completed, Mack asked if Franklin might be interested in running for the seat in the state assembly that represented Hyde Park. Though Democrats were a rare specie in rural Dutchess County, Mack was confident that Roosevelt, a Democrat, could win. The Roosevelts were a highly respected family in the county, and both Franklin's father and grandfather had been active in the local Democratic Party. Moreover, the two most popular politicians in the district, District Attorney Mack and Poughkeepsie mayor John Sague, were Democrats who counted on the support of the city's solidly Democratic Irish and Italian wards.

Mack told Roosevelt that Lewis Chanler, the Democrat who held the assembly seat under discussion, was not expected to seek reelection. It was widely assumed that Chanler, who had campaigned successfully for lieutenant governor in 1906 and unsuccessfully for governor in 1908, would retire from his lowly assembly seat. Would Franklin be interested in that seat? Yes, he replied enthusiastically. But before he could think seriously about his campaign, he received the deflating news that Chanler had reconsidered and would, indeed, stand for reelection.

By this time, Franklin had made the decision to begin a career in politics. The problem was that the only elective office open to him at the time, a seat in the State Senate representing Columbia, Dutchess, and Putnam counties, had been held by a Democrat only once since the Republican Party emerged in 1856. The current Republican occupant, John Schlosser, was a respected lawyer and popular representative who had carried the district by a margin of two to one over his Democratic opponent in 1908. Mack told Franklin that his chances of defeating Schlosser were no better than one in five.

Before coming to a final decision, Franklin discreetly inquired, through Theodore Roosevelt's sister, Bamie, whether the former president[*] planned to campaign for Republican candidates in the district. If he did, and made a disparaging remark about his distant cousin, Franklin's chances for election would be destroyed. Franklin should run, TR replied, though he wished he would do so as a Republican.

All that remained was for Franklin to receive the blessing of the Dutchess County Democratic chairman, Edward Perkins. This was no easy task since Perkins, a hard-bitten veteran with close ties to New York City's Tammany machine, viewed Franklin as an aristocratic dilettante who had no serious business running for office. Perkins's distaste for Roosevelt was captured by this story: Franklin arrived at a Democratic Party meeting three days before the nominating convention wearing riding breeches and boots. Perkins told him to go home and put on some regular pants. Reluctantly, Perkins acquiesced in Franklin's candidacy, in part, no doubt, because the Roosevelt family could be expected to foot a large part of the campaign bill.

On October 6, 1910, Franklin accepted his party's nomination for state senator and promised a vigorous month-long campaign against the Republican incumbent. He spoke in lofty platitudes, pledging to follow in his father's footsteps in fighting for corruption-free government. To underscore

---

[*] Roosevelt's chosen successor, William Howard Taft, had been elected president in 1908.

his promise of an aggressive campaign, Franklin took the fight to Senator Schlosser in his hometown of Fishkill Landing. He charged that Schlosser had aided the party bosses in Albany in thwarting Governor Charles Evans Hughes's reform agenda. Did Roosevelt support the reform measures of the Republican governor? he was asked. "You bet I do," Roosevelt replied. "I think he's one of the best governors the state has ever had." And if Hughes hadn't been opposed by reactionaries in his own party like Senator Schlosser, he added, he would have accomplished even more.*

Roosevelt made the critical decision to hire Harry Hawkey, a piano tuner, and his bright red Maxwell touring car at $20 a day. The Maxwell, bedecked with American flags, chugged along at 22 miles an hour, which enabled Roosevelt to cover virtually every inhabited rural acre of the district.† Averaging more than ten speeches a day, FDR stopped wherever he spotted a farmer—at every hay wagon, dairy farm, and grange hall—to make his pitch. His speeches were not especially memorable, but his delight in shaking hands was unforgettable. Smiling broadly, he approached each potential voter as a friend, and only later asked for his vote.

He never missed an opportunity to remind voters that he was related to TR. The words "deelighted" and "bully" entered his vocabulary. "I'm not Teddy," he told one crowd. "A little shaver said to me the other day that he knew I wasn't Teddy—I asked him why, and he replied: 'Because you don't show your teeth.' " Both FDR and his audience roared with pleasure.

He also aligned himself with the progressive policies of his illustrious distant cousin—and against the entrenched bosses. He took special aim at Lou Payn, who was a Republican committee chairman from Chatham in Columbia County and well known to be a loyal lieutenant to William Barnes, Jr., the state Republican Party's most powerful boss—and an old TR nemesis. Lumping Payn and his opponent, Schlosser, together, Franklin accused them of being out of touch with ordinary voters. "Whether it is that [Schlosser] has represented the Sage of Chatham [Payn] by long distance 'phone, or whether it is that he has represented nobody at all except himself I don't know," he declared. "I do know that he hasn't represented me and I do know that he hasn't represented you."

---

* Hughes had, by then, resigned as governor to accept his appointment to the U.S. Supreme Court.

† Roosevelt did not campaign in the city of Poughkeepsie, confident that he could count on its traditionally Democratic majority.

On election night, Franklin and his family awaited the returns at Springwood, with Sara carefully tabulating the votes from each precinct on her personal stationery. By late evening, it was clear that Franklin had won a decisive victory in an overwhelmingly Democratic election year. He defeated Schlosser by 1,140 votes, winning the rural areas and Poughkeepsie by margins far exceeding those of the newly elected Democratic governor, John Dix. At the age of twenty-eight, his career in politics was launched.

On January 1, 1911, Franklin, Eleanor, their three children (Anna, James, and Elliott), and a large staff of nurses and servants moved into a three-story brownstone at 248 State Street, just a short walk to Albany's Capitol. Franklin had rented the large house for four months at $400 a month, more than his annual salary as a state senator. Unlike most of his fellow legislators, who needed to return to jobs in their home districts when the legislature was not in session, Franklin intended to make the Senate his full-time occupation—and wanted everyone in Albany to know it.

Within weeks, he was embroiled in a political donnybrook that pitted Franklin and a small band of insurgents against the powerful downstate Democrats, led by Charles Murphy, the shrewd boss of Tammany Hall.* The issue was the selection of the next U.S. senator from New York. Although there had been increasing calls by reformers of both parties for the direct election of senators (including a failed proposal by former Governor Hughes), the process in New York still required that the selection be made by the state legislature. The term of Republican senator Chauncey Depew was due to expire in March. With Democrats in the majority of both the state assembly and the Senate, it was a foregone conclusion that the next senator would be a Democrat. Tammany's Murphy endorsed William ("Blue-eyed Billy") Sheehan, a utilities magnate and major contributor to the Democratic Party. Franklin promptly announced his opposition to Sheehan, vowing to fight "against the boss rule system." His choice was Edward Shepard, who, like Sheehan, had strong ties to major corporations (he was counsel to the Pennsylvania Railroad). But Shepard, un-

---

* Five years earlier, Murphy had been attacked by another reform politician, Charles Evans Hughes, who had linked him to his 1906 gubernatorial opponent, William Randolph Hearst, in Hughes's campaign against boss rule.

like Sheehan, had long been an advocate for clean government in New York City and, crucially for Franklin, was not the handpicked candidate of Tammany.

Murphy controlled enough Democrats in the legislature to guarantee Sheehan's selection, so long as all Democrats in the Assembly and Senate showed up for the party's caucus in which all were bound by the majority's vote. But Franklin and his cohorts refused to participate in the caucus, effectively blocking Sheehan's nomination. Though Franklin had not been the originator of the rebellion against Tammany, he quickly became the rebels' leader. They met twice daily in Roosevelt's library, leaving in the late evening after Eleanor had served crackers, cheese, and beer.

When not huddling with his anti-Sheehan compatriots, Franklin courted the press and always, it seemed, was good for a printable quote. "There is nothing I love as much as a good fight," he told *The New York Times*. "I never had as much fun in my life as I am having right now." Overnight, Roosevelt and his rebellious colleagues had become the center of attention. "Never in the history of Albany have 21 men threatened such total ruin of machine plans," reported Louis Howe for the *New York Herald*. Franklin, more than anyone else, enjoyed the adulation of the press. One newspaperwoman rapturously observed that "with a well set up figure he is physically fit to command. His face is a bit long but the features are well modeled, the nose is Grecian in its contour, and there is the glow of country health in his cheeks."

While reporters were enamored with Franklin's dash and loquacity, veteran lawmakers in Albany held a contrary view. Al Smith, the Democratic leader of the state assembly, wrote him off as a "damned fool." An impatient Robert F. Wagner, the Democratic leader of the Senate, exhorted Roosevelt to finish one headline-grabbing oration so that the legislative body could move forward with its serious business.

Whatever their private views of Roosevelt, the major players in the drama—Murphy and Sheehan—eventually made appointments to meet with him. On January 30, 1911, Roosevelt's twenty-ninth birthday, Murphy conferred with the young legislator. After exchanging pleasantries, Murphy said, "I know I can't make you change your mind unless you want to change it. Is there any chance of you and the other twenty men coming around to vote for Sheehan?" Roosevelt's answer was a polite but firm no. At Murphy's suggestion, Roosevelt invited Sheehan to lunch at his home to tell him why he opposed his nomination. Afterwards, FDR reiterated his opposition for reporters. "Mr. Sheehan is delightful personally, but that is one thing, the senatorship fight is another."

Sheehan fought back furiously, accusing Roosevelt of anti-Catholic bigotry, a charge supported by the Catholic bishop of Syracuse. But Sheehan's candidacy was doomed, and no one knew that better than Charles Murphy. Quietly, Murphy began to explore alternatives to Sheehan and, at the same time, put indirect pressure on the renegades less affluent than Roosevelt. Suddenly, local banks called in loans of recalcitrant legislators, merchants withdrew their support, and legislative leaders shelved their pet projects. By late March, Murphy had transferred his support to a state trial judge, James Aloyius O'Gorman, a former grand sachem of Tammany. Despite his close affiliation with Tammany, O'Gorman had built a reputation for honesty and competence on the bench. The combination of pressure on the renegades and Murphy's endorsement of a more appealing candidate than Sheehan assured O'Gorman's senatorial nomination.

When Roosevelt entered the legislative chamber for the vote, he was greeted by derisive chants of "Tam-ma-nee, Tam-ma-nee/ Franklin D., like Uncle 'The,' Is no match for Tam-ma-nee." To a chorus of hisses and groans, he announced that he and his associates had done their duty and, as a result, "the Democratic Party has taken an upward step." He then cast his vote for O'Gorman.

When he returned to his district, Roosevelt realized, to his surprise and delight, that his futile stand against Tammany had resonated with his rural constituents. And his celebrity extended far beyond Columbia, Dutchess, and Putnam counties. In assuming the mantle of reformer, he was linked to the newly elected governor of New Jersey, Woodrow Wilson, who had similarly attacked boss rule in his state. Even more flattering, he was compared to Cousin Teddy who, as a first-term New York assemblyman a generation earlier, had forced an investigation of a scandal that reached the highest echelons of New York City's financial world as well as the state judiciary. Like young TR, Franklin was a fighter, noted the *Cleveland Plain-Dealer*: "A known fighter is always well on the road to being taken for a popular hero. Franklin D. Roosevelt is beginning his public career fully as auspiciously. . . . If none of the colonel's sons turn out to be fit objects for popular adoration may it not be possible that this rising star may continue the Roosevelt dynasty?"

A few weeks after the O'Gorman nomination, Franklin introduced a resolution endorsing an amendment to the U.S. Constitution providing for the direct election of U.S. senators. The resolution easily passed, as did a similar measure in the assembly. Two years later, the proposal, ratified by thirty-six states, became the Seventeenth Amendment to the Constitution.

Roosevelt's proposed reforms consistently reflected the interests of his rural constituents. As chairman of the Senate's Forest, Fish, and Game Committee, he tried unsuccessfully to pass a comprehensive conservation measure that would have protected both public and private forests from destruction by timber companies. His commitment to the environment was a hallmark of his agrarian progressivism; it was also a product of his lifelong concern for the protection of the natural environment. The same could not be said for his public Puritanism. Though personally enjoying liquor, he publicly favored Prohibition. He also reflected the values of the voters in his district in opposing legalized horse racing, legalized boxing, and Sunday baseball.

At first, Roosevelt withheld support for social and economic reforms that primarily benefitted the state's urban voters. He did not initially support a bill limiting work to fifty-four hours a week for boys ages sixteen to twenty-one and insisted on consulting his constituents before taking a position on women's suffrage. He was not involved in the legislature's investigation of the tragic fire at the Triangle shirtwaist factory on March 25, 1911, that swept the top three floors of the supposedly fireproof building on Washington Place in New York City, killing 148 people (mostly young women between the ages of sixteen and thirty-five). Nor did he have a significant role in the factory safety reform legislation that followed. He always appeared too busy to listen to Frances Perkins, the young lobbyist for the Consumer League, who wanted to win his endorsement for a broad range of reforms concerning the wages, hours, and working conditions of women. She recalled his annoying habit of "throwing his head back" and "looking down his nose." He was an arrogant young man, she concluded, who "really didn't like people very much."

Emboldened by the rave reviews for his fight against Tammany, Roosevelt pledged to continue the battle until boss rule had been eliminated "root and branch."* But away from the limelight, Franklin showed a willingness to work with Tammany and downstate Democratic legislators,

---

* Roosevelt's version of his fight with Tammany improved over the years. In 1928, he reminisced with an old acquaintance: "Do you remember the old Sheehan fight of 1911?

voting to shift patronage jobs from Republicans to Democrats. He finally supported the fifty-four-hour workweek for boys and later recommended a women's suffrage amendment. And he became a vigorous advocate for improved safety conditions in Adirondack iron mines. Overall, he compiled an admirably progressive voting record that transcended the narrow interests of his rural constituents.

His first term in the Senate also served as an important learning experience. Aside from his talent for making headlines, he began to understand the essential ingredients for translating reform ideas into tangible legislation. In a speech that he delivered on March 3, 1912, in Troy, New York, Roosevelt outlined his basic political philosophy, which required a substantial government role in working for the common good: "Every new star that people have hitched their wagon to for the past half century, whether it be anti-rebating, or anti-trusts, or new fashioned education, or conservation of our natural resources or State regulation of common carriers, or commission government . . . [is a step] in the evolution of the new theory of the liberty of the community."

After his election in 1910, Governor Woodrow Wilson of New Jersey shook the legislature in Trenton out of its lethargy, transforming the state from one of the nation's most backward to a model of progressive government. New legislation provided for a direct primary election, workmen's compensation, corrupt practices regulations, and a public utilities commission with rate-setting authority. With his progressive record firmly established, Wilson instantly became a leading candidate for the Democratic nomination for president in 1912. Aspiring Democratic reform politicians, including New York State senator Franklin D. Roosevelt, rushed to Trenton to meet the governor.

At Roosevelt's first meeting with Wilson at the governor's mansion in the fall of 1911, Wilson asked the young state senator to assess Wilson's chances of winning the New York delegation's votes at the party convention, scheduled for the following June. Not good, Roosevelt candidly replied. Although he estimated that Wilson had the backing of thirty New York delegates, their support would come to naught since the ninety-

---

When the final Murphy surrender came, the flag of truce was brought to me by Assemblyman Alfred E. Smith, Assemblyman Jim Foley and State Senator Bob Wagner."

member delegation was bound by majority rule. And Tammany boss Charles Murphy, no friend of New Jersey's reform governor, controlled the votes of a majority of the delegates. Roosevelt and Wilson continued their conversation when Franklin accompanied the governor and his personal secretary, Joseph Tumulty, by train to Wilson's home in Princeton. Despite the long odds against success, Roosevelt pledged to rally New York's upstate reform Democrats around Wilson's candidacy in another challenge to Tammany's rule.

Franklin was now a committed Wilson man, though his first political hero, Cousin Teddy, was already planning to challenge the incumbent, President William Howard Taft, for the Republican nomination. By the fall of 1911, whatever goodwill had existed between TR and his chosen successor, President Taft, had disintegrated into a crossfire of bitter and personal recriminations. Even with a string of primary victories in 1912, TR had no chance of winning the Republican nomination, since the overwhelming number of delegates at the convention in Chicago belonged to the party's old guard and were pledged to Taft. After the president was nominated for a second term, TR declared himself to be as fit as a "bull moose," and ready to lead a third-party crusade against the stand-pat Taft administration. Stunned, the phlegmatic Taft vowed to meet the challenge. "I don't want to fight," he said, "but even a rat in a corner will fight."

Years later, Franklin compared the political skills of Theodore Roosevelt to Wilson's. TR "succeeded in stirring people to enthusiasm over specific individual events," he said, but lacked Wilson's "appeal to the fundamental and failed to stir, as Wilson did, the truly profound moral and social convictions." In temperament, Franklin was much closer to his ebullient cousin than to the dour, moralistic Wilson. But Wilson, like Roosevelt's father, and the Reverend Peabody, preached a stern Protestant ethic that appealed to Franklin. While he continued to admire TR, he irrevocably cast his political lot with Wilson and the reform wing of the Democratic Party.

The split between Taft and TR virtually guaranteed a Democratic victory in November 1912. The scramble for delegates among the Democratic presidential aspirants therefore took on an exhilarating urgency in the months preceding the party's convention in Baltimore. Committed as he was to Wilson's candidacy, Roosevelt's efforts were futile. Tammany's control of the state delegation was never in serious doubt, and, in the process, Roosevelt suffered two public humiliations. In April, he had invited upstate

New York reform Democrats to a dinner at the Belmont Hotel the night before the opening of the Democratic State Convention in New York City; out of twenty who responded, seventeen sent their regrets. Shortly before the national convention, Roosevelt was reminded of his low standing with state party regulars when he failed to be named a delegate or alternate in the New York delegation.

If Roosevelt was discouraged, he did not show it. With two other couples, he and Eleanor rented a house in Baltimore for the convention, and Franklin proceeded to plot his next move on Wilson's behalf. From the convention's gallery, Franklin and 150 other New York supporters of Wilson boisterously shouted their candidate's name to the delegates below. Roosevelt also managed to sneak his troops onto the convention floor where they paraded with Wilson banners before a nonplused New York delegation.

House Speaker Champ Clark of Missouri led in the early balloting but was far short of the required two-thirds vote to win the nomination. Charles Murphy had kept the New York delegation pledged to conservative Governor Judson Harmon of Ohio in the early voting. After the tenth ballot, Murphy made his move to become the convention's kingmaker. He instructed the New York delegation to shift their votes from Harmon to Clark, giving Clark a majority of 11 votes. But other delegations did not rush to Clark, and Wilson remained very much in contention. The first break came on the fourteenth ballot when William Jennings Bryan, the party's previous presidential nominee, announced that his Nebraska delegation, earlier pledged to Clark, would switch to Wilson. In abandoning Clark, Bryan declared that he could not vote for any man "willing . . . to accept the high honor of the Presidential nomination at the hands of Mr. Murphy." Slowly, the drumbeat of support for Wilson grew louder. Finally, on the forty-sixth ballot, Wilson, with 990 votes, won the nomination.

Franklin was euphoric. ALL MY PLANS VAGUE SPLENDID TRIUMPH, he wired Eleanor, who had left Baltimore and gone to Campobello.

Roosevelt's plans for reelection to the State Senate were complicated by the presidential race. He not only had to contend with a Republican opponent but also a reform candidate running under the banner of Teddy Roosevelt's Progressive Party. He had problems, moreover, within his own party. In a reconnaissance trip through his district in the summer, he discovered that Tammany allies were working to deny him his party's nomination. He suspected that Ed Perkins, the Dutchess County Democratic committee chairman with close ties to Tammany, was behind the dump-Roosevelt movement. But Roosevelt, buoyed by his continued popularity with his rural constituents, took defiant notice of his problem: "Perkins has no spine," Roosevelt said, "but he knows now that if he listens to orders from 14th Street [Tammany headquarters] he will have a perfectly delightful little fight on his hands that will not stop easily or quickly."

Roosevelt's opponents backed down, and he won his party's unanimous endorsement for a second term. But shortly after a brief vacation with his family at Campobello, Franklin suffered a severe, potentially fatal blow to his political career. Returning by boat from Campobello, both Franklin and Eleanor thoughtlessly brushed their teeth with what proved to be contaminated water that had been poured into pitchers in their state room. After they arrived at the house on East 65th Street, they went to bed with low fevers. Eleanor soon recovered, but Franklin did not and was later diagnosed with typhoid fever. The bedridden Franklin's plans to campaign in the critical month of October were no longer possible. On his instructions, Eleanor wired Louis Howe, the Albany stringer for the *New York Herald*, who had met and admired Franklin during his anti-Sheehan fight with Tammany. Would Howe come to New York immediately to run Roosevelt's campaign? Howe agreed and rushed to Franklin's bedside from his vacation cottage in southern Massachusetts. From that day forward, until Howe's death in 1936, he would serve as Roosevelt's indispensable political strategist.

Howe was forty-one years old when he took command of Roosevelt's State Senate campaign. He addressed Roosevelt in a 1912 letter, only half-facetiously, as "Beloved and Revered Future President." Without their shared ambitions for Franklin, the team of Roosevelt and Howe was utterly incongruous.

Howe was barely five feet tall and scrawny, with a large nose, bulging eyes, and a cigarette usually dangling precariously from his lower lip. His slightly uncouth appearance was accentuated by an oversized, stiff, white-collared shirt that was always frayed and dirty. By his own admission, he was extremely ugly.

He was born in Indianapolis, Indiana, the son of Captain Edward Howe, a local insurance executive who lost everything in the Panic of 1873. When Louis was five, his father moved the family to Saratoga

Springs, New York, where he scraped together the funds to buy the weekly *Saratoga Sun*. Edward Howe was an outspoken Democrat in this wealthy Republican stronghold, and neither his editorials nor his temperament were conducive to financial success. In Saratoga, the Howes did not earn much money or respect.

As a child, the sickly Louis read voraciously, favoring the heroic writings of Thomas Carlyle. He composed romantic poetry and acted in local theater productions, but never in a leading role. As a teenager, he worked for his father's newspaper and later for the *New York Herald*, reporting on two of his abiding interests: horse racing and politics. Though he never attended college, he was a gifted writer and intrepid researcher, admired by his journalistic colleagues for his shrewd analysis of Albany politics and his ability to mine archival facts that gave his stories freshness and depth. When Howe received Eleanor Roosevelt's telegram in September 1912, he was unhappily married, with two children, and broke. Overnight, he found his real-life hero and calling, both named Franklin D. Roosevelt.

Howe quickly devised a campaign theme: Roosevelt, the indefatigable champion of farmers' rights. In full-page newspaper ads, the media-savvy Howe declared war (in Roosevelt's name) on unscrupulous commission men in New York City whose fees cheated farmers of a fair price for their produce. "FARMERS! ATTENTION!" one of Howe's ads proclaimed. "The time to put a stop to the ROBBERIES of dishonest commission merchants is NOW! . . . When Franklin D. Roosevelt says he will fight for a thing, it means he won't quit until he wins—you know that." Howe shrewdly turned Roosevelt's illness into an asset. In written correspondence under Franklin's signature, the candidate candidly acknowledged that typhoid fever prevented him from meeting face-to-face with his constituents. He urged the voters nonetheless to help him bring agricultural reform to Albany. One of Howe's letters appeared to be personally signed by Roosevelt, though it was multigraphed, and was sent to more than 11,000 of the district's rural voters. It solicited suggestions to help the candidate improve upon a proposed agricultural reform bill he would introduce at the beginning of the next legislative session when he became chairman of the Senate Agricultural Committee. The letter conveniently included a stamped, self-addressed envelope for responses, which Roosevelt received by the bundle.

Throughout the campaign, Roosevelt was relegated to the role of passive spectator. While he remained in the Upper East Side town house,

Howe ran ads and circulated letters to burnish the candidate's rural re-form image. He opposed higher license fees for Hudson River shad fisher-men and supported a standard apple barrel to prevent shady buyers from supplying oversized containers. All the while, Howe roamed the district, vigilantly protecting Roosevelt's interests while attacking his Republican opponent for failing to campaign in Columbia County. Of course, Roose-velt did not campaign in any of the three counties in his election district.

The peripatetic Howe ran the whole show, though he always checked with Franklin before implementing his latest idea. Before placing one newspaper ad, he wired Roosevelt: "As I have pledged you in it, I thought you might like to know casually what kind of a mess I was getting you into." Roosevelt never objected, and Howe had the time of his life. "I am having more fun than a goat," he wrote his boss, signing the telegram: "Your slave and servant."

Roosevelt won reelection with a plurality of 15,590 votes, greater than the total he had received two years earlier, even though his opposition to Tammany cost him some Democratic votes. His margin of victory was provided by Republican and independent voters, attracted to his reform message, refined to perfection by the inimitable Louis Howe.

When he returned to Albany in January 1913, Franklin rented a small apartment, in contrast to the grand three-story house he had leased for himself and his family during his first Senate term. His more modest ac-commodations suggested that Franklin's ambitions no longer were focused on the state legislature. Before contracting typhoid fever, he had worked tirelessly for Woodrow Wilson among upstate reform Democrats. After Wilson won the presidency, thanks to the split between Taft and Teddy Roosevelt, Franklin waited patiently for a call from the president-elect. Meanwhile, he vigorously followed up on his campaign promises, introduc-ing five agricultural reform bills, highlighted by proposed regulations on commission merchants through licensing and inspection. In mid-January, he received a telegram from Joseph Tumulty, Wilson's secretary, requesting that Roosevelt visit the president-elect in Trenton. At the meeting Roo-sevelt offered his recommendations for patronage jobs in New York and expressed his interest in joining the new administration in Washington.

Three days before Wilson's inauguration, Roosevelt went to Wash-ington, where he met Wilson's new Secretary of the Treasury, William McAdoo. Would Franklin accept the position of Assistant Secretary of the Treasury, asked McAdoo, or alternatively, Collector of the Port of

New York? Roosevelt declined both offers, though the collectorship would have nicely positioned him to build a reform constituency in the bowels of Tammany's home base. On the morning of the inauguration, Roosevelt received the offer that he had been waiting for when he met Wilson's Secretary of the Navy, Josephus Daniels, in the lobby of the Willard Hotel.

"How would you like to come to Washington as Assistant Secretary of the Navy?" Daniels asked.

Roosevelt beamed. "How would I like it?" he responded. "I'd like it bully well. It would please me better than anything in the world."

At the age of thirty-one, Roosevelt had even outdone Cousin Teddy in becoming the youngest Assistant Secretary of the Navy in history. With the appointment, he climbed to the second rung on the ladder he had envisioned for himself when he discussed his political ambitions with his fellow law clerk, Grenville Clark, at Carter, Ledyard only six years earlier.

Since childhood, Roosevelt had loved ships, and so, not surprisingly, he took unmitigated pleasure in the privileges of his new office. He gloried in the 17-gun salute fired when he boarded a battleship and in his inspection of the ship's officers assembled in crisp dress uniforms to greet him. He designed his own flag to be flown during his nautical visits, and from time to time commanded a yacht or destroyer from the fleet. On one occasion, he ordered the destroyer *Flusser* to take him on an inspection of naval installations at Frenchman Bay, Maine. With the nervous commander at his side, he guided the ship through the strait between Campobello Island and the mainland.*

Pomp aside, Roosevelt was a serious student of naval history and well understood the heavy responsibilities of the department in which he now served. In 1913, the U.S. Navy was the nation's first line of defense. With an annual budget of almost $144 million (roughly 20 percent of the federal budget), the Navy Department supervised a large fleet, including thirty-nine battleships and heavy cruisers, and employed 63,000 officers, sailors, and Marines. It was vastly superior to the American navy of a quarter century earlier, but still woefully inferior to Great Britain, the world's great naval power, as well as to the naval forces of Germany and France. At a

---

* The commanding officer of the *Flusser* was a young admiral named William "Bull" Halsey.

time when there was anxious talk of war in Europe, Roosevelt was convinced that the United States, and that meant the navy, must be prepared for war. "[W]e are confronted with a condition—the fact that our nation has decided in the past to have a fleet, and that war is still a possibility," he told the Navy League in April 1913. It was necessary, he continued, that the United States maintain "a fighting force of the highest efficiency."

Roosevelt's immediate job was to oversee the civilian workforce in the navy yards across the country. The mutual antipathy between commanding officers and civilian laborers at the yards was palpable. Franklin managed, with crucial help from his assistant, Louis Howe, to placate labor without antagonizing their employers. Just as Howe had done in Franklin's Senate campaign, he became Roosevelt's eyes and ears in the navy yards. In advance of the Assistant Secretary's visits, he met with civilian workers and listened to their grievances. When he returned to Washington, Howe briefed Roosevelt on his findings, which invariably were sympathetic to labor. He also urged Roosevelt to set aside substantial time on his tours of the yards to meet directly with labor representatives. Franklin took Howe's advice, and as a result maintained exceedingly cordial relations with labor. But unlike Howe, Roosevelt also earned the respect of the naval officers in charge of the yards, demonstrating his intimate knowledge of ships as well as sympathy for their challenges.

Roosevelt was a hands-on administrator, not only in meeting personnel in the yards, but in making close inspections of the equipment. He wanted to know how the machinery worked and did not hesitate to get his hands dirty testing oily wheels and levers. He often made inspections in which he was accompanied by reporters, usually producing favorable stories in local papers the next day. He also informed local Democratic officials in advance of his tours and regularly shared with them his thoughts about possible improvements of naval facilities in their districts. Insisting on multiple bids from private contractors, he made a practice of awarding contracts to the lowest bidder. But there were exceptions. When a Canadian firm submitted the low bid for a flag and bunting contract, he gave the job to an American firm. Cost-efficiency had its limits, particularly when influential congressmen might accuse the Assistant Secretary of being unpatriotic.

Franklin's career appeared to be humming along when, in the late summer of 1914, he made a careless misstep, announcing that he would be a candidate for the U.S. Senate in the Democratic primary in New York. "My senses have not yet left me," he wired Howe, who was on vacation. But Howe must have wondered, since Franklin had not made his peace with Tammany, and Charles Murphy had yet to announce his own candidate. There was a persistent rumor that Murphy would endorse William Randolph Hearst, who had lost the gubernatorial race, despite Tammany backing, to Charles Evans Hughes in 1906. Roosevelt salivated at the prospect of running against Hearst. "I have been offering my prayers," he wrote from Campobello. "It would be magnificent sport and also magnificent service to run against him." But, alas, Murphy had a better idea. He chose a loyal member of Tammany, James Gerard, the U.S. ambassador to Germany, who enjoyed a reputation as an honest, wealthy, and liberal public servant. Gerard remained in Berlin during the primary, busy helping to rescue Americans stranded at the outbreak of the First World War. It was no contest. Gerard swamped Roosevelt, winning New York City 4–1 and Franklin's upstate stronghold by a margin of 2–1. Unfortunately for Gerard, the internecine warfare between Roosevelt's upstate reformers and Tammany enabled the Republican senatorial candidate, James Wadsworth, to easily win the general election.

Roosevelt had been demanding a larger, more modern naval force since his first weeks in office at the Navy Department. By the early months of 1914, he had ratcheted up his rhetoric to capture the public's attention. "You can't fight Germany's and England's dreadnoughts with United States gunboats, strange as it may seem," he said in an interview with the *Milwaukee Sentinel*, "and the policy of our congress should be to buy and build dreadnoughts until our navy is comparable to any other in the world." He was convinced that only a strong naval force, capable of defeating any enemy on the open sea, could adequately protect the nation. In formulating his outspoken views, he was influenced by the writings of Admiral Alfred Thayer Mahan, whose books on naval history he had devoured since he was a student at Groton. His perception of his own large role in setting naval policy was, no doubt, inspired by the precedent set by his predecessor, Theodore Roosevelt, fifteen years earlier. With his boss away, TR had ordered Commodore Dewey to attack Manila in the event of war with Spain. Franklin, with his superior, Secretary Daniels, absent for a few days, took notice of his cousin's bold action. "There's a Roosevelt on the job today," he told reporters with a grin. "You remember what happened the last time a Roosevelt occupied a similar position?"

In dealing with Secretary Daniels, Franklin faced a superior far more adept at managing his staff than the Secretary of the Navy in TR's day. Daniels was the former populist editor of the *Raleigh News and Observer*, and looked every inch the rural southern newspaper editor. He wore string ties and rumpled white suits, and kept his speech as simple as his attire. But behind the hayseed facade, Daniels was a sophisticated politician who skillfully maneuvered through the Washington corridors of power. He was also an able administrator who knew how to get the best work out of the employees in his department, including Assistant Secretary Roosevelt, who only many years later appreciated his boss's considerable talents.

Daniels did not share Roosevelt's militant, big-navy perspective. In fact, he was a pacifist who, like his close friend Secretary of State William Jennings Bryan, believed that the world's conflicts could only be solved by diplomacy. The headstrong young Assistant Secretary bristled under Daniel's rein. His frustration deepened in the summer of 1914, shortly after Archduke Franz Ferdinand of Austria was assassinated in Sarajevo, Bosnia, the spark that ignited the First World War. After Germany declared war on Russia, Roosevelt immediately understood the cataclysmic consequences of these fast-moving events. "These are history-making days," he wrote only hours after Germany's declaration. "It will be the greatest war in the world's history."

News of Germany's declaration of war reached Roosevelt in Reading, Pennsylvania, where he was dedicating an anchor from the battleship *Maine*. He rushed back to Washington expecting a Navy Department abuzz with excitement and activity. But he was shocked to find a business-as-usual attitude in the department, presided over by a very calm Secretary Daniels. FDR vowed to do everything in his power, short of insubordination, to prepare the navy for the critical days ahead. Daniels was "feeling chiefly very sad that his faith in human nature and civilization and similar idealistic nonsense was receiving such a rude shock," Roosevelt wrote scornfully, "so I started in alone to get things ready and prepare plans for what ought to be done by the Navy end of things."

Unfortunately for Roosevelt, President Wilson, like Daniels, did not share his sense of urgency. From the beginning of the conflict, Wilson declared that the United States would remain neutral and issued pointed instructions to the Navy Department to make no public comment on the military or political situation "on the other side of the water." Roosevelt seethed privately, writing contemptuously of the two prominent pacifists in the Wilson cabinet, Bryan and Daniels. "These dear good people like W.J.B. and J.D. have as much conception of what a general European war means as Elliott [his four-year-old son] has of higher mathematics," he complained to Eleanor. "They really believe that because we are neutral we can go about our business as usual." In speeches, he continued to advocate a bigger, better equipped navy to cope with the potential danger to the United States posed by the conflagration sweeping Europe.

In urging the United States toward greater military preparedness, Franklin was not alone. He received strong support from Rear Admiral Bradley Fiske, aide for Naval Operations, and several other militant officers in the Navy Department, as well as Alfred Thayer Mahan, who wrote Roosevelt letters of encouragement. He could also count among his allies Theodore Roosevelt, who by the fall of 1914 regularly expressed disgust with the Wilson administration's policy of neutrality. In Congress, the ranking member of the Senate Naval Affairs Committee, Henry Cabot Lodge, offered his own outspoken criticism of Wilson's policy, as did Lodge's son-in-law, Congressman Augustus Gardner, chairman of the House Military Affairs Committee.

In October, Gardner delivered an incendiary speech on the House floor, charging that U.S. armed forces were woefully unprepared to defend the nation's interests. Implicit in Gardner's attack was condemnation of Secretary Daniels's leadership. Amid the furor created by the speech, Acting Secretary of the Navy Roosevelt* handed the press a lengthy memorandum essentially undercutting his boss's position that the navy was prepared to meet any crisis. Roosevelt's statement asserted that thirteen of the navy's second-line battleships were useless unless Congress authorized appropriations for an additional 18,000 sailors to operate them. He sent a copy of his memorandum to Eleanor with a note: "The enclosed is the truth and even if it gets me into trouble I am perfectly ready to stand by it. The country needs the truth about the Army and Navy instead of a lot of soft mush about everlasting peace which so many statesmen are handing out to a gullible public." Reporters quickly pointed out discrepancies between Daniels's public statements and his Assistant Secretary's memorandum, forcing Roosevelt to retreat behind a strained parsing of the language of his memo. He had not "recommended" additional men, he told the press lamely, for that was a policy decision left to Secretary Daniels.

---

* Secretary Daniels was away for a few days.

A few weeks later, however, Roosevelt was at it again, pressing his preparedness message. This time, he responded to an address by the pacifist president of Stanford University, David Starr Jordan, who had advocated disarmament and labeled opponents "warmongers." Roosevelt offered a spirited rebuttal, calling for a military draft and defending it as "just plain common sense." He denied that he was in favor of war. Quite the contrary. "Many of us who want to keep the peace believe that $250,000,000 a year for the Navy, which amounts to only one-half of one percent of our national wealth, is merely good insurance."

Three days later, President Wilson, in his annual address to Congress, reiterated his policy of neutrality. "We are at peace with the world," he said, and rejected calls for a compulsory military draft, an increase in the regular army, or expansion of the reserves. As to an accelerated construction program for the navy, that would require further study. "We shall not alter our attitude because some amongst us are nervous and excited," he said. A day later, as if on cue, Secretary Daniels reassured the House Naval Affairs Committee that the U.S. Navy was operating at top efficiency. It could successfully defend the nation against any other naval force in the world, he testified. The navy's warships in reserve could be ready for action within a matter of days with the addition of less than 5,000 men.

Roosevelt testified before the same committee a week later and, without explicitly contradicting Daniels, furnished facts and figures on naval vessels and manpower that cast doubt on the Secretary of the Navy's assurances. He cited Naval War College estimates that 30,000 to 50,000 additional men would be needed to make all of the navy's warships fully operational. Training the new men and preparing the ships for combat would take many months, not days, Roosevelt said, casting further doubt on Daniels's optimistic projections. And while he did not openly challenge Daniels's claims of high efficiency for the navy, he suggested that the navies of both Great Britain and Germany were superior to the naval forces of the United States. Throughout the five hours of his testimony, Roosevelt studiously avoided discussing broad naval policy, despite constant prodding by committee members. That, he said, was his boss's job.

His testimony received rave reviews in the New York newspapers. The *Sun* exclaimed that Roosevelt "had exhibited a grasp of naval affairs that seemed to astonish members of the committee who had been studying the question for years." The *Herald* reported that he "had made a most complete study of the problems of national defense." Franklin was no less impressed than others with his performance. When committee members "tried to quiz me and put me in a hold," he wrote his mother, "I was able not only to parry but to come back at them with thrusts that went home." Best of all, he added, he was able to put forward his own views "without any particular embarrassment to the secretary."

Roosevelt's testimony earned him the gratitude of Congressman Gardner, who publicly praised the Assistant Secretary for his courage in providing his committee with "the truth and nothing but the truth." But it did nothing to jolt the Wilson administration into action. The president only began to reconsider his neutrality policy after May 7, 1915, the day that a torpedo from a German U-boat destroyed the British passenger ship *Lusitania* in the Irish Sea. The huge ocean liner sank in eighteen minutes; nearly 1,200 passengers drowned, including 128 Americans. At first, Wilson responded timorously. "There is such a thing as a man being too proud to fight," he said. But Americans across the country were outraged, accusing the German Imperial Navy of "wanton murder on the high seas." Prodded by public opinion, Wilson sent two notes of protest to the German government, the second holding Germany to "strict accountability" for its actions. Secretary of State Bryan was so fearful that Wilson's second note would draw the United States into the war that he resigned in protest.

Roosevelt welcomed Bryan's resignation, and hoped, in vain, that Secretary Daniels's would follow. He also sent the president a longhand note of support: "I want to tell you simply that you have been in my thoughts during these days and that I realize to the full all that you have had to go through—I need not repeat to you my own entire loyalty and devotion—that I hope you know. But I feel most strongly that the Nation approves and sustains your course and that it is *American* in the highest sense." Wilson responded that Franklin's note "had touched me very much" and that "such messages make the performance of duty worth while."

By the summer of 1915 Wilson was advocating preparedness, and asked Secretary Daniels to create a task force within the Navy Department to draw up plans for a naval program to submit to the next Congress. Daniels appointed Roosevelt to the task force, though Franklin did not have as large a role in the formulation of new naval policy as he would have liked. The task force nonetheless recommended the immediate construction of 176 ships at a cost of $600 million, the largest peacetime construction in the nation's history. Wilson approved the plan, and Daniels's effective lobbying helped guide the legislation through Congress.

In a series of public addresses, Roosevelt returned to his theme of military preparedness, though he toned down his language to conform with Wilson's moderate approach. In fact, he began to identify more closely with the president's cautious policies. He was not unduly disappointed, for example, when Wilson rejected his recommendation for a Council of National Defense. Wilson might accept his proposal later, Roosevelt wrote, but understood that "the President does not want to 'rattle the sword' while Germany seems anxious to meet us more than half way."

By the spring of 1916, presidential politics vied for headlines with news of the war in Europe. It was a foregone conclusion that Wilson would seek a second presidential term. But Republicans were optimistic, sensing that the president was particularly vulnerable on the preparedness issue. They only had to avoid a repeat of the 1912 debacle when TR's third-party candidacy allowed Wilson to eke out a Democratic victory. Theodore Roosevelt still harbored presidential ambitions, but the party's old guard adamantly opposed him. A united party would win the presidency, Republican leaders concluded, and Associate Justice Charles Evans Hughes was the man to lead them to victory.

Anticipating their theme for the fall campaign, Republicans began to attack the naval policies of Secretary Daniels. Roosevelt, who had been so dismissive of his boss's policies, rushed to Daniels's defense. He insisted that the Navy Department was operating far more efficiently than it had in past administrations, and suggested that criticism of past failings was not in the national interest. The nation's attention should be focused on the present danger, not past errors, he told delegates to the Navy League convention. To make his point more vivid, he chose the metaphor of a raging fire. It made no sense, he said, to "indulge in a slanging match as to who was responsible for the rotten hose or the lack of water at the fire a week ago."

On Flag Day, June 14, 1916, President Wilson, carrying an American flag over his shoulder, marched at the head of a preparedness parade in downtown Washington. Not far behind him, Franklin Roosevelt led the Navy Department contingent. Later, he joined Wilson on the reviewing stand and proudly stood next to the president while photographers snapped their picture for the next day's newspapers. Later that week, delegates to the Democratic Convention in St. Louis unanimously nominated Wilson for a second presidential term.

3

"Common Sense Idealism"

One late weekday afternoon in the fall of 1915, Associate Justice Charles Evans Hughes was observed briskly walking down Capitol Hill, head erect, full beard gently swaying in the breeze, a man "at peace with the world." It was obvious to all who knew Hughes that he was happily engaged in the intellectual work of the Supreme Court. He was satisfied that he had put an end to his political career in 1912 when he refused to have his name considered for the Republican presidential nomination. He had even stopped voting in New York, concerned that the train trip would cost him precious time away from the Court.

But admirers in the Republican Party continued to write to Hughes, expressing their hopes that he would reconsider his decision to give up politics, especially as the 1916 election approached. If Wilson were reelected, they argued, both the Republican Party and the nation could be irreparably harmed. Hughes was unmoved. In answer to an inquiry from former Governor Edward Stokes of New Jersey, Hughes wrote, "It seems to me very clear that, as a member of the Supreme Court, I have no right to be a candidate, either actively or passively." Stokes interpreted Hughes's letter to mean that he would not, under any circumstances, be a candidate for the presidency in 1916. Others were not so easily dissuaded. In Nebraska, a petition was circulated to put Hughes's name on the ballot for the state's presidential preference primary. When his refusal to accept the nomination did not deter his supporters, he threatened court action to keep his name off the state ballot.

Neither Hughes's words nor his actions discouraged the press from speculating on his potential presidential candidacy. "[N]o man can keep himself out of it [his party's presidential contest] if the people want him in," *The Washington Post* commented. "It is not Hughes the judge who is discussed as a candidate," wrote *The New York Times*, "but Hughes the fearless investigator, Hughes the Governor who put moral courage into his reforms . . . Hughes the campaign speaker of 1908 who deeply impressed himself on the country as a man who carried heavy guns."

The most persuasive brief in favor of Hughes's candidacy came in the form of a lengthy letter to the justice from former President William Howard Taft. "What is the country's great need?" asked Taft. "It is the restoration of the Republican party to power to do the constructive work needed in carrying out a policy of reasonable preparedness which involves financial and economic preparedness," he answered. The party could not afford another split between Republicans and Progressives that doomed his own candidacy in 1912. Taft then proceeded to discuss the merits of each potential nominee (e.g., "Mr. Roosevelt is thundering . . . but I cannot think it in the cards for him to win"). Only Hughes, Taft concluded, could unite the party. The former president summed up as if making closing arguments to a jury: "You will certainly be elected if you accept the nomination and you will reunite the only party from which constructive progress can be expected at a most critical time in the country's history. Your opportunity as President to guide the country through the trial bound to come after the war will be as great as Washington's or Lincoln's. You are equal to it. Strong men will respond to your call because you are yourself so satisfying in strength and in your political courage and patriotism."

In a postscript, Taft said that he did not expect a response from Hughes. The next day, he sent an addendum to his arguments. He anticipated that Hughes would hesitate to leave the Court and have Wilson fill the vacancy. True enough, Taft conceded, but "think of the vacancies he is likely to fill if he is to be re-elected. He can almost destroy the court." In Taft's opinion, Hughes really had no choice but to accept his party's nomination. The alternatives were intolerable. Roosevelt, should he overcome what Taft considered to be overwhelming odds against him, would likely take the country to war. But a second term for Wilson, "whom I regard as the greatest opportunist and hypocrite ever in the White House," was even worse. "As I conceive it," he concluded, "the exigency presented to you is whether you will save the party from Roosevelt and the country from Wilson."

Under increasing pressure from his party, Hughes sought the advice of Justice Willis Van Devanter, a Republican from Wyoming, who had been appointed to the Court by Taft. While he sympathized with Hughes's efforts to oppose the use of his name as a candidate, Van Devanter said that if the Republican Party nominated him, he "could not rightly decline." Chief Justice Edward White, a Democrat, referring to persistent newspaper reports of Hughes's likely nomination, offered the same advice as Van Devanter: if nominated, he should accept.

"I was torn between two profound desires," Hughes recalled, "one to keep the judicial ermine unsullied, and the other not to fail in meeting what might be a duty to the country."

Meanwhile, rumors circulated that if Hughes remained on the Court, he would soon replace White as Chief Justice. A member of Wilson's cabinet, Interior Secretary Franklin Lane, took Hughes aside at a dinner party and strongly hinted that he would be the president's choice to succeed White. And Chief Justice White himself approached Hughes shortly before the Republican Convention to deliver the same message. Before Hughes made a decision to leave the Court, the Chief Justice told him, he should know that White planned to retire. If Hughes did not resign, he would succeed him.

"Why, President Wilson would never appoint me Chief Justice," Hughes exclaimed.

"Well, he wouldn't appoint anyone else, as I happen to know," White replied.

Hughes told the Chief Justice that his decision would not be influenced by the suggestion that he would succeed White. Hughes was not naive. He was aware that Republicans and Democrats alike, including the president, considered him a stronger presidential candidate than Theodore Roosevelt. If he remained on the Court and was then appointed Chief Justice, it would be seen as a deal between Hughes and Wilson. Even if no deal were made, his succeeding White, rather than accepting the Republican nomination, would be widely perceived as a seamy backroom bargain. Either way, Hughes wanted no part of it.

The Hughes bandwagon picked up speed. Republican polls consistently showed him to be the first choice of members of his party. Michigan Republicans named Hughes as their candidate at the state party convention. He won the Vermont and Oregon Republican primaries. Frank Hitchcock and Eugene Meyer, Taft's managers of his successful 1908 campaign, began to line up delegates for Hughes, an increasingly easy task. During this period of frenzied activity on his behalf, the justice remained silent.

Republican nominations for president began on June 9, 1916, the third day of the party's convention in Chicago. After the Alabama delegation passed, Arizona yielded to New York. "We bring you today the name of a man trained for battle for the truth," New York governor Charles Whitman intoned. "We have seen him the man of action, the champion of the people, the idol of the electorate, the faithful public servant, the profound thinker on national affairs." Whitman then placed in nomination the name of Associate Justice Charles Evans Hughes, New York's "noblest and best."

Hughes led on the first ballot with 253½ votes, more than twice as many as the man in second place, Senator Elihu Root of New York. Theodore Roosevelt trailed badly with only 65 votes. By the second ballot, Hughes added another 75 to his total, but was still 170 votes short of a majority. The next day, on the third ballot, Hughes won the nomination easily. While New York governor Whitman led a triumphant procession around the coliseum, an important question still remained unanswered: Would Hughes accept the nomination?*

Hughes was having lunch with his family in the dining room of his town house on 16th Street in Washington when news of his nomination reached him. He walked downstairs to meet with the scores of reporters who had crowded in front of the entrance to his home. With tears in his eyes, he said that he would accept his party's nomination, thereby becoming the first member of the Supreme Court in American history to be the presidential nominee of a major political party. He promptly sent the president a one-sentence letter of resignation and then drafted a telegram

---

* A similar question was asked at the Progressive Party's convention, held in Chicago at the same time as the Republican Convention, after Progressives nominated Theodore Roosevelt: Would TR accept their nomination? To the consternation of the delegates, he declined. The party then nominated Hughes.

to the Republican delegates in Chicago. "I recognize that it is your right to summon and that it is my paramount duty to respond," he wrote them. The Republican Party demanded a "dominant, thoroughgoing Americanism with firm protective upbuilding policies, essential to our peace and security." He could not fail to answer their call for his service to his country.

Woodrow Wilson expected his party to nominate him for a second presidential term at the Democratic Convention in St. Louis held the week following Hughes's nomination. He anticipated a vigorous campaign defending his progressive domestic record (e.g., low-cost loans for farmers, a ban on products in interstate commerce manufactured by child labor, federal regulation of trade), and his new resolve to stand up for American rights jeopardized by the war in Europe. But the Democratic Convention chairman, Senator Ollie James of Kentucky, offered a very different strategy for victory in November. James introduced Wilson to the convention as the nation's courageous peacemaker, who stood up for America "without orphaning a single American child, without widowing a single American mother, without firing a single shot, without shedding a single drop of blood. . . ." The delegates followed James's lead. After nominating Wilson by acclamation, Democrats hoisted their campaign banner: "He Kept Us Out of War."

In many ways, Wilson and Hughes were mirror images of each other. Both men were sons of Protestant clergymen and projected a strict sense of public morality. Both had been brilliant students and university professors before entering politics as reform-minded idealists. Both forged records as progressive governors of northeast states, challenging entrenched political and financial interests.

Though Wilson was the incumbent, Hughes began the presidential campaign as the bookmakers' heavy favorite. The calculation was based on history and math, more than Hughes's prowess as a politician. The Republican Party had dominated the presidency for more than fifty years. Only two Democrats, Grover Cleveland and Woodrow Wilson, had occupied the White House since Lincoln took the oath of office in 1861. And Wilson's victory in 1912 was only made possible by the disastrous rift between Taft and Roosevelt. Republicans were confident that 1916 would be different. They believed that Hughes's moderate, reform record, superb intellect, and personal integrity assured unity and victory for the party in November.*

Once Hughes had made the excruciating decision to leave the Court, his first order of political business was to bring together the two competing factions in his party. In late June, he dined separately with Roosevelt and Taft. Roosevelt had declared his wholehearted support for Hughes shortly after the Republican and Progressive conventions, but TR was not good at hiding his true feelings. He had never really warmed to the stiff, independent Hughes, once referring to him as the "bearded iceberg." The bellicose Roosevelt was also suspicious that Hughes was "another Wilson with whiskers" who, like the president, would continue to appease the German military machine. Hughes was much more comfortable with Taft, meeting him for lunch at the former president's summer home in Bridgehampton, Long Island. Taft was, of course, delighted that his gentle hectoring had produced the Republican candidate of his choice. He awaited orders to serve Hughes as the candidate wished.

Hughes prepared for the fall campaign as he had done for every other professional challenge, with total concentration and careful attention to detail. He immersed himself in the relevant political literature, devouring stacks of government reports and issues of the *Congressional Record*, as well as hundreds of magazine and newspaper articles on every relevant domestic and foreign policy issue.

On July 30, he set the lofty tone for his campaign when he delivered his formal acceptance speech in New York City's Carnegie Hall. Before a capacity, sweltering crowd of 3,000 people, he chose the theme "America First and America Efficient" to plead for national unity in perilous times. For the next hour and a half, Hughes offered a program of domestic reforms and the promise that he would protect America's interests abroad. He concluded by calling for the creation of an international tribunal and world organization at war's end that could impose disarmament on the industrial nations and produce an enduring peace. Though his speech was indisputably sincere and high-minded, it raised two problems for Hughes in the upcoming campaign. Substantively, Hughes's positions did not differ significantly from those of the president. His oration, moreover, failed

---

* Republicans were further encouraged by widespread public disapproval of Wilson's recent marriage to Edith Galt, the widow of a Washington jeweler, whom the president had begun to court less than seven months after his first wife's death.

to heed Theodore Roosevelt's admonition that "a campaign speech is a poster, not an etching."

Hughes held his first major rally in Detroit, where he addressed 10,000 workers before attending a Detroit Tigers baseball game, leaping over a railing to shake hands with the team's star outfielder, Ty Cobb. Always accompanied by his wife, Antoinette, Hughes sat for scores of interviews and gamely smiled through a blur of daily luncheons and receptions in his honor. He made as many as ten extemporaneous speeches a day, from Chicago to Seattle, drawing on his photographic memory to recite the details of his policy positions for each audience. To show that he was a regular fellow, he stopped abruptly to pose in front of a little boy's camera. He and Antoinette donned waterproof slickers to descend to the depths of a copper mine in Butte, Montana, and climbed to Bear Lake, 10,000 feet up in the Rockies. But the candidate never quite escaped the image of a distinguished Supreme Court justice awkwardly masquerading as a politician.

In a formal gesture of party solidarity, Roosevelt and Taft dutifully posed together for photographers, but no one was fooled. Their animosity toward each other had not dissipated, and the hostility permeated the ranks of the Progressive and Republican parties. Hughes's choice of a campaign manager, William Willcox, did not help in healing the rift. Willcox had served competently under Governor Hughes as the first head of the Public Service Commission in New York City. But he was a political neophyte who was ill-equipped to deal with the infighting between Progressives and old guard Republicans.

The rivalries flared up in California after Hughes arrived to campaign in the state. Governor Hiram Johnson, who had run in 1912 on the Progressive ticket with TR as the party's vice-presidential candidate, was challenging Willis Booth, a Republican backed by Taft regulars, for a seat in the U.S. Senate. Hughes should have anticipated that his visit would provoke a vicious turf battle between the state's Progressives and the Republican establishment. But neither he nor his campaign manager, Willcox, made a concerted effort to bring the two sides together behind his candidacy.

The bitter climax to the feud occurred after Hughes had completed a full day of campaigning in Southern California. Late in the afternoon, Hughes and his entourage stopped for a rest at the Virginia Hotel in Long Beach. Unknown to Hughes, Governor Johnson entered the hotel and asked why there was such a commotion in the lobby. Learning for the first time that the Republican presidential candidate was in the same hotel,

Johnson waited impatiently for an invitation to meet with Hughes. When he did not hear from Hughes, he abruptly departed.

Why Hughes was not informed that Johnson was in the same hotel was never explained, though Progressive supporters of Johnson suspected that old guard Republicans on Hughes's staff had purposely kept the information from him. When Hughes heard that he and Johnson had missed each other, he immediately attempted to make amends. He wired the California governor suggesting that Johnson introduce him at a rally in Sacramento, and that they exchange mutually supportive telegrams. Johnson declined both invitations, and Hughes left the state with California's governor nursing his bruised feelings.

Throughout the campaign, Hughes advocated a more muscular foreign policy than Wilson's, claiming that he would be firmer in dealing with the Germans. But he always spoke in generalities. Confident that he would win the presidency, he did not want to make commitments that would bind him when he assumed office. Meanwhile, an uninhibited Teddy Roosevelt barnstormed through the Midwest, demanding immediate action against German aggression and virtually promising a declaration of war if Hughes were elected.

On the stump, Hughes was no match for the president, who bristled with kinetic energy in defending his administration's policies. At the same time, Wilson's surrogates exploited TR's bombast, reminding voters that the president "Kept Us Out of War." They drove their point home by distributing enormous posters throughout the country, luridly depicting the ravages of war with a mother and her children looking on in horror. Below the picture was the caption: "He has protected me and mine."

Republicans countered the Democrats' propaganda by denouncing the president's lack of preparedness, lumping Wilson with Navy Secretary Daniels in billboards proclaiming that "A Vote for Wilson is a Vote for Daniels." Hughes also took aim at Daniels, blaming the Secretary for not giving sufficient attention to the pressing business of military preparation.

Hughes's charge brought as instant retort from Assistant Secretary of the Navy Franklin Roosevelt, campaigning for Wilson in New York: "I can show him [Hughes] an organization that would not break down in case of war. I can show him long-range shooting with big guns that has surprised and delighted every officer in the fleet. . . . All it [the navy] needs now is boosting and not knocking."

*   *   *

On election day, November 7, professional gamblers in New York City made Hughes a 5–3 favorite to win the presidency. As the Hughes family dined in their suite at the Astor Hotel, supporters interrupted them with good news. Hughes had carried New York by 100,000 votes. Bulletins from every other state in the Northeast reported Hughes victories, and early returns from the West were promising. The bright lights of Times Square flashed a Hughes triumph, repeated in several of the city's newspapers. Reporters demanded a victory statement from the apparent president-elect. "Wait til the Democrats concede my election," a cautious but confident Hughes replied; "the newspapers might take it back." When Hughes went to bed at midnight, he had reason to believe that he would awake as the next president of the United States. A gloomy Franklin Roosevelt, watching the same returns until midnight at the Democratic headquarters in the Biltmore Hotel, came to the same conclusion.*

By morning, the race had tightened. Wilson swept the South. And in the Midwest, pacifist sentiment, particularly among large German-American communities, inexorably moved electoral votes into the Democratic column.

"The most extraordinary day of my life," Franklin wrote Eleanor, who was at Hyde Park. "After last night, Wilson may be elected after all."

In the end, the election was decided by the state of California. Wilson carried the state by less than 4,000 votes, while Governor Hiram Johnson, running on the Republican ticket with Hughes, won a Senate seat by nearly 300,000 votes. With California's 13 electoral votes, Wilson's reelection was assured: 277 electoral votes for the president to Hughes's 254.†

---

* Wilson himself was so discouraged by the early returns that he had to be persuaded by Joseph Tumulty not to concede the election to Hughes. The president nonetheless anticipated his defeat and devised a plan to provide for Hughes's immediate succession without waiting for his inauguration in March. Under the plan, Wilson would immediately appoint Hughes Secretary of State, then both he and the vice president would resign, so that Hughes could at once become commander in chief.

† In his analysis of his narrow defeat, Hughes refused to blame what he termed "the misadventure in California." Instead, he pointed to the effectiveness of Democratic speakers, particularly in the Midwest, "in spreading the notion that if I were elected Colonel Roosevelt would be the leading spirit in my administration and we should be brought into the war."

*   *   *

In late January 1917, Franklin Roosevelt talked Secretary Daniels into approving his inspection of the Caribbean island of Hispaniola, where U.S. Marines maintained order and protected U.S. interests in both Haiti and the Dominican Republic. The trip was billed as government business, but Franklin viewed it as a marvelous opportunity to have fun while doing his duty. For his adventure into what he termed the "Darkest Africa of the West Indies," he was accompanied by Major General George Barnett, the Marine commandant, as well as John McIlhenny, Franklin's frequent golf partner and chairman of the Civil Service Commission, George Marvin, a heavy-drinking old friend, and Livingston ("Livy") Davis, a Harvard classmate who always seemed to be available to share a good time with Franklin.

After a brief visit to Havana, where Franklin made a formal call on the Cuban president, Mario Garcia Menocal, and, with his cohorts, partied late into the night, they sailed on the destroyer USS *Wainwright* into the harbor of Port-au-Prince. At dawn the next day, Franklin stood on the bridge of the *Wainwright* to inspect the entire Atlantic Fleet, seventy-two ships strong, which greeted the Assistant Secretary of the Navy with a booming salute of their guns. Once he had disembarked, Franklin, dressed in top hat and cutaway, delivered a speech in French to the welcoming Haitian delegation. Unknown to him, the delegation did not include the island's highest-ranking officials, so Franklin made the same speech a second time to the mayor of Port-au-Prince, and, finally, a third time, to the Haitian president and his cabinet in the plush drawing room of the presidential palace. Franklin loved retelling the story of his thrice-given speech, as indeed he loved his entire Caribbean adventure. He and his entourage were wined and dined extravagantly in Port-au-Prince, between serious discussions with Haitian officials and U.S. Marine officers in charge of island security. Afterward, Franklin led a four-day horseback trek through the mountainous northern region of the island, escorted by 50 Marines and 150 Haitian policemen.*

After Franklin and his companions sailed from Haiti to the Dominican

---

* The heavily armed escort was thought necessary because of the threat of *cacos* (bandits) who sporadically fought the Marines. Franklin later remembered that he had heard the sound of gunfire in the distance, but no one else in the party had a similar recollection.

Republic in early February, they dined in the beautiful courtyard of an old Spanish colonial house at Santiago de los Caballeros as the guests of the Marine commandant for the Dominican Republic and his wife. Toward the end of the meal, an orderly handed Franklin a coded message, which he read after excusing himself. It was from Secretary Daniels: BECAUSE OF POLITICAL SITUATION PLEASE RETURN WASHINGTON AT ONCE. AM SENDING SHIP TO MEET YOUR PARTY AT PUERTO PLATA TOMORROW MORNING. Franklin returned to the table and gravely reported that political conditions made it necessary for him to leave immediately for the United States. He later recalled that the commandant's wife looked at him in horror and said, "What can political conditions mean? It must be that Charles E. Hughes has led a revolution against President Wilson." Franklin replied dryly, "My dear lady, you have been in the tropics too long!"

Actually, there was not much mystery to the political conditions to which Franklin referred. Tension between the United States and Germany had been building for almost a month. The European war had stalemated on the battlefields of France. The Allies' lines were stretched thin but refused to break. At the same time, the British naval blockade was effectively cutting the flow of supplies to the German people. The German high command concluded that it must quickly knock Great Britain out of the war by the only means available—unrestricted submarine warfare. Within six months, German military leaders estimated, their U-boat onslaught in the Atlantic and North Sea would force an isolated Great Britain to withdraw from the war. By the time the United States came to the Allies' defense, which the German military anticipated, it would be too late to stop Germany's march to victory.

On January 9, 1917, Kaiser Wilhelm had ordered unrestricted submarine attacks to begin on February 1. On the third day in February, after a German U-boat had sunk the American freighter *Housatonic*, President Wilson went before Congress to announce that he had broken off diplomatic relations with Germany. The next day, on his voyage home from the Dominican Republic on the collier USS *Neptune*, Roosevelt thought it probable that the two countries were at war. His impression was reinforced as his ship sailed north toward the naval installation at Hampton Roads, Virginia. He observed that "no lights were showing, the guns were manned and there was complete radio silence."

When he arrived in Washington, Roosevelt was ready for action. But he discovered, as he had after Germany's declaration of war in the summer of 1914, that the Navy Department was operating as if it were just another ordinary day of bureaucratic business. He found "no excitement, no preparations," not even an order to bring the Atlantic Fleet back from the Caribbean to prepare for war. The department's lackadaisical pace reflected the attitude of Roosevelt's boss, Secretary Daniels, who clung to the belief that the United States could stay out of the war. More important, the surface calmness served President Wilson's cautious approach to the crisis. The president still held out hope that handing German ambassador Count von Bernstorff his passport would persuade the German government to rescind its order of unrestricted submarine warfare. But Wilson's policy of watchful waiting withered under the pressure of mounting evidence that Germany was intent on winning the war at all costs. In February alone, German submarines destroyed more than 700,000 tons of Allied shipping. On March 1, a furious Wilson released to the press a decoded telegram from Berlin to the German ambassador in Mexico City with instructions to inform the Mexican government that Germany would value Mexico as an ally in the event that the United States entered the war against the central powers. To entice the United States's southern neighbor, Germany offered Mexico the victor's spoils of its lost territories of Texas, New Mexico, and Arizona.

During the first week of March, Acting Secretary of the Navy Roosevelt met with President Wilson to urge the immediate recall of the Atlantic Fleet stationed at Guantánamo Bay, Cuba, to refit the ships with guns in preparation for war. The president quietly but firmly rejected the younger man's advice. As Roosevelt was leaving, Wilson stopped him at the door to explain: "I want history to show not only that we have tried every diplomatic means to keep out of the war; to show that war has been forced upon us deliberately by Germany; but also that we have come into the court of history with clean hands." By then Wilson, like Roosevelt, believed that the U.S. entry into the war was inevitable. But the president nonetheless was reluctant to make the historic decision, fearing that the monumental military effort required would eviscerate his domestic reforms and seriously impede the nation's progress in the postwar era.

Roosevelt shared none of Wilson's dread of war and made no secret of his unvarnished militancy. He advocated an immediate increase in the size of the navy and army at a dinner meeting in New York City attended by leading politicians and private citizens, including Theodore Roosevelt. TR challenged Senator Elihu Root's defense of the Wilson administration, demanding a more aggressive policy of preparedness. "I backed T.R.'s theory," Franklin later wrote in his diary. In public, his outspoken position struck a responsive chord with a national press that was increasingly impatient with the go-slow policies of Franklin's boss. "Mr. Daniels has one, only one, virile-minded, hardfisted, civilian assistant," observed an editorial writer for the *Chicago Post*. "Uncuriously enough his name is Roosevelt."

German aggression finally pushed Wilson to the brink of making the momentous decision to send the nation to war. On March 18, three American merchant ships, the *City of Memphis*, *Illinois*, and *Vigilancia*, were torpedoed by U-boats. Two days later, the president met with his cabinet to ask their advice on the administration's next step. One by one, the members of his cabinet recommended that Wilson go before Congress to call for a declaration of war against Germany. The final man to speak, a visibly shaken Secretary Daniels, made the recommendation unanimous.

That evening, six hundred influential members of the Republican Party, including their defeated 1916 presidential candidate, Charles Evans Hughes, met behind closed doors at New York City's Union League Club and demanded a declaration of war on Germany. "Let us not delude ourselves," Hughes told his fellow Republicans. "Germany is making war upon the United States, making war with ruthless barbarity." He regarded the attacks as "an onslaught on liberty and on civilization itself." Together with others at the meeting, including TR and Senator Root, he voted for a resolution that "begged the President to give the people a chance to defend themselves." Afterward, Hughes joined Roosevelt and Root at a nearby café for further discussion. The fifty-nine-year-old Roosevelt, blind in one eye and hearing-impaired, vowed to lead a brigade to fight with the Allies. His voice heavy with emotion, TR turned to Hughes and Root, pleading with them to speak to the president on his behalf. "I must go," he said, "but I will not come back." For a moment, there was respectful silence. Root then spoke up with brave good humor. "Theodore, if you can make Wilson believe that you will not come back, he will let you go."

The president was escorted by a cavalry battalion to Capitol Hill on the cold, damp evening of April 2 to ask Congress to declare war on the Imperial German Government. The House chamber was packed with members of Congress, the Supreme Court, the president's cabinet, and other high-ranking administration officials. Franklin Roosevelt sat next to Secretary

Daniels while Eleanor peered down anxiously from the gallery. Wilson entered the chamber to thunderous applause, then spoke somberly and directly to the American people. The United States believed in peace and had no quarrel with the German people, he said. But the nation could not stand by idly when the German government was "guilty of throwing to the winds all scruples of humanity." Under those intolerable circumstances, Americans had no option but to fight for peace and justice and to make the world "safe for democracy." He asked Congress to draft 500,000 men for combat and to take all necessary measures to prepare the U.S. Army and Navy for war. At the end of his speech, his voice rose for the first time. "It is a fearful thing to lead this most peaceful people, into the most terrible and disastrous of all wars, civilization itself seeming to be in the balance," he said. But America must spill her blood for her principles. "God helping her, she can do no other."

The audience stood as one in exuberant agreement with the president, waving the small American flags that had been given to them upon entering the chamber. As Wilson made his way slowly down the aisle after his speech, his inveterate political opponent, Republican senator Henry Cabot Lodge, told him: "Mr. President, you have expressed in the loftiest manner possible the sentiments of the American people." Eleanor Roosevelt had listened "breathlessly" to the address and "returned home still half dazed by the sense of political change."

With a burst of patriotic fervor, Franklin declared that he would resign his post to enlist, as his Cousin Teddy had advised. But Wilson would not hear of it, telling Secretary Daniels to reason with his assistant. "Tell the young man to stay where he is," the president said to Daniels,* who agreed that Franklin was far more valuable to the country serving in the Navy Department.

Franklin assumed responsibility for building the navy arsenal to combat efficiency, a herculean task given the fact that on April 6, 1917, the day that Congress declared war on Germany, the naval fleet numbered slightly more than two hundred ships. Roosevelt attacked his new job with characteristic energy and decisiveness. Within six months, he had quadrupled the number of combat-ready ships needed to transport Allied troops to the battle zones of Europe. His eagerness to back British and French forces sometimes caused him to pledge military assistance without consulting the

---

* Wilson also rejected TR's request to return to active duty.

president, Secretary Daniels, or key members of Congress. It did not seem to matter, since Franklin was never reprimanded for his determination to cut red tape and unnecessary delay. By all accounts, he did a superb job. At war's end, only a year and a half after the United States had joined the Allied cause, the U.S. naval fleet had increased to more than 2,000 ships.

In addition to his official duties at the Navy Department, Roosevelt promoted a host of creative ideas to advance the Allied cause. Some were slightly harebrained, such as Franklin's proposal to build a fleet of 50-foot motorboats to patrol the Atlantic coast. Roosevelt thought that the small boats could, at the very least, serve as an early warning system for roving enemy submarines. A skeptical Daniels asked: "How much of that sort of junk shall we buy?"

But one of Roosevelt's pet projects—laying a vast mine field in the North Sea to destroy German submarines—proved to be strategically useful. Though the mine barrage was not originally Franklin's idea, he pushed it aggressively. The joint U.S.-British venture eventually laid 70,000 mines at a cost of $80 million. The number of submarines actually destroyed by the mines was relatively small, but the threat of mines may have contributed, as Franklin later contended, to the mutiny of the demoralized German Navy shortly before the armistice.

Roosevelt's greatest disappointment during the war was his failure to see active service. In June 1918, he came closest to realizing his ambition. Either he or Secretary Daniels, Franklin had insisted at that time, must consult with the Allies and go to the front lines to get a firsthand look at the war. Otherwise, their strategic planning would be akin to playing chess in the dark, he suggested. Since the president needed Daniels at meetings in Washington, Franklin was given the assignment. Rather than taking ordinary transport, he set the dramatic tone by boarding a new destroyer, the USS *Dyer*, bound for the war zone. During the voyage, he made the commander's cabin his own and dashed to the bridge in his pajamas during two nocturnal alarms. The *Dyer* zigzagged across the ocean and managed to avoid German submarines, though Franklin reported that the destroyer remained in imminent danger. When the *Dyer* stopped in the Azores for repairs and refueling, he wrote Eleanor: "A German submarine was off this port yesterday, but did not dare attack!"

After landing at Portsmouth, Roosevelt was driven in a Rolls-Royce to a magnificent suite at London's Ritz Hotel as the guest of the British Admiralty. On his first morning of business in London, Roosevelt met with the First Lord of the Admiralty, Sir Eric Geddes, for a briefing on the Allies' prosecution of the war. Geddes complained that the Italian Navy had failed to engage the enemy and asked Franklin to persuade Italian military leaders to take a more aggressive role in the conflict. While in England, Roosevelt inspected British and American military installations, was given a forty-minute private audience with King George V, met with the British prime minister, David Lloyd George, and honored British war ministers at a dinner at Gray's Inn where he was introduced to the minister of munitions, Winston Churchill.*

On the last day of July, Franklin sailed from Dover to the northern coast of France on a British destroyer flying the flag of the Assistant Secretary of the Navy. At Dunkirk, he observed bombed-out buildings that had been the targets of constant German attacks. En route to Paris, he and his party passed freshly dug trenches and barbed-wire fortifications.

In Paris, Franklin stayed as the guest of the French government in the luxurious Hôtel Crillon and conferred with a succession of French leaders. He was most impressed with the vigor and courage of the seventy-seven-year-old premier, Georges Clemenceau: "I knew at once that I was in the presence of the greatest civilian in France. . . . He [Clemenceau] said—'Do not think that the Germans have stopped fighting or that they are not fighting well. We are driving them back because we are fighting better and every Frenchman and every American is fighting better because he knows he is fighting for the Right and that *it* can prevail only by breaking the German Army by force of arms.' "

Roosevelt was determined to witness heavy fighting, angrily brushing aside a naval subordinate's itinerary that would have shielded him from the dangers of the front. At Mareuil-en-Dole, he watched an American gun battery shell German soldiers only seven kilometers away while antiaircraft guns shot at German planes overhead. At Verdun, wearing a French helmet and gas mask, he was again under fire. Later, he took cover at Fort Douaumont and felt the reverberation of German shells exploding outside. He was more thrilled than scared by his battle experience, though it reminded him sadly that his wartime service was largely confined to an office in Washington.

He traveled on by private railroad car to Rome, where, as he had prom-

---

* Decades later, when FDR and Churchill were world leaders, Roosevelt recalled their first meeting and was disappointed that Churchill had no memory of it.

ised Sir Eric Geddes, he prodded risk-averse Italian military leaders to take the battle to the enemy. He urged the Italian Navy to confront the Austrian Navy in the Adriatic, but was told that was impossible since both navies remained in their respective harbors. "We feel sufficiently superior to defeat them if they should decide at any time to come out of harbour to meet us," an Italian naval official told the bemused Assistant Secretary, who termed the attitude "a naval classic" of inertia.

Roosevelt made strenuous return trips to England and France for more high-level meetings and field inspections, and, in the tiny sliver of Belgium territory held by the Allies, came under continuous German artillery fire. His exhausting pace took its toll on his health. By the time he collapsed on his bunk on the *Leviathan* on the passage home, he was seriously ill, suffering from a virulent strain of influenza as well as double pneumonia. After the ship docked in New York Harbor, he was rushed in an ambulance to his mother's town house.

When Eleanor Roosevelt unpacked her ailing husband's suitcase, she discovered a cache of love letters to Franklin from Lucy Mercer, whom Eleanor had hired in 1914 to be her social secretary. It is unlikely that Eleanor's discovery of a romantic liaison between Franklin and Lucy came as a complete surprise. Correspondence between Franklin and Eleanor during the summers of 1916 and 1917 suggested that the couple had grown apart both emotionally and physically. Eleanor and their children* had spent the summers at Campobello while Franklin remained in Washington. In her letters to Franklin, Eleanor expressed frustration at being away from him for such long periods of time. Franklin responded with lighthearted banter, assuring her that he wanted nothing more than to be with his wife "and the chicks," but that his work required that he forgo summer vacations in Maine with his family. What Franklin did not tell Eleanor was that, in his wife's absence, he was spending many evenings and most weekends in the company of Lucy Mercer.

Eleanor had hired Lucy at the suggestion of her Auntie Bye (TR's sister, Bamie) to lighten her responsibilities as the wife of the gregarious Assistant Secretary of the Navy. Lucy was perfectly suited for the job, smart, well-

---

* On March 13, 1916, Eleanor and Franklin's fifth and last surviving child, John Aspinwall Roosevelt, was born.

bred, charming, and effortlessly efficient in imposing order on Eleanor's crammed social calendar. Her parents were descendants of old, wealthy southern families, but the family fortunes had been squandered by the time Lucy came to work for Eleanor. Her father, Carroll Mercer, was a hard-drinking career military man who rose to the rank of captain in the army. After his retirement, he continued to drink heavily and lived primarily off the dwindling funds of his wife, Minnie Tunis Mercer, a beautiful Washington socialite. When Lucy was twelve, the couple separated. Minnie moved to New York City with Lucy and her older sister, Violetta, and marketed her good taste as an interior decorator for wealthy clients. She returned to Washington in 1912 and made a modest living advising young congressmen on tasteful paintings for their residences.

In the winter of 1914, when Lucy was twenty-three years old, she began to work three mornings a week for Eleanor Roosevelt in the family's rented mansion on N Street. She was a devout Catholic whose education had been modest and sheltered, primarily at a convent in Melk, Austria. But she had inherited her mother's natural grace and beauty, and fit comfortably within the Roosevelt household. The children loved her easy manner and warmth, and the entire family was captivated by her radiant smile. At first, she appeared to serve as both Eleanor's social secretary and the children's informal governess. Franklin's earliest written reference to "Miss Mercer" suggested the formal relationship of master to servant. That relationship changed irrevocably over the next three years.

By the summer of 1916, when Eleanor was at Campobello with the children, Lucy was Franklin's frequent companion on cruises up the Potomac River on the navy yacht *Sylph*. Franklin always arranged for the couple to be surrounded by family members and friends. But he did not report other excursions to Eleanor, including his many automobile trips into the Virginia countryside, in which he and Lucy took long walks and picnicked alone.

Neither Franklin nor Lucy ever publicly admitted their love affair, but it is not difficult to understand their mutual attraction. At thirty-four, Franklin was eleven years older than Lucy, but retained his youthful vitality. He was an influential member of the Wilson administration by day, and a gay, effervescent spirit on the Washington social circuit at night and on weekends. Lucy offered Franklin a freshness and quiet understanding that his overburdened wife could not. She was tall, like Eleanor, but displayed none of her physical awkwardness or discomfort in the society that

Franklin so enjoyed. She was fun-loving, witty, and, most of all, delighted in Franklin's company.

Eleanor must have suspected that Franklin's attention had wandered from his family when she wrote to him from Campobello in July 1917, imploring him to join her. He responded: "I really can't stand that house all alone without you, and you were a goosy girl to think or even pretend to think that I do not want you here *all* the summer, because you know I do! But honestly *you* ought to have six weeks straight at Camp, just as *I* ought to, only you can and I can't!" Later that summer, Eleanor returned to Washington to nurse Franklin, who was hospitalized with a serious throat infection. After he recovered, she issued a polite ultimatum: he *must* come to Campobello. And he did.

By then, the affair was a poorly kept secret in Washington. Franklin's friend Nigel Law, a young diplomat at the British Embassy, regularly fronted for the couple, pretending to be Lucy's escort. Those who made capital gossip their business were not diverted. "I saw you twenty miles out in the country," Alice Roosevelt Longworth chided Franklin.* ". . . Your hands were on the wheel, but your eyes were on that perfectly lovely lady." Franklin replied, "*Isn't* she perfectly lovely."

Earlier that summer, Lucy had joined the navy as a yeoman, undoubtedly with Franklin's knowledge and approval. She was assigned to secretarial duties at the Navy Department, where she and Franklin could see each other every day. Secretary Daniels, a confirmed family man who loved Franklin as a son, tried to take paternal control of what he perceived to be a dangerous situation. In October, Lucy was summarily dismissed from her Navy Department job without explanation. But the two could not be kept apart, at least until Franklin's departure on the *Dyer* for Europe in June 1918.

In the fall of 1918, Eleanor confronted Franklin over Lucy's love letters. She offered to give him a divorce, but warned him of the destructive effect that would have on their children. When Franklin's mother was told of the affair, she was appalled at the prospect of such a public scandal in her family. If Franklin divorced Eleanor, Sara told her son, he would not receive another penny from her, nor would he inherit the family's estate at

---

* Alice, TR's married daughter, later arranged for Franklin and Lucy to have dinner at her house when Eleanor was out of town. "He *deserved* a good time," she explained. "He was married to Eleanor."

Hyde Park. Louis Howe also strongly opposed a divorce. If he left Eleanor, Howe told him, Franklin's political career was over.

After much soul-searching, Eleanor agreed not to divorce Franklin if he broke off his affair and promised never to see Lucy again. He accepted Eleanor's conditions. Eleanor never slept in the same bedroom with her husband again. Her trust in the men she had loved—first her adored father, who had abandoned the family, and now Franklin—was shattered. While Franklin's infidelity destroyed the marital bonds at the deepest level, it did not prevent Eleanor from serving as his companion and valued political confidante in the years ahead. Eleanor's decision to cut the most intimate emotional ties with Franklin, moreover, liberated her from the conventional role of mother and supportive spouse. She had been intensely unhappy in her marriage, overwhelmed by her child-rearing responsibilities and increasingly distant from her inexhaustible husband.

Even before she knew of Franklin's affair, Eleanor had taken the first steps toward a fully engaged, satisfying life outside her home. After the United States entered the war in 1917, she helped Josephus Daniels's wife organize the Navy Red Cross. She worked three days a week at the Red Cross canteen at Washington's Union Station, wrapping sandwiches and pouring coffee for young recruits headed for Europe. On the other two weekdays, she visited veterans at Washington's naval hospital, all the while busily knitting sweaters, scarves, and socks for the Comforts Committee of the Navy League. From those wartime days of public service, Eleanor developed into an extraordinarily independent and outspoken woman who would achieve iconic status as a feminist voice for liberal causes.

Soon after her breakup with Franklin, Lucy became governess to the six children of Winthrop Rutherfurd, a wealthy widower and sportsman. They developed a close emotional bond when his eldest son, Lewis, was dying of an undisclosed ailment. During the vigil, Lucy agreed to marry him. Winthrop, almost twice Lucy's age, provided his young wife with a varied and interesting life of leisure. They traveled abroad frequently, attended fashionable parties, and resided in turn at one of Winthrop's three homes—his country estate in Allamuchy, New Jersey, his town house in New York City, or his winter residence in Aiken, South Carolina. Lucy was devoted to his children and helped raised them, as she did the couple's own daughter.

Despite Franklin's promise to Eleanor, he remained in touch with Lucy. When he was president, he arranged for her to watch his inaugurations from a White House limousine. During the Second World War, the White House switchboard was given instructions to put calls from Mrs. Rutherfurd through to the president. Later, Franklin and Lucy began to see each other again, taking rides together in Washington's Rock Creek Park and dining at the invitation of the Roosevelts' daughter, Anna, when Eleanor was out of town. When Roosevelt died at Warm Springs, Georgia, in 1945, Lucy, not Eleanor, was there.*

After his narrow defeat in the 1916 presidential election, Charles Evans Hughes sold his Washington residence and moved his family back to New York City, where he planned to return to the private practice of law. He received an offer from the Guggenheim Brothers organization to do its legal work (at $50,000 a year plus expenses) as well as a partnership in the prominent law firm of Cadwalader, Wickersham & Taft. Turning both suitors down, he chose to resume his practice with his former partners in their small firm, which was renamed Hughes, Rounds, Schurman & Dwight. For Hughes, there was one gratifying addition to the firm: his son, Charles Junior, who had served as editor-in-chief of the *Harvard Law Review*, was now an associate.

While practicing law, Hughes also gave unstinting public support to the president and Congress in the nation's fight against the central powers. He coined the phrase "the fighting Constitution" in a speech to the American Bar Association, imploring Wilson and the Democratically controlled Congress to read their war powers broadly. "The power to wage war," he said, "is the power to wage war successfully." To Hughes, that meant that the federal government must have the necessary military and economic tools to vanquish the enemy. Under his interpretation of the Constitution, Congress could impose a compulsory military draft, ration the nation's food supply, and regulate its industrial plants.

Shortly after the nation's entry into the war, Hughes became totally involved in the war effort. He was appointed the chairman of New York City's draft appeals board, which turned out to be an onerous and emotionally draining experience. The board received 4,000 letters a day drawn from a draft pool of 600,000 registrants. Hughes worked day and night reviewing the appeals. Aware that the board's decision could mean life or

---

* By then, Lucy was a widow. Winthrop Rutherfurd had died in 1944 after a long illness.

death to an applicant, Hughes insisted on personally signing the papers, in quadruplicate, of every man who came before the board.*

At President Wilson's request, Hughes agreed to serve as special investigator of the aircraft industry amid charges that the industry's wartime bureaucracy was fraught with incompetence, inefficiency, and possible corruption. He resigned from the draft appeals board and returned to Washington to begin hearings behind closed doors. As part of his assignment, he also traveled to Dayton, Detroit, New Brunswick, and Buffalo to inspect aircraft factories, examine company books, and question executives. His investigation soon produced evidence of widespread waste and lax supervision. He forced one government administrator to cancel a trip to Paris to make an on-site inspection of the aircraft industry's books; at Hughes's request, Secretary of War Newton Baker was able to gather the information by cable. In all, Hughes called 280 witnesses over a five-month period, and produced 17,000 pages of testimony, documenting inefficiencies up and down the aircraft production line. Even before Hughes had written his final report, news of his investigation exerted indirect pressure on nervous industry administrators, who began to achieve markedly improved production quotas.

Hughes saved his most intense grilling for Colonel E. A. Deeds, who, as head of the Signal Corps' Equipment Division, assumed overall responsibility for the aircraft program. In his interrogation, Hughes showed that Deeds had helped business associates organize an aircraft company, then, as government administrator, awarded the company highly profitable contracts while remaining a confidential adviser to his former associates. Though Deeds himself did not profit from the contracts, Hughes recommended disciplinary measures to Attorney General T. W. Gregory, who found Deeds "guilty of censurable conduct." When Hughes's report on the aircraft industry was completed, *The New York Times* concluded that probably "there has never been a more searching and thorough investigation under the direction of the Government."

After the armistice, Hughes returned to his law practice, representing a broad range of clients and causes. He was hired by John D. Rockefeller to modify his will to limit the fees of his executors. He represented large

---

* Charles Junior left his law firm to enlist as a private, although as the father of two young children he was unlikely to have been drafted. He served with the 305th Field Artillery and rose to the rank of regimental sergeant major.

bond companies in the U.S. Supreme Court, arguing successfully that the Federal Farm Loan Act, which provided that tax-exempt bonds could be issued under the statute, was constitutional. His client list also included striking members of John L. Lewis's United Mine Workers (UMW) union who had been sued under the Sherman Anti-Trust Act for triple damages for destroying company property. Hughes argued, again successfully, that the UMW strikers could not be punished under the statute since their destructive action had no relation to interstate commerce and was not, therefore, covered by the federal statute. And he served as counsel to the state of New York in its effort to prevent New Jersey and the Passaic Valley Sewerage Commissioners from polluting the Upper Bay of New York Harbor.

Hughes could have earned a large fee from liquor interests that wanted him to challenge the constitutionality of the Eighteenth Amendment that made Prohibition the law of the land. As a matter of policy, Hughes believed that the amendment was unwise and impracticable. But he turned down the retainer and, instead, filed a brief as *amicus curiae* on behalf of twenty-one state attorneys general in support of the amendment. In his brief, Hughes cited records from the 1787 Constitutional Convention in Philadelphia to show that the Framers had placed no limits on changes that Congress and the states could make through the amendment process. No matter how wrongheaded the amendment might be, it could only be corrected through the same amendment process that had imposed Prohibition in the first place. Otherwise, Hughes maintained, the very fabric of the constitutional system would be undermined—a position that the Supreme Court adopted.*

At the height of the postwar hysteria over suspected subversives, the so-called Red Scare, Hughes defended, without fee, five Socialist members of the New York Assembly who had been ousted for their unpopular political views. Though all five members had been duly elected, they were summoned by the assembly speaker, denied their seats "pending investigation," and banished from the legislative chamber by the sergeant at arms. Hughes filed a brief charging that the assembly's action had deprived the Socialists of their legal rights in "a reversal of the rule applicable to the meanest criminal." He concluded: "We have passed beyond the state in political

---

* The same amendment process did, in fact, repeal the Eighteenth Amendment when the Twenty-first Amendment was passed in 1933.

development when heresy-hunting is a permitted sport. . . . If a majority can exclude the whole or a part of the minority because it deems the political views entertained by them hurtful, then free government is at a end."* Harvard law professor Zechariah Chafee, Jr., author of a seminal work on free speech, credited Hughes's written defense of the Socialists with breaking the national fever of intolerance against political minorities.

In addition to his busy law practice, Hughes served as president of the city's Legal Aid Society as well as the New York State Bar Association. His most abiding postwar public concern, however, was the terms of the peace treaty. As a presidential candidate in 1916 and later, after the United States had entered the war, Hughes had urged the great powers to devise a comprehensive postwar peace plan. His expressed interest in the peace process, as well as his prominence in the Republican Party, should have made Hughes a leading candidate for U.S. membership on the Peace Commission that was created after hostilities ended. But President Wilson named only members of his own party to the commission except for Henry White, a professional diplomat. Wilson's decision was symptomatic of his determination to control the U.S. delegation and, hopefully, the outcome of the peace negotiations in Paris in January 1919.

On January 2, 1919, Franklin and Eleanor Roosevelt were escorted to their suite on the USS *George Washington*, docked in New York Harbor and bound for France. Franklin had lobbied tirelessly with his superior, Secretary Daniels, to send him to Europe to supervise the demobilization of the vast U.S. Navy establishment, which included fifty-four shore bases, twenty-five port offices, and millions of dollars' worth of supplies and munitions. The transatlantic voyage was the first for Eleanor and Franklin together since their honeymoon fourteen years earlier and came only a few months after Franklin had broken off his affair with Lucy Mercer.

The stormy Atlantic crossing caused the *George Washington*'s crew to lash the lifeboats with heavy ropes. But the inclement weather did nothing to dampen Franklin's spirits or slow his energetic pace. He made a thorough

---

* A few days later, Roosevelt quietly reprimanded the commandant of the Boston Navy Yard, who had discharged three navy machinists on loyalty grounds for being members of the Socialist Party. "Now my dear Admiral," Roosevelt wrote the commandant, "neither you nor I can fire a man because he happens to be a Socialist. It so happens that the Socialist Party has a place on the official ballot in nearly every State in the Union."

inspection of the ship, joined Yale's football coach, Walter Camp, for daily exercises, played shuffleboard, and addressed guests at a gala dinner. Meanwhile, Eleanor spent long hours reading *The Education of Henry Adams*, a tale of disillusionment over the course of American history. On January 6, Eleanor and Franklin were shocked and saddened by the news that Theodore Roosevelt had died in his sleep at the age of sixty-one. "Death had to take him in his sleep," said Vice President Thomas Marshall. "If Roosevelt had been awake, there would have been a fight."

Throughout the voyage, the central topic of conversation was the impending Paris Peace Conference. Both Eleanor and Franklin were swept up in the excitement of the historic moment, their anticipation heightened by the presence on board of the Mexican and Chinese delegations to the conference. After the ship dropped anchor near Brest, Franklin hosted a luncheon in honor of the conference-bound delegations.

While Eleanor and Franklin settled into their suite at the Ritz in Paris, diplomats in the lobby below huddled in intense conversations about the negotiations. The official delegations to the conference held talks behind closed doors in the chambers of the French Foreign Ministry, leaving the Roosevelts and the world at large to guess about their progress. The city itself was a study in contrasts: the Roosevelts and other dignitaries dined in splendor at elegant restaurants, while on the sidewalks crippled soldiers begged for change, and war widows, shrouded in black, mourned their dead husbands.

With confidence and skill, Roosevelt began discussions with his French counterpart, André Tardieu, to sell the U.S. Navy's large radio transmitter, which had been set up near Bordeaux, though construction was not yet completed. Tardieu told Roosevelt that his government could not afford to buy the transmitter. If that were the case, Roosevelt responded, then he supposed the navy would have to dismantle it, part by part, and ship it back to the United States. Tardieu capitulated, agreeing to pay the U.S. government $4 million for the transmitter.

Franklin was less successful in his negotiations with Herbert Hoover, who headed the Allied postwar relief effort. Roosevelt attempted to convince Hoover to buy surplus naval uniforms, but Hoover declined. He chose to purchase an inferior quality of clothing at a lower price from another vendor and also rejected Franklin's offer to sell thousands of tins of navy rations, preferring to buy only the bare necessities—condensed milk, beans, and flour.

Roosevelt left most of the navy's negotiations over buildings and supplies in France to his staff. Meanwhile, he and Eleanor were driven through the battle-torn villages and fields of northern France. Once they had crossed the English Channel, scenes of the war's devastation disappeared. When Franklin made his tour of naval facilities in Great Britain, he discovered that Admiral William Sims had not only laid the groundwork for the demobilization but had virtually completed the negotiations. Sims's work left Roosevelt ample time to meet Eleanor for pleasant lunches and afternoon teas with friends and high-level government officials.

After returning to Paris, the Roosevelts boarded a train to Brest in mid-February for their return voyage on the *George Washington*. Despite having spent six weeks in Europe, much of it in Paris, they knew no more about the details of the peace negotiations than the ordinary newspaper reader. Franklin read the terms of the proposed Covenant of the League of Nations for the first time when a *New York Times* correspondent who was on the same train to Brest showed him a draft of the agreement. Only then did he learn of the controversial Article 10 of the document that obligated every member of the proposed League of Nations to come to the defense of other signatories, even though post–World War One boundaries had not been settled.*

Franklin hoped that he might learn more about the proposed agreement directly from the president, who, with his wife, were among his fellow passengers on the ship. Although Wilson kept out of public view during most of the voyage, Franklin was extremely pleased to receive an invitation to meet with the president in his cabin to discuss the League. Shortly after their meeting, Franklin and Eleanor were invited to be the president's guests at a small luncheon. "The United States must go in [to the League] or it will break the heart of the world," Wilson told his guests, "for she is the only nation that all feel is disinterested and all trust."

After his return to the United States, Roosevelt gave a series of speeches vigorously supporting the League of Nations. Only a year earlier, he admitted, he had considered such an international organization a uto-

---

* Article 10 provided: "The members of the League undertake to respect and preserve as against external aggression the territorial integrity and existing political independence of all Members of the League. In case of any such aggression or in case of any threat or danger of such aggression the Council shall advise upon the means by which this obligation shall be fulfilled."

pian dream. But his firsthand observations on the battlefields of Europe during the previous summer had convinced him that the Allies not only were determined "to beat the Hun" but desired something more than a peace treaty at the end of the conflict. "This is a time of idealism," he said, and the League embodied "the high purpose with which we came into this war." He also was convinced that the United States must join the League to maintain its deserved place as a world leader. It was no longer possible for the United States, or any other great power, to erect "an old Chinese wall policy of isolation."

It would take a second trip by Wilson to France and an additional four months of negotiations before he could return to Washington with the formal Treaty of Versailles. The treaty, he said, was not the negotiators' work but that of "the hand of God who has led us into this way." Members of the Senate did not feel so divinely inspired. A small group of conservative Republicans (labeled "the Irreconcilables") adamantly opposed the treaty. Most Democrats supported the president and were prepared to vote for the treaty without amendments. In the middle were a critical group of Republicans who would determine the outcome. They were led by Senator Henry Cabot Lodge, who wanted to ratify the treaty but with changes to Article 10 that would protect the sovereignty of the United States.

Hughes followed the Senate debate closely. When he had first read about Article 10 in his morning newspaper, he said to his wife that the American people "will never stand for that." Later, he told a Union League audience that the guarantee in Article 10 was "a trouble-breeder and not a peace-maker." To Wilson's declaration that Article 10 was the heart of the treaty, Hughes replied that if that were so, then it was suffering from a bad heart. As opposition to Article 10 built among Republicans in the Senate, Hughes suggested a compromise that would allow the United States to join the League of Nations but not bind the nation to Article 10. Under Hughes's proposed terms, Congress would determine in each case whether the nation had an obligation under the treaty, and, if so, how it should be met.

But Hughes's proposal did not satisfy the Republican "Irreconcilables." Nor did it sway the president, who continued to ignore the Republican victories in the 1918 congressional elections that gave them control of both houses of Congress. He insisted that Article 10 was essential, and non-negotiable. Yet even ardent Wilson supporters, like Franklin Roosevelt, acknowledged the need for compromise.

"I have read the draft of the League three times," Roosevelt said, "and always find something to object to in it, and that is the way with everybody." The goal must be to agree on the general concept of the League and then work out the controversial details. After all, he reasoned, the United States' governing document, the Constitution, was the product of compromise among contentious men of good faith. But neither Roosevelt nor Hughes had the ear of the increasingly isolated president. His insistence that the Senate must approve every provision, including Article 10, lost crucial Democrats, who favored U.S. entry into the League of Nations, as well as Republicans. The Senate refused to ratify the treaty.

In the fall, the president began a cross-country campaign in hopes of rallying the nation to his rigid position. On September 25, after making a speech in Pueblo, Colorado, in support of the Covenant, Wilson suffered a total physical breakdown. He canceled the remainder of his national campaign for the League and returned to Washington. A week later, he suffered a severe stroke that paralyzed his left side and left him near death. He never fully recovered. Sick, bitter, and disillusioned, the president was a shell of the man who had campaigned so vigorously for his reelection four years earlier. It was painfully obvious that Wilson, who had proved highly proficient in mobilizing the nation's resources in the war effort, was incapable of forging a viable peace plan.

By the early months of 1920, Republicans brimmed with optimism about their chances of winning the presidency. The name of Charles Evans Hughes immediately resurfaced as a possible candidate for the Republican nomination. He had, to be sure, lost the 1916 election, but he had done so narrowly, primarily as a result of the Democrats' winning slogan that Wilson had kept the nation out of war. Since his defeat, Hughes had maintained a high profile as a lawyer in private practice, arguing twenty-five cases before the U.S. Supreme Court. In his public statements, he had demonstrated a sophisticated understanding of the peace treaty that the Senate had failed to ratify. And he had suggested a pragmatic solution to overcome the political impasse that had eluded President Wilson.

The chairman of the Republican National Committee, Will Hays, proposed that Hughes accept the temporary chairmanship of the party's convention to be held in Chicago in June and deliver the keynote address. Hughes was concerned that if he agreed to take a central role at the convention, his presidential nomination could follow. He declined the invitation. Later, several powerful Republican members of the Senate, including Henry Cabot Lodge, made their presidential preference for Hughes known. He did not respond to their entreaties.

Though Hughes was weary of elective politics, his decision to reject all political overtures was personal. He was devastated by the tragic death of his beloved eldest daughter, Helen, who died in the late winter of 1920 at the age of twenty-eight. After graduating from Vassar College in 1914, Helen had dedicated her life to helping others. She volunteered for service with the YWCA, first organizing friendship groups for high school girls and later working as a member of the organization's War Work Council in Boston. While acting as a hospital aide, she fell seriously ill with influenza, which soon turned into pneumonia. In the summer of 1919, after recuperating at the family's New York home, she attended her fifth college reunion in Poughkeepsie. But she was soon again bedridden with an advanced case of tuberculosis that led to her death.

In June, shortly before the Republicans convened in Chicago to nominate the party's candidate for president, several influential Republican senators sent an envoy to Hughes to ask him if he would permit his name to be placed in nomination. Tears welled in Hughes's eyes. "I beg of you to believe me," he said. "Since our daughter died, Mrs. Hughes and I are heartbroken. I don't want to be President of the United States. I request that my name not even be mentioned in the convention."

Hughes's wishes were honored. The Republicans nominated a U.S. senator from Ohio, Warren G. Harding, for president and Governor Calvin Coolidge of Massachusetts for vice president. Instantly, the Harding-Coolidge ticket became the odds-on favorite to win the election against the Democrats, who nominated Ohio governor James Cox and his vice-presidential running mate, Franklin Delano Roosevelt.

Despite the demands of his wartime duties, Roosevelt had kept in close touch with the New York politicians who could serve his future ambitions in the Democratic Party. It was no coincidence that he gave special attention to personal requests from Congressman John Fitzgerald, the powerful head of the House Ways and Means Committee, who also happened to be Tammany Hall's most prominent representative in Washington. With oversight responsibility for the nation's shipbuilding, Roosevelt also steered government contracts to the Navy Yard in Fitzgerald's Brooklyn district.

Franklin's attention to Fitzgerald appeared to reap tangible results in the summer of 1917 when he was asked to deliver the oration at Tammany's 128th annual Independence Day anniversary. His patriotic address was a rousing success. Afterward, he glad-handed the faithful and joined in a spirited rendition of "Tammany Forever." It was enough to satisfy even Franklin's old nemesis Charles Murphy, who stood stiffly for a photograph at Roosevelt's side wearing his society's ceremonial sash. The New York press reported that Tammany was considering Roosevelt as the organization's gubernatorial candidate in 1918. Franklin denied any interest in returning to New York to run for governor. His denials were sincere and primarily based on his commitment to his work at the Navy Department during the war. But it did not escape his trained eye that 1918 was likely to be a Republican year. In any case, he was at the center of the action in wartime Washington and could postpone his political career.*

Once the war had ended, Roosevelt was more outspokenly partisan in his public addresses. His first major postwar opportunity to excoriate the Republican Party, and implicitly call attention to his own progressive Democratic principles, came in a speech to the Democratic National Committee in Chicago in May 1919. The keynote speaker was Attorney General A. Mitchell Palmer, who hoped that his widespread raids of suspected subversives (known as "Palmer raids") would be just the credential to take him to the White House. But Roosevelt, who followed Palmer to the podium, stole the show with a blistering attack on the Republicans.

Roosevelt warned that the choice for voters in the 1920 presidential election was stark, and foreboding: either the conservative, reactionary policies of the Republican Party or the liberal, progressive policies of the Democrats. He charged that the new Republican majority in Congress favored high tariffs for "pet groups of manufacturers" and low taxes "to lighten the burden of those unfortunate individuals who have incomes of $1,000,000 a year or more." In foreign affairs, he accused Republican

---

* Franklin's prediction that the Democratic gubernatorial candidate in 1918 would go down to defeat was wrong. Tammany's candidate, Al Smith, scored an upset victory over the popular incumbent Republican governor, Charles Whitman.

senator Henry Cabot Lodge, the chairman of the Foreign Relations Committee, of charting his party's misguided direction only after reading the morning newspaper to learn what President Wilson had said or done—and then "his policy for the next 24 hours becomes the diametrical opposite." The Democratic Party, in contrast, had guided the nation "through the most stupendous war in history," and had done so after passing unprecedented progressive legislation "for the good of the whole population." The Republican Party stood for "special privilege, partisanship, destruction," while Democrats offered "common sense idealism, constructiveness, progress."

"Oh, Franklin!" wrote Arthur Vandenberg, the editor of the Republican *Grand Rapids* [Michigan] *Herald*, "even so good a man . . . occasionally falls into sophistry when he turns into a plain, every-day politician." But Democrats rejoiced in their handsome, aggressive young leader. Ohio's Governor Cox, frequently mentioned as a front-runner for the Democratic presidential nomination, was impressed. So was the *Chicago Tribune*, which announced in a front-page headline: PALMER LOSES PLACE IN SUN TO ROOSEVELT.

Roosevelt burnished his political image as a "common sense idealist," subtly putting distance between himself and his party's unpopular leader, President Wilson. Whereas Wilson stubbornly stuck to his all-or-nothing approach to the Covenant of the League of Nations, Roosevelt presented himself as a pragmatist who recognized the need for compromise. And though Roosevelt had worked in the federal bureaucracy for both terms of the Wilson administration, he publicly deplored the government's inefficiencies. He called on Congress to adopt a business model to eliminate the gross mismanagement that he had observed, advocating a national budget and greater centralized authority in the executive departments, including the Navy Department. He did not spare the U.S. Congress in his criticism, asserting that it was "just about 100 years behind modern American conditions." If Congress were a private business, he said, "it would be in the hands of a receiver in a week." He further mocked Congress in an address to students at Harvard in February 1920, recommending the *Congressional Record* for comic relief, and reporting congressional hearings where committee members "talk and talk endlessly, and then adjourn to allow the stenographers to catch up with the records."

Roosevelt was too young and inexperienced to be considered a serious contender for his party's presidential nomination. But second place on the national ticket was a possibility, first seriously raised with Franklin by his old *Harvard Crimson* colleague Louis Wehle, who had served as general counsel to the War Finance Corporation. Wehle suggested that a Hoover-Roosevelt ticket was perhaps the only combination that could lead to a Democratic victory. Hoover was recognized as a superb wartime food administrator, enjoyed a reputation as a progressive, and favored the Versailles Treaty with minor alterations. Roosevelt offered youth, a stellar record as Assistant Secretary of the Navy, and the incomparable Roosevelt name. Together, they would begin the campaign with an immediate strategic advantage: California (Hoover's home state) and New York (Roosevelt's) were critical to a Democratic electoral victory.

Franklin was excited about the prospect of running with Hoover, whom he called "a wonder," and the best qualified man in the country to become president. He was aware, of course, that being elected vice president after having served as Assistant Secretary of the Navy was exactly the political track that had led his cousin to the White House. And if the Democrats should lose, Franklin would have positioned himself nicely for a later run for president. There was only one problem: no one seemed to know whether Hoover was a Republican or Democrat. And the tight-lipped Hoover did nothing to discourage the guessing game. Roosevelt attempted to learn Hoover's political affiliation at a dinner in late winter 1920, but came away no more enlightened than when the evening began. Finally, at the end of March, Hoover announced that he was a progressive Republican, had been a registered member of the party for more than twenty years, and had proudly cast a ballot for Theodore Roosevelt in 1912.

Even with the bad news about Hoover, Franklin did not rule out the possibility of becoming his party's vice-presidential nominee. He knew that no one campaigned for vice president, but he nonetheless prepared for the day that he might be tapped for the national ticket. In May, he returned to his old insurgency ways against Tammany, declaring his opposition to the unit rule for the New York delegation at the convention. The move at once established his independence from the New York City machine but did not irrevocably alienate Boss Murphy. He invited old political allies and friends to accompany him on the 3,000-mile train trip to the San Francisco convention in late June, including his two earliest Dutchess County mentors, Thomas Lynch and John Mack, and Lathrop Brown, his Harvard roommate and former congressman. After arriving on the west coast, he ingratiated himself with Tammany delegates by inviting them to be his guests on a visit to the battleship *New York*, anchored in San Francisco Harbor.

Each of the three major contenders for the Democratic Party's presidential nomination—Attorney General Palmer, Governor Cox, and former Secretary of the Treasury William McAdoo—posed serious problems. Palmer's reckless raids had alienated the party's labor-liberal wing. Cox, the candidate of the Democratic bosses, was competent enough but lackluster. And McAdoo, conspicuously, did not have the endorsement of his father-in-law, President Wilson.

Before the voting began, Roosevelt captured the convention's attention with typical dramatic flair after a large oil portrait of President Wilson was unveiled. Delegation after delegation spontaneously joined in a procession honoring the president. But the Tammany-controlled New York delegation remained in their seats. An outraged Roosevelt and his fellow upstate delegate, Mayor George Lunn of Schenectady, forcibly wrested the state placard from a Tammany delegate, then triumphantly joined in the parade on the convention floor.

Tammany's Charles Murphy expected to hold a tight rein on the majority of New York delegates, instructing them to vote for the state's favorite son, Governor Al Smith, in the early balloting.* Later, he hoped to tip the scale decisively toward his first presidential choice, Governor Cox. After the seventh ballot, Murphy gave the order to shift the majority of New York delegates to Cox, who eventually won the nomination on the forty-fourth ballot.

Less than twelve hours after the Cox nomination, the delegates reassembled to pick a vice-presidential candidate. Roosevelt's friends had already circulated among the delegates to promote their man. A leader of the Ohio delegation, Judge Timothy Ansberry, told Cox that Roosevelt would make a good running mate. Cox agreed, saying that young Franklin would add three valuable assets to the ticket: he was from New York, an independent, and offered the Roosevelt name. But Cox did not want to

---

* Roosevelt retained sufficient goodwill with Tammany to be asked to make a seconding speech for Smith.

cross Boss Murphy, and, through his manager, Edmund Moore, sought to clear the Roosevelt nomination with the Tammany leader.

"I don't like Roosevelt," Murphy told Moore, "but, Ed, this is the first time a Democratic nominee for the presidency has shown me courtesy." With the Ohio governor's gesture of respect, Murphy said, "I would vote for the devil himself if Cox wanted me to. Tell him we will nominate Roosevelt on the first ballot as soon as we assemble."

After several states had nominated their favorite sons, Florida yielded to Ohio, prompting Judge Ansberry to go to the podium. "The young man I am going to suggest," he told the delegates, "is but three years over the age of thirty-five prescribed by the Constitution . . . but he has crowded into that short period of time a very large experience as a public official. . . . His is a name to conjure with in American politics . . . Franklin D. Roosevelt." The nomination was seconded by the Indiana and Kansas delegations; the favorite sons quickly withdrew, and Roosevelt was nominated by acclamation.

Shortly after noon on a hot day in early August, Roosevelt addressed a crowd of 5,000 well-wishers who had assembled under the giant oak trees at Springwood to hear his speech formally accepting the Democratic Party's nomination for vice president. His mother was seated next to Franklin on the front porch of the family estate, while Eleanor and their two oldest children, Anna and James, sat nearby in the bright sunshine. Many in the audience were old friends and longtime admirers of the Roosevelt family from Hyde Park. But there was more than a sprinkling of prominent politicians, including the governor of New York, Al Smith, former Secretary of the Treasury William McAdoo, and Franklin's boss, Josephus Daniels.

Roosevelt repeated the themes that he had introduced in his speeches in the months preceding the Democratic Convention—the need for U.S. leadership in the international community and efficient, progressive government at home. He did so with more polish than in his earlier efforts, thanks to the editing help of his friend Franklin Lane, the Secretary of the Interior. In supporting the League of Nations,* FDR said, "Today we are

---

* Earlier that summer, Cox and Roosevelt had pledged their support for the League in a sad meeting at the White House with the incapacitated president, who appeared in a wheelchair, his paralyzed left side covered by a shawl.

offered a seat at the table of the family of nations to the end that smaller peoples may be truly safe to work out their own destiny, to the end that the sword shall not follow on the heels of the merchant, to the end that the burden of increasing armies and navies shall be lifted from the shoulders of a world already suffering under the weight of taxation." He concluded: "It is the faith which is in me that makes me very certain that America will choose the path of progress and set aside the doctrines of despair, the whispering of cowardice, the narrow road to yesterday."

Both in word and cadence, Roosevelt exuded confidence that his party would lead the nation to future greatness. But his upbeat speech belied the pervasive feeling that nothing could save the Democratic ticket from disaster in November, even the party's high-spirited vice-presidential candidate. "His [Roosevelt's] nomination was a compliment," editorialized the *Poughkeepsie Eagle*, "his defeat a certainty."

Two days after his Hyde Park speech, Roosevelt embarked on the first of two whirlwind national tours that would take him 8,200 miles through eighteen states in twenty days. He did so in style, aboard the private railroad car, the *Westboro*, which was attached to regularly scheduled passenger trains according to a carefully laid out campaign plan.* He was accompanied by a staff that included two men who would work for him at the White House after FDR was elected president: Stephen T. Early, a former Associated Press reporter who served as the vice-presidential candidate's advance man, and Marvin McIntyre, who had handled public relations at the Navy Department. Roosevelt's campaign schedule frequently began shortly after dawn when he delivered the first of seven or eight formal speeches, interspersed with dozens of informal, extemporaneous remarks, and ended after midnight, usually followed by a game of poker with his staff and friends.

His dashing, peripatetic image differed markedly from both candidates on the Republican ticket. His vice-presidential opponent, Governor Calvin Coolidge of Massachusetts, was a man of remarkably few words and somber demeanor. And Senator Warren Harding, who headed the Republican ticket, studiously followed the sedentary strategy of another suc-

---

* Before he started campaigning, Roosevelt demonstrated that his love of an adventure in high style could overwhelm his judgment, as happened when he piloted the destroyer *Hatfield* from Boston to Campobello in late July. The *New York Journal* was incensed that taxpayers were paying for FDR's expensive commute to his vacation home, burning "up coal enough to heat the homes of fifty families all winter to carry his 165 pounds. . . ."

cessful Ohio politician, the late Republican president William McKinley, conducting most of his campaign from his front porch in Marion, Ohio. Harding, the genial former editor of the *Marion Star*, had claimed his party's presidential nomination without displaying much energy or discernible talent. With the political tide coursing strongly in the Republicans' favor, he and his manager, Harry Daugherty, calculated that the candidate could afford to sit back and remind voters that he was not the crippled, unpopular Democratic president. Harding was against "Wilson's League of Nations" and for "a return to normalcy," leaving the electorate to define that felicitous, open-ended phrase.

Undaunted by the challenge, Roosevelt hammered away at Harding, invoking the incandescent name of his late cousin, Teddy, to remind voters of his family's progressive pedigree. "I do not profess to know what Theodore Roosevelt would say were he alive today," he told one audience, "but I cannot but help think that the man who invented the word 'pussyfooter' could not have resisted the temptation to apply it to Mr. Harding." He scattered his speeches with TR phrases like "bully" and "square deal" and assured voters that he and Governor Cox, not Harding and Coolidge, would carry on in the nation's progressive tradition.

"Franklin is as much like Theodore as a clam is like a bear-cat," groused the *Chicago Tribune*. The Republican Party recruited TR's son, Theodore, Junior, to refute Franklin's claim that he was the heir to his father's political legacy. "He [Franklin] is a maverick," said young Theodore. "He does not have the brand of our family." Franklin brushed aside his cousin's attack, lamenting that personal vilification was a fact of political life, all the while continuing to link himself inextricably to TR with receptive western audiences.

In Deer Lodge, Montana, Franklin's exuberant defense of the League of Nations resulted in his worst gaffe of the campaign. To counter Republican charges that the Covenant would give Great Britain (with the certain votes of five of its colonies) an unfair advantage over the United States, Franklin assured his audience that the United States would control the votes of the Central American states. He then went beyond hyperbole to outright falsehood. "You know I have had something to do with the running of a couple of little republics," he said. "The facts are that I wrote Haiti's Constitution myself and, if I do say it, I think it is a pretty good constitution." His boast, which he repeated in two later speeches, was pure nonsense. After the statement was published, he insisted that he had been misquoted. But more than a dozen members of the press who had heard Roosevelt's remarks signed a statement attesting to the accuracy of their reporting. The *coup de grâce* was leveled by Governor Harding in a statement issued from Marion: "I will not empower an Assistant Secretary of the Navy to draft a constitution for helpless neighbors in the West Indies and jam it down their throats at the point of bayonets borne by United States Marines."

Franklin never admitted that he had lied and continued to take the attack to the Republicans.* He regularly defended the League even though his advance man, Steve Early, reported that the rank-and-file were more concerned about "their bread baskets" than "their war allies." He declared his support for farmers, labor, and schoolteachers, reminding a St. Paul audience that the Democrats were the party of ordinary Americans. In Centralia, Washington, he demonstrated that he was not above rank demagoguery, telling the crowd that he considered his visit to their town as "a pilgrimage to the very graves of the martyred members of the American Legion who had given their lives in the sacred cause of Americanism." What he did not say was that the legionnaires' deaths came after their unprovoked attack on the local labor union headquarters of the radical International Workers of the World.

In early October, Roosevelt thought that Harding made a serious, perhaps fatal, mistake when he appeared to oppose the League of Nations under any circumstances. He knew that unqualified opposition to the League contradicted the position of moderate leaders of Harding's own party, including Charles Evans Hughes.

Hughes had met with Harding in Marion in August en route to St. Louis, where he was scheduled to address the American Bar Association. After their meeting, Hughes issued a statement endorsing Harding's candidacy, declaring that his election was the best assurance that the United States would assume its proper leadership role in international relations. His discussion with the candidate had convinced Hughes that Harding was committed to the League of Nations, though not to Article 10. After Harding's statement in October appeared to renege on that commitment, Hughes joined thirty other Republican leaders in signing a statement of support for the League with changes to the controversial Article 10.

---

* Eight years later, after *The Nation* referred to the "Roosevelt Constitution," he protested that he had never claimed to have written the Haitian constitution.

"[T]o bring America into an effective league to preserve the peace," they concluded, "we can only look to the Republican Party and its candidate."

Despite the apparent split between Harding and the moderate leadership of his party over the League, late polls showed the Harding-Coolidge ticket ahead of Cox and Roosevelt by more than three to one in six critical states, indicating that the Republicans might sweep into office by a landslide. Roosevelt, returning to Hyde Park after the grueling campaign, expressed confidence in a Democratic victory. But no one around him was sure that even he believed what he was saying.

On election day, Harding received 61 percent of the popular vote (16 million votes to Cox's 9 million) and captured 404 electoral votes to the Democrats' 127. "This is not a landslide," concluded President Wilson's secretary, Joseph Tumulty; "it is an earthquake."

Roosevelt took the resounding defeat in stride. "I do not feel in the least bit downhearted," he said. "It seems to me that everything possible was done during the campaign, and no other would have been either honorable or successful." Behind his cheerful stoicism lay the promising reality that he was now a national leader of his party. Campaign-tested, he could call on leaders in every state that he had visited who believed that he represented the party's best hope to return to the White House, perhaps as early as 1924.

After the Republican victory, President-elect Harding asked Charles Evans Hughes to come to Marion to confer with him on "the problem we have to solve in dealing with our new world relationship." Harding had more than a friendly discussion in mind. He offered Hughes the most challenging cabinet position in his administration, that of Secretary of State, charged with developing the nation's foreign policy in the perilous postwar world. Would Hughes, who was still distressed over the tragic death of his eldest daughter, accept? Yes, Hughes told Harding, he would be honored to serve.

4

Searching for the Next Jefferson

R oosevelt was honored at a posh black-tie dinner at Delmonico's
in New York on January 7, 1921, by a select group of the nation's
most successful corporate titans. Attendees included Edward Stet-
tinius of U.S. Steel, Daniel Willard of the Pennsylvania Railroad, Owen
Young of General Electric, and Adolph Ochs, publisher of *The New York
Times*. The master of ceremonies for the evening was William P. G. Harding, the governor of the Federal Reserve Board, who predicted that stable
business conditions would return to postwar America, assuring the nation's
steady economic prosperity. Roosevelt heartily applauded with the other
guests who had much to gain if Harding's prediction proved accurate.

For the first time in his career, Roosevelt faced daunting financial problems. All five of his children were enrolled in expensive private schools,
while at the house on East 65th Street a large staff of servants continued
to provide for the family's domestic needs. Franklin eagerly anticipated
joining the ranks of the "younger capitalists," and fortunately Van-Lear
Black, a major contributor to the Democratic Party and a longtime Roosevelt admirer, gave him the opportunity. Black hired Franklin to be vice
president in charge of the New York office of Fidelity & Deposit Company.
Known as F&D, the company was the nation's fourth largest surety bonding concern, whose business was to insure contracts for both government

and private industry. Roosevelt's salary was $25,000 a year, five times what he had earned as Assistant Secretary of the Navy. He knew very well that he had not been hired for his expertise in the bonding business but rather to bring in large new accounts through his vast political network. He relished the challenge and immediately contacted old political allies and recipients of Navy Department contracts during the Wilson administration to inquire if they or their colleagues might need insurance with F&D. In many cases, they did, and Franklin's boss, Van-Lear Black, was enormously pleased.

Roosevelt's lucrative position at the bonding company only required that he be in the office on weekday mornings. That left his afternoons free to practice law and renew alliances in the Democratic Party. He had formed a law partnership with two old friends, Grenville Emmett and Langdon Marvin, but soon discovered that the practice, even limited to afternoons, held no greater interest for him in 1921 than it had at Carter, Ledyard & Milburn more than a decade earlier. Keeping his hand in Democratic politics, both at the state and national level, was another matter. His name was already prominently mentioned as a candidate for the U.S. Senate in 1922.

With the help of a devoted, attractive young secretary, Marguerite ("Missy) Le Hand,* who had first worked for him during his vice-presidential campaign, Roosevelt maintained a steady correspondence with leaders of the New York Democratic Party as well as those whom he had met while stumping across the country for the Cox-Roosevelt ticket. He first addressed the need to rebuild the party's upstate organization after the 1920 debacle. Convinced that the party must unite to be successful, he devoted great energy to the task of preaching cooperation between upstate and Tammany leaders.

At the same time, he began to take moderate positions on national issues that contrasted with his reformist zeal during his eight years in the Wilson administration. His more cautious approach to public policy was a tacit acknowledgment that the Republicans' lopsided presidential victory accurately reflected the country's conservative mood. In international affairs, he quietly abandoned his advocacy of U.S. entry into the League of Nations, supporting, instead, a separate peace with Germany and ne-

---

* She was given the nickname "Missy" by one of the Roosevelt children who had difficulty saying "Miss Le Hand."

gotiations with other world powers to reduce armaments. He no longer demanded a large navy, but agreed with President Harding's Secretary of State, Charles Evans Hughes, that there must be a drastic reduction in naval armaments among the great miliary powers.

As a private citizen, Roosevelt's daily appointment calendar was as crammed as it had been when he served in the Navy Department. When not calling on potential clients for F&D or meeting with a valued political ally, he worked feverishly for a variety of civic causes. He served as chairman of the Greater New York Committee of the Boy Scouts of America, director of the Seaman's Church Institute, member of the executive board of the Near East Relief Committee, chairman of a $2 million fund drive for Lighthouses for the Blind, and overseer of Harvard University.

Despite his busy schedule, Franklin always found time for fun with friends, often accompanied by good food and drink. One spring evening, while Eleanor was out of town, he attended a reunion of his college class at the Harvard Club. When Eleanor returned the next day at noon, she was told by the maid that Franklin was still in bed. She rushed to his bedside, frantic that he might be seriously ill. She discovered that he was merely suffering from a bad hangover "after a wild 1904 dinner & party."

Though Roosevelt had successfully made the transition from official Washington to the private sector, his intention to run for high elective office was never in doubt. There was one piece of unfinished business from his work at the Navy Department, however, that seriously threatened his political future. In 1919, both Roosevelt and Secretary Daniels had become alarmed by reports that sailors at the naval base at Newport, Rhode Island, were being corrupted by drugs, prostitutes, and homosexual procurement.

Just how much Roosevelt knew about the details of the scandal or how involved he was in supervising the U.S. Navy sting operation that followed has never been clearly established. He certainly was informed about the problems at Newport and approved of the general effort to clean up the mess. But Roosevelt never admitted that he authorized the naval unit, under Lieutenant Erastus Hudson, that asked sailors to solicit sexual favors from suspected homosexuals and then have them arrested. When stories of the entrapment efforts became public, Daniels ordered an internal investigation. The result was a report that exonerated Roosevelt of primary responsibility for the operation. Issued in late February 1921, only a week before Warren Harding's presidential inauguration, the report concluded only that the Assistant Secretary had been "ill-advised" when he "either directed or permitted the use of enlisted personnel to investigate perversion." Franklin resented even that conclusion. "Frankly, I must decline to be made in any way the scapegoat for things which had their inception among the regular navy officers concerned," he said.

Franklin worried that those involved in the Newport operation could still be brought up on criminal charges, precipitating a new round of bad publicity about the scandal. He urged Daniels to submit the legal question to the U.S. Attorney General before the Republicans took office. On the night before Harding's inauguration, Wilson's Attorney General ruled that the officer in charge, Lieutenant Hudson, and his agents, should be censured but allowed to resign honorably from the navy.

The Attorney General's ruling was not the final word on the Newport scandal, as both Daniels and Roosevelt had hoped. In the spring of 1921, a three-member subcommittee of the Senate Naval Affairs Committee (composed of two Republicans and one Democrat) resumed its investigation of the Newport scandal that they had begun in the last year of the Wilson administration. Roosevelt had testified briefly before the subcommittee in February 1920, but despite his request, had not been invited back to give a fuller account of his knowledge of the scandal.

In July 1921, while Roosevelt was vacationing with his family at Campobello, he received a telegram from Josephus Daniels informing him that the Senate subcommittee was ready to issue its report on Newport the following Monday, and that it was "libelous." Roosevelt wired the chairman of the subcommittee, Republican Senator L. Heisler Ball of Delaware, demanding that he be given the opportunity to respond to the committee's findings at a hearing, which, he said, had been promised.

Roosevelt rushed back to Washington to defend himself. But when he arrived at the Capitol, the two Republican members of the subcommittee told him that his testimony was unnecessary, since he had provided all necessary information in the navy's internal report. They did agree to give Roosevelt a few hours to examine the fifteen volumes of the report, including 6,000 pages of testimony before the committee, and to submit a statement by 8 p.m. that evening. Roosevelt was furious, but nonetheless retreated to a hot, airless room in the Navy Department to sift through the massive report. As he thumbed through the pages, pencil in hand, his worst fears were realized. His repeated denials of responsibility for the scandal were rejected as "unbelievable" and "incredible." He must have known and approved of the "most deplorable, disgraceful and unnatural" activities at Newport, the report concluded.*

Even with the assistance of Steve Early and Missy Le Hand, Roosevelt knew that he had no time to rebut the accusations against him. Instead, he went on the offensive, attacking the report as unfair and politically motivated. He accused the subcommittee's two-member Republican majority of "deliberate falsification of evidence" and "perversion of facts." Most deplorable of all, he wrote, as "an American, irrespective of party, one hates to see the United States Navy . . . used as the vehicle for cheap ward politics." He was certain, he added, that the attacks would "boomerang" on his accusers. But, in fact, Roosevelt was extremely concerned that the report would do serious and perhaps permanent damage to his reputation. His anxiety only deepened when he read the headline in *The New York Times*:

LAY NAVY SCANDAL TO F. D. ROOSEVELT
DETAILS ARE UNPRINTABLE

Roosevelt returned to New York to take care of business at his Wall Street office, still fuming over his treatment by the two Republicans on the Senate subcommittee. He wrote to one of them, Senator Henry Keyes of New Hampshire, who was a fellow Harvard alumnus, that he had been privileged over the years to know thousands of graduates of their alma mater. "Of the whole number I did not personally know one whom I believed to be personally and willfully dishonorable," he noted. "I regret that because of your recent despicable action I can no longer say that." He did not send the missive, but filed it in a cabinet with the notation—"Not sent—what was the use? FDR."

A week later, he joined a group of prominent community leaders on a cruise up the Hudson to celebrate the work of more than 2,000 Boy Scouts from the city who were attending summer camp at Bear Mountain, New York. Though still fatigued from his Washington ordeal, Roosevelt showed no outward sign of stress. He marched at the front of a parade, admired the Scouts' skills in tying sailor knots, and served as toastmaster at a campfire dinner. He also acted as prosecutor in the mock trial of New York City's

---

* The Democratic member of the subcommittee, Senator William King of Utah, filed a minority report defending Roosevelt, writing that the attacks on him were "unjust, entirely unwarranted and not supported by the record."

police commissioner, another honored guest, who was accused of imbibing an alcoholic beverage from a hollow cane. Franklin sniffed the suspicious liquid, declared it to be harmless vanilla extract, and grandly dismissed the case, evoking peals of laughter from the delighted audience.

In that long, seemingly carefree day with the Scouts, Roosevelt almost certainly was infected with a virus that would change his life and the nation's destiny.

On August 5, Franklin set sail from New York for a delayed reunion with his family at Campobello on Van-Lear Black's 140-foot yacht, the *Sabalo*. When he arrived at the family's summer home three days later, Eleanor and their five children, as well as their house guests, the Louis Howe family, stood on the dock to greet him. The three-day voyage from New York had not rid Franklin of his fatigue, but he was sure that his time-honored prescription—nonstop physical activity—offered the best remedy.

Franklin led his children through a constant regiment of sailing, fishing, swimming, and foot-racing around the island. On the third day, with Franklin at the helm of the family's small sailboat, the *Vireo*, they saw smoke rising on one of the nearby islands, the familiar sign of a forest fire. Franklin expertly piloted the craft close to the island so that the family could wade ashore. Soon enough, they found the fire. Franklin tore boughs from pine trees and distributed them to the family to smother the fire, which took several hours. Dirty and exhausted, they headed home.

When they arrived at Campobello about four o'clock in the afternoon, Franklin felt unusually tired and decided that he needed a swim in a nearby pond to invigorate himself. With his family in tow, Franklin yelped and splashed and swam to the other side of the pond. He then climbed a low ridge and jumped into the frigid Bay of Fundy. He was disappointed that the plunge failed to give him "the glow I'd expected."

He returned to the family cottage more exhausted than ever. He sat in his wet swim trunks reading the mail, "too tired even to dress." He admitted, "I'd never felt quite that way before." An hour later, he began to shiver and excused himself to go to bed. It must be a cold, he thought. Eleanor covered him with a heavy wool blanket, but he continued to tremble uncontrollably. After a restless night, he swung his legs over the side of the bed and headed for the bathroom. His left leg buckled. Steadying himself, he awkwardly made his way to the bathroom for a shave. His head throbbed, his back ached, and he began to lose feeling in his right leg. He nonetheless managed to return to his bed unassisted. Eleanor took his temperature: 102 degrees.

She summoned Dr. E. H. Bennet, an elderly local physician, who had treated the Roosevelt children and other summer residents for sore throats and broken bones. He told Franklin that he had a bad cold and would check back the next day. But the paralysis worsened and his temperature rose. Franklin was sure that the country doctor's diagnosis was wrong, though he did not know what had befallen him. By the end of the week, both of his legs were useless. He could not stand up and was paralyzed from the waist down. His thumbs were numb, so that he could not hold a pen. Increasingly alarmed, Eleanor and Louis Howe sought a second medical opinion. Howe canvassed every resort on the Maine coast to find a specialist who was willing to interrupt his vacation to examine Franklin. At Bar Harbor, Howe contacted Dr. William Keen, a renowned eighty-four-year-old Philadelphia surgeon, who agreed to come to Campobello.

After his examination, Keen concluded that Franklin's paralysis was the result of a blood clot in the lower spinal cord. He recommended constant massages to increase blood circulation until the clot dissolved and voiced optimism that the patient's health would improve within a few months. He sent a bill of $600 for his services, which infuriated Eleanor. She and Louis Howe nonetheless followed Dr. Keen's instructions, constantly rubbing Franklin's paralyzed legs, which turned out to be both excruciatingly painful and counterproductive. Roosevelt's condition deteriorated. The paralysis spread to his hands and arms, his fever spiraled upward, and he lost control of his bodily functions. Eleanor slept on a couch in his room, massaging his legs, brushing his teeth, and administering catheters and enemas.

Finally, Howe, an inveterate skeptic, wrote Roosevelt's uncle, Frank Delano, in New York expressing his doubts about Dr. Keen's diagnosis. After describing Franklin's symptoms to Delano, Howe asked him to consult with experts in New York and Boston. Franklin, his uncle learned, almost certainly had been stricken by infantile paralysis. Dr. Robert Lovett, professor of orthopedic surgery at the Harvard Medical School faculty and the nation's leading expert on infantile paralysis, was contacted at his summer home in Newport and agreed to come to Campobello.

Dr. Lovett arrived at Campobello on August 25, exactly two weeks after Franklin had lost the use of his legs. The doctor, a tall, elegant man with a carefully waxed gray mustache, gently moved his hands over Franklin's body. It was "perfectly clear," he concluded, that Franklin was the victim of infantile paralysis. He offered a glimmer of hope, telling the patient that he had seen much worse cases, and that he might well regain the use of the paralyzed parts of his body. Franklin accepted the diagnosis silently, without any visible trace of emotion. Lovett told Eleanor that the massages must stop immediately, and, out of earshot of Franklin, warned that the patient would likely become depressed and irritable.

For Eleanor, the doctor's warning was unnecessary. Only days after Franklin had experienced the paralysis, she reported that he was not just depressed but temporarily delirious. Franklin later recalled that for the first time in his life he questioned his belief in a caring God. In addition to his spiritual crisis, he also contemplated a temporal future unlike anything he had ever known: no vigorous physical activity, no frantic juggling of business appointments, no raucous good times at the Harvard Club or luxurious trips abroad. After his temperature subsided and he reported some feeling in his thumbs, his innate optimism returned. In reality, his progress was illusory.

Soon after Dr. Lovett had departed from the island, an alarmed Dr. Bennet, who had been left in charge of Franklin's daily care, wired him: ATROPHY INCREASING POWER LESSENING CAUSING PATIENT MUCH ANXIETY ATTRIBUTED BY HIM TO DISCONTINUANCE OF MASSAGE CAN YOU RECOMMEND ANYTHING TO KEEP UP HIS COURAGE AND MAKE HIM FEEL THE BEST IS BEING DONE.

To the outside world, meanwhile, Franklin's confinement appeared to be due to nothing more serious than a bad cold. Eleanor, Louis Howe, and Missy Le Hand, who had come up from New York, conspired to perpetuate the ruse. They answered his mail, routinely forging his signature. In one letter sent to an old friend, Franklin cheerfully conceded only "a severe chill," which he attributed to the "vagaries of the Bay of Fundy climate." While he was flat on his back and in almost constant pain, his surrogates volunteered his services as a new member of the board of trustees of Vassar College and the executive committee of the New York State Democratic Party. His correspondence never mentioned that he had been stricken with polio.

Franklin, Eleanor, and Louis Howe were committed to the deception about the true nature of his illness until the prognosis was clearer. Howe was designated dissembler-in-chief and energetically assured curious wire service reporters that Roosevelt was improving daily, and that it was only a matter of days until he would be strolling about Campobello. Meanwhile, Franklin's temperature spiked again and his muscles showed no sign of recovery. Despite Franklin's impatience, Dr. Lovett advised that complete bed rest was critical.

If he must remain in bed, Franklin decided that he should do so in New York City, where he could be treated at Presbyterian Hospital and be near his friends and business interests. Uncle Frank arranged for Franklin to travel to Manhattan by a private railway car waiting at nearby Eastport, Maine, while Louis Howe made sure that no reporters were informed of his departure. On Tuesday morning, September 13, Franklin was gingerly lifted from his bed by six men, who placed him on a stretcher, carried him downstairs, through the living room, and down the slope of the Campobello estate to a motorboat ready to take him to Eastport.

"Don't worry chicks," he told his anxious children. "I will be all right."

Three days later, *The New York Times* broke the true story of Franklin's illness on the front page:

F. D. ROOSEVELT ILL OF POLIOMYELITIS
BROUGHT ON SPECIAL CAR FROM CAMPOBELLO,
BAY OF FUNDY, TO HOSPITAL HERE

Though Roosevelt's illness was now a matter of public record, Dr. George Draper, his physician at Presbyterian Hospital (and a protégé of Dr. Lovett), insisted in the *Times* report that his patient could expect a full recovery. "[H]e definitely will not be crippled," Dr. Draper said. "No one need have any fear of any permanent injury from this attack."

That was just the prognosis that Franklin craved. His good spirits immediately returned and were reflected in a letter that he dictated to his friend, *Times* publisher Adolph Ochs: "While doctors were unanimous in telling me that the attack was very mild and that I was not going to suffer any permanent effects from it, I had, of course, the usual dark suspicion that they were just saying nice things to make me feel good. But now that I have seen the same statement officially made in *The New York Times* I feel immensely relieved because I know of course it must be true."

Draper's optimism quickly turned to concern when Roosevelt's paralyzed muscles refused to respond to treatment. The patient's insistent good cheer for the six weeks he remained at Presbyterian Hospital belied his serious condition. He greeted his children every afternoon with a wide grin and invitation to join him on his bed. When his anguished former boss, Josephus Daniels, paid a visit, Franklin good-naturedly punched him in the stomach. "You thought you were coming to see an invalid," he joked. "But I can knock you out in any bout!"

Roosevelt had trained for a lifetime for this bravura performance. As a boy, he was taught by his mother to hide pain or sadness. He quickly became adept at sparing his fragile father, who suffered from a chronic heart condition, any unpleasant news. When young Franklin badly cut his forehead, he asked his mother to clean the wound and put a hat over it before his father could see it. Later, after James's heart condition had worsened, his son's letters from Groton were relentlessly upbeat.

In Roosevelt's own life, when events did not turn out exactly as he would have liked, he confidently rededicated himself to success. After being rejected in his first attempt to make the *Harvard Crimson* staff, he worked harder, was selected, and eventually rose to the top editorial position. He stumbled occasionally in his otherwise meteoric political career—failing miserably in his bid for the U.S. Senate in 1914 and as the Democratic Party's vice-presidential candidate in 1920. Both setbacks, he was sure, were temporary. He would come back stronger than ever.

Polio was different. The disease posed problems for Franklin that he had never confronted before. He could not will his improvement by an indomitable spirit. Nor could he rid himself of the paralysis by sheer hard work and determination. And he faced a formidable psychological challenge, Dr. Draper realized, in addition to fighting his debilitating illness. "He has such courage, such ambition," Draper wrote Lovett, "and yet at the same time such an extraordinarily sensitive emotional mechanism, that it will also take all the skill which we can muster to lead him successfully to a recognition of what he really faces without utterly crushing him." When Roosevelt left the hospital after six weeks, his chart read: NOT IMPROVING.

Franklin was moved up three flights of stairs to the quietest bedroom in the family town house. But it was never calm in the Roosevelt household once he returned. Eleanor dedicated herself to Franklin's recovery and prodded him, sometimes to his irritation, to follow doctors' orders. Louis Howe was given sixteen-year-old Anna's bedroom as his temporary home, much to the teenager's displeasure. Howe continued to insist that Franklin would someday be elected president and assiduously courted reporters, feeding them stories of Roosevelt's improving health and political viability.

Next door, Sara planned for her invalid son's imminent retirement from politics. He would, she assumed, live the rest of his life at Springwood under her loving supervision, as had her husband James.

Eleanor and Louis were natural allies in this tense tug-of-war over Franklin's future. For her part, Sara continued to provide critical commentary of Eleanor as both wife and mother. She was always ready to take the children's side in any dispute with their mother, as she did in sympathizing with Anna after she was forced to relinquish her bedroom to Howe. Sara had no use for Howe, whom she described as "that dirty, ugly little man."

At the center of this perfect domestic storm lay Franklin who, besides wanting to please everybody, concentrated on making his body whole again. To assist him, Kathleen Lake, a trained physiotherapist, was hired to administer massages to his lifeless legs. Every morning except Sunday, the efficient and humorless Mrs. Lake placed a board across Franklin's bed, covered it with oilcloth, then carefully moved one leg onto the wood. Slowly, laboriously, she lifted the leg, stretched the sensitive muscles, returned it to the board, and repeated the exercise with the other leg. The routine was painful for Franklin and did not change. He never complained.

Meanwhile, with the indispensable help of Eleanor, Louis, and Missy Le Hand, Franklin projected a vigorous public image of a polio patient on the inevitable road to a complete recovery. He continued to serve on the boards of the Boy Scout Foundation of Greater New York and the Cathedral of St. John the Divine. Every Tuesday afternoon, he presided at a strategy session for F&D in the family library. And he vigilantly maintained a steady correspondence with state Democratic leaders and was pleased to read newspaper reports that he was a likely candidate for the U.S. Senate in the midterm elections.

Roosevelt also refused to give up his role as paterfamilias. At Christmastime, he read Dickens's *Christmas Carol* aloud and carved the holiday turkey, though he did so for the first time from a sitting position in his wheelchair. And he forced the five children to confront his paralysis, making a sport of pointing to each affected muscle and quizzing them on the correct medical term.

In February 1922, Roosevelt was given crutches and fitted for steel braces that weighed 14 pounds and extended from his hips to his heels. For the first time since August, he could stand up, though not in a way that he had ever known. He was exhilarated nonetheless and eagerly followed instructions on how he might move forward unassisted. It required him to lean heavily on his crutches, use his neck muscles to thrust his head for-ward, tipping his body so that he could drag the heavy braces slowly across the floor. He then threw his head back, taking the weight off his crutches just long enough for him to shift them to a forward position. He became highly adept at this awkward maneuver, all the while making a great effort to hide the enormous strain that it demanded.

It was just as well that Roosevelt did not know about the progress re-port that Draper sent to Lovett. Though the patient was walking success-fully with his crutches and braces and seemed to be gaining power in his hip muscles, Draper wrote, "below the knee I must say it begins to look rather hopeless." Draper also expressed concern about the effect on the patient of the tensions within the Roosevelt household. In late May, they recommended that Roosevelt be moved to Springwood for the summer, to Sara's obvious delight.

Sara ordered ramps built for his wheelchair and reactivated James's old elevator to take Franklin to his bedroom on the second floor. She instructed her staff that her son must have absolute quiet unless she de-creed otherwise. He slept late every morning except for the three days a week that Mrs. Lake came to Springwood to massage his legs. After he was served breakfast in bed, he exercised his upper body on rings hanging from the ceiling. Later, he read, worked on his stamp collection, whittled on model boats, and dined with his mother. It was soon apparent, even to Sara, that Franklin was restless and bridled under her tight rein. He hated the solitude.

In June, Eleanor and the children joined him, as did two frequent visi-tors, his cousins Laura Delano and Margaret Suckley. Parallel bars were constructed on the south lawn at the level of Franklin's shoulders to build his upper torso. He worked on the bars every day, simultaneously carrying on an unbroken monologue on trivia or world events for whomever was available to keep him company. He eagerly accepted an invitation from a wealthy Dutchess County neighbor, Vincent Astor, to use his heated swim-ming pool to exercise his withered legs.

Politics was never far from Franklin's mind. While Howe continued to keep his name in the newspapers, Eleanor began a conscious effort to serve as her husband's surrogate, taking a leadership role in state Demo-cratic women's organizations, making speeches whenever invited. She was carefully tutored on her new role by Howe and found, to her surprise and pleasure, that she was good at it.

Even though Al Smith had lost the governorship in the Republican landslide of 1920, he remained the most popular Democrat in the state. But in 1922 Smith was enjoying prosperity for the first time in his life as a trucking industry executive and serving on several corporate boards, earning five times his gubernatorial salary. He was reluctant to return to elective politics, but was prodded in that direction by William Randolph Hearst's announcement that he would seek the Democratic nomination for governor. Smith loathed Hearst, never having forgiven the publisher for his newspapers' vicious (and baseless) attacks on him during the 1918 gubernatorial campaign. State Democratic leaders, fearing a Hearst defeat in the general election, persuaded Smith to challenge the newspaper publisher. Smith sought a prominent Protestant upstate party leader to call publicly for his nomination, and turned to Roosevelt, who happily obliged. In a public letter, he urged Smith to run "in the name of countless thousands of citizens of upstate New York." Hearst withdrew from the race, and Smith won a resounding victory in the November general election.

Roosevelt returned to New York in the fall of 1922, determined to resume a normal professional life. He had not been to F&D's office since he had been stricken with polio. In the late morning of October 9, he was driven by his chauffeur in the family Buick from his Upper East Side house to the bond company's Wall Street office. After the car stopped at the curb, the driver came over to the back door and helped him out. Perspiring heavily, Franklin made his way slowly, painfully, into the lobby and began to cross the slick marble floor. Suddenly, he lost his balance and crashed to the floor. Onlookers were stunned. They watched him awkwardly pull himself up to a sitting position, never losing his frozen grin, and summon two sturdy young men nearby to help him to his feet. He then made his way to the elevator, laughing at his momentary collapse. The doors closed, and the dreaded moment when his helplessness was fully exposed was over. Later, he assured his boss, Van-Lear Black, that his first day at the office had been "a grand and glorious occasion." He did not mention his fall in the lobby. But he did not return to the Wall Street office for two months. And never again would he allow his paralysis to subject him to public humiliation.

With his valuable support for Smith in the gubernatorial election, Roosevelt again was a force in state Democratic politics, though he was limited to a symbolic role. His primary goal was to rehabilitate his ravaged body. He received hundreds of letters of encouragement, many accompanied by advice on how he might overcome the paralysis. He carefully read every suggestion and searched on his own for a remedy. He became convinced that extended exposure to the sun would heal his paralyzed legs. Accompanied by Eleanor and Missy Le Hand, he vacationed in Southern Florida in February 1923 to take advantage of the hot, sunny weather. He rented a houseboat, the *Weona II*, and invited old friends to keep him company while he fished, swam, and sunbathed. Eleanor quickly tired of the languorous pace and returned to New York and her now active public life.

Missy stayed on board, catering to Franklin's every need, as she would do until 1941, when her own health began to fail. She devoted her life to Franklin, serving as a surrogate wife and inseparable companion. On the *Weona II*, she fished with him, served his favorite cocktails, and prodded him to tell his favorite jokes, all the while taking care of his demanding physical needs. They were joined for weeks at a time by old Roosevelt friends, including fellow Harvard alums Livy Davis, Lewis Ledyard, Jr., and John Lawrence. "I have been in swimming four times and it goes better and better," Franklin wrote his mother. "I'm sure this warmth and exercise is doing lots of good."

The following winter, he and John Lawrence purchased a houseboat, which they christened the *Larooco* (taking the first letters of the two owners' names and the abbreviation of "company"). The boat proved to be only intermittently seaworthy, requiring a never-ending series of repairs. But that did not spoil Franklin's fun. With Missy and a new wave of friends joining him off the Florida Keys, Franklin delighted in his winter vacation, certain that it was helping to restore his paralyzed legs to health. After a day of fishing and sunbathing in February 1924, he wrote his mother, "I know it is doing the legs good, and though I have worn the braces hardly at all, I get lots of exercise crawling around and I know the muscles are better than ever before."

Roosevelt's doctors did not share his optimism. Before Franklin left for Florida, he was examined by Dr. Draper. "I am very much disheartened about his ultimate recovery," Draper wrote Lovett. "I cannot help feeling that he has almost reached the limit of his possibilities." Nothing Franklin did in Florida or anywhere else changed that prognosis.

As the presidential election year of 1924 approached, it appeared that the Republicans were vulnerable. The administration of the genial but ineffectual Warren Harding was rocked by scandal. Albert Fall, the Secretary of the Interior, had secretly leased federal oil reserves, intended to provide the U.S. Navy with petroleum, to two private corporations in exchange for huge bribes. Fall would go to prison for his part in the Teapot Dome scandal (named for the Wyoming reserve at the heart of the scandal), indelibly tainting the Republican administration.

When Harding died unexpectedly in the fall of 1923, succeeded by Vice President Calvin Coolidge, Franklin Roosevelt thought the Democrats were presented with a ripe opportunity to regain the White House. "I cannot help feeling that Harding's unfortunate taking off has helped rather than hurt the Democratic Party," he wrote. The conservative Coolidge was no "world beater," Roosevelt continued, but his nomination appeared certain, which meant that "we must nominate a Progressive without fail."

In the winter of 1924, the leading Democratic candidate was William McAdoo, Woodrow Wilson's son-in-law and former Secretary of the Treasury. Although McAdoo was a transplanted New York corporate lawyer living in California, he enjoyed the broad support of the party's rural constituencies in the South and West that favored Prohibition. In addition to the "Drys," McAdoo's candidacy was championed by the increasingly powerful Ku Klux Klan (KKK). But McAdoo's chances were seriously undermined when it was disclosed that he had been paid $250,000 for his influence with the Harding administration by Edward Doheny, one of the oil company executives who had bribed Secretary of the Interior Fall.

The immediate beneficiary of the reported McAdoo-Doheny connection was New York governor Al Smith, McAdoo's chief rival for the Democratic presidential nomination. Smith, the candidate of the urban eastern wing of the party, opposed Prohibition and proudly embraced his Catholic faith, thus assuring him the enmity of both rural Drys and the KKK. Roosevelt supported Smith. But his optimism about Democratic prospects for a November victory, expressed only a few months earlier, vanished as he anticipated a debilitating convention fight between McAdoo and Smith delegates.

In an attempt to broaden his appeal, Smith, the tough, Tammany-educated, streets–of–New York candidate, asked the upstate, patrician Roosevelt to head his campaign committee. Franklin accepted, flattered and pleased to reemerge for the first time since his paralysis as a key player in the party. Despite his public embrace of Roosevelt, Smith never really liked him. He still clung to his early impression when both men were in the state legislature: too pretentious and opportunistic for his political tastes. Smith, nonetheless, reluctantly asked Roosevelt to nominate him at the Democratic Convention scheduled to convene at Madison Square Garden in late June.

Smith's close adviser, Judge Joseph Proskauer, had already written a draft of Smith's nominating speech, complete with a quote from a Wordsworth poem,* when Roosevelt was asked to place the New York governor's name in nomination. Franklin did not like Proskauer's draft and would have preferred to write his own. In the end, he used the judge's draft but changed certain passages, including the Wordsworth quote, to suit his style and cadence.

Shortly before noon on June 26, 12,000 Democratic delegates waited in tense anticipation for Roosevelt's speech. They watched as the crippled Roosevelt made his way slowly up the aisle, leaning heavily on the right arm of his tall, athletic son James, now sixteen, and using his shoulders to pivot his crutches and braces forward. Father and son engaged in loud, forced banter to ease the tension. Determined to reach the podium unassisted, Franklin had carefully measured out the 15 feet from the back of the platform to the speaker's stand the previous night in his library. When the moment came, he left James at the back of the dais and maneuvered toward the podium. Sweating profusely, he clutched the lectern, threw his head and shoulders back, and greeted the audience with the broad, reassuring grin that would become familiar to all Americans eight years later.

Roosevelt spoke for thirty minutes in his warm tenor voice, concluding that Smith "has a power to strike at error and wrongdoing that makes his adversaries quail before him. He has a personality that carries to every hearer not only the sincerity but the righteousness of what he says. He is the 'Happy Warrior' on the political battlefield."

The crowd erupted with a thunderous ovation that lasted for three minutes while Smith delegates flooded the aisles. But the wild clapping and shouting was as much a tribute to Roosevelt, for his courage under immense pressure, as to the man he had nominated.

Roosevelt's speech was the highlight of the convention. As he had predicted, McAdoo and Smith delegates fought each other to a futile standstill. Finally, Democrats nominated a compromise candidate, John

---

* This is the Happy Warrior, this is he
  Whom every man in arms should wish to be.

W. Davis, a Wall Street attorney and former ambassador to Great Britain. Long after Davis had lost the presidential election to Calvin Coolidge, Democrats savored the dominant image of their convention, the mesmerizing presence of Franklin D. Roosevelt at the podium.

Former President Woodrow Wilson privately referred to "the bungalow mind" of his successor, Warren G. Harding. Wilson's contempt for Harding might not have seriously offended the new president, even if he had been aware of the insult. Harding had never aspired to be more than a small-town newspaper editor turned amiable politician and all-around good fellow. Shortly before the Republican Party nominated him to be president, Harding was dismissed as "the best of the second-raters." His presidency proved that dim compliment excessive.

The Republican power brokers had chosen Harding because he was attractive, genial, and, most of all, malleable. And Americans voted for him in droves. They were tired of Wilson's puritanical lectures and idealistic exhortations. Harding was the anti-Wilson. He did not preach or offer any substantive ideas, though he admitted that he loved to "bloviate," his term for speaking in grand generalities. He prided himself on his back-slapping good humor and talent for making friends. As president, he transformed Wilson's austere White House into a swell fraternity party for his cronies. High-stakes poker games were played in the president's study, the room thick with cigar smoke, the card table strewn with chips and whiskey glasses.

Even before the revelations of widespread excess and corruption in his administration, Harding acknowledged that his friends posed his most serious problem. He recalled that his father had once said that it was fortunate that Warren was not a girl. "You'd be in the family way all the time," he said. "You can't say No." After his election to the presidency, Harding appointed friends to his cabinet, like Attorney General Harry Daugherty, his old campaign manager, and the soon-to-be disgraced Albert Fall, Secretary of the Interior. They called him by his first name or his nickname, "Wernie." But Harding also appointed several first-rate men to his cabinet whose ability and integrity were unquestioned, including Secretary of Commerce Herbert Hoover, Secretary of Agriculture Henry C. Wallace (the father of FDR's future cabinet member), and Secretary of State Charles Evans Hughes.

Hughes never uttered an unkind word about his new boss, whom he described as "a most agreeable Chief, always accessible, anxious fully to understand each problem as it arose." He had no cause for complaint, since the president allowed Hughes to run the State Department and U.S. foreign policy pretty much as he wished. He met with the president almost every day, usually slipping in a side door so that he would not have to wait in the reception area with the multitude of Harding friends in line for favors. In the Oval Office, Harding sometimes put his arm around his Secretary of State and said with bemused awe, "Hughes, this is the damndest job!"

Once the two men sat down, Hughes was all business. He provided the president with the facts of a particular international problem as he saw it, then proposed a clear plan of action. Harding routinely followed Hughes's advice without objection.

But even the brilliant Hughes found the answer to the first international problem confronting the Harding administration elusive. In March 1921, the United States still had not signed the Versailles Treaty and therefore was not a member of the League of Nations. Hughes's position on the treaty and the League was well known. In 1919, he had supported the treaty and U.S. participation in the League, suggesting only that the controversial Article 10 be modified so that the United States would not be obligated to defend a signatory against any act of aggression. During the presidential campaign of 1920, he had been one of thirty-one prominent Republican leaders who supported the League, even though the party's candidate, Senator Harding, was noticeably noncommittal on the issue. The Democratic presidential candidate, Governor James Cox of Ohio, had made support of the League central to his campaign, and he was trounced.

The election returns showed that the overwhelming majority of Americans were no more enthusiastic about the League than Harding. And even if Harding had shared his Secretary of State's position on the League, opponents remained in power in the Senate, guaranteeing, at the very least, a brutal fight. Hughes nonetheless initially planned to ask the Senate to vote in favor of U.S. membership in the League, though on more modest terms than had been demanded by President Wilson. To lay the groundwork, Hughes invited senators opposed to the League to meet with him at the State Department, where he argued that United States' membership in the organization would best serve the nation's interests in international affairs.

An outraged Senator Frank Brandegee of Connecticut, one of the original "Irreconcilables," returned to the Senate from his meeting with Hughes and reported to his conservative colleagues that they faced a new challenge from the "whiskered" Secretary of State, who would soon try to force the country into the League of Nations. Hughes decided that a fight against intransigent senators like Brandegee was not worth making. Not only would the League go down to another defeat, he concluded, but any hopes of progress by the administration in other critical areas of international affairs would be doomed.

President Harding announced his official surrender to the Senate's "Irreconcilables" in a message to Congress in April. "[T]here will be no betrayal of the deliberate expression of the American people in the recent election," said the president. "[T]he League Covenant can have no sanction by us." Less than six weeks into office, the president had abandoned one of Hughes's early foreign policy objectives.

If Hughes was demoralized, he did not show it. The defeat was different from his losing battles as the reform governor of New York with entrenched interests in the state legislature. He was not the chief executive in Washington, but was obligated to serve the president. And members of the U.S. Senate, unlike the bosses he had fought in Albany, were bound by the Constitution to ratify international treaties by a two-thirds vote. The votes were not there, and Hughes was ready to move on.

Disappointed advocates of the League demanded that the Harding administration explore alternatives. Hughes, in fact, had done so, but had concluded that any such initiative would be counterproductive. When one prominent League supporter, A. Lawrence Lowell, chairman of the executive committee of the World Peace Foundation, proposed U.S. participation in a new association of nations, Hughes responded in a curt letter of rebuttal. A new association would require a definite plan, he wrote, and it was "impractical to suggest a plan at this time." He continued, "If there are those who think that they should renew a barren controversy, that is their right. Nothing good will come of it, and very likely it will stand in the way of much that might otherwise be accomplished."

After Chief Justice White died in May, Hughes was prominently mentioned as his likely successor, the third time that he had been considered to lead the Court. The appointment had first been suggested by President Taft in 1910 when he dangled the possibility as an enticement to Governor Hughes to accept his invitation to join the Court as an associate justice. Six years later, Edward White, whom Taft had chosen to lead the Court rather than Hughes, told Hughes that he could expect to succeed him if he did not accept the Republican nomination for president. In the spring of 1921, when Hughes was again reported to be considered for the chief justiceship, he immediately squelched the rumor. He did not want to be diverted from his cabinet duties and sent word to President Harding by way of Under Secretary of State Henry Fletcher, a close personal friend of the president, that he would not accept the appointment if it were offered. Harding soon nominated former President Taft.

Hughes turned his attention to the immediate problem posed by the Senate's refusal to ratify the Versailles Treaty: how could the United States protect its postwar interests in Germany? In late summer, Congress had attempted to solve the problem by passing a joint resolution declaring the war with Germany to be at an end, and claiming "all rights, privileges, indemnities, reparations, or advantages" to which the nation was entitled under the armistice and Treaty of Versailles. But Hughes was convinced that U.S. claims under the joint resolution were not secure without a separate treaty with Germany.

Hughes persuaded President Harding of the need for a separate treaty. When the president ran into stiff resistance in the Senate, he invited key senators to a conference at the White House and asked his Secretary of State to win over the skeptics. It would be folly, Hughes told the senators, to rely upon a joint congressional resolution to protect U.S. interests. Unconvinced, the senators warned Hughes and the president that the proposed treaty with Germany would likely meet the same fate in the Senate as had the Versailles Treaty. The Secretary of State did not want to risk another rebuke. What to do?

One restless night shortly after the conference at the White House, Hughes awoke with a solution that was as ingenious as it was simple. His brainstorm was to incorporate critical language from both the Versailles Treaty and the congressional resolution that would satisfy Germany as well as the U.S. Senate. His proposed treaty would include provisions in the Versailles Treaty guaranteeing rights and privileges that benefited the United States. Germany would have to accept these provisions, he reasoned, since it had already agreed to the terms when it signed the treaty. At the same time, Hughes inserted verbatim language from the joint congressional resolution, so that the Senate would have nothing to fight about. The result was a treaty giving the United States all the benefits accruing to any power under the Versailles Treaty, but imposing none of the responsibilities assumed by the other victorious nations. "This gives us a footing that is practically unassailable," Hughes wrote his son, "and while it may be swallowed with a wry face, it is privately recognized by all those who have sense enough to appreciate the facts that it is the best that could be done." Germany signed the new treaty in late August 1921, and the Senate ratified it two months later.

Hughes began a typical ten-hour workday of appointments with Senator Henry Cabot Lodge, chairman of the Senate Foreign Relations Committee, followed by a briefing for President Harding at the White House, a trip to Capitol Hill to testify before the House Foreign Affairs Committee, and several back-to-back meetings with important U.S. ambassadors and foreign ministers. When he had a few spare minutes, Hughes summoned his male secretary, William Beck, who took dictation at more than 200 words a minute. As Beck read his notes back, Hughes rapidly inserted punctuation, corrected errors, and provided addenda to his original thoughts. He also held daily news conferences for the press in which he displayed a daunting command of international issues as well as a surprisingly robust sense of humor, which had been missing in his strained, self-conscious public appearances of earlier years.

At noon, he often took a brisk walk home for a light lunch with Antoinette, promptly returned to his office, swallowed a dyspepsia tablet, and pressed the buzzer for his staff to bring him more work. More often than not, the buzzer went unanswered, since his staff took a full lunch break even if their driven boss refused to. Most evenings, when he was not in his study reading reports from State Department divisions or dispatches from U.S. embassies abroad, Hughes, accompanied by Antoinette, attended dinners at foreign embassies or entertained diplomats at home. He considered even these gayer aspects of his job useful. "I seldom went to a dinner party," he said, "without gaining information which helped me in my work." His weekends were hardly less stressful than his official workweek. On Saturday nights, he cleared his desk by taking home a suitcase or two full of papers for Sunday reading.

A top priority for Hughes was to address the urgent need for the United States, fated to remain outside the League of Nations, to find other channels to assert its influence in the dangerous postwar period. The First World War had reduced Germany to a weak debtor nation. France and Italy, severely battered by the conflict, were no longer first-rank powers. Russia was just emerging from the throes of a revolution. This left Great Britain,

Japan, and the United States as the most powerful nations in the world. Great Britain and Japan had formally forged an alliance twenty years earlier, but the United States had no pact with either nation. The immediate challenge, as Hughes saw it, was to impose limits on the formidable navies of the three major powers.

Thanks to the enormous shipbuilding program of the U.S. Navy during the Wilson administration, spearheaded by the aggressive Assistant Secretary of the Navy, Franklin D. Roosevelt, the United States possessed a potent arsenal of warships. By war's end, the U.S. Navy had under construction or authorized enough dreadnoughts and battle cruisers to add nearly 750,000 tons and 152 16-inch guns to the fleet. In March 1921, Great Britain announced plans to build fighting ships that would be equal to or superior to any other navy. In the Pacific, Japan was straining its resources in an attempt to keep pace.

How, Hughes wondered, could the three great powers be persuaded to stop the naval arms race? Fortuitously, the huge costs of continued construction of warships had begun to dampen the ambitions of all three postwar governments. Congress cut naval appropriations by more than $330 million. Led by Senator William Borah of Idaho, it also passed a resolution calling for the Harding administration to negotiate with Great Britain and Japan to halt the naval race. Leaders in Great Britain knew that, despite the resumption of naval construction, their nation's war-strained economy could not sustain an arms race. And in Japan, where the government was spending nearly half of its revenues on the military, there was increasing demand for fiscal restraint.

Hughes closely monitored the encouraging developments in all three countries. In July, shortly after Congress had passed the resolution calling for a negotiated halt to the arms race, Hughes cabled the U.S. ambassadors in Great Britain, Japan, France, and Italy,* instructing them to inquire whether those governments would agree to participate in a conference to limit naval armaments. The conference, the Secretary of State suggested, would be held in Washington at a mutually convenient time. Though the responses were positive, Hughes was immediately confronted with what he considered a serious obstacle to a successful conference. The British foreign minister, Lord Curzon, had proposed a conference in London among

---

* Though the naval resources of France and Italy were inferior to the three superpowers, Hughes thought it important that both nations be parties to any disarmament agreement.

Dominion nations to discuss their mutual problems in the Far East. The Washington conference, Curzon suggested, could follow.

Hughes firmly rejected Curzon's proposal. If a London conference on the Far East preceded the Washington conference, he feared that it could very well preempt the issues to be discussed in Washington. The arms issue must be dealt with all at once in Washington under American leadership, he insisted. Hughes prevailed, and the Washington conference was scheduled to begin on November 12, following the president's dedication of the Tomb of the Unknown Soldier on Armistice Day.

The conference required careful planning, beginning with Hughes's selection of the official U.S. delegation. Hughes did not want to repeat the mistake of the ill-fated U.S. delegation to the Paris Peace Conference. President Wilson had made it clear that he intended to dictate the terms of the American position and, conspicuously, refused to name a prominent Republican to the delegation. Hughes, to be sure, chose to lead the U.S. delegation at the Washington Conference, but he also selected the Senate's Democratic minority leader, Alabama's Oscar Underwood. They were joined by Republican senator Henry Cabot Lodge, chairman of the Foreign Relations Committee, and the respected elder statesman Elihu Root, former U.S. senator, Secretary of State, and Secretary of War.

In preparing for the November meeting, Hughes pondered the one question that would have to be answered affirmatively for the conference to be a success: Was there a formula for limiting naval armaments that would satisfy all of the delegations? He well knew that the admirals in the competing navies would seek military advantage and not voluntarily give up existing warships or plans to build new ones. For this reason, he did not want to rely on the recommendations of each nation's naval leadership, even his own. They would insist that any disarmament be based on need, and once "need" became the criterion, there would be no end to the bickering. Devouring data on the navies' comparative strengths, Hughes devised a workable formula: each nation must stop naval armaments *at once*. The delegations could then agree to the relative strengths of each nation and use those numbers as the operating ratios for the future.

A subsidiary but crucial issue was to determine the basis on which the strengths of the existing navies were to be calculated. It would not do, Hughes quickly surmised, to rely on the number of warships that existed in each navy. The only measure that was both practicable and subject to verification was ship tonnage. Reliable information on capital ships (bat-

tleships and cruisers) of all three navies furnished by the Navy Department suggested a rough tonnage ratio among the three great powers of ten
(U.S.): 10 (Great Britain): 6 (Japan).

Hughes was confident that Congress would accept his proposal, despite anticipated protests from top U.S. naval officers. After all, naval
appropriations had been slashed only a few months earlier. In fact, there
was not nearly enough money in the navy's budget to complete the warships planned or under construction. If the United States agreed to abandon shipbuilding plans and even ship construction in progress under the
Hughes plan, Great Britain and Japan could be persuaded to follow its
lead. Hughes believed that his formula was not only realistic but fair to
all, and stood a good chance of being adopted. He was bolstered by the
enthusiastic support that his proposal received from every member of the
U.S. delegation.

As the opening ceremony approached, Hughes worried that his proposal would be leaked to the press, diffusing its dramatic impact on the
foreign delegations. Originally, President Harding had been scheduled to
address the delegates on Saturday, November 12, with the plenary sessions
to begin the following week. Hughes met with the president to express his
concern. "I had not planned to make our proposal on the opening day," he
told Harding, "but I am so afraid that a leak or some other development
might spoil its effect that I think I should get it off right away."

"Oh, that's all right," replied the accommodating president. "Go
ahead."

On a chilly, blustery November day the conference opened in Continental Hall, the elegant white-marble building dedicated to the heroes
of the American Revolution. The dismal weather did not tamp down the
excitement swirling around the historic meeting attended by prominent
statesmen from around the world. Arthur James Balfour, the tall, distinguished veteran diplomat, led the British delegation; Admiral Baron
Tomosaburo Kato, minister of the navy, headed the Japanese delegation;
and Premier Aristide Briand represented France. The delegations were
arranged around a large walnut table, shaped in a U, with Secretary of
State Hughes seated at the bottom. Senators Lodge and Underwood and
former Secretary of State Elihu Root sat to his right and the British delegation to his left. French premier Briand objected to the arrangement
because he was not given a place at the *table d'honneur*. Hughes denied
that there was any such arrangement but nonetheless asked each delegate

to move one seat to the left, so that Briand faced in the same direction as the U.S. delegates. That small gesture satisfied the French leader.

The gallery was filled with dignitaries, including Vice President Coolidge, Mrs. Harding, and a large contingent of congressional leaders. Chief Justice and Mrs. Taft attended the first session, as did Justices Holmes and Brandeis. William Jennings Bryan wore a silk hat and old-fashioned cape. The large press corps of three hundred reporters included the veteran international reporter Henry Nevinson of the *Manchester Guardian*, the noted author H. G. Wells, and William Allen White, the respected editor of the *Emporia* (Kansas) *Gazette*. Journalist Mark Sullivan, who covered Hughes in the State Department, noted that the Secretary of State was unusually composed. For Sullivan, the telltale sign of Hughes's calm state of mind was his perfectly groomed beard, "every hair . . . at a satisfactory upward angle."

After Hughes called the session to order, he announced: "The President of the United States." Harding then entered the room, appearing slightly embarrassed by all of the attention. He bowed to his audience, then proceeded to deliver one of the best speeches of his life. He began with a moving reference to the ceremony that he had attended at Arlington Cemetery the previous day: "Here in the United States we are but freshly turned from the burial of an unknown American soldier, when a nation sorrowed while paying him tribute. Whether it was spoken or not, a hundred millions of our people were summarizing the inexcusable causes, the incalculable cost, the unspeakable sacrifices, and the unutterable sorrows; and there was the ever-impelling question: How can humanity justify or God forgive?" He concluded with a challenge to the conference: "I can speak officially only for the United States. Our hundred millions frankly want less of armament and none of war."

Dropping his paper and pencil, William Jennings Bryan leapt to his feet and led the applause for the president. Hughes grasped Harding's hand and shook it vigorously. And then the president was gone as quickly as he had entered the room. It was time for Hughes to take control.

In the first part of Hughes's written address to the conference, which he had kept in a locked cabinet at the State Department, he welcomed the delegates, recounted the laborious preparations for the conference, and made a pointed reference to the failed earlier disarmament conference convened by Tsar Nicholas of Russia at The Hague twenty-three years earlier. His delivery was formal, lawyerlike, and boring, so much so that many reporters lost their focus and idly wrote irreverent notes to each other poking fun at individual delegates.

Once Hughes had completed the obligatory opening remarks, his delivery surged with energy as he introduced his proposal to limit naval armaments. "We can no longer content ourselves with investigations, with statistics, with reports, and with the circumlocution of inquiry," he began. "The time has come and this Conference has been called, not for general resolutions of mutual advice, but *for action*." The only adequate way out of the interminable cycle of rearmament "is to end it now," he exclaimed. "It is proposed that for a period of not less than ten years there should be no further construction of capital ships."

The full import of Hughes's stunning proposal had not settled in the delegates' minds when he recited the specific number of ships and tonnage that America was prepared to abandon or destroy. The United States would scrap *all* capital ships, including six battle cruisers and seven battleships under construction, as well as two battleships already launched. That made a total of fifteen capital ships with a combined tonnage of 618,000 tons. The United States, moreover, would discard fifteen older battleships with a total tonnage of 227,740 tons.

When Hughes paused for effect, the delegates applauded heartily, assuming that his speech had reached its commendable end. But the U.S. delegates looked stonily ahead, aware that the Secretary of State would soon demand *quid pro quos* from Great Britain and Japan. He turned first to the British delegation and told them that the Royal Navy should abandon plans to construct four new super "Hoods," giant battleships weighing nearly 50,000 tons a piece, then listed the existing ships to be destroyed, including the *King George V.* Admiral Sir Ernle Chatfield "turned red and then white, and sat immovable."

In equally bold terms, Hughes instructed the Japanese delegates that he expected their navy to make comparable sacrifices, beginning with the destruction of the pride of the Japanese fleet, the *Mutsu*, as well as the requisite number of battleships and cruisers to match the depleted tonnage of the U.S. and British fleets.

Hughes ended his speech on an idealistic note. The acceptance of his proposal, he said, would mean that the vast sums that had been spent on battleships could be invested in programs "to aid the progress of civilization." While his plan would allow each nation to meet the demands of national defense, the "preparation for offensive naval war will stop now."

Wild applause broke out in the gallery. Hats and handkerchiefs were waved in celebration. Total strangers exchanged handshakes and hugs of joy. Tears streamed down the cheeks of William Jennings Bryan. William Allen White later wrote that it was the most "intensely dramatic moment I have ever witnessed." Ring Lardner left in mock disgust. "I'm going home," he declared. "This is going to be a bum show. They've let the hero kill the villain in the first act."

Overnight, Hughes became a national hero, saluted in newspapers across the country for his "master stroke," his "astounding and stupendous move," and his "practical idealism." Justice Holmes wrote his old friend, "This is simply to say that I was proud of your dignity and thrilled by what you said yesterday." In London, Winston Churchill told U.S. Ambassador George Harvey that "he could not find words to express his rejoicing as an Englishman and his pride in his American ancestry. His hat was not only off but as high as he could throw it."

The speech was the easy part of Hughes's task. Now he had to make his proposal a reality by hard negotiations with Great Britain and Japan. Fortunately for Hughes, he had developed a warm, respectful friendship with the leading British delegate, Arthur Balfour. When Balfour later addressed the conference, he said that he counted himself "among the fortunate of the earth" in being present for Hughes's speech, adding that he considered the opening day "one of the landmarks in human civilization." More important than his accolades for Hughes, Balfour was intent on keeping his disgruntled admirals in tow, making sure that the British delegation adhered to the ship and tonnage limitations called for.

The problem was Japan. Baron Kato, like Balfour, accepted Hughes's proposal in principle, but with "a few modifications." Those modifications soon turned into an outright challenge to Hughes's proposal. Kato argued that Japan was entitled to a more favorable calculus, adjusted to 10:10:7. Limiting Japan to anything less than 70 percent of the tonnage allotted to the United States and Great Britain, he said, would undermine his country's national security. He claimed that Hughes had miscalculated the strength of the Japanese Navy relative to the United States, refusing to count American ships under construction. In addition to his demand for an adjusted ratio for battleships and cruisers, Kato insisted that Japan maintain parity with the United States and Great Britain in aircraft carriers and that its new battleship, the *Mutsu*, be retained.

The negotiations dragged on for more than a month. Hughes responded to Baron Kato's demands with cold logic, backed by facts and figures. To Kato's contention that the United States should not include ships under construction in the ratio calculation, Hughes replied that a warship that was 90 percent completed would be an important asset in a naval emergency. Similarly, he argued that a ship 70 or even 50 percent completed was "so much naval strength in hand." The American people would never consent to a calculation that ignored more than $300 million of their tax dollars spent on ships under construction. If Baron Kato doubted Hughes's claims, he was welcome to have Japanese experts examine U.S. naval records on the progress of the ships under construction.

Kato finally accepted Hughes's argument on U.S. ships under construction, but remained adamant that the *Mutsu* must be protected. The ship, then fully manned, had become a source of national pride, he said. Schoolchildren had contributed to the vessel's building fund. To destroy it would deal a devastating blow to the nation's morale and possibly bring down the government. Reluctantly, Hughes acquiesced. He told Kato that retention of the *Mutsu* would mean that the United States, in order to preserve the agreed-upon 10:10:6 ratio, would be entitled to complete two battleships under construction, the *Washington* and the *Colorado*.

Hughes's concession to Japan provoked a mutiny by British admirals. If Japan could keep its most formidable ship, they demanded that Great Britain be permitted to construct at least two of its super Hoods to maintain parity. This demand posed a new challenge for Hughes. Neither the United States nor Japan, even counting the *Mutsu*, had a ship that weighed more than 35,000 tons; the super Hoods were nearly one-third heavier. Balfour reminded Hughes that the British had already expended substantial sums on planning construction of the super Hoods. His admirals would be willing to scrap five older ships in order to build two super Hoods.

Baron Kato agreed to the British plan, but Hughes balked. As he considered the British proposal, he became increasingly alarmed at the prospect of two colossal battleships on the high seas, substantially larger than any warship ever built. If Great Britain were allowed its two super Hoods, Hughes was convinced that it was only a matter of time until its rivals would renew the naval arms race.

"How could we possibly defend such a decision before our peoples?" Hughes asked Balfour at a meeting in his State Department office. "They are looking to us to curtail naval strength. We cannot be content with agreement upon mathematical formulas. No matter how we might try to justify the building of warships of such colossal size, most of the moral and psychological impact of the conference would be lost."

Visibly shaken, Balfour excused himself to consult with Admiral Chatfield. When he returned, he told Hughes that the admiral refused to reduce the size of the two super Hoods. "But I think you are right," he told Hughes. "I do not like to act without consulting my government, but what you have proposed is so manifestly just, and I am so impressed with the importance of avoiding further delay, that I will take the responsibility of accepting the scheme under which Great Britain would have the right to build two new ships of not more than 35,000 tons."

Balfour's concession was the dramatic highlight of the negotiation. After the meeting at the State Department, the United States, Great Britain, and Japan announced their agreement to the world. They had accepted the 10:10:6 ratio and a ten-year naval holiday, except for two American and two British ships to offset Japan's retention of the *Mutsu*.

With the benefit of historical hindsight, it is easy to disparage the achievement of the Washington Conference. After all, only two decades later the world was convulsed in the Second World War. In 1941, Germany, not even a party to the conference, had conquered much of Europe and its submarines were wreaking havoc in the Atlantic Ocean. And in the Pacific in December, Japan bombed most of the U.S. Fleet at Pearl Harbor to smithereens.

But in 1922, when the Washington Conference officially adjourned, none of these events could have been foreseen. Indeed, the conference was pronounced a major success and tangible proof that great powers, acting in good faith, could secure a lasting peace. More than a decade later, world leaders still referred to the conference as a model of international diplomacy. President Franklin D. Roosevelt, in a letter to the chairman of the American delegation to the 1935 naval conference, wrote: "The Washington Naval Conference of 1922 brought to the world the first important voluntary agreement for limitation and reduction of armament. It stands out as a milestone in civilization. . . . The important matter to keep constantly before your eyes is the principle of reduction—the maintenance of one of the greatest achievement of friendly relations between nations."

In his successful negotiations of the Naval Arms Limitation Treaty, Hughes had thrust the United States into a major role in international affairs despite operating outside of the League of Nations and against the strong tide of isolationism prevalent in Congress and the nation at large. He did so cautiously and pragmatically, never losing sight of the limitations imposed by a suspicious Congress. Before the Washington Conference closed, Hughes had also committed the United States to two more international treaties, later ratified by the Senate. The first, the Four Power Treaty, enlarged the previous Anglo-Japanese Alliance to include the United States and France and called for peaceful resolution of disputes among the parties involving their Pacific island possessions. At first, the United States alone had been offered entry into the alliance. But Hughes, concerned that Great Britain and Japan might exercise undue pressure, insisted on bringing France into the alliance to give the United States greater leverage in resolving disagreements. Hughes also committed the United States to a third international agreement, the Nine Power Treaty, which guaranteed China's territorial integrity and pledged the signatories to an open door policy to China's commercial markets.*

Turning his attention to the western hemisphere, Hughes was determined to recalibrate U.S. relations with Latin America. Too often in the past, he believed, U.S. diplomacy with Central and South American nations had been conducted at the point of a gun. When possible, he strived to replace the old Yankee imperialism that had so alienated Latin American nations with diplomacy, built on mutual respect and cooperation. Toward that end, he initiated a plan, later implemented, to withdraw U.S. troops from the Dominican Republic and Nicaragua,† and provide for the election of independent governments. He hoped to duplicate that achievement in every country that was still occupied by American troops. But he was a realist and recognized that conditions in other island nations, like Haiti, were not yet conducive to the withdrawal of U.S. troops. Given the poverty and frequent upheavals in Haiti, he concluded that U.S. Marines were still needed to prevent a bloody revolution.

Hughes also aggressively used his office to settle incendiary boundary disputes. The night after Harding's inauguration, he took home the voluminous State Department files on a bitter boundary dispute in the Coto

---

* The nations signing the treaty were the United States, Great Britain, Japan, France, Belgium, China, Italy, the Netherlands, and Portugal.

† Later, after Hughes had left office, President Coolidge again sent Marines to Nicaragua to protect U.S. interests when the government was overthrown.

region between Costa Rica and Panama that threatened to precipitate open warfare between the two small Central American countries. The dispute had been arbitrated by Chief Justice White, who made a ruling favorable to Costa Rica. Both countries signed the agreement, but Panama later refused to honor it. Costa Rica retaliated by sending troops to the disputed boundary to challenge Panamanian forces.

Having pored over the documents, Hughes concluded that White's ruling was both legally sound and fair. Even though U.S. strategic interests were more closely aligned with Panama (i.e., the Panama Canal), he took immediate action to see that the award favoring Costa Rica was enforced. He sent notes to both countries demanding that they stop fighting and despatched two warships to the region to protect U.S. interests. Costa Rica immediately withdrew its troops, but Panama did not. After Hughes informed Panama that a reasonable time had elapsed to withdraw its troops, U.S. Marines were sent to the Canal Zone. Panama then evacuated the disputed district, and the White award went into effect.

Though the challenges in Asia and Latin America were formidable, the economic crisis in Europe overshadowed every other foreign policy problem that Hughes faced during his term as Secretary of State. Dispatches to Hughes in 1922 from the U.S. ambassador in Berlin, Alanson Houghton, described the desperate conditions in Germany as "a sort of quiet bleeding to death." The German people were suffering extreme hardship, Houghton reported, "insufficiently nourished, unprotected against the bitter cold of the approaching winter." Ominously, Houghton wrote, armed groups in Germany were "working toward dictatorship." The most dangerous was a group of 30,000 men led by a young Austrian named Adolf Hitler. "By his vehemence and fanaticism, he was rapidly becoming leader of a whole movement . . . following the pattern of the Fascisti in Italy," Houghton noted. "These people seem to me to be slowly going mad."

The German economy had no chance of recovery under the weight of the billions of dollars demanded in reparations by the victorious Allies. Other European nations were also struggling, burdened by the $10 billion that they owed in war debts to the United States. Recognizing these irrefutable facts, economists on both sides of the Atlantic recommended the cancellation of Germany's reparations as well as the war debts of all European countries. But politicians like French premier Raymond Poincaré, still smoldering with rage over his country's destruction, were determined to collect every franc of the tens of billions owed to France by Germany.

Meanwhile, in the United States, Congress refused to forgive the war debts owed by twenty European countries.

Hughes understood that Europe's problems were also America's and spoke candidly of the challenge. "We cannot dispose of these problems by calling them European," he said in an address to the American Historical Association in New Haven in December 1922, "for they are world problems and we cannot escape the injurious consequences of a failure to settle them." If Germany did not recover economically, then neither could the other European nations. Hughes proposed that a committee of experts, drawn from the best financial minds in Europe and the United States, study Germany's economy with the goal of determining the amount of reparations that would be accepted throughout the world as both realistic and authoritative.

The Reparations Commission created a committee of experts, along the lines suggested by Hughes, to analyze economic conditions in Germany and recommend ways to balance the nation's budget and stabilize the currency. General Charles Dawes, President Harding's director of the federal budget, was Hughes's choice to head the committee. In its first report, the Dawes Committee recommended the creation of a bank as depository and fiscal agent of the German government and annual payments by Germany to the Allies of $250 million the first year (increasing in subsequent years). The payments would be drawn from income earned from the country's railroads and industry and from loans, including an additional $200 million from Allies.

At a reparations conference in London in 1924, all of the committee's recommendations were accepted. The conference "has reestablished harmony among the Allies over the principal problem of Europe," reported *The Times* (London). "The first tentative suggestion of Mr. Hughes in his famous speech at New Haven some 18 months ago . . . has now borne splendid fruit."

Hughes's proposal, translated into action at the London conference, served only as a temporary palliative in the futile effort to revive Germany's economy. Nothing was done about the war debts to keep the other European nations solvent, and the high U.S. tariffs only exacerbated the problem. And neither the U.S. Secretary of State nor any one else foresaw the world depression of the thirties and the calamitous events that followed.

Before leaving office, Hughes argued passionately in support of U.S.

participation in the International Court of Justice (ICJ). He believed that
the Court offered a direct, practical method of peaceful resolution in the
dangerous modern world. Chiding critics who opposed the judicial settle-
ment of international controversies, Hughes reminded an audience of the
Society of International Law that the U.S. government had accepted such
settlements since the early days of the republic. "If you are to treat participation in a permanent court of international justice as an entanglement
foreign to our institutions," he asserted, "you must rewrite American history." But alas, his plea failed to convince a skeptical, isolationist Senate.
Indeed, the United States did not join the ICJ until the United Nations
was created after the Second World War.

The Times called Hughes "the most compelling figure among the Foreign Ministers of the post-war period." While President Calvin Coolidge,
who succeeded Harding, worked well with Hughes, he did not consider
him indispensable. Responding to Hughes's letter of resignation in January
1925, Coolidge wrote that "you are personally entitled, after twenty years
of public service, to seek some of the satisfactions of private life." It was
true that Hughes was worn out from his arduous four years as Secretary of
State and looked forward to a vacation with his family and the return to his
law practice. But secretly, he had hoped that Coolidge might try to change
his mind. "Much as I wish to return to private life," Hughes said, "if he
had said to me, 'Hughes, I earnestly ask you to stay,' I don't think anything
could have driven me from the job!"

Franklin Roosevelt tirelessly pursued a cure for his paralyzed legs. He ped-
aled furiously on an adult tricycle that his mother had bought in Europe.
It did not help. Then he began a regular schedule of horseback riding, but
invariably ended up being led because his legs were of no use. He always
returned to the two remedies that he was convinced had restorative powers: swimming and sunbathing. He was therefore intrigued by the story of
the rehabilitative powers of naturally warm, mineral-laden springs fed into
a large swimming pool at a resort hotel in rural Georgia that had brought
about the miraculous recovery of one young polio victim.

Roosevelt first heard of the pool from George Foster Peabody, a friend
and major contributor to the Democratic Party, at the party's 1924 convention. Later that summer, Peabody, a wealthy New York banker who had
invested in the Georgia resort, told Roosevelt about Louis Joseph, who had

been paralyzed and confined to a wheelchair since childhood. Joseph had exercised daily in the pool for three years and could now walk, assisted only by a cane. Roosevelt made plans for an on-site visit in the fall.

In early October, Franklin, Eleanor, and Missy Le Hand arrived at the Meriwether Inn, which he described as "a perfectly good down-at-the-heels summer resort and nothing else." He was altogether too generous in his assessment. Even with the fresh coat of paint hastily ordered by Peabody, the ramshackled old building creaked with age. Eleanor peered disapprovingly through cracks in the thin, pine walls of one of the nearby cottages to grounds overrun with weeds.*

The resort's woeful state of disrepair did not concern Franklin. His singular focus was the swimming pool. Helped on with his swimsuit, he eased himself into the pool without his braces. The 88-degree water, flowing at a rate of 1,800 gallons a minute from the depths of nearby Pine Mountain, soothed his lower body while the mineral salts kept him buoyant. "I don't think I'll ever get out," he exclaimed. Encouraged by Louis Joseph, whom he had met the first morning, Franklin was able to slightly lift his right foot for the first time since being paralyzed more than three years earlier. He was ecstatic.

A reporter from the *Atlanta Journal*, Cleburne Gregory, came to observe the resort's famous visitor. In an article entitled "Franklin Roosevelt Will Swim to Health," Gregory described Franklin's daily routine. For two hours every morning, Roosevelt, alone in the pool, "swims, dives, using the swinging rings and horizontal bar over the water and finally crawls out on the concrete pier for a sun bath that lasts another hour." By the end of the month, Roosevelt reported, "I walk around in water 4' deep without braces or crutches almost as well as if I had nothing the matter with my legs."

Soon enough, as a result of Gregory's nationally syndicated newspaper article, Franklin was joined at Warm Springs by ten polio victims from around the country. None of the cottages was habitable, nor was there a physician who could supervise the new arrivals. Roosevelt took charge, finding lodging for the visitors in a nearby village until the cottages could be repaired and collaborating with local physicians to set up a polio clinic.

---

* Eleanor was appalled by the resort's decrepit conditions and shocked by the poverty that she observed in the surrounding area. She left the next day for New York to resume her active role in Al Smith's gubernatorial campaign.

And every morning, he happily led them through improvised water exercises in the pool.

Roosevelt gave special attention to one large lady who could not get both of her legs down to the bottom of the pool. "Well, I would take one large knee and I would force this large knee then I would say, 'Have you got it'?" he recalled, "and she would say, 'Yes,' and I would say, 'Hold it, hold it.' Then I would reach up and get hold the other knee very quickly and start to put it down and then number one knee would pop up. This used to go on for half hour at a time." But by the end of her stay, Franklin's patient could get both legs down to the bottom of the pool, thanks to his good-natured persistence.

Before he returned to New York in the spring of 1925, Franklin had already laid out plans for a complete renovation and expansion of the Georgia resort. By his own proud admission, he was not only resident physician (referring to himself as "Old Doctor Roosevelt") and physiotherapist, but also consulting architect and landscape engineer. His grand vision included new water and sewage systems, a spruced-up dance hall, tearoom, picnic grounds, and two championship golf courses. Warm Springs provided exhilarating therapy for Roosevelt's spirit as well as his body. "I sometimes wish I could find some spot on the globe where it was not essential and necessary for me to start something new—a sand bar in the ocean might answer," he wrote his friend Livy Davis, "but I would probably start building a sea wall around it and digging for pirate treasure in the middle."

He had a cottage built for himself at Warm Springs and bought a farm of 1,750 acres on a summit near Pine Mountain where he raised cattle. Rejecting Eleanor's advice, he purchased the Warm Springs hotel, cottages, and 1,200 acres of land in 1926 for $200,000, which represented two thirds of his fortune. He was confident that he could operate a luxury resort at a sufficient profit to pay for a world-class rehabilitative center for polio victims next door. It did not work out that way. Wealthy patrons resented sharing their vacations with polio sufferers, and their numbers soon diminished, as did Franklin's plans (the two golf courses were never built).

Warm Springs became exclusively a therapeutic haven for polio victims, who enjoyed four spring-fed swimming pools (three constructed after Roosevelt took over) and renovated facilities managed by a hotel management professional. Roosevelt recruited Dr. Leroy Hubbard, an orthopedic surgeon attached to the New York State Department of Health, who supervised a staff of physical therapists. And on any given day, the patients might have the pleasure of swapping stories with Roosevelt himself.

Despite Roosevelt's initial euphoria over the restorative powers of the Warm Springs pool, he never regained the use of his legs. But for the rest of his life, the resort served as a life-affirming refuge where he could relax, enjoy the pools and, perhaps most important, help other victims of polio.

With the slogan "Keep Cool with Coolidge," Calvin Coolidge, the dour, former Massachusetts governor who had succeeded Warren Harding as president, easily won the 1924 presidential election. He beat his Democratic opponent, John W. Davis, by more than 7 million popular votes, taking 382 electoral votes to the Democrat's 136. Probably no Democrat could have won the election, given the heady postwar prosperity, but Davis's uninspired campaign did not even offer a serious challenge. Republicans also retained control of both houses of Congress by wide margins.

After the election, Roosevelt sent out letters to thousands of delegates who had attended the Democratic Convention calling upon their party to agree upon a set of principles that would lead to victory in the future. For his part, Roosevelt offered what he considered the self-evident truths about the two parties. The Republican leadership "stands for conservatism, for the control of the social and economic structure of the nation by a small minority of hand-picked associates," he wrote. In contrast, the Democratic Party was "unequivocally the party of progress and liberal thought."

Later, in an article in the journal *Foreign Affairs*, Roosevelt attacked the foreign policies of both postwar Republican administrations (Harding and Coolidge), claiming that their reactionary policies had isolated the United States from the world diplomatic community. He did not spare Secretary of State Hughes in his sweeping condemnation. "It will always be a regret to fair-minded Americans that, except in one instance [the Washington Naval Disarmament Conference], the Secretary of State, Charles Evans Hughes, allowed his great ability and high ideals to be wholly smothered by the caution and smallness of the President's mind and the provinciality and ignorance of most of his professional political advisors."

Roosevelt's criticism of Hughes (who by then had resigned) was neither fair nor accurate. In fact, Secretary Hughes's policies encouraged international diplomacy and were consistent with Roosevelt's views. In addition to support for the Naval Arms Limitation Treaty, both Hughes and

Roosevelt advocated closer ties with Japan, an end to U.S. imperialism in Latin America, and U.S. membership in the International Court of Justice.

In his outspoken criticism of the Republicans, Roosevelt returned to his theme that the Democratic Party was the natural heir to Jefferson, while the Republicans supported the Hamiltonian philosophy of government for and by the wealthy. "We are approaching a period similar to that from 1790–1800 when Alexander Hamilton ran the federal government for the primary good of the chambers of commerce, the speculators, and the inside ring of the national government," he wrote. "He was a fundamental believer in an aristocracy of wealth and power—Jefferson brought the government back to the hands of the average voter, through insistence on fundamental principles and the education of the average voter." The Democrats needed "a similar campaign of education today," he continued, and suggested that "perhaps we shall find another Jefferson." He was not so presumptuous as to suggest that he might be the party's next Jefferson. But he continued to exhort Democrats to return to their Jeffersonian roots.

Roosevelt's name was prominently mentioned as the Democrats' strongest candidate to run for a seat in the U.S. Senate from New York in 1926. He was not interested, primarily because "my legs are coming back to such fine shape that if I devote another two years to them I shall be on my feet again without braces." He had another reason, kept private, for resisting a Senate draft in 1926. Both he and Louis Howe believed that the next two presidential elections would probably be won by the Republicans. Roosevelt would only be fifty-two years old in 1932, when they expected him to run for governor. If he won, he could then make a serious run for the presidency in 1936.

In 1928, when others in the party were promoting him to run for president, he tried a different tack to discourage his candidacy. He spoke glowingly of *his* presidential candidate, Governor Al Smith, and provided a masterful section-by-section analysis of the electoral map to show that Smith had a far better chance than he did to capture to White House that year. And he followed his analysis with the speech placing Smith's name in nomination at the 1928 Democratic Convention, as he had done four years earlier. He approached the podium on the arm of his son Elliott, smiled broadly at the delegates, and delivered the first of many superb speeches especially written for a radio audience. Al Smith, he said, had "the quality of soul" essential to a national leader, "the quality of sympathetic understanding of the human heart, of real interest in one's fellow man." Roosevelt, a polio victim for seven years, was no longer the cocksure vice-presidential candidate of 1920, but a genuinely compassionate leader whose words could just as well have described himself.

After Smith won the nomination on the first ballot, Roosevelt thought that he had neatly postponed his run for elective office. But as the fall presidential campaign approached, he felt increasing pressure to run for governor. Democratic leaders feared that Smith would be beaten by his Republican opponent, Secretary of Commerce Herbert Hoover, even in New York. If Smith lost the state's 45 electoral votes, he could not win the election. Only Roosevelt, they concluded, could assure Smith's victory in his home state by joining him on the ticket as the party's candidate for governor.

In September, a tense, extended telephone conversation began between the reluctant Roosevelt, happily ensconced in Warm Springs, and Smith and his advisers in New York. Roosevelt opposed running for elective office in 1928 for the same reasons that had caused him to discourage supporters in 1926. He wanted more time in Georgia to restore the use of his legs. Both he and Louis Howe, moreover, believed that his best chance of victory in a race for governor was four years away.

But as Smith's campaign languished, the telephone calls from Democratic headquarters in New York to Warm Springs became more urgent. Smith assigned Ed Flynn, the Bronx political boss and a close friend of Roosevelt's, the task of persuading FDR to run. Each time Flynn called, Roosevelt said no. But Flynn detected a subtle shift in Roosevelt's responses, suggesting that he might accept a draft. Finally, the day before the state Democratic Convention, Smith came on the line:

"Frank, I told you I wasn't going to put this on a personal basis, but I've got to."

Roosevelt tried to reassure Smith that he could win without him on the ticket.

"I just want to ask you one more question," said Smith. "If those fellows nominate you tomorrow and adjourn, will you refuse to run."

Roosevelt hesitated.

"All right," said Smith. "I won't ask you any more questions."

Within minutes, it was all arranged. The next day, New York mayor Jimmy Walker placed Roosevelt's name in nomination for governor, and the delegates voted his nomination by acclamation.

Before Roosevelt's nomination, his Republican opponent, New York attorney general Albert Ottinger, had been heavily favored to win the election, largely on the basis of his outstanding record in prosecuting loan sharks, fraudulent stock dealers, and food profiteers trading in impure products. But Roosevelt's name alone lowered the odds of a Republican victory. And rural and small-town voters immediately responded to his progressive message—aid to farmers, state development of water power, reform of the judicial and administrative system.

Republicans made the foolish error of spreading the rumor that Roosevelt was in such fragile health that he could possibly die in office, if elected. Roosevelt's rebuttal was to stand up in the back of his campaign automobile, his braces locked in place, flash his famous grin, and lash out at the do-nothing Republicans. "Too bad about that unfortunate sick man," he said, mocking his Republican critics. And the crowds loved it. He honed his message (delivered in more than a dozen speeches a day) to include support for the underprivileged—regulated hours and work conditions for women and children, appointment of a minimum wage advisory board, extension of the state workmen's compensation act, and help for those in need who could not help themselves.

In supporting government assistance for crippled children, Roosevelt offered a poignant, personal testimonial. "I suppose that people readily will recognize that I myself furnish a perfectly good example of what can be done by the right kind of care," he told an audience in Rochester. What the Roosevelt fortune had done for him, he declared, should be done by the state for those less fortunate.

On November 6, Roosevelt went to the Biltmore Hotel in New York to receive the returns. By early evening, it was obvious that Smith would lose badly to Hoover in the presidential race, even in New York, and that Roosevelt was likely to be buried in the Republican avalanche. Roosevelt left Democratic headquarters convinced that he had lost. But as the late returns from upstate trickled in, Ed Flynn realized that Roosevelt might just squeak by, if the upstate results were tallied before Republican bosses could tamper with the returns. At 2 a.m., Flynn issued a press statement that he was sending 1,000 lawyers upstate to challenge irregularities. Flynn's threat was largely bluff (only a small number of lawyers were sent), but it worked. Upstate votes came in more rapidly. Roosevelt won by 25,000 votes—out of more than 4 million cast.

Roosevelt was elected governor four years earlier than he and Howe had planned. They would soon adjust their timetable for Roosevelt's presidential run—to 1932.

Immediately after resigning his office as Secretary of State, Hughes, his wife, and college-age daughter, Elizabeth, embarked on an extended vacation, the first that the family had taken in many years. First, they sailed to Bermuda for two months of relaxation; then they returned to New York's Lake George for the summer. In the fall, Hughes joined his old law firm for a practice that was, in his words, "large, varied, and lucrative." He represented some of the nation's largest corporations, and his annual income soared to $400,000 (in contrast to the $12,000 a year he had earned as Secretary of State).

But Hughes, who turned down roughly half the cases that he was offered, also accepted legal assignments that he deemed to be in the public interest. The most important was his appointment by the U.S. Supreme Court to serve as special master in a dispute among several states arising from the Chicago Sanitation District's practice of using waters from the Great Lakes to flush the city's sewage into the Mississippi River. Hughes was authorized to take evidence and make findings of fact, conclusions of law, and recommendations for a binding legal decree. After more than a year and a half of work, he presided at hearings that produced more than 10,000 pages of testimony. Hughes concluded that the Chicago Sanitation District had improperly drawn more than 8,500 cubic feet of water per second from Lake Michigan, significantly lowering the level of the Great Lakes, and causing substantial damage to the navigation and commercial interests in the Great Lakes states. Relying heavily on the Hughes report, the Court entered a decree that compelled Chicago to end its illegal drainage.*

In addition to his busy law practice, Hughes resumed his leadership role in the larger community, serving as president of the American Bar Association (ABA), head of Legal Aid of New York City, and cofounder of the Conference of Christians and Jews. As ABA president, he delivered

---

* Justice Holmes, in charge of compensation for the special master, asked counsel in the case for recommendations, which ranged from $60,000 to $125,000; Hughes refused to accept such a high fee and ultimately agreed to receive $30,000 for his services.

a timely lecture on civil liberties, deploring "the intolerant spirit" spreading across the country that was reflected in a Nebraska law forbidding the teaching of German in the public schools and Tennessee's attempt to suppress the teaching of evolution (at issue in the famous Scopes trial). "[F]reedom of learning is the vital breath of democracy and progress," he declared. The columnist Walter Lippmann wrote that Hughes had made "about the most useful speech that anyone has undertaken to make in America for a long time."

As a private citizen, Hughes quickly resumed an exhausting work schedule, usually rising before 5 a.m. to compose a speech or a university lecture before heading to his law office. He gave three highly acclaimed university lecture series, later published, on topics on which he was an expert. At Princeton he spoke on "Our Relations to the Nations of the Western Hemisphere" and at Yale on "Pan American Peace Plans."

His most significant lectures were given at Columbia University in 1927 on "The Supreme Court of the United States," in which he offered a detailed description of the Court's history and work. He expressed admiration for all members of the Court, concluding that they consistently demonstrated "a capacity for independence, impartiality and balanced judgment."* The justices did not judge the wisdom of legislation, he said, nor question Congress's motives.

While Hughes's discussion of public policy issues after his resignation as Secretary of State was nonpartisan, he remained a loyal member of the Republican Party. His commitment to the party as well as his distinguished career made him, once again, an attractive potential Republican candidate for office. In 1926, he was approached to run for both the U.S. Senate and governor of New York (to challenge Al Smith). He declined both invitations, but campaigned for each of the unsuccessful Republican candidates. When President Coolidge's popularity declined in 1927, and Hughes's name was raised as a possible presidential nominee in 1928, he issued a statement intended to put an end to speculation about his candidacy: "I

---

* Hughes criticized only three decisions, which he termed "self-inflicted wounds," because they undermined public confidence in the Court. The first was the *Dred Scott* decision in which the Court, composed of a majority of southerners, declared that African-Americans had no constitutional rights and that Congress could not prohibit slavery in the territories. The other "self-inflicted wounds," he said, were decisions in which new appointees provided crucial votes to reverse rulings on the constitutionality of paper currency legislation during the Civil War and, later, the federal income tax.

am too old to run for President and I would neither seek nor accept the nomination."

Still, interest in Hughes as a presidential candidate persisted. After Coolidge declined to run for reelection and his Commerce Secretary, Herbert Hoover, was actively seeking the nomination, the Republican national committeeman for New York announced that the state delegation would go to the convention prepared to back Hughes. Again, Hughes refused to become a candidate and, as he had done in 1920, also rejected an invitation to make the keynote address, concerned that it could lead to a draft. After Hoover was nominated, Hughes waged a vigorous campaign on his behalf in several key midwestern and northeastern states, culminating in a radio address the night before the election.

Hoover urged Hughes to return to Washington as Secretary of State, but Hughes, despite the president-elect's repeated entreaties, declined the appointment. Earlier in the year, he had accepted a two-year appointment to replace John Bassett Moore as a judge on the International Court of Justice. He believed deeply in the mission of the ICJ and hoped that his judicial work at The Hague might help persuade Congress to formally vote for U.S. membership in the tribunal. He had hardly begun work on the Court and did not want to leave after so short a tenure.

But a year later, Hughes felt compelled to reconsider his decision to complete his term at the ICJ. The health of his old friend Chief Justice Taft had deteriorated badly and rumors circulated in January 1930 that he would soon resign. When Taft was president and had appointed Hughes to be an associate justice in 1910, he had said that he was likely to promote him to Chief Justice during his presidential term. Taft chose Edward White instead, thinking that there would be time enough for Hughes, who was only forty-eight years old in 1910, to succeed the sixty-five-year-old White. Now, two decades later, Taft wanted to make good on his early pledge. He sent word to the White House that he wished Hughes to succeed him as Chief Justice. Besides his enormous admiration for Hughes, Taft had two additional reasons for urging his appointment, both having to do with the possibility that Hoover would nominate his close friend, Associate Justice Harlan Fiske Stone, rather than Hughes. "Stone is not a leader," Taft wrote his son Robert, "and would have a great deal of trouble in massing the court." He also feared that Stone, a frequent dissenter on the conservative Taft Court, would lead the justices in a more liberal direction.

Late in January, Taft's family abandoned all hope for his recovery and reported the Chief Justice's desperate condition to the White House. At the same time, members of the Supreme Court informed Attorney General William Mitchell that the Chief Justice would resign as soon as the president had decided on a successor. Mitchell's choice was the same as Taft's: Hughes. But Mitchell did not want to make the recommendation to the president until he was sure that Hughes would accept. The Attorney General asked two members of the Court, Associate Justices Willis Van Devanter and Pierce Butler, to dine with Hughes in his New York apartment to determine his willingness to return to the Court as Chief Justice. They did so on January 28, and reported to Mitchell the next day that Hughes would likely accept the nomination if it were offered.

At an early breakfast at the White House on January 31, Hoover told Hughes that as soon as he received Taft's resignation, he proposed to name him Chief Justice "to prevent all the political pulling and hauling that takes place over a vacancy." After thanking the president for the great honor, Hughes gave Hoover several reasons why he should nominate someone else. He was almost sixty-eight years old—too old, he suggested, to take on the rigorous responsibilities of Chief Justice. He was also reluctant to interfere with the career of his son, Charles Junior, whom Hoover had appointed Solicitor General of the United States (the government's chief advocate before the Supreme Court) only eight months earlier. "Finally," he said, "I think I've earned the right to finish life in peace."

Hoover patiently listened to Hughes's objections, then told him why he should accept the nomination. Hughe's argument that he was too old for the job was betrayed by the energy with which he pursued his wide-ranging professional activities. As to his concern about his son, the president assured Hughes that he intended to keep Charles Junior in the government at a high level comparable to that of solicitor general. He should also consider the Chief Justice's wishes. Taft would more readily resign, Hoover argued, if he knew that Hughes was to be named his successor. Finally, he appealed to Hughes's patriotism. "It is your duty to take it," he said.

Hughes agreed to accept the nomination. Three days later, the president received Chief Justice Taft's letter of resignation. Later that afternoon, Hoover held a press conference to announce that he would nominate Hughes to be the eleventh Chief Justice of the United States.

5

"An Emergency More Serious Than War"

Herbert Hoover was elected president in 1928 by one of the largest margins in American history, shattering the once solid Democratic South and winning every other state in the Union except Massachusetts and Rhode Island. He owed his victory in large part to postwar prosperity under two Republican administrations, as well as to the hapless candidacy of his Democratic opponent, Al Smith, whose Catholicism and outspoken opposition to Prohibition gave rural voters in his party ample excuse to stay home on election day or vote for Hoover.

But Hoover also deserved considerable credit for his lopsided victory. When he campaigned for the presidency, he was perhaps the most admired man in the nation. Trained as an engineer, he had retired as a partner in an international mining company at the age of forty, having amassed a fortune of $4 million. He then devoted himself to public service. During the First World War, he had demonstrated both efficiency and compassion in organizing the massive food relief effort in Belgium and, later, serving as President Wilson's wartime food administrator. Little wonder that both Republican and Democratic leaders (including Franklin Roosevelt) hoped that he might head their party's future presidential ticket. After Hoover announced that he was a Republican, he became the energetic and far-sighted Secretary of Commerce in both the Harding and Coolidge administrations. He convened a presidential conference on unemployment and promoted trade associations with the purpose of stabilizing prices, protecting employment, and rationalizing industrial production. In all of these initiatives, Hoover adhered to his core belief in enlightened, voluntary cooperation between private business and the federal government.

As president, Hoover was determined to guide the nation toward even greater achievement and prosperity with his progressive policies. "In no nation are the fruits of accomplishment more secure," he proclaimed in his presidential inaugural address on March 4, 1929. Shortly after taking office, he called a special session of Congress and successfully lobbied for the Agricultural Marketing Act, the first major legislation to cope with the agricultural depression that had persisted for almost a decade. The statute created the Federal Farm Board with capital of $500 million to promote agricultural cooperatives and stabilization corporations to bring order to the markets of depressed commodities such as cotton and wool.

But even as a confident Hoover pursued his agenda in the early months of his presidency, there were ominous signs that the economy was in trouble. The gap between the rich and ordinary wage earners widened. Mass-produced automobiles rolled off the assembly lines, but fewer and fewer Americans could afford them. Production was cut, but steel and automobile inventories continued to mount. At the same time, the once booming housing market spiraled downward. And the agricultural depression deepened. All the while, astronomical paper profits were being made on Wall Street where speculators bid stocks ever higher. Finally, in late October, the bottom fell out of the stock market. On Wednesday, October 23, more than 6 million shares changed hands, destroying $4 billion in paper value. Six days later, more than 16 million shares were bought and sold, precipitating an historic monthlong decline. By mid-November, $26 billion, about one third of the stock value in September, had disappeared.

Despite the terrible news from Wall Street, Hoover remained convinced that his policies would contain the damage and ultimately lead the nation to unprecedented prosperity. In November, he summoned an elite group of the nation's corporate leaders to the White House, exhorting them to maintain wages to encourage consumer spending in the sliding economy. They agreed. A month later, he announced that railway and public utilities executives would expand their building and maintenance programs and that state and local governments, responding to his request, would accelerate construction projects.

Given his early successes, Hoover was not concerned about political opposition to his nomination of Charles Evans Hughes to be Chief Justice. Hughes himself was not so sure. In their discussion at the White House on January 31, 1930, Hughes reminded the president of his prominent role in the Republican Party for more than two decades. "If you are convinced that the nomination will be confirmed by the Senate without a scrap," Hughes told the president, "I will accept it. But I don't want any trouble about it." The president assured Hughes that there would be no trouble.

Less than two weeks later, both the president and Hughes realized that they had badly miscalculated. On February 8, 1930, after the Senate Judiciary Committee had voted the Hughes nomination favorably out of committee, Republican senator George Norris of Nebraska, the committee's chairman, announced that he had changed his mind and would oppose the nomination. He handed the press a list of fifty-four cases in which Hughes had appeared as counsel before the Supreme Court since 1925; the overwhelmingly majority of the nominee's clients had been large corporations and wealthy individuals. Norris's purpose was clear. As leader of the progressive wing of the Republican Party, he hoped to use the Hughes nomination to ignite a populist rebellion against his party's dominant conservatism.

"We have reached a time in our history when the power and influence of monopoly and organized wealth are reaching into every government activity," Norris declared. "Perhaps it is not amiss to say that no man in public life so exemplifies the influence of powerful combinations in the political and financial worlds as does Mr. Hughes." He called the Hughes nomination "one of the most significant developments in the political life of this nation in many years," charging that Hughes shared the oligarchical philosophy of his wealthy clients. "His viewpoint is clouded," Norris said. "He looks through glasses contaminated by the influence of monopoly as it seeks to get favors by means which are denied to the common, ordinary citizen."

Neither Norris nor any other progressive opposing the nomination presented evidence that Hughes's views coincided with his wealthy clients. Nor did they discuss his role in representing the public interest, whether early in his career as special counsel to the New York legislature in investigating vested corporate interests or, more than two decades later, in serving as special master in the Great Lakes sewage dispute. And they said nothing about his advocacy of unpopular causes, such as defending the Socialists expelled from the New York legislature in 1919. Their overriding concern was that Hughes, like former Chief Justice Taft, would skillfully lead the pro-business Court majority. Hughes's confirmation, said Senator William Borah of Idaho, would result in "great economic oppression to the people of the United States."

Senator Robert LaFollette, Jr., of Wisconsin, following Norris and Borah, attacked the conservative economic decisions of the Taft Court, including a decision announced a few weeks before the Hughes nomination. In that January 1930 decision, the Court struck down a Maryland regulation limiting the rate charged by United Railways & Electric Co., the company that operated a streetcar monopoly in Baltimore. The state-imposed rate would have allowed United Railways an annual profit to 6¼ percent. That was confiscatory, wrote Associate Justice George Sutherland for a six-member majority, depriving the company of its "liberty" of contract without due process of law under the Fourteenth Amendment.* If the Senate confirmed Hughes, LaFollette asserted, it would effectively endorse "the Supreme Court's usurpation of power," and strip "the government of the States and the government of the nation of all power to regulate these utilities and public service corporations."

Insurgent Republicans were joined in opposition to the Hughes nomination by conservative Democrats, like Carter Glass of Virginia, who objected to Hughes's resignation from the Court in 1916 to run for the presidency, compromising, in their view, the independence of the judiciary. In the end, Hughes won confirmation handily, 52–26, buoyed by his reputation for personal integrity, legal brilliance, and outstanding public service. But the insurgents had served notice: they would challenge future nominees whom they suspected would further solidify the conservative Court majority on economic and social issues.

Shortly after Hughes's confirmation, Justice Stone, who regularly joined Justices Brandeis and Holmes in dissent, wrote approvingly of the Senate debate over the Court's role in the nation's social and economic affairs. "There is a very surprising but I think wholesome interest in what

---

* The amendment provides that no state shall "deprive any person of life, liberty, or property without due process of law." The conservative majority interpreted "liberty" in the clause to implicitly protect liberty of contract. Justice Brandeis, joined by Justices Holmes and Stone, dissented, writing that "a net return of 6¼ per cent upon the present value of the property of a street railway enjoying a monopoly in one of the oldest, largest, and richest cities on the Atlantic seaboard would seem to be compensatory."

the Court is doing and a disposition to study and discuss it with real intelligence," he noted to his friend Professor Felix Frankfurter of the Harvard Law School. Stone did not view the debate as "a contest between conservatism and radicalism" so much as it is "a difference arising from an inadequate understanding of the relationship of law to the social and economic forces which control society."

Progressive Republicans lashed out again a month later when President Hoover nominated a federal appeals court judge, John J. Parker, to replace Associate Justice Edward Sanford, who had been a reliable conservative vote on the Court. They accused Parker of being anti-labor, pointing to one of his judicial opinions that upheld the constitutionality of a so-called yellow dog contract that required workers to sign contracts agreeing not to join a union. They also accused Parker of being a racist, quoting a statement that he had made a decade earlier while running as a Republican candidate for governor of North Carolina that "[t]he participation of the Negro in politics is a source of evil and danger to both races." This time, the Senate voted down the nominee, 41 to 39.

Ironically, Hoover's next nominee, Owen Roberts, a prominent corporation lawyer from Philadelphia with a record on social and economic issues not discernibly different from Parker's, was easily confirmed two months later to replace Sanford. Though Roberts had many wealthy corporate clients, he had also represented labor leaders for a nominal fee, escaping the anti-labor label that had sunk Parker's nomination. Progressives were also impressed with Roberts's record as Special Deputy Attorney General under President Coolidge in prosecuting wrongdoers in the Teapot Dome scandal that had besmirched the Harding administration.

When the first full term of the Hughes Court convened in the old Senate chamber of the Capitol on the first Monday in October 1930, the new Chief Justice's daily work pattern was already well established. Rising early in the morning in his large, commodious residence on R Street, he ate a light breakfast at 7:30 a.m., then walked a mile along Massachusetts Avenue. By eight thirty he was at his desk making notes on cases to be argued at the Court or writing opinions.* On argument days, he left his home at

---

* As Chief Justice, Hughes assigned majority opinions when he was a member of the majority. He could also write concurring opinions and dissents, as could his colleagues.

11:30 a.m. and, after arriving at the Court, attended to any pressing administrative matters. At 11:55, he took his place in the anteroom where the justices assembled and, by tradition, shook hands and chatted informally with each other. Hughes then announced: "Brethren, the time has come." At precisely the stroke of twelve, two Court pages parted the drapes and the nine members of the Court took their seats on the bench.

Hughes was well acquainted with many of his judicial colleagues, including the senior member of the conservative judicial bloc, seventy-one-year-old Associate Justice Willis Van Devanter. He had known Van Devanter since the two men had served on the Court together during Hughes's earlier term as an associate justice. Van Devanter had been appointed to the Court in 1910 by President William Howard Taft after a successful career as an attorney in Cheyenne, Wyoming, representing the Union Pacific Railroad and specializing in land use transactions. He had parlayed his service as chairman of the Wyoming Republican Party into appointments as Assistant Attorney General in the Interior Department in charge of public lands and Indian affairs and later as a federal appeals court judge.

In his early years on the Court, Van Devanter could not be rigidly categorized as conservative, voting consistently, for example, in favor of broad government power to regulate the railroads. Though respected for his fastidious attention to the details of a case, Van Devanter suffered from what his colleague, Justice Sutherland, termed "pen paralysis," rarely producing more than three or four judicial opinions a term. But in conference, Van Devanter was remarkably effective in building majority coalitions, always for a conservative result in the later years of his tenure, a talent that Justice Brandeis likened to that "of a renaissance cardinal."

Associate Justice James McReynolds, sixty-eight years old, was born in Elkton, Kentucky, near the Tennessee border, to parents who belonged to the fundamentalist Campbellite sect. Tall and broad-shouldered, he was a serious, puritanical young man who did not drink, smoke, or play sports. After graduating valedictorian of his class at Vanderbilt and studying law at the University of Virginia, he practiced law in Nashville, representing large corporations such as the Illinois Central Railroad. He also taught commercial law at the Vanderbilt Law School, but found time in his busy schedule to join the campaign to rid Nashville of gambling and prostitution. Appointed Assistant Attorney General under President Theodore Roosevelt, he zealously prosecuted the tobacco trust, which he considered "essentially wicked." He briefly served in President Wilson's cabinet as Attorney General, continuing his trust-busting prosecutions, before he was appointed to the Court in 1914.

On the Court, McReynolds proved to be a dependable conservative vote, consistently reading federal government power narrowly and corporate property rights expansively. He was also the most irascible and openly prejudiced member of the Court. When a woman lawyer appeared before the justices, he loudly muttered, "I see the female is here again." And he made no secret of his virulent anti-Semitism, burying himself in a daily newspaper rather than witness the swearing-in of Justice Benjamin Cardozo, who was Jewish.

Former U.S. Senator George Sutherland of Utah, another conservative stalwart on the Court, had been one of Warren Harding's closest political advisers during the 1920 presidential campaign before his judicial appointment in 1922. A genial and handsome man, with a neatly trimmed white beard, Sutherland, sixty-eight years old, had succeeded in law and politics in the West much as had Van Devanter, building a thriving corporate law practice and smoothly climbing the ladder of Republican politics in Utah. He was elected the state's sole member of the House of Representatives in 1900 and five years later to the U.S. Senate. After he lost his reelection bid in 1916, he was elected president of the American Bar Association. As the head of the ABA, he attacked government regulation of the business community, which he said was "beset and bedeviled with vexatious statutes, preying commissions, and governmental meddling of all sorts." Committed to the status quo, he defended "the methodical habits of the past," and warned against "careering after novel and untried things."

Sutherland, like Van Devanter, used his trenchant skills as a lawyer to argue in favor of a conservative result in virtually every case. In 1923, for example, he wrote the majority opinion in *Adkins v. Children's Hospital* that struck down a law passed by Congress for the District of Columbia prescribing minimum wages for women. Liberty of contract, he declared, could not be subjected to "a naked, arbitrary exercise" of legislative power.*

The fourth member of the conservative bloc, Associate Justice Pierce Butler, sixty-four years old, was raised by Irish immigrants on a farm in

---

* For Sutherland and the other Court conservatives, the due process clause of the Fifth Amendment protected private contracts from federal economic legislation just as the due process clause in the Fourteenth Amendment provided protection against the states.

rural Minnesota. As a boy, Butler rode each day on horseback to a one-room schoolhouse. At fifteen, he was already over six feet tall and an accomplished wrestler when he began to teach in the same school he had attended. A rough-and-tumble taskmaster, Butler once bloodied the nose of one of his students, poured a pail of water over him, then resumed his lesson. He attended Carleton College, paying his expenses by working at a nearby dairy, then studied law in a St. Paul firm. Early in his legal career, he served as prosecuting attorney for Ramsey County, which included St. Paul, winning the greatest number of criminal convictions in the county's history. For the next thirty years, he built a reputation as an outstanding corporate lawyer, representing some of the nation's largest railroads. An acknowledged expert on the accounting procedures necessary to calculate railroad values and rates, he argued with notable success before the Interstate Commerce Commission that the value of his clients' railroad properties should be raised so that they could charge higher rates.

Butler was a partner in one of Minnesota's most prosperous corporate law firms when he was appointed to the Court by President Harding in 1923. He was a gruff, intimidating presence on the Court, as he had been in private practice. Hughes had observed Butler firsthand as a courtroom advocate when he argued the *Minnesota Rate Cases* before the Court in 1912. Almost two decades later, Justice Butler, accompanied by his colleague Willis Van Devanter, dined in Hughes's New York apartment, where the two conservative members of the Court gauged Hughes's willingness to accept the chief justiceship.

Justice Oliver Wendell Holmes, Jr., the venerable dissenter on the conservative Court, was born in 1841 in Boston, the scion of a distinguished New England family. His father was a celebrated surgeon and man of letters; his mother was the daughter of a justice of the Supreme Judicial Court of Massachusetts. After graduating from Harvard College in 1861, Holmes joined the Union Army as a second lieutenant in the 20th Massachusetts Regiment. He served for three years and was wounded three times in battle (at Ball's Bluff, Antietam, and Fredericksburg). Mustered out as a captain in 1864, he entered the Harvard Law School, graduating in 1866, and went on to practice law in Boston. Although a successful practitioner, Holmes pursued his wide-ranging intellectual interests as well, becoming a founding member of the Metaphysical Club that included the renowned philosopher William James. In 1881, he wrote *The Common Law*, which was immediately recognized as a seminal work of legal philosophy. "The life of the law has not been logic," Holmes noted. "It has been experience." In the book, he rejected a coherent, all-inclusive rule-based system of law in favor of a more pragmatic, utilitarian analysis. He was appointed to the State Supreme Court in 1882 and later became chief justice, writing more than 1,300 judicial opinions. President Theodore Roosevelt appointed Holmes to the U.S. Supreme Court in 1902.

Tall, spare, with aquiline features and a magnificent thick mustache, Holmes was an imposing physical presence. He was also the Court's most elegant stylist. In 1905, he wrote one of his most famous dissents, rejecting the conservative majority's opinion that New York's regulation of the maximum hours that bakers could work was a violation of the liberty of contract between employee and employer guaranteed by the Fourteenth Amendment. "[A] constitution is not intended to embody a particular economic theory," he lectured the Court majority, "whether of paternalism and the organic relation of the citizen to the State or of laissez faire." After Hughes was appointed an associate justice in 1910, he and Holmes developed a warm friendship, exchanging jocular notes in the margins of their draft opinions and often voting together in support of the constitutionality of broad federal legislative power as well as the protection of individual civil liberties. After Secretary of State Hughes organized the Washington Disarmament Conference in 1921, Holmes attended the first session and wrote his former judicial colleague a note of congratulations on his accomplishment.

Louis Brandeis's parents immigrated to the United States from Bohemia and settled in Louisville, Kentucky, where Brandeis's father prospered as a grain merchant. The Brandeis home in Louisville became a meeting place for intellectuals and talented musicians. Louis was a brilliant student, attending a pre-university academy in Dresden at sixteen, skipping college, and entering Harvard Law School at the age of eighteen. He completed his legal studies in two years, reportedly earning the highest grades ever recorded, and opened a law practice in Boston that was wide-ranging and highly profitable. Though he represented many large corporations, Brandeis also used his great skills as a advocate on behalf of reform causes, including minimum wage and maximum hour legislation. In what became known as "the Brandeis brief," he furnished judges with mountains of facts and statistics to support his legal arguments. In the early 1900s, he attacked vested interests in Boston's utilities and insurance industries, as did his friend and counterpart in New York, Charles Evans Hughes.

When Brandeis was nominated to the Court by President Wilson in 1916, seven former presidents of the American Bar Association, including William Howard Taft and George Sutherland, opposed the appointment, charging that Brandeis was too radical to sit on the highest court in the nation.* Once confirmed, Brandeis often joined Holmes in opposition to a Court majority that considered private property and contract rights virtually inviolate under the due process clauses of the Constitution. Brandeis, like Holmes, did not consider those rights beyond the reach of government regulation. In contrast to the gracious, convivial Holmes, Brandeis, seventy-three years old, projected the image of an ascetic, gaunt in physical appearance and austere in his tastes and lifestyle. And whereas Holmes was a skeptic who distrusted judge-made law, Brandeis was a moralist who believed that the Court should be a national teacher, using judicial opinions to explicate complex social and economic issues.

Harlan Fiske Stone, the son of a New Hampshire farmer, attended Amherst College, where he first demonstrated his talent for advocacy. Young Stone successfully argued that the dismissal of a fellow undergraduate by a faculty decree should have been reversed because the action was not approved by the student senate. After graduating from Amherst and the Columbia Law School with high honors, Stone divided his professional time for twenty-five years between teaching and practicing law in New York City. He served as dean of the Columbia Law School for thirteen years before President Coolidge appointed him U.S. Attorney General in 1924, succeeding Harding's crony, Harry Daugherty. A year later, Coolidge appointed Stone to the Supreme Court.

As a member of the Court, Stone, now fifty-eight years old, counseled judicial restraint, objecting to both conservative and liberal justices who, he believed, too often substituted their policy preferences for constitutional analysis. Though he was a lifelong Republican, Stone concluded that government power was necessary to meet the changing social and economic conditions of the twentieth century. He therefore was often aligned with Holmes and Brandeis in dissent in cases in which the conservative majority struck down social and economic regulations. In January 1930, Stone was deeply disappointed when President Hoover, a close personal friend and fishing companion, passed over him for the chief justiceship. He believed the rumor, spread by Joseph Cotton, Hoover's Under Secretary of

---

* An undercurrent of anti-Semitism also fueled opposition to the Brandeis nomination.

State, that the president had expected to appoint him after extending the invitation to Hughes only as a courtesy.*

The only justices whose views on the constitutionality of economic and social legislation were not well known were the Court's two newest members, Chief Justice Hughes and Associate Justice Roberts. Roberts owed his easy confirmation in large part to the fact that he had said and written virtually nothing on the subject. Hughes, on the other hand, had said and written a great deal about the need for social and economic reform. He first captured the public's attention as special counsel to state legislative committees investigating corruption and mismanagement in the utilities and insurance industries. Later, he served two terms as a reform governor of New York. And as an associate justice for six years, from 1910 to 1916, he often sided with Holmes in challenging the conservative majority. But that progressive record would have to be balanced against Hughes's loyal service in the cabinets of two conservative Republican presidents, Harding and Coolidge. In addition, Hughes could be expected to act with prudence as Chief Justice in an effort to emulate his mentor, former Chief Justice Taft, in "massing the Court."

When the Hughes Court heard the first arguments of the October 1930 term, the economy continued to plunge. During the year more than 1,300 banks closed their doors, twice the failures of the previous year. Gross national product sank by 12.6 percent of its 1929 level. The first federal census of unemployment reported that 3 million Americans could not find work. And "Hoover blanket," a sardonic reference to the newspaper covering those who slept on park benches, entered the nation's vocabulary.

When Franklin Roosevelt was pressed by New York Democratic leaders in 1926 to run for the U.S. Senate, he said that he preferred to work in the executive branch of government. And though it took considerable arm-twisting from Governor Smith and Ed Flynn to persuade FDR to accept his party's nomination for governor in 1928, once elected, he appeared

---

* Stone had an additional reason to believe that he was Hoover's choice. Presidential secretary George Akerson walked into the White House press room on February 3, 1930, and whispered, "It's Stone." Akerson's statement was wired to newspapers across the country before Hoover corrected the false report and announced that he would nominate Hughes to be Chief Justice.

supremely confident in his abilities to serve as chief executive of the nation's most populous state.

That confidence was not shared by his predecessor, Al Smith, who rented a suite of rooms in Albany's DeWitt Clinton Hotel so that he could be available to tutor FDR on the intricacies of running the complicated state machinery. Smith also expected FDR to retain two of his most trusted lieutenants, Belle Moskowitz and Robert Moses. Though Moskowitz's title was secretary to the governor, she served as his chief of staff, principal speechwriter, and key political strategist. Moses was secretary of state under Smith, and, like Moskowitz, exercised power far beyond his official job description.

Shortly before Roosevelt was to take the oath of office, Smith told him that he needn't bother writing his inaugural address; Mrs. Moskowitz was already preparing the speech. The governor-elect thanked Smith, but told him that he intended to write his own speech. He would be happy to show a draft to Mrs. Moskowitz, he said, but he never did. As for Moses, FDR had taken a visceral dislike to him when he had tangled with Smith's headstrong Secretary of State over funding for the Taconic State Parkway when Roosevelt was the parkway's chairman.

Roosevelt ignored Smith's advice to retain Moskowitz and Moses, and brought in his own team. Missy Le Hand and Grace Tully shared secretarial duties. A young lawyer, Sam Rosenman, became his chief speechwriter, a position he had first filled during the gubernatorial campaign. Eleanor Roosevelt served as her husband's trusted political ally (insisting that he drop Mrs. Moskowitz), and Louis Howe remained his indispensable strategist. Ed Flynn, the astute Bronx boss, replaced Moses as secretary of state.

As if to reassure Smith of their continued political alliance, Roosevelt began his inaugural address on January 1, 1929, with effusive praise for his predecessor, calling him "a public servant of true greatness." But his public accolades for Smith were not followed up with phone calls seeking the former governor's advice. A resentful Smith soon realized that FDR intended to forge an independent course as governor, and that his services would not be needed. After Roosevelt's inauguration, the two men, never close friends, grew further apart. Smith became so embittered by Roosevelt's perceived lack of respect for him that he challenged him for the Democratic presidential nomination in 1932 and eventually made a clean break, denouncing Roosevelt's New Deal policies during the 1936 presidential campaign.

In his inaugural address as governor, Roosevelt proposed an ambitious progressive agenda that called for reforms across a broad economic, social, and political spectrum. At the top of his list was the need to harness New York's water resources to produce and distribute electricity cheaply and efficiently throughout the state.* "The water power of the state should belong to the people," he declared, and called for the state to build new dams, install power stations, and construct transmission lines so that power could be distributed to tens of thousands of homes and factories. He also vowed to help struggling farmers who had suffered through the decade's agricultural depression, proposing lower taxes, better rural roads to get their products to market, and a marketing cooperative for dairy farmers to stabilize the price of milk.

A day later, Roosevelt delivered his first annual address to the state legislators, seeking their cooperation in promoting his ambitious goals. In addition to his public power and agricultural proposals, he asked lawmakers to help him clean up inefficient (and often corrupt) county and town court systems, improve prison conditions, impose tougher maximum hour work restrictions for women and children, extend workmen's compensation, and explore the need for old age pensions.

In all of his efforts, Roosevelt operated simultaneously on two levels— setting his idealistic goals broadly while preparing to do gritty battle with recalcitrant legislators on a daily basis. Privately, he marveled at how little the hidebound legislature had changed since he had served as a state senator eighteen years earlier. He knew that his challenge was formidable: he not only had to contend with entrenched committee chairmen, but also faced a Republican majority in both houses that was emboldened by the party's sweeping victories in the 1928 election. Another reform-minded governor, Charles Evans Hughes, had faced similar problems two decades earlier. But whereas Hughes's battles with the legislature had not only proved frustrating but also jeopardized his health, Roosevelt appeared energized by the challenge, writing a friend that he was in "one continuous glorious fight with the Republican legislative leaders."

Republican legislators tested the new governor's mettle early in the

---

* Roosevelt asked Louis Howe to study former Governor Charles Evans Hughes's efforts to regulate the state's utilities and later publicly acknowledged Hughes's initiative.

term, insisting that they controlled his spending options even after they had passed the annual budget. Roosevelt sent back the budget bill, vetoing all of the large, lump-sum items (amounting to $54 million). The legislature returned the identical bill to the governor's desk, accompanied by nine hundred other bills that killed all of his progressive initiatives. Roosevelt again vetoed the lump-sum items, forcing a court test, which he eventually won in the highest state court. Except for that victory, Roosevelt's ambitious agenda was undercut regularly by the defiant Republican legislature.

Unfazed, Roosevelt took his progressive message directly to the people in speeches around the state and in Sunday night fireside chats broadcast from his Albany office. In his reassuring, conversational tone, he explained complicated public policy in everyday terms that his listeners could easily understand. Lobbying for cheaper electricity, Roosevelt noted that a housewife in Ontario, Canada, cooked, ironed, and listened to the radio for a fraction of the price per kilowatt charged to a housewife in Buffalo or Brooklyn. The difference, Roosevelt explained, was that the Canadian government sold electricity on a strictly cost basis while loosely regulated privately owned utilities companies in New York were allowed to earn large profits.

Though his message went unheeded in Albany, Roosevelt was already attracting considerable attention outside New York as a potential Democratic candidate for the presidency in 1932. After the state legislature adjourned in April 1929, he spoke at the national press corps's Gridiron Dinner in Washington (other guests: President Hoover and Chief Justice Taft) and was serenaded:

> Oh, Franklin, Franklin Roosevelt,
> Is there something in a name?
> When you tire of being Governor
> Will you look for bigger game?
> Will you wish for something higher
> When at Albany you're through?
> When you weary of the State House
> Will the White House beckon you?

Roosevelt, always the good sport, heartily joined in the laughter over the presumptuous ditty. But he had no plans to seek the presidency, at least not in 1932. He and Howe assumed that Hoover would be elected to a second term, unless some catastrophe punctured the economic bubble of prosperity. In the spring of 1929, their sights were still on 1936. And so Governor Roosevelt emphatically issued denials of his presidential ambitions. Even after the market crashed, he was reluctant to challenge Hoover's policies. He, like the president, thought the market would correct itself in short order, and that the nation would return to prosperity.

In late January 1930, FDR was forced to reconsider his original judgment on the crash and its aftermath. After the president announced that employment was beginning to rebound, Roosevelt's industrial commissioner, Frances Perkins, held a news conference to cite Labor Department statistics on unemployment that proved the president wrong. A slightly anxious Perkins then called her boss to report on her news conference; he assured her that he approved. Roosevelt soon added new items to his progressive agenda, pegged to the deepening economic crisis. He created a state commission to stabilize employment and became the first governor in the nation to endorse unemployment insurance.

By the spring, Roosevelt was openly challenging the president, ridiculing Hoover's optimistic forecasts that defied the basic economic law of supply and demand. And he returned to one of his favorite themes: Republicans governed on behalf of the wealthy. "If Thomas Jefferson were alive," he told guests at the National Democratic Club's Jefferson Day Dinner, "he would be the first to question this concentration of economic power." The keynote speaker at the dinner, progressive Democratic senator Burton Wheeler of Montana, followed Roosevelt to the podium and unexpectedly endorsed FDR for president in 1932. "As I look about for a general to lead the Democratic party, I ask to whom we can go. I say that, if the Democratic party of New York will re-elect Franklin Roosevelt governor, the West will demand his nomination for president and the whole country will elect him."

Roosevelt wrote Senator Wheeler that he was gratified by the endorsement of "one of the real leaders of progressive thought and action in this country." But he confessed that talk of his candidacy in 1932 put him "in a somewhat difficult position" since he "had no personal desire to run for a national office." He was also concerned that "the more I get into the national limelight the more it is going to hurt my present work as governor of New York." He was disingenuous in denying any presidential ambitions. But he was sincere, and surely correct, in telling Wheeler that talk of his seeking the presidency could only detract from his work in Albany. He knew, moreover, that he must be reelected later that year to enhance his presidential prospects.

Roosevelt and Howe carefully planned the reelection campaign to focus on the policies he had championed in his first term: public power, agrarian reform, and full employment. But his Republican opponent, Charles Tuttle, the U.S. Attorney for the southern district of New York, attempted to make Tammany Hall corruption the central issue of the campaign.

"Never let your opponent pick the battleground on which to fight," Roosevelt told Sam Rosenman. "If he picks one, stay out of it and let him fight all by himself." And so, while Tuttle railed against crooked judges controlled by Tammany, FDR pushed for tighter state regulation of electricity rates. "It takes the same number of kilowatts to cook a beef stew in Toronto as it does in Syracuse," he told an upstate audience, demanding that New York emulate the Canadian government in the effective regulation of utilities companies.

Though Roosevelt resolutely campaigned on state issues, President Hoover was his unannounced Republican opponent. He taunted Hoover for his optimistic pronouncements on the sagging economy as "a desperate and futile attempt to restore prosperity by means of proclamations from Washington." He was fully prepared to take on three members of Hoover's cabinet, Secretary of State Henry Stimson, Secretary of War Patrick Hurley, and Under Secretary of the Treasury Ogden Mills when they came to New York to campaign for his opponent. He had no personal complaint against "these three eminent gentlemen," he said. But one, Secretary of War Hurley, was a carpetbagger from Oklahoma who knew nothing about New York's problems. The other two were New Yorkers, but both of them, Roosevelt noted, had run for governor and lost. "The people did not believe in them then," he said, "and they will not believe in them or in their issues now."

In the last week of the campaign, Roosevelt finally acknowledged that there might be a problem of corruption in New York City's courts. "If there are corrupt judges still sitting in our courts, they shall be removed by constitutional means, not by inquisition, not by trial in the press, but by trial as provided by law," he said. "That is justice. That is America. That is right."

Roosevelt won reelection by 725,000 votes, the largest plurality in a gubernatorial race in the state's history. Thanks largely to the grassroots organizational skills of Jim Farley, the big, jovial secretary of the state Democratic committee, he carried three times as many upstate counties as his Republican opponent. And Tammany produced a prodigious majority for Roosevelt in New York City.

At the suggestion of Louis Howe, Farley held a news conference the day after the election. "I do not see how Mr. Roosevelt can escape becoming the next presidential nominee of his party," he told reporters, "even if no one should raise a finger to bring it about." After the news conference, Farley called Roosevelt in Albany to report what he had said.

"Whatever you said, Jim, is all right with me," Roosevelt replied, laughing.

Three years before he was appointed Chief Justice, Charles Evans Hughes had declared that leadership on the Supreme Court depended on "strength of character" and "ability," carefully observed, "in the intimate relations of the judges." A Chief Justice's influence, he had said in his 1927 lectures on the Court, rose in direct proportion to his colleagues' perception of his "[c]ourage of conviction, sound learning, familiarity with precedents, [and] exact knowledge due to painstaking study of the cases under consideration." Members of the Court quickly sized up the strengths and weaknesses of their brethren, including the Chief Justice, Hughes suggested, undoubtedly drawing on his own experience serving for six years as an associate justice. He said that Chief Justice John Marshall's "preeminence was due to the fact that he was John Marshall, not simply that he was Chief Justice." Marshall was "our most illustrious judicial figure," Hughes observed, because of his magisterial opinions defining the broad contours of the Constitution, and was not dependent on his being Chief Justice.

Another lesson in his lectures on the Court offered a cautionary warning to Hughes himself after he became Chief Justice. It was essential, Hughes had said, that the Court project an institutional image of objectivity; the justices should be perceived by the public as men of integrity, who were above partisan politics. When the Court's rulings appeared to be based on the justices' political biases, the Court's authority was diminished by a "self-inflicted wound." That occurred, Hughes had suggested, in the disastrous *Dred Scott* decision, when a Court dominated by justices from slave states excluded African-Americans from the protections of the Constitution.

At the time Hughes gave his Columbia lectures, the conservative Taft

Court majority was accused by critics of voting their political values in rejecting government economic regulation of private enterprise. But their decisions did not jeopardize the Court's public standing, because they were consistent with the prevailing ethos in the 1920s, reflected in the popular, pro-business presidential administrations of Harding, Coolidge, and Hoover (before the market crash). The Taft Court, moreover, appeared institutionally stable, since the Chief Justice was successful in "massing the court" by regularly producing six-man majorities for his conservative views.

But in 1930, after Hughes became Chief Justice, the fresh precedents of the Taft Court were not only challenged by the three dissenters (Justices Brandeis, Holmes, and Stone) but increasingly by restive progressive politicians calling for greater government intervention in response to the worsening economic depression. Hughes's prescription for leadership on the Court, so carefully laid out in his Columbia lectures, therefore carried a special urgency when he greeted his brethren in October 1930 for the first full term of the Hughes Court.

The new Chief Justice was well aware of the philosophical cleavage on the Court. The four conservative holdovers from the Taft Court—Justices Butler, McReynolds, Sutherland, and Van Devanter—were "all able men of high character," he later wrote, who "generally acted together." Justices Brandeis, Holmes, and Stone, he knew, disagreed with their colleagues' interpretation of the due process clauses of the Fifth and Fourteenth amendments that made private contracts between employer and employee impregnable. To the dissenters, popularly elected legislators, not life-tenured justices, should determine the limits of social and economic regulation, so long as those regulations were reasonable.

In what direction would Hughes attempt to lead the Court? With his appointment and that of Associate Justice Owen Roberts, liberals had high hopes that the conservative juggernaut, so dominant during the Taft Court years, would, at last, be stopped. After all, nothing in Hughes's or Roberts's records suggested that either held rigidly ideological views on the sanctity of private contracts or opposed economic and social regulation. In Hughes's long career of public service, however, he had always moved his progressive agenda forward cautiously and with careful attention to the political limitations imposed on him, whether as governor of New York or U.S. Secretary of State. And now, as Chief Justice, he faced a serious institutional problem: If he attempted to lead the Court in a progressive direction, he would undoubtedly roil the tough-minded conservative bloc and could jeopardize the Court's public image of stability during an unprecedented national crisis.

Even with the formidable challenge of leading a sharply divided Court, Hughes could always rely on his extraordinary legal talents when he presided at the justices' conference on Saturdays to discuss the cases that had been argued earlier in the week. As Chief Justice, Hughes spoke first, stating the facts, legal issues, and how he thought the case should be decided. Always well prepared, he exhibited a sure command of the judicial record and an incisive mind that appeared to sift effortlessly through the fog of conflicting legal claims. By temperament, he was self-contained, seemingly detached. He considered his presentations in judicial conference to be his primary means of persuading his colleagues to agree with his point of view on how a case should be decided. He avoided appeals to his colleagues' emotions and rarely lobbied for his position outside the justices' conference room.

Despite his minimalist approach to advocacy among his brethren, Hughes made a powerful impression on his colleagues. "Hughes has real energy and intelligence," observed Louis Brandeis, shortly after Hughes became Chief Justice. Harlan Fiske Stone wrote that Hughes fulfilled his responsibilities with "painstaking care and unflagging energy." And Justice Roberts recalled that the Chief Justice's stamina in presiding at the intense Saturday conferences, sometimes lasting more than six hours, "was always a matter of wonder and admiration to me."

It did not take long for the Court to confront the most contentious constitutional provision that divided the justices: the due process clause of the Fourteenth Amendment. On October 30, 1930, the Hughes Court heard the case *O'Gorman & Young v. Hartford Insurance Co.*, in which an insurance agency challenged a New Jersey statute that limited commissions for the sale of fire insurance to 20 percent of premiums. Lawyers for the insurance agency argued that the state's limitation on commissions was arbitrary price-fixing that interfered with the private contract between the insurance company and its agent, violating the Constitution. The state responded that the statutory limitation on commissions was constitutional because it was rationally related to New Jersey's legitimate interest in maintaining the financial stability of insurance companies and controlling the costs of premiums.

Hughes voted to support New Jersey's position that the statute was reasonable and therefore constitutional. But he left no notes on the conference in which the justices discussed *O'Gorman*, or any other written record indicating how strongly he expressed his views on the merits of the case. In his conclusion, he was joined by the newest associate justice, Owen Roberts, as well as the three liberal holdovers from the Taft Court, Justices Brandeis, Holmes, and Stone. The four conservatives dissented. The Chief Justice, as a member of the majority, was responsible for assigning the Court's opinion; he gave it to Brandeis.

In his opinion for the razor-thin majority, Justice Brandeis appeared sensitive to the danger of displeasing either Hughes or Roberts, whose views on the due process clause were not well established and who might be uncomfortable with an expansive discussion of the constitutional issue. He wrote a short, cautious opinion that tracked closely to the state's argument. The limitation on agents' commissions was a reasonable regulation in the public interest, Brandeis concluded, in preventing exorbitant fire insurance rates and discouraging discriminatory premiums among policyholders.

Justices Butler, McReynolds, Sutherland, and Van Devanter filed a joint dissent, which reiterated their long-held position that the due process clause forbid such government regulation of private contracts. "This Court has steadfastly upheld the general right to enter into private contracts and has definitely disapproved attempts to fix prices by legislative fiat," they wrote. "The right to contract about one's affairs is a part of the liberty of the individual protected by this clause."

In this early test of Hughes's and Roberts's views on the due process clause, both had disagreed with their conservative brethren. But the rejoicing in liberal legal quarters was muted, since it was only one decision, and neither Hughes nor Roberts had expressed his individual opinion on the explosive constitutional issue. As a member of the majority, the Chief Justice could have assigned the Court opinion to himself or written a concurring opinion revealing his views. He did neither. But in three other high-profile cases during his initial full term as Chief Justice, Hughes wrote extensive opinions. All dealt with important issues of civil liberties, a subject on which Hughes had been outspoken for more than twenty years, dating back to his terms as governor of New York.

The first case involved Yetta Stromberg, a nineteen-year-old counselor at a Young Communist League youth camp in the foothills of California's San Bernardino Mountains. Every morning, Stromberg led her campers in a salute to a red flag bearing the hammer and sickle (the official flag of the Soviet Union and the U.S. Communist Party) and a pledge of allegiance "to the workers' flag and cause for which it stands." She was arrested and convicted for violating a state statute that made it a crime to display a red flag in a public or meeting place as a symbol of opposition to organized government, support for an anarchistic act, or for propaganda that is "of a seditious character." In leading the camp ceremony, Stromberg, a U.S. citizen, said that she was exercising her constitutional right to free expression.

Hughes was a member of a seven-member majority (Butler and McReynolds dissented) that ruled in favor of the defendant, and this time he assigned the Court opinion to himself. In his opinion, he focused exclusively on the first prong of the statute that made it a crime to display a red flag as a symbol of opposition to organized government. One could participate in a red flag ceremony that violated the broad language of the statute that would nonetheless be protected speech, he wrote. A member of a political party out of power, for example, could take part in such a ceremony in peaceful protest against the party in power. If it were a peaceful demonstration, without anarchistic or seditious intent, he reasoned, it was protected by the Constitution.

The Chief Justice's opinion was dry and legalistic, quoting extensively from both the state statute and lower court opinions that favored his position. In concentrating on the language of the statute, he stripped it of all emotional content. The first provision of the statute, he concluded, was so vague and over-broad that it could cover constitutionally protected conduct. Stromberg's conviction was overturned.

In a decision announced a week after *Stromberg*, a five-member Court majority (Roberts joined the four conservative justices) declared that the federal government was justified in rejecting the application for U.S. citizenship of Dr. Douglas Macintosh, a Yale University professor of theology who was born in Canada. In his naturalization application, Dr. Macintosh, who had served as a chaplain for the Canadian government during the First World War, had written that he would only take up arms for the United States in a war that he considered moral.

Hughes wrote a long dissent, focusing on Congress's intent in writing the statutory requirements for citizenship. He observed that the statute providing that applicants for citizenship take an oath to support and defend the Constitution and the laws of the United States was substantially the same as that required for civil officers (including members of Congress), which did not require a pledge to bear arms. These oaths should be read in the context of the country's long history of protecting the freedom of conscience. Conscientious objectors were excused from military service, he noted, an indication that Congress had not intended to subordinate one's religious beliefs to civil power. "There is abundant room for . . . maintaining the conception of the supremacy of law as essential to orderly government, without demanding that either citizens or applicants for citizenship shall assume by oath an obligation to regard allegiance to God as subordinate to allegiance to civil power," he concluded.

A week after Hughes filed his *Macintosh* dissent, the Court announced its opinion in *Near v. Minnesota*, an historic challenge to the constitutional protection of freedom of the press. The case posed the painful question of whether freedom of the press covered the bigoted rantings of the publisher of the *Saturday Press*, a tiny scandal sheet, which claimed that a Jewish gangster controlled gambling, bootlegging, and racketeering in Minneapolis with the tacit consent of city officials. After repeated warnings, the state shut down the publication under a law that made it a public nuisance to publish "malicious, scandalous and defamatory" newspapers or magazines. Under the statute, truth was a defense, but only if it could be shown that the article was published "with good motives and for justifiable ends." Further publication was punishable by imprisonment for contempt of court.

The case had attracted national attention as it proceeded through the Minnesota courts. The *Saturday Press*'s publisher, Jay Near, whose hatred of blacks, Jews, and labor unions was well documented, had successfully solicited the financial support of the American Civil Liberties Union, the liberal organization dedicated to the protection of individual liberties. The defendant also received backing from the publisher of the conservative *Chicago Tribune*, Colonel Robert McCormick, who had a professional stake in fighting the Minnesota "gag law." If the Minnesota law was upheld, then the Illinois legislature might pass its own version, jeopardizing the *Tribune*'s own freewheeling investigations of official corruption. In addition to common journalistic interests, McCormick shared Near's prejudices against blacks, Jews, and labor unions.

When the case was argued before the Court on January 30, 1931, the four conservative members appeared ready to support the state's defense of the statute. Although they remained zealous in their defense of the "liberty" in the Fourteenth Amendment when it protected private contracts, they had never interpreted the clause to cover press freedom. But the Chief

Justice indicated early in the oral argument that he did not agree with his conservative brethren on that crucial constitutional issue. He interrupted Minnesota's deputy attorney general when he attempted to argue that the liberty clause did not protect freedom of the press. He need not argue the point further, said Hughes, because the case *did* raise the issue.

Justice Brandeis, the only Jew on the Court, then suggested to counsel that the anti-Semitic attacks in the *Press* may have served a legitimate purpose. "How else can a community secure protection from that sort of thing [official corruption] if people are not allowed to engage in free discussion of such matters?" he asked. He did not wait for an answer from the state's attorney. "You cannot disclose evil without naming the doers of evil. It is difficult to see how one can have a free press and the protection that it affords in the democratic community with the privilege this act seems to limit."

At the Saturday conference in which *Near* was discussed, the justices divided 5–4 to strike down the law, with the four conservatives dissenting. Hughes would have been justified in assigning the majority opinion to Justice Brandeis, whose intense questioning of the state's counsel at oral argument reflected his strongly held belief in freedom of the press. Earlier in the term, the Chief Justice had assigned the *O'Gorman* opinion to Brandeis, who was also the Court's most outspoken advocate for broad state authority to pass economic legislation. But whereas Hughes chose Brandeis to write the majority opinion in *O'Gorman*, he kept the Court's opinion in *Near v. Minnesota* for himself.

On June 1, 1931, the last day of the term, Hughes read his *Near* opinion from the bench in a strong, resonant voice. In it, he approached the critical constitutional issue with the same attention to statutory detail that had characterized his *Stromberg* opinion. Stating at the outset that there was no absolute right to freedom of the press, he conceded that censorship was justified in exceptional circumstances. The government could suppress the publication of the sailing dates of troops during wartime, for example, or attacks in print that incited violence. The Minnesota statute, however, was not limited to those narrow exceptions that would justify shutting down a newspaper's press. The *Saturday Press*, however scurrilous its charges, was ostensibly attempting to expose official corruption. And the state law, in demanding proof of truth "with good motives and for justifiable ends," allowed the government to suppress a publication that might uncover official corruption. That was "the essence of censorship," Hughes declared, and was a violation of the Constitution.

Toward the end of his opinion, Hughes wrote about the critical importance of freedom of the press. A free press was a cornerstone of America's
constitutional democracy, he emphasized, tracing that belief back to James
Madison, the architect of the First Amendment. If probing journalists were
essential to holding government accountable in colonial times, they might
be even more important in the twentieth century. As big-city governments
become more complex, there was greater opportunity for official corruption, and a need for a "vigilant and courageous press." He concluded: "The
fact that the liberty of the press may be abused by miscreant purveyors of
scandal does not make any the less necessary the immunity of the press
from previous restraint in dealing with official conduct."

The New York Times called the decision "weighty and conclusive."
Colonel McCormick declared, "The decision of Chief Justice Hughes will
go down in history as one of the greatest triumphs for free thought." Mc-
Cormick also wrote Hughes a personal letter reiterating his high praise. To
make Hughes's opinion a permanent reminder to his staff of the role of a
free press, McCormick ordered that a long passage be etched in marble in
the lobby of the Tribune Building.

With widespread public acclaim for the Chief Justice's *Near* opinion,
the first full term of the Hughes Court had ended on a very high note for
Hughes. Equally important, he had met one of the key elements of Court
leadership, "ability," as he had defined it in his 1927 lectures at Columbia.
He presided with quiet authority at oral argument. And in the Saturday
conferences, he earned his brethren's respect with his comprehensive presentations of the cases and his calm demeanor in leading the justices' discussions.

Liberals on the Court and in the academic world were encouraged by
the Chief Justice's strongly worded opinions favoring civil liberties as well
as his vote in the *O'Gorman* decision that gave constitutional sanction to
New Jersey's regulation of fire insurance commissions. Justice Stone expressed satisfaction with the term's work, noting that neither Holmes nor
Brandeis had written a single dissenting opinion. "The Court is not to
stand in the way of experimentation," an editor of the *Yale Law Journal*
wrote approvingly. "The addition of two vigorous thinkers to the bench
[Hughes and Roberts] has carried the day for pragmatism and liberal toler-
ance of legislative experiment with control for the purpose of advancing a
larger capacity for individual freedom."

Despite those early victories for the liberal wing of the Hughes Court, the conservative justices had reason to think that the Chief Justice might yet join them in vigorously protecting private contract rights. In his most celebrated opinion of the term, *Near v. Minnesota*, the Chief Justice, in discussing the "liberty" in the Fourteenth Amendment that protected press freedom, wrote that "this Court has held that the power of the State stops short of interference with what are deemed to be certain indispensable requirements of the liberty assured, notably with respect to the fixing of prices and wages." In support of that statement, Hughes cited the Taft Court's decision in *Adkins v. Children's Hospital*, which struck down the District of Columbia's minimum wage law for women as a violation of an employer's due process rights.*

During the term, Oliver Wendell Holmes, Jr., celebrated his ninetieth birthday. In a radio tribute, Hughes saluted his legendary colleague, recognizing his wisdom and zest for life. He ended his public remarks on an uncharacteristically emotional note. "We honor him, but, what is more, we love him," he said. "We give him tonight the homage of our hearts."

At ninety, the remarkable Holmes remained intellectually vibrant and engaged in the Court's work. He continued to take copious notes on the bench and write jaunty messages of approval in the margins of Hughes's draft opinions. After the Court convened for the fall term in October 1931, however, Hughes noticed that Holmes's health had deteriorated badly. It was evident to Hughes that his colleague lacked the energy to write his fair share of opinions, so the Chief Justice discreetly reduced his assignments. During oral argument, Holmes dozed off, his head drooping until it almost touched the desk in front of him. Holmes's colleagues feared that the great man's condition, so publicly on display, could undermine confidence in the Court.

Finally, in January 1932, a majority of the justices urged the Chief Justice to ask for Holmes's resignation. Hughes was well aware of the Court's history on such demands. Shortly after the Civil War, Justice Stephen Field was a member of a delegation designated to request the resignation of the failing Justice Robert Grier before the closely divided Court voted in a highly controversial case. Years later, when an aging Justice Fields was

---

* When Brandeis questioned the citation in Hughes's draft opinion, the Chief Justice replied that he wanted "to expose the inconsistency of the dissenters" on their application of the due process clause. The citation nonetheless appeared to reaffirm the validity of the *Adkins* decision, which Brandeis and the other dissenters considered wrong.

approached by Justice Harlan on a similar mission, Harlan reminded Fields of his earlier visit to Grier. "Yes! And a dirtier day's work I never did in my life," an indignant Fields replied.

On Sunday, January 11, Hughes dutifully arranged to visit Holmes at his residence. Once they were seated in Holmes's study, the Chief Justice slowly, awkwardly, came to the point of his visit. The burdens of the Court's work had become too great for Holmes, he suggested. Then, with tears in his eyes, he asked for his old friend's resignation. Without a hint of resentment, Holmes requested that Hughes go to his bookshelf and find the applicable statute setting out the procedure for his resignation. The disagreeable deed was then quickly done.

A month later, President Hoover nominated Justice Benjamin Cardozo, the chief judge of New York's Court of Appeals, to replace Holmes. In nominating Cardozo, a Democrat, the beleaguered president received a rare and hearty round of bipartisan applause. Democratic senator Clarence Dill of Washington, who had opposed Hughes's nomination, called the nomination "the finest act of his [Hoover's] career as President." New York governor Franklin D. Roosevelt also congratulated the president: "I know of no jurist in the law more liberal in its interpretation, more insistent that simple justice must keep step with the progress of civilization and the bettering of the law of the average individuals who make up mankind." Cardozo was confirmed by a unanimous voice vote in the Senate on February 24, 1932.

Chief Justice Hughes wrote his son, who had clerked for Cardozo, that he was "delighted" with the appointment. No member of the Court could have seriously objected to the appointment of the eminently qualified Cardozo except the anti-Semitic Justice McReynolds, who now had two Jewish brethren to resent. Cardozo was a brilliant judge and philosopher of law. On the bench, he had written groundbreaking opinions in the areas of tort and contract law that forced courts to rethink old common law theories and adjust, as Cardozo did, to the realities of modern life and law. While serving on New York's highest court, he had also delivered the Storrs Lectures at Yale, later published in book form as *The Nature of the Judicial Process*, which was recognized as a classic work of judicial philosophy.

Cardozo joined his new judicial colleagues too late to hear arguments in another controversial due process case that tested the constitutional limits of a state's regulation of private business. Oklahoma had passed a law that required those in the business of manufacturing and selling ice to be licensed. After obtaining a license, the New State Ice Company invested $500,000 to build a plant and sell ice in the state. When a freelance businessman, Ernest Liebmann, started his own ice business in competition with New State Ice without obtaining a license, New State Ice sued him for operating in violation of the law. Liebmann responded by charging that the Oklahoma regulation violated his liberty protected by the due process clause of the Fourteenth Amendment.

The critical constitutional issue came down to whether the ice business was "affected with a public interest," and could therefore be regulated by the state. The Court had traditionally recognized certain businesses as "affected with a public interest," including railroads, public utilities, and, as demonstrated in the O'Gorman decision of the previous term, the insurance industry. The ice business was different, wrote Justice Sutherland for a six-man majority that included Hughes and Roberts, ruling that the state legislature had exceeded its constitutional authority. Sutherland conceded that Oklahoma had legitimately regulated the production of cotton, the chief industry of the state, even though it did not fit within the traditional category of a business "affected with a public interest." The state did not depend on the ice business for its prosperity, he noted, as it did cotton. "It is a business as essentially private in its nature as the business of the grocer, the dairyman, the butcher, the baker, the shoemaker or the tailor," he wrote. Sutherland said that Liebmann had rightly invoked the constitutional principle of "liberty" protected by the due process clause. "The principle is imbedded in our constitutional system that there are certain essentials of liberty with which the state is not entitled to dispense in the interests of experiments."

George Sutherland's reference to "experiments" was undoubtedly aimed at Justice Brandeis's long, heavily documented, and passionate dissent pleading for the Court to allow elected legislators, not life-tenured judges, to decide the economic regulations that were "affected with a public interest." Brandeis, who ordinarily opposed monopolies, suggested that Oklahoma's lawmakers could have been responding to unique economic circumstances that justified curtailing competition. By imposing the licensing requirement, the state may have prevented waste and inefficiency in an industry that was vital, especially during the state's hot summers when ice was necessary to preserve perishable food. He noted that when the due process clause was ratified in the difficult economic times after the Civil War, at least two states regulated the price of bread, reaching "the baker" that Sutherland had declared off-limits in his majority opinion. The Court should be mindful that economic circumstances change, Brandeis wrote, and presume the validity of a state economic regulation, so long as it was reasonable.

As he had done as both lawyer and judge, Brandeis then linked the constitutional issue to the economic facts of the day. In 1932, as the nation slipped deeper into the Great Depression, Brandeis observed that free market economics, and especially the venerable law of supply and demand, did not work. Past economic emergencies were caused by the scarcity of goods, but in 1932 the problem was not scarcity but overabundance: "The long continual depression has brought unprecedented unemployment, a catastrophic fall in commodity prices and a volume of economic losses which threatens our financial institutions."

"The people of the United States are confronted by an emergency more serous than war," Brandeis declared, and it was time for the Court to allow legislatures "to do their part to remold through experimentation our economic practices and institutions to meet changing social and economic needs." Brandeis refused to believe that the framers of the Fourteenth Amendment, or the states that ratified it, "intended to deprive us of the power to correct the evils of technological unemployment and excess production capacity." He concluded with a pointed warning to the Court's conservative bloc: "This court has the power to prevent experimentation. . . . But in the exercise of this high power we must be ever on our guard, lest we erect our prejudices into legal principles."

Only Justice Stone joined Brandeis's dissent and later explained his vote. "While I doubt the wisdom and efficacy of much attempted regulation of business, I think those are questions to be determined by the legislature and not by the Supreme Court," he wrote John Bassett Moore, the former judge on the International Court of Justice. "I have never been able to persuade myself that the Fourteenth Amendment was ever intended to preclude the legislature from regulating business where regulation could not be said to be palpably arbitrary and unreasonable."

Chief Justice Hughes, who joined Sutherland's opinion for the majority in New State Ice Company v. Liebmann, never explained why he voted to strike down the Oklahoma regulation. Years later, he told his biographer, Merlo Pusey, that "the case was near the border line." But it is difficult to understand why Hughes, who prided himself on making decisions based on the facts of a case without ideological predilections, did not conclude, like Brandeis and Stone, that the Oklahoma regulation was a reasonable response to an economic crisis. He may have made the pragmatic decision to contribute a sixth vote to the conservative majority to reinforce the Court's image of legitimacy, even if he found the dissenters' constitutional interpretation more persuasive. But if his vote was primarily based on that institutional consideration, then he would seem to have forsaken one of his proclaimed attributes of individual leadership on the Court—"courage of conviction."

Hughes's vote in *Liebmann* was even more puzzling after he discussed his view of permissible state economic regulations in an address to a conference of federal judges shortly after the Court term was over. In his speech, he appeared to support Brandeis's broad constitutional view of appropriate economic regulation. Discussing the principles of liberty under the Fourteenth Amendment, Hughes said that the Constitution "demands freedom for state authority to meet local needs. It demands opportunities for experimentation and progress." But in the next paragraph he pulled back from that expansive statement, declaring that there were boundaries to regulation which legislatures must respect. It was the Court's responsibility to define those boundaries: "It is a highly difficult, but I think not an impossible task, to escape the errors of the extreme constructions which either would nullify, or would extend beyond their fundamental purpose, the great guarantees of individual liberty." He did not, however, take the opportunity to explain his vote in *Liebmann* supporting the Court majority's judgment that Oklahoma's regulation of the ice business exceeded those constitutional boundaries.

If Hughes's speech raised more questions than it answered about his interpretation of the due process clause, it nonetheless underscored his centrist position on this most controversial constitutional issue. His task, it seemed, was to balance the two warring philosophies on the Court and still maintain the stability of the institution, which he conceived to be one of his primary responsibilities as Chief Justice. Meanwhile, the nation suffered through the third year of the depression: 86,000 businesses had failed, 2,294 banks suspended operations in 1931 alone (nearly twice as many as the previous year), farm income dropped by 50 percent, and unemployment stood at over 12 million. When the state and federal legislatures passed more sweeping measures to stimulate the economy, their initiatives were challenged by opponents as unconstitutional. And Hughes's task of holding the Court together became exponentially more difficult.

*   *   *

The deepening financial crisis was especially devastating in New York, where a quarter of the nation's bank deposits, roughly $17 billion, were located but largely unprotected by state law. Only weeks before Roosevelt's second gubernatorial inauguration, the Bank of the United States closed its fifty-seven branch offices in four boroughs, representing the worst bank failure in the nation's history. The Bank's frozen assets directly affected almost a half million depositors and indirectly caused financial hardship to one third of the city's population. The overwhelming number of the 450,000 depositors were New Yorkers of modest means, many of them Jews working in the garment district who kept less than $400 in their unprotected thrift accounts.

When the crusading Socialist Norman Thomas wrote to Roosevelt demanding protection for thrift accounts, the governor pointed an accusing finger at the Republican-controlled legislature. "Confidentially, for your information I was greatly disappointed that [the] last legislature did nothing about thrift accounts," he wrote Thomas. "I expect to recommend such action to this legislature."

Roosevelt was less than candid in suggesting to Thomas that he bore no responsibility for the appalling lack of protection for the vast majority of depositors. After the failure of the first large New York bank, City Trust, a year and a half earlier, acting Governor Herbert Lehman appointed Robert Moses to investigate the debacle.* Moses uncovered a trail of incompetence, reckless speculation with depositors' funds, and outright corruption. He recommended drastic reform legislation. Roosevelt ignored the recommendations and chose, instead, to create a commission to study the problem. Had the legislation that Moses recommended passed, the Bank of the United States and its depositors might have been saved.

Roosevelt's cautious approach to banking reform reflected his confidence in the leaders of New York's major banks, many of whom he had known and respected when he served as vice president of Fidelity & Deposit Company. He publicly condemned the banking industry for the first time in March 1931, when he sent a special message to the legislature urging reform. "By merely blocking all reform, as they [the banking interests] appear to be doing this year," he said, "they discredit any claims that their

---

* Roosevelt was vacationing at Warm Springs.

efforts are accompanied by any sincere desire to protect the depositors of the State." Though now fully committed to reform, the governor could not stir the legislature to act.

Roosevelt was more alert to the alarming increase in the unemployment rolls in the state. Six months into his first term in office, he had appointed a commission to stabilize employment, the first governor to do so, and later made himself an expert on the subject. By the spring of 1931, he was ready to transform his study into law. Still, his approach to legislation was essentially conservative, as it had been in response to the banking crisis. He insisted on avoiding "the dole," his term for government-operated unemployment insurance in Great Britain. Instead, he proposed a program run by the private insurance industry with the payment of premiums shared by employers and employees. Even this cautious proposal was not signed into law while Roosevelt was governor.

Meanwhile, the destitute huddled in makeshift shanties in New York State's cities and towns and stood in lengthening bread lines. Roosevelt realized that neither private charities nor conventional public measures were adequate to feed the hungry and shelter the homeless. In June 1931, he told a Conference of Governors at French Lick, Indiana, that there was a pressing need for government to intervene "to protect its citizens from disaster." "Old remedies have not worked," he said. "A new economic and social balance calls for positive leadership and definite experiments."

Two months later, he demanded action at a special session of the state legislature. "Modern society, acting through its government," he said, "owes the definite obligation to prevent the starvation or the dire want of any of its fellow men and women who try to maintain themselves but cannot." It was not a matter of charity, he declared, but of government's social duty to its citizens.

He backed up his words with an innovative proposal: the creation of a new state agency, the Temporary Emergency Relief Administration (TERA), which would distribute $20 million of relief funds throughout the state. The relief effort would be paid for by raising the state income tax by 50 percent, a soundly conservative means of financing.* Though

---

* The proposed tax increase was not onerous, even for the 300,000 New Yorkers who paid state income taxes. Under the proposal, a wage earner with two dependents making $10,000 annually would pay an additional $26; one making $100,000 would pay an additional $1,128.

the Republican majority initially resisted, Roosevelt publicly exposed their blatantly political opposition, shaming them into passing the measure. The governor then appointed Jesse Straus, the president of Macy's department store and a major contributor to the Democratic Party, to head the agency. Straus, in turn, hired an intense and energetic young social worker named Harry Hopkins to serve as the agency's executive director. By year's end, TERA was providing relief for nearly 10 percent of the families in the state.

In implementing TERA, Roosevelt demonstrated a sensitivity to the suffering masses and a willingness to commit government to a major rescue effort on their behalf. In contrast, President Hoover seemed to be tinkering at the crisis's edges. He remained convinced that the nation would work its way out of the economic catastrophe largely by individual initiative and volunteerism.

Roosevelt denied that he aspired to any higher political office well into his second gubernatorial term. Repeatedly, he rejected all suggestions that he was running for the presidency. "I am giving no consideration or thought or time to anything except the duties of the Governorship," he told reporters shortly after Jim Farley had announced Roosevelt's certain presidential nomination in 1932. And he stuck to that pledge publicly. But he did not take his denial of interest in the nomination as his last word on the subject. He was performing a delicate political minuet, bowing deeply to his suitors, but refusing to declare his true intentions. He nonetheless kept himself fully informed of the elaborate campaign being organized on his behalf by Louis Howe and Jim Farley, aided by shrewd behind-the-scenes advice from Ed Flynn.

Soon after Roosevelt's triumphant reelection, Howe rented several rooms in a midtown Manhattan office building, where he and a small staff of secretaries churned out hundreds of letters to newspapers and potential supporters across the country promoting Roosevelt's presidential candidacy, signed by "Friends of Roosevelt." Howe worked from a constantly updated roster of key county and state Democratic officials and party contributors, touting Roosevelt's stellar credentials. At the same time, Farley shook hands and made friends for Roosevelt wherever he traveled, from the rural hamlets in upstate New York to cities on the Pacific coast. The hearty, hail-fellow Farley, who did not smoke or drink, was Roosevelt's goodwill ambassador to the party's convention delegates, while his exact opposite, the chronically irritable Howe, plotted their campaign's next strategic move from his cigarette-strewn office in New York City.

By the spring of 1931, Roosevelt was the clear favorite to win his party's presidential nomination. Jesse Straus, a committed Roosevelt supporter, reported the results of two polls he had taken with Democrats critical to a candidate's success. The first showed that a majority of delegates to the party's 1928 convention who voiced a presidential preference named Roosevelt; the same poll had Roosevelt leading in thirty-nine of forty-four states. In the second poll, Democratic businessmen and professionals also favored Roosevelt. A few months later, Farley came to the same happy conclusion after talking to leading Democrats during an eighteen-state tour through the midwestern and western states. In Seattle, he announced that "the name of Roosevelt is magic."

The good news stirred a strong reaction from Roosevelt's enemies, who whispered ominously that he was not physically fit to serve as president. Roosevelt quietly arranged for Earle Looker, a journalist and professed Republican, to challenge him to be examined by a committee of medical experts. Roosevelt promptly agreed to the examination by medical specialists selected by the director of the New York Academy of Medicine. In addition, he asked Looker to observe him in unannounced visits as he went through his arduous workdays in Albany. The medical committee reported to Looker that Roosevelt's "health and powers of endurance are such as to allow him to meet any demands of private and public life." Looker's reported observations were equally positive. "In so far as I had observed him," he wrote in Liberty magazine, "I had come to the conclusion that he seemed able to take more punishment than many men ten years younger."

Despite his early front-runner status, Roosevelt's nomination was far from inevitable. His first problem was the convention rules, which required that a candidate win two thirds of the delegates to receive the nomination. Even assuming that Straus's polls were accurate, Roosevelt still fell substantially short of the necessary two-thirds vote for nomination. The two-thirds rule, moreover, favored spoilers: favorite sons as well as compromise and dark horse candidates waiting for the front-runner to falter. And there was no dearth of presidential hopefuls, alert to the first signs that the Roosevelt bandwagon was stalled. Favorite sons from important states abounded: William McAdoo of California; Texas's John Nance Garner, the Speaker of the House of Representatives; and former Secretary of War Newton Baker of Ohio. But the greatest threat to the Roosevelt candidacy was the party's 1928 standard-bearer, former New York governor Al Smith.

Smith had insisted that he would not be a presidential candidate in

1932, even when old allies, like Ed Flynn, pressed him before declaring their support for Roosevelt. But Smith's smoldering dislike for Roosevelt now burned with white-hot intensity. With predictions of a Roosevelt victory circulating widely, Smith retreated into a sullen silence, no longer issuing emphatic denials of his interest in the nomination.

John Raskob, chairman of the Democratic National Committee, acting on Smith's behalf, made the first official move to undermine Roosevelt's candidacy. Raskob called for a special meeting of the committee with the intent of committing the party to the protectionist Smoot-Hawley Tariff Act and repeal of Prohibition. Smith favored both policies. Roosevelt opposed Smoot-Hawley and was considered "damp" on Prohibition, in favor of repeal but leaving the final decision to the states. Raskob's ploy was designed to force Roosevelt into a politically tenuous position. If he opposed Smith on the issues, he risked losing support in the East. But if he publicly joined Smith, he would undermine his potential support from farmers and other "Drys" in the South and West.

Roosevelt first appealed to Smith to stop the Raskob maneuver, contending that the party's platform should be decided at the presidential convention, as it had in the past, not at a closed-door meeting of the national committee. Though he focused on the decision-making process, Roosevelt was understandably concerned that the policies supported by Raskob and Smith would split the party, leading to disastrous results in the 1932 general election as it had in 1924 and 1928.

Smith did not respond to Roosevelt directly, but a few days later, he said at a news conference that he saw no reason to discourage the Democratic National Committee from passing resolutions on party policy. Roosevelt knew that he must fight back. He called an early morning meeting with Howe, Farley, and Flynn to draft a resolution for the New York Democratic Committee opposing the Raskob proposal. The state committee quickly adopted the resolution, which stated that the national committee had no authority to commit the party to any issue before the national convention. Roosevelt sent Farley, armed with the resolution, to Washington to make his case. He also called Senator Cordell Hull of Tennessee, an influential member of the national committee who, like other southerners, opposed Smith and other "Wets" in the East. He assured Hull that he would back him in the battle against the Smith-Raskob forces.

Roosevelt, Howe, and Flynn then manned the telephones to line up proxies of members of the national committee who could not attend the meeting. By the time Farley arrived by train at Washington's Union Station, he claimed to have enough proxies to defeat Raskob by at least two to one. Facing sure defeat, Raskob backed down, leaving the party's platform to be decided at the convention.

In December 1931, Clark Howell, the publisher of the *Atlanta Constitution* and a friend of both Roosevelt and Smith, wrote Roosevelt to report on a disturbing meeting he had recently held with Smith. Howell told Roosevelt that he had not minced words with Smith. "Governor, you hold in the palm of your hand the assurance of an overwhelming Democratic victory next year."

"How?" asked Smith.

"By your attitude toward Franklin Roosevelt," Howell replied. "With your support of him all opposition to him will vanish, and his nomination will be a mere formality. The country expects you to support him, and it will not believe that you can possibly do otherwise."

"The hell I can't!" Smith retorted. "I am for the party first, above any man," he told Howell, "and I will support the man who seems best for the party."

The next month, Roosevelt made his candidacy official by simply authorizing the Democratic Central Committee of North Dakota to enter his name in the preferential party primaries. Two weeks later, Smith announced that he would be available to accept the nomination if it were offered to him.

In addition to Smith and other potential challengers, Roosevelt faced the unrelenting hostility of the nation's most respected syndicated columnist, Walter Lippmann of the *New York Herald Tribune*. Lippmann doubted that Roosevelt had the intellectual heft or convictions to be president. "Governor Roosevelt belongs to the new post-war school of politicians who do not believe in stating their views unless and until there is no avoiding it," he wrote. Reviewing the governor's three-year record in Albany, Lippmann concluded: "Franklin D. Roosevelt is no crusader. He is no tribune of the people. He is no enemy of entrenched privilege. He is a pleasant man who, without any important qualifications for the office, would very much like to be President."

As if to emphasize Lippmann's opinion that he lacked conviction, Roosevelt backed away from his early support for U.S. participation in the League of Nations. His retreat came after William Randolph Hearst launched a crusade in his newspapers against any Democratic presidential contender who favored such U.S. participation. Roosevelt explained that the League had changed, not him, and that it now operated exclusively for the political interests of the European nations. He contended that it was no longer in the nation's best interests to join.

Roosevelt also waffled on another issue that Lippmann held dear: removing corrupt officials in Tammany-controlled New York City. The governor was conspicuously slow to act as evidence mounted that bribes were an everyday way of doing business that infected city operations, including the office of the dandy, high-stepping mayor, Jimmy Walker. He took a middle course, refusing to remove Walker, but authorizing a wide-ranging investigation that soon presented incontrovertible evidence of the mayor's corruption.

Lippmann's attacks notwithstanding, Roosevelt continued to burnish his liberal credentials shortly before the Democrats met in Chicago to select a presidential nominee. He delivered an ambitious speech at Oglethorpe University in Georgia on May 22, 1932, articulating his vision of greater government responsibility for its citizens' welfare. Though the speech was drafted by Ernest Lindley, a former reporter for the *New York Herald Tribune*, it accurately reflected Roosevelt's belief that government must devise new solutions to meet the unprecedented challenges of the Great Depression: "The country needs and, unless I mistake its temper, the country demands bold, persistent experimentation. It is common sense to take a method and try it: If it fails, admit it frankly and try another. But above all, try something."

Roosevelt's Oglethorpe speech demanding experimentation was delivered the same month that Justice Brandeis read his dissent aloud from the bench in *New State Ice v. Liebmann*, pleading with the conservative Court majority to allow state governments to develop new remedies to meet the economic catastrophe.

Louis Howe planned for Roosevelt's victory at the Democratic Convention down to the smallest detail. He imported Roosevelt's switchboard operator from Albany to avoid telephone leaks, paid off convention attendants to provide locked rooms for secret conferences between Roosevelt supporters and key undecided delegates, and assigned Roosevelt loyalists to every important convention committee. For his part, Farley foraged for uncommitted delegates, escorting them to Roosevelt's headquarters in the lobby of the Congress Hotel, where he proudly pointed to a map of the United States with a large swath of states coded in red that supported

Roosevelt. Later, Farley joined Flynn upstairs in Howe's suite, which was connected by a telephone line to Roosevelt's small study in Albany's executive mansion. Critical delegates were then treated to a conversation with the candidate. "My friends from Nebraska" (or Ohio or Maryland), Roosevelt would greet the startled visitors, then deliver a warm, personal message giving reasons for them to support his candidacy.

When the Democratic Convention officially opened in the new, air-conditioned Chicago Stadium on June 27, Roosevelt could count on a majority of delegates to support his nomination for the presidency. Still, he was slightly more than 100 votes short of the necessary two thirds, and it was not clear how he would close the gap. Smith, though far behind in delegate count, controlled about 200 votes and was determined to stop Roosevelt. The California and Texas delegations appeared to hold the key to victory, but neither had shown any interest in putting Roosevelt over the top. The chairman of the California delegation, William McAdoo, had thrown his state's support behind Texas's John Nance Garner, giving the Speaker of the House 90 votes from those two large state delegations.

Despite the discouraging math, Farley bravely predicted a first ballot victory for Roosevelt. His prognosis was built on the debatable assumption that Roosevelt's nomination was inevitable and would succeed in jarring loose the necessary additional delegates. But after more than an hour and half of polling, Roosevelt was still short by 104 votes. All of the delegations with favorite sons held firm, so a second ballot was taken, and then a third, without conclusive result.

Farley had met secretly with Texas congressman Sam Rayburn, Garner's manager, raising the possibility of a vice-presidential nomination for Garner if his delegates switched to Roosevelt. The cordial Rayburn made no commitment. He had been told by California's McAdoo that his delegation was behind Garner "until Hell freezes over if you say so." But Garner, who remained in Washington, was not interested in a desperate last stand. In fact, he was perfectly content to keep his job as Speaker, and did not find the lure of second place on a Roosevelt-Garner ticket attractive. The problem was that the Texas delegation, stubbornly loyal to the Speaker, would only support Roosevelt if Garner was his vice-presidential running mate.

Garner finally made the decision to support Roosevelt (and join the ticket as vice-presidential nominee) because he dreaded a deadlocked convention and the prospect of another Democratic defeat in the general election. Convinced that Roosevelt could be a winner, he instructed Rayburn to caucus the Texas delegation and release them to support the New York governor. At the caucus, a narrow majority of the Texas delegation (54–51) voted to support Roosevelt. Rayburn, fearing a revolt on the convention floor by die-hard Garner supporters, asked McAdoo to break the logjam on the fourth ballot by announcing both California's and Texas's switch to Roosevelt.

When the chairman of the convention, Senator Thomas Walsh of Montana, reached California in the roll call of states, McAdoo jumped to his feet. "California came here to nominate a President," he shouted. "She did not come here to deadlock this convention or to engage in another disastrous contest like that of 1924."*

With McAdoo's announcement that the California and Texas delegates were voting for Roosevelt, pandemonium broke out on the convention floor while the organist played a spirited rendition of "Happy Days Are Here Again," Roosevelt's newly adopted theme song.†

"Good old McAdoo," Roosevelt exclaimed, listening to his radio in Albany.

The bandwagon for Roosevelt quickly shifted into high gear, with Illinois, Maryland, and Ohio following California and Texas's lead. At 10:32 on the evening of July 1, Walsh announced that Roosevelt had received 945 votes, more than enough to make him the Democratic nominee for president of the United States.

Only Al Smith spoiled the euphoria of the Roosevelt victory. He sat in his hotel room, hurt and bitter, refusing to release his delegates to make Roosevelt's nomination unanimous.

For weeks, Roosevelt had planned to shatter tradition by appearing before convention delegates the night after his nomination to deliver his

---

* McAdoo's reference was an angry swipe at Al Smith who, eight years earlier, had refused to release his delegates to McAdoo, denying the nomination to the former Secretary of the Treasury.

† "Anchors Away" was played when Roosevelt's name was first placed in nomination. Ed Flynn thought it sounded funereal and suggested a change to the peppy "Happy Days Are Here Again," taken from a 1929 Hollywood musical.

acceptance speech.* He intended his dramatic appearance to convey to the delegates and the nation that old customs and failed policies of the past would be replaced with fresh ideas and bold new national leadership. And so, at 7:25 a.m. on July 2, Roosevelt, accompanied by Eleanor, his sons Elliott and John, Sam Rosenman, secretaries, and bodyguards, boarded an American Airlines trimotored airplane in Albany and headed for Chicago's Municipal Airport (with scheduled refueling stops in Buffalo and Cleveland). Buffeted by strong headwinds, the plane tossed unpredictably, stretching Roosevelt's flight time to eight hours. Unperturbed, the nominee kept busy revising his speech with Rosenman.

When he appeared at the podium of Chicago's Stadium before 30,000 screaming delegates, Roosevelt was buoyant, beaming and fully in charge. He spoke movingly to his countrymen "in these days of crushing want," but the policies he offered were strictly pragmatic (public works, lower tariffs, home mortgage refinancing, securities regulations). The substance of his message was less important than the energy and confidence with which it was delivered: "I pledge you, I pledge myself, to a new deal for the American people. Let us all here assembled constitute ourselves prophets of a new order of competence and of courage. This is more than a political campaign; it is a call to arms. Give me your help, not to win votes alone, but to win in this crusade to restore America to its own people."

Roosevelt instantly became the heavy favorite to win the presidential election in November, more than a month before President Hoover formally accepted the Republicans' nomination to run for a second term. He had electrified the convention and the nation with his surprise appearance and rousing speech in Chicago. He symbolized hope to a weary and dispirited America while the president, isolated in the White House, appeared exhausted and beaten.

Hoover did not help his already slim reelection prospects in July with his handling of the so-called Bonus Army, the thousands of bedraggled veterans of the First World War who had converged on Washington to pressure Congress to accelerate the payment of their bonuses for wartime

---

* Typically, the party's presidential candidate formally accepted the nomination long after the convention had ended. Charles Evans Hughes, the Republicans' presidential nominee in 1916, for example, gave his acceptance speech in New York more than a month after he had been nominated at the party's convention in Chicago.

service (due in 1945). The president signed a bill to pay the veterans' rail fare home, but refused to meet with their leaders. Many remained in the capital in noisy, restless protest. When they refused to leave vacant buildings on Pennsylvania Avenue, an ugly riot erupted, and District of Columbia police shot two Bonus marchers dead. Hoover then ordered Army Chief of Staff General Douglas MacArthur to take charge. MacArthur, resplendent in dress uniform with medals gleaming, responded as if he were attacking a German-held village on the Marne. Heavy tanks rumbled forward and infantrymen, wearing gas masks and brandishing fixed bayonets, lobbed tear gas at the helpless veterans. The troops chased the veterans from the office buildings and, for good measure, set fire to their shanty town erected in southeast Washington. MacArthur had exceeded the president's instructions in torching the shanties, but was satisfied that he had suppressed "a bad looking mob."

Hoover, like MacArthur, believed that the army had quelled a potentially dangerous insurrection. But Hoover, unlike the army commandant, was running for political office. And unfortunately for the president, the spectacle of heavily armed soldiers chasing defenseless, retreating veterans was caught by newspaper photographers and newsreel cameramen for the entire nation to see. The images only reinforced the public's perception of Hoover as an insensitive chief executive who did not understand or care about the suffering of ordinary Americans.

While Hoover's image was further tarnished, Roosevelt seized an opportunity to improve his own in an area where he had been particularly vulnerable. On August 11, Roosevelt summoned New York mayor Jimmy Walker to appear before him in Albany's executive chamber to answer charges of corruption that had been leveled by special investigator Samuel Seabury. The date selected by Roosevelt to open the hearings coincided with Hoover's acceptance speech at the Republican Convention, diverting the national press's attention from the president to the suddenly intrepid New York governor investigating official wrongdoing. Throughout the hearings, the calm and dignified Roosevelt bore in on the fidgeting mayor, asking question after tough question. By the end of the grueling three-week hearing, Roosevelt was widely perceived as a serious, vigilant public servant. Best of all for Roosevelt's political fortunes, Mayor Walker submitted his resignation on September 1.

While Roosevelt was conducting the public's business, Howe and Farley set up his presidential election headquarters in Manhattan's Biltmore Hotel. Both men were fully prepared and eager to assume their critical roles in the campaign. Howe accelerated his highly successful personal letter-writing barrage, connecting the candidate to prominent governors and members of Congress as well as to curious citizens from small towns and cities across the country who had questions for the candidate. Each response was tailored to the inquiry, with those to the most influential correspondents signed personally by Roosevelt. Farley, meanwhile, kept in constant communication with a vast network of party regulars, sending campaign pamphlets and personal letters to thousands of Democrats in the field, from state chairmen to local volunteers. "The fellow out in Kokomo, Indiana, who is pulling doorbells night after night," Farley said, "gets a real thrill if he receives a letter on campaigning postmarked Washington or New York."

At a nearby midtown hotel, Roosevelt's policy advisers, known as the Brain Trust, prepared speeches on the major issues of the campaign. Headed by Raymond Moley, a Columbia political scientist professor and able administrator, the core group included two of Moley's faculty colleagues, the economist Rex Tugwell and Adolph Berle, Jr., a law professor specializing in corporate finance, as well as Roosevelt's speechwriter, Sam Rosenman. Their liberal views were balanced by retired Brigadier General Hugh Johnson and the conservative financier Bernard Baruch. Others, like Harvard Law School's Felix Frankfurter, contributed to the intellectual mix. In all, as many as twenty-five policy advisers, drawn from academia, business, and politics, could be involved in composing a single speech, sometimes contributing wildly divergent, even contradictory, points of view. Roosevelt welcomed the crossfire of ideas but retained absolute control of the final product.

Roosevelt's inclusive approach to the campaign extended to erstwhile opponents, like Al Smith. When Smith greeted Roosevelt warmly at the New York State Democratic Convention, he replied, "Hello, Al, I'm glad to see you too—and that's from the heart." Smith later stumped vigorously for the Roosevelt-Garner ticket. Roosevelt also won the endorsement of one of Smith's strongest allies at the convention, Jersey City boss Frank Hague. In late August, Hague hosted a gigantic rally for Roosevelt at the New Jersey governor's summer home in Sea Girt. More than 100,000 people sat on the governor's lawn, enjoying a brass band and comedians, gawking at airplanes swooping overhead, and, finally, hearing the Democratic presidential candidate call for the repeal of Prohibition.*

Republican leaders privately conceded that Hoover could win only if the economy suddenly revived or Roosevelt made a serious mistake during the campaign. Though business activity increased modestly in the summer months, other dismal economic indicators (high unemployment, more bank closings, burgeoning relief rolls) suggested that a full-scale recovery by the November election was virtually impossible.

That left a Hoover victory dependent on a major Roosevelt miscue. But Roosevelt, the consummate politician, refused to be pinned down on controversial issues like farm policy and tariffs that could give Hoover a critical boost in the polls. Instead, he attacked the Hoover administration relentlessly, offering an Alice-in-Wonderland parody of the failed Republican policies. He avoided personal attacks on the president, aware that they might jeopardize his chances to win over independents and Republicans. "He [Hoover] is personally flat," he said, "and we can safely leave him there."

In September, Roosevelt embarked on a strenuous coast-to-coast campaign trip by train, concentrating much of his energy on the farm states in the West which, he calculated, he must win. His speech in Topeka, Kansas, was billed as his major address on agricultural policy. Having gone through the grinder of the Brain Trust, the speech appeared to offer something for every farmer, without seriously offending anyone. As a farmer himself, Roosevelt said, he understood the intolerable conditions that they had suffered as a result of disastrous Hoover administration policies. He promised easier credit, lower taxes, voluntary cooperatives, and equal treatment for agricultural commodities with industrial products in the East. But he did not present specific programs. When he was later asked at rallies in Sioux City, Iowa, Springfield, Illinois, and Atlanta, Georgia, to provide details on his farm policy, he referred his audiences to his Topeka speech.

When it came to tariff policy, Roosevelt was similarly inscrutable. After Moley presented Roosevelt with two versions of a speech on tariff policy, one protectionist, the other advocating low tariffs, the candidate

---

* Roosevelt was advised by farm belt supporters not to worry that his opposition to Prohibition would undermine his standing among "Drys" in the West and South. Their overriding concern was the economy.

told his incredulous adviser to mold the two into a coherent final draft. In his major public address on tariffs, Roosevelt reiterated his opposition to the most extreme protectionist policies of the Smoot-Hawley Tariff Act. At the same time, he refused to support lower tariffs on agricultural commodities from abroad that could undercut U.S. farmers. Roosevelt's studied ambivalence on the tariff issue gave his glum opponent a rare opportunity to respond with biting humor. Hoover said that Roosevelt's tariff policy was "like a chameleon on Scotch plaid."

Hoover was so despondent that he did not even begin active campaigning until October. Roosevelt's elusive positions on farm policy and tariffs frustrated him. But what was truly infuriating to the president was Roosevelt's suggestion that he alone was capable of meeting the nation's economic crisis with innovative programs. Though Hoover had been slow to break away from traditional Republican policies, he had done so dramatically earlier in the year when he proposed, and Congress created, the Reconstruction Finance Corporation (RFC), a federal agency capitalized at $500 million and authorized to borrow up to $1.5 billion more to provide emergency loans to banks, building and loan societies, railroads, and agricultural stabilization corporations. *BusinessWeek* called the RFC "the most powerful offensive force [against the depression] that governmental and business imagination has, so far, been able to command." But no one, it seemed, gave Hoover credit, or scrutinized Roosevelt's vague promises. In desperation, the president ordered his cabinet to rebut Roosevelt's daily attacks, but his loyal Secretary of State, Henry Stimson, refused, complaining that the rapid-response mandate was both undignified and exhausting.

Roosevelt never broke stride. In Seattle, he waved to huge crowds (estimated at between 75,000 and 100,000) standing on curbs shouting "Hurrah for Franklin" as his motorcade passed by. His engineer stopped the campaign train at every small town and village. Roosevelt, on the arm of his eldest son, James, appeared on the back platform, grinned broadly, bantered pleasantly with the crowd for a few minutes, and waved joyfully as the train pulled away. In the cities and large towns where he had delivered major addresses earlier in the day, he held open house at his hotel, shaking hands and making small talk until midnight. Early the next morning, he was fresh and ready for another round of speeches, handshakes, and strategy sessions with state and local Democratic chairmen.

On issues where he had built a long progressive record, such as government regulation of private utilities, he did not equivocate. Private utilities served as trustees for the public, he said, and were entitled to a reasonable return on their investment, but nothing more. He also supported government-owned and operated utilities when private service was inadequate or rates exorbitant. This pleased western progressives, like Republican senator George Norris, who crossed party lines to support Roosevelt. He was a liberal, Roosevelt declared over and over in the West, invoking the hallowed names of Jefferson and Woodrow Wilson. In this uncharted era of oversupply and underconsumption, he said, government was justified in reining in entrenched economic oligarchies. Wealth and products must be distributed more equitably, he told a San Francisco audience, so that existing economic organizations served the people more efficiently. "The day of the enlightened administration," he declared, "has come."

Upon his return to the more conservative East, he tacked abruptly to the right. He promised in Pittsburgh to balance the federal budget and put a stop to the profligate spending of the Hoover administration. The federal budget had increased by approximately $1 billion between 1927 and 1931, Roosevelt charged, representing "the most reckless and extravagant past that I have been able to discover in the statistical record of any peacetime government anywhere, anytime." If elected, he would insist on an austerity budget. "I shall approach the problem of carrying out the plain precept of our Party, which is to reduce the cost of current Federal government operations by 25 per cent," he said. The only exception would be to save Americans from starvation or other dire need.

In the final days of the campaign, Roosevelt continued to slash away at the Hoover administration, declaring in Baltimore that he was waging a war against the "Four Horsemen" of the Republican leadership: "Destruction, Delay, Deceit, Despair." In his prepared text, he attacked Congress and the president, but in ad-libbed remarks he included the Supreme Court.

Hoover called Roosevelt's attack on the Court an "atrocious slur," revealing his opponent's reckless demagoguery and subversive attitude toward the nation's highest judicial tribunal. But it was no use; by then, Roosevelt's election was a foregone conclusion.

Even Roosevelt's longtime critic, Walter Lippmann, was convinced that the country desperately needed a change in leadership. "It'll be a great relief to have the election over, and to me at least, though I have the deepest reservations about Franklin Roosevelt, a relief to be rid of the present administration," he wrote. "It's so utterly discredited that it no longer has any usefulness as an instrument of government. And even assuming that Roosevelt isn't any better than Hoover, a new man for a little while will be better than a man who's worn out and used up."

On the eve of his election, Roosevelt spoke to friends and supporters in Dutchess County, as he had done at the end of each of his previous campaigns for public office. This time, there were microphones in front of him that broadcast his message to millions of radio listeners across the country. Solemnly, he anticipated the challenge ahead: "To be the means through which the ideal and hopes of the American people may find a greater realization calls for the best in any man. I seek only to be the humble emblem of this restoration."

Roosevelt carried forty-two states and won in the electoral college, 472 to Hoover's 59. He received 22,800,000 popular votes, representing 57.4 percent of all the ballots cast.

After receiving the returns at the Biltmore Hotel with jubilant supporters, Roosevelt returned to the family town house. Before he retired for the night, reporters overheard the president-elect tell his mother, "This is the greatest night of my life."

6

"Black Monday"

The morning after his presidential election, Roosevelt was served breakfast in bed and prepared to respond to the avalanche of congratulatory telegrams. He addressed his old Navy Department boss, Josephus Daniels, as "my dear Chief," and assured him "[t]hat title still stands! And I am still Franklin to you." To Justice Benjamin Cardozo, who sent congratulations from "my place of exile in Washington," he replied that he looked forward to the same "delightful relations with the Supreme Court" that he had enjoyed as governor with the state's highest court when Cardozo served as its chief judge.

Roosevelt did not respond so breezily to a telegram from President Hoover, who had pledged himself to cooperate with the president-elect "[i]n the common purpose of all of us." On the back of Hoover's telegram, Roosevelt jotted in pencil that he stood "in readiness to cooperate with you in our common purpose." But then he crossed out the phrase and substituted "ready to further in every way" their common purpose. After conferring with Raymond Moley, Roosevelt again revised his reply, writing that he joined "in your gracious expression of a common purpose in helpful effort for our country."

Roosevelt's subtle alterations reflected a distrust and growing antipathy toward the man he would succeed as president. His admiration for

Hoover more than a decade earlier—when FDR said that the Democrats should make him their presidential nominee in 1920—had totally disappeared. Roosevelt had voiced increasingly sharp criticism of Hoover's policies as president, especially after the Great Depression had undermined the American economy and psyche. But he also resented Hoover personally. He had not forgiven the president for what he considered to have been a purposefully cruel attempt to expose his physical disability the previous spring when Roosevelt, already the leading candidate for the Democratic nomination, joined other governors for a meeting with Hoover in the White House. For nearly an hour, Roosevelt had stood painfully in his heavy braces, perspiring visibly, waiting in a receiving line for the president, who arrived late without explanation. In the summer, Roosevelt was disgusted by Hoover's brusque handling of the Bonus Army veterans. Afterward, he told Rex Tugwell that he regretted ever having recommended Hoover for the presidency. "There is nothing inside the man but jelly," he said. "Maybe there never had been anything."

Hoover returned Roosevelt's animosity in kind. He expressed his utter disdain for FDR in both private conversations with cabinet members and his public speeches. He considered Roosevelt a lightweight and demagogue whose policies would destroy the country. Prior to the Democratic Convention, he told Secretary of State Henry Stimson that Roosevelt's nomination would probably precipitate a national panic. During the campaign, he warned that Roosevelt's election would mean that "the grass will grow in the streets of a hundred cities, a thousand towns; the weeds will overrun the fields of a million farms." This was not merely campaign rhetoric; Hoover believed every word.

There were, in fact, honest policy differences between the two men. Hoover believed that the source of the Great Depression was the First World War and its devastating economic impact on postwar Europe. Roosevelt viewed the depression as domestically driven by overproduction and underconsumption. In 1931, Hoover had initiated a one-year moratorium on all postwar debts and reparations. After Roosevelt's election, Hoover continued to believe that the remedy to the worldwide depression required international cooperation to keep the dollar strong, maintain the gold standard, and reduce pressure on European nations by postponing their billions of dollars in debt service to the United States. International policy was secondary to President-elect Roosevelt, whose focus was on legislation to stabilize the domestic economy.

Two weeks after the election, Hoover invited Roosevelt to the White House to discuss a common approach to the pressing problem of the immense debt still owed to the United States by the economically prostrate European nations. Secretary of State Stimson agreed with most international economists that the world depression could only be overcome by the cancellation of war debts as well as Germany's reparation payments. But to the reigning Democratic conservatives in Congress, like House Speaker Garner, the billions in debt owed to the United States were both a financial and moral obligation. President Hoover took a middle position: the debts ought to be postponed, but, in return, the United States should be able to extract concessions from the European debtor nations on trade and disarmament issues. After Roosevelt's election, U.S. policy on debt service became more urgent when the British asked for a suspension of their $95 million debt payment due to the United States on December 15.

Hoover was determined to pressure Roosevelt into supporting his position that the debt payments should be postponed in the economic interests of both the United States and the European nations. The president knew, of course, that any agreement to postpone debt service would meet with immediate and vocal opposition from Democratic leaders in the House, whom Roosevelt was counting on to support his domestic agenda. Hoover "could scarcely have chosen a field in which there was less probability of sympathetic cooperation between the two administrations," Moley wrote.

On November 22, a wary Roosevelt nonetheless agreed to meet with Hoover "as a private citizen" and listen "objectively" to the president's views on the debt issue. He called attention to his objectivity by asking Vice President-elect Garner, a certain opponent of debt postponement, to accompany him to the White House meeting. After he heard of Roosevelt's invitation to Garner, an agitated Hoover telephoned Stimson to vent his displeasure—and was relieved when the Texan declined to accompany Roosevelt to the meeting. Hoover was so distrustful of Roosevelt, fearing that he would renege on any agreement that might emerge from their meeting, that he insisted that Secretary of the Treasury Ogden Mills be present as a witness (Roosevelt brought Moley).

At the White House meeting, Hoover nervously puffed on a cigar while Roosevelt, equally anxious, smoked a cigarette. Once the president launched into his lengthy analysis of the debt crisis, he demonstrated a masterly command of the details of the complex issue. Throughout his presentation, he virtually ignored Roosevelt, alternately staring at the carpet in front of him or focusing his attention on Moley. Hoover proposed that he and Roosevelt jointly support the creation of a new bipartisan commission composed of Republican and Democratic members of Congress as well as appointees of the outgoing and incoming administration. The commission would be modeled on the bipartisan Dawes Committee that had dealt with the same postwar issues of European debts during the Harding administration. Hoover suggested that the commission should begin negotiations with the debtor nations immediately and continue into the Roosevelt administration.

During the discussion, Roosevelt maintained a surface cordiality and, as was his habit when listening to a proposal, broke his silence with an occasional "yes, yes." To Roosevelt, this meant that he understood the president's proposal. Hoover, however, thought that Roosevelt's "yes, yes" indicated his willingness to support the president's plan. Less than a hour after the meeting, Hoover told Stimson that he had spent most of his time in the discussion "educating a very ignorant" president-elect. The president nonetheless came away assured that Roosevelt had understood his tutorial well enough to promise to support the debt commission. Roosevelt's adviser Moley was just as certain that Roosevelt had made no such promise.

Hoover should have known that Roosevelt would not tie his hands on any issue before he took office, and certainly not one as complicated and freighted with political dynamite as the debt question. Shortly after his meeting at the White House, Roosevelt told newspapermen that he would not attempt to exert pressure on Congress on the issue and that the responsibility for debt negotiations rested entirely with the Hoover administration. The next day, Roosevelt met with Democratic leaders of Congress and assured them that he had made no commitments at his meeting with the president, and that there would be no request of Congress to suspend the December 15 debt payments.* He then spent the remainder of his meeting with the congressional leaders discussing domestic legislation.

During the four months between Roosevelt's election and his presidential inauguration, Americans sunk ever deeper in the morass of the Great Depression. In 1933, the stock market was worth one quarter of its pre-crash 1929 value. National income was cut in half. Five thousand banks were shuttered, and one in every three workers was unemployed. Farm prices continued to fall, crops rotted, and cattle languished unsold.

---

* Great Britain paid its debt installment; France defaulted.

While the lame-duck president struggled futilely to bend his successor and a recalcitrant Congress to his will, Roosevelt spent much of his time trading ideas with a myriad of advisers, including Louis Brandeis, and politicians of every persuasion. In a conversation with Brandeis, Roosevelt disagreed with the justice, who said that the United States should relent on the European nations' war debts. But Brandeis was pleased to hear that the president-elect, after excoriating irresponsible bankers, vowed to lead a proactive administration that would welcome innovative ideas to solve the nation's economic problems. The justice concluded from their conversation that Roosevelt understood the fundamental challenges that faced the nation and would forge a liberal coalition, even if it meant losing his conservative supporters. Brandeis advised him to create a new political alignment drawn from progressive members of both parties.

Everyone Roosevelt spoke to appeared to be pleased with what he heard. "When I talk to him, he says 'Fine! Fine! Fine!' " drawled Huey Long, the populist senator from Louisiana. "But Joe Robinson [the conservative Democratic senator from Arkansas] goes to see him the next day and again he says 'Fine! Fine! Fine!' Maybe he says 'Fine!' to everybody." The exasperated Long's comment was more accurate than he realized. During the interregnum, Roosevelt replicated the approach he had taken toward his Brain Trust during his presidential campaign. He effortlessly blended the ideas of his advisers—an unwieldy assortment of idealistic liberals, pragmatic moderates, and hard-nosed conservatives—and served them up to his audiences with incomparable brio.

And just as he had done during his campaign, Roosevelt presented himself to the public as the supremely optimistic leader who would bring change and hope to a downtrodden nation. As if he did not have a care in the world, he joined his Hyde Park neighbor, the millionaire Vincent Astor, and a small party of friends and family on the Astor yacht, the *Nourmahal*, for an eleven-day cruise off the coasts of Florida and the Bahamas one month before his inauguration. "I am getting a marvellous rest—lots of air and sun," he wrote his mother. "When we land [in Miami] on the 15th [of February] I shall be full of health and vigor."

After the *Nourmahal* docked in Miami the evening of February 15, 1933, Roosevelt rode in a green Buick convertible to Bayfront Park, where he was scheduled to attend a reception and make brief remarks. Tanned and happy, he waved to the thousands of people standing on Biscayne Avenue en route to the park. When he reached the park, his bodyguard helped him to sit on the top of the backseat of the car in front of the bandstand. He spoke to the crowd for less than two minutes about his trip (glorious sun, fish stories they would not believe). After he slid down to his seat, Chicago mayor Anton Cermak, who was vacationing in Florida, walked up to the side of Roosevelt's car to offer his good wishes. Suddenly, shots rang out—*pop, pop, pop* (Roosevelt later said the shots sounded like firecrackers)—and Cermak slumped over. A woman on the bandstand was also hit, as were two other bystanders. But remarkably, Roosevelt, the target of the attempted assassination, was unscathed.

Hearing the shots, Roosevelt's driver instantly pushed down on the accelerator pedal. But after the vehicle had gone only 15 feet, Roosevelt ordered him to stop. Secret Service agents shouted to get Roosevelt out of the crowd. After the driver had driven another 30 feet, Roosevelt again told him to stop the car. He had seen Cermak being carried away and insisted that the wounded mayor be lowered into the backseat next to him. He was alive, but Roosevelt did not think he would survive. He put his left arm around Cermak and offered steady, encouraging words all the way to the hospital. "Tony, keep quiet—don't move," he said. "It won't hurt you if you keep quiet." No words or treatment could save Cermak; he died a few weeks later.

After leaving Cermak at the hospital, Roosevelt returned to the *Nourmahal* for the night. His companions expected him to be exhausted and traumatized by the horrific experience. They were stunned to find him as calm and upbeat as ever. "There was nothing—not so much as the twitching of a muscle, the mopping of a brow, or even the hint of a false gaiety—to indicate that it wasn't any other evening in any other place," recalled Moley, who had accompanied him back to the yacht. "Roosevelt was simply himself—easy, confident, poised, to all appearances unmoved." A concerned Secret Service agent posted outside Roosevelt's state room during the night peeked in to check on him periodically. Each time, he found Roosevelt sound asleep.

The gunman was thirty-two-year-old Giuseppe Zangara, a diminutive unemployed New Jersey bricklayer who opposed all heads of government "and everybody who is rich." After he had read in the newspaper that Roosevelt was to appear at Miami's Bayfront Park, he had bought a pistol for $8 and arrived at the park early so he could get a seat close to where the president-elect was scheduled to speak. Others were already standing on the first two rows of benches, so Zangara climbed onto the bench behind them. When those in front of him sat down, he opened fire. But just as he pulled the trigger, the bench wobbled. The handbag on the arm of a housewife standing next to him apparently jostled the gunman, spoiling his aim. A Miami carpenter on the bench behind Zangara grabbed the gunman's arm, and he was quickly subdued.* Still, he was able to fire five shots, killing Cermak and wounding three others. Later, he was convicted of murder and executed.

Roosevelt's valor under fire was an inspiration to the nation. The dramatic series of events in Miami was best told to the press by the president-elect himself, who provided the harrowing details with the natural storyteller's gift for narrative and the superb politician's self-assurance that his near-death experience would rally the public to his side in the tense days ahead. He also visited the wounded victims and wrote a personal thank-you note to the housewife whose handbag had bumped Zangara's arm, praising her "unselfish courage and quick thinking." The day after the attempted assassination, Roosevelt boarded a train for his return trip to the East. He showed nary a sign of strain when he arrived in New Jersey and was escorted to New York by 1,000 police officers who were assigned to protect him. "I'm feeling fine," he said, "and I've had a fine trip."

Two days later, Roosevelt appeared in good humor at a dinner in the Astor Hotel as he enjoyed skits performed by the "Inner Circle," a group of New York reporters who poked irreverent fun at the politicians they covered. At eleven o'clock, a Secret Service agent approached the president-elect and discreetly handed him a large brown envelope bearing the seal of the president of the United States. Inside, Roosevelt found a second envelope, also sealed, containing a ten-page, handwritten letter from President Hoover. "A most critical situation has arisen in the country of which I feel it is my duty to advise you confidentially," the president's letter began. Hoover urged Roosevelt to issue a public statement announcing two or three policies of the new administration that he felt would boost the "steadily degenerating confidence in the future which has reached the height of general alarm."

Writing as if he had won the 1932 presidential election, Hoover challenged virtually every position that Roosevelt had taken during the

---

* The forty-eight-year-old housewife, Lillian Cross, was celebrated as a national hero. But several eyewitnesses maintained that the Miami carpenter, Thomas Armour, was primarily responsible for saving Roosevelt's life.

campaign. He insisted on his version of the causes of the crisis (the First World War and its disastrous economic aftermath in Europe), credited his administration's policies for reviving the economy the previous summer, and blamed the Democratically controlled Congress for blocking further progress toward recovery. He implored Roosevelt to publicly commit to the continuation of the Republican administration's conservative economic policies. There should be "no tampering" with the currency, which, to Hoover, meant that the nation must remain on the gold standard—a position that Roosevelt had conspicuously refused to take during the campaign.

Roosevelt calmly read Hoover's letter at the dinner, then passed it under the table to Moley. When he, Moley, and other advisers returned to the town house after midnight, they discussed Hoover's letter for more than an hour. Outwardly, the president-elect showed no anxiety over the state of affairs that Hoover had described, nor did he seem irritated by the president's presumptuous analyses and demands.* But neither did he commit himself to any response.

Meanwhile, Hoover assumed that he had checkmated his successor, congratulating himself on his clever maneuver in a letter that he wrote to Republican senator David Reed of Pennsylvania a few days later. "I realize that if these declarations be made by the President-elect, he will have ratified the whole major program of the Republican Administration; that is, it means the abandonment of 90% of the so-called new deal," he wrote. "But unless this is done, they [Roosevelt and the Democratically controlled Congress] run a grave danger of precipitating a complete financial debacle." He waited in vain for Roosevelt's expected capitulation.

Roosevelt did not reply to Hoover's letter for ten days. When he finally did so, he apologized for the delay, saying that his secretary had inadvertently misplaced it.† He enclosed the earlier draft as well as a fresh letter, dated February 28, in which he expressed his appreciation for "your fine spirit of co-operation." He agreed with the president that there was a growing financial crisis, "but my thought is that it is so very deep-seated that

---

* Later, Roosevelt called Hoover's letter "cheeky."

† He almost surely was not telling the truth. The reply that he said had been drafted shortly after receipt of Hoover's letter contained information on the deteriorating financial crisis that Roosevelt could not have known at the time he said he had written his original response. The stenographic notes for both letters, moreover, appeared to have been taken on the same day; and the date originally written at the top was crossed out, with the 20th inserted.

the fire is bound to spread in spite of anything that is done by way of mere statements." He promised to call a special session of Congress to deal with the crisis early in *his* administration.

The banking crisis had become desperate by late February. In Michigan, long-idle auto workers withdrew what was left of their meager savings so that their families would not have to join the bread lines. Michigan governor James Couzens tried to persuade Henry Ford to come to the rescue with private financing to bolster the state banks. But Ford refused, even after he received a special plea from Under Secretary of the Treasury Arthur Ballantine, who rushed to Detroit with a promise of a maximum loan from the Reconstruction Finance Corporation. On February 14, Governor Couzens proclaimed an eight-day banking holiday. A week later, depositors in Baltimore withdrew $13 million, $6 million the last day before Maryland's governor declared a three-day bank holiday. More holidays were imposed by governors in states across the country. By the morning of Roosevelt's inauguration, thirty-eight states, including New York and Illinois, had closed their banks. The New York Stock Exchange had shut down, as had the Chicago Board of Trade—for the first time since 1848.

Who was to blame? Hoover had no doubt that the culprit was Roosevelt, who refused to take the action that he had urged. Roosevelt was just as sure that Hoover was responsible for making a bad situation worse by dallying ineffectually, all the while attempting to dragoon the president-elect into supporting his failed policies. Both had a point. In the short term, the financial crisis might not have deteriorated so precipitously had Roosevelt shared ownership of Hoover's policies. But Roosevelt had to weigh any temporary salve that his cooperation might have accomplished against the political costs to his aspirations for his administration. If he agreed to accept the burdens of governing in the last days of the Republican administration, he knew that he would also receive his share of the blame. And he would not have solved the nation's colossal problems. Better to start fresh after his inauguration, he concluded, and make a clean break with the past, a message emphatically delivered by the voters who had elected him.

Roosevelt made detailed preparations for his inauguration on March 4. He wrote the clerk of the Supreme Court requesting that he be sworn in on an old Bible printed in Dutch ("very large and heavy folio"), which had been in his family's possession for nearly three hundred years. He also inquired whether he might recite the entire oath of office, instead of simply saying, "I do," as previous presidents-elect had done. He then wrote Chief Justice Hughes to say that in addition to "our long time friendship and to my admiration and respect for you, I think it is interesting that a governor of New York is to administer the oath to another governor of New York."

In his reply, Hughes readily agreed to Roosevelt's suggestion that he repeat the oath in full as "the more dignified and appropriate course." He wished Roosevelt "a most successful administration," reciprocated "the sentiments of friendship," and concluded that "I especially prize the opportunity of being associated with you in our great American enterprise."

By the time Roosevelt had exchanged cordial letters with Hughes, he had already revised the first draft of his inaugural address, written by Moley, making his changes in longhand on yellow-lined paper. The final version was typed on March 3, ready for delivery the next day.

Hoover invited Roosevelt to afternoon tea at the White House on March 3, but not to dinner, as had been the custom for many years of presidential transitions. At four o'clock on the 3rd, Franklin, Eleanor, James and his wife were ushered into the Red Room for tea with the president. Roosevelt was unaware that Hoover intended to transform the social occasion into a working session in which he planned to make one final effort to coax Roosevelt into taking joint action with him to deal with the banking crisis. The president-elect was informed by Ike Hoover, the White House chief usher (no relation to the president), that Secretary of the Treasury Mills, the governor of the Federal Reserve Board Eugene Meyer, and President Hoover awaited him to discuss the ongoing crisis. Roosevelt immediately sent for Moley, who was napping in his room at the Mayflower Hotel. After a brief discussion, Hoover asked Roosevelt to join him in a joint proclamation to regulate withdrawals from the nation's banks.

An irate Roosevelt refused, saying that he would have to consult with his advisers on any action. He then announced that his family's visit to the White House was over. In a feigned effort at politeness, he told Hoover that he need not reciprocate with a call on Roosevelt that evening.

"Mr. Roosevelt," Hoover replied, "when you are in Washington as long as I have been, you will learn that the President of the United States calls on nobody."

Roosevelt was indignant. "That was that," he recalled. "I hustled my family out of the room. I was sure Jimmy wanted to punch him in the eye."

The next morning, Roosevelt and his family attended services at

St. John's Episcopal Church, across Lafayette Square from the White House. At Roosevelt's request, the Reverend Endicott Peabody, now seventy-six years old, participated in the service. After reading selections from the Book of Common Prayer, Peabody blessed his former student: "O Lord . . . most heartily we beseech Thee, with Thy favor to behold and bless Thy servant, Franklin, chosen to be President of the United States." Roosevelt remained on his knees in private prayer for several minutes, his face cupped in his hands.

After the service, Roosevelt returned to the Mayflower Hotel for last-minute discussions on the banking crisis with Moley and his designated Secretary of the Treasury, William Woodin, a New York industrialist. He scribbled a few final notes on banking to be inserted into his inaugural speech. Shortly before eleven o'clock, Roosevelt, wearing the traditional striped pants, cutaway coat, and silk top hat, was driven to the porticoed north entrance of the White House, where he waited in the open limousine for President Hoover to join him in the backseat. Hoover, stiff and unsmiling, looked straight ahead as they were driven down Pennsylvania Avenue to the Capitol. In an attempt at small talk to break the uncomfortable silence, Roosevelt commented lamely about the "lovely steel" in the construction of the new Department of Commerce building. Hoover did not respond.*

After the inaugural ceremonies, Roosevelt and Hoover never saw each other again, ending the most acrimonious presidential transition since President John Quincy Adams had left Washington, D.C., on March 4, 1829, headed for his Quincy, Massachusetts, home, avoiding altogether the inauguration of his detested successor, Andrew Jackson.

Shortly after one o'clock, under gray, foreboding skies, a bugle sounded and the Marine Corps Band played "Hail to the Chief." Roosevelt, on James's arm, walked slowly down a maroon-carpeted ramp to the rostrum where Chief Justice Hughes, wearing his black robes, awaited him. Roosevelt placed his left hand on his family's Dutch Bible, which was opened to the

---

* Before they arrived at the Capitol, however, Hoover requested that Roosevelt find a position in the federal government for Walter Newton, his White House liaison with Congress. The president-elect complied, appointing Newton to the inactive Federal Home Loan Bank Board.

page in Corinthians he had marked: "And now abideth faith, hope, charity, these three; but the greatest of these is charity." Raising his right hand, he repeated the oath after the Chief Justice: "I, Franklin Delano Roosevelt . . . will, to the best of my ability, preserve, protect and defend the Constitution of the United States. So help me God."

In his fifteen-minute address (short by inauguration standards), Roosevelt spoke in a somber voice. "This is a day of national consecration," he began, imbuing the quadrennial event with religious purpose. To the 150,000 spectators spread out on the 40-acre mall in front of him and the millions of Americans listening on the radio, he proclaimed that a new political order—bold and confident—was now in charge. "This great Nation will endure as it has endured, will revive and will prosper," he intoned. "So, first of all, let me assert my firm belief that the only thing we have to fear is fear itself—nameless, unreasoning, unjustified terror which paralyzes needed efforts to reconvert retreat into advance."* He attacked the "practices of the unscrupulous money changers" and promised strict regulation of banking and investments. And he vowed to put the unemployed back to work, raise farm prices, prevent home foreclosures, and provide for "an adequate but sound currency." Voters had demanded "direct, vigorous action," he said. If Congress did not take the necessary action, he would ask for broad executive authority to confront the economic crisis that was as dangerous as any military foe. The American people "have made me the present instrument of their wishes. In the spirit of the gift," he concluded, "I take it."

The three-hour parade that followed was hardly in the simple Jeffersonian spirit that Roosevelt had originally proposed. But the Democrats had been out of power for twelve years and nothing, not even the worst depression in the nation's history, was going to spoil their celebration. Bands from forty-eight states strutted down Pennsylvania Avenue while a hundred planes and the dirigible *Akron* flew overhead. On the reviewing stand, Roosevelt gaily waved his approval as contingent after happy contingent marched in his honor, including Jim Farley, the new Postmaster General of

---

* Louis Howe was later credited with inserting the sentence into FDR's inaugural address after the speech had been typed. But Eleanor Roosevelt claimed that her husband might have taken it from an anthology of Thoreau's works that had been given to him by a friend of hers while they were staying at the Mayflower Hotel. The debilitating effect of fear had been a literary topic for centuries in the works, for example, of Shakespeare and Francis Bacon in the early seventeenth century.

the United States; Al Smith, proudly sporting his Tammany Hall sash (and tipping his brown derby to the crowd); and a small, giddy group of African-Americans pushing lawn mowers in mock defiance of Hoover's warning that grass would grow in the streets of a Roosevelt presidency.

That evening, after hosting a gala White House reception, Roosevelt quietly went upstairs to the Oval Office where his cabinet waited to be officially sworn in. For the occasion, FDR had asked his friend Benjamin Cardozo to administer the oaths. The president called the names, one by one: Cordell Hull, Secretary of State; Henry Wallace, Secretary of Agriculture; William Woodin, Secretary of the Treasury; Frances Perkins, Secretary of Labor; Homer Cummings, U.S. Attorney General . . . "No cabinet has been sworn in before in this way," Roosevelt told them, and promised that it would not be the last time he broke with the past.

Roosevelt knew that he must deal immediately with the banking crisis. On the morning of his inauguration, hours before he and President Hoover rode uncomfortably together to the Capitol, he had already directed his Attorney General–designate, Homer Cummings, to quickly research the legal question whether, as president, he could declare a national bank holiday and impose an embargo on trade in gold and silver under the Trading with the Enemy Act, a statute passed during the First World War. The answer from Cummings was affirmative, delivered to the president early that evening shortly before Cummings was officially sworn into the Roosevelt cabinet.

That same morning, Roosevelt had asked William Woodin to begin work on emergency banking legislation to be sent to Congress the next week that would allow banks to reopen in an orderly way. Roosevelt did not object when Woodin, a conservative corporation executive (and registered Republican), sought the counsel of President Hoover's key financial advisers, Ogden Mills and Eugene Meyer of the Federal Reserve Board (both men had sat with Hoover at tea on March 3 when the president made one last attempt to persuade Roosevelt to act jointly with him on the crisis). That was fine with Roosevelt, who had never been antagonistic toward responsible bankers, only to those "unscrupulous money changers" he blamed for the crisis. At the suggestion of Hoover's Treasury Secretary Mills and Under Secretary Ballantine, he invited leading bankers from New York, Chicago, Philadelphia, Baltimore, and Richmond to come to Washington to advise his administration on banking policy.

On Sunday afternoon, March 5, Roosevelt officially convened his cabinet for the first time and described the banking crisis and attendant legal problems in comprehensive detail. That evening, he met with key congressional leaders in the White House and explained why it was necessary for him to issue a proclamation closing all of the banks the next day. Though details of his policy were noticeable sparse, the legislators pledged their support. Later the president drafted a proclamation that declared a four-day bank holiday, embargoed the transfer of gold and silver, and prohibited the exchange of dollars into foreign currency, effective Monday morning. He also called a special session of Congress to convene on Thursday, March 9 (to allow the return by train of west coast representatives), to validate his bank holiday and approve the emergency legislation that Secretary Woodin was still struggling to draft amid cacophonous advice from liberal and conservative congressmen and private bankers.

Roosevelt, meanwhile, conducted the campaign for support of the emergency legislation with pitch-perfect skill. He met with congressional leaders of both parties, all forty-eight governors, his cabinet, and Hoover cabinet holdovers, all the while maintaining an uncanny buoyancy. Senator Hiram Johnson, the progressive Republican from California, confessed that he did not fully understand the intricacies of the proposed legislation, but marveled at Roosevelt's "readiness to assume responsibility and his taking that responsibility with a smile."

On Wednesday morning, March 8, shortly after ten o'clock, Roosevelt held his first press conference as president. Nearly 125 reporters crammed around his desk for the first give-and-take news conference at the White House. Presidents Coolidge and Hoover had insisted on written questions submitted in advance and conducted the sessions with detached formality. In contrast, the always convivial Roosevelt treated the reporters as equals in what he considered their joint enterprise of informing the public of the president's thoughts and actions. It was a role he had perfected through his years as Assistant Secretary of the Navy and governor of New York. The president set the ground rules. Reporters could ask whatever questions they chose, but he would decide if they were too sensitive or hypothetical to answer, and whether his opinions were for background only or strictly off the record. Any direct quotations from the president would have to be given in writing by his press secretary, Steve Early. Reporters were delighted with the arrangement, and thus began a twelve-year love affair between Roosevelt and the Washington press corps.

Late on Wednesday afternoon, Roosevelt, at the suggestion of Felix

Frankfurter, visited Justice Oliver Wendell Holmes, Jr., who was celebrating his ninety-second birthday. Accompanied by Eleanor and James, Roosevelt called on the justice at his Georgetown home—a social courtesy that President Hoover had told him was simply not done by the nation's chief executive. During the half-hour visit, the president listened to the great jurist's opinions on the boxer John L. Sullivan, his Civil War experiences, and the challenge of the presidency. He advised Roosevelt to attack the economic crisis like a general sending his troops into battle. Blow the trumpet and charge, he said. "And that's exactly what you are doing," he continued. "You are in a war, Mr. President, and in a war there is only one rule, 'Form your battalion and fight!' "

Roosevelt met for more than four hours that evening with Woodin, Cummings, Moley, and key members of Congress to discuss the draft of the legislation that he expected to send to Capitol Hill the next morning. They labored over the bill past midnight, but the final version of the legislation was still not completed. After consulting with Federal Reserve governor Meyer the next morning, Roosevelt wrote out the terms of the proposed bill in longhand only fifteen minutes before Congress was scheduled to convene. It provided that financially sound banks would open for resumption of business as soon as possible and authorized the executive branch of the federal government to supervise the banks to protect depositors. It was a conservative bill, reflecting the philosophy of its major author, William Woodin, who had rejected demands from liberal congressmen to nationalize the banks. He had also vetoed the idea of the government issuing unsecured scrip in favor of printing additional currency, backed by the assets of the Federal Reserve Board. "It won't look like stage money," Woodin told Moley. "It'll be money that looks like money. And it won't frighten people."

The House "debated" the bill for only thirty-eight minutes before approving it unanimously by voice vote. The Senate discussed the bill for several hours, primarily because of objections from progressive senators like Wisconsin's Robert LaFollette, Jr., who worried that the legislation would encourage predatory practices of the big New York banks; Louisiana's Senator Huey Long complained that the bill would not protect vulnerable depositors in state banks. Despite their objections, the Senate easily passed the legislation, 71–7, early in the evening. The bill was on Roosevelt's desk for signature in less than an hour, and he signed it into law at 8:37 p.m.

Three days later, Roosevelt held the first of his Sunday evening fire-

side chats as president and explained the banking legislation to his immense radio audience (estimated at 60 million listeners) with the same
easy assurance and plainspoken language that he had used as New York's
governor to justify the need for the state's regulation of private utilities. "I
want to talk for a few minutes with the people of the United States about
banking—with the comparatively few who understand the mechanics
of banking but more particularly with the overwhelming majority who use
banks for the making of deposits and the drawing of checks," he began. He
then discussed the nature of the crisis and how the new legislation would
help bring it under control. "It needs no prophet to tell you that when the
people find that they can get their money—that they can get it when they
want it for legitimate purposes—the phantom of fear will soon be laid,"
he said. "I can assure you that it is safer to keep your money in a reopened
bank than under the mattress."

Over the next three days, more than 70 percent of the federal banks
reopened. Americans did just as their new president advised, depositing
twice as much money in the banks as they withdrew. On the morning
after Roosevelt's fireside chat, when official foreign exchange resumed,
the dollar surged while the franc and pound dropped in value. When the
stock markets reopened on Wednesday, March 15, volume reached a six-
month high. At the same time, Treasury certificates worth $800 million
were snapped up by eager reopened banks. "Last week marked an end to
three years of a nation's drifting from bad to worse," the *Wall Street Journal*
declared. "For an explanation of the incredible change which has come
over the face of things here in the United States in a single week we must
look to the fact that the new Administration in Washington has superbly
risen to the occasion."

Not everyone was impressed. "The President drove the money-changers
out of the Capitol on March 4th, and they were all back on the 9th," one
liberal congressman complained. A day after Roosevelt had signed the
emergency banking legislation, he stunned liberals with a second block-
buster proposal to slash government spending: a request that Congress give
him authority to cut more than $500 million from the federal payroll. His
effort to balance the budget should have come as no surprise, since he had
pledged to do so during his presidential campaign. What no one could
have anticipated were the prime targets for his drastic belt-tightening measures. Four fifths of the cuts ($400 million) would come from reductions in
veterans' benefits; another large chunk ($100 million) would be realized

by a cut of as much as 15 percent in all government salaries, including those of the congressmen whom Roosevelt expected to pass the legislation. "Too often in recent history liberal governments have been wrecked on the rocks of loose fiscal policy," he admonished.

The economy bill was essentially the work of Lewis Douglas, Roosevelt's thirty-nine-year-old, Amherst-educated director of the budget. Douglas's family had made a fortune in copper in Arizona, but he rejected an easy life of leisure in favor of public service, having twice been elected to the House of Representatives. In Congress, he had earned high marks from his colleagues for his intelligence and natural charm. When it came to fiscal matters, he was strictly business. In taking on the powerful veterans' lobby as well as his former colleagues, Douglas appeared to have signed a suicide pact. But he was a First World War veteran himself (cited for bravery by General John Pershing) and had mastered the budgetary numbers. He was an immediate favorite of FDR, who claimed that he was "in many ways the greatest 'find' of the administration."

While Douglas adroitly defended his line-by-line calculations, Roosevelt took care of the politics of pushing the legislation through Congress. He worked with conservative Democrats in the House, especially John McDuffie of Alabama, the chairman of the House Economy Committee. But they faced a formidable challenge from the American Legion, which had organized a massive letter-writing campaign to pressure representatives to defeat the bill. There was, as a result, nothing close to the remarkable unanimity that had propelled the emergency banking bill through the House in less than hour only a few days earlier. Liberal Democrats broke ranks with the president and voted against the legislation. But conservatives in both parties favored the bill. It passed 266 to 138.

Roosevelt shrewdly avoided a Senate filibuster on the bill by suddenly sending up a vastly more popular proposal—an amendment to the Volstead Act making beer of 3.2 percent alcoholic content and wine legal. "I think this would be a good time for beer," Roosevelt had joked with friends the night before he sent his seventy-two-word message on the liquor bill to the Senate. He knew that the upper house could not approve the bill to legalize beer and wine until the senators had voted on the economy legislation. The budget bill passed. So did the Beer-Wine Revenue Act, which was projected to increase government revenues by more than $100 million. In St. Louis, the hometown of Budweiser, steam whistles blew and sirens screamed in celebration. Bands played "Happy Days Are Here Again" in

Times Square, while six sturdy brewery horses pulled a wagon to the curb of the Empire State Building, where a case of beer was presented to Al Smith.

In the first two weeks of his administration, Roosevelt had sent three ambitious bills to Congress, and he had signed each into law. He was understandably pleased and ready for more. Though he had originally thought he would terminate the special congressional session at the end of March, his success emboldened him to press forward. "We are all keeping our fingers crossed and hoping to get in some real work while the temper of the country and Congress is so pleasant," he wrote the financier Joseph Kennedy, a New Deal supporter. But whereas his early deflationary measures (closing the banks; drastically cutting the federal budget) appealed to conservatives, he predicted that his "banker friends may be horrified" by his next set of proposals, which, he conceded, would be inflationary.

While the final details of the economy bill were still being worked out in the Senate, FDR instructed Secretary of Agriculture Henry Wallace and his deputy, the liberal economist Rex Tugwell, to draft major legislation to help the nation's long-suffering farmers. For his entire political career, Roosevelt had championed agricultural interests, dating back to his days as chairman of the agricultural committee in the New York Senate. During his presidential campaign, he had called for a national agricultural policy that offered economic parity with the industrial sector. He suggested a limit on domestic crop allotments to reduce agricultural surpluses. Though he was conspicuously vague on details, the purpose behind his proposal was clear enough. By limiting production, farm prices would rise, farmers would then have money to feed and clothe their families, buy new equipment and other manufactured goods, thereby spurring both the agricultural and industrial sectors of the economy.

Roosevelt did not have to be told that the plight of the farmer was desperate. Two months before his inauguration, Edward O'Neall, the president of the powerful Farm Bureau Federation, had said, "Unless something is done for the American farmer we will have revolution in the countryside within twelve months." But how could the Roosevelt administration draft effective legislation for "the American farmer," when the term itself encompassed such a broad range of agricultural workers, from the Alabama cotton farmer to the Montana cattle rancher, from fruit growers in California to dairymen in upstate New York?

In early March, Secretary Wallace invited leaders of major farm organizations to Washington for a bill-drafting conference. Roosevelt's only instruction to participants: reach a consensus. After four days and nights of wrangling, an omnibus agriculture bill was produced that offered something for everyone. The centerpiece was a domestic allotment provision that paid midwestern and southern farmers to leave hundreds of thousands of acres fallow with revenues from a tax on food processors (millers, canners, packers). But the bill also contained a provision appealing to conservatives who opposed production limits—government assistance in dumping surpluses abroad.

The day before Roosevelt sent the bill to Congress, he told reporters that his agricultural policy was a work-in-progress. "My position toward farm legislation," he said in an off-the-record session, "is that we ought to do something to increase the value of farm products and if the darn thing doesn't work, we can say so quite frankly, but at least try it." His message to Congress, however, was drafted in more urgent, hortatory language. The bill was "a new means to rescue agriculture," he wrote, and would be "of definite, constructive importance to our economic recovery." The bill sailed through the House after less than a week of debate. But it met stiff headwinds in the Senate, where food processors and conservative farm lobbyists had time to organize opposition to the most far-reaching provisions of the bill.

It took all of Roosevelt's charm, guile, and blunt intimidation to transform the bill into law. His first tactical challenge was to prod the chairman of the Senate Agriculture Committee, Ellison ("Cotton Ed") Smith, into action. Smith, a conservative South Carolinian and proud racist ("Cotton is king and white is supreme"), did not like the liberal tilt of the legislation and was in no hurry to complete hearings on the bill. The president summoned Smith's entire committee to the White House for some tough talk on the urgency of farm legislative. But he also confided in Smith that he would not appoint a liberal member of his administration (i.e., Wallace or Tugwell) to head the new administrative agency overseeing agricultural policy.* Smith promptly sprung the bill from his committee for floor debate.

By the time the Agricultural Adjustment Act (AAA) was passed two months later, Roosevelt had agreed to significant changes to attract a Senate majority. He promised a new agency, the Farm Credit Administration,

---

* Roosevelt kept his word, appointing the conservative George Peek, president of the Moline Plow Company, who opposed domestic allotments in favor of marketing agreements and dumping surpluses overseas.

to provide federal funding to refinance farm mortgages threatened with foreclosure. And he publicly took the nation off the gold standard to stave off a hyperinflationary amendment to the bill introduced by Oklahoma senator Elmer Thomas, which would have authorized coining silver and issuing $3 billion in greenbacks. Roosevelt's more moderate proposal prohibited most overseas shipments of gold and allowed the dollar to float downward. Congress backed FDR's initiative by passing legislation abrogating provisions in public and private contracts that required payment in gold. Budget director Douglas was appalled. "This is the end of western civilization," he told a friend after the president's announcement. But most Americans, including the Wall Street titan J. P. Morgan, supported the policy.

From the outset, the president had conceded that the final version of the Agricultural Adjustment Act was less important to him than the broad contours of the legislation and, of course, its passage. But he justifiably claimed pride of authorship in the Civilian Conservation Corps (CCC), which Congress authorized in late March. He had preached conservation for decades, both as a politician and a private citizen (he supervised annual planting of more than 20,000 saplings on the family's Hyde Park estate). The CCC quickly hired more than a quarter million unemployed young men between the ages of eighteen and twenty-four to work in the national forests and parks, building firebreaks and lookout towers, clearing trails and campsites, thinning millions of acres of trees, and planting saplings of cedar, hemlock, and poplar to revive eroded hillsides and mountaintops. They were paid $30 a month, and were required to send $25 of that home to their families. Roosevelt considered the income less important than "the moral and spiritual value of such work," and savored the idea of transporting tens of thousands of hopeless Americans walking city streets to the countryside to do healthy, invigorating labor.

The CCC put more than 3 million idle young men to work over the next decade, providing them with meaningful jobs and their impoverished families with steady income. Besides cutting the nation's unemployment lines, the CCC also proved enormously successful as a conservation measure. More than half of all forest planting in the United States was done by the Corps.

Shortly after the CCC's founding, Roosevelt transformed another of his core convictions into a glittering New Deal achievement. Harnessing water power for the public good had been a Roosevelt goal since his first term as governor of New York. When he visited Wilson Dam at Muscle Shoals, Alabama, in January 1933, he had imagined the myriad potential uses of the Tennessee River that flowed through Alabama and six other southern states. He was accompanied that day by progressive Senator George Norris of Nebraska, who had fought unsuccessfully for years to make the Wilson Dam, originally constructed during the First World War to produce nitrates for explosives, a federal operation to control floods and generate electricity for the seven-state region. In Roosevelt, Norris found an eager acolyte. "He is more than with me," Norris told a reporter, "because he plans to go even farther than I did."

At FDR's urging, Congress created the Tennessee Valley Authority (TVA), a public corporation authorized to generate cheap, abundant hydroelectric power from Muscle Shoals, construct more dams on the Tennessee River for flood control and additional generating capacity, manufacture fertilizers, combat soil erosion and deforestation, and dig a 650-mile navigable waterway from Knoxville to Paducah, Kentucky. Roosevelt's plan for the region went far beyond electric power and conservation. The Muscle Shoals development, he promised, would serve as an unprecedented experiment in national planning to serve the impoverished, underdeveloped region. He expected the TVA to attract industry, create jobs, clean up abysmal sanitary conditions, offer improved health services, and introduce innovative educational programs for the largely illiterate population. Even Norris was stunned by the president's audacious vision. "What are you going to say when they ask you the political philosophy behind TVA?" Norris asked Roosevelt. "I'll tell them it's neither fish nor fowl," he answered, "but whatever it is, it will taste awfully good to the people of the Tennessee Valley."

Roosevelt built on his early successes with the confidence of a pocket billiards champion intent on running the table. He asked Congress to create a new agency, the Federal Emergency Relief Administration (FERA), to coordinate and channel $500,000 million in direct federal unemployment assistance to the states. To head the agency, the president appointed Harry Hopkins, the curt, chain-smoking former social worker who had efficiently administered FDR's state relief program from Albany. On the president's recommendation, Congress also established the Home Owners' Loan Corporation (HOLC), which rescued small urban homeowners facing foreclosure, as the farm mortgage bill had done for farmers. HOLC set long-term repayment schedules at low interest rates, eventually refinancing one out of every five mortgaged private dwellings in urban America.

Turning to a prime target in his inaugural address, Wall Street excess, Roosevelt recruited an elite group of Harvard law graduates (all recommended by Professor Frankfurter) to draft the Securities Act of 1933. The law required that accurate information on all stock offerings be posted for the public. Untruthful corporate officers faced both civil and criminal penalties for violations. "To the ancient rule of *caveat emptor*," Roosevelt warned, the new legislation added the further doctrine: "let the seller beware." The Glass-Seagall banking bill, which separated commercial banking from investment, quickly followed. Toward the end of the special session, Roosevelt proposed, and Congress enacted, a railroad reorganization bill to revive and streamline the nation's rail network.

All along, Roosevelt had planned major legislation to prime the industrial sector in much the way that he expected the Agricultural Adjustment Act to restore the rural economy. And the president approached the task of melding the contentious parties, business and labor, as he had the disparate interests involved in the Agricultural Act negotiations. He told drafters of the legislation to lock themselves in a room and emerge only when they had reached an agreement.

By the time a draft agreement was presented to Roosevelt, populist Senator Hugo Black of Alabama had preemptively undercut the president by introducing his own thirty-hour workweek bill. Black claimed that the mandatory thirty-hour workweek requirement would produce 6 million jobs. Roosevelt predicted that the bill, if enacted into law, would be declared unconstitutional by the conservative Supreme Court.* The president also considered the bill impractical, since it could not adapt "to the rhythm of the cow," preventing farmers from attending to their necessary chores.

In response to Black's thirty-hour bill, Roosevelt proposed federal regulation of maximum hours and minimum wages in selected industries. Another labor-friendly provision in the president's proposal gave indus-

---

* Roosevelt's prediction was based on a 1918 Court decision, *Hammer v. Dagenhart*, that had struck down a federal statute prohibiting products of child labor to be transported across state lines. The Court ruled that Congress had exceeded its authority to regulate interstate commerce under Article I of the Constitution.

trial workers the right to organize and collectively bargain through their representatives. The legislation also created the National Recovery Administration (NRA) to supervise production, codes of fair competition, and wages-price regulations under government-sanctioned industrial compacts. As a concession to business, most of the nation's antitrust laws were suspended. The bill's final component established the Public Works Administration (PWA) to oversee a massive public works program that would pump $3.3 billion into the nation's clogged economic arteries.

After Congress enacted the bill, known as the National Industrial Recovery Act (NIRA), Roosevelt's critics accused him of abandoning laissez-faire capitalism. "If that philosophy hadn't proved to be bankrupt," he replied, "Herbert Hoover would be sitting here right now."

Several years later, Raymond Moley, who had by then become disillusioned with the New Deal, dismissed the notion that there was a coherent theme to the flurry of legislation passed in the early days of the Roosevelt administration. "To look upon these policies as the result of a unified plan," he wrote, "is to believe that the accumulation of stuffed snakes, baseball pictures, school flags, old tennis shoes, carpenter's tools, geometry books, and chemistry sets in a boy's bedroom could have been put there by an interior decorator."

But Moley missed the point. Roosevelt never aspired to be the nation's interior decorator. He did not expect everything that he proposed to fit neatly into a preordained design. He was an avowed experimenter, more akin to a collagist than a designer. He produced bold colors and jagged cutouts, sometimes painting over sections and ripping out others. The result was not tidy, but it was satisfying to millions of demoralized Americans in 1933 who craved a president offering dynamic, innovative leadership.

On June 16, 1933, the special session of Congress adjourned. In the first one hundred days of his administration, Roosevelt had sent fifteen legislative messages to Congress, and each had become law. It was a dazzling achievement and demonstrated an astonishing spirit of cooperation between the president and Congress. But the third co-equal branch of the federal government, the Supreme Court of the United States, had yet to pass judgment on the historic legislation.

While the president adroitly balanced conservatives and liberals to push through New Deal legislation, Chief Justice Hughes was not so fortunate in bringing harmony to a badly polarized Court. The Hughes Court was an-chored by strong-willed men on both ends of the ideological spectrum. Jus-tice Pierce Butler, a moralistic, dogmatic member of the conservative bloc, was an intimidating presence in the justices' conferences, who defended private property rights with unwavering conviction. Justice Brandeis was just as tough-minded in arguing for his interpretation of the Constitution, which allowed an active, socially conscious government to regulate for the common good. Butler was sometimes so ill-tempered in his attacks on Brandeis that Hughes had to intervene, gently admonishing him to restore a judicial tone to the discussion.

Hughes's task was further complicated by the resentment of Harlan Fiske Stone, who believed that he, not Hughes, should have been ap-pointed Chief Justice. Though he had stoically accepted Hughes's appoint-ment, Stone was convinced that he could do a better job than Hughes in leading the Court. To make matters worse, he felt unappreciated by the Chief Justice, whom he believed purposely gave him picayune assignments. Hughes's shifts between the two wings of the Court was viewed by Stone as an attempt to placate both sides and avoid an open break. But Stone concluded that the Chief's overriding concern for stability sacrificed any consistent constitutional principles. After two years on the Hughes Court, Stone was so demoralized that he considered resigning to return to private practice.

In the Chief Justice's struggle to achieve consensus, or at least a strong Court majority to support his views, he faced another daily challenge that the president was spared. Unlike FDR's handpicked cabinet, the associate justices of the Supreme Court held life-tenured appointments and felt no loyalty to the Chief Justice. That message could be delivered to Hughes in blistering dissents to his opinions. Or in more mundane ways, as As-sociate Justice McReynolds reminded him one weekday morning shortly before the Hughes Court was to convene for oral arguments. An impatient Hughes sent a page to James McReynolds's chambers to inform the justice that his colleagues were assembled, and waiting for him. "Tell the Chief Justice I don't work for him," McReynolds snapped.

The justices' reactions to Roosevelt's presidential campaign and elec-tion divided, predictably, along ideological lines.* The four conservatives

---

* Neither Hughes nor Roberts, the Court's swing justices, expressed any recorded opin-ion on the presidential campaign or Roosevelt's election.

supported Hoover and rued the prospect of a Roosevelt presidency. "I am praying that Roosevelt and his demagogic cohorts will not succeed," Willis Van Devanter wrote his sister. Justice Sutherland, Van Devanter added, "thinks Roosevelt unfitted and unsafe for the presidency." Justice Brandeis, on the other hand, was enthusiastic about Roosevelt's campaign and applauded his election.

Only Stone, among the justices, appeared conflicted. He assisted his fellow Republican and close friend, President Hoover, during the campaign. "I am with the President 100 per cent in this address," he wrote Hoover's presidential secretary, who had sent the justice one of the president's campaign speeches for comment. He was nonetheless philosophical, even hopeful, after Roosevelt's election. "I cannot see in Roosevelt and his entourage any improvement over Hoover," he wrote. "Nevertheless the overturn may not be without benefit."

Roosevelt and Hughes demonstrated distinctly different styles of leadership, but shared one dominant trait: extraordinary self-control. Outwardly jovial and welcoming of all opinions, Roosevelt's conviviality hid an inner reserve and implicit trust in his own judgment to make difficult decisions. Hughes was always cordial, but never effusive in his relations with friends and colleagues. Throughout his adult life, he rarely confided in anyone outside his immediate family. Like Roosevelt, he kept his own counsel on important professional decisions, including the business before the Supreme Court. As Chief Justice, he usually avoided even genteel arm-twisting of colleagues; he rarely sent memos or engaged in extended conversations to bring them around to his point of view. He worked intensely to prepare each case in meticulous detail for the justices' conferences. But once he had expressed his opinion on the merits, he considered that his primary task of persuading his colleagues was completed, and turned to the next case.

In the fall of 1933, Felix Frankfurter, an enthusiastic New Deal supporter as well as an eminent constitutional scholar, nervously focused his attention on the Hughes Court. In a letter to Justice Stone, the Harvard professor noted that the Chief Justice appeared to resent close scrutiny of the Court's work. "Why people should resent constant criticism upon their labors—particularly people who have ultimate power—I have never been able to understand," he wrote. "But perhaps the answer is that they *have* ultimate power." Frankfurter was convinced of the constitutionality of the New Deal legislation, but not eager to have the statutes challenged before the Court. With seven Republicans and only two Democrats (Brandeis and Cardozo) on the Court, he was not confident that the desperate economic times dictated liberal judicial results. "I can assure you that there is no right to any such hope under the leadership of Hughes, let alone the others," he wrote a fellow liberal.

Frankfurter and other New Dealers did not have long to wait to learn how the justices might rule on the historic legislation. On November 8, the Hughes Court heard arguments in a constitutional challenge to the Minnesota Mortgage Moratorium Act of 1933, a measure that had been rushed through the Minnesota legislature to provide temporary relief to the tens of thousands of homeowners who faced foreclosure in the state. The Minnesota law, like most major New Deal legislation, was conceived as an emergency measure. It was passed under duress in April 1933 by lawmakers who deliberated while several thousand farmers, threatened with the loss of their homes, milled restlessly outside the legislative chamber. The governor, meanwhile, issued an executive order directing all sheriffs to refrain from conducting foreclosure sales until the legislative session had ended.

Six months later, the justices calmly listened to the constitutional challenge to the state law made by the attorney for Minnesota's Home Building and Loan Association, which held the defaulted mortgage of John and Rosala Blaisdell. Under the mortgage moratorium statute, the Blaisdells had been given an additional two years to make good on their mortgage payments. The state law was unconstitutional, the mortgage company's attorney argued, because Article I of the Constitution forbade any state to pass a law "impairing the obligation of contracts." Like earlier challenges under the due process clause of the Fourteenth Amendment, the *Blaisdell* case invited the justices to answer an essential question of constitutional interpretation: Does the Constitution allow a state to pass economic legislation for the general welfare of its citizens even though it may impinge upon private contract or property rights?

Chief Justice Hughes answered the question affirmatively for a narrow 5–4 Court majority that included Roberts and the three liberals (Brandeis, Cardozo, and Stone). His opinion focused on the dire economic circumstances surrounding the emergency legislation. "While an emergency does not create power," he wrote, "an emergency may furnish the occasion for the exercise of the power." Just as a state may act to give temporary relief to citizens devastated by a natural disaster such as a fire, flood, or earthquake, he reasoned, it may meet an urgent public need produced by an economic depression. Earlier Court decisions, he observed, confirmed that "there has been a growing appreciation of public needs and of the necessity of finding ground for a rational compromise between individual rights and public welfare." He emphasized that the Minnesota statute did not destroy the agreement between the mortgagee and the Blaisdells, but only modified the conditions to accommodate the economic reality of the depression. Finally, he responded to Justice Sutherland's charge in dissent that the Court majority had disregarded the Framers' intent. "It is no answer to say that this public need was not apprehended a century ago," he wrote, "or to insist that what the provision of the Constitution meant to the vision of that day it must mean to the vision of our time."

Great political significance was attached to Hughes's opinion in the press and especially the fact that the Chief Justice had joined the Court's liberals. The decision, the *New York Herald Tribune* reported, might quell reports that the president "entertained the thought of enlarging the court to shift the balance of power from 'conservative' to 'liberal' if necessary to insure approval of his recovery program." With the Chief Justice lining up with the Court "liberals" in the Minnesota case, the *Herald Tribune* continued, "the decision was interpreted as giving the President reason to believe he would have the Supreme Court backing he has openly requested without the necessity of reconstituting the court."

Though Roosevelt made no public statement, he "was exceedingly gratified and happy" with the decision, according to his Attorney General, Homer Cummings. He was further encouraged two months later when the same five justices upheld a New York law that authorized a state board to set minimum retail milk prices. Just as the Minnesota law had responded to pressure from homeowners facing foreclosures, so had the New York statute attempted to meet the demands of dairy farmers whose livelihood had been threatened by depressed milk prices. The board had fixed the retail price of milk at 9 cents a quart. In defiance of the regulation, Leo Nebbia, a Rochester grocer, sold two quarts of milk and a 5-cent loaf of bread for 18 cents. Nebbia's sale triggered the constitutional argument by the grocer that the state price regulation violated his rights to due process under the Fourteenth Amendment.

Justice Roberts, who wrote the majority opinion in the *Nebbia* case, reportedly paced the floor of his home until the early morning hours before deciding how he would cast his vote. He and Hughes had joined the conservative bloc in the *Liebmann* decision handed down only two years earlier that denied Oklahoma the authority to regulate the manufacture and sale of ice. The ice business, according to Justice Sutherland's majority opinion in *Liebmann*, was "not affected with a public interest." Neither was the sale of necessities, such as groceries or dairy products, he had added. How, then, could the New York law pass constitutional muster under the due process clause in view of the *Liebmann* decision?

Without overruling *Liebmann*, Justice Roberts's *Nebbia* opinion simply ignored Sutherland's definition of what constituted business "affected with a public interest." The phrase, Roberts wrote, meant only that "an industry, for adequate reason, is subject to control for the public good." And there was no doubt, Roberts emphasized, that the New York law regulating the retail price of milk promoted the public welfare. The milk industry was a paramount industry in the state and milk was an essential staple in every family's diet. With milk prices below the costs of production, a legislative committee had reported that there was a danger that desperate dairy farmers would cut corners and send contaminated milk to market. The state regulation was a reasonable effort to protect consumers against a legitimate health threat. While private contract and property rights were fundamental, Roberts conceded, they were not immune from reasonable government regulation. "Equally fundamental with the private right," he concluded, "is that of the public to regulate it in the common interest."

The *Nebbia* decision, *The Washington Post* reported, "appears to mark another historic liberalization of the Court's construction of the Constitution, another 'modernization' of judicial interpretation." Jerome Frank, general counsel of the Agricultural Adjustment Administration, applauded the decision as a clear indication that the Court was sympathetic to the New Deal. "The Supreme Court lays down, once and for all, that a legislative body may, when economic conditions warrant it, regulate any business," he said.

While not as optimistic as Frank, Roosevelt admitted that the *Blaisdell* and *Nebbia* decisions had given him "a glimmer of hope that the Supreme Court would take a broad view of the Constitution." But challenges to the New Deal were yet to come, and lawyers in the administration were notably reluctant to press the justices for decisions on the constitutionality of the federal legislation. In the spring of 1934, the first potential test case, a challenge to the authority of the National Recovery Administration, had been postponed at the urgent request of the Justice Department. "Why are you so anxious for a decision," Professor Frankfurter asked one of his impatient students, "until you are sure of getting the right one?"

But selecting a case that would produce Frankfurter's "right" decision was a daunting challenge for Roosevelt's Justice Department. Part of the difficulty was the unpredictable pace of constitutional litigation. A second and more intractable problem was that much of the early New Deal legislation had been hastily drafted and was, therefore, vulnerable to legal attack. One of the most complex and poorly constructed pieces was the National Industrial Recovery Act, and the enabling statute creating the National Recovery Administration, which gave the president sweeping powers to bring order to the floundering industrial economy. The so-called hot oil provision of the NIRA, as it turned out, became the first constitutional challenge to New Deal legislation to be heard by the Hughes Court.

The petroleum code, like NIRA codes in other vital industries, was designed to curb excessive production to boost prices. In 1933, the oil industry was the third largest in the nation, but profits were disastrously undermined by overproduction and vicious competition, often by renegade wildcatters who ignored state production quotas and flooded the interstate market with cheap oil. With the price of oil sinking as low as 2½ cents a gallon, Congress inserted a section in the law that attempted to stanch the flow of illegal "hot oil" by setting quotas on the amount that could be transported across state lines. Under the statute, the president was given virtually unlimited authority to determine federal petroleum policy and impose sanctions "as he may see fit."

The legal challenge to the code's "hot oil" provision was brought by the Panama Refining Company, a small, bootleg oil production business that had profited from lax enforcement of state quotas in the East Texas oil fields. The lawsuit had been filed after a Panama official was arrested for violating the quota provision of the law. The company's attorney charged that the open-ended language of the code was an unconstitutional delegation of congressional power to the president, and that the law exceeded Congress's authority to regulate interstate commerce.

Shortly before his Court appearance to defend the law, Assistant Attorney General Harold Stephens discovered that the penalty section of the petroleum code had been inadvertently omitted from the final bill. He informed the justices of the unfortunate oversight, but his embarrassing admission did not relieve him of the unenviable task of defending the government's arrest, indictment, and imprisonment of the defendant when the penal provision could not be found in the code.

Panama's counsel seized on the point at oral argument, protesting that his client had been jailed for several days for violating a law that did not exist.

Had his client seen a copy of the code? he was asked.

Only one copy, he replied, and that was in the "hip pocket of a government agent sent down to Texas from Washington."

Even Justice Stone, who harbored no hostility to the New Deal, was incredulous. "It is a rather extraordinary situation," he wrote his brother about the case. "Executive orders, purporting to have the force of law, violation of which was a crime, not being published or authenticated in any way so that those charged with criminal offenses could tell whether or not their acts were prohibited. Strange doings!"

Justice Brandeis, an unabashed admirer of FDR, was visibly agitated by the lack of specific administrative procedures in the code.

"Is there any official or general publication of these executive orders?" Brandeis asked.

"Not that I know of," Stephens replied.

"Well, is there any way by which one can find out what is in these executive orders when they are issued?"

"I think it would be rather difficult," Stephens conceded.

The vote at the justices' conference was 8–1 to strike down the "hot oil" section of the statute as an unconstitutional delegation of congressional power. Only Justice Cardozo dissented, contending that the law provided sufficient guidelines to the president to conserve natural resources and protect law-abiding petroleum dealers from unfair competition from lawbreakers.

Hughes assigned himself the opinion for the Court and wrote with his usual workmanlike efficiency. For more than a century, he wrote, the Court had recognized that Congress could confer on the executive branch the power to make regulations to implement the law. But there were limits, he added, and the "hot oil" section of the petroleum code exceeded those limits by giving the president "unfettered discretion." The result was to invest in the president "an uncontrolled legislative power." If the code provision was held valid, he concluded, "it would be idle to pretend that anything would be left of limitations upon the power of the Congress to delegate its law-making function."

Hughes enjoyed the pleasant, and unusual, experience of receiving enthusiastic comments on his draft opinion from both liberal and conservative colleagues. "Yes Sir," Brandeis wrote. "Clear, convincing, and written with careful discrimination," Sutherland added.

The arch conservative *Chicago Daily Tribune* saluted the opinion of the "distinguished" Chief Justice for "put[ting] the brakes on the development of a dictatorship in the United States." *The New York Times*'s Arthur Krock was more tempered in his assessment of the Court's decision: "[T]he highest tribunal has set a semaphore along the crowded legislative thoroughfare of the New Deal. 'Stop—look—listen' will be heard a good deal more in Washington."

Official reaction to the opinion in the Roosevelt administration was cautious and not altogether negative. The president set the tone, telling reporters that Hughes's opinion had done nothing more than deliver a bracing lecture to Congress to do a better job of drafting future legislation. That message was reinforced privately by Owen Roberts in a conversation with Interior Secretary Harold Ickes at a small dinner at the Danish ambassador's home. Roberts told Ickes that he was sympathetic to New Deal efforts to control "hot oil" and encouraged the administration to write new legislation to overcome the Court's objections. But other New Dealers, like the young Treasury Department attorney Robert Jackson, admitted that the decision had caused "profound anxiety."

Only one day after the "hot oil" decision was announced, the justices heard oral arguments in cases that posed infinitely greater dangers to the New Deal. "[T]he whole American economy was haled before the Supreme Court," Jackson wrote. At issue was Congress's constitutional authority, under a joint resolution passed in June 1933, to invalidate both public and private contracts requiring payment of debts in gold. The resolution, enacted shortly after FDR had taken the nation off the gold standard, effectively immunized the federal government and private debtors from language routinely written into bonds, mortgages, and ordinary contracts guaranteeing payment in gold coin. Enforcement of those contracts would have required payment of $1.69 in the devalued currency of 1933 for every $1.00 in debt assumed in the original agreements. On January 8, 1935, when the Court heard arguments, gold obligations in the United States were estimated at $100 billion; the U.S. Treasury held only a small fraction of that amount in gold reserves. If the Hughes Court ruled against the administration, the federal government would face bankruptcy and, undoubtedly, the teetering economy would be thrown into chaos.

Plaintiffs in the gold clause cases argued that the sanctity of contract, not the solvency of the federal government, should be the Court's overriding concern. One petitioner was a railroad bondholder whose private contract, by its written terms, obligated the corporate debtor to pay him in gold coin. John Perry, the plaintiff in a second case, had bought a $10,000 Liberty bond during the First World War and demanded that the U.S. government pay him $16,931.25, the amount owed in gold, as guaranteed on the face of the bond.

Generations of Justice Department lawyers have calculated their chances of success in arguments before the Court based on the prior judicial opinions of individual justices. For Homer Cummings, who headed the legal team representing the Roosevelt administration in the gold clause cases, the nine justices provided him with the narrowest opportunity to prevail. The four conservatives—Butler, McReynolds, Sutherland, and Van Devanter—almost certainly would reject his argument that Congress's action had been necessary to revive the domestic economy and make American business competitive abroad. These justices (known collectively as "the Four Horsemen") had voted virtually in lockstep to preserve private contract and property rights threatened by government regulation.

Cummings would, therefore, have to win the votes of all five of the remaining justices. Had he been privy to the private correspondence of the three liberal members of the Court, Brandeis, Cardozo, and Stone, he would have had additional cause for concern. All three expressed anxiety about the policy, if not the constitutionality, of the nation's abandoning the gold standard. In the late spring of 1933, Brandeis had written Frankfurter that the president's action "is terrifying in its implications." Cardozo worried that the policy treated creditors unfairly. And Stone wrote his friend John Bassett Moore that "[t]o countenance the repudiation of solemn obligations is abhorrent to me."

Attorney General Cummings, dressed in formal morning coat, made an impassioned defense of the congressional resolution, asserting that contractual obligations must give way to the nation's "power of self preservation." He described in dramatic detail the necessity of the congressional resolution to protect the fragile U.S. economy. If Congress had not acted, he said, the United States would have been reduced to "a cripple among the nations of the earth." A Court ruling unfavorable to the government, he warned, would lead to an economic collapse that would "stagger the imagination."

Chief Justice Hughes did nothing to calm the nerves of Cummings and other New Dealers when he later questioned the assistant solicitor general about the *Perry* case: "Here we have a bond issued by the United States government . . . in time of war . . . a bond which the government promised to pay in a certain kind of money. Where do you find any power under the Constitution to alter that bond, or power of Congress to change that promise?" The government lawyer's reply, that it resided in Congress's authority to regulate the currency, was hardly reassuring.

After the three days of arguments, several weeks went by without any word of a Court decision. Chief Justice Hughes, acutely aware of the enormous impact that the Court's decisions would have on the markets, issued an unprecedented statement on Saturday, February 2, two days before Court decisions were usually announced, that "the Court is not ready." He repeated that cautionary message a week later.

A restless Roosevelt pondered his response should the justices rule against the administration. In talks with Cummings, Secretary of the Treasury Henry Morgenthau, and other members of his administration, he considered a wide range of options, including packing the Court with new appointees* or outright defiance of the decision. On February 8, when the justices dined at the White House "on the President's gold plates," no one dared spoil the evening by discussing the pending decision. But the next day, Roosevelt summoned Cummings and Donald Richberg, director of the National Recovery Administration, to the White House and, in their presence, dictated his answer to what he assumed would be an adverse decision.

In the first section of his prepared statement, Roosevelt vigorously defended his policy of taking the country off the gold standard. Had his administration insisted on holding all debtors to the gold standard, he said, the result would have been "universal bankruptcy." He then described in

---

* Roosevelt was intrigued with President Grant's effective solution to a Supreme Court ruling declaring legal tender legislation unconstitutional. Grant appointed two new justices, one to fill a vacancy, the other a new seat created by Congress. In his 1927 Columbia lectures, Hughes had condemned the new majority's ruling reversing the legal tender decision as a "self-inflicted wound" that diminished the Court's standing in the country.

personal, conversational terms the catastrophic consequences that ordinary Americans would face as a result of the putative Court decision. Consider, he said, the plight of the individual who has bought a home for himself and his family: "If there is a gold clause in his mortgage—and most mortgages contain that clause—this decision would compel him to increase his payments 69% each month from now on." No homeowner, whether city worker or farmer, could meet that demand. Under the Court's ruling, corporate bondholders (including one of the petitioners in the gold clause cases) would reap an unconscionable, "wholly unearned profit" and, in the process, bankrupt virtually every railroad in the country.

Turning to U.S. savings bonds, Roosevelt recounted the story of "an old lady [who] came to see me the other day. She is dependent heavily on the income from government bonds (about $800 a year). Being the right type of citizen, she volunteered to tell me that she does not consider herself entitled to more than the $10,000 which she had saved and invested."

Roosevelt did not doubt that "the distinguished members" of the Court had decided the cases "in accordance to the letter of the law as they read it." But that could not be the end of the matter for the American people, he insisted, since the decision would have disastrous consequences for the nation. He quoted Lincoln's challenge in 1857 to the Court's pro-slavery *Dred Scott* decision. If the vital questions affecting the nation, such as slavery, are irrevocably fixed by the Court, Lincoln had said, then "the people will have ceased to be their own rulers, having to that extent practically resigned their government into the hands of that eminent tribunal." Lincoln had not called for a Court-packing plan or open defiance of the justices' ruling, but only suggested that voters elect a president committed to the appointment of justices who would reverse the *Dred Scott* decision.

Roosevelt was more combative than Lincoln. He said that, as president, he shared responsibility with Congress to protect the American people from "intolerable burdens involuntarily imposed." Otherwise, he suggested, the executive and legislative branches of the federal government would be guilty of malfeasance. "To stand idly by and to permit the decision of the Supreme Court to be carried through to its logical, inescapable conclusion," he said, would "imperil the economic and political security of this nation." Those were fighting words, and, as Attorney General Cummings scrawled at the top of his copy of the speech, "for use if needed."

On Saturday, February 16, when there was no word from the Court about the gold clause cases, Roosevelt knew that the decisions would be announced the following Monday. By late morning on the 18th, every seat in the courtroom was filled and latecomers stood against the wall in the back. At one minute after noon, Hughes ended the suspense when he began reading the first of his opinions for the Court.

Speaking for a five-member majority—Hughes, Brandeis, Cardozo, Roberts, and Stone—the Chief Justice declared that Congress had the constitutional authority to nullify private contracts. For Hughes, this conclusion was neither exceptional nor unprecedented. As an associate justice more than two decades earlier, he had written an opinion making the same constitutional point. And in his *Blaisdell* opinion the previous Court term, he had written that a state government could adjust the terms of a private contract in an emergency. He was even more forceful in asserting the power of Congress. "Contracts may create rights of property, but when contracts deal with a subject matter which lies within the control of the Congress," he wrote, "they have a congenital infirmity."

Whether the federal government could alter the explicit terms of public contracts, such as U.S. savings bonds, was a more difficult issue for the Chief Justice, as he had indicated at oral argument. Like his brethren Brandeis, Cardozo, and Stone, he found the idea of the U.S. government reneging on its word to be repugnant. While it was true, as the assistant solicitor general had argued, that Congress had the constitutional power to regulate money, to break the promise to investors in U.S. savings bonds was immoral. It was also unconstitutional, he concluded. If Congress could "disregard the obligations of the government at its discretion," he wrote, "the credit of the United States was an illusory pledge." The Constitution forbade such a policy. Congress could not alter or destroy the "binding quality of the promise of the United States."

Did Hughes's opinion obligate the federal government to pay out additional billions of dollars in gold coin to savings bonds investors? If so, it would cause an inevitable run on the gold-deficient U.S. Treasury. His surprising answer was no. In rejecting petitioner John Perry's claim, Hughes's reasoning came very close to that expressed by Roosevelt in his dictated statement. For Perry and every other owner of a $10,000 bond to collect $16,931.25 would constitute "unjustified enrichment," Hughes wrote. Perry had made no attempt to prove that he had suffered any loss. There was no showing, moreover, that his purchasing power was diminished by Congress's action. Perry, in effect, was no different from the old lady in FDR's story who had told him that she was not entitled to more than the

$10,000 she had saved and invested. That was the fair result, the president had said, and that conclusion was reinforced by Hughes's opinion for the Court majority.

James McReynolds wrote a bitter dissent for the four conservatives, deploring the government's "loss of reputation for honorable dealing," which, he predicted, would lead to "legal and moral chaos." From the bench, he unleashed an extemporaneous blast at the Chief Justice's majority opinion and, not so subtly, at the president. "This is Nero at his worst," he said. "The Constitution is gone." His outburst was so vitriolic that it was excised from the official reports of Court decisions.

The Court's decision "swept away the biggest barrier before the New Deal," *The Washington Post* reported, "and obviated counter action for which the New Deal was warily, uneasily prepared had the verdict gone the other way." *The New York Times* called it a "golden ruling," while the *San Francisco Chronicle* observed, "The Constitution has been stretched, perhaps, but not beyond its limit of elasticity."

"In history the name of Hughes will be greater than that of Marshall," an admirer wrote to the Chief Justice. Linking Hughes to Marshall surely pleased the Chief Justice, for he, like every other serious student of the Court, considered Marshall to be the greatest leader in the Court's history. Constitutional scholars later gave their own reasons to compare the two Chief Justices. The unexpected turn at the end of Hughes's *Perry* opinion (concluding that the plaintiff was right as a matter of constitutional law, but that the government owed no damages) was reminiscent of Marshall's famous opinion in *Marbury v. Madison*. Marshall had lectured President Jefferson and his Secretary of State, James Madison, for failing to deliver a judicial commission, but then avoided retribution from the president or the Jeffersonian Republican–controlled Congress by denying that the Court had jurisdiction of the case. Hughes, it was suggested, accomplished a similar feat by reprimanding the New Deal Congress for its joint resolution which disregarded the solemn obligation of the U.S. government to savings bond investors, but did not require additional payments that would have provoked a national economic crisis or risk retaliation from Congress or the president of the United States.

The White House released a terse statement: "The President is gratified by the decision of the Supreme Court." It was a gross understatement; Roosevelt was elated. "As a lawyer it seems to me that the Supreme Court has at last definitely put human values ahead of the 'pound of flesh' called for by a contract," he wrote Joseph Kennedy one day after the decision had been announced. "[T]he Nation will never know what a great treat it missed in not hearing the marvelous radio address the 'Pres' had prepared for delivery to the Nation Monday night if the cases had gone the other way."

Roosevelt was so proud of his undelivered radio address that he appended an excerpt to his letter to Kennedy and read a portion at a White House luncheon with several cabinet members. Not surprisingly, choice passages from the address were leaked to the *Times* and appeared on its front page later in the week. Had FDR given the radio speech, Arthur Krock wrote, "it would have marked the most sensational and historic episode in the Court's history since Andrew Jackson said of a Supreme Court ruling: 'John Marshall has made this decision; now let him enforce it.' "* If New Deal legislation fared poorly in later constitutional challenges, Krock mused, an angry Roosevelt might yet deliver "in revised form the speech he has now laid aside."

Roosevelt's goodwill toward the Hughes Court lasted less than three months. On May 6, Justice Roberts, writing for himself and the four conservatives, struck down the Railroad Retirement Act of 1933 that provided a compulsory retirement and pension system for workers in the railroad industry. For New Dealers, the result was bad enough, but Robert's vehement attack on the statute was shocking. His opinion expressed contempt for the legislation, ridiculing the notion that the promise of security in old age could boost workers' morale and therefore increase their efficiency and enhance railroad safety. If the Court accepted that rationale, he wrote, Congress could also provide employees' medical care or, more absurdly in his view, shelter, food, or housing for their children. Such social welfare legislation might "relieve the employee of mental strain and worry," he conceded sarcastically. But it exceeded Congress's power to regulate interstate commerce and deprived railroad corporations (required to contribute to the pension fund) of their property without due process of law.

This was the same justice who, only a year earlier, had written the Court's expansive *Nebbia* opinion that upheld the reasonableness of New

---

* Modern constitutional historians have questioned the authenticity of the Jackson quote. There is no doubt, however, that Jackson resented Marshall's opinion in *Worcester v. Georgia* (1832) in which the Chief Justice took the state of Georgia to task for ignoring the terms of a federal treaty with the Cherokee Indians.

York's regulation of milk prices. And Roberts, only two months earlier, had assured Harold Ickes privately that he was sympathetic to the New Deal Congress's regulation of "hot oil," suggesting only that it craft a better statute.

Robert's biting opinion in the railroad pension case provoked a strong, indignant dissent from Hughes, the first time that the Chief Justice had publicly squared off against his colleague in their four years on the Court together. Hughes accused Roberts of failing to distinguish between a perfect or even wise statute, and one that was constitutional. In previous Court decisions, he pointed out, the Court had found no constitutional flaw in state worker compensation laws. By the same reasoning, Hughes wrote, the Court should have recognized Congress's broad power to regulate the railroad industry. "The fundamental consideration which supports this type of legislation is that industry should take care of its human wastage, whether that is due to accident or age," he wrote.* "That view cannot be dismissed as arbitrary or capricious. It is a reasoned conviction based upon abundant experience."

"Rotten," was the word Roosevelt used to describe the Court's decision. He had not been an enthusiastic supporter of the Railroad Retirement Act when it was passed, having admitted publicly that it was "crudely drawn." He nonetheless signed the bill, and urged Congress to revise it in the future. The president had not insisted on a model bill or even an especially good one. But he, like Chief Justice Hughes in his dissent, firmly believed that the imperfections in the statute did not make it unconstitutional.

Three weeks later, on May 27, the Court dealt three more body blows to Roosevelt and the New Deal. In one decision, the justices scolded the president for exceeding his authority in firing a recalcitrant Republican member of the Federal Trade Commission. In a second decision, they ruled that Congress had acted unconstitutionally in changing the federal bankruptcy law to give immediate relief to farmers facing foreclosures. But the third decision, on "Black Monday," was the most devastating of all, eviscerating the National Recovery Administration, which Roosevelt had

---

* In a long letter to Hughes before he had drafted his dissent, Justice Cardozo, after consultation with Stone, had suggested the analogy between state workers' compensation laws and the Railroad Retirement Act. "What is the distinction between compensating men who have been incapacitated by accident (though without fault of the employer) and compensating men who have been injured by the wear and tear of time, the slow attrition of the years?" Cardozo asked.

hailed as the "most important and far-reaching legislation in the history of the American Congress."

When the shaken president received news of the decisions, he demanded a breakdown of the votes.

"What about old Isaiah [Brandeis]?" he asked.

"With the majority," replied one of his legal advisers.

"Where was Ben Cardozo? Where was Stone?"

"They too were with the majority."

All three decisions were unanimous.

Hughes had been so concerned about the staccato impact of the decisions that he had asked Brandeis if the Court should spare the administration such trauma on a single day. No, Brandeis replied. Though Brandeis admired Roosevelt as a progressive leader, he abhorred centralized power, whether in the private sector or government. He later proclaimed May 27 to be "the most important day in the history of the court and the most beneficent."

The Chief Justice selected Justice Sutherland to deliver the tongue-lashing to Roosevelt for sacking William Humphrey, the intrepidly pro-business member of the Federal Trade Commission. Brandeis was given the opinion that tossed out the federal statute that had mandated debt restructuring for farmers who could not pay their mortgages. But Hughes kept the most controversial assignment for himself, the opinion in *Schechter Poultry Corporation v. United States*, the decision that ended the New Deal's most ambitious experiment, the National Recovery Administration.

Joe Schechter and his three brothers operated a thriving wholesale kosher poultry business in Brooklyn, despite cutthroat competition and intimidation by racketeers. The Schechters, like other small businessmen, had welcomed the NRA in 1933 with its promise of stabilized prices and robust profits. The banner of the Blue Eagle, emblem of the NRA, was hoisted in parades and hung proudly in the windows of small wholesalers and large retailers from coast to coast. General Hugh Johnson, the first director of the NRA, confidently predicted that the compact between government and industry would return prosperity to workers and employers alike and restore "the kind of a country that we knew in happier years." When the economy did not revive, public enthusiasm for the NRA waned. Johnson nonetheless was stuck with the administration of hundreds of unwieldy industrial codes that not only covered national industries like steel and textiles but also corncob pipes and burlesque theaters.

By 1935, Roosevelt had replaced the ineffective Johnson with a five-member board that oversaw the prosecution of hundreds of businesses that flouted the NRA's codes and practices. One suit named the Schechters as defendants, charging the brothers with violations of the NRA's wage and hours standards as well as the trade-practice provisions of the "Live Poultry Code," including the accusation that they had illegally sold thousands of pounds of diseased chickens at 4 to 8 cents a pound below market price. The Schechters' attorneys mounted a two-pronged constitutional defense. They contended that the Live Poultry Code, like the petroleum code in the "hot oil" case, was an improper delegation of congressional authority to the president. Congress, they also claimed, had exceeded its authority to regulate interstate commerce in dictating wages and hours for the Schechters' workers.

At their three-week trial in federal district court in Brooklyn, the defendants were found guilty on seventeen counts, given brief jail time, and fined $7,425. On appeal, a three-judge circuit court, which included the revered Learned Hand, reversed the convictions on wages and hours violations, agreeing with the Schechters' lawyers that Congress's power to regulate interstate commerce did not reach the brothers' wholesale poultry business. But the court upheld the constitutionality of the Live Poultry Code, sustaining the multiple charges against the defendants.

The decision of Justice Department lawyers in early April 1935 to appeal the circuit court's *Schechter* decision had been made reluctantly, and only after they had abruptly requested that the Court dismiss an earlier appeal from a federal court decision in Alabama that had ruled against the NRA. In early January, government attorneys had directly appealed the Alabama federal district court decision that had declared the NRA's lumber code unconstitutional. The lower court decision was a victory for William Elbert Belcher, a lumber mill owner in Bibb County, Alabama, who had ignored the NRA's wage and price regulations, claiming successfully that they constituted an unconstitutional delegation of congressional power to the president, and that Congress had exceeded its authority under the commerce clause in regulating his lumber business.

Three days after the Justice Department had appealed the district court's *Belcher* decision, Chief Justice Hughes delivered the Court's opinion declaring that the "hot oil" section of the NRA's petroleum code was an unconstitutional delegation of congressional power. That decision provoked a two-month debate among Justice Department lawyers whether to maintain the *Belcher* appeal. Finally, on March 25, less than three weeks before the case was scheduled for oral argument, the Court granted the quickly drafted request by administration lawyers to dismiss the case.

Though belated, the government's decision to defend the NRA in *Schechter* rather *Belcher* offered strategic advantages. Whereas the Alabama district court decision in *Belcher* had ruled against the NRA on both delegation and commerce clause grounds, the prestigious circuit court in New York had upheld every provision of the fair practices code challenged in *Schechter*. The poultry industry, moreover, indisputably affected the national economy, providing the administration with a stronger argument that Congress had not exceeded its authority to regulate interstate commerce.

"The case was far from ideal as a test case," Robert Jackson admitted, but "as the Schechters were carrying it to the Supreme Court [on the code violations], there was no real choice but to make it the test case there." Among other New Dealers, there was genuine panic that *Schechter* would be the death knell of the NRA. Frankfurter urged delay and instructed his protégé Tommy Corcoran to wire Roosevelt (who was enjoying a week-long fishing trip) that the *Schechter* appeal was "most impolitic and dangerous." It was too late; Attorney General Cummings had already filed the appeal.

At oral argument, Frankfurter's warning appeared prescient. A hostile Justice McReynolds pressed Solicitor General Stanley Reed to defend the code's guidelines.

"What does unfair competition mean?" he asked Reed. "Is it anything industry says is unfair?"

"The only standard is what industry considers unfair," Reed replied, "plus the judgment of the President as to whether they are fair trade practices."

McReynolds, after hearing a few more unsatisfactory answers from Reed and his co-counsel, the NRA's Donald Richberg, ceremoniously snapped a rubber band around the briefs, dropped them to the floor, and shut his eyes.

The other justices were more attentive but no less skeptical. They laughed when the Schechters' attorney, Joseph Heller, described a few of the more opaque provisions of the poultry code in his thick Brooklyn accent. And they listened intently when Heller's co-counsel, the distinguished Wall Street attorney Frederick Wood, suggested that if the commerce clause applied to the Schechters' poultry business, then Congress would soon be "in charge of all human activity."

Richberg attempted to revive the government's case, making a last plea to the justices in his summation. "The NRA law was enacted for the purpose of checking the progressive destruction of industry, to make possible an orderly advance by industry rather than a disorderly retreat," he said. "Only Congress could deal effectively with the cause contributing to this breakdown of interstate commerce." Much more was at stake, he asserted, than punishing the illegal activities of a kosher chicken business in Brooklyn. "For the court to pass on this case only as if it fitted into the Schechter poultry case would be like trying to diagnose a case of scarlet fever by examining one small spot on the skin."

Three weeks later, Richberg and Reed sat in the courtroom nervously awaiting the Court's decision. "I feel as though I were waiting for a jury to come in—guilty or not guilty," Richberg said.

Chief Justice Hughes appeared cheerful as he entered the courtroom, but his demeanor turned deadly serious as he began to read his *Schechter* opinion. Speaking slowly, occasionally stroking his beard, Hughes methodically dismembered the NRA. "Extraordinary conditions may call for extraordinary remedies," he conceded, but "extraordinary conditions do not create or enlarge constitutional power." Congress had provided no meaningful standards under the NRA's fair practices mandate, he said, so that individual industries were free to make codes as they pleased. The president could then approve the codes, discard them, or substitute his own version at will. "Such delegation of power is unknown to our law," said Hughes, "and utterly inconsistent with the constitutional prerogatives and duties of Congress."

Had the Chief Justice stopped there, the NRA might have survived. If Congress were guilty of unconstitutional delegation of authority to the president, it could correct the flaw by drafting better guidelines in a revised statute. This was the remedy suggested by Roosevelt in January after the Court had thrown out a section of the petroleum code in the "hot oil" case.

But Hughes stifled any life that might have remained in the NRA when he turned to the argument that the NRA's rules, backed by criminal prosecutions, exceeded Congress's constitutional authority to regulate interstate commerce. He conceded that congressional authority was broad, citing his own 1914 opinion recognizing the Interstate Commerce Commission's authority to regulate a state's discriminatory intrastate railroad rates that affected interstate railroad traffic. But he drew a fundamental distinction between the *direct* effect on interstate commerce of the discriminatory intrastate railroad rates, and the *indirect* effect of the Schechters' poultry operation. The line between direct and indirect might change from decade to decade, he conceded, but it was readily discernible by the Court.

Hughes's direct-indirect distinction was puzzling, since that formulaic line drawing had been discredited by constitutional scholars and largely abandoned by the Supreme Court shortly after it was first introduced in an 1895 decision. In that earlier decision, the justices had ruled that the Sherman Act prohibiting monopolies did not apply to the American Sugar Refining Company, whose purchase of four smaller companies gave it control of 98 percent of all sugar refined in the United States. Congress could not constitutionally reach a monopoly in the manufacturing of sugar under its commerce clause power, the Court ruled, since it only *indirectly* affected interstate commerce. Ironically, Hughes had not applied the direct-indirect test in his 1914 *Shreveport Rate Case* opinion, adopting instead an analysis that emphasized the practical physical or economic effects of intrastate activities on interstate commerce. In *Schechter*, Justice Cardozo, joined by Stone, wrote a brief concurrence putting distance between themselves and Hughes's direct-indirect analysis. "The law is not indifferent to considerations of degree," Cardozo wrote, suggesting that Hughes's test imposed an artificial constitutional standard.

Hughes acknowledged that more than 90 percent of the chickens purchased by the Schechters were transported from other states. He made the critical judgment, however, that the flow of commerce had stopped once the chickens arrived at the defendants' Brooklyn plants. If Congress could reach their wholesale poultry operation, he concluded, "there would be virtually no limit to the federal power and for all practical purposes we should have a completely centralized government."

Late that afternoon, Roosevelt summoned Reed, Richberg, and Cummings to the White House to study and discuss Hughes's *Schechter* opinion. After the two-hour meeting, Richberg announced to reporters: "This decision of the Supreme Court makes all codes of fair competition unenforceable as a matter of law." He then returned to his office and wired orders to suspend immediately all enforcement of NRA codes.

Roosevelt said nothing publicly about the decision for four days, breaking his official silence at a morning press conference in his office at eleven o'clock on Friday, May 31.

Surrounded by two hundred reporters, he lit a cigarette, then lashed out at the Court's *Schechter* decision in an eighty-five-minute diatribe. He began by first reading excerpts from telegrams he had received from businessmen across the country protesting the Court's decision. "The implications of this decision," he said gravely, "are much more important than any decision probably since the *Dred Scott* case." He did not object to the Court's judgment on the delegation doctrine, which, he said, could easily be remedied by Congress's revising the statute. But he warned that Hughes's interpretation of the commerce clause would have disastrous consequences for the New Deal's regulatory efforts to lift the nation out of the depression. "Does this decision mean that the United State Government has no control over any national economic problem?" he asked. "We thought we were solving it, and now it has been thrown right straight in our faces and we have been relegated to the horse-and-buggy definition of interstate commerce."

As Roosevelt prepared to end the conference, a reporter asked if he had spoken to anyone about limiting the powers of the Supreme Court. No, he said firmly, but added jokingly that he had received "about fifty different suggestions" for improving the federal government that ranged from "abolishing the Supreme Court" to "abolishing the president." Everyone laughed.

FDR's inveterate sense of humor was, as usual, on public display. But privately, he did not consider the Hughes Court a laughing matter.

7

"A Stratosphere of Icy Certainty"

"As soon as Chief Justice Hughes had finished reading the opinion," wrote the respected journalist Henry Pringle in *The New Yorker*, "there *was* no NRA in law or in fact." The *Schechter* decision demonstrated the awesome power of the Supreme Court, Pringle observed. It also underscored the importance of judicial review of federal legislation, which "may well prove our most important contribution to the science of government." He marveled at the Court's unchallenged authority, notwithstanding the controversial decisions handed down on May 27. No serious voice had been raised in Congress or anywhere else to pack the Court with pro–New Deal jurists. "[E]ven the wildest Brain Truster would shrink from any proposal to do so," he reported.

The first of Pringle's three long, admiring articles on Chief Justice Hughes appeared in *The New Yorker* a month after Black Monday. They traced in detail Hughes's early career in New York as fearless investigator of the utility and insurance industries, two-term reform governor, associate justice of the Supreme Court, Republican presidential candidate, and Secretary of State. Most of Pringle's attention, naturally, focused on Hughes's six years as Chief Justice, "the crown of a distinguished career." He described Hughes as a brilliant, impartial leader, dedicated to preserving the integrity of the Constitution and the Supreme Court of the United States.

To underscore Hughes's non-ideological approach, Pringle cited the Chief Justice's civil liberties opinions as well as those recognizing government's broad scope to regulate economic affairs. He concluded that "[Hughes] has ruled against capital, against labor, against the farmer and for the farmer, against Congress and for Congress, against the President and for him. Each time he has been loudly praised or privately damned. Such, perhaps, is the proper role for the Chief Justice of the United States."*

While Hughes was portrayed to be above politics, one of his brethren, Louis Brandeis, was fully engaged in a fierce, if indirect, argument with President Roosevelt over his New Deal policies. Immediately after the decisions were handed down on Black Monday, the seventy-eight-year-old Brandeis summoned two of Frankfurter's protégés, Benjamin Cohen and Thomas Corcoran, to the anteroom of the Court clerk's office. Visibly agitated, he told the young attorneys that "[t]he President has been living in a fool's paradise." He demanded that Frankfurter arrange an immediate meeting with Roosevelt and instruct the president that "these three decisions change everything." The president must be told that "[a]ll of the powers of the States cannot be centralized in the Federal government."

A few weeks later, Brandeis expanded on his theme in an off-the-record interview with two reporters at his vacation home in Chatham on Cape Cod. He denounced bigness in government and angrily hurled back Roosevelt's dismissive "horse-and-buggy" criticism of the Court. The three decisions on Black Monday did not return the Court to "horse-and-buggy" days, he said, but "compelled a return to human limitations." The NRA was an unseemly example of bloated government. The great advances in economic and social regulation had emerged from the states and localities, he said, not from the federal government. Far from delivering a destructive blow to the nation, the Court had performed a great public service in halting the centralizing tendencies of the Roosevelt administration.

Shortly after Roosevelt's attack on the *Schechter* decision at his May 31 press conference, he received a letter from former Secretary of State Henry Stimson expressing alarm that the president might push for a constitutional

---

* Hughes was generally satisfied with *The New Yorker* profile, taking exception only to Pringle's repetition of the widely circulated rumor that Hoover had preferred Justice Stone to be Chief Justice and only offered the position to Hughes on the assumption that he would decline. In his autobiographical notes, Hughes, still smarting from the rumor, quoted from Pringle's profile and followed it with a long quotation from a letter that Hoover later wrote him explicitly denying the rumor.

amendment to take ultimate authority in economic matters away from the Court. Stimson told Roosevelt that he had been unfair to the Court, which, in a series of decisions, had carefully developed the law to allow the federal government to deal with national economic problems. If the Court had ruled in favor of the government in *Schechter*, Stimson added, he did not see what principled limits could be imposed on federal power over the economy.

In a cordial reply, Roosevelt sought to assure Stimson that he remained open to sensible solutions to the problems posed by the Hughes Court. Reporters had taken his remarks out of context, he said. His major complaint with the *Schechter* decision was the "dictum" (a statement not essential to the decision) that appeared to severely limit the federal government's ability to regulate commerce with direct interstate implications. "[I]f the dictum is followed in the future," he wrote Stimson, "the Court would probably find only ten per cent of actual transactions to be directly in interstate commerce." He did not endorse a constitutional amendment or any other drastic action. Instead, he assured Stimson "that I am trying to look at several angles and that I hope something practical can be worked out."

Even before he wrote Stimson, the president's focus had turned from the Court to Congress. In a June 4 memorandum to Democratic legislative leaders, he listed in caps nine "must" bills that should be passed before the first session of the Seventy-fourth Congress adjourned for the summer. Congressmen, desperate to escape hot, steamy Washington, protested vociferously. But the president whipped them forward, determined to recapture the momentum of the first six months of the congressional session. FDR's ambitious agenda included passage of the Social Security Act; the Wagner Act, which created the National Labor Relations Board and mandated industry's collective bargaining with labor; the Wealth Tax Act, which increased income and estate tax rates and imposed a tax on corporate income (known to readers of the conservative Hearst newspapers as "Soak the Successful"); and the Public Utilities Holding Company Act, whose purpose was to regulate and ultimately eliminate giant utility holding companies.

Justice Brandeis, recent outspoken critic of the NRA, was Roosevelt's most enthusiastic ally in fighting the massive lobbying effort mounted by utility companies to defeat the holding company bill. "F.D. is making a gallant fight," Brandeis wrote the crusading liberal editor Norman Hapgood, "and seems to appreciate fully the evils of bigness."

Throughout the whirl of legislative activity, Roosevelt did not lose sight of the threatening shadow of the Hughes Court. He attempted to assuage the constitutional concerns of nervous congressmen considering the Guffey-Snyder bill to regulate the troubled bituminous coal industry. The proposed legislation established an NRA-like regulatory scheme for the coal industry aimed at stabilizing prices, wages, and production levels, and imposing industrial codes. Roosevelt wrote Congressman Samuel Hill, chairman of the subcommittee of the Ways and Means Committee charged with reporting on the bill: "Manifestly, no one is in a position to give assurance that the proposed act will withstand constitutional tests. [But] the situation is so urgent and the benefits of the legislation so evident that all doubts should be resolved in favor of the bill, leaving to the courts, in an orderly fashion, the ultimate question of constitutionality." In an apparent conciliatory gesture toward the Court, he added: "A decision by the Supreme Court relative to this measure would be helpful as indicating [the] constitutional limits within which the Government must operate." Meanwhile, the president suggested, Hill's subcommittee should not permit doubts about the bill's constitutionality, "however reasonable," to block the suggested legislation. The bill was reported out of committee and narrowly passed in the House and Senate.

When Congress finally adjourned on August 27, 1935, FDR could claim a remarkable record of achievement in what historians later labeled the "Second Hundred Days" (actually eighty-five days). Every significant bill he favored was enacted into law. Brandeisians were elated that the president appeared to finally be moving away from centralized planning and toward reform to shrink the size of business. Conservatives in Congress and the press continued to accuse FDR of dictatorial ambitions. Even if Roosevelt were inclined to impose some grand label on his accomplishments (he was not), he was too exhausted to boast. "I was so tired," he told Henry Morgenthau, Jr., "that I would have enjoyed seeing you cry or would have gotten pleasure out of sticking pins into people and hurting them."

Though he had assured Stimson in June that he had no plans to introduce a constitutional amendment to curb the Court's power, he never fully abandoned the idea. During the summer, he encouraged the exchange of ideas on a proposed amendment with Homer Cummings, Stanley Reed, and Felix Frankfurter.* Roosevelt was confident that whatever course of

---

* The columnist Walter Lippmann, meanwhile, discouraged any further talk of a constitutional amendment. A new amendment, he wrote, would either achieve "1) an intolerable centralization of power or 2) a meaningless jumble of weasel words." He was convinced that the Court, if presented with carefully drafted legislation based upon thorough investigation and full debate, "will act very differently than it did in the *Schechter* case."

action he ultimately decided to take would be supported by the American people. Voters would not stand by idly while an obstructive Court frustrated the popular will. "If the Court does send the AAA [Agricultural Adjustment Act] flying like the NRA," he told a Justice Department official, "there might even be a revolution."

In early September, Roosevelt floated the idea of a constitutional amendment through a surrogate, George Creel, the Washington's correspondent for the weekly magazine *Collier's*, and an old friend from the Wilson administration. "It is the deep conviction of Franklin D. Roosevelt," Creel's article began, "that the Constitution was never meant to be a 'dead hand,' chilling human aspiration and blocking humanity's advance, but that the founding fathers conceived it as a living force for the expression of the national will with respect to national needs." After the Court convened on the first Monday in October, Creel conceded that the justices could well strike down more New Deal statutes, pummeling the president with yet another "licking." Creel then delivered Roosevelt's message, and warning: If the Supreme Court continued to hold the present generation "powerless to meet social and economic problems that were not within the knowledge of the founding fathers," he wrote, "then the President will have no other alternative than to go to the country with a Constitutional amendment that will lift the Dead Hand, giving the people of today the right to deal with today's vital issues."

The article stirred no groundswell of support for a constitutional amendment, as Roosevelt had hoped. A Gallup poll published the same month that Creel's article appeared showed that 53 percent of respondents opposed a curb on the Court's power to invalidate congressional legislation, only 31 percent favored it, and the rest had no opinion. At the same time, Gallup reported, Roosevelt's popularity had continued to drop at a rate of one percentage point a month for more than a year. In September 1935, just over 50 percent of Americans polled by Gallup supported the president, his lowest approval rating since he had taken the presidential oath.

Charles Evans Hughes and Antoinette always looked forward to their summer vacations together. In Hughes's first year as Chief Justice, the couple had traveled through Europe, motoring in France, Germany, and Switzerland, before returning to France for a final few days in Paris. The next year they chose a Mediterranean route, spending a week in Sicily, then journeying to Rome, and north by car to Florence, Siena, Bologna, and the northern lakes. Beginning in 1932, they limited their travel to the United States and Canada, delighting in the spontaneity of their choices for lodging. If they spotted an inn that looked comfortable and attractive, they stopped and stayed for the night. In June 1935, shortly after Hughes had read his *Schechter* opinion to a packed courtroom, he and Antoinette drove to New Hampshire's White Mountains, took a steamer through the Great Lakes, then headed west, visiting Yellowstone and Glacier national parks, before boarding an eastbound train that took them across the continent. They ended their summer adventure in Montreal.

When Hughes returned to Washington in late September, he anticipated presiding at the October 1935 Court term in a spectacular new judicial home. For seventy-five years, the Court had heard oral arguments in the intimate old Senate chamber of the Capitol. Beginning in October, they would meet in an imposing four-story white-marble building constructed behind the Capitol at a cost of $10 million. The enormous modern-day Greek temple, replete with towering Corinthian columns and a pediment frieze above the entrance, was the dream of Hughes's predecessor, Chief Justice Taft.

The marble alone cost more than $3 million, transported from Spain and Italy and from quarries in Sylacauga, Alabama. Builders boasted that the new Supreme Court building contained more marble than any structure in the world. In the triangular pediment above the huge Corinthian columns, the sculptor Robert Ingersoll Aitken carved a roster of heroes. Chief Justice Hughes was seated, contemplatively, with one elbow resting on his knee, reminiscent of Rodin's *The Thinker*. Chief Justice Marshall was depicted as a boy, and a plump William Howard Taft as a student at Yale.*

Most of the justices were embarrassed by the grandeur of the building and their spacious three-room suite of offices. Brandeis vowed to continue to do all his work at home. The elaborate new judicial home reminded

---

* The sculptor of the frieze included himself in the pantheon of heroes, as well as Cass Gilbert, the architect of the building. Adding to the incongruity, Elihu Root, a distinguished public servant who did not serve on the Court, was there. But no other justice made the final cut, not even the legendary Oliver Wendell Holmes, Jr. Although Hughes was the chairman of the Supreme Court Building Commission, he expressed surprise when he discovered his sculpted presence on the frieze.

one Justice of a faux Taj Mahal. "On the first day we hold court there," he said sourly, "the Chief should go in on an elephant and the rest of us on stilts."

The Chief Justice did not call attention to the Court's sumptuous new quarters on October 7, the first day of the new term. He opened the proceedings at noon, as usual, without taking any official notice of the new building. After swearing in a host of new attorneys to the Supreme Court bar, Hughes and his brethren began what promised to be another tumultuous term. Already on the docket was a challenge to the Agricultural Adjustment Act, the second major pillar of FDR's ambitious legislative edifice to revive the economy (the first, the NIRA, was already in ruins, as a result of the Court's *Schechter* decision). The justices also had agreed to hear arguments in a case challenging the constitutionality of the Tennessee Valley Authority. And though the Guffey-Snyder Act regulating the bituminous coal industry had been passed in the late summer, there was rising anxiety among New Dealers that the justices would later add a case to their calendar challenging that legislation.

When the term began, a disconsolate Justice Stone had more serious concerns to brood about than what he considered to be the needlessly ostentatious new Court building. He worried that the Court majority, led by the four conservative ideologues and abetted by Hughes and Roberts, would run roughshod over every piece of New Deal legislation that came before them. Emboldened by last term's devastation of Roosevelt's New Deal, they would forsake the judicial craft, he feared, and act as a super legislature to strike down any law that did not comport with their conservative political values. An obscure tax case from Vermont, argued during the second week of the term, deepened his anxiety.

At issue in *Colgate v. Harvey* was a Vermont tax assessment on out-of-state loans that was higher than the rate from loans originating within the state. The primary question addressed in the lawyers' briefs and at oral argument was whether Vermont's discriminatory tax was a violation of the equal protection clause of the Fourteenth Amendment. Stone's ire was immediately raised at the justices' Saturday conference following the oral arguments when Chief Justice Hughes presented the case "in his usual fashion of greatly over-elaborating the unimportant details of the case and disposing, by *ipse dixit*, in a sentence of two of the vital question."

But Stone was much less aggravated by Hughes's presentation than by the justices' vote. Hughes and Roberts joined the four conservatives in striking down the Vermont law as a violation of the equal protection clause. Stone, Brandeis, and Cardozo, in dissent, argued that no Court precedent supported the majority's conclusion that the equal protection clause restrained Vermont's power to tax the income of a citizen derived from sources outside the state. Stone prepared to write a blistering dissent—a factor, he thought, that Hughes considered when he assigned the majority opinion to Justice Sutherland. It was another example, in Stone's mind, of the risk-averse Chief Justice avoiding "any unnecessary exposure to attack."

Stone's dissent was so sharp, asserting that there was no basis in constitutional law for striking down the Vermont law on equal protection grounds, that Sutherland redrafted his original opinion. In a later draft, Sutherland pinned the constitutional violation on the privileges and immunities clause of the Fourteenth Amendment.* The problem with that interpretation was that the privileges and immunities clause had been rendered a dead letter by the Court almost immediately after the amendment had been ratified in 1868. In more than fifty years, the Court had never struck down a state law as a violation of the clause.

Sutherland's new draft was even more infuriating to Stone than his first one. The argument that the Vermont law violated the privileges and immunities clause had not been made at oral argument or discussed at the justices' conference. Stone was appalled by the shoddy judicial process that resulted in Sutherland's revised majority opinion, which was supported by the same five members who had voted to strike down the Vermont law at conference on equal protection grounds.

The Court's decision in the Vermont tax case did not, of course, have anything to do with New Deal legislation. But Stone saw an ominous pattern in the new majority's decisions that threatened to bury more New Deal legislation and, at the same time, undermine the integrity of the Court. "The Court suffered in the case [*Colgate v. Harvey*], as it has in a good many recent ones, from an overstimulated inventive genius," he wrote Frankfurter shortly after the decision was printed. "If the opinion had rested on the equal protection clause it would have merely added another bad

---

* The Fourteenth Amendment provides, in part: "No State shall make or enforce any law which shall abridge the privileges and immunities of citizens of the United States . . . nor deny to any person within its jurisdiction the equal protection of the laws."

decision to a considerable group. This way of dealing with constitutional questions is even more alarming than the results themselves."

After the *Colgate* decision was announced, Frankfurter wired Stone: "Gosh, it is unbelievable. Apparently history and precedents mean nothing. I don't think I have ever been more shocked."

Frankfurter considered the *Colgate* decision an unfortunate contribution to a disturbing series of ill-conceived Hughes Court rulings. In an article that he co-authored with his fellow Harvard professor, Henry Hart, Jr., Frankfurter attacked Hughes's *Schechter* opinion for resurrecting the direct-indirect commerce clause test. The Court, he maintained, could have struck down the NRA on the single ground that Congress had unconstitutionally delegated authority to the president. "Constitutional theory and practice of a century and a half united in protest against such advisory pronouncements," he and Hart wrote in their article reviewing *Schechter* and other Court's recent decisions. They advised the Court to confine itself to the narrowest possible constitutional grounds, so as to leave as much congressional power as possible intact.*

Frankfurter and Stone would soon have the opportunity to further test their theory that the Hughes Court majority appeared ready to destroy the New Deal, regardless of the soundness of its judicial method. On December 9, the Court heard arguments in *United States v. Butler*, the first major challenge to the New Deal of the October 1935 term. At stake was the survival of the Agricultural Adjustment Act, the legislative core of FDR's strategy to revive the agricultural economy.

As the Democratic presidential candidate in the fall of 1932, Roosevelt had promised to introduce an innovative agricultural program aimed at dealing with the crucial problem of depressed farm prices and mounting surpluses. He had been vague on the details during the campaign, but the Agricultural Adjustment Act, passed by Congress in May 1933, provided federal regulations to transform FDR's promise into tangible results. Under the statute, farmers were paid directly by the federal government not to

---

* Frankfurter and Hart's criticism of *Schechter*, though carefully argued for an academic readership, was not so different from Roosevelt's. The president had complained of the unnecessary "dictum" in Hughes's opinion and, more generally, that the Court had not shown appropriate deference to Congress.

produce crops beyond an allotment set by the Secretary of Agriculture. The allotment payments were funded by a processing tax levied against millers, meatpackers, canners, and textile manufacturers. The purpose of the acreage limits was to cut production and raise commodity prices on the open market.

The AAA was one of Roosevelt's proudest achievements. In the first two years of its existence, farm incomes and food prices doubled. But the legislation was no panacea; the agricultural economy did not return to the prosperity that had immediately followed the First World War. Meanwhile, opponents, outraged by the act's centralized planning, took their complaints to court. By the fall of 1935, more than 1,700 law suits had been filed in federal district courts across the country challenging the constitutionality of the legislation.

Despite the proliferating lawsuits, Roosevelt continued to vigorously defend the act. He told a Fremont, Nebraska, audience on September 28, 1935, that the legislation, despite its "imperfections," had brought enormous benefits to farmers. Estimated farm income in 1935, he said, would total $5 billion more than in 1932. The Agricultural Adjustment Act was not just good policy, he proclaimed, but reflected the high national purpose envisioned by the Framers. "I like to think that agricultural adjustment is an expression, in concrete form, of the human rights those farmer patriots sought to win when they stood at the bridge at Concord, when they proclaimed the Declaration of Independence, and when they perpetuated these ideals by the adoption of the Constitution." In passing the act, the New Deal Congress had understood that "the true function of government under your Constitution [is] to promote the general welfare." The president reiterated his defense of the act in an address to the American Farm Bureau Federation in Chicago on December 9, the day the Court began to hear arguments in *United States v. Butler*, which challenged the constitutionality of the legislation.

The case before the Supreme Court had been initiated by William Butler, former Republican senator from Massachusetts, manager of Calvin Coolidge's presidential campaign in 1924, and past chairman of the Republican National Committee. He sued on behalf of Hoosac Mills, a Massachusetts cotton textile manufacturing firm that had once turned a handsome profit (and made Butler rich), but now faced bankruptcy primarily as a result of competition from southern textile mills. Butler, as a receiver in the Hoosac Mills bankruptcy, went to federal district court in Boston to prevent the government from collecting the $20,000 a month AAA processing fee levied against the cotton textile corporation. The district court rejected Butler's argument, but the federal appeals court reversed, declaring the Agricultural Adjustment Act unconstitutional. That appellate decision set up the showdown in the Supreme Court on December 9.

Butler's attorney for the Court argument was George Wharton Pepper, Philadelphia's most eminent attorney and a close friend of Justice Roberts. Pepper, who taught Roberts law at the University of Pennsylvania, had recommended him to President Coolidge to serve as special prosecutor investigating the Teapot Dome scandal. In 1930, he had urged President Hoover to appoint Roberts to the Supreme Court.

All 238 seats in the new courtroom were filled for the two days of oral arguments in the *Butler* case. Those lucky enough to be seated included a dozen U.S. senators, former Democratic presidential candidate John W. Davis, the Archbishop of York, scores of New Dealers and anti-New Dealers, and the popular crooner Rudy Vallee. Another 2,000 people waited outside the chamber, the greatest crowd that Court officials could remember.

At the outset of his argument for the government, Solicitor General Stanley Reed described the broad purposes of the Agricultural Adjustment Act as part of a "concerted effort to bring about recovery." He adopted Roosevelt's argument in his Fremont speech that the act's benefit payments to farmers was an appropriation by Congress "to be in the general welfare."* But the continuity of Reed's argument was quickly destroyed by a barrage of hostile questions from three of the Court's most conservative members, Justices Butler, McReynolds, and Sutherland. The fourth conservative, seventy-six-year-old Justice Van Devanter, said little.

Justice Sutherland interrupted Reed to suggest that regulating agricultural production was not within Congress's authority. "Isn't there a distinction between a public purpose of the United States and a local public purpose?" he asked pointedly.

---

* Article I, section 8, provides: "The Congress shall have Power To lay and collect Taxes . . . [to] provide for the common Defence and general Welfare of the United States. . . ." After the *Schechter* decision, Reed was understandably reluctant to argue that the act could be justified as a congressional regulation of interstate commerce.

Justice McReynolds then began quizzing Reed in an intimidating tone of voice.

"Who fixes the tax, Mr. Solicitor?" McReynolds asked curtly.

Reed replied that Congress devised the formula, and he began reading provisions of the statute relating to the processing tax.

"The farmer buys all sorts of things," McReynolds retorted sarcastically. "He buys silk stockings and woolen coats. Which is it that controls the tax?"

Reed, clearly disconcerted by McReynolds's questioning, responded that the processing tax was determined by a complicated formula based on statistics compiled in the Department of Agriculture.

Justice Brandeis came to the struggling Reed's rescue, as a law professor might guide a floundering student. He asked the Solicitor General to read the Secretary of Agriculture's proclamation fixing the rate of the processing tax on cotton at 4.2 cents per pound.

"Is that a very definite finding?" McReynolds asked.

"It is a finding by the Secretary of Agriculture on certain information in the Department of Agriculture," Reed replied tentatively.

"It is a determination of the rate—a finding as a basis of administrative action," Brandeis interjected emphatically.

Justice Butler probed further, asking Reed for the exact method used for determining the processing tax.

Reed could not answer Butler's question, referring the justice to the method outlined in the government's brief.

Again, Brandeis broke in to elicit from Reed the fact that the method used by the Department of Agriculture to calculate the processing tax was one used by other departments in statistical determinations.

On the second day of arguments, when Reed was also forced to defend a second New Deal statute, the Bankhead Cotton Control Law, he collapsed in his chair from physical exhaustion, the apparent victim of the constant, withering questions from the bench. Out of concern for the Solicitor General's health, Chief Justice Hughes adjourned the proceedings for the day.

In contrast to Reed's ordeal, his opponent in the *Butler* case, George Wharton Pepper, sailed through his argument virtually without interruption. He followed up on Justice Sutherland's point that agricultural policy could only be set by the states and local governments, not by Congress. He contended that the processing tax was a regulation disguised as a reve-

Franklin D. Roosevelt, age nineteen, with his parents, James and Sara, posing for a formal portrait in Poughkeepsie, New York, in 1899. His parents doted on their only child.

Charlie Hughes, age four, with his parents, the Reverend David Charles Hughes and his wife, Mary Catherine, about 1866. Hughes's parents hoped that their son would follow the Reverend Hughes into the ministry.

At Groton, Franklin competed earnestly in athletics but did not excel. He became manager of the prep school's baseball team and is pictured here (in straw hat) with team members.

4

At Brown University Hughes was elected to Phi Beta Kappa in his junior year. He graduated third in his class in 1881 and is shown here in his graduation photograph.

Franklin and Eleanor Roosevelt sitting together at Hyde Park, N.Y., in 1906. It was one year after their wedding.

Antoinette and Charles Evans Hughes, photographed at the time of their wedding in 1888. Hughes adored his wife, writing love poems to her on her birthday and their wedding anniversary during their more than fifty years of marriage.

Hughes campaigning for governor of New York in 1906. He successfully ran as a reform-minded Republican against his Democratic opponent, the publishing magnate William Randolph Hearst, whose newspapers, he charged, ignored reason and dispassionate discussion.

FDR in his first political campaign shaking hands with voters in Dutchess County in his successful race for a seat in the New York Senate in 1910. His victory was the first step in his ambitious plan to emulate his distant cousin, Theodore Roosevelt, who had won a seat in the New York legislature and later served as assistant secretary of the navy before being elected president of the United States.

Republican presidential candidate Hughes campaigning in 1916. He ran a lackluster campaign and lost California by less than 4,000 votes, allowing President Woodrow Wilson to eke out a re-election victory.

Secretary of State Hughes, center, taking a break from meetings with other world leaders at the Washington Disarmament Conference in 1921. Left to right, Prince Tokugawa of Japan, Arthur James Balfour of Great Britain, Hughes, Premier Aristide Briand of France, Baron de Cartier of Belgium, Senator Schanzer of Italy, and Viscount d'Alte of Portugal. The conference was a triumph for Hughes, who led negotiations that resulted in a treaty imposing strict limits on warship tonnage of the major naval powers.

Roosevelt, the Democratic vice presidential candidate in 1920, in Billings, Montana. Left to right, Louis Howe, Tom Lynch, Roosevelt, and Marvin MacIntyre. Howe was FDR's indispensable political strategist from 1912 until his death in 1936. Lynch, a Dutchess County Democratic leader, gave critical support to FDR during his first campaign for the state senate. MacIntyre served as Roosevelt's press secretary during his vice presidential campaign and continued to work for him as president.

Democratic presidential candidate Governor James Cox of Ohio and Roosevelt marching in a parade in Dayton, Ohio, during the 1920 campaign. They were trounced in the election by U.S. Senator Warren G. Harding of Ohio and his vice presidential running mate, Governor Calvin Coolidge of Massachusetts.

Roosevelt speaking in Topeka, Kansas, during his presidential campaign in 1932. As part of his pledge of a "new deal for the American people," FDR promised farmers in Kansas and other agricultural states that the federal government would provide major assistance to ease credit, lower taxes, and bolster depressed farm prices.

Roosevelt and President Herbert Hoover being driven to FDR's inauguration on March 4, 1933. The two men, who detested each other, barely spoke during the ride to the Capitol. After the ceremony they never saw each other again.

President Roosevelt being sworn in by Chief Justice Hughes for his second term during a torrential rain storm on January 20, 1937. When Hughes recited the oath to "support the Constitution," FDR recalled he felt like saying, "Yes, but it's the Constitution as I understand it, flexible enough to meet any new problem of democracy—not the kind of Constitution your Court has raised up as a barrier to progress and democracy."

Chief Justice Hughes, seated in the center, poses with his brethren for a formal portrait of the Supreme Court in 1932. Front row, Louis Brandeis, Willis Van Devanter, Hughes, James McReynolds, and George Sutherland. Back row, Owen Roberts, Pierce Butler, Harlan Fiske Stone, and Benjamin Cardozo. Within a two-year period (1935–36), a Court majority struck down major New Deal statutes, leading FDR to propose his Court-packing plan in early 1937.

Roosevelt discussing his Court-packing plan in a fireside chat on March 9, 1937. The point had been reached as a nation, he told his radio audience, "where we must take action to save the Constitution from the Court and the Court from itself."

"To Furnish The Supreme Court Practical Assistance."

THIS ACT SHALL TAKE EFFECT ON THE 30TH DAY AFTER THE DATE OF ITS ENACTMENT.

CONGRESS

Great Social Changes Sweep World Today

An editorial cartoon depicting the effect of Roosevelt's Court-packing plan, with six new appointees in the president's image standing behind the nine sitting justices, providing "practical assistance."

A political cartoon, entitled "Bull's Eye," showing the devastating effect of Chief Justice Hughes's seven-page letter to the Senate Judiciary Committee demonstrating that, contrary to Roosevelt's claim, the justices were fully abreast of their judicial work. Roosevelt later said, in grudging admiration, that Hughes was the best politician in the country.

Hughes addressing a joint session of Congress on March 4, 1939, to commemorate the sesquicentennial of the meeting of the first Congress. At the time, Hughes was suffering from a bleeding ulcer and could hardly walk to the podium unassisted. He nonetheless completed his speech and insisted that his colleagues join him for a judicial conference that afternoon.

Roosevelt addressing a joint session of Congress on December 8, 1941, reporting that Japanese planes had bombed the U.S. fleet at Pearl Harbor in what he declared was a day that would "live in infamy." FDR had dictated his short speech to his secretary, Grace Tully, the previous afternoon after he learned of Japan's surprise attack.

Hughes and his wife, Antoinette, leaving the White House following Roosevelt's funeral on April 14, 1945.

nue measure, and beyond Congress's constitutional powers. He questioned the voluntary nature of the domestic allotment plan, comparing it to a poll of college students "to see if they favored the continuance of fathers' allowances."

Pepper ended his argument in a crescendo of emotion: "I believe I am standing here today pleading the cause of the America I love. I pray Almighty God that not in my time will the land of the regimented be substituted for the land of the free." After sitting down at counsel's table, he sobbed.

Four days later, Chief Justice Hughes and five of his colleagues joined President Roosevelt at the Gridiron Dinner for an evening of irreverent skits performed by the national press corps. "Is it not true that the Constitution is what the judges say it is?" asked a citizen in one skit, paraphrasing the Chief Justice's often misinterpreted opinion expressed when he was governor of New York. "It's supposed to be," another replied, "but what those judges say ain't necessarily so," said another, as a chorus continued the dialogue in song to the tune of Gershwin's "It Ain't Necessarily So." A darker skit portrayed the four Jewish Schechter brothers bringing their "most famous chickens in the world" to the 1936 Olympic Games in Berlin. "Heil Hitler!" one shouted. "Heil Roosevelt!" said another. "Heil with 'em all!" said a third. In the final skit, nine journalists dressed as Athenian soldiers were presented as "the nine wisest men in the entire world." They turned out not to be the justices of the U.S. Supreme Court but members of the conservative Liberty League. The justices in attendance smiled bravely.

In his closing remarks, Roosevelt joked, "I suppose I should be in a mood of appropriate humility and contrition for all the sins I have committed and all the wisecrack statesmanship which I have failed to display." But then his mood turned serious. "I am not one who fears for the survival of our political institutions," he said, "or of the broad structure of our national economic life. I believe that part of the genius of our form of government is its adaptiveness to the needs of changing times. The wise and sound general principles upon which our government rests, and from which our peace and happiness are derived, were not intended to become rigid formulae, inflexible, resistant to the stresses and strains . . . out of which true progress arises."

Afterward, Chief Justice Hughes, who sat only one chair away, leaned toward the president and warmly congratulated him.

Roosevelt's informal remarks offered a more eloquent defense of the Agricultural Adjustment Act than the battered Solicitor General Reed had managed in Court a few days earlier. But it was too late. Only a few hours before the Gridiron Dinner, the justices had met in conference to decide the fate of the act.

At the justices' Saturday conference, Hughes had begun the discussion of the *Butler* case by stating his opinion that the statute should be overturned as an improper delegation of congressional authority. On the merits, Hughes said that the act was a regulation of agriculture that invaded the reserve rights of the states under the Tenth Amendment.* He emphasized that farmers could only receive payments from the processing tax by signing contracts with the Secretary of Agriculture to restrict production.

The four conservatives and Roberts objected to basing the Court's opinion on the delegation issue, as Hughes had suggested. Instead, they seized upon the Chief Justice's view that the AAA was an unconstitutional regulation of agriculture. Stone was annoyed that there was no discussion of Hughes's view that the tax was an unconstitutional federal regulation. He was even more aggravated that there was no discussion of the question whether the processing tax was coercive, an issue that he thought crucial to the Court's decision. His view, which he expressed to his colleagues, was that there was no coercion and that a careful analysis of the relationship of conditional grants or the AAA contracts to the spending power would have proved his point. He later complained privately that Hughes had rushed the justices through the *Butler* discussion without adequate consideration of his argument.

The justices voted 6–2 to strike down the Agricultural Adjustment Act, with Justice Brandeis, a day later, joining the other two liberals, Cardozo and Stone, in dissent.

Hughes assigned the majority opinion in the *Butler* case to Justice Roberts. Neither Roberts nor the Chief Justice had said much during the oral arguments, apparently content to let Butler, McReynolds, and Sutherland fire away at the embattled Solicitor General. After the justices' conference, Hughes had suggested to Roberts that he include in his majority opinion a discussion of the historical interpretation of Congress's authority to tax and spend for "the general welfare," with particular attention to the view of Alexander Hamilton. Taking Hughes's advice, Roberts pointed out in his

---

* The Tenth Amendment states: "The powers not delegated to the United States by the Constitution, nor prohibited by it to the States, are reserved to the States respectively, or to the people."

draft opinion that the two principal architects of the Constitution, Madison and Hamilton, had disagreed on how Congress's power to tax and spend for the general welfare should be interpreted. Madison had insisted that Congress could only promote "the general welfare" by exercising the explicit authority subsequently granted, such as regulating interstate commerce, establishing post offices, or supporting the military services. Hamilton took a more capacious view of Congress's power, arguing that legislation was constitutional so long as it promoted the nation's welfare, even if the law was not tethered to a specific constitutional grant of authority.

If Roosevelt could have peered over Robert's shoulder while the justice wrote about the Madison-Hamilton disagreement, he would have been encouraged. Roberts contended that Hamilton was correct in his more expansive interpretation, suggesting that the Court might well find the Agricultural Adjustment Act constitutional. After all, as Roosevelt had argued, the statute was enacted to solve a national economic problem by increasing farmers' persistently depressed incomes and raising agricultural prices throughout the country. And as he had pointed out in his Fremont speech, both farm income and agricultural prices had increased dramatically since the New Deal legislation was passed.

Unfortunately for Roosevelt and the New Deal, after Roberts embraced the Hamiltonian interpretation of congressional authority, he proceeded to condemn the act for a variety of constitutional sins. In his full-fledged attack on the legislation, Robert's opinion tracked closely to the arguments made in open court by his old Pennsylvania friend, George Wharton Pepper. His discussion of Hamilton's broad interpretation of Congress's taxing and spending authority was largely irrelevant, he wrote, since the act "invades the reserve rights of the states." Just why Roberts was so certain in arriving at this conclusion was not self-evident. His constitutional source, the Tenth Amendment, provides only that whatever powers not given the federal government are retained by the states. But nothing in that amendment or anywhere else in the Constitution forbids Congress from regulating agricultural production, as Roberts so confidently proclaimed.*

---

* Roberts's stark delineation between federal and state constitutional authority made a mockery of his professed approach to constitutional interpretation in *Butler*. According to Roberts, his task was simple: "When an act of Congress is appropriately challenged in the courts . . . the judicial branch of the government has only one duty; to lay the article of the Constitution which is invoked beside the statute which is challenged and to decide whether the latter squares with the former."

Roberts summarily dismissed the government's argument that the processing tax was constitutional. It was not really a tax at all, he maintained, because it expropriated "money from one group for the benefit of another." It was a regulation to control agricultural production, he wrote, echoing Pepper's argument. He also rejected the administration's contention that the acreage allotment plan was voluntary: "The power to confer or withhold unlimited benefits is the power to coerce or destroy." The tax was forced regimentation by another name, as Pepper had contended. With scant textual or historical documentation, Roberts rejected as fanciful the idea that the Framers "by a single clause gave power to the Congress to tear down the barriers, to invade the states' jurisdiction, and to become a parliament of the whole people, subject to no restrictions save such as are self-imposed." It was the Court's duty to rein in this renegade Congress, he concluded, and declare the Agricultural Adjustment Act unconstitutional.

Justice Stone spent most of New Year's Day, 1936, working on his dissent in the *Butler* case. Roberts's dogmatic majority opinion spurred him to mount a fierce counterattack. Challenging Roberts's claim that the act was an infringement of state power, Stone described Congress's broad constitutional power to tax and spend for the general welfare in a succinct, carefully reasoned narrative. Congress's use of money for the general welfare, he wrote, is a substantive power granted in general and unambiguous terms, similar to Congress's authority to coin money or declare war. Just as Congress may choose the means to support the armed forces or to provide the nation's currency, he continued, it may choose the means to meet the nation's economic challenges. Justice Roberts's assertion that states' rights imposed constitutional limits on Congress's authority to tax and spend for the general welfare, he wrote, "do not find their origin in any express provision of the Constitution."

Stone gave short shrift to Roberts's claim that Congress's processing tax was unlawfully coercive. It was a contradiction is terms, he wrote, to say that "there is power to spend for the national welfare, while rejecting any power to impose conditions reasonably adapted to the attainment of the end which alone would justify the expenditure." He charged that Roberts's flawed reasoning would lead to absurd results, and he offered a few examples. Should the government give seeds to farmers, but not be able to condition the gift upon their being planted in places where they are most needed or even planted at all? Could Congress provide money for the unemployed and not require that they shall give their labor in return?

Had Congress acted unconstitutionally in passing the Morrill Act, which encouraged the teaching of the science of agriculture by offering grants to state educational institutions on the condition that they be used to fulfill Congress's purpose?

Stone conceded that there were a wide range of opinions on the wisdom of the Agricultural Adjustment Act. The Court's role was not to pass on the wisdom of the legislation, he admonished, but only to decide if Congress had the constitutional authority to enact it. Stone himself had serious reservations about the wisdom of the act. But he suggested that Roberts, in attacking the New Deal Congress, had pointed an accusing finger at the wrong branch of government. "Courts are not the only agency of government that must be assumed to have capacity to govern," he noted. He reprimanded the Court majority, not Congress, for failing to exercise constitutional restraint. In a final swipe at the *Butler* majority, Stone reminded his fellow life-tenured justices that "the only check upon our own exercise of power is our own sense of self-restraint."

Roberts resented the vehemence of Stone's dissent and complained to the Chief Justice. Hughes refused to intervene, suggesting that Roberts take up the matter with Brandeis, who perhaps could mediate between the two justices. Brandeis refused, saying that he approved of Stone's dissent. "I join in a fine job," he wrote on Stone's circulating draft.

If Roberts was bruised by Stone's attack, he did not show it on January 6, 1936, when he recited his *Butler* opinion in a firm, deliberate voice before a crowded courtroom. Turning from left to right, as a experienced lecturer might address his audience, Roberts scarcely glanced at his written text as he delivered his twenty-page opinion from memory. It was a dazzling display of the justice's retentive powers, if not his talent for illuminating constitutional analysis. Reporters did not wait for Roberts to reach the end of his opinion. Once he had said that the Agricultural Adjustment Act was unconstitutional, they sent the news by pneumatic tube to the basement newsroom where the decision was wired to the waiting outside world.

After Roberts had finished his recitation, Stone read his dissent, trying unsuccessfully to hide his emotions. "There was fire there that flashed," wrote *The Washington Post's* Karl Schriftgiesser, "futile fire perhaps, but fire that came from deep down inside the man. There was bitterness, too, and scorn. You could not miss it."

At a winter cabinet meeting, Attorney General Cummings shared a tantalizing piece of gossip about the Court's deliberations in *Butler*. Cummings said, "There was a report to the effect that Chief Justice Hughes was willing to go either way in the AAA case." Cummings added that "the Chief Justice does not like five-to-four opinions and if Justice Roberts had been in favor of sustaining AAA, the Chief Justice would have cast his vote that way also."

Cummings's report that Hughes had been willing to change sides during the Court's *Butler* deliberations was wrong, as Stone's memorandum on the justices' conference confirmed. At the outset of the conference, Hughes said that the AAA should be struck down as unconstitutional. The Chief Justice, in fact, later applauded at least one aspect of Robert's majority opinion that doomed the act. He wrote that "the most significant and important ruling in the *Butler* case" was the majority's adoption of Hamilton's broad interpretation of the general welfare clause. Hughes's post-conference conversation with Roberts, in which he took Hamilton's position, was based on an opinion that he had written for a private client in 1919. The Chief Justice said nothing, however, about Roberts's abandonment of Hamilton's position immediately after stating it in his *Butler* opinion. Nor did he explain why he signed on to Roberts's exceedingly narrow interpretation of the general welfare clause in *Butler*.

"What bothers me most is the Chief Justice's role in all this business," Frankfurter wrote Stone shortly after the *Butler* decision had been announced; "something deep in me just balks at that assumption of obtuseness in Hughes."

Stone's reply to Frankfurter was not reassuring. "[P]erhaps it can be summed up in two phrases which you have doubtlessly heard me repeat before: 'lack of vision' and the unwillingness of certain gentlemen [Hughes and Roberts] to trust their own intellectual processes. The worst of it is that the one that you find it most difficult to understand is the one chiefly responsible." The problem, Stone concluded, was a failure of leadership by the Chief Justice.

Farm prices dropped precipitously after the *Butler* decision. In Iowa, the six justices in the majority were hanged in effigy. Roberts's opinion was labeled "a political stump speech" by Senator John Bankhead of Alabama. And Governor George Earle of Pennsylvania dismissed the Court as a "political body," accusing the six members in the majority of supporting the policies of the conservative Liberty League.

The Court's most outspoken and improbable defender was former New York governor Al Smith. Dressed in white tie and tails, Smith delivered a rousing anti–New Deal speech to 2,000 well-heeled members of the Liberty League in the banquet hall of Washington's Mayflower Hotel. He praised the Court, which had been forced to work overtime "throwing the alphabet out the window three letters at a time" to uproot the Roosevelt administration's socialistic policies. "It is all right with me if they want to disguise themselves as Norman Thomas or Karl Marx, or Lenin, or any of the rest of that bunch," he shouted, "but what I won't stand for is allowing them to march under the banner of Jefferson, Jackson and Cleveland."

Publicly, the president seemed unperturbed by the *Butler* decision or the savage attack by his former Democratic ally, Al Smith. He said nothing about the Smith speech. Nor did he express outrage at Roberts's *Butler* opinion, as he had at Hughes's majority opinion in *Schechter*. For the time being, he saw no need to upbraid the justices or declare war on the Court, as he had done at his news conference following the *Schechter* decision.

Privately, however, he was not so serene. In a "Memorandum for AAA file," he wrote that "the decision virtually prohibits the President and the Congress from the right, under modern conditions, to intervene reasonably in the regulation of nation-wide commerce and nation-wide agriculture." The *Butler* decision was arrived at by "a special technique," based on "the private, social philosophy of a majority of the nine appointed members of the Supreme Court," without regard to the views of the popularly elected members of Congress or the president of the United States.

Roosevelt's memorandum reflected his long-simmering hostility to a conservative Court that he felt was frustrating the popular will. At a cabinet meeting one week before *Butler*, Roosevelt had led a discussion of ways to curb the Court's power. According to Harold Ickes, the president told his cabinet that the idea of "packing the Supreme Court" was "distasteful." He also rejected the possibility of a series of constitutional amendments as too cumbersome. He then asked his cabinet to "very carefully" consider a single amendment: it would grant the Court explicit authority to declare an act of Congress unconstitutional, but permit Congress, after a congressional election, to reenact the law. The new law could not be struck down by the Court. The amendment, Roosevelt reasoned, would provide a popular referendum that effectively countermanded the Court's decision.

Typically, Roosevelt's thinking was not confined to a single means of accomplishing his desired goal—to restrain the Court. "What was the

McArdle case?" he asked Attorney General Cummings a week after *Butler*. "I am told that the Congress withdrew some act from the jurisdiction of the Court."*

Late in January 1936, Roosevelt told his cabinet that he did not object "to the Supreme Court declaring one New Deal statute after another unconstitutional." He anticipated that the Court's decisions would ultimately prove politically advantageous for his New Deal agenda. The president, Ickes reported, "believes that the Court will find itself pretty far out on a limb before it is through with it and that a real issue will be joined on which we can go to the country." The anti–New Deal Court decisions, he believed, "cast a deep shadow of doubt upon the ability of Congress ever at any time to protect the Nation against catastrophe by squarely meeting modern social and economic maladjustments."

Five days later, Roosevelt told Ickes that a federal statute to check the Court's power, rather than an amendment, was more attainable and could accomplish his objective. Even if the Court struck down a law enacted by Congress that undercut the justices' authority, Roosevelt said, he "would carry out the will of Congress through the offices of the United States Marshals and ignore the Court."

The president's threatened defiance of the Supreme Court's authority was startling. But he had made a similar threat a year earlier when he drafted a written response to anticipated adverse Court decisions in the gold clause cases. His intended public challenge to the Court in February 1935 had not been necessary, since the decisions in the gold clause cases did not, as he feared, undermine Congress's devaluation of the currency. But his public response in 1936 to additional Court decisions striking down New Deal legislation might be different. In late winter, Roosevelt awaited Court decisions in cases challenging other New Deal measures, including the Tennessee Valley Authority and the Guffey Act regulating the bituminous coal industry.

In mid-February, the president was mildly encouraged when the Court gave the New Deal a small victory by sustaining the validity of a contract

---

* Roosevelt's reference was to the 1868 Court decision, *Ex parte McCardle*, in which the justices had ruled that the Court lacked jurisdiction to hear the habeas corpus petition of a Mississippi newspaper editor imprisoned for violating a Reconstruction statute prohibiting the publication of "incendiary and libelous articles." When it appeared that the Court would hear the case, Congress had abruptly passed another law withdrawing the Court's appellate jurisdiction to review the original statute.

between the Tennessee Valley Authority and a private power company for the sale of excess power generated by TVA's Wilson Dam at Muscle Shoals, Alabama. Chief Justice Hughes, writing the majority opinion, rejected the claim by minority shareholders in the private power company that TVA, as a government agency, had no constitutional right to sell electricity. The dam was constructed to provide power for national defense and to improve the navigability of interstates waterways, Hughes wrote, both purposes well within Congress's authority to regulate interstate commerce.

Hughes's opinion was only a tepid victory for the administration, however, since it was carefully limited to the specific contract at issue. The Court did not decide the larger question of whether the ambitious multifaceted TVA program, which included massive soil reclamation, flood control, and electric power development programs, was constitutional. It seemed that the Court, even when rendering a ruling favorable to the administration, was determined to keep the New Deal on a very tight leash. "There was gratification in Administration circles that the threatened annihilation of its power policy had at least been postponed," Robert Jackson wrote. "But there was no assurance of the future projects other than the Wilson Dam, and every transaction by a corporation with the government was now subject to the risk of a law suit by a stockholder, whether as a stalking horse or otherwise."

Anxiety over the Court's direction prompted extensive discussions among New Deal congressmen and within the administration of imposing age limits on the members of the Supreme Court, either by statute or constitutional amendment. In March, the influential *New York Times* columnist Arthur Krock lent his imprimatur to the idea, quoting none other than Chief Justice Hughes. "Probably the faults of the system could be reduced if there were an age limit for justices who have served more than a certain number of years," Krock wrote. Citing the "eminent" author, Charles Evans Hughes, Krock noted that the Chief Justice had once suggested that an age limit of seventy-five might be salutary to rid the bench of judges who had "stayed too long."

Hughes wrote Krock in response to his column, but did not seem annoyed that the words from his 1927 lecture on the Supreme Court had been taken out of context. In fact, Hughes had supported the idea of keeping experienced judges who maintained their intellectual rigor on the bench. His concern was for judges whose tenure exceeded their physical and mental capacities. "I am glad you found my 'favorite author' a useful source," Hughes replied to Krock. Without reproving the columnist for his inaccuracies, the Chief Justice made his point in another way. The Court's oldest justices, Brandeis (seventy-nine) and Van Devanter (seventy-six), "are still going strong."

The Chief Justice continued to vigilantly protect the Court's public image. "I am happy to report that the Supreme Court is still functioning," he archly told members of the American Law Institute in early May. For two minutes he basked in uninterrupted applause from a predominantly conservative audience. Brushing aside criticism of his often divided Court, he asked why the justices, any more than others engaged in resolving complex issues, should be unanimous in their opinions. "In the highest ranges of thought—in theology, philosophy and science—we find differences of view," he observed. On profound legal issues, "we do not suddenly rise to a stratosphere of icy certainty."

As if to underscore the message of Hughes's speech to the American Law Institute, the Court announced two of its most fractured decisions in the last two weeks of the term. In each case, the Four Horsemen joined by Roberts prevailed, while the dissenters—Brandeis, Cardozo, and Stone—attacked both the majority's decisions and, more broadly, their conservative philosophy. Chief Justice Hughes was caught in the middle, writing an opinion only for himself, buffeted by the gale-force winds from his right and left.

Justice George Sutherland, writing for the five-member conservative majority, struck down the Guffey Coal Act, passed only nine months earlier by Congress to bring relief to the nation's distressed bituminous coal industry. When the bill was stalled in committee in July, Roosevelt had lobbied tirelessly for the legislation. In speaking to skeptical congressmen, he had conceded that the legislation would be challenged in court. But the need was great, he argued, and, at the very least, the Supreme Court could usefully draw the parameters of permissible federal regulation of vital national industries.

Roosevelt's unfulfilled hope that the Guffey Act would survive the Court's scrutiny was based on the fact that the coal industry was a far cry from the Schechter brothers' poultry business in Brooklyn. Ninety-seven percent of all coal mined in the United States was transported in interstate commerce. The history of the industry, moreover, was rife with problems that affected the national economy. For twenty years, Congress had studied and tried to cure the industry's chronic ailments: cutthroat competition, drastic ebbs and flows in production, unstable prices and wages, costly and often bloody labor strikes. The Guffey Act attempted to stabilize the industry by establishing a fair competition code, collective bargaining, and regulation of miners' wages and hours as well as the price of coal. Anticipating the Court challenge, the bill specifically severed the labor provisions from the price regulations, so that a decision declaring one provision unconstitutional would not necessarily affect the other. The case challenging the statute was brought by James Carter, the president of the Carter Coal Company, who sought an injunction to prevent his own company from complying with the statute. The complex lawsuit was further complicated because the labor provisions of the Guffey Act had not yet gone into effect.

Neither Congress's separation of the law's major provisions nor the arguably premature challenge to the labor sections mattered one iota to Justice Sutherland, who, with a broad brush, swept away the entire statute. Taking up where Justice Roberts left off in *Butler*, Sutherland's majority opinion erected an impregnable wall between federal and state authority. Coal mining, like farm production, he contended, was local activity and therefore off-limits to congressional regulation: "The local character of mining, of manufacturing and of crop growing is a fact, and remains a fact, whatever may be done with the products."

Citing Hughes's opinion in *Schechter*, Sutherland drew a distinction between a direct and indirect effect on interstate commerce. "If the production by one man of a single ton of coal intended for interstate sale and shipment, and actually sold or shipped, affects interstate commerce indirectly," he wrote, "the effect does not become direct by multiplying the tonnage, or increasing the number of men employed, or adding to the expense or complexities of the business, or by all combined." There may be evils to be corrected in the coal industry's troubled history of labor relations, Sutherland conceded, but "the evils are all local evils over which the federal government has no legislative control." His doctrinaire opinion gave further credence to Roosevelt's accusation that the Court had regressed to the "horse-and-buggy" era of constitutional law.

The majority's bright line direct-indirect distinction was challenged convincingly in a dissent written by Benjamin Cardozo, joined by Justices Brandeis and Stone. Great principles of constitutional law, Cardozo wrote, could not be reduced to a few adjectives. The Court's approach should be more nuanced, placing the facts of a case in a larger, practical context. The devastation of the coal industry had profound national implications. "Congress was not condemned to inaction in the face of price wars and wage wars so pregnant with disaster," he observed. "Mining and agriculture and manufacturing are not interstate commerce considered by themselves," he conceded, "yet their relation to that commerce may be such that for the protection of the one there is need to regulate the other."

To support his practical approach, Cardozo cited the Court's majority opinion in the *Shreveport Rate Case*, written in 1914 by Associate Justice Charles Evans Hughes. *Shreveport* showed that "the causal relation in such circumstances is so close and intimate and obvious as to permit it to be called direct without subjecting the word to an unfair or excessive strain." Just as Texas's intrastate railroad rates had a close and substantial relation to interstate rates in *Shreveport*, "there is a like immediacy here." "The prices for intrastate sales of coal have so inescapable a relation to those for interstate sales," he reasoned, "that a system of regulation for transactions of the one class is necessary to give adequate protection to the system of regulation adopted for the other." As to the labor provisions of the statute, Cardozo said that it was premature to decide their constitutionality since they had yet to take effect.

The Chief Justice put to rest, at least temporarily, the criticism that he facilely tacked to the right or the left to solidify the Court's majority, regardless of the constitutional principle at stake. In the *Carter* decision, he wrote a separate opinion splitting the difference on the commerce clause issue between the majority and dissenters. He agreed with the majority's view that mining was not commerce, and that the labor provisions of the statute exceeded Congress's commerce power. But he supported Cardozo's analysis of the price regulations (based on his own approach in his *Shreveport* opinion), and found them constitutional. He suggested further that the people might wish to enact a constitutional amendment to "give Congress the power to regulate industries within the State." *

On June 1—the last day of the Court's term—the same five-member

---

* Hughes joined the three liberal dissenters in another late-term decision in which the five-member majority, speaking through Justice McReynolds, struck down the Municipal Bankruptcy Act on the grounds that Congress had violated state sovereignty by permitting local governments to declare bankruptcy. Stone complained in a letter to Frankfurter that the decision was so obviously political that it constituted "a form of indecent exposure."

conservative majority in *Carter* struck down New York's minimum wage law for women, defending the old substantive due process philosophy that had reigned during the Taft Court years of the 1920s. The New York law had been passed after Governor Roosevelt's second term expired. Shortly after his presidential inauguration, Roosevelt had recommended the progressive New York statute as a model for other states. That high ambition came tumbling down with the Court's decision in the New York case, *Morehead v. Tipaldo*, which effectively barred states from passing progressive social and economic legislation, just as the Court's *Schechter*, *Butler*, and *Carter* decisions had applied a brake to the New Deal.

Ironically, it had been the Court's liberals who pushed to have the New York minimum wage case placed on their calendar. They viewed it as an opportunity to overrule the Taft Court's 1923 decision, *Adkins v. Children's Hospital*, which had struck down a similar statute in the District of Columbia on substantive due process grounds. Congress had no power to regulate minimum wages for adult women in the District of Columbia, the Court had held in *Adkins*, because it interfered with the employer's liberty of contract under the due process clause of the Fifth Amendment. But once the Court heard arguments in *Tipaldo* on the merits, Justice Roberts joined the four die-hard conservatives to strike down New York's law *and* preserve *Adkins*.

"In making contracts of employment," Justice Butler wrote for the majority in *Tipaldo*, "the parties have equal rights to obtain from each other the best terms they can by private bargaining." The state, he continued, "was without power by any form of legislation to prohibit, change or nullify contracts between employers and adult women workers as to the amount of wages to be paid." As a result of the Court's opinion, women working long, arduous hours in factories in Buffalo, Rochester, and New York City were now free to bargain with their employers, unencumbered by the state's minimum wage law.

The enforced bargain outraged Justice Stone who, joined in dissent by Brandeis and Cardozo, noted: "There is grim irony in speaking of the freedom of contract of those who, because of their economic necessities, give their services for less than is needful to keep body and soul together." Attacking the conservatives' laissez-faire philosophy, Stone charged: "It is difficult to imagine any grounds, other than our own personal economic predilections, for saying that the contract of employment is any the less an appropriate subject of legislation than are scores of others, in dealing with which this Court has held that legislation may curtail individual freedom in the public interest,"

Hughes, speaking only for himself, wrote that he could "find nothing in the Federal Constitution which denies to the State the power to protect women from being exploited by overreaching employers through the refusal of a fair wage as defined in the New York statute and ascertained in a reasonable manner by competent authority." But, unlike Stone, he refused to condemn the *Adkins* decision, relying on a technical distinction between the District of Columbia and New York statutes in calculating minimum wages.

Stone deplored the Chief's hair-splitting distinction. It was "a sad business to stand only on differences of the two statutes," he wrote Frankfurter, adding that he could not understand why the Chief Justice "felt it necessary to so limit his opinion." Stone had made a similar complaint after Hughes had filed his separate opinion in *Carter*. When Stone expressed exasperation at Hughes's opinion, Louis Brandeis offered an explanation. "He [Hughes] is deeply unhappy," he said. "He has no control over the Court."

In only a year, the towering image of the Chief Justice leading the Court had evaporated. His major triumphs—in the "hot oil" decision, the gold clause challenges, and especially *Schechter*—appeared to be relics of a distant judicial past. Even Hughes's speech to the American Law Institute back in April already seemed woefully out of date. He had ridiculed the idea that the justices could decide complex constitutional issues with "icy certainty." To be sure, the justices' gaping divisions underscored his point that the Court was no monolith. But the more crucial truth—that the conservative majority was cruising in "a stratosphere of icy certainty"—was undeniable.

Reaction to the Supreme Court's *Tipaldo* decision was swift and uniformly negative. "The majority decision will leave the states at sea regarding how they are to deal with the exploitation of women in industry," *The New York Times* editorialized. The *Boston Herald* called it "a shocking blow to enlightened conservatives," and Republican congressman Hamilton Fish, a strident critic of the administration, condemned what he termed this "new *Dred Scott* decision."

Justice Stone, a registered Republican, cheerfully noted the bipartisan criticism. "It seems to be dawning on a good many minds," he wrote his Democratic colleague, Justice Brandeis, "that after all there may be something in the protest of the so-called liberal minority." Brandeis replied, "Yes, the consternation of the enemy is encouraging."

At the presidential news conference held the day after *Tipaldo* decision was announced, Roosevelt was asked if he saw any way New Deal objectives "can be reached within the present framework of the Constitution." He responded by recommending that the American people read all three opinions in *Tipaldo* (Butler's, Stone's, and Hughes's). Together, he said, they make "one fact fairly clear." It was that there exists a "no man's land," defined by the current Court majority, "where neither state nor federal government may function."

"How can you meet that situation?" a reporter asked.

"I think that is about all there is to say," Roosevelt replied. He knew instinctively that the public's adverse reaction to *Tipaldo* made another incendiary "horse-and-buggy" presidential attack on the Court unnecessary.

After *Tipaldo*, Republicans, not the president, felt pressure to question the Court's power. At the Republican National Convention a week after Roosevelt's press conference, delegates repudiated the *Tipaldo* decision, recommending that New York's minimum wage law for women be restored.

Justice Cardozo could not stifle his mischievous delight. "We would be less than human," he wrote Stone during the Republican Convention, "if we failed to sit back in our chairs with a grin on our face as we watch the response to the minimum wage decision."

Roosevelt launched his reelection campaign on the third day of 1936 in a fighting speech before both houses of Congress. Over the loud protests of Republicans, he insisted that his State of the Union address be delivered to the nation at night to maximize his radio audience. Opening with a sober warning of dictators abroad, he quickly turned to threats at home from what he termed "the resplendent economic autocracy." The New Deal's struggle to return government to the people had "earned the hatred of entrenched greed," he said. "Autocrats in small things, they seek autocracy in big things. They steal the livery of great national constitutional ideals to serve discredited special interests. Give them their way and they will take the course of every autocracy of the past—power for themselves, enslavement for the public."

Without knowing his Republican opponent, Roosevelt was confident that he would win a second presidential term. Every major economic indicator pointed in his direction. Since 1933, national income had risen more than 50 percent, unemployment had been cut by almost half, large corporations, such as U.S. Steel and General Motors, anticipated huge profits, and the Dow Jones industrial average was 80 percent higher than when Roosevelt took office.

Still, the president took nothing for granted, and carefully plotted his reelection strategy. He relished the fight against his chosen enemy, "the economic autocracy," but counted every other American as a potential vote for a second Roosevelt administration. He emphasized "the rounded picture"—his term for the interdependence of various regions in the country. Reasonable city dwellers would not complain about the rise in the price of pork chops, he said, once they understood the pig farmer's problems and his need for a fair return on his livestock and labor. He rejected "the frame of mind which talks about 'your group' and 'my group' among Liberals." While he said that Justice Brandeis was "one thousand per cent right in principle" in opposing monopolies, he also thought that "in certain fields there must be a guiding or restraining hand of Government." He relied on "the human element" to get his message across to individual voters. "Don't tell them in Georgia what is being done in Alabama," he counseled. "Take the nearest project to where you are speaking in Georgia and tell them about that."*

The Republican front-runner was Governor Alfred Landon of Kansas, the only governor of his party to survive the Democratic tidal wave in 1934. He owed his political success to a mild, agreeable personality, resolute fiscal conservatism, and a surprising streak of social progressivism. He proudly boasted that he had balanced his state's budget, though he did not call attention to the $400 million in federal stimulus funds that made the feat possible. He endorsed many other New Deal initiatives, especially those that benefitted his state. A former Bull Mooser, he also compiled an admirable civil liberties record and fought the Ku Klux Klan.

---

* For the first time since 1910, Roosevelt did not have the shrewd, indefatigable Louis Howe to advise him. Howe, who suffered from congestive heart problems, died at Washington's Naval Hospital in April at the age of sixty-four. Roosevelt ordered American flags to fly at half-mast and arranged for a state funeral in the White House. A special funeral train carried the president and his wife to Fall River, Massachusetts, where Howe was buried. At the graveside service, Roosevelt grieved for his old friend in silence, oblivious to everyone around him.

Republicans counted on Landon's "just folks" sincerity to overcome the recurrent problem of his soporific speeches. Democratic national chairman Jim Farley caused a furor when he referred to Landon as "the governor of a typical prairie state." Roosevelt, who wanted to run against the Kansas governor, quickly rebuked him. "[N]o section of the country should be spoken of as 'typical,' " he wrote Farley. "If the sentence had read 'One of those splendid prairie States,' no one could have picked us up on it, but the word 'typical' coming from any New Yorker is meat for the opposition."

Landon received his party's nomination at the Republican Convention in Cleveland, but it was former President Herbert Hoover, not the Kansas governor, who electrified the delegates. Pounding the speaker's podium, Hoover painted an apocalyptic vision of the United States if Roosevelt were reelected. The nation could expect "the succeeding stages of violence and outrage by which European despotism have crushed all liberalism and all freedom." The New Deal had piled up an enormous national debt, which two generations of Americans could not repay. "If this is to continue," he warned, "the end result is the tears and anguish of universal bankruptcy."

Hoover whipped the crowd into a frenzy when he asked: "[H]ave you determined to enter in a holy crusade for liberty which shall determine the future and the perpetuity of a nation of free men?"

"Yes," they shouted.

"Thus can America be preserved," he replied. "Thus you will win the gratitude of posterity, and the blessing of Almighty God."

The delegates cheered and waved ecstatically to the former president, who received their adoration with a half smile on his face.

Landon's best chance for election depended on the vitality of the third-party candidacy of Congressman William Lemke, an agrarian populist from North Dakota who was expected to siphon off millions of votes from Roosevelt. Though Lemke, the Union Party's candidate, had no hope of victory, he was endorsed by two anti-Semitic demagogues, Father Charles Coughlin (the "radio priest") and the Reverend Gerald L. K. Smith. Father Coughlin immediately warmed to his task, ripping off his coat and clerical collar to denounce the president as "the great betrayer and liar." Smith, in his Louisiana drawl, explained his stump-speech appeal: "Religion and patriotism, keep going on that. It's the only way you can get them really 'het up.' " Lemke was also supported by Dr. Francis Townsend, whose pension plan promised to pay every citizen over sixty years old $200 a month.

Roosevelt issued orders that the Democratic Party platform should be short and uncomplicated. There would be no call for a constitutional amendment to restrain the conservative Supreme Court, he decided. His political intuition told him that ordinary American voters would not be able to understand the need for an amendment. "There's one issue in this campaign," Roosevelt told Raymond Moley shortly before Democratic delegates convened in Philadelphia. "It's myself, and people must be either for me or against me."

As the president had instructed, the Court was not mentioned in the party's platform. But that did not stop one spellbinding orator, Senator Alben Barkley of Kentucky, from lambasting the justices in his impassioned keynote address. "Over against the hosannas of Hoover for the tortured interpretation of the Constitution of this nation," he thundered, "I place the tortured souls and bodies" of the nation's workingmen, women, and children. The Democratic Party expected the Court to treat the Constitution "as a life-giving charter," he proclaimed, "rather than an object of curiosity on the shelf of a museum."

"Is the Court beyond criticism?" Barkley asked rhetorically.

"No!" the delegates roared.

"May it be regarded as too sacred to be disagreed with?"

"No! No!"

On the evening of June 27, the night that Roosevelt was scheduled to accept his party's nomination for a second presidential term, more than 100,000 men and women filled every seat in the huge outdoor stadium at the University of Pennsylvania's Franklin Field. The Philadelphia Orchestra, conducted by Leopold Stokowski, played Tschaikovsky, and the Metropolitan Opera's Lily Pons sang "Song of the Lark." Shortly before 10 p.m., spotlights trained on the presidential limousine as it entered the stadium, and the orchestra broke into a highbrow version of "Hail to the Chief." The crowd burst into applause as Roosevelt, on the arm of his son James, stiffly made his way onto the stage.

Smiling broadly on the podium, Roosevelt waved to Edwin Markham, the bearded eighty-four-year-old poet whose "Man with a Hoe" had immortalized "the forgotten man" of TR's era. As Markham came forward to greet the president, the crowd surged behind him, causing the poet to jostle the president. Roosevelt's steel brace holding his right leg snapped out of position, and he fell heavily to the floor. Instantly, the presidential bodyguard, Gus Gennerich, knelt down and forced the brace back into place.

Roosevelt's face was ashen, his confidence shaken. "Clean me up," Roosevelt angrily told his aides. He also ordered those around him to keep their feet off "those damned sheets," the scattered pages of his prepared acceptance speech. "I was the damnedest, maddest white man at that moment you ever saw," he later recalled. "It was the most frightful five minutes of my life."

Once he was helped up, his balance and his composure restored, Roosevelt noticed a stricken Markham cowering anxiously nearby. The president smiled and warmly clasped the poet's hand. He was again in control.

Roosevelt stood triumphantly, his shoulders erect, his high-wattage grin radiating to the adoring crowd. While Senator Joseph Robinson made his formal introduction, the president calmly rearranged the smudged pages of his speech in sequential order. Once the tumultuous ovation died down, he delivered one of the best speeches of his career. Returning to the theme of his State of the Union address, he derided "the economic royalists [who] complain that we seek to overthrow the institutions of America. What they really complain of is that we seek to take away their power." In mesmerizing cadence, he then summoned the nation to join his cause:

> Governments can err, Presidents do make mistakes, but the immortal Dante tells us that divine justice weighs the sins of the cold-blooded and the sins of the warm-hearted in different scales.
>
> Better the occasional faults of a Government that lives in a spirit of charity than the consistent omissions of a Government frozen in the ice of its own indifference.
>
> There is a mysterious cycle in human events. To some generation much is given. Of other generations much is expected. This generation of Americans has a rendevous with destiny.*

For ten minutes the crowd was on its feet, clapping and cheering deliriously. Roosevelt and his family stood on stage while the Philadelphia Orchestra played "Auld Lang Syne." The president liked the rendition so much that he requested an encore. This time, the Roosevelts and everyone else in the stadium sang lustily.

---

* Two White House aides, the former journalist Stanley High, and the Frankfurter prótegé Tommy Corcoran, contributed memorable phrases to the speech: "economic royalists" was High's and "rendevous with destiny" was Corcoran's.

Once his campaign began, Roosevelt hurled himself into the fray with cyclonic force, delivering more than two hundred speeches in sixty days. Everywhere he toured, the crowds were enormous, cramming sidewalks and pressing close to the rear platform of the presidential train. More than 150,000 people filled Boston Common and admirers lined the streets of New York City and its environs for thirty miles. In Chicago, five days after Landon had been driven through near-empty streets in a pouring rain, Roosevelt arrived on a balmy night and the same streets were packed. The president always appeared to be having the time of his life, waving, exchanging greetings and banter with the crowds, even bursting into song, as he did in Syracuse when he joined an American Legion chorus in a robust rendering of "Pack Up Your Troubles in Your Old Kit Bag."

His campaign theme was reduced to a single question to voters: Are you better off today than four years ago? Often his audience provided an unrehearsed punch line. "He saved my home," yelled one. "He gave me a job," shouted another. Roosevelt beamed with pleasure, and offered facts and figures to back up the New Deal recovery. Six million jobs had been created in three years, and industrial output had doubled. Retail businesses were booming; in August, Montgomery Ward reported its largest sales in history.

Roosevelt insisted that his was a nonpartisan campaign. He mentioned the Democratic Party only a few times and never referred to his Republican opponent by name. When he met Landon at a midwestern governors conference, he was the model of cordiality, suggesting to the Kansas governor that they should meet after the election, no matter who won. Campaigning in Emporia, Kansas, the home of the eminent Republican newspaper editor and New Deal critic William Allen White, he wished out loud that "his very old friend" was in the crowd. When told that White was, indeed, in attendance, the president summoned him to the platform. "Hello, Bill, glad to see you," Roosevelt said. "I hope I shall be able to come back to Emporia," he told the audience, "and, when I get back, it may be in one of those three-and-a-half-year periods when Bill White is with me." He and White shook hands warmly while the crowd applauded.

Behind all the campaign hoopla, Roosevelt was building a daunting new Democratic coalition. The masses in the northern cities formed the base, enlarged by the critical support of the nation's largest labor unions. The United Mine Workers' John L. Lewis, who had voted for Hoover in

1932, called Roosevelt "the greatest statesman of modern times." Lewis backed his words of praise with an astonishing contribution of $770,000 from UMW and Congress of Industrial Organizations (CIO) coffers (roughly $10 million in today's dollars). The powerful garment unions and key chapters of the American Federation of Labor quickly followed suit. One North Carolina millworker explained the president's appeal. "Mr. Roosevelt is the only man we ever had in the White House who would understand that my boss is a sonofabitch," he said.

FDR campaigned vigorously in the Midwest, reminding his rural audiences that the New Deal had saved tens of thousands of farms from foreclosure and had boosted farm prices to pre-depression highs. Though he spent little time in the South, he was confident that the region, home of the Tennessee Valley Authority, would remained staunchly Democratic. He actively sought the votes of three new constituencies: African-Americans, women, and Republican progressives. African-Americans had consistently supported the party of Lincoln since the passage of the Fifteenth Amendment in 1870 guaranteed them the vote. But in 1936, Eleanor Roosevelt was a passionate advocate for civil rights, backed by the president, who told a Howard University audience that "among American citizens there should be no forgotten men and no forgotten races." And thanks again largely to Eleanor, women turned to Roosevelt in record numbers. The final piece of the gigantic Democratic mosaic was provided by Republican progressives who could not turn against a president who had championed so many of their causes. Senators Robert LaFollette and George Norris campaigned for Roosevelt. The president, in a grand nonpartisan gesture, returned the favor by endorsing Norris against his Democratic opponent.

On the last day of his campaign, Roosevelt was welcomed with cowbells, horns, a band playing a boisterous version of "Happy Days Are Here Again," and a thirteen-minute ovation from a shrieking, overflow crowd in Madison Square Garden. The president again attacked big business, telling his audience that the forces of "organized money are unanimous in their hate for me—and I welcome their hatred."* In the first Roosevelt administration, he said, "the forces of selfishness and of lust for power met their

---

* Not all businessmen opposed Roosevelt. The reform-minded merchant Edward Filene enthusiastically supported the president, as did such innovative entrepreneurs as Thomas Watson, president of International Business Machines.

match." When the work of his anticipated second-term administration was completed, he told the roaring crowd, he should have it said that these same forces "met their master."

On November 2, Roosevelt won the greatest presidential victory since the early nineteenth century, carrying all but two states, Maine and Vermont. He polled 27,476,673 million votes to Landon's 16,679,583, capturing 61 percent of the vote. Lemke was a distant third, with a paltry 892,492 votes. Roosevelt's triumph was the most decisive since 1820 when James Monroe coasted to victory. Democrats trounced Republicans in congressional races, taking more than 75 percent of the seats in both the House and Senate. The new margin in the Senate was so great (76–20) that twelve freshmen Democrats had to take their seats on the traditionally Republican side of the aisle.

Only one branch of the federal government, the Supreme Court of the United States, remained outside of FDR's orbit. Roosevelt had conspicuously ignored the Court during his presidential campaign. But a week after his overwhelming victory, his thoughts again turned to the Hughes Court. A short holiday "will give me a chance to re-study the problem created for the Nation by the Supreme Court," he wrote the *New York Daily News*'s Joseph Patterson. "It is a mighty difficult one to solve but one way or another I think it must be faced. And it can be faced and solved without getting away from our underlying principles."

8

The "Most Dangerous, Implacable Enemy"

I n June 1936, Chief Justice Hughes was despondent. The five-member conservative majority had ended the Court's term with a vengeance, striking down two New Deal statutes as well as New York's minimum wage law for women. They had repudiated his leadership, which was bad enough, but what troubled him more was his fear that they had inflicted fresh wounds upon the prestige of the Court. He was particularly chagrined that the majority had rejected his compromise in the New York minimum wage decision, *Morehead v. Tipaldo*. He had written a separate opinion, supported by no other justice, contending that the New York statute was constitutional, but refusing to overrule the Court's 1923 *Adkins* decision that had struck down a similar minimum wage law in the District of Columbia. Hughes was concerned that the Court's *Tipaldo* decision left New York and other state governments impotent to pass progressive legislation. Whether consciously or not, the conservative majority had created a political vacuum in which no government could act, regardless of social or economic conditions.

Hughes's earlier warning that the Court must avoid "self-inflicted wounds" had gone unheeded. The conservative justices were widely perceived to be voting their political biases, which threatened to bring harsh retribution from President Roosevelt and the New Deal Congress. The

Chief Justice had heard the persistent rumors that the Roosevelt administration planned to pack the Court with new liberal appointees to outvote the conservative bloc. He was also aware of the flurry of legislative proposals introduced in Congress to curb the Court's powers. This Court was under attack, it seemed, from all directions.

Hoping to recharge his sagging spirits, Hughes and his wife embarked on their annual summer vacation, driving to picturesque St. Andrews, New Brunswick. After the couple returned to the United States, they visited Justice Owen Roberts and his wife at the Robertses' large country estate in rural Pennsylvania. The Chief Justice almost surely had more in mind than simply enjoying the scenery and his colleague's hospitality. Roberts, who had earlier joined Hughes at the center of the polarized Court, appeared to have taken a sharp turn to the right. He had abandoned Hughes in all of the controversial conservative decisions at the end of the term, including *Tipaldo*, which was of the greatest concern to the Chief Justice. Public reaction to *Tipaldo* had crossed party lines, drawing the ire of delegates to the Republican Convention. Whatever slender hope that existed for the incipient "Roberts for President" boomlet was quickly squelched. The party's presidential nominee, Governor Landon, explicitly denounced the *Tipaldo* decision.

The Hugheses' visit to the Roberts farm lasted barely twenty-four hours, but the Chief Justice used several of those hours to engage his colleague in intense conversation. Roberts's wife, Elizabeth, watched her husband and the Chief Justice pace back and forth across the terrace, deep in conversation; they continued their talk after dinner in Roberts's library. Mrs. Roberts and Antoinette Hughes, meanwhile, were forced to conduct their own long, unplanned conversation, discussing their children, servants, gardens, the weather, and Washington gossip. While the two men talked on and on, Elizabeth Roberts admitted that she and Mrs. Hughes "got to the end of our rope." So far as Mrs. Roberts knew, neither her husband nor the Chief Justice ever shared the topic of their extended conversation with anyone. But critical agreement between the two justices in several important decisions during the next Court term suggests that their summer discussion covered more than the joys of vacation and the beauty of the Pennsylvania countryside.

*   *   *

The 1936 Supreme Court term promised to be as controversial as the previous two. The docket was stocked with new challenges to New Deal legislation, as well as an important case questioning the president's authority in foreign affairs. Shortly after the Court convened in early October, Hughes was beset by two additional problems.

On October 12, Harlan Fiske Stone was stricken by a debilitating attack of bacillary dysentery and was bedridden for more than two months in his Washington home. Hughes knew that Stone's illness would make the Court's work more difficult, possibly creating 4–4 deadlocks in contentious cases. But he never let that impending problem interfere with his genuine concern and attention to his ailing colleague. He told Stone's wife, Agnes, that if her husband's extended illness caused them financial problems, he was ready to come to their assistance. When Stone's health began to improve, Hughes sent word of his "rejoicing in your steady and satisfactory progress." He nonetheless counseled Stone not to rush his recovery. "Don't try to come back too soon—we need you—but we need you in full vigor," he wrote.

Two weeks after the Chief Justice learned of Stone's illness, *The Nine Old Men*, a scathing indictment of the Hughes Court, was published. The book was written by the widely known columnists Drew Pearson and Robert Allen, who began their extended diatribe against the Court with a quote from a 1908 speech by former New York governor Hughes. "When there is muck to be raked, it must be raked," Hughes had said, "and the public must know of it, that it may mete out justice." The authors then unleashed a relentless assault on the character, motives, and work of the justices. They described the Chief Justice as "the No. 1 high aerial acrobat of Big Top politics [who] swung back and forth from liberalism to economic stultification with greater ease than the daring young man on the flying trapeze," adding that "it is only now, at the zenith of his career, that he shows signs of losing his nerve and balance." Don't be misled by "his stately bearing," they warned. "Charles Evans Hughes today is the most pathetic figure on the Supreme Court."

The phrase "Nine Old Men" soon entered the popular vocabulary to define the antiquated, isolated members of the Supreme Court. Despite the irreverent tone and many inaccuracies in the book, *The Nine Old Men* quickly rose on the nation's best-seller lists and was serialized in newspapers across the country.

One week after the book's publication, Roosevelt won reelection by the greatest margin in modern presidential history, and New Deal Democrats were elected to Congress in record numbers. Would the Court follow the election returns, as the Irish humorist Finley Peter Dunne's "Mr. Dooley" had famously observed?

In their first post-election arguments before the Court, government attorneys sensed that the conservative justices were less hostile toward them than in past terms. But no one in the Roosevelt administration was willing to predict that the more congenial courtroom atmosphere would translate into favorable judicial results. Early decisions were encouraging, though not definitive. On November 23, the Court upheld a New York Court of Appeals decision sustaining the state's unemployment law. The New York statute had been enacted in response to the Social Security Act, another major New Deal measure whose constitutionality had yet to be decided by the Hughes Court. The justices divided 4–4, with Hughes and Roberts joining Brandeis and Cardozo to uphold the law. The Court's tie vote preserved the state court decision.

Had Stone participated, New Dealers were confident that the vote would have been 5–4 in favor of the constitutionality of the state law. Democratic senator Joseph O'Mahoney of Wyoming immediately announced that "Mr. Dooley seems to be right." But other New Dealers were less sanguine. There were differences between the state and federal unemployment laws, a cautionary sign to administration attorneys who had not forgotten the technical distinction made by Hughes in *Tipaldo* between the New York and District of Columbia minimum wage laws for women.

Unknown to the president or the public, a stunning vote at the justices' conference in mid-December augured well for the Roosevelt administration. Only three weeks after a divided Court had upheld the New York unemployment law, the same four justices—Hughes, Roberts, Brandeis, and Cardozo—voted to preserve Washington State's minimum wage law for women. After Roberts told Hughes in a private conversation how he would vote in the case, the Chief Justice felt like hugging his unpredictable colleague. Roberts, of course, had cast the decisive fifth vote with the conservative bloc only six months earlier that had doomed New York's minimum wage statute.

The Washington law was almost identical to the New York statute that Roberts and the four conservative justices had struck down in *Tipaldo*.

Hughes could have formally recorded the 4–4 vote, as he had done in the state unemployment law case a few weeks earlier, which would have upheld the Washington law without calling for a Court opinion. But he shrewdly held the case over until Stone's anticipated return in February 1937. If Stone voted to uphold the Washington statute, as Hughes anticipated, the Chief Justice could assign a full-fledged majority opinion that presumably would overrule *Tipaldo*. This unexpected development was, for the time being, unknown outside the justices' chambers.

A week later, on December 21, the Court announced a decision on the scope of executive power that was both surprising and highly favorable to the president. In *United States v. Curtiss-Wright Export Corp.* the justices broadly construed the president's authority to conduct the nation's foreign affairs. At issue was the constitutionality of a joint congressional resolution that authorized President Roosevelt to prohibit the sale of arms to Bolivia and Paraguay, which were engaged in a conflict over the Chaco region claimed by both nations. In his opinion for eight members of the Court, Justice Sutherland conceded to the president virtually unlimited constitutional authority to conduct the nation's foreign policy. Congressional legislation in the field of international affairs "must often accord to the president a degree of discretion and freedom from statutory restriction which would not be admissible were domestic affairs alone involved," he wrote. The president, not Congress, "has the better opportunity of knowing the conditions which prevail in foreign countries, and especially is this true in time of war." Only Justice McReynolds dissented.

Administration lawyer Robert Jackson called the *Curtiss-Wright* decision "a Christmas present to the President," noting that the Court had given Roosevelt more power over foreign affairs than government attorneys had asked for. But the administration's enthusiasm was necessarily muted. Sutherland had emphasized that the Court's interpretation of the president's authority in domestic affairs was narrowly circumscribed, as Roosevelt had bitterly learned when the Court ruled in 1934 that he had illegally fired William Humphrey, a Republican member of the Federal Trade Commission.

In early January 1937, Chief Justice Hughes wrote an opinion for a unanimous Court that signaled the justices were not irresolutely hostile to the New Deal Congress. The decision upheld a 1934 federal law that had banned from interstate commerce the sale of harnesses manufactured by convicts.* The decision in *Kentucky Whip and Collar Co. v. Illinois Central Railroad Co.* was significant, because it undercut one of the most notorious conservative rulings of the twentieth century, *Hammer v. Dagenhart.*

In 1918, the Court in *Hammer* had ruled that Congress exceeded its power to regulate interstate commerce when it prohibited the products of child labor to be transported across state lines. The products of child labor at issue in *Hammer* were "harmless," wrote Justice William Day for the Court, and could not be regulated indirectly by the federal government. Justice Holmes wrote a famous dissent, arguing that Congress's power to regulate interstate commerce was given in unqualified terms, and that the majority's distinction between "harmless" and "harmful" products manufactured within a state was constitutionally meaningless.

In his *Kentucky Whip* opinion, Hughes wrote that Congress had the authority to prevent the transportation in interstate commerce of harnesses manufactured by convicts, even though they could be termed "harmless" products. His opinion discredited the reasoning of *Hammer* and implicitly endorsed Holmes's dissent. But he continued to enhance his centrist image by refusing to overrule the 1918 precedent. Just as he had done in his separate opinion in *Tipaldo*, the Chief Justice strained to preserve a Court precedent that had been the target of harsh criticism from constitutional scholars. He claimed that the child labor law at issue in *Hammer* had unconstitutionally placed local production under federal control, which distinguished it from the 1934 congressional statute. As a result, he did not appear to be altering constitutional doctrine.

Hughes's refusal to write an opinion in which he advocated overruling *Hammer* deprived him of the opportunity to lead the Court in an unmistakably progressive direction. His decision to keep the discredited *Hammer* precedent on the books may have persuaded his conservative colleagues to support his opinion. This allowed him to project the institutional image of a unanimous Court sustaining a New Deal law. But the cost to him was an unnecessarily labored reading of Congress's broad power to regulate

---

* On the same day that Hughes announced the Court's decision in *Kentucky Whip*, he also spoke for a unanimous Court in upholding the constitutionality of a provision of a federal bankruptcy law that subordinated the claims of landlords of bankrupt corporations to those of shareholders, again demonstrating that the justices were not rigidly opposed to legislation that effectively altered contractual obligations.

interstate commerce.* The 1934 statute was much the same in its effect on interstate commerce as the 1916 statute that had been struck down in *Hammer*. Hughes's opinion in *Kentucky Whip*, moreover, was inconsistent with the Court's decision of the previous term, in which the conservative majority had refused to recognize the substantial effect on interstate commerce of labor and price regulations in the coal industry.

On the same day that his *Kentucky Whip* decision was announced, the Chief Justice wrote a landmark civil liberties decision for a unanimous Court that overturned the conviction of Dirk De Jonge, a labor organizer and Communist Party member, who had been sentenced to seven years in prison for violating Oregon's syndicalism statute. At a Communist Party meeting, De Jonge had criticized the Portland police for harassing striking maritime workers, deplored conditions in the county jail, and called for greater efforts to increase Party membership. Hughes said that Oregon's syndicalism statute, which punished advocacy of the violent overthrow of the government, swept too broadly in the defendant's case. The meeting called by De Jonge and other members of the Communist Party, he noted, was a peaceful assembly for a lawful purpose and, therefore, protected by the Constitution.

The *De Jonge* decision was applauded by civil libertarians because the Court, for first time in its history, relied on the protection of an individual's freedom of assembly to invalidate a state conviction. But Hughes carefully limited his opinion to the facts in the case and did not strike down the syndicalism statute, which Oregon, like other states with similar laws, used to prosecute political radicals. Had he written a more expansive opinion, he would have been celebrated unconditionally in the liberal community, but would almost certainly have lost the votes of the Court's conservatives.

With the early decisions in the term, Hughes appeared to be reemerging as the leader of a modestly progressive Supreme Court. The press nonetheless remained skeptical. "The judges are trying very hard to present a united front to a hostile public opinion," *The Nation* observed. *The New York Times*, while praising the *De Jonge* decision, commented on the irony that "this splendid vindication of a fundamental American right" was pro-

---

* Hughes could have written an opinion for the Court advocating the reversal of *Hammer*, even if he did not have the required five votes to overrule the precedent. He then would have laid the groundwork for a later reversal. Four years later, a unanimous Court with six Roosevelt appointees officially overruled *Hammer*. Hughes assigned the Court's opinion to Justice Stone, who approvingly cited Holmes's dissent in *Hammer*.

vided by judges "who so often have been described as narrow-minded reactionaries." And the *Washington Daily News* asked, "Is the Court Shifting?"
adding that it hoped the Court would continue to "mend its opinions."

On November 3, Roosevelt received the election returns in the family
home at Hyde Park—a tradition that dated back to his first run for political office in 1910. After absorbing the extraordinary dimensions of his victory, he returned to the capital, where 200,000 admirers lined the streets,
welcoming him as the nation's conquering political hero. In his open presidential limousine, he waved his hat, grinned broadly, and nodded apprecia-
tively to the exuberant crowds.

"Now that the election is over," a reporter asked the president, "will
you discuss your attitude toward amending the Constitution?"

"Why spoil another happy day?" Roosevelt replied cheerily.

Roosevelt's jaunty, outward calm betrayed a private determination
to deal decisively with the Supreme Court, the unspoken target of the
reporter's question. The conservative Court majority had confounded his
most ambitious plans for lifting the country out of the Great Depression.
Their decisions had struck at the very heart of the New Deal, claiming as
major fatalities the National Industrial Recovery Act and the Agricultural
Adjustment Act. It was only a matter of time, the president believed, before
the Court buried the Social Security Act and the Wagner Act, which had
created the National Labor Relations Board. Braced by his sweeping reelection victory, Roosevelt prepared to meet the Court's challenge head-on.

For almost two years, he had mulled over the means to combat the
reactionary Court conservative majority. At first, he had favored a constitutional amendment to restrain the justices. But neither he nor his advisers
could agree on language that would effectively curb the Court's authority
to declare social and economic legislation unconstitutional. And even if
they were successful in drafting satisfactory language, a contorted interpretation of the amendment by a conservative Court majority could render it
useless.

After his reelection, Roosevelt considered an additional reason to oppose an amendment. The process was simply too cumbersome and time-
consuming. It required a vote of two thirds of both houses of Congress and
three quarters of the state legislatures. The amendment process could not
realistically be completed in less than two or three years, virtually exhaust-

ing his second presidential term. And the results, he knew, were by no means assured. "Give me ten million dollars," he said, "and I can prevent any amendment to the Constitution from being ratified by the necessary number of states."

Two days after his return to Washington, Roosevelt presided at a cabinet meeting and made clear that the Court was very much on his mind. He told Solicitor General Stanley Reed (attending in place of the vacationing Attorney General Cummings) to press forward with the Justice Department's constitutional defense of key New Deal legislation, including the Social Security Act and the Wagner Act. He joked that he expected Justice McReynolds (who reportedly vowed "never [to] resign as long as that crippled son-of-a-bitch is in the White House") to be on the bench when he was one hundred and five years old. In a more serious vein, the president predicted that the conservative majority would declare more New Deal statutes unconstitutional, accelerating what he considered the inevitable confrontation between his administration and the Hughes Court. He told his cabinet that he would use the decisions as the basis "for an appeal to the people over the head of the Court."

But just how Roosevelt would challenge the Court was still undecided. Only when Homer Cummings returned from a golfing vacation to the capital on November 15 did the two men begin to seriously concentrate on what Cummings later referred to as their "constitutional problems." They talked at length about proposed constitutional amendments and congressional statutes, including Cummings's suggestion of a measure aimed at "possible changes in the Supreme Court *or additions thereto*." It was the Court-packing suggestion, which Roosevelt had deemed "distasteful" less than a year earlier, that became the focus of their renewed attention.

By the time FDR and his Attorney General met in the White House in mid-November, they had established a comfortable, trusting relationship. On the surface, Cummings seemed an unlikely choice to be Roosevelt's chief adviser in his fight against the Court. He did not possess the analytical brilliance of Frankfurter or the drafting skills of Frankfurter protégés, Ben Cohen and Tommy Corcoran. He had not even been Roosevelt's first choice for Attorney General. But after his Attorney General—designate, Senator Thomas Walsh, died suddenly before the presidential inauguration in 1933, FDR chose Cummings, whom he had known since they were young Woodrow Wilson Democrats in the predominantly Republican northeast.

A Yale graduate, Cummings had been a popular mayor of Stamford, Connecticut, who rose to prominence in the Democratic Party, serving as chairman of the Democratic National Committee. He was also an early supporter of Roosevelt, acting as a floor manager for his nomination at the 1932 Democratic Convention. Throughout his term as Attorney General, he had demonstrated a trained eye for political advantage and an insatiable drive to find a practical solution for the president's Court problem.

Cummings had been trawling for ideas for almost two years. He had raised the possibility of changing the Court's makeup with Roosevelt earlier, after both agreed that the problem was not the Constitution, but the conservative Court majority interpreting it. When he and the president met on November 15, Cummings had already been actively exploring ideas. One was proposed by Judge William Denman of the U.S. Court of Appeals for the Ninth Circuit, who had lobbied Roosevelt to revitalize the federal judiciary by adding new federal judges. Denman's plan was limited to the lower courts, but Roosevelt and Cummings were willing to rework the concept to include the Supreme Court.

A second and related idea was raised by constitutional scholar Professor Edward Corwin of Princeton, an outspoken Supreme Court critic who accused the justices of usurping the legitimate powers of the other branches of the federal government. Corwin, who had consulted other academics, suggested several possible remedies, including a constitutional amendment or federal statute imposing an age limit on Supreme Court justices. In the final article of a series scheduled for publication in December in the *Philadelphia Record*, Corwin boldly concluded that no federal judge should hold office beyond his seventieth birthday.

Cummings prepared a thick packet of Court materials for Roosevelt before the president sailed on November 18 for a four-week tour of South America. The ostensible purpose for the trip was for FDR to attend a peace conference of Latin American nations in Buenos Aires, but the voyage coincidentally served as a restful cruise after his arduous campaign. He luxuriated in the warm days at sea on the USS *Indianapolis*, deep-sea fishing, sunbathing, and drinking martinis at cocktail hour. At every port, he received despatches from Cummings—memos, clippings, and more expert opinions—on ways to dislodge the Court from its conservative moorings.

On December 22, Cummings wrote Roosevelt that he was "bursting" with ideas, and requested a meeting. By then, the Attorney General had read a sixty-five-page document analyzing the president's Court options written by Warner Gardner, a twenty-seven-year-old Justice Department attorney and former clerk for Justice Stone. Gardner had examined several plans, including one to increase the number of justices, though he worried about "the superficial character of the remedy—the problem would occur, probably every decade."

Cummings discovered another useful court reform proposal that had been recommended in 1913 to President Wilson by his Attorney General. To bring fresh talent into the federal judiciary, Wilson's AG had proposed that lower federal court judges retire at full pay at the age of seventy. If they refused, a new federal statute would authorize the president to appoint another judge, "who would preside over the affairs of the court and have precedence over the older one." Cummings could easily envision the proposal applying to Supreme Court justices. An added attraction: the delicious irony that the author of the twenty-three-year-old proposal was Justice McReynolds!

While Cummings was Roosevelt's chief strategist, the president also pursued his Court mission independently. In early December, he had once again commissioned his old friend, *Collier's* editor George Creel, to act as his surrogate in appealing "over the head" of the Court to the American people. Roosevelt had concluded, after studying the Court's powers under Article III of the Constitution, that the justices did not have the authority to override an act of Congress.* So why, he asked Creel, shouldn't Congress attach a rider to each bill reminding the Court that all legislative power vested in Congress, and that the Constitution explicitly authorized the federal legislature to provide for the general welfare? What if the Court ignored the riders and continued to declare legislation unconstitutional? Creel responded. Then, said Roosevelt, his face taut in anger, "Congress can enlarge the Supreme Court, increasing the number of justices so as to permit the appointment of men in tune with the spirit of the age."

Creel's article was published under the title supplied by the president, "Roosevelt's Plans and Purposes," in *Collier's* December 26 issue. But this

---

* Roosevelt did not appear concerned that virtually every constitutional scholar disagreed with his conclusion that Chief Justice John Marshall in 1803 had overstepped his judicial authority in declaring a congressional statute unconstitutional in *Marbury v. Madison.*

Roosevelt-Creel collaboration, like their last co-authored *Collier's* article more than a year earlier, did not have the desired effect. There was no public outcry against the Court.

Cummings, meanwhile, prepared to move forward with a specific plan, which he discussed at length with the president in a late afternoon meeting the day after Christmas. The Attorney General conceded that there was "substantial objection in the country to a deliberate addition to the Supreme Court for the purpose of meeting the present situation." But what if the president proposed a judicial *reform* bill whose purpose was to revitalize the entire federal bench, including the Supreme Court, with the appointment of younger, vigorous new judges? Cummings did not record in his diary any reaction from Roosevelt to his proposal. But the president almost certainly approved, since Cummings immediately began to draft legislation along the lines that he had discussed at his White House meeting.

For the next week and a half, Cummings, aided by Gardner and other young Justice Department lawyers, worked on the legislation. They borrowed generously from the ideas of Judge Denman, Professor Corwin, and former Attorney General McReynolds. By January 3, 1937, Cummings had written five drafts of a bill to overhaul the federal judiciary. The most eye-popping provision called for the possible increase in the membership of the Supreme Court to a maximum of fifteen justices. If any member of the Court did not retire within six months of his seventieth birthday, the president could appoint another justice to share his responsibilities. The proposed legislation would give Roosevelt *six* new appointments to the Supreme Court, either to replace or sit with the present justices over seventy years old, including Chief Justice Hughes.

On December 29, at his last cabinet meeting of the year, Roosevelt said nothing about the Court-packing plan in the works. But he again invited discussion of the Court, referring to the "constitutional difficulties in the way of certain social reforms which the country ought to have." He noted that the justices had recently remanded an important labor law case to the district court for a new trial, and wondered if the Court was "trying to tire us out, or it may be delaying in the hope that there will be a shift in public sentiment at the congressional elections two years hence." His unspoken message: time was of the essence in dealing with the Supreme Court.

In the early drafts of his 1937 State of the Union address, Roosevelt did not hide his hostility toward the Court. He deplored the wholesale demolition of the NRA and considered quoting Hughes (out of context, as usual) on the malleability of the Constitution by willful judges. But by the time he read the final draft to his cabinet on the afternoon of January 5, he had toned down his references to the Court. Secretary Ickes was pleased with the speech, which "raised the Supreme Court issue very clearly and very cleverly but very inoffensively." The president's final draft invited the Court to cooperate with him and Congress, but suggested that the legislative function should be left to Congress, as the Constitution intended. At the cabinet meeting, Ickes asked the president if he was still considering a constitutional amendment to restrain the Court. According to Ickes, the president replied that "his message didn't close the door on any method that it might be necessary to employ in order to put the Supreme Court in its place."

Roosevelt was greeted with loud applause when he entered the House chamber the next day on James's arm. His State of the Union address, as his cabinet had learned the previous day, made indirect but unmistakable references to the obstructive decisions of the conservative Court majority. Citing debates at the Constitutional Convention, he insisted that the Supreme Court was obligated to accept Congress's broad powers to meet national problems, as the Framers had intended. Though he issued no explicit threat, he warned that "[m]eans must be found to adapt our legal forms and our judicial interpretation to the actual present national needs of the largest progressive democracy in the modern world." He concluded: "We do not ask the Courts to call non-existent powers into being, but we have a right to expect that conceded powers or those legitimately implied shall be made effective instruments for the common good."

With obvious satisfaction, the president reported on his public chiding of the justices to his old friend Claude Bowers, the U.S. ambassador to Spain. "I had a little fun in presenting the message on the State of the Union," he wrote Bowers. "None of the nine highest members of our Judicial branch were present for the occasion, but I have received some intimation that they at least read the remarks which pertained to them. I hope so!"

The conservative *New York Herald Tribune* reacted cautiously to Roosevelt's speech. "It is possible to interpret these paragraphs as a warning to the Court," the editorial began. But it then chose a more reassuring interpretation that "the good temper and restraint of the whole passage seems to us such a vast improvement on the 'horse and buggy episode.' . . . We prefer to accept it as the promise of new wisdom rather than as an exhibition of old wounds." But the liberal *New Republic* expressed impatience with the president for not pledging aggressive action against the Supreme Court after his huge reelection victory. Instead of interpreting the election as a mandate to demand a constitutional amendment or legislation to override the Court, the magazine complained, the president appeared to be coddling the two pivotal members, Hughes and Roberts, with a too-subtle lecture on the proper role of the Court in a constitutional democracy. "Do we . . . dare to make our way in the future on the resolute legs of the people themselves," it asked, "or do we prefer to cut them off and hobble along on crutches provided by the Supreme Court?"

On inauguration day, January 20, the Capitol was drenched in a wind-driven torrential rain. Shortly after noon, Roosevelt repeated the entire presidential oath after Chief Justice Hughes, as he had done at his inauguration in 1933. A soaked Harold Ickes noted that the president spoke slowly and with particular emphasis when he vowed to protect and defend the Constitution of the United States.* The sight of seven members of the Court (only Brandeis and Stone were absent) sitting in their black gowns during the downpour prompted a wicked joke: Since Roosevelt had failed to give the justices apoplexy with his message on the State of the Union, he was now trying pneumonia.

Despite the inclement weather, Roosevelt delivered a brisk, eloquent speech, deploring the condition of "one-third of a nation ill-housed, ill-clad, ill-nourished." Though he did not mention the Court by name, he demanded that *every* agency of the federal government be used to carry out the will of the people. Sam Rosenman, who helped polish the president's speech, was watching Hughes when Roosevelt implored all three branches to work together. "There was no doubt that the Chief Justice understood what the President meant," Rosenman recalled.

In their discussions before the inauguration, Roosevelt and Cummings had agreed that the president's Court-packing plan should be sent to Congress in three separate, reinforcing communications. The bill itself would be ac-

---

* After the ceremony, Roosevelt provided his version of the oath-taking. "When the Chief Justice read me the oath and came to the words 'support the Constitution of the United States,' I felt like saying: 'Yes, but it's the Constitution as *I* understand it, flexible enough to meet any new problem of democracy—not the kind of Constitution your Court has raised up as a barrier to progress and democracy.' "

companied by a presidential message explaining the pressing need for legislation to reinvigorate the federal judiciary. Roosevelt's message would, in turn, be underscored by a letter from the U.S. Attorney General providing specific statistics emphasizing the dual problems of federal court backlogs and an aging judiciary. No reference would be made in any of the documents to the six Supreme Court justices over seventy years old.

Roosevelt insisted that the final details of the plan be developed in secret. The covert operation was due, in part, to the president's penchant for springing dramatic surprises on friends, and the nation. The secrecy was also necessary to guard against leaks that might tip off opponents. Cummings was involved from the beginning. So was the anxious Solicitor General, Stanley Reed, who was scheduled to defend the constitutionality of the Social Security and Wagner acts before the justices, who would, by the time of his oral arguments, be fully aware of the Court-packing proposal. Other Justice Department lawyers were sent scurrying for information on court delays and birth dates of long-serving federal judges, but were not told the purpose of their assignments. No member of the cabinet, except Cummings, knew of the plan. No member of Congress, not even the chairmen of the House and Senate Judiciary committees, were informed of the proposal. Frankfurter received only a cryptic warning from FDR in mid-January. "Very confidentially, I may give you an awful shock in about two weeks," the president wrote. "Even if you do not agree, suspend final judgment and I will tell you the story."

Absolute secrecy of a plan promising such profound consequences for the nation was virtually impossible. Cummings, who took singular pride of authorship, intimated the broad outlines of the proposal to his friend Breckenridge Long, the U.S. ambassador to Italy, who was in Washington for a brief visit in early January. After the inauguration, Donald Richberg, the former NRA director who had been asked by Roosevelt to join the task force, told the journalist Ray Clapper that the president was considering a Court-packing proposal and was "determined to curb the Court and put it in its place." On January 24, Irving Brant, chief editorial writer for the St. Louis Star-Times, wrote Roosevelt that he had been told by several senators that the president would make an announcement on the Supreme Court in a few days.

Members of Congress, meanwhile, had introduced dozens of new proposals for constitutional amendments to restrain the Court. And Congressman Emanuel Celler, a member of the House Judiciary Committee, announced in a radio address that Congress would "pack the Court" if the justices threw out more New Deal legislation.

Roosevelt realized that he must move quickly to head off competing Court proposals. In his best cloak-and-dagger style, he belatedly asked his favorite speechwriter, Sam Rosenman, to join the team working on his plan. On Saturday, January 30, after Rosenman had arrived from New York to attend the presidential birthday party that evening, he received a call from Missy Le Hand inviting him to the White House for an important pre-lunch meeting with the president. He was not told the purpose of the meeting. When he arrived, he was escorted to a table set for five in the Oval Office. Joining the president for lunch, besides Rosenman, were Cummings, Reed, and Richberg. The luncheon conversation, so far as Rosenman could discern, had no purpose or theme, though Cummings, Reed, and Richberg seemed especially appreciative of the president's well-spun story of a camouflaged combat ship during the First World War that suddenly opened fire on a surprised German submarine. After the dishes were cleared away and the doors closed, Roosevelt began to read slowly to the assembled team the latest draft of his proposal to reorganize the federal judiciary, including the Supreme Court.

The team worked furiously over the weekend, composing draft after laborious draft, to nail down the final wording of the bill, the president's message, and Cummings's letter. Roosevelt held the group to a tight deadline: the proposal must be announced by Friday, February 5. He wanted his plan unveiled in advance of oral arguments in cases challenging the constitutionality of the Wagner Act, scheduled for February 9, so that he did not appear to be pressuring the Court. He anticipated that the bill would move quickly through committee and floor debate in both House and Senate before passage, which he never doubted. His new appointments to the Court, he hoped, could be confirmed shortly after the bill's passage.

When the president hosted his annual dinner in honor of the justices of the Supreme Court on Tuesday evening, February 2, he was in noticeably good spirits. Before the guests of honor arrived at the White House, Roosevelt had mischievously considered whether he should have one cocktail, and not mention his Court-packing plan, or lay out mimeographed copies of the Court bill beside each justice's plate, in which case he would fortify himself with three cocktails. At the appointed hour of 7 p.m., the eighty-five guests began to arrive. Roosevelt and a jovial Chief Justice Hughes greeted each other with their usual good-natured salutation—"Governor."

The president was no less cordial in welcoming his other guests, including six associate justices (Brandeis did not accept dinner invitations; Stone was still recuperating from his serious illness), Congressman Hatton Sumners, chairman of the House Judiciary Committee, and his Senate counterpart, Henry Fountain Ashurst, as well as Mrs. Woodrow Wilson, the ex-heavyweight champion Gene Tunney, and all four of the president's co-conspirators. A convivial Roosevelt lingered after dinner to converse with the Chief Justice and Justice Van Devanter, which reminded a suspicious William Borah of "the Roman Emperor who looked around his dinner table and began to laugh when he thought how many of those heads would be rolling on the morrow."

On Friday, February 5, the White House secretarial staff reported to work at 6:30 a.m., as ordered by the president. They were instructed to mimeograph copies of the Court bill, as well as Roosevelt's and Cummings's related attachments, for distribution at the special cabinet meeting, which the president had scheduled for ten o'clock. Roosevelt had invited House Speaker William Bankhead, House majority leader Sam Rayburn, Senate majority leader Joe Robinson, and Judiciary Committee chairmen Sumners and Ashurst to attend the meeting. Neither the congressional leaders nor the cabinet had been informed of the agenda.

Roosevelt entered the room hurriedly, bid everyone a genial good morning, and waited for the mimeographed materials to be distributed. The meeting must be brief, he said, since he had scheduled a press conference in an hour. He then explained that the documents before them presented a plan to reorganize the federal judiciary. He read out passages from his message and the bill, looking up occasionally to offer brief explanations. He did not ask for comments, apologized for his haste, and promised that all members of Congress would learn the details of the proposed legislation at noon when the documents were scheduled to be delivered to Capitol Hill.

At his press conference in the Oval Office, Roosevelt was more expansive. With nearly two hundred reporters standing in a semicircle around his desk, the president leaned back, clutched a sheaf of papers, and announced he had "a somewhat important matter" to discuss. He then proceeded to read Cummings's letter, his own message to Congress, and highlights of the proposed legislation. The problem of overcrowding in the federal courts was extremely serious, he said, noting that 87 percent of all cases presented by private litigants were turned down by federal courts without explanation. That is an "amazing statement," he continued, and "brings forward the question of aged or infirm judges—a subject of delicacy and yet one which requires frank discussion." He looked up to see if the reporters caught his sly innuendo. They did, and spontaneously broke out in laughter.

The president was cheerful throughout the session, smiling constantly, playing for laughs, sometimes at the justices' expense. He credited former Attorney General McReynolds with an admirable judicial reform proposal. Guffaws all around. He also quoted "a very important judge" (Hughes)* on the inability of some aging members of the judiciary to recognize their infirmities and retire. "You will have to find out who said it," he teased. "I am not going to tell you." At the end of the session, he became serious, making his closing argument that a "constant and systematic addition of younger blood will vitalize the courts and better equip them to recognize and apply the essential concepts of justice in the light of the needs and facts of an ever-changing world."

Roosevelt's proposal was greeted with shrieks of outrage from the Republican press. "It was the French King, Louis XIV, who said 'L'état, c'est moi—I am the state,' " snorted the *New York Herald Tribune*. "The paper shell of American constitutionalism would continue if President Roosevelt secured the passage of the law he now demands. But it would only be a shell." The moderate Republican editor of the *Emporia Gazette*, William Allen White, wrote, "Surely Mr. Roosevelt's mandate was to function as President, not as *Der Fuehrer*." Invoking the recurrent theme of dictatorship, the columnist Mark Sullivan added, "We are going down the road to fascism."

On the day after Roosevelt sent his message to Congress, former President Hoover phoned Republican senator Arthur Vandenberg from New York's Waldorf-Astoria "eager to jump into the fray." But Vandenberg, Borah, and Senate minority leader Charles McNary, all opponents of the president's legislation, concluded that their fight against the overwhelming Democratic majority (75–23) could not afford Hoover's public opposition; he was still "poison" in the minds of American voters.†

---

* Roosevelt used the same quote from Hughes's lecture in 1927 on the Court that had appeared in an April 1936 column by Arthur Krock. Roosevelt, like Krock, took the quote out of context, as Hughes explained in a letter to Krock.

† Hoover remained muzzled only temporarily. Two weeks later, he offered "a watchword" to his Union League Club of Chicago audience—"Hands off the Supreme Court."

Roosevelt serenely received the news of Republican opposition, secure in the huge Democratic majorities in both the House and Senate. More important than the reassuring congressional math, the president firmly believed the voters were on his side. "The people are with me," he said. "I know it."

But the thousands of letters inundating congressional offices and newspapers across the country told a different story. "As a boy I was taught to honor and revere the Supreme Court above all things," wrote a New Orleans insurance man. Whether the justices' decisions were right or wrong, the Supreme Court, as an institution, commanded respect. One prominent Catholic layman compared the Court to the Pope. "To all intents and purposes," he wrote, "our Supreme Court is infallible."

Besides tinkering with a revered institution, Roosevelt's proposal alienated septuagenarians and their younger defenders. An aged Clemenceau led France to victory in the First World War, one constituent wrote his Florida congressman, and Justice Holmes served with distinction on the Court at ninety. Goethe completed *Faust* at eighty, Tennyson wrote "Crossing the Bar" at eighty-three, and Titian painted his *Battle of Lepanto* at ninety-eight, noted a letter writer to *The Washington Post*. "Can you calculate the loss to the world if such as these had been compelled to retire at 70?"

Roosevelt was accused of rank duplicity, his so-called reform plan widely viewed as a brazen attempt to remake the Supreme Court in his political image. At the same time, civil libertarians rallied to the Court's defense, fearing that a weakened Court would mean less protection for personal liberties. They pointed to decisions by the Hughes Court, several written by the seventy-four-year-old Chief Justice, protecting individual rights.

The president's approval rating, which had stood at 65 percent before the legislation was announced, began to drop. Shortly after he sent his message to Congress, the Gallup poll reported that 51 percent of Americans disapproved of his Court proposal, and that number rose steadily.

Roosevelt had made the first blunder even before he announced his proposal. Democratic congressional leaders were kept in the dark while Roosevelt and Cummings hatched their plan. These proud, powerful men were given no advance warning of the legislation that the president presumed they would efficiently guide through Congress. The first defector was Hatton Sumners, chairman of the House Judiciary Committee. "Boys, here's where I cash in my chips," he told his fellow congressional leaders in their ride to the Hill after meeting with Roosevelt on February 5. A majority of Democrats on Sumners's committee joined him in opposition to the bill, forcing Speaker Rayburn and majority leader Bankhead to make a difficult decision. Were they willing to engage in divisive arm-twisting to achieve the two-thirds vote necessary to bypass Sumners's committee in order to bring the legislation directly to the House floor? They were not. The bill, therefore, was sent to the Senate first, which held its own pitfalls for the president.

Roosevelt had not anticipated the furor over his proposal. But he did not wait for Senate hearings to prepare a spirited counteroffensive, appealing directly to voters. In two speeches spaced five days apart, he abandoned the judicial reform rationale of his message to Congress and bluntly admitted that the fight was about the survival of the New Deal. It was also about his leadership, which had been emphatically affirmed by more than 27 million Americans who voted for him in November.

On March 4, exactly four years since his first inauguration, the president reminded 1,300 Democrats at a $100 plate dinner in the Mayflower Hotel's grand ballroom (and a half million more of the party faithful connected by radio hookup at similar "victory" dinners in forty-three states) that theirs was the majority party obligated to do the people's business. That was impossible when one institution of the federal government—he did not name the Court—struck down major New Deal statutes designed to help ordinary Americans. The Agricultural Adjustment Act was meant to help farmers in distress, he said, but "[y]ou know who assumed the power to veto, and did veto that program." He repeated the refrain for the NIRA, the Railroad Retirement Act, and the Guffey Coal Act. "If three well-matched horses are put to the task of plowing up a field where the going is heavy, and the team of three pull as one, the *field . . . will . . . be . . . plowed*," he said, bobbing his head up and down in cadence with his words. "If one horse lies down in the traces or plunges off in another direction, the *field . . . will . . . not . . . be . . . plowed!*" His audience cheered and whistled their approval.

In his eighth fireside chat as president, given five days after his fiery Mayflower harangue, Roosevelt delivered a quieter speech, assuring the millions in his radio audience that he was not a power-hungry dictator, as charged by the Republican press, but a president defending democracy's noblest aspirations. Reread the Constitution, he instructed, just as he encouraged his listeners to read the Bible again and again. The Court had created a problem for the nation, because it was "reading into the Constitution words and implications which are not there and which were never intended to be there." The point had been reached as a nation, he said, "where we must take action to save the Constitution from the Court and the Court from itself."

Privately, Roosevelt employed his superior communication skills to convince wavering Democrats in Congress that his Court plan was reasonable and necessary. He summoned them to the White House individually and in small groups, treating them gently, as he might have calmed a nervous horse in his early riding days. He discussed the salient points in the legislation without asking for commitments. But his unspoken appeal was to their party loyalty and the threat to the New Deal's success posed by the conservative Court majority.

He could count on stalwart New Deal loyalists, like the populist Senator Hugo Black of Alabama. But other usually reliable Roosevelt men, such as Senator Joseph O'Mahoney of Wyoming, who was also a vocal Court critic, balked. He criticized the bill for failing to limit the Court's power of judicial review and did not think it was an effective remedy for aging justices or divided Court decisions. Conservative Democratic senator Carter Glass of Virginia did not mince words in his opposition to the bill. "There has been no mandate from the people to rape the Supreme Court or tamper with the Constitution," he said.

More troubling to Roosevelt than either O'Mahoney's or Glass's opposition was that of the progressive Democratic senator Burton Wheeler of Montana. A prominent liberal voice in the Senate for more than a decade, Wheeler had given Roosevelt his first important endorsement for the presidency, spearheaded the drive for his nomination among northwest liberals at the 1932 convention, and helped draft one of the signature measures of the Second Hundred Days, the Public Utilities Holding Act. Despite his thoroughgoing support for Roosevelt and the New Deal, Wheeler never felt that he had been treated as an administration insider, a status that he thought he had earned. His opposition to Roosevelt's Court bill went beyond personal pique. He believed it undermined a healthy balance of power among the three federal branches of government, dangerously skewing it toward the White House. Wheeler's stance deprived Roosevelt of the argument that reactionaries alone wanted to defeat the bill.

Shortly after Roosevelt sent his message to Congress in early February, the president's gadabout young lieutenant, Tommy Corcoran, learned of the vehemence of Wheeler's opposition to the bill when he and Wheeler met for lunch at the Dodge Hotel near the Capitol. The two men, who had been allies in drafting the Public Utilities Holding Company Act, began arguing about the bill. Finally, Corcoran pounded the table and said, "It's going to pass."

"I tell you it isn't going to pass," Wheeler answered with equal fervor. "And what's more I'm going to fight it with everything I've got."

Wheeler kept his word, spearheading opposition in the Senate on both sides of the aisle. He worked with Democratic conservatives, New Deal liberals, anti-Roosevelt Republicans, and fellow progressives, like William Borah of Idaho. A vaunted legislative infighter, he was adept at using obscure parliamentary rules to advance his cause. And though not a great orator, his speeches could deliver a punch. "I speak to you tonight as a lifelong liberal," he told a radio audience. "A liberal cause was never won by stacking a deck of cards, nor by stuffing a ballot box, nor by packing the court."

At 10:30 a.m. on the morning of March 10, Henry Fountain Ashurst, Chairman of the Senate Judiciary Committee, convened hearings on S. 1392, "a bill to reorganize the judicial branch of government." To accommodate the demand for seats, Ashurst had moved the sessions from the small corner room on the ground floor of the Capitol to the ornate Senate Caucus Room. Spectators filled all four hundred chairs, while dozens of reporters and photographers crowded in front of the long rectangular table of the eighteen-member committee.

The administration's first witness was Attorney General Cummings, who, unlike the president, defended the original rationale for the bill—overcrowded dockets and worn-out, elderly judges. For the justices to keep abreast of all briefs and lower court records, he said, "would be like reading *Gone with the Wind* before breakfast every morning."

Once Cummings had read his prepared statement, an impatient Senator Borah, speaking out of turn, asked, "Suppose after the six additional members of the Supreme Court are appointed, the Court should divide seven to eight, this entire plan would fall, would it not?"

"It would depend upon which side the seven were on," Cummings responded with a knowing grin, "and upon which side the eight were on."

Cummings was followed by Assistant Attorney Robert Jackson who, with the president's knowledge, had dropped judicial reform arguments in favor of a direct attack on the conservative Court majority. The New Deal was perilously close to "being lost in a maze of constitutional metaphors," he warned. The justices should be bound by their sense of self-restraint, as Justice Stone had pleaded in his *Butler* dissent. But "self-restraints are proving no restraints," he lamented.* He then used former New York governor Hughes's often misconstrued 1907 quotation on the Court to support the administration's argument for additional justices: "If the Constitution is what the judges say it is, then we should have something to say about who the judges are." †

Senator Wheeler, who was scheduled to be the first committee witness opposing the bill, hoped to enlist the Chief Justice in his cause. On Thursday, March 18, Wheeler, accompanied by the ranking Republican on the Judiciary Committee, Warren Austin of Vermont, and the second-ranking Democrat, William King of Utah, called on Hughes at his home to ask if he would testify before the committee.

"I was entirely willing to do this for the purpose of giving the facts as to the work of the Court," Hughes recalled. But he told the senators that he thought it advisable that he be joined by a colleague, preferably Louis Brandeis, "because of his standing as a Democrat and his reputation as a liberal judge." Brandeis adamantly refused, and told Hughes that no member of the Court should appear before the committee. Van Devanter, whom Hughes also consulted, agreed with Brandeis.

The next day, Hughes placed phone calls to Wheeler and King, informing them of "the very strong feeling" among his colleagues that no justice should testify. But he added, "On matters relating to the actual work of the Court, I should be glad to answer in writing giving the facts."

Wheeler later recounted the events leading to his next meeting with Hughes the following day. They began with a visit by Alice Brandeis, the justice's wife, to the Alexandria home of Elizabeth Colman, Burton Wheeler's daughter. Justice Brandeis and Senator Wheeler, both progressive Democrats, and their wives had been close friends since the Wheelers

---

* Justice Stone wrote his sons that Jackson had given "a powerful exposition" for the popular view that "the Court has misused its powers," a view that he had often expressed in his dissents. But he also noted "a strong popular feeling" that the Supreme Court should not "get its law from Presidential messages."

† Shortly after Jackson's testimony, Hughes wrote a letter of thanks to Ogden Reed, publisher of the *New York Herald Tribune*, for an editorial that explained the context of his 1907 quotation which had been misinterpreted by Jackson and Roosevelt.

first arrived in Washington more than a decade earlier. Mrs. Brandeis's visit appeared to be a purely social call to celebrate the birth of Senator Wheeler's grandson, six-week-old Tommy Colman. But before leaving, Mrs. Brandeis said to Mrs. Colman, "Tell your father, the justice is in favor of his fight against the Court bill."

Wheeler's daughter immediately conveyed the message to her father, who decided to make a late afternoon call on his old friend Louis Brandeis. The justice, after reiterating his view that no member of the Court should testify before the Judiciary Committee, told Wheeler, "You call the Chief Justice and he'll give you a letter." Wheeler hesitated, at which point Brandeis led him to the telephone and dialed Hughes's number. When Hughes came on the line, Wheeler asked if he might pay the Chief Justice another visit, this time without Senators Austin and King. Hughes immediately invited him to his house, which was only a few blocks from Brandeis's apartment.

After Hughes greeted Wheeler warmly, the senator told him that Brandeis had said he would give him a letter.

"Did Brandeis tell you that?" he asked. Wheeler's recollection may have been slightly enhanced for dramatic effect. By Hughes's own account, he could not have been surprised by Wheeler's request on that Saturday afternoon, since he had told Wheeler and King a day earlier that he was willing to furnish a report in writing on the Court's workload.

"When do you want it?" Hughes asked.

Wheeler said that he would like to have the letter by Monday morning when he was scheduled to testify before the Judiciary Committee. On Sunday afternoon, Hughes called Wheeler and asked him to come to his home. When he arrived, Hughes handed him a seven-page letter.

"The baby is born," the Chief Justice said with a broad smile.

After Roosevelt announced his Court proposal on February 5, the National Broadcasting Company telegraphed Chief Justice Hughes with an offer to make its radio facilities available "to any member of the Supreme Court to discuss the proposal to Congress made by the President today." Hughes's secretary wired back that the Chief Justice "thanks you but does not care to take advantage of it." Hughes also declined an invitation from The New York Times to discuss the president's proposal. Later, CBS's

Edward R. Murrow tried a different tact, suggesting that he come to Washington to interview Hughes about the president's plan. Again, Hughes's secretary declined on his behalf, saying that he did "not wish to put you to the inconvenience of coming to Washington."

The Chief Justice remained silent about Roosevelt's proposal, despite every aggressive effort by the press to pry open his true feelings. But no one familiar with Hughes's record or views on the Court could doubt that he deeply resented and disapproved of the plan.* The president's proposal threatened his most cherished institutional values, the Court's integrity and independence, subjects that he had written about long before he was appointed Chief Justice. Roosevelt's charge that the Court was behind in its work was especially insulting to Hughes. He took great pride in his efficient disposition of the Court's business. The plan, moreover, seriously undercut Hughes's status as the leader of the Court, as Harold Ickes acknowledged. "The proposal of the President is a distinct slap in his [Hughes's] face," Ickes wrote in his diary. "What a blow this will be to the prestige of Chief Justice Hughes."

No wonder, then, that Hughes enthusiastically welcomed Senator Wheeler's invitation to defend the Court's work. Wheeler rejoiced in what he described as his unexpected good fortune in securing Hughes's letter. But Wheeler's version differed from Hughes's own account, which was supported by transcriptions of his telephone conversations with Wheeler and King. Those conversations took place the day before Wheeler phoned the Chief Justice from Brandeis's apartment. The Chief Justice had expressed an eagerness to rebut Roosevelt's charges before he met alone with Wheeler.

When Wheeler appeared before the committee on the morning of March 22, he conducted himself with the easy confidence of a poker player who had successfully drawn to an inside straight. He first testified that he had been a great supporter of the president and New Deal legislation and had only reluctantly decided to oppose his Court proposal. He then pulled out Hughes's letter from his inside coat pocket. The letter, which had been read and approved by both Brandeis and Van Devanter, was a sharp rejoinder to every major premise in Roosevelt's judicial reform bill.

---

* Years later, Hughes confirmed in writing that he considered Roosevelt's plan an assault on the independence of the judiciary.

"The Supreme Court is fully abreast of its work," Hughes's letter began. With characteristic attention to detail, the Chief Justice then provided facts and figures to support his opening statement. "When we rose on March 15 (for the present recess) we had heard arguments in cases in which certiorari had been granted only 4 weeks before—February 15. . . . There is no congestion on our calendar." He assured the senators that this "gratifying condition" had been present for several years. There was no backlog or lack of careful consideration of cases meriting the justices' review. Roosevelt's proposed increase in the membership of the Court would actually impair efficiency, he contended. "There would be more judges to hear, more judges to confer, more judges to discuss, more judges to be convinced and decide." He concluded, "The present number of Justices is thought to be large enough so far as the prompt, adequate, and efficient conduct of the work of the Court is concerned."

Though Hughes's letter was dispassionate, its careful phrasing suggested that the Chief Justice sought tactical advantage in his battle with Roosevelt. By writing that he was "confident that it is in accord with the view of the Justices," Hughes gave the distinct impression that his letter had the unanimous support of his colleagues when, in fact, only Brandeis and Van Devanter had seen it. A statement by a unanimous Court would have had the most powerful impact on the senators and the public, as Hughes surely knew. The day after Wheeler read Hughes's letter, the Chief Justice met with the other justices and explained his reason for failing to consult all of them. He had planned to solicit their approval, he said, but found it impossible, given the brief time he had to prepare the letter. He hoped that they all approved of what he had written. Several assured him that they did. But Justice Stone resented what he considered Hughes's high-handed tactic and later made his disapproval known to other members of the Court.

The letter was only the first of three explosive Hughes missiles that jeopardized Roosevelt's Court-packing plan. The second blast, his strong opinion for the Court upholding the Washington minimum wage statute, was announced only a week after Senator Wheeler had read his letter to a hushed audience in the Senate Caucus Room. After Stone had returned to the Court the first week in February, he cast his vote, as expected, to uphold the minimum wage law. Hughes promptly assigned himself the majority opinion. But he delayed announcing it at the height of the uproar over the Roosevelt's proposal in an effort to avoid the insinuation that the Court had been intimidated by the president.

On the bright Monday morning of March 29, the day Hughes chose to announce the Court's minimum wage decision, the nation's capital was crammed with tourists for the Easter holidays. Four thousand visitors, many carrying cameras and Easter baskets, had been admitted to the imposing new Supreme Court building an hour before the Chief Justice was scheduled to convene the Court. Shortly after noon, those fortunate enough to be admitted to the session heard Hughes announce the decision in *West Coast Hotel Co. v. Parrish*, which he said "presents the question of the constitutional validity of the minimum wage law of the State of Washington."

The Chief Justice waited for the excited bustle of the crowd to subside before reading his opinion. Never one to scrimp in his recitation of the facts of a case, he then told the compelling legal story of Elsie Parrish, a chambermaid at the Cascadian Hotel in Wenatchee, Washington. Late in the summer of 1933, she had begun cleaning toilets and sweeping rugs at the hotel for an hourly wage of 22 cents, later raised to a quarter. She was discharged from her job in May 1935 and audaciously demanded $216.19 in back pay, the difference between her weekly pay and what she was entitled to under the state's minimum wage law. She refused the offer of the Cascadian, which was owned by the West Coast Hotel Corporation, to settle for $17. After consulting a local attorney, she sued.

The presiding judge of the superior court of Chelan County ruled against her, citing the U.S. Supreme Court's *Adkins* decision, which held that the District of Columbia's minimum wage law for women violated the liberty of contract. On appeal, the State Supreme Court overturned the lower court decision, claiming that *Adkins* involved a congressional statute and was not binding on the states. At the time, the Court had never struck down a state minimum wage law, though that was soon rectified by the conservative majority that invalidated New York's statute in *Tipaldo*, decided only six weeks after the decision by Washington State's Supreme Court.

To uphold Washington's minimum wage law and rule in favor of Elsie Parrish, Hughes knew that he must either distinguish the Court's *Tipaldo* decision or overrule it. He chose to distinguish the cases, which reflected his cautious judicial approach and may also have been calculated to give Roberts, the critical fifth vote for his majority, cover for his *Tipaldo* vote. In *Tipaldo*, Hughes observed, the Court had agreed with the New York Court of Appeals decision that *Adkins* was controlling precedent and, therefore, the state statute was invalid. In *Parrish*, he noted, the highest court in Washington State had explicitly denied that it was bound by *Adkins*.* The conflict between the two State Supreme Court decisions, the narrowness of the *Adkins* majority (5–4), and the desperate economic conditions, he said, justified the Court's reexamination of its ruling in *Adkins*.

His review of *Adkins* began with a careful reexamination of the freedom of contract, the constitutional foundation for the Court's 1923 decision. "What is the freedom of contract?" Hughes asked, his voice rising. "The Constitution does not speak of freedom of contract," he said. The liberty safeguarded by the Fourteenth Amendment's due process clause was not absolute, but allowed a state legislature to reasonably protect the health, safety, morals, and welfare of its people. "[E]ven if the wisdom of the policy be regarded as debatable and its effects uncertain, still the legislature is entitled to its judgment," Hughes noted, echoing Roberts's 1933 majority opinion in *Nebbia*, which upheld New York's milk-pricing statute.

Addressing Washington's minimum wage law, Hughes took "judicial notice of the unparalleled demands for relief which arose during the recent period of depression and still continue to an alarming extent despite the degree of economic recovery which has been achieved." The Constitution did not prevent a state from protecting the economic exploitation of workers from employers' "selfish disregard of the public interest." With language worthy of the most passionate reformer, he concluded that "[t]he Legislature was entitled to adopt measures to reduce the evils of the 'sweating system,' the exploiting of workers at wages so low as to be insufficient to meet the bare cost of living, thus making their very helplessness the occasion of a most injurious competition." Elsie Parrish, therefore, was entitled to her $216.19 in back pay, as required by her state's minimum wage law.

Heartening as was the chambermaid's victory, the Court decision had vastly more important implications. *Adkins*, the substantive due process decision that had haunted reformers for more than a decade, was overruled. With his majority opinion, Hughes pointed the Court in a direction that

---

* Roberts later explained his apparently contradictory votes in the New York and Washington State cases, offering a rationale slightly different from that of Hughes in his *Parrish* opinion. In the New York case, he voted to strike down the statute because the state's attorney had not made the necessary argument that the *Adkins* precedent must be overruled in order to sustain the state law. In the Washington case, Roberts contended, incorrectly, that the state had asked the Court to overrule *Adkins*. Roberts wrote, therefore, that he felt free to vote to overturn *Adkins* and uphold the state law.

promised to accommodate progressive legislation passed in the states and by the New Deal Congress. It was a constitutional development that had appeared all but impossible only a year earlier.*

Though New Dealers were gratified by the Court's *Parrish* decision, they nonetheless attributed cynical motives to the pivotal Justice Owen Roberts. "[W]ith the shift by Roberts," Frankfurter wrote Roosevelt, "even a blind man ought to see that the Court is in politics, and understand how the Constitution is 'judicially' construed. It is a deep object lesson—a lurid demonstration—of the relation of men to the 'meaning' of the Constitution." Frankfurter added a sneering comment about the Chief Justice, questioning Hughes's motives in writing his letter to the Judiciary Committee. "*That* was a characteristic Hughes performance—part and parcel of that pretended withdrawal from considerations of policy, while trying to shape them, which is the core of the mischief of which the majority have so long been guilty."

Pundits later joined Frankfurter in his contemptuous assessment of Roberts's vote in *Parrish*, dubbing it "the switch in time that saved nine." Feeling the heat of Roosevelt's Court-packing plan, Roberts, they concluded, caved in to political pressure.† Both Roberts and Hughes knew that explanation was wrong, since Roberts had voted to overturn the Washington minimum wage statute more than a month before Roosevelt announced his Court-packing plan.

The public demeaning of Roberts infuriated Hughes. He not only resented the false accusation, but also was appalled by the implicit attack on his colleague's character. He knew that the sixty-two-year-old Roberts (who would not have been affected by Roosevelt's plan) had no intention of quietly bending to the president's will. After the plan was announced, Roberts vowed to resign in protest if the proposal became law. Unlike Roberts, Hughes never considered resignation. "If they want me to preside over a convention," he said defiantly, "I can do it."

Two weeks after reading his *Parrish* opinion, Hughes delivered his third searing rebuttal to Roosevelt's Court-packing plan. On the heels

---

* On the same day, the Court announced three other opinions favorable to the New Deal. One upheld the National Firearms Act; a second sustained a redrafted federal statute providing mortgage insurance to farmers; and a third found the collective bargaining requirements of the Railway Labor Act constitutional.

† After his appointment to the Court, Frankfurter regretted his judgment on his colleague's motivation in *Parrish* and later wrote an article defending Roberts's vote.

of his letter to the Judiciary Committee and his *Parrish* opinion, he announced the Court's decision sustaining the constitutionality of the action of the National Labor Relations Board (NLRB), a critical component of the Wagner Act. In doing so, Hughes, writing for the same five justices as in *Parrish*, rejected the claim that the NLRB had invaded the reserve powers of the states. His majority opinion further exposed the weakness of Roosevelt's argument that the current justices were determined to destroy the New Deal.

The Chief Justice's comprehensive opinion in *NLRB v. Jones & Laughlin Steel Corp.* demolished the direct-indirect commerce clause analysis that had been championed by conservative justices for more than forty years. Devoid of the precious technical distinctions that had marred his opinions in *Carter v. Carter Coal* and *Tipaldo* the previous term, he wrote with a confident mastery of the facts and law in the case.

At the outset, he described in detail the far-flung operations of Jones & Laughlin, the nation's fourth largest steel producer. Though its major plants manufacturing iron and steel were located in Pittsburgh and nearby Aliquippa, Pennsylvania, the corporation was what Hughes termed "a completely integrated enterprise." It operated ore, coal, and limestone properties, lake and river transportation facilities, and terminal railroads located at the manufacturing plants. Its commercial interests spread across Michigan and Minnesota, where it owned or controlled mines, and included four ore ships operating on the Great Lakes. In addition to the steel and iron manufacturing plants in Pennsylvania, the corporation owned coal mines in the state and operated tugboats and steam barges used to carry the coal to its factories. Approximately 75 percent of the corporation's products were shipped out of Pennsylvania to warehouses in Chicago, Detroit, Cincinnati, and Memphis.

Hughes approvingly quoted an NLRB report that analogized Jones & Laughlin's operations in Pennsylvania "to the heart of a self-contained, highly integrated body." Extending the metaphor, the report compared the corporation's supply lines to arteries that drew raw materials from four states, transformed the materials, then pumped them out to all parts of the nation.

Having provided the factual context in telling detail, Hughes addressed Jones & Laughlin's argument that the NLRB's order, which reinstated ten workers who had been discharged for union activity, was beyond the reach of the federal government. Whether the NLRB had the constitutional authority to cite Jones & Laughlin for an unfair labor practice depended on the Court's interpretation of Congress's power to regulate interstate commerce. "It is the effect on commerce, not the source of the injury," he wrote, that defines the boundary of congressional authority. He posed the constitutional question in practical terms: Did the activity have a close and substantial relation to interstate commerce? It was an approach that Hughes had first articulated as an associate justice in his 1914 *Shreveport Rate Case* opinion. Once he endorsed the "close and substantial" analysis, he had no difficulty identifying the necessary nexus between the NLRB's order and its effect on interstate commerce.

Experience, not theory, must guide the Court in its interpretation of the commerce clause, he insisted, and "[e]xperience has abundantly demonstrated that the recognition of the right of employees to self-organization and to have representatives of their own choosing for purpose of collective bargaining is often an essential condition of industrial [peace]." The federal government rightfully assumed oversight of labor relations at Jones & Laughlin, whose complex corporate operations fanned out to states far beyond its Pennsylvania base. "When industries organize themselves on a national scale, making their relation to interstate commerce the dominant factor in their activities," he concluded, Congress had the power to protect interstate commerce "from the paralyzing consequences of industrial war."

In two other decisions announced the same day, the slim majority of five justices sustained the constitutionality of the National Labor Relations Act in two smaller industries, holding that Congress's power to regulate interstate commerce extended to the manufacturing of trailers and clothes. Though the operations at issue were smaller than Jones & Laughlin's, the Court concluded that both businesses obtained substantial amounts of raw materials from other states and shipped most of their products for sale across state lines.

The liberal *Nation* magazine responded enthusiastically, describing the decisions as "nothing short of a miracle," and applauding the new Court majority as "a stabilizing force in our national life." But a fellow liberal publication, the *New Republic*, cautioned that champagne bottles should remain corked. "Who knows when Mr. Justice Roberts will do another flop?" the editor asked.

*   *   *

The day after Senator Wheeler read Hughes's letter to the Judiciary Committee, the political cartoonist for the *Christian Science Monitor* depicted a large cannonball smashing through the center of Roosevelt's written claim that the Court was overworked. The caption underneath the cartoon read: "Chief Justice Hughes's Letter Makes Its Mark."

If the president was distraught over Hughes's statement, he did not show it. On the morning of Wheeler's testimony, March 22, Roosevelt was basking in natural spring waters in a swimming pool at Warm Springs, Georgia. Afterward, he rested in his cottage before receiving a delegation from the literary society at the University of Georgia that made him an honorary member. When he phoned Harold Ickes later in the week, he was his usual cheerful self. He seemed more concerned about the effects of proliferating sit-down strikes, which had idled more than 160,000 workers in industries across the country, than the political fallout from Hughes's letter. He told Ickes that Senate majority leader Joe Robinson and some others on Capitol Hill "were jittery about the sit-down strike situation" and its effect on his Court fight. But Ickes assured him that the labor strife only strengthened the administration's argument that such disturbances were exacerbated by a Court "that isn't up to date on social and economic questions."

Roosevelt made no comment to Ickes on Hughes's letter, according to the secretary's diary. For his part, Ickes grudgingly gave the Chief Justice high marks for "good tactics," conceding that "Hughes chose to fight his skirmish where we were weakest." The Interior Secretary, nonetheless, remained optimistic about prospects for the success of the president's plan. He noted that the administration had long abandoned the court reform argument that was the target of Hughes's letter. Ickes's observation was strangely at odds with that of another cabinet member, Homer Cummings, whose recent testimony before the Judiciary Committee had made reorganization of the federal judiciary its primary focus.

Just as Roosevelt appeared to ignore Hughes's letter, he was similarly undaunted by an attack on his Court-packing plan by an old friend, Harvard University's treasurer Jerome Green. In a letter to *The New York Times*, Green asserted that it was "impossible not to recognize that the packing of the Supreme Court as exactly what a dictator would adopt as his first step," adding that the president "may not know where he is going, but he is on his way." Roosevelt thanked Green for sending him a copy of his *Times* letter, but repeated his familiar refrain that "unless this nation continues as a nation—*with three branches of government pulling together to keep it going*—you might find yourself unable to write to the paper a quarter of a century hence."

Even after Chief Justice Hughes announced the Court's *Parrish* decision that upheld Washington's minimum wage law, Roosevelt was unmoved. "Mr. President, do you think the Supreme Court is curing itself?" a reporter asked Roosevelt at a press conference the next day. The president shrugged. "I don't think there is any news in it [the *Parrish* decision]," he replied. "To tell you the honest truth, I haven't even had time to read the opinions." He said only that he would ask Attorney General Cummings to advise him on whether Hughes's *Parrish* opinion revived the District of Columbia's minimum wage law that had been invalidated in *Adkins*. If that was Cummings's conclusion, another reporter persisted, "would you explore the possibility of having other laws, such as NRA and AAA . . ." Roosevelt cut him off. "You are getting too 'iffy," he said.

On the Senate floor, majority leader Robinson attempted to turn Hughes's *Parrish* opinion to Roosevelt's advantage. "From 1922 until a few hours ago, it was unconstitutional for a state to have a minimum-wage law for the protection of women and children from oppressive conditions," he told his colleagues. "Now within the last few hours, it has become entirely constitutional." This turnabout suggested to Robinson that "what Mr. Justice Hughes said is in a sense correct (i.e., that 'the Constitution is what the judges say it is')." It was time, therefore, to bring new justices onto the Court, he contended. But Senator Wheeler immediately challenged Robinson's supposition. With decisions by the new Court majority upholding progressive legislation, there was no need for Roosevelt's Court-packing plan, he asserted.

In the midst of the Court fight, Roosevelt, dressed in white tie and tails, joined Chief Justice Hughes and five hundred other VIPs who attended the Gridiron Club Dinner in the Willard Hotel ballroom. To the tune of "March of the Soldiers," fifteen journalists, dressed in robes and sporting miniature straw hats, entered the room carrying a giant rubber stamp and sang:

Nobody knows the opinions I sign,
Nobody knows but Franklin . . .

Holding their noses, the chorus belted out another ditty to a popular Cole Porter melody:

> It's delib'rate, it's deceptive,
> It's deplorable, it's delirious . . .

Both Roosevelt and Hughes joined in the laughter.

At the end of the evening, Hughes was serenaded with "Happy Birthday," in honor of his seventy-fifth birthday, only hours away. The president unabashedly joined in the happy salute, even though the Chief Justice's advanced age (and leadership) were central targets of his Court plan. After listening to the birthday greeting and receiving a standing ovation, Hughes rose and bowed graciously to the cheers and applause, but said nothing.

Two days later, he found his public voice, triumphantly reading his opinion in *NLRB v. Jones & Laughlin* to the capacity crowd in the courtroom. Roosevelt, too, had much to say about Hughes's opinion a few hours later, though in private conversation. He was furious that the opinion, which broadly interpreted Congress's commerce clause power, deprived him of the jolt he needed to prod the Senate toward passage of his bill. He blamed the Chief Justice for attempting to defeat his bill. "It was political, purely," he said of the Court's decision. "It was engineered by the Chief Justice," whom he considered his "most dangerous, implacable enemy."

The president's mood improved appreciably the next day when he joked with reporters about the Court's decision during an off-the-record press conference. He had been "chortling all morning," he said, and was particularly amused by the editorial in the *New York Herald Tribune* trumpeting the Court's "great" *Jones & Laughlin* decision. At his request, his press secretary Steve Early had found a previous editorial in that "elegant, establishmentarian New York daily" when the Wagner Act had passed— denouncing it as unconstitutional! The Court seemed to have abandoned its "no man's land of regulation,"* he said, and "we are now in Roberts' Land."

The president could have his fun with reporters, but his point man on the Judiciary Committee, chairman Henry Ashurst, was increasingly unhappy. Opponents of the legislation had dominated press coverage for

---

* FDR's reference was to his denunciation of the Court's decision in *Tipaldo* that invalidated New York's minimum wage for women.

weeks with testimony vociferously objecting to the president's plan. The chairman felt the political ground shifting under him. When the hearings finally ended on April 23, Ashurst concluded that the majority of his committee opposed the bill and would support a report criticizing it.

Roosevelt summoned Ashurst to the Oval Office. "At the White House today the mercury of his manners toward me registered zero," Ashurst recalled. The president told him that he wanted the bill reported out of the Judiciary Committee without recommendation. He then handed Ashurst a memorandum with data to be included in the report. That afternoon, Ashurst showed Roosevelt's memo to Robinson. Both Democratic Senate leaders concluded that it would not be possible to report the bill out of committee without recommendation, as the president desired.

Even with Ashurst's pessimistic report, Roosevelt insisted that the Senate votes were still there for passage of the legislation. "It is quite clear that the utter confusion of our opponents among themselves means success for us," he wrote Frankfurter, "even though it may be deferred until June or July." He was encouraged in his assessment by the optimistic projections of supporters, like Ickes, who reported from his sources inside the Republican National Committee that the GOP could rely on only 37 votes against the legislation (49 was a majority). The president agreed, based on his own calculations. The problem for Roosevelt was that there remained 17 uncommitted votes. And despite his rosy forecast that he could count on at least twelve of those uncommitted senators to vote in favor of the legislation, it was by no means a foregone conclusion.

Still, there was no talk of compromise from the president, even after three previously uncommitted Democrats on the Judiciary Committee announced their opposition to the bill. Now it was Senator Wheeler, leader of the opposition, who talked tough. "We're all taking the president at his word," he told reporters. "He said, 'No compromise.' We will not accept any compromise. We will vote against any and all amendments and against the bill."

Ashurst, a reluctant champion of the legislation, continued to serve as the administration's good soldier in his public pronouncements. He scoffed at reports that his committee would produce a negative report. And even if it did, he told reporters, an "unfavorable report would in no sense be a fatal blow."

At ten o'clock on the morning of May 18, the members of the Senate Judiciary Committee filed into their committee room for final deliberations before voting on their recommendation to the full Senate on the president's proposal. The closed-door session began with a series of six votes on amendments, each proposed by Roosevelt's supporters searching for a compromise. All failed. The committee voted 10 to 8 against reporting the president's proposal favorably out of committee.

Fifteen minutes before the Judiciary Committee convened to vote on the president's plan, Roosevelt's valet brought him a letter on a tray while he was reading the morning papers in bed. It was from Justice Willis Van Devanter, informing the president that he would retire on June 2, the last day of the Court's term. Roosevelt asked his valet for pencil and paper and scrawled a reply. It had been a privilege to know the justice for many years, he wrote, and he extended every good wish for his retirement. Before leaving Washington for the summer, he added, he hoped Van Devanter "would come in to see me."

The timing of Van Devanter's letter was not a coincidence. At the request of Van Devanter's close friend, William Borah, the justice had delayed writing his retirement letter for more than a month. Borah, who vehemently opposed Roosevelt's Court plan, wanted it to coincide with the deliberations of the Senate Judiciary Committee for maximum impact on the debate. The justice's retirement, Borah reasoned, would provide another strong argument for senators to oppose the bill, since the departure of the first of the Four Horsemen significantly diminished the influence of the Court's formidable conservative bloc.

The seventy-eight-year-old Van Devanter had spoken to colleagues for several years about his desire to retire. But he had been discouraged by Congress's action in 1933, after Justice Holmes retired, that cut retiring justices's pensions to half of their full salaries of $20,000. During Congress's winter session in 1937, Hatton Sumners, chairman of the House Judiciary Committee and a friend of Van Devanter's, sponsored a bill to restore the justices' pensions at their pre-1933 level. After the bill passed on March 1, Van Devanter made his decision to retire, but was persuaded by Borah to delay his announcement.

Van Devanter's retirement would, under normal circumstances, have pleased the president, giving him the opportunity to nominate a Supreme Court justice for the first time in more than four years in office. Instead, it complicated the turbulent politics surrounding his Court plan. Opponents immediately seized upon the vacancy to argue that it made the president's proposal superfluous. The vacancy also posed a delicate political problem for Roosevelt. It was common knowledge on Capitol Hill that during his first one hundred days in office he had promised the first Court appointment to Senate majority leader Robinson. But Robinson, while a loyal New Dealer, was also a friend to utility companies in his native Arkansas and suspected of latent conservative tendencies. And he was sixty-four years old, hardly the picture of the young, vigorous judicial talent that Roosevelt had promised to send to the Court.

Robinson considered the nomination to be his, as did his Senate colleagues. After the announcement of Van Devanter's retirement, Republicans and Democrats alike swarmed around him on the Senate floor, giving him congratulatory hugs and slaps on the back, and addressing him as "Mr. Justice."

At a news conference on May 21, Roosevelt was asked: "Do you intend to confirm the Senate nomination of Senator Robinson to the Supreme Court?"

"I have not considered the Supreme Court vacancy at all," Roosevelt replied. "And I don't expect to for some time."

Robinson made no secret of his disappointment in the president's dilatory tactics. "Everybody's told me they're for me except that fellow in the White House," he grumbled.

Three days after Roosevelt's press conference, the Court announced two decisions that upheld the Social Security Act. Both majority opinions were written by Justice Cardozo, who distanced the Court from its *Butler* decision the previous term that had struck down the AAA. In his first opinion (for the now familiar five-member liberal majority), Cardozo found the unemployment compensation provisions of the act constitutional. Under the statute, a payroll tax was imposed on employers of eight or more workers, but the employers were entitled to a credit of up to 90 percent of the federal tax for any contributions to a comparable state unemployment fund. Cardozo distinguished the payroll tax, which went into general funds, from the processing tax ruled unconstitutional in *Butler*. Unlike the tax in *Butler*, there was no showing that "the tax and the credit in combination are weapons of coercion, destroying or impairing the autonomy of the states." He also noted that the impoverished states could not afford to pay for the relief. "[There] was need of help from the nation if the people were not to starve," he wrote.

In the companion case, the Court upheld the old age benefits provisions of the Social Security Act. Relying on *Butler*'s endorsement of the broad Hamiltonian interpretation of the spending clause, Cardozo admitted that there was a constitutional line to be drawn, but that discretion belonged to Congress unless its choice was clearly wrong. Here, it was not. He again acknowledged that the problem was "plainly national," well beyond the financial means of the states. "Only a power that is national can serve the interests of all," he concluded.

In upholding the constitutionality of the Social Security Act, Cardozo deftly distinguished the cases from the conservative majority's precedent of the previous term (*Butler*). The approach was similar to that employed by Hughes in his *Jones & Laughlin* opinion, which distinguished but did not overrule *Carter v. Carter Coal*. The advantages to these somewhat strained interpretations of recent precedents were obvious. They reinforced the Court's institutional image of maintaining continuity with past decisions, a cherished judicial value. They also attracted the support of Justice Roberts, who had voted with the conservatives in the earlier decisions.*

The Chief Justice, meanwhile, continued to wage low-key, judicious warfare against the president's legislation. In May, he delivered a speech to the American Law Institute, reiterating the claims of his letter to the judiciary committee. "[T]he Court is fully up with its work," he said, adding, "I am happy to say that it is true of the current term." He also suggested that society was better served by "the processes of reason as opposed to tyranny of force." If society chose to be governed by the processes of reason, he continued, "it must maintain the institutions which embody those processes." No one in the audience could doubt his meaning.

During the Court's term, the justices upheld every New Deal statute that had been challenged. "[T]he New Deal's victory was complete," declared *The Washington Post*. But Justice Stone, who had voted with the majority in every one of those decisions, wrote Frankfurter that he questioned "the permanence of sudden conversions."

Frankfurter was even warier than Stone of the unexpected turn of the Court. Though he favored the results, he did not trust the process,

---

* Robert's vote was crucial to form a five-man majority in the first decision upholding the Social Security Act as well as in *Jones & Laughlin*. In the second Social Security Act case, concerning old age pensions, there was a seven-man majority, with only Justices Butler and McReynolds dissenting.

"because of the political somersaults (for such they are) of the Chief and Roberts." He saved his most savage criticism for Hughes. "When I see how a synthetic halo is being fitted upon the head of one of the most politically calculating of men," he wrote Stone, "it makes me, in the sanctified language of the old gentleman [Holmes], 'puke.' "

Roosevelt waited two weeks before reaching out to the disenchanted Senate majority leader, Joe Robinson. During that time, his tiny circle of high-powered intellectual advisers (Corcoran, Cohen, and Jackson) urged him to abandon his Court-packing plan for the remainder of the congressional session. The president should declare victory and publicly take credit for the Court's newly minted liberal majority, Jackson advised, then reschedule debate on a far-reaching judicial bill for the next congressional term. But Roosevelt was not easily persuaded to back down, even temporarily, on a plan that he believed was necessary to preserve the New Deal and was supported by the voters. He nonetheless considered an alternative to the Jackson strategy, one that required the political savvy and clout of Senator Robinson.

Roosevelt asked his son James, now officially ensconced in the White House as his personal secretary, to pay a friendly visit to Robinson at his office on Capitol Hill, ostensibly to discuss a patronage matter important to the senator. James turned on the Roosevelt charm, assuring the majority leader of the president's boundless goodwill toward him. "Father's been wishing you would come to see him, Senator," James said. "In fact he's rather hurt that you've stayed away so long." Robinson replied gruffly that he did not want to appear to be seeking Van Devanter's seat on the Court. The president would never think Robinson so crass, James said. With those assuring words, James, by prearrangement with his father, grabbed the phone on Robinson's desk and dialed the president's private number. FDR immediately answered and asked Robinson to come by the White House that evening.

They talked for two hours, primarily about the chances for passage of the president's Supreme Court plan. Robinson said that he did not have the votes to pass the original proposal, but that he should be able to convince a majority of his colleagues to support a compromise. Roosevelt agreed to give Robinson complete control over the Senate fight, cutting off Corcoran, Cohen, and Jackson. In addition, the president, though not making an explicit commitment, strongly suggested that he would nominate the majority leader to replace Van Devanter on the Court. When Robinson left the White House, he hinted to waiting reporters of a compromise on the president's Court proposal. He was a happy man, they observed, beaming with good cheer and optimism.

"Tell us about your conversation with Senator Robinson last night," a reporter asked Roosevelt at his weekly press conference. Without responding directly, the president engaged the press corps in his usual friendly jousting, assuring them that it was "just plain silly" to think that he had abandoned his court reform proposal. He returned to his complaint about case backlogs from federal district courts all the way to the Supreme Court. While on the subject, he told them that he was concerned that the constitutionality of important legislation, such as the Public Works Administration and regulation of power companies, remained unresolved. He had done a little research and found out that, while the Supreme Court was required by statute to begin the term on the first Monday in October, nothing prevented the justices from cutting short their four-month summer holiday to eliminate needless delays.* When asked about the number of new justices he would demand under a compromise measure, he good-naturedly scolded reporters for concentrating on the "trees" (nominees) and losing sight of the "forest" (reform). "How many trees make a forest?" a reporter persisted. The president ignored the question.

While the president bantered with reporters, Senator Robinson huddled with influential Democratic colleagues to craft a compromise on Roosevelt's Court plan. Senator Charles Andrews of Florida proposed a revised plan that would have created an expanded Court of eleven justices, ten associate justices representing each of the federal judicial circuits, and a Chief Justice appointed at large. Robinson was unenthusiastic about Andrews's proposal, since it would have effectively excluded him from the Court (Justice Butler represented Robinson's circuit and had expressed no interest in retirement). A second proposal, more to Robinson's liking, was put forward by Senator Carl Hatch of New Mexico. Under Hatch's plan, a

---

* Roosevelt's criticism was misleading. The Court had disposed of every case on its docket that was adequately prepared for argument. Before the recess, the justices had ordered rearguments in four cases in which the government had vital interests but had not been represented in the first argument. They also agreed to hear two cases involving the rights of government to finance municipal power plants, which had not been ready for argument when the Court adjourned.

new seat would be added to the Court for every justice who refused to retire at the age to seventy-five (raised from seventy under FDR's proposal) but limited to only one a year.

Even Hatch's compromise proposal was a hard sell. Wheeler and other opponents smelled victory and were in no mood to retreat. Other Democrats openly questioned Roosevelt's stubborn refusal to withdraw his plan. "Why run for a train after you've caught it?" asked Senator James Byrnes of South Carolina.

In mid-June, Robinson's plan to forge an acceptable compromise among his Democratic colleagues was dealt a severe blow when Vice President Garner announced that he was leaving Washington to take his first vacation during a congressional session in more than thirty years. As vice president, Garner presided over the Senate and continued to wield influence in both chambers of Congress. No one asked Garner to spell out the reasons for his abrupt departure. It was well known, however, that he detested Roosevelt's proposal. Rather than assisting Robinson, he preferred to go fishing in a lake near his Uvalde home in South Texas.

A few days after Garner's announcement, the Senate Judiciary Committee released its final report, which provided a devastating critique of the president's proposal. It rejected Roosevelt's assertion that his proposal was truly a judicial reform bill and said that it was intended to persuade justices over seventy years old to resign. It castigated the president for presenting "a needless, futile, and utterly dangerous abandonment of constitutional principles." The bill's ultimate purpose "would be to make this government one of men rather than one of law, and its practical operation would be to make the Constitution what the executive or legislative branches of the government choose to say it is—an interpretation to be changed with each change of administration." The report's final sentence was the most damaging of all: "It is a measure which should be so emphatically rejected that its parallel will never again be presented to the free representatives of the free people of America."

While Congress remained in session in sultry Washington, the Chief Justice and his wife rested quietly in a small bungalow belonging to a small hotel in Littleton, New Hampshire. They spent long hours reading, taking walks, and enjoying daylong excursions by automobile. Though the couple ate in the hotel dining room, Hughes rarely spoke to anyone except his wife. Once a reporter reached him by telephone and asked if he would comment on the Court proposal. "No," he replied tersely.

But the Chief Justice willingly gave two speeches in late June, and his words could readily be deciphered to render harsh judgment not only on the rise of totalitarianism in Europe, but also on a domineering president's Court plan at home. On June 19, after attending the graduation ceremony of his grandson, Henry Stuart Hughes, from Amherst College, he told a luncheon audience of college alumni that "[w]e come to you with youthful hearts, with spiritual arteries not yet hardened." Though it was not appropriate for him to discuss contemporary political questions, he said, he worried that the institutions of democracy were threatened by an authoritarian philosophy. "[C]rusaders may have more fervor than wisdom, and extreme demands may create an intolerable civil strife," he observed. "Where shall we look for the balanced judgment, the sane appraisales and the reasonable methods by which civilized society may attain its purposes without surrendering the democratic principle to a regime of force?"

Two days later, he returned to the theme of authoritarianism at Brown University, where another of his grandsons, Charles Evans Hughes III, received his A.B. degree. "The question is no longer one of establishing democratic institutions but of preserving them," he told a group of alumni. "The question is not one of the adequate power of government, designed to keep clear the highways of honest endeavor," he said, "but how that power shall be used." Wise and responsible use of liberty was the effective antidote to "the arch enemies of society . . . who know better but by indirection, misstatement, understatement and slander seek to accomplish their concealed purpose or to gain profit of some sort by misleading the public."

At the end of June, Roosevelt made one last, grandiose effort to create a spirit of unity among congressional Democrats who had been torn apart by his Court proposal. He played genial host to more than 150 of his party's lawmakers for a three-day picnic on a small island in the Chesapeake Bay, four miles from Maryland's Eastern Shore. The president, wearing old linen slacks and a shirt open at the collar, presided under an apple tree, swapping tall tales with Democratic colleagues and watching them toss horseshoes, swim, shoot skeet, and roast hot dogs. It was all great fun, but did not soften the tense relations between the president and opponents of his plan.

Roosevelt and Senator Wheeler, the leader of the opposition, exchanged cheerful greetings at the beginning of the holiday, but did not speak again until they bid each other farewell at the end of the long weekend.

When Joe Robinson stepped ashore in Annapolis at the end of the weekend, he insisted to waiting reporters that the holiday activities had been strictly social. He nonetheless announced that he and other Democratic Senate leaders had conferred with the president and intended to open debate on a Court bill after the Fourth of July holiday. After the compromise measure (actually Senator Hatch's proposal) reached the floor of the Senate, opponents harassed Robinson and other supporters, interrupting them with constant objections.

In a final attempt to win over Wheeler, Roosevelt invited him to the White House for a friendly chat. Appealing to party loyalty, he assured the Montana senator that he wanted to modernize the federal judiciary, not destroy the Supreme Court. Wheeler ignored the president's plea and returned to the Court-packing issue. For most Americans, he said, the Court was sacred. The legislation not only jeopardized a revered institution, he argued, but would destroy the achievements of the Roosevelt presidency. The choice, Wheeler said, was between "coming out as a great President or a bad one." At meeting's end, neither man had budged.

An exhausted Robinson still counted enough votes to pass the compromise bill, but Wheeler's threat of a filibuster hung heavily over the Senate chamber. The bill suffered a decisive setback on the morning of July 14 when the majority leader was found dead on the floor of his apartment, the victim of a heart attack.

When John Nance Garner returned to Washington from attending Robinson's funeral in Little Rock, Arkansas, he met with the president to discuss the Court bill. How do you want to hear the bad news, the vice president inquired, "with the bark on or the bark off?" He preferred the unvarnished truth, Roosevelt replied. "You are beat, Capt'n," said Garner. "You haven't got the votes." On July 22, the Senate voted 70–20 to return the bill to the Judiciary Committee, effectively burying it.

Roosevelt later claimed that he lost the Court battle but won the war. He was only half right. He certainly lost the battle over his Court-packing plan. Throughout the arduous process, Hughes proved to be a shrewder politician than the president. His letter to the Judiciary Committee was instrumental in its defeat, as Robert Jackson later conceded. But Hughes, not Roosevelt, was also the victor in the larger war. With a critical assist from Justice Roberts, he astutely steered the Court away from outmoded constitutional interpretations that had obstructed progressive social and economic legislation. The Chief Justice also demonstrated that he was a wiser statesman than Roosevelt. With dignity, he successfully defended his institution's integrity and independence, withstanding taunts and repeated attacks by the most popular president in modern American history.

9

"The Great Arsenal of Democracy"

Roosevelt claimed victory at his weekly press conference the day after the Senate had resoundingly rejected his Court-packing plan. He recalled an earlier reformer, his beloved Cousin Teddy, who had railed against conservative judges during his Bull Moose presidential campaign in 1912. For two decades, beginning with TR's ill-fated 1912 campaign, progressives' agitation for judicial reform had produced "some pretty effective results," he said. "The courts listened and they *legislated*," he continued. Realizing his Freudian slip, he joined in the reporters' laughter. "I mean they decided, it is the same thing," he corrected. "They made their decisions more on judicial lines than on legislative lines."

His 1937 Court plan, he contended, simply advanced the progressives' judicial agenda. His intention all along had been to improve the judicial system, he said, and he had largely succeeded in his objective. To prove his point, he compared Supreme Court decisions before and after February 5, 1937 (the day he announced his Court plan). Prior to February 5, the Court had held minimum wage laws unconstitutional; after his proposal had been sent to Congress, the Court declared Washington State's minimum wage law constitutional. As a result of his proposal, he suggested, the Court had also reversed itself to uphold the Wagner Act (in *Jones & Laughlin*) and expand Congress's authority to spend for the general welfare in the

Social Security Act decisions. Though these achievements were laudable, they were only temporary, he warned. "We are getting somewhere," he concluded, "but we have a long way to go."

Roosevelt's sunny assessment may have been good political theater, but it was flawed judicial history. Early demands by progressives for a more liberal federal judiciary went largely unheeded, though there were modest reforms at the lower federal court level. The Supreme Court under Chief Justice Edward White was somewhat more moderate than in previous years. Still, the Court's liberal dissenters, Associate Justices Holmes and Hughes often pleaded in vain for more judicial deference to the popularly elected branches of government. In the 1920s, under Chief Justice Taft, the conservative Court majority more insistently blocked progressive legislation, including the District of Columbia's minimum wage law for women that was struck down in the *Adkins* decision.

The president's analysis of the salutary effects of his Court-packing plan was also overstated. The justices voted to uphold Washington's minimum wage law more than six weeks before he had announced his Court plan, though Roosevelt did not know it at the time. He was certainly not alone in suggesting that the Court wilted under his political pressure to uphold the Wagner and Social Security acts. Both Justice Stone and future Justice Frankfurter, among others, privately agreed with him.

But the authors of the major Wagner and Social Security Act opinions, Hughes and Cardozo, provided a plausible counter narrative. Both went to extraordinary lengths to distinguish their majority opinions from the conservative precedents of the previous term. Hughes insisted that Jones & Laughlin Steel Corporation's huge, multistate enterprise justified a different constitutional result from that reached in *Carter v. Carter Coal*, which dealt with the production of coal in a single state. And Justice Cardozo, in his opinion for a five-man majority upholding the unemployment benefits provisions of the Social Security Act, took pains to point out the critical difference between the "coercive" processing tax ruled unconstitutional in *Butler* and the tax that went into general funds for unemployment benefits.

Though Roosevelt smiled throughout his July 23 press conference, he was, in fact, furious over the defeat of his Court proposal. At his first cabinet meeting after the legislative debacle, he berated Vice President Garner for his ineffectual leadership in pushing the administration's legislative agenda. "He [Roosevelt] doesn't overlook any chance to send a pointed barb, albeit with a laugh, in the direction of the Vice President," Ickes noted in his diary.

Shortly afterward, when Ickes joined Roosevelt for a fishing trip on the Potomac, he observed that the president's face was heavily lined and gaunt, the toll taken, he surmised, from the brutal Court battle. Despite the draining experience, Roosevelt was already thinking ahead to his first chance to solidify what he had termed the temporary liberal swing on the Court. During the fishing trip, Roosevelt confided in Ickes that he was seriously considering two liberal senators, Sherman Minton of Indiana and Hugo Black of Alabama, both ardent supporters of his Court-packing plan, to replace retired Justice Van Devanter. The short list of potential Court nominees drawn up by Homer Cummings also included Solicitor General Stanley Reed, the able, if uninspired, Kentucky lawyer.

All three men satisfied the four essential criteria required by Roosevelt: unquestioned loyalty to the New Deal; relative youth (Minton was forty-seven, Black fifty-one, Reed fifty-two); residents of judicial circuits underrepresented on the Court; and easily confirmable by the Senate. On the last point, the nomination of Black or Minton would benefit from the unwritten rule of senatorial courtesy; the soft-spoken Reed enjoyed extremely good relations with members of the Senate.

Roosevelt had reservations, nonetheless, about each of the candidates. Reed, he felt, lacked the evangelical fire that he sought in his first liberal nominee. He did not think Black was as able a lawyer as Minton. But Minton was much more of a team player in the Senate than Black, and could perform valuable service in promoting the president's agenda during the remainder of what promised to be a fractious term.

On August 9, Minton made the president's choice easier when he asked Cummings, a close friend, to withdraw his name from consideration. In defending Roosevelt's Court-packing plan, Minton had viciously attacked the justices for what he considered their blatant anti–New Deal politics disguised as judicial opinions. The prospect of spending the remainder of his professional life in the company of the men he had so denigrated was not appealing. He also worried that his presence on the Court might cause further judicial retaliation against the New Deal. Besides, his political career was on the rise. When he told Cummings of his decision, Minton strongly recommended that Roosevelt nominate Black.

Even without Minton's endorsement, Roosevelt was increasingly drawn to Black. If nominated, the Alabama senator would be a highly unorthodox choice for the nation's highest Court. Hugo Black grew up in the dusty hill country of northern Alabama, the son of a struggling shop-keeper. He was largely self-educated, though he studied law for two years at the University of Alabama and graduated at the top of his small class. He made his reputation as a brilliant prosecutor and trial lawyer in Bir-mingham before successfully running for the Senate in 1926. During that campaign, he received the indispensable endorsement of the powerful Ku Klux Klan and was widely rumored to have been a member of that racist organization for a brief time. But in his two terms in the Senate, Black's record was unwaveringly liberal, even left-wing. He pushed aggressively for wage and price legislation, which was anathema to mainstream southern politicians. He was also one of the Senate's true intellectuals, reading vora-ciously in the fields of American history, philosophy, and political theory. Records at the Library of Congress showed that Black checked out more books than any other member of the Senate. And he took copious notes on his reading, annotating, for example, the complete works of Thomas Jefferson.

Roosevelt had no doubt that Black would bring his fiery liberal con-victions to the Court and considered his combative nature, demonstrated in his unyielding committee interrogations of corporate lobbyists, another asset. He knew, moreover, that Black was concerned about the severe hear-ing problems of his son, Sterling, and that a Court appointment would allow him to spend more time at home. FDR also factored in a cold politi-cal calculation: he thought Black was too liberal for his state and would face a tough reelection campaign in 1938. Better to secure this liberal New Dealer's service on the Court than risk his defeat at the polls. Black's nomi-nation would, finally, enable the president to settle a score with the Senate. Black was a loner in the Senate and despised by many of his colleagues. The president savored the thought of so many senators who had defied him during the Court fight grudgingly confirming their unpopular colleague. "Father was very angry at the Senate—hopping mad, almost," recalled James Roosevelt. "He wanted to get back at them, stick it to them."

The president took no one into his confidence during his final de-liberations on the nomination. On the afternoon of August 11, he made his decision and invited Black to meet him in the White House that evening. When Black was escorted to FDR's upstairs office, he thought the president might want to talk to him about pending wages and hours legislation. Roosevelt greeted Black warmly, but said nothing about the purpose of the meeting. He did not ask the senator a single question about his background or qualifications to serve on the Supreme Court. Instead, he showed him an official form for presidential nominations to be sent to the Senate. He had written in the words "Associate Justice of the Supreme Court of the United States" and, breaking into a broad smile, pointed to the blank space for the nominee's name. "Hugo, I'd like to write your name here," he said. After Black, as expected, agreed to be nominated, Roosevelt filled in his name, placed the commission in an envelope, and sealed it.

Roosevelt kept his latest secret from his press secretary, Steve Early, who told reporters the next morning that the Court nomination would probably be delayed for two weeks. At noon, a White House messenger was despatched to the Senate with the sealed envelope. At the rostrum, Vice President Garner ripped open the envelope and announced to the astonished senators that Hugo L. Black of Alabama had been nominated to sit on the Supreme Court. Most of Black's colleagues sat in mute silence. Only a tiny band of Black's liberal colleagues, like Senator LaFollette, rushed over to congratulate him. Senator Ashurst, recovering quickly from the stunning news, stood to ask that Black's nomination be confirmed by acclamation. But Hiram Johnson of California rose to object and the nomination was referred to the Judiciary Committee. After several days of largely perfunctory deliberations, which included a delicate discussion of Black's purported KKK membership, the nomination was reported favorably to the Senate. On August 17, Black's nomination was confirmed 63–16 (with seventeen senators not voting).

Roosevelt exulted in Black's confirmation. In a fighting speech the next day, he excoriated those who placed supreme power in a democracy with an elite, educated class "deeply interested in the security of property." He did not mention Black's detractors or the conservative justices he was expected to join on the Court, but his point was meant to sting all of them.

The president's feisty defense of Black did not make his first Court appointment secure. Widely circulated rumors of Black's reputed membership in the KKK suddenly became very public on Monday, September 13, when the *Pittsburgh Post-Gazette* published the first in a series of articles by investigative reporter Ray Sprigle that began: "Hugo Lafayette Black, associate justice of the United States Supreme Court, is a member of the hooded brotherhood that for 10 long blood-drenched years ruled the Southland with lash and noose and torch, the Invisible Empire Knights of the Ku Klux Klan. He holds his membership in the masked and oath-bound legion as he holds his high office in the Nation's Supreme Tribunal—for life."

The president was taken by surprise by the revelation of Black's ties to the Klan, though it had long been common knowledge in Washington. Not only had it been openly discussed in the Senate cloakroom, but Charles Michelson, the director of publicity for the Democratic National Committee, had written a series of articles in 1926 for the *New York World* on Black's Klan connection. In Roosevelt's meeting with Black on August 11, he had not asked the senator about his prior affiliations or anything else of substance. And Black, who had long since abandoned any tie to the Klan (Sprigle was wrong about his lifetime membership), considered it a distant and irrelevant chapter in his rise to national prominence as an outspoken southern liberal.

The president told reporters that he would have no comment on the *Post-Gazette* story until Black and his wife, Josephine, who were vacationing in Europe, returned to Washington. The unspoken message: Black was on his own to save or lose his Court appointment.

At the height of the furor over Black's Klan membership, Roosevelt rekindled his simmering feud with the Court. On the 150th anniversary of the signing of the U.S. Constitution—September 17—he told a crowd of 65,000 people at the Washington Monument that the language of the Constitution was intended to adapt to the changing needs of the American people. This original understanding had obviously been ignored by the recent conservative Court majority, he said. Once again, he ridiculed the Court's constitutional conversions on minimum wage laws and the Wagner Act immediately after he had sent to Congress his message "on the rejuvenation of the judiciary." Americans wanted the three branches of the federal government to work together, he said, and they saw "nothing more sacred about that branch furthest removed from the people than about either of the others, which are nearest to the people." Americans should celebrate the Constitution "not because it is old, but because it is ever new."

At 9 p.m. on Friday, October 1, three days before Hugo Black was scheduled to take his seat for the new term of the Supreme Court, he sat erect in an antique chair in the living room of his friend Claude Hamilton, poised to make the most important speech of his life. Before a battery of six microphones and fifteen radio announcers and technicians, he admitted to 30 million radio listeners that he had been a member of the Robert E. Lee Chapter of the Ku Klux Klan in Birmingham, Alabama. In a tense eleven-minute talk, he said that he had joined the Klan in 1923 but had resigned from the organization before he had campaigned for the Senate in 1926. His confession of Klan membership accounted for barely a minute of his speech. The former trial lawyer devoted far more time to an attack on religious bigotry in the United States and pledged his continued support for civil rights and liberties for all Americans.

"It was a grand job," Roosevelt declared privately. "It did the trick. You just wait and see." Within days, Roosevelt's political judgment was confirmed. The first Gallup poll taken after Hugo Black's radio address showed that a majority of Americans thought that he had vindicated himself and deserved his appointment. Black took his seat for the new Court term, as scheduled, on the first Monday in October.

Roosevelt's image of invincibility, magnified by his great 1936 reelection victory, broke into tiny shards during the bruising fight over his Court-packing plan. Conservative Democrats who had supported the New Deal, both out of loyalty to Roosevelt and fear of reprisal, suddenly realized that they could join Republicans in opposing his most cherished initiatives. And progressives of both parties, whom he had counted on for his most ambitious social and economic experiments, were still angry at his roughhouse tactics. By the end of the August congressional session, only one of the administration's measures, a low-cost housing statute, had been passed, and that success was more a tribute to the efforts of the bill's sponsor, Senator Wagner, than to the president's influence. The other bills—to reorganize the executive branch, regulate wages and hours, revise the farm program, and create a set of regional TVAs—stalled in committees.

The Court-packing plan was only the most conspicuous of the president's miscalculations. He committed an unforgivable breach of protocol by refusing to attend the funeral of the popular Senate majority leader, Joe Robinson. And then he unwisely meddled in the election of Robinson's successor, putting pressure on Democratic senators to support Alben Barkley of Kentucky over Mississippi's Pat Harrison. Barkley had actively supported the Court proposal; Harrison had been passive. Barkley won by a single vote, but his victory alienated Harrison, the powerful chairman of the Senate Finance Committee, and many of his friends in the Senate.

Even before the Court-packing debacle, the president's usually superb political skills failed him. He appeared paralyzed by indecision during a rash of disruptive labor strikes. After diemakers at General Motors' Flint plant sat down and refused to leave the factory floor, virtually bringing production at the nation's largest automaker to a halt, he asked plaintively: "Why can't these fellows in General Motors meet with the committee of workers?" GM soon agreed to union representation, as did U.S. Steel. But the so-called Little Steel companies, like Republic, refused to go along. Industrial violence erupted at Republic's South Chicago plant, where police shot ten protesters dead (seven in the back), and later at plants in Youngstown and Masillon, Ohio.

Pressure built on Roosevelt to intervene. Still, the president refused to take sides, which satisfied no one. Attacks on Roosevelt from his favorite enemy, big business, were expected. But he now faced criticism from his once dependable constituency, the urban middle class. They originally supported the labor movement, but were now frightened by its radical turn. The president's neutrality also offended the CIO's John L. Lewis, one of his most generous supporters during the 1936 presidential campaign. "It ill behooves one who has supped at labor's table," said the grandiloquent Lewis, "to curse with equal fervor . . . both labor and its adversaries when they become locked in deadly embrace."

Meanwhile, the economy, which had steadily improved since 1933, began to spiral downward. Continuing labor strife undoubtedly contributed to declining industrial production. But Roosevelt's decision to cut government spending on public works and farm subsidies was at the core of the problem. He wanted to honor his early campaign pledge to balance the budget, and thought it was time to turn off the federal spigot. His cost-cutting reduced the deficit from $4.3 billion in 1936 to $2.7 billion in 1937. But, simultaneously, prices on the New York Stock Exchange dropped ominously to levels not seen since 1929. Critics labeled it the "Roosevelt Recession," but the president blamed the market decline on a small number of people "who insist on continuing to speculate with margin accounts."

Undeterred by the dismal economic reports, Roosevelt called a special session of Congress for November and embarked on a whistle-stop tour of the Northwest to promote his agenda. Again, he was in his element, chatting happily from the rear platform of his presidential train and warmly clasping the hands of local politicians. But he pointedly snubbed Democratic senators Wheeler and O'Mahoney, who had opposed his Court plan. Promising more New Deal achievements, including an expanded farm program and wages and hours legislation, he drew inspiration from the people "who respond to simple common-sense words." At a cabinet meeting shortly after his return to Washington, he was still elated by the large, enthusiastic crowds that had greeted him. His suggestion to cut federal expenditures "met with pretty general approval," he said, and he noted that "even on the Court issue the majority of the western states would be carried."

In his message for the special congressional November session, Roosevelt acknowledged the marked recession in industrial production and purchases, but said the poor economic numbers were no cause for alarm. Congress needed to pass legislation to halt the recession and lay the foundation for a permanent recovery. But none of his recommendations, which consisted of leftover legislation from the summer session, rivaled in scope his original New Deal proposals. Even these modest requests were rejected by Congress. When the lawmakers adjourned a few days before Christmas, not one of Roosevelt's proposals had passed.

The special session was not only an embarrassing legislative failure for Roosevelt but also sparked an outright rebellion by conservatives in his own party. In the final days of the session, a group of conservative congressmen, dominated by southern Democrats, issued a ten-point "Conservative Manifesto." Drafted primarily by Senator Josiah Bailey of North Carolina, it called for lower federal taxes and a balanced budget, extolled states' rights, and warned against a permanently dependent welfare class. It was "a kind of founding charter for modern conservatism," the historian David M. Kennedy has written.

In early January 1938, Senator Wagner exacerbated southern resentment by reintroducing anti-lynching legislation that he had first proposed in 1934. Since 1933, eighty-three African-Americans had savagely been put to death in the South by public hanging. But enraged southerners, blind to the facts, glimpsed only the dreaded specter of a second Reconstruction. "I believe in white supremacy," declared Louisiana senator Allen

Ellender, "and as long as I am in the Senate I expect to fight for white supremacy." The legislation was an attempt "to lynch the last remaining evidence of States' rights and sovereignty," said Senator Richard Russell of Georgia. And Josiah Bailey called it "the forerunner of a policy studiously cultivated by agitators, not for the purpose of preventing lynching, but for the purpose of introducing the policy of Federal interference in local affairs." He then hurled a veiled threat at Roosevelt: "[N]o administration can survive without us."

When Wagner's bill was brought to the Senate floor for debate, southern Democrats mobilized for an around-the-clock filibuster. Roosevelt was asked at his next press conference if he favored the bill. "I have not referred to it at all," he responded. "I should say there was enough discussion going on in the Senate." His silence on the issue appeared to validate Bailey's claim: he needed the support of southern congressmen (whose seniority on key committees allowed them to wield power far beyond their numbers) to pass legislation more important to him than the anti-lynching bill. "I did not choose the tools with which I must work," he later told the NAACP's Walter White. "But I've got to get legislation passed to save America." In mid-February, Senator Wagner withdrew his bill.

The economy continued to falter. By the end of March 1938, every economic index, including farm prices, had plunged. Roosevelt was caught in a crossfire between his conservative advisers, led by Treasury Secretary Henry Morgenthau, Jr., counseling fiscal austerity, and liberals, like the WPA's Harry Hopkins and Interior Secretary Harold Ickes, urging a return to massive federal spending. The liberals won the argument, and Roosevelt asked Congress for an emergency appropriation of $3.4 billion. Funds were restored for the WPA ($1.4 billion), public works ($1 billion), and millions more for slum clearance, farm subsidies, and low-cost housing. By the end of the year the economy would begin to revive, but Roosevelt's budget-balancing exercise had exacted a heavy toll. The economy regained only half of the ground it had lost in jobs and industrial production.

When the Seventy-fifth Congress adjourned in June 1938, Roosevelt could claim no greater success in bending Congress to his will than in the previous year. The farm bill that finally passed was essentially a revised AAA, which now seemed safe from constitutional challenge. The one major legislative success, the passage of the Fair Labor Standards Act (FLSA), had been bandied about and watered down since Senator Hugo Black had first introduced it in May 1937. The statute prohibited child labor, established a minimum wage of 40 cents an hour, and a forty-four-hour workweek in American industries (but not in agriculture or domestic service). "That's that," said a relieved Roosevelt, when he signed the bill. Though he did not know it at the time, the FLSA would be the last significant New Deal measure to be enacted into law.

Roosevelt attempted to regain the momentum by orchestrating primary challenges to conservative Democrats who had defied him. His first target was Senator Guy Gillette of Iowa, who had actually supported most New Deal legislation but had committed the unpardonable sin of opposing his Court proposal. At the president's behest, Harry Hopkins recruited a liberal congressman, Otha Wearin, to challenge Gillette in the Democratic primary. Gillette charged that his opponent was the White House's handpicked candidate, not Iowa's, and easily won reelection.

In three other Democratic primaries, Roosevelt personally injected himself into the attempted purge of recalcitrant conservative Democrats. When he dedicated a new rural electrification project in Barnsville, Georgia, near Warm Springs, he used the occasion to laud a young U.S. attorney from Atlanta, Lawrence Camp, who was trying to unseat three-term conservative Senator Walter George. With both George and Camp on the platform, Roosevelt said that he preferred Camp. Though his "personal friend" Senator George was "a scholar and a gentleman," the president said that he was too conservative to carry out "the people's will" in Washington. "Mr. President," George replied, "I want you to know that I accept the challenge." He trounced Camp and won a fourth term in the Senate.

In South Carolina, the president fared no better. The administration convinced Governor Olin Johnston to take on the race-baiting Senator "Cotton Ed" Smith. Johnston announced his candidacy from the steps of the White House, which handed Smith, like Gillette in Iowa, a ready-made carpetbagger issue. Even though Roosevelt campaigned for Johnston, Smith beat his opponent by 10 percentage points. After the election, Smith was asked if Roosevelt was his own worst enemy. "Not as long as I am alive," he snapped.

In Maryland, Roosevelt barnstormed over the Labor Day weekend for liberal Congressman David Lewis, who was challenging the arch-conservative Senator Millard Tydings. Again, the president called for the election of a true New Deal Democrat. And again the voters returned the conservative incumbent. Tydings defeated Lewis by 60,000 votes.

The president's futile efforts only deepened the divide between liberals and conservatives within his party, paving the way in the November general election for major Republican gains: eighty-one seats in the House, eight in the Senate, and thirteen governorships. The Democrats still retained control of both houses of Congress, but Roosevelt could no longer count on a committed New Deal majority. Entering the final two years of his term, he appeared to be a demonstrably weak, lame-duck president.

Early on the rainy morning of Monday, October 4, 1937, Hugo Black drove his car into the basement entrance of the Supreme Court Building, avoiding the hundreds of demonstrators in front of the building protesting his appointment. In the robing room, he met most of his new colleagues for the first time. He was personally acquainted only with Brandeis, whom he had befriended during his first Senate term, and Cardozo, who had visited him after his appointment was announced.

Once the justices had taken their seats in the courtroom, with Black, as the junior justice, assigned the chair to the far left of the Chief Justice, Hughes announced the confirmation of "Hugo L. Black, of Alabama, a former member of the Senate of the United States." Shortly afterward, those in the courtroom, including Black's wife, Josephine, were reminded of the controversy surrounding his appointment. Two formal motions were presented to the Court claiming that Black was unlawfully seated; the motions were dismissed.

Black was especially nervous about how he would be treated by the Chief Justice. As a senator, he had voted in 1930 to reject Hughes's nomination to head the Court. But Hughes greeted Black as if he were the most distinguished jurist ever to be appointed. "When I viewed his Jovian countenance and heard the warmth of his greeting," Black recalled, "I was overwhelmed." Hughes personally escorted Black through the building, introducing his colleague to his new professional home. There was nothing awkward or insincere about Hughes's cordiality. "What would you expect?" Hughes asked indignantly. "I was the Chief Justice."

The furor over Black's appointment dismayed Harlan Fiske Stone, who was convinced that, after so many recent terms of tumult and public scrutiny, the Court dearly needed "a season of peace and quiet." Black's admission of Klan membership instantly shattered Stone's hope of institutional serenity. But, like Hughes, Stone extended his hand in friendship to his new colleague, assuring Black that "the Court is a great tribunal doing its work with extraordinary thoroughness and fidelity," and adding that "the preservation of most of its traditions is worthy of our best efforts." Black replied that Stone had "no warmer admirer," and that he intended to seek his guidance.

Less than three months later, Black circulated a long dissent that made it alarmingly apparent to Stone that Black was no acolyte. Nor, it seemed, was he interested in preserving the Supreme Court's traditions. The case in which Black challenged the judicial wisdom of Stone and his seven other colleagues, as well as several decades of Court precedents, dealt with the rate-making valuation of the Indianapolis Water Company. The company had asked the federal courts to set aside the rate established by a state regulatory commission, claiming that it was so low as to be confiscatory. In an unsigned opinion, eight members of the Court sided with the utility company, sending the case back to the federal district court for a new rate-making analysis with the clear directive to consider the water company's rising costs.

Black's nineteen-page dissent questioned the competence of judges, including members of the Supreme Court, to review state utility rates. In a further act of judicial heresy, he asserted that the water company, like other corporations, should not be protected by the Fourteenth Amendment's due process clause. His constitutional position challenged Court precedents dating back to 1873. The Alabama populist was again taking the side of the little guy, in this case the consumer, against the utility company monopoly and what he perceived to be the corporation-friendly Supreme Court.

Stone wrote Chief Justice Hughes that he was "a good deal troubled" by Black's dissent. Though full of bold ideas and searing criticism of the status quo, it made Stone uneasy for a number of reasons. First of all, Black had dissented from an unsigned opinion supported by all eight of his colleagues. By tradition, that simply was not done. Much of Black's dissent, moreover, was based on arguments that had not been raised by counsel in the case. Black's raw intellect was not to be denied, but Stone was concerned that he lacked reverence for the judicial method. Stone was, nonetheless, sufficiently impressed with his new colleague's cogent analysis* that he asked Hughes to either schedule a reargument of the case to address Black's criti-

* Stone suspected that Black's dissent was ghostwritten by Tommy Corcoran, a major draftsman of the Public Utilities Holding Company Act.

cism or, alternatively, allow him time "to make a more adequate study of the whole case."

Hughes rejected Stone's requests. The Court's *per curiam* opinion and Black's dissent came down, as scheduled, on January 3, 1938.

Black soon served notice that his dissent in the utilities case was not a neophyte's stumbling, inadvertent mistake. In a second dissent a few weeks later, he wrote a small treatise following up on his earlier opinion that the Fourteenth Amendment did not protect corporations. His position was disarmingly straightforward. The amendment, Black wrote, "followed the freedom of a race from slavery," and when it was submitted to the people, they "were told that its purpose was to protect weak and helpless human beings and were not told that it was intended to remove corporations in any fashion from the control of state governments."

In late January, Stone was joined in his early morning walk by the journalist Marquis Childs and freely admitted that he was concerned about Black's opinions. His observations were published under Childs's by-line in the *St. Louis Post-Dispatch*. Confiding that his article represented "an inside view of the Court," Childs wrote that a "new man on the bench who has had no judicial experience and only a comparatively limited legal experience is not a help to his colleagues in the first two or three years." Stone was so pleased with the article that he suggested that Childs expand on the theme for a national audience, which he did with a May article in *Harper's* magazine. In the meantime, Stone visited Black's chambers to point out deficiencies in his opinions. He also recruited his friend, Felix Frankfurter, to participate in his tutorial.

"Do you know Black well?" Stone asked Frankfurter. "He needs guidance from someone who is more familiar with the workings of the judicial process than he is."

Frankfurter enthusiastically accepted his new assignment. "I used to say to my students," Frankfurter wrote Black, "that legislatures make law wholesale, judges retail." In other words, he was advising Black to show a little judicial humility and tone down his opinions.

While Stone and Frankfurter were earnestly trying to enlist Black in a self-improvement program, the Chief Justice extended every courtesy to his new colleague, never suggesting by word or action that he was inadequately prepared for the Court. Hughes had written the unsigned utilities company opinion, but did not resent Black's brash dissent. He believed that dissents were vital to the Court and helped sustain the public's confidence in the independence of judges. Besides treating Black with professional respect, Hughes also cultivated his friendship. In late December 1938, for example, he left the Court early to drive to Blacks' home, where, bent down on his hands and knees, he helped place gifts under the family Christmas tree.

Black always spoke of Hughes with admiration and affection. He never felt the same way about Stone, whom he had admired above all other justices when he joined the Court. After Childs's article appeared in *Harper's*, Stone was identified as his confidential source. An embarrassed Stone apologized to Black and insisted that his views had been distorted by Childs. Black coolly assured Stone that he was "not disturbed in the slightest."

Midway through the Court term, Justice George Sutherland retired from the Court, providing Roosevelt with his second opportunity to replace one of the conservative Four Horsemen. Every early indication suggested that Black, who had replaced Van Devanter, was the outspoken liberal voice that Roosevelt had sought. For his next appointment, the president played it safe, sending steady, workmanlike Stanley Reed to the Court. As Solicitor General, Reed had been a reliable spokesmen for the administration in many tense arguments before the Court. He was no Brandeis, or even Black, but he would do.

By the spring of 1938, New Deal legislation appeared to be safe from Court tampering. Just how far the Supreme Court had traveled in its deference to Congress was demonstrated in a case testing the constitutionality of a federal statute prohibiting interstate shipment of skimmed milk infused with unhealthy additives. In rejecting the due process challenge, the majority opinion, written by Justice Stone, virtually removed the Court from oversight of federal economic and social legislation. So long as a federal statute was rational, it was constitutional. The Court, wrote Stone, would *assume* the existence of facts to support the law based "on some rational basis within the knowledge and experience of the legislators."

In a famous footnote, Stone heralded a new Court era in which the justices would concentrate on their special role in protecting individual rights and liberties. Social and economic regulations, which had been subject of such close judicial scrutiny in *Butler, Carter v. Carter Coal,* and *Tipaldo,* would henceforth presumed to be constitutional. But he warned that the

Court would apply a more exacting review of legislation that restricted the right to vote or assemble or that discriminated against "discrete and insular" religious or racial minorities.

True to Stone's word, the Court broadly interpreted congressional commerce power, generously construed government's authority to tax and spend for the general welfare, and firmly rejected the once potent doctrine of substantive due process that protected laissez-faire economic values. With only Justices Butler and McReynolds resisting the liberal tide, federal and state laws that only two years earlier would have been subjected to the most demanding review were declared constitutional.

Hughes did his part to usher in the new constitutional era, expanding the Court's commerce clause doctrine, which he had announced in *Jones & Laughlin* the previous term. While he often took more cautious positions than the Court's expanding liberal wing, he appeared more assured than ever in his leadership. Writing for a seven-man majority, he declared that the unfair labor practices of a fruit-canning company that shipped only 37 percent of its products out of state could be reached by the National Labor Relations Act. In applying the constitutional standard of a "close and substantial relation to interstate commerce," he disdained "mathematical or rigid formulas." Only Butler and McReynolds dissented.

Soon after southern Democrats in Congress talked the anti-lynching bill to death, the Hughes Court quietly assumed the role of the nation's primary protector of civil rights. The Court's most important work in the field, of course, lay in the future. But in 1938, the Chief Justice wrote a majority opinion that represented a modest but essential first step toward dismantling the system of segregated public schools. The lawsuit was brought by Lloyd Gaines, an African-American, who applied for admission to the all-white law school at the University of Missouri. He was told that he was ineligible to study at the law school because of his race. At the same time, Missouri offered Gaines a tuition "scholarship" at a desegregated state university law school in an adjacent state. This scholarship policy, the state of Missouri argued, satisfied the constitutional requirement of equal protection under the Fourteenth Amendment.

When Dean Charles Houston of the Howard Law School began his argument on behalf of Gaines before the Supreme Court, Justice McReynolds contemptuously turned his back and stared at the wall. But Dean Houston, who also served as the NAACP Legal Defense Fund's first director, did not expect to win McReynolds's vote. He and his young assistant,

Thurgood Marshall, directed their arguments at open-minded members of the Court who, they hoped, would recognize the glaring disparities in opportunities offered to whites and African-Americans in higher education. Marshall, who succeeded Houston as director of the Legal Defense Fund, later explained, in his salty fashion, the reason that he and Houston chose to begin their legal assault on segregated public schools at the graduate level. "Those racial supremacy boys think that little kids of six or seven are going to get funny ideas about sex and marriage just from going to school together," he said, "but for some equally funny reason, youngsters in law school aren't supposed to feel that way."

Seven members of the Hughes Court agreed with Houston and Marshall that Missouri's refusal to admit Gaines to its state law school violated the equal protection clause. The state's offer to send Gaines to an out-of-state desegregated law school on "scholarship" did not satisfy the constitutional mandate, Hughes concluded. Missouri was obligated to provide residents of all races in-state training in the law. The offer to send Gaines across the border for law school, Hughes wrote, "may mitigate the inconvenience of the discrimination but cannot serve to validate it." The decision was the first Court victory for the NAACP Legal Defense Fund and was delivered over the rancid dissent of McReynolds (joined by Butler), who predicted that a desegregated law school in Missouri would "damnify both races."

Throughout Roosevelt's first six years as president, domestic economic policy was his consuming priority. To be sure, he watched with growing concern as Adolf Hitler systematically, and with appalling brutality, trampled on the last hopes for an enduring peace in Europe. But he concentrated on the persistent problems of the Great Depression, expending little energy or political capital on international affairs. His focus accurately reflected the wishes of Congress and the American voters, who were in a pronounced isolationist mood.

He deplored Italy's invasion of Ethiopia in 1935 and Germany's march into the Rhineland in 1936 in flagrant violation of the Treaty of Versailles. But he took no action. In December 1937, after Japanese warplanes sunk a U.S. gunboat, the *Panay*, anchored in China's Yangtze River, the administration downplayed the incident, quickly accepting an apology and restitution from the Japanese government.

Roosevelt would have preferred more flexibility in dealing with belligerents than a series of neutrality laws (first enacted in 1935) allowed. But he did not seriously consider challenging the overwhelmingly isolationist Congress. The statutes reaffirmed the mandatory ban on arms and loans to countries at war, which, as Roosevelt's knew, favored aggressors like Germany's Hitler and Italy's Benito Mussolini.

The president was skeptical of Britain's prime minister, Neville Chamberlain's, assurance at Munich in September 1938 of "peace in our time" after Britain and France ceded Czechoslovakia's industrially rich Sudetenland to Germany. But the president did nothing to deter Germany when it later gobbled up the rest of the country. He recalled the American ambassador to Berlin after receiving reports of Nazi storm troopers' rampage against Jews on the night of November 10, 1938, in response to a Polish Jewish refugee's shooting of a German diplomat in Paris. Dozens of Jews were murdered, 20,000 arrested and sent to concentration camps, 200 synagogues burned, more than 7,000 shops looted, and countless homes destroyed. FDR told reporters that he "could scarcely believe that such things could occur in a twentieth-century civilization." But when asked if he would relax immigration restrictions on Jewish refugees, he replied, "We have a quota system." *

In his State of the Union address in January 1939, Roosevelt finally spoke bluntly to the American people about the threat posed by foreign aggression to the nation's values as well as its security. He warned of "storms from abroad" directly challenging religious freedom, an obvious reference to the Nazis' persecutions of Jews. "There comes a time in the affairs of men when they must prepare to defend not their homes alone but the tenets of faith and humanity on which their churches, their government and their very civilization is founded." As a first step, he called for revision of the neutrality statutes, which, he said, "may actually give aid to an aggressor and deny it to the victim."

In April, a month after Germany had completed its conquest of Czechoslovakia, Roosevelt sent Hitler and Mussolini (whose troops had invaded Albania) a message seeking a guarantee that they would not at-

---

* In contrast to his public position on immigration quotas, Roosevelt worked quietly behind the scenes to help Jewish refugees. After Hitler annexed Austria in March 1938, the president evaded the strict U.S. quotas on European refugees by combining the quotas for Germany and Austria and expediting Jewish visa applications, which resulted in the escape of some 50,000 Jews from the Nazis. By presidential order, he also extended the visas of some 15,000 German and Austrian nationals, including that of Albert Einstein.

tack thirty-one countries that he listed by name. By then, both dictators had taken the measure of the American president and concluded that he was all bluster. Hitler responded in a harangue before the Reichstag in which he mocked Roosevelt's request. Germany was the victim, not the aggressor, he claimed, and only sought to correct the injustices perpetrated by the Versailles Treaty. He then taunted Roosevelt, comparing their records of achievement since both men had taken office in the winter of 1933. He himself had "conquered chaos," he boasted, increasing factory production, building major roads and canals, and finding useful work for 7 million unemployed. "You, Mr. Roosevelt, have a much easier task in comparison," he said. "From the outset you stepped to the head of one of the largest and wealthiest States in the world," and now have "the time and leisure to give your attention to universal problems." His world, Hitler concluded with masterful guile, "is unfortunately much smaller."

Isolationists in Congress, led by progressive Republicans, agreed with Hitler that Roosevelt should keep his nose out of Europe's business. "Gad, what a chance Hitler has!" exclaimed an admiring Senator Borah. "If he only moderates his religious and racial intolerance, he could take his place beside Charlemagne." Responding to Hitler's Reichstag speech, Hiram Johnson of California thought the president had justifiably received his comeuppance. He "put his chin out, and he got it resoundingly whacked," said Johnson. "He asked for it," agreed Gerald Nye of North Dakota.

Roosevelt's plea to revise the neutrality laws received a predictably hostile response in Congress. The House voted to retain the arms embargo. The Senate followed suit, despite an impassioned plea from Roosevelt at a White House meeting with Senate leaders. The decision to revise the law, the president told them, "may well affect not only the people of our own country, but also the peoples of the world." William Borah, who was at the White House meeting, dismissed such desperate talk of war. "There's not going to be any war this year," he said. "All this hysteria is manufactured and artificial."

At 2:50 a.m. on September 1, 1939, Roosevelt was awakened by a phone call from U.S. Ambassador William Bullitt in Paris. Bullitt reported that German planes had bombed Warsaw and several divisions had already driven deep into Polish territory.

"Well, Bill," Roosevelt replied. "It has come at last. God help us all!"

*   *   *

After Chief Justice Hughes presided at the justices' Saturday conference in late February 1939, he sat alone at the conference table, pale and perspiring. Wiping his brow, he told the Court clerk, Charles Cropley, that he was ill and asked to be helped to a nearby couch. He closed his eyes and instructed the clerk to remain with him. When he felt better, he sat up and asked the clerk not to mention the incident to anyone. He refused to allow Cropley to accompany him home, fearing that it would raise questions about his health and his ability to remain in office.

Though feeling weak, he continued to work at home on the speech he was scheduled to deliver to a joint session of Congress on March 4 to commemorate the sesquicentennial of the meeting of the first Congress. On the morning of the 4th, an unsteady Hughes, accompanied by Antoinette, gathered with the other justices and their wives in the old Supreme Court chamber in the basement of the Capitol. Seeing Cropley's anxious expression, Hughes whispered to the clerk: "I'm all right." His assurance was sheer bravado. He was so weak that he was not sure that he could walk unassisted to the rostrum in the House of Representatives. But he did so, summoning all of his energy to deliver his speech, sometimes haltingly, from memory.

Hughes praised the democratic principles that "have given our government both stability and capacity for orderly progress in a world of turmoil and revolutionary upheavals." His theme—the strength of American constitutional government when European democracies were under siege—resonated throughout the chamber. Under the Constitution's system of checks and balances, he said, the Supreme Court formed a great partnership with Congress and the president to make democracy workable. All three branches were dedicated to the spirit which pervades the nation's institutions: "exalting the processes of reason, seeking through the very limitation of power the promotion of the wise use of power, and finding the ultimate security of life, liberty, and the pursuit of happiness, and the promise of continued stability and a rational progress, in the good sense of the American people."

Once the ceremony was over, Hughes's concerned colleagues urged him to postpone their regularly scheduled conference. "Oh, Chief Justice, you have done enough today," said Justice Roberts. "Let the conference wait until next week." Other justices immediately seconded Robert's suggestion.

Hughes adamantly refused. "Well, come on, brethren," he said. "We have work to do." Even in his weakened condition, he not only presided at the long afternoon conference, but also at a large dinner party that he and Mrs. Hughes hosted that evening in their home. When he went to bed, he was totally drained of strength. Two days later, he learned from his physician that he had a bleeding duodenal ulcer and had sustained a serious loss of blood. For several weeks he was confined to his bed, but he then returned to the Court to complete the term.

During the term, Hughes had welcomed two new colleagues to the Court. The first was Felix Frankfurter, nominated by Roosevelt to replace Benjamin Cardozo, who had died the previous summer after a long illness. In early January, the president placed a telephone call to Frankfurter in his Cambridge apartment to inform him of his decision. The Harvard professor answered the call in his underwear. "All I can say is that I wish my mother were alive," said the usually voluble Frankfurter.

Frankfurter's appointment was applauded by liberal Democrats and anti–New Deal Republicans alike, and ranked, according to *The New York Times*, as one of FDR's most popular appointments during his entire presidency. The Harvard don offered all of the tangible judicial credentials that Black and Reed lacked—legal scholarship, deep understanding of Court history, and breadth of vision built over years of study and hard experience as adviser to three presidents (TR, Wilson, and FDR). He was also a dedicated libertarian, having been a founder of the American Civil Liberties Union and the author of a searing criticism of the murder convictions of the Italian anarchists Nicola Sacco and Bartolomeo Vanzetti.

Frankfurter dressed casually in an alpaca coat and slacks for his first Saturday judicial conference. Upon entering the well-appointed conference room, he was chagrined to find that all his new colleagues wore suits. At the lunchtime break, Frankfurter rushed home, changed into a suit, and returned for the afternoon session. He was greeted by Chief Justice Hughes, who had also made a lunchtime change of dress, and now wore *his* alpaca coat. With that gracious gesture, Hughes disarmed the man who had called him "the most politically calculating of men" during Roosevelt's Court-packing fight. Frankfurter was soon effusively praising Hughes's leadership skills, comparing him to Arturo Toscanini in his mastery of the Court's business.

Two months after Frankfurter's appointment, the great Justice Brandeis, eighty-two years old, informed Roosevelt that he was retiring from the Court. The president chose William O. Douglas, the brash, brilliant young chairman of the Securities and Exchange Commission (SEC), for his fourth nominee to the Court in less than two years. Douglas had grown up in Yakima, Washington, in the shadow of the Cascade Mountains. He nonetheless shared more than his impeccable New Deal credentials with Frankfurter, the Austrian immigrant, and Black, the southern populist. Like Frankfurter, Douglas had compiled a distinguished academic record, first as a superb student at Columbia Law School and later as an innovative business law professor at the Yale Law School. And like his fellow liberal, Hugo Black, Douglas deeply distrusted corporate power. As the head of the SEC, he had rigorously enforced new government securities regulations against some of Wall Street's most prominent bankers and securities traders.

With both Hughes's and Roberts's support, the Court accelerated the speed with which it distanced itself from the conservative rulings of 1935 and 1936. The Chief Justice wrote the opinion for the Court that upheld the Tobacco Inspection Act of 1935, which required federal inspection and certification of tobacco sold at auctions for interstate sales. He dismissed arguments that the regulation impinged on state activity beyond the authority of Congress. "The fact that intrastate and interstate transactions are commingled on the tobacco market does not frustrate or restrict the congressional power," he noted. He similarly rejected the argument that Congress had unconstitutionally delegated authority to the Secretary of Agriculture to establish standards for the inspection of tobacco. "We have always recognized that legislation must often be adapted to conditions involving details with which it is impracticable for the legislature to deal directly."

Demonstrating just how far the Court had come in three years, the new majority also sustained the constitutionality of the Agricultural Adjustment Act of 1938. Justice Roberts, the author of the *Butler* opinion that had struck down the first AAA statute, wrote a brief opinion declaring that the statute regulated interstate commerce rather than production and was therefore constitutional. Only Justices Butler and McReynolds dissented.

Whatever enmity existed between Roosevelt and Hughes over the Court-packing plan had disappeared by 1939. Hughes denied that his relations with the president had ever been less than cordial. And Roosevelt, by the spring of 1939, had no reason to complain about the Chief Justice. The Supreme Court was no longer an obstacle to his legislative ambitions, which was more than he could say for rebellious conservative Democrats in Congress.

The friendly relations between Roosevelt and Hughes were vividly illustrated in June 1939, when the president prepared to welcome King George VI and Queen Elizabeth to Washington. Roosevelt had issued the invitation to the king in September 1938, at the height of the Munich crisis, as a goodwill gesture to solidify relations between the two nations. The president planned every detail of the royal couple's visit, from the parade to the White House to the weekend menu at Hyde Park, which included hot dogs on the lawn. Chief Justice and Mrs. Hughes were invited to the state dinner, but Hughes, who was undergoing two days of medical tests, had to decline. Roosevelt personally called Antoinette Hughes to express his regrets that her husband could not attend. He urged her to attend the dinner without the Chief Justice and promised to seat her next to the king, if she did. She attended the dinner, and the president kept his promise.

Shortly before noon on September 1, 1939, Roosevelt met with the press in the Oval Office, just nine hours after Ambassador Bullitt's transatlantic phone call had interrupted his sleep with news of Germany's invasion of Poland.

"Can we stay out of this?" a reporter asked.

"I not only sincerely hope so," the president replied, "but I believe we can and every effort will be made by this Administration to do so."

German troops and tanks had, by then, cut deeply into the Polish countryside and Nazi dive-bombers continued to pulverize Warsaw. Two days later, Great Britain and France declared war on Germany, formally igniting the Second World War. That Sunday evening, Roosevelt addressed the nation in a fireside chat, assuring his radio audience that the United States would remain a neutral nation. But he did not insist, as President Wilson had done in 1914 at the outbreak of the First World War, that Americans must remain neutral in thought as well as action. "Even a neutral has a right to take account of facts," he said. "Even a neutral cannot be asked to close his mind or his conscience."

The president's sympathies were decidedly with the Allies, as were the vast majority of the American people's. A Gallup poll showed that 84 percent of respondents favored the Allies and only 2 percent supported

Germany. For Roosevelt, the first order of business was to repeal the arms embargo provision of the 1939 Neutrality Act. In an address to Congress, he emphasized that repeal was not a partisan issue, but necessary to keep America out of the war. By making belligerents pay for arms on a "cash and carry" basis, he said, the United States would remain neutral and serve the cause of peace. He knew, of course, that the embattled Allies would be the sole beneficiaries of the repeal, since the formidable military arsenal of the Third Reich had no need for the war materials that the United States could offer.

Roosevelt faced vocal opposition from Republican isolationists in the Senate like Idaho's Borah, as well as from the young American aviation hero Colonel Charles Lindbergh. "This is not a question of banding to-gether to defend the white race against foreign invasion," said Lindbergh, who had recently been decorated by Field Marshal Hermann Goering with one of Germany's highest medals. "This is simply one of those age-old struggles within our own family of nations."

The best strategy, Roosevelt decided, was to maintain a low profile and let congressional Democrats do the work. Ironically, he received strong support from conservative southern Democrats, including Georgia's Sena-tor Walter George, the target of Roosevelt's failed purge in 1938. During the repeal debate, the president was so nervous that he asked the Governor General of Canada, Lord Tweedsmuir, to postpone his official visit until after the vote had been taken. "I am almost literally walking on eggs," he explained. At the end of October, a month after the Germans had overrun Poland, the Senate voted to repeal the arms embargo, 63–30, as did the House, voting along comparable party lines.

Both Germany and the Allies dug in for the long winter, producing a ghostly calm across Europe. An hour before dawn on April 9, 1940, Ger-man warplanes, troops, and armor shattered that calm, invading Denmark with lightning speed. A half hour later, German destroyers emerged out of a snowstorm in the port of Narvik to fire on Norwegian gunboats while thousands of German infantry poured out of barges and troopships. Den-mark surrendered in days, Norway in weeks.

On May 10, a blizzard of German parachutists landed in the fields of Holland and Belgium, seizing strategic airfields and bridges. At the same time, thousands of Luftwaffe bombers pummeled Rotterdam and destroyed Dutch ground fortifications. More than one hundred German infantry di-visions and armored units stormed across the borders of the Low Countries.

Prime Minister Winston Churchill, who had succeeded Neville Chamberlain, sent a desperate cable to Roosevelt. "The scene has darkened swiftly," he wrote. "The small countries are simply smashed up, one by one, like matchwood." He anticipated an imminent German invasion of Great Britain and pleaded for help. "I trust you realize, Mr. President, that the voice and force of the United States may count for nothing if they are withheld too long."

The next day, Roosevelt spoke to a joint session of Congress, his voice steady, his hands tightly gripping the podium. "The brutal force of modern offensive war has been loosed in all its horror," he said. "No defense is so strong that it requires no further strengthening and no attack is so unlikely that it may be ignored." He asked Congress for $1.2 billion for a supplemental defense appropriation and set a goal of 50,000 warplanes a year (the United States had just 2,806 aircraft, most of them outmoded). The president's request was met with rousing cheers and quick passage.

Three days later, 1,800 German tanks slashed through the thinly defended Ardennes forest and began a dash across northern France toward the English Channel. On May 20, the 350,000 men of the British Expeditionary Force and the French First Army were pinned down on the beaches of the northern coastal town of Dunkirk. Holland had already surrendered; Belgium would fight only another week. Between May 29 and June 2, most of the British force and 100,000 French troops were miraculously evacuated across the Channel by a motley armada of cruisers, destroyers, and small sailboats. The Allies left behind 7,000 tons of ammunition, 90,000 rifles, and 120,000 vehicles. On June 5, the German juggernaut turned south, smashing through France's defenses with deadly efficiency.

On Monday, June 10, Franklin and Eleanor boarded a train at Union Station headed for Charlottesville, Virginia, where the president was scheduled to give the commencement address at the graduation of Franklin Junior from the law school at the University of Virginia. Shortly before boarding the train, Roosevelt was stunned by reports that Mussolini had declared war on France. He had worked assiduously to keep Mussolini out of the conflict, offering to mediate differences between the Allies and Italy. In his formal remarks at the commencement, Roosevelt promised to "extend to the opponents of force the material resources of this nation." But at the end of his speech, still furious over Mussolini's action, he charged that "the hand that held the dagger has struck it into the back of its neighbor." Roosevelt's angry rhetoric heartened Churchill. But nothing could help

France. German troops entered Paris on June 14 and immediately hoisted the swastika on the Eiffel Tower.

On the sunny afternoon of June 21, Hitler's big Mercedes arrived in the little clearing in the woods of Compiègne, the site of the armistice ceremony that had ended the First World War. The Führer walked slowly to the commemorative monument and read the inscription: HERE ON THE ELEVENTH OF NOVEMBER 1918 SUCCUMBED THE CRIMINAL PRIDE OF THE GERMAN EMPIRE—VANQUISHED BY THE FREE PEOPLES WHICH IT TRIED TO ENSLAVE. His face was "afire with scorn, anger, hate, revenge, triumph," observed the journalist William Shirer. Stepping back from the monument, Hitler snapped his hands on his hips, arched his shoulders, and spread his feet wide apart in a gesture of contempt and triumph. He then entered the same railway car that had served as the scene for the armistice twenty-two years earlier, dictated harsh terms for France's total surrender, and left.

For the Gridiron Dinner in December 1939, the press corps built an eight-foot papier-mâché sphinx with FDR's face and signature cigarette holder tipped at a jaunty angle. Roosevelt loved it and later had it displayed in his presidential library at Hyde Park. The point of the huge, inscrutable image was that Roosevelt adamantly refused to divulge his future plans, even as aspiring Democratic and Republican presidential candidates actively devised their own.

Roosevelt was, in fact, undecided as to whether to seek a third term. No president had ever successfully done so—a tradition, if challenged, that could produce a formidable political backlash. The fifty-eight-year-old president genuinely looked forward to a productive, relaxing retirement on the family estate. He delighted at the thought of living in his hilltop "dreamhouse," which was being built to his specifications, including wide doors to accommodate his wheelchair. Construction was also near completion on his presidential library, where he expected to edit his papers, work on his memoirs, and engage in other writing projects. In January 1940, he signed a contract with *Collier's* magazine to serve as contributing editor after leaving office for a fee of $75,000 a year, the same as his presidential salary.

In the winter of 1940, Roosevelt balanced his plans for retirement against reasons to seek another presidential term. He was concerned that only he could see the New Deal through to a satisfactory conclusion. The

European crisis also weighed heavily on his mind. If it got worse, he might consider it his duty to lead the nation. "I do not want to run," he told Henry Morgenthau, Jr., "unless between now and the convention things get very, very much worse in Europe."

The president kept his options open throughout the winter months and into the early spring. He encouraged several potential Democratic candidates, including former Indiana governor Paul McNutt, Secretary of State Cordell Hull, and Postmaster General Jim Farley. His open-mindedness gave each candidate ample opportunity to undercut his rivals' support, leaving the field to Roosevelt, should he choose to run. Roosevelt had already arranged for the party's convention to be held in Chicago, where he expected the city's boss, Mayor Edward Kelly, to pack the galleries with Roosevelt loyalists. And he quietly made sure that delegates pledged to him would be entered in important Democratic primaries, like California and Texas, which he won handily. At the same time, the president's approval ratings climbed steadily, as anxious Americans, aware of the Allies' disastrous losses in Europe, rallied around their leader.

On June 19, five days after the German Army had entered Paris, Roosevelt announced the creation of a bipartisan war cabinet to contend with the ominous events in Europe, naming two prominent Republicans to key positions. Seventy-three-year-old Henry Stimson, who had served in the Taft and Hoover cabinets, was appointed Secretary of War, replacing the stubborn isolationist Harry Woodring. He was joined by Colonel Frank Knox, an old Rough Rider, publisher of the *Chicago Daily News*, and Governor Alf Landon's running mate in 1936, who was named Secretary of the Navy. Both men advocated a military draft and massive aid to the Allies.

Roosevelt's announcement of a war cabinet came less than a week before Republican delegates convened in Philadelphia to nominate a presidential candidate. When the balloting began, three men were in serious contention: the isolationists' candidate, Senator Robert Taft of Ohio; the racket-busting New York District Attorney, thirty-eight-year-old Thomas Dewey; and Wendell Willkie, an Indiana lawyer turned corporate executive, who served as the president of Commonwealth & Southern, the nation's largest utility holding company. On the sixth ballot, the delegates made the improbable choice of Willkie, an internationalist and recent Republican convert who had voted for Roosevelt in 1932.

Two weeks later, when Democrats gathered in Chicago, Roosevelt still had not indicated if he would accept a draft. By then, any momentum for three potential rivals—McNutt, Vice President Garner, and Secretary of State Hull—had fizzled. Only big, bluff Jim Farley, FDR's stalwart lieutenant in his earlier presidential campaigns, stood between Roosevelt and a draft. On a hot day in early July, the two men met at Hyde Park, each cautiously gauging the other's intentions. Roosevelt said he did not want to run and waited, expectantly, for Farley to urge him to do so. Farley refused. Instead, he raised concerns about an unprecedented third term and suggested that the president could issue an unequivocal statement, as General William Tecumseh Sherman had famously done, that he would not run if nominated nor serve if elected. Neither man gave ground. Once the convention started, Roosevelt tried again, phoning Farley from the White House, pointing out that there would be no need for a ballot if, as he implied, he were drafted by the delegates. "That's perfectly silly," Farley replied, and the matter was dropped.

With Roosevelt's intentions still unknown, the delegates wandered listlessly around the convention floor. Most assumed that the president would accept the nomination, but were frustrated by what they perceived as his cat-and-mouse game. They prepared to accept Roosevelt's nomination "with the enthusiasm of a chain gang," observed the *Chicago Daily News*. Ickes pleaded with the president to declare his candidacy. THIS CONVENTION IS BLEEDING TO DEATH, he wired Roosevelt from Chicago. YOUR REPUTATION AND PRESTIGE MAY BLEED WITH IT.

By prearrangement with Roosevelt, Senator Alben Barkley, at the end of another spellbinding speech extolling New Deal accomplishments, announced that the president had informed him the delegates were free to cast their votes for the candidate of their choice. The puzzled delegates momentarily groped for the president's meaning. Suddenly, from loudspeakers around the convention hall, a loud voice boomed repeatedly: "WE WANT ROOSEVELT." Delegates erupted in celebration, parading through the aisles while the Chicago police band marched and played "Happy Days Are Here Again." Roosevelt won on the first ballot with 946 votes; Farley was a distant second, with 72. The Postmaster General dutifully moved to make the vote unanimous. Later, the source for the initial Roosevelt rallying cry was identified as Mayor Kelly's superintendent of sewers, Thomas Garry, who had sat for hours in front of a microphone in a cramped basement office waiting for his cue.

Roosevelt basked only momentarily in his victory before turning to the selection of a vice-presidential candidate. He had hoped that his running mate would be his Secretary of State, but Hull had turned him down. He then settled on his Secretary of Agriculture, Henry Wallace, a dependable liberal who might help overcome isolationist sentiment in the rural Midwest. He sent word of his choice to Chicago and immediately received a hostile reaction from Democratic leaders, already furious that they had been manipulated to support his "draft." Eleanor Roosevelt flew to Chicago to deliver a conciliatory speech, pleading with delegates to support her husband's choice. But opposition to Wallace persisted. Many were rebelling against Roosevelt's willful control of the convention. Others complained that the Secretary of Agriculture was politically naive, a mystic, and a former Republican, hardly credentials to secure the party's victory in November. They insisted on an open convention to pick the party's vice-presidential candidate. Roosevelt, just as insistently, demanded Wallace and scribbled on a pad a statement refusing to accept the nomination if his choice for vice president was denied.

On the first ballot, the lead fluctuated between Wallace and House Speaker William Bankhead of Alabama, an unreconstructed southerner whose conservatism contrasted starkly with Wallace's liberalism. At the end of the roll call, Bankhead held the lead. Roosevelt sat by a radio in the Oval Office, anxiously listening to the results. When several urban states that had passed during the initial roll call belatedly recorded their votes for Wallace, he overtook Bankhead to win the nomination. The president had prevailed.

Once Wallace's victory was assured, Roosevelt put on a fresh shirt and prepared to address the convention from the White House. He told the delegates of his reluctance to abandon his plans for retirement in January 1941. "These plans, like so many other plans, had been made in a world which now seems as distant as another planet," he said. "Today all private plans, all private lives, have been in a sense repealed by an overriding public danger." If elected to a third term, "I say to you, in the utmost simplicity, I will, with God's help, continue to serve with the best of my ability and with the fullness of my strength."

When Chief Justice Hughes greeted his brethren at the beginning of the new judicial term in October 1939, the Supreme Court was no longer a source of national controversy. The decisions in 1935 and 1936 that struck down New Deal statutes had been effectively neutralized by later rulings in which the Court majority treated economic and social regulations with conspicuous deference. Just as telling, Congress, with southern Democrats and Republicans opposing virtually every presidential initiative, showed no appetite to pass ambitious economic legislation.

Roosevelt no longer held a grudge against the Court. His reasons for complaint against a conservative Court majority had, literally, disappeared. Hughes and Roberts had joined the Court's three liberals to sustain important New Deal legislation in the spring of 1937. And that fragile five-member majority was bolstered by Justices Black and Reed, who replaced conservatives Van Devanter and Sutherland. Roosevelt's third and fourth appointments, Justices Frankfurter and Douglas, added vitality and intellectual firepower to the liberal wing of the Court. Frankfurter, in addition, continued to advise Roosevelt on a variety of pressing issues, including U.S. foreign policy. On Frankfurter's recommendation, Roosevelt had appointed Henry Stimson to be Secretary of War. Justice Douglas also remained a valued adviser and friend, and a regular player in Roosevelt's weekly poker game at the White House.

Many of the important cases during the 1939 term involved civil rights and liberties, just as Justice Stone in his *Carolene Products* footnote had anticipated. Hughes had built an outstanding judicial record opposing racial discrimination long before Stone's footnote suggested that the Court would scrutinize laws depriving minorities of their constitutional rights. In Hughes's first major opinion as an associate justice in 1911, he had written an outspoken dissent insisting that the Thirteenth Amendment prohibiting involuntary servitude and the Civil Rights Act of 1866 protected a poor African-American farm hand in Alabama from conviction under a state peonage law. And three years later, he wrote the majority opinion for a deeply divided Court that struck down a state law permitting railroads to furnish sleeping and dining cars only for whites as a violation of the Fourteenth Amendment's equal protection clause.

Twenty-five years later (and two years before the *Carolene Products* decision), Chief Justice Hughes had expressed outrage at the coerced confessions extracted by police from three young, ignorant African-American men accused, and later, convicted of murder in Mississippi. In his opinion for a unanimous Court, Hughes reversed the convictions of the defendants, who had been tortured by police until they confessed. One of the men had been hanged from a tree, then systematically beaten until he signed a statement that was dictated to him. The other two were brutally beaten with buckles on the ends of leather straps. Hughes said that the trial transcript read like an account from medieval times, not a record produced in a presumably enlightened constitutional government. "The rack and torture chamber may not be substituted for the witness stand," he wrote. "It would be difficult to conceive of methods more revolting to the sense of justice than those taken to procure the confessions of these petitioners." It was the first decision in which the Court struck down a state criminal conviction on the basis of a coerced confession.

On January 4, 1940, the Court again heard arguments in a case involving young African-American defendants who had been convicted of murder, in part, based on coerced confessions. The defendants were tenant farmers in rural southeast Florida, who had been arrested by police for the murder of an elderly white man and interrogated for six days without interruption. Finally, after an all-night session, the young men confessed. After oral arguments in the case, seven justices, including Hughes, voted to overturn the convictions. It would have been appropriate for the Chief Justice, the author of the earlier coerced confession decision, to assign the opinion to himself. Instead, he asked Justice Black to write the opinion in *Chambers v. Florida*.

"I think Chief Justice Hughes assigned *Chambers* to me because I was a Southerner," Black recalled. Hughes undoubtedly considered more than Black's southern heritage. His assignment offered Black, the former member of the Ku Klux Klan, a unique opportunity to put the rumors of his latent prejudice to rest. "At first I didn't want to [write the opinion]," Black recalled. "He [Hughes] said, 'Don't worry, I'll get the Court for you.' " In the end, the Chief Justice was true to his word; Justices McReynolds and Reed, who had originally opposed reversing the convictions, joined Black's opinion.

In his *Chambers* opinion, Black reviewed the facts of the case with rising indignation. "From virtually the moment of their arrest until their eventual confessions," he wrote, "they never knew when just any one would be called back to the fourth floor room, and there, surrounded by their accusers and others, interrogated by men who held their very lives— so far as these ignorant petitioners could know—in the balance." Declaring that the defendants had been deprived of their due process rights under the Fourteenth Amendment, he concluded: "Under our constitutional system, courts stand against any winds that blow as havens of refuge for those who might otherwise suffer because they are helpless, weak, outnumbered, or because they are non-conforming victims of prejudice and public excitement."

The Court's *Chambers* decision was announced on Lincoln's birthday and provided a striking antidote to Hitler's racist rants. The justices similarly demonstrated the strength of the Constitution's protection of religious minorities, as shocking stories of the Nazis' persecution of Jews emerged from Germany. A unanimous Court overturned the conviction of a Jehovah's Witness who had been arrested for inciting a breach of the peace while proselytizing in New Haven, Connecticut. The Witness, Jesse Cantwell, had been arrested after going into an overwhelmingly Roman Catholic neighborhood of the city and playing a phonograph recording that virulently attacked Catholicism. One of two men who had initially given Cantwell permission to play his record was so angered, once he heard it, that he told Cantwell "he felt like hitting him." The other man advised Cantwell that he'd "better get off the street before something happened to him." Cantwell stopped playing his phonograph, gathered his books, and walked up the street.

In reversing the conviction, Justice Roberts's opinion for the Court noted that Cantwell was proselytizing on a public street where he had a right to peacefully express his views to others. There had been no showing at his trial that he was "noisy, truculent, overbearing or offensive." The sound of his record did not disturb neighborhood residents, draw a crowd, or impede traffic. Roberts conceded that the record could have been highly offensive to some listeners, as it obviously was to the two men who testified at the trial. But the defendant was exercising his constitutionally protected rights to free speech and the practice of his religion in "an effort to persuade a willing listener to buy a book or to contribute money in the interest of what Cantwell, however misguided others may think him, conceived to be true religion."

In a later Jehovah's Witnesses' case that term, the justices were faced with a more excruciating constitutional challenge involving Lillian and William Gobitis, ages twelve and ten. The Gobitis children had refused to join their public school classmates in saluting the American flag before classes began each weekday morning in the small community of Minersville, Pennsylvania. To engage in that patriotic exercise, they had been taught, was to worship false idols prohibited by God's command. The refusal to participate in the early morning patriotic exercise resulted in the children's expulsion from school. In a lawsuit brought on their behalf by their father, the

Gobitis children claimed that their expulsion violated their constitutional right to the free exercise of religion. In 1937, a federal district court judge ruled in their favor and that decision was upheld by an appeals court.

When the Supreme Court listened to oral arguments in the *Gobitis* case in April 1940, the Western world had been radically transformed by Hitler's violent ambitions. The Nazis had already conquered large chunks of Europe. In those portentous times, the Minersville School Board's defense of its compulsory flag salute had an especially poignant appeal.

At the judicial conference following oral argument in the case, Chief Justice Hughes spoke first. "I come up to this case like a skittish horse to a brass band," he said. "I am disturbed that we have this case before us. There is nothing that I have more profound belief in than religious freedom, so I must bring myself to view this case on the question of state power." Having posed the question skillfully, Hughes concluded that "the state can insist on inculcation of loyalty. It would be extraordinary if in this country the state could not provide for respect for the flag of our land."

Justice Black and the newest Roosevelt appointee, Frank Murphy, the passionately liberal former Michigan governor,* expressed doubts about the wisdom of the school board regulation. But these two justices, as well as Roosevelt appointees Douglas and Reed, eagerly awaited the views of Felix Frankfurter. The former Harvard law professor, an eminent constitutional scholar and celebrated civil libertarian, told his judicial colleagues that the Court was confronted with two clashing constitutional rights: the individual's right to the free exercise of religion and the state's right to teach patriotism. For Frankfurter, the Court's only foreign-born citizen, an American public school's prerogative to nurture national loyalty was constitutionally unassailable. Every other Roosevelt appointee agreed with him. The vote was 8–1 in favor of upholding the compulsory flag salute; only Justice Stone, who had been appointed by President Calvin Coolidge, dissented.

Hughes assigned the majority opinion to Frankfurter because of his "moving statement at conference on the role of the public school in instilling love of country in our pluralistic society." The Chief Justice was also surely aware that a Court opinion written by a founder of the ACLU could

---

* Roosevelt appointed Murphy to the Court in January 1940, succeeding Justice Butler, who had died in November 1939. The president had appointed Murphy to serve as U.S. Attorney General, replacing Homer Cummings, after the Michigan governor lost his bid for reelection in 1938.

soften criticism from civil libertarians upset by the majority's rejection of the constitutional claims of Lillian and William Gobitis.

On the morning of June 3, 1940, the large crowd in the courtroom was abuzz with the rumor that Frankfurter would read his *Gobitis* opinion aloud. They were disappointed when Frankfurter chose simply to announce the result. But Justice Stone, hunched forward in his seat, read his dissent with heavy emotion. "History teaches us that there have been but few infringements of personal liberty by the state which have not been justified, as they are here, in the name of righteousness and the public good, and few which have not been directed, as they are now, at politically helpless minorities." He concluded: "This seems to me no less than the surrender of the constitutional protection of the liberty of small minorities to the public will."

One of Frankfurter's New Deal protégés, Benjamin Cohen, shunned his mentor and wrote a letter of congratulations to Stone. "When a liberal judge holds out alone against his liberal brethren," Cohen wrote, "I think he ought to know when he has spoken not for himself alone, but has superbly articulated the thoughts of his contemporaries who believe with him in an effective but tolerant democracy."

Frankfurter had his supporters, not the least being the president of the United States. While Roosevelt mixed cocktails for Felix Frankfurter and his wife, Marion, at Hyde Park a few weeks after the *Gobitis* decision, he approvingly explained the justice's position to a skeptical Eleanor Roosevelt. The Minersville School Board had acted stupidly, he said, but not outside its legal authority.

Eleanor listened patiently and did not question the constitutional argument of her husband and Justice Frankfurter. But there was something profoundly unsettling, she said, about a Supreme Court decision that made children in public schools salute the American flag in violation of their religious beliefs. The first lady added that such official intolerance could well encourage a cruder variety in the public at large. Her concern proved prophetic. Mobs attacked Witnesses in Litchfield, Illinois, and Rockville, Maryland; other beatings and burnings of Jehovah's Witnesses' property were reported in Maine, Texas, and California. A Justice Department study later traced the lawlessness directly to the Court's *Gobitis* decision.*

---

* Three years later, the Court reversed the *Gobitis* decision, upholding the constitutional rights of Jehovah's Witness students in West Virginia who had refused to salute the flag in public school ceremonies.

*   *   *

After Democrats had nominated Roosevelt for a third presidential term, he somberly informed the party's delegates in Chicago that perilous events abroad demanded that he eschew a traditional campaign. His first priority must be to fulfill his responsibilities as commander in chief. During the fall, he would therefore remain in the White House or nearby, where he could maintain contact with Europe or Asia by telephone and be at his desk quickly to respond to new developments. "I shall not have the time or the inclination to engage in purely political debate," he declared in his acceptance speech.

The president's above-the-fray pledge was a good political strategy, but also a fair assessment of his critical role in protecting U.S. foreign policy interests. By mid-July 1940, the Japanese military had won control of that nation's cabinet. A month earlier, Winston Churchill had pointedly reminded Roosevelt and the rest of the free world that their survival was at stake in the imminent aerial Battle of Britain. "Hitler knows that he will have to break us in this island or lose the war," he told the House of Commons. "But if we fail, then the whole world, including the United States, including all that we have known and cared for, will sink into the abyss of a new Dark Age." Four weeks later, after Germany had sunk or damaged eleven British destroyers, Churchill appealed directly to Roosevelt. For Britain to survive, he said, the United States must supply the Royal Navy with fifty or sixty old, reconditioned American destroyers. "Mr. President," he wrote, "with great respect I must tell you that in the long history of the world this is a thing to do *now*."

Roosevelt was intent on helping Churchill, but considered new legislation necessary to send U.S. destroyers to Great Britain. At a cabinet meeting on August 2, he raised the destroyer issue—and the problem posed by Republican isolationists in Congress who could defeat the proposed bill or delay it interminably. That opposition might be overcome, he said, if he could obtain support for the legislation from his Republican challenger, Wendell Willkie, who had advocated aid to Great Britain before his nomination. The president called William Allen White, a friend of both candidates, and asked him to speak to Willkie about the proposed legislation. He stressed to White "the importance of having the issue acted on without regard to party politics in any way." White reported back to the president that Willkie had agreed not to make the legislation a campaign issue. But he refused to publicly support the president on the issue, aware that such a bipartisan position could alienate isolationists in his party and jeopardize his election prospects.

In mid-August, relays of German bombers and fighters flew over the English Channel heading toward England in the first of a barrage of air assaults that destroyed British radar stations and airfields and wreaked incendiary havoc on London's buildings. One result of the Luftwaffe's onslaught was a dramatic spike in Americans' support for aid to Britain, reflected in public opinion polls. With pressure building, Roosevelt proposed sending the warships Churchill had requested in exchange for British naval bases in Newfoundland and Bermuda and ninety-nine-year leases on additional bases in the British West Indies.

To convince Senator David Walsh, the isolationist chairman of the Naval Affairs Committee, that he was driving a hard bargain with the British, Roosevelt recounted his recent conversation with a Dutchess County farmer. "Say, ain't you the Commander in Chief?" the farmer asked. "If you are and own fifty muzzle-loadin' rifles of the Civil War period, you would be a chump if you declined to exchange them for seven modern machine guns—wouldn't you?"

No folksy Dutchess County wisdom could sway Walsh, who, unbending as ever, refused to cooperate. Finally, Roosevelt, taking a considerable political risk, decided to bypass Congress altogether. He was backed by the legal opinion of several prominent lawyers, including Dean Acheson and Charles Burlingham, who contended in a carefully argued letter published in *The New York Times* that the destroyer deal could be consummated under existing legislation. On September 3, Roosevelt announced the terms of the deal during a war plant inspection tour in Charleston, West Virginia.

Two weeks later, the president signed into law the first compulsory peacetime draft in the nation's history. Roosevelt could not claim credit for the legislation, which received widespread bipartisan support. His first public statement on the bill, supporting it as essential for national defense, had come on August 2, well over a month after the legislation had been introduced in Congress. Willkie's endorsement quickly followed. On October 16, more than 16 million American men between the ages of twenty-one and thirty-five registered for the draft. Later that month, a blindfolded Secretary of War Stimson retrieved a capsule from a huge fishbowl and handed it to Roosevelt, who announced the first man called to duty.

The president shrewdly promoted his image as the resolute commander in chief, making well-publicized defense inspection tours arranged to pass through as many towns as possible. He also visited military bases, receiving officers' salutes while his long cape flapped dramatically in the wind. And he extended long-distance congratulations to the thousands of workers streaming into aircraft plants from California to Connecticut. By the end of the year, new defense contracts had shrunk the nation's unemployment rolls to the lowest level in ten years.

Roosevelt effectively co-opted the defense issue from a frustrated Wendell Willkie, who continued to search for a winning political issue. In late September, Willkie struck hard and often on a new theme: the president was a warmonger whose reelection would inevitably draw the United States into the raging conflict abroad. "If his promise to keep our boys out of foreign wars is no better than his promise to balance the budget," he shouted, "they're already almost on the transports." Late in the campaign, he ratcheted his rhetoric a notch higher: "On the basis of his past performance with pledges to the people, if you re-elect him you may expect war in April 1941." Willkie's attacks appeared to be working; polls showed him rapidly cutting into the president's once formidable lead.

In late October, Roosevelt retaliated in a flurry of speeches to correct what he charged were his opponent's gross distortions and outright falsehoods. In his first campaign foray in Philadelphia, he proclaimed: "I am an old campaigner, and I love a good fight." No one in the large, delighted crowd could doubt him as he responded to Willkie, by turns, with biting sarcasm or righteous indignation. He gave his solemn assurance that there was no secret treaty, no commitment, and no understanding with any government "to involve this nation in any war or for any other purpose." In Madison Square Garden five days later, he accused Republicans of "playing politics with national defense." And in Boston, he responded to Willkie's charge that his reelection would mean war within six months: "I have said this before, but I shall say it again and again and again: Your boys are not going to be sent into any foreign wars."*

On election night at Hyde Park, Roosevelt was unusually nervous. He worried that his rebuttals to Willkie's warmongering charges might have come too late to halt his opponent's late surge in the polls. He sat at the

---

* Roosevelt carefully modified his earlier promises, which always contained the caveat "except in case of attack." It wasn't necessary, he decided. "If we're attacked," he said, "it's no longer a foreign war."

family dining-room table, his coat off and tie loosened, sweating freely. Large tally sheets were spread before him. He instructed his bodyguard, Mike Reilly, to keep everyone out of the room, including Eleanor and his old Dutchess County neighbor, Henry Morgenthau, Jr., who had bustled in and out with early, fragmentary returns.

When returns began to pour in from the large urban areas, it became clear that working-class and lower-middle-class workers, bulwarks of Roosevelt's New Deal coalition, had stood by the president. He carried every city in the nation with a population of 400,000 or more, except Cincinnati, and all of the great industrial states in the East and Midwest. A relaxed Roosevelt invited friends and family to join him in the dining room to celebrate. He had won a third term, beating Willkie by almost 5 million in the popular vote and more decisively in the electoral college, 449 to 82. The victory was an impressive personal triumph for Roosevelt, but nonetheless represented the lowest majority of a winning presidential candidate since Woodrow Wilson had narrowly defeated Charles Evans Hughes in 1916. After midnight, Roosevelt happily greeted Hyde Park well-wishers who had paraded from the village center to FDR's front lawn in what had become a local election victory tradition.

In early December, Roosevelt boarded the USS *Tuscaloosa* for a postelection cruise in the Caribbean. He spent his days deep-sea fishing and sunbathing, and his nights playing poker, watching movies, and bantering with Harry Hopkins and his small personal staff. That restful interlude was interrupted on December 9 when a navy seaplane landed next to the *Tuscaloosa*, anchored off Antigua, and delivered an urgent letter to the president from Winston Churchill.

The British prime minister had drafted and redrafted his letter to carefully set the tone, emphasizing the close bond between the two men and their nations, then making an unavoidably bold request. By Churchill's calculation, the United States was two years away from a fully operational modern military force. In the meantime, he assured Roosevelt that Great Britain would "hold the front and grapple with Nazi power until the preparations of the United States are complete." There were two critical obstacles, Churchill noted, to their nations' successful joint defense of the free world. Nazi bombers and U-boats prowling the Atlantic were destroying military aid to Great Britain at an alarming rate. His country, moreover, was almost bankrupt, a desperate financial plight that led Churchill to the underlying purpose of his letter. Britain could not pay for the necessary munitions and ships that the United States was sending under the existing "cash and carry" regulations. It would be wrong, he wrote, if "Great Britain were to be divested of all saleable assets so that after victory was won with our blood, civilization saved and time gained for the United States to be fully armed against all eventualities, we should stand stripped to the bone."

Roosevelt lounged alone in his deck chair for the next two days mulling over Churchill's letter. When he returned to Washington a week later, sun-tanned and rested, he knew exactly how he would respond. He laid the framework at a press conference on December 19. The nation's security interests, he told reporters, were inextricably tied to Great Britain's success in defending itself. He then suggested that U.S. aid to Britain should not be bound by the "cash and carry" provisions of the Neutrality Act. "Now what I am trying to do," he said with calculated jocularity, is to "get rid of the silly, foolish old dollar sign." He analogized the nation's position to that of a homeowner helping a neighbor whose house was on fire. "If he can take my garden hose and connect it up with his hydrant, I may help him to put out his fire," he said. It would be silly for a good neighbor to demand the immediate repayment of the cost of the hose. "I don't want $15—I want my garden hose back after the fire is over." His conclusion: "If you lend certain munitions and get the munitions back at the end of the war . . . you are all right."

Ten days later, Roosevelt drove his point home forcefully in a fireside chat to the nation. "If Great Britain goes down, the Axis powers* will control the continents of Europe, Asia, Africa, Australasia, and the high seas—and they will be in a position to bring enormous military and naval resources against this hemisphere," he warned. "It is no exaggeration to say that all of us, in all the Americas, would be living at the point of a gun." To prevent that tragic result, the United States "must be the great arsenal of democracy," quickly and abundantly supplying Great Britain with ships, planes, tanks, and guns to save Americans "the agony and suffering of war." The president clung tenuously to his campaign pledge to shield

---

* Japan had officially joined the Axis by signing the Tripartite Pact with Germany and Italy in September 1940.

young American men from the armed conflict. But in his call for unconditional help to Great Britain, he pushed the United States one step closer
toward outright war against the Axis powers.

The final iteration of Roosevelt's emerging plan to give unqualified
support to Great Britain was delivered in his State of the Union address to
Congress on January 6, 1941. His theme of the "Four Freedoms"—freedom
of speech and religion, freedom from want and fear—drew a principled link
between the New Deal of his first two presidential terms and the daunting
challenge of his third, to marshal all of America's vast material and human
resources to repel the Axis powers. He announced that he would send a
Lend-Lease bill to Congress to serve as the legislative girding for his new
foreign policy, effectively removing the strictures of "cash and carry." Like
the good neighbor in his fire scenario, the United States, under the legislation, could rush military assistance to Great Britain and settle financial
accounts after the war.

On Monday, January 20, 1941, a clear, cold, and windy day in the
nation's capital, Roosevelt's third term officially began. As had been his
custom at each of his inaugurations, FDR attended midmorning services
at St. Johns Church, across Lafayette Park from the White House. Afterwards, he was driven to the Capitol flanked by motorcycle escorts and eight
Secret Servicemen riding on the running board of his car. Friendly crowds
lined Pennsylvania Avenue while sidewalk salesmen did a brisk business
hawking badges saying: "To Hell with Hitler." Shortly before noon, the
president emerged from the shadows of the Capitol rotunda on the arm of
James, now a captain in the Marine Corps smartly attired in his red, gold,
and blue uniform. For the third time in eight years, Chief Justice Hughes
stepped forward to administer the presidential oath. Just as the president
had done at his previous inaugurations, he repeated the entire oath after
Hughes. "So help you God?" asked Hughes. "So help me God," Roosevelt
answered firmly.

In his inaugural address, Roosevelt exhorted Americans to be vigilant
in the face of the Axis threat. "There are men who believe that . . . tyranny
and slavery have become the surging wave of the future—and that freedom
is an ebbing tide," he said. "But we Americans know that this is not true."

When Hughes presided at the opening of the Supreme Court term in October 1940, he lacked his usual robust energy. He nonetheless sat erect

in the center chair, his full white beard and stern visage projecting the worldly image of God.

Shortly after the judicial term began, former President Hoover attempted to lure the Chief Justice into the increasingly nasty presidential campaign, naturally on the side of the Republican presidential candidate, Wendell Willkie. "I am about to make a suggestion that may impress you as fantastic," Hoover wrote Hughes. "I would not do it if I did not believe that the whole future of the American people hangs upon the decision of this election." Hoover suggested that Hughes resign from the chief justiceship "with a declaration to the country of the complete necessity for a change in the Administration." Hughes declined.

The Court's calendar included cases raising important questions about the meaning of the equal protection clause and First Amendment and the boundaries of congressional power to regulate interstate commerce. The Chief Justice tried to keep pace, but found it increasingly difficult to carry his customary full load. He began to think of retirement, recalling the admonition that he had delivered in his 1927 lectures on the Court: elderly justices should be sensitive to their loss of physical or mental capacity and retire before they become a burden to their colleagues.

Hughes gamely assigned himself two significant civil rights and liberties opinions during the term. The first case involved Arthur Mitchell, an African-American congressman from Illinois, who had been forced to move from a first-class Pullman car into a second-class segregated coach as the train approached the Arkansas border. Hughes wrote the opinion for a unanimous Court, which ruled that railroads traveling across state lines must provide first-class accommodations for African-American passengers. He reminded the nation's railroads, just as he had the state of Missouri in the 1938 *Gaines* decision, of their obligation to take seriously the second part of the "separate but equal" doctrine (established in the Court's 1896 decision, *Plessy v. Ferguson*). The discrimination against Congressman Mitchell, wrote Hughes, was "palpably unjust."

Hughes also wrote an opinion for a unanimous Court that limited the discretion of public officials to issue permits for public parades and marches as to "time, place, and manner." The Court's limitation effectively prevented town or city authorities from denying permits to groups whose causes they disapproved of. The defendant Jehovah's Witnesses had not applied for a permit, which was required by New Hampshire law, and were arrested after marching on busy city sidewalks carrying signs bearing such slogans as "Religion is a Snare and a Racket." The Court concluded that local officials had acted properly since there was no evidence that they had administered the statute in an unfair or discriminatory manner.

A unanimous Court sustained the Fair Labor Standards Act of 1938, which forbade shipment in interstate commerce of goods produced in violation of federal wages-and-hours standards. The sweeping commerce clause decision, *U.S. v. Darby*, would have been unimaginable five years earlier. Hughes assigned the opinion to Justice Stone, who wrote that Congress could enforce the federal statute by excluding lumber from interstate commerce that was produced in Georgia under substandard labor conditions. He brushed aside the argument that states' rights under the Tenth Amendment prevented Congress from controlling labor conditions within a single state. The Tenth Amendment "states but a truism," wrote Stone, namely, that individual states retain all powers not surrendered to the federal government. But Congress, in prescribing the rules by which interstate commerce was governed, was exercising its legitimate authority to deny the channels of interstate commerce to goods produced in violation of federal standards. Stone came to the "inescapable" conclusion that the Court must overrule *Hammer v. Dagenhart*, the 1918 decision that had struck down a congressional statute prohibiting goods produced by child labor to be transported in interstate commerce.

When the justices made their annual pilgrimage to the White House for dinner in January 1941, Hughes appeared to be in good spirits. Attorney General Robert Jackson, who also attended the dinner, heard Hughes mischievously tell Roosevelt, "I hope you won't mind, after I administer the oath to you the third time, if I lean over and quietly ask, 'Governor, is this getting to be a habit?' " Both Roosevelt and Hughes broke out in hearty laughter.* In the same convivial spirit, the president congratulated Hughes on his seventy-ninth birthday in April. Sending "affectionate regards," he added, "You are not a day older—mentally or physically than I am—just 59!"

Hughes's apparently carefree mood at the White House dinner betrayed his true state of mind. Antoinette, who was in poor health, urged him to

---

* Years later, Hughes recalled the incident slightly differently: the conversation occurred after the inauguration, when the two men were sitting on a sofa in the president's library after dinner. Hughes confessed to Roosevelt, "I had an impish desire to break the solemnity of the occasion by remarking, 'Franklin, don't you think this is getting to be a trifle monotonous!' "

leave the Court, so that they could spend their remaining years traveling at their leisure and enjoying their family and each other. The Chief Justice had, by this time, made his decision to retire. But James McReynolds's announced retirement in February caused him to postpone his own. He did not want to leave the Court with two vacancies during the term.

In the spring, Hughes kept to as brisk a schedule as his energy would allow. He delivered a state-of-the-judiciary speech to the American Law Institute that closed with a burst of patriotic fervor, contrasting the vitality of the American constitutional system with the deteriorating human conditions under fascism. "The lamps of justice are dimmed or have wholly gone out in many parts of the earth," he observed, "but these lights are still shining brightly here." The United States was "engaged in harnessing our national power for the defense of our way of life. "But that way is worthwhile only because it is the pathway of the just." The Court, he concluded, would help turn the tide against fascism by demonstrating to the world the nation's high constitutional standards of justice.

Roosevelt was preoccupied with defense policy during the spring months. In March, he successfully fought off opposition to his Lend-Lease bill by die-hard isolationists. Burton Wheeler, his old nemesis from the Court-packing fight, called the legislation "the New Deal's triple 'A' foreign policy—it will plough under every fourth American boy." The president retorted angrily at his next press conference, "I regard [it] as the most untruthful, as the most dastardly, unpatriotic thing that had ever been said. Quote me on that." The measure passed overwhelmingly in both the House and the Senate. In Parliament, Churchill praised the legislation as "the most unsordid act in the history of any nation."

The war continued to go badly for the British, who struggled to retain control of shipping lanes in the Mediterranean and protect vital Middle East oil reserves. The Germans quickly defeated Yugoslavia and expelled the British Army from Greece, while General Erwin Rommel's Afrika Korps tanks roared across North Africa. Roosevelt, by this time, was convinced that Great Britain could not defeat the Axis powers alone, and that the United States' entry into the war was inevitable. But he also knew that the nation was not yet prepared militarily and did not want to provoke Hitler into a declaration of war.

On June 2, the last day of the Court's term, Roosevelt received a brief letter from Hughes announcing that for reasons of health and age he would retire on July 1. The president immediately wrote his reply in longhand: "This comes to me, as I know it will to the whole Nation, as a great shock for all of us had counted on your continuing your splendid service for many years to come. My every inclination is to beg you to remain; but my deep concern for your health and strength must be paramount."

Roosevelt invited Hughes to have lunch with him the next week at the White House, where the two men talked—"Governor" to "Governor"; President to Chief Justice; American to American.

Epilogue

The choice of Hughes's successor dominated the luncheon conversation between Roosevelt and Hughes the week after the Chief Justice had announced his retirement. Two potential nominees were discussed: Attorney General Robert Jackson and Associate Justice Harlan Fiske Stone. Hughes respected Jackson but strongly recommended that the president nominate Stone. For Hughes, Stone's long judicial experience tipped the balance toward his colleague. He also advised Roosevelt to consult Felix Frankfurter, who, as a valued Roosevelt confidant, would undoubtedly have been consulted whether Hughes suggested his counsel or not. Frankfurter too recommended Stone, telling the president that the appointment of Stone, a Republican, would promote the spirit of bipartisanship as the nation edged ever closer toward war.

Hughes was determined to take his retirement seriously. He rejected an invitation to be the guest of honor at the American Bar Association's meeting in Indianapolis in September 1941, even though Roosevelt urged him to accept. The president thought the invitation presented an opportunity for Hughes to call public attention to the danger of Nazi domination in Europe. "As you know," Roosevelt wrote Hughes, "it is a task of the utmost difficulty to make people realize what the effect of a German victory would be, and I know of nothing more effective than a speech broadcast by you." Hughes replied: "I feel that the time has come when I should be excused from preparing addresses and be spared the fatigue of public performance. I must leave to others the effort to inform, clarify and persuade."

Only once during his retirement did Hughes made an exception to his rule of refusing to be drawn into public policy discussions. In 1944, at Secretary of State Cordell Hull's request, he reviewed the draft of the United Nations Charter and made several pragmatic suggestions to improve the governance of the proposed international organization. He recalled France's sensitivity to snubs from the great powers during the 1921 Washington Conference and suggested that that country be invited to join the proposed four permanent members of the Security Council (The United States, Great Britain, the Soviet Union, and China). He also recommended that membership of the Security Council be expanded from the proposed eight to eleven members to include additional small nations. Both of Hughes's recommendations were incorporated into the UN Charter.

Secretary Hull asked Hughes's advice on the most contentious issue facing the Roosevelt administration in signing the Charter: the role and conditions under which the United States would join a UN force in any international conflict. Hughes told Hull that presidents throughout American history had acted to defend the nation's security interests without asking Congress for a declaration of war. The president had ample constitutional authority as commander in chief to order U.S. troops to join a military force under the auspices of the United Nations, he said.* When Hull informed Hughes that Senate leaders of both parties were being consulted on vital provisions of the Charter, the former Secretary of State heartily approved. He recalled the disastrous go-it-alone strategy employed by President Wilson, which had resulted in the Senate's voting down the Versailles Treaty. When the UN Charter was adopted at the San Francisco Conference in 1945, Hughes pronounced it "a beacon in a darkened world."

During the early years of his retirement, Hughes's attention was primarily focused on his family, especially his beloved wife, Antoinette. They traveled to favorite vacation spots, like Jasper Park, Arizona, but happily returned to their quiet life in their R Street home. In frail health, Antoinette required two operations in 1941 at the Johns Hopkins Hospital in

---

* President Truman would invoke that authority less than a decade later when U.S. troops fought as part of a UN force in the Korean War.

Baltimore. Hughes visited her every day; their daughter Catherine fretted that her father's daily commute to the hospital would wear him out. "Don't you worry," he replied. "How could I get tired going to see my best girl!"

Hughes's devotion to Antoinette was constant and often expressed with the romantic ardor of a young swain. On her eightieth birthday, September 14, 1944, he wrote:

> *Happy Birthday to my best beloved!*
> *We "climbed the hill together"*
> *And, now that we are going down*
> *On the other side, we find the*
> *Slope gentle and beautiful!*
> *And so we go hand in hand—*
> *In the eighties!*

By her eighty-first birthday, Antoinette's health had badly deteriorated, and a few months later, her husband sat at her bedside preparing for the inevitable. On December 5, 1945, he wrote Catherine: "Today is our 57th wedding anniversary! I am trying to fix my thought upon our long and beautiful companionship, a perfect union with a radiant spirit." The next morning, while he was eating breakfast, a nurse informed Hughes that his wife was dying. He rushed upstairs in a panic and saw that she was unconscious. He placed a phone call to Catherine in New York. "Mother is sinking rapidly," he said, barely controlling his emotions. Antoinette Hughes died that evening.

Hughes, who died three years later, never fully recovered from the loss of his wife. He insisted that their living room remain precisely as Antoinette had left it. His children and grandchildren attempted to fill the emotional void, but with limited success. He joined them during the summers at their cottage on Cape Cod, and they visited him at his winter home in Florida. Fortunately, he had almost completed his memoirs before Antoinette died. He worked at home, dictating what he originally entitled "Biographical Notes," aided by the materials compiled by Henry Beerits, a young Princeton graduate who had earlier prepared extensive memoranda on Hughes's ancestry, childhood, and career.

In a prefatory note, Hughes wrote that his memoirs might be of interest to his children and grandchildren and useful to others who wished accurate information on his life. Though he intended no apologia, he was well aware that his effort represented his final summation on his place in American history. It was, therefore, no surprise that he devoted the greatest space in the chapter on his years as Chief Justice to two contentious episodes.

The first raised the issue of whether President Hoover had wanted to appoint Hughes to be Chief Justice in 1930. Hughes offered a fresh rebuttal to the rumor at the time of his appointment that Hoover had only made the offer to him as a formal courtesy, expecting Hughes to decline so that he could appoint his first choice, Associate Justice Stone. Hughes quoted verbatim Hoover's letter of February 19, 1937, which corroborated Hughes's recollection that the president had offered him the chief justiceship in good faith and with the expectation that he would accept it.

The second issue, which Hughes dealt with at length, was his role in opposing Roosevelt's Court-packing plan. He devoted several pages to the decisions leading up to the president's proposal, taking care to show that five of the Court's so-called anti–New Deal decisions were unanimous and two others were supported by an eight-man majority. He defended two of the most controversial Court decisions in which he joined Owen Roberts and the four conservatives in declaring unconstitutional the McGuffey Coal Act (*Carter v. Carter Coal*) and the Agricultural Adjustment Act of 1933 (*U.S. v. Butler*).

He vigorously denied Roosevelt's claim that the Court had succumbed to pressure from his Court-packing plan when the justices sustained the Washington minimum wage law (*West Coast Hotel Co. v. Parrish*). To demonstrate that FDR was wrong, Hughes revealed the justices' votes at their conference in December 1936, in which they upheld the law two months *before* the president announced his Court proposal. As to the plan itself, he wrote that it "was justly regarded as an assault upon the independence of the judiciary." After recounting the circumstances leading to his letter to the Senate Judiciary Committee defending the Court, he concluded that "the letter appears to have had a devastating effect by destroying the specious contention as to the need of additional justices to expedite the work of the Court."

Hughes's legacy as Chief Justice, naturally, encompassed far more than his role in defending the Court against Roosevelt's Court-packing plan. It was not quite as pristine a judicial record as Hughes himself suggested in his autobiographical notes. His stalwart defense of virtually every anti–New Deal Court decision was not always persuasive. He could easily justify decisions striking down poorly drafted bills, such as the National Industrial Recovery Act; the statute's weakness was underscored by the justices' unanimity in declaring it unconstitutional in *Schechter Poultry Corporation v. United States*. But he was less successful in defending other decisions driven by the conservative bloc, such as *Carter v. Carter*, in which Hughes and Roberts joined "the Four Horsemen" in striking down the McGuffey Coal Act. The majority's rigid line drawing between direct and indirect effects on interstate commerce was a throwback to an earlier constitutional era that Hughes himself had discredited as an associate justice in his 1914 *Shreveport Rate Case* opinion. As his critics have charged, Hughes's vote with the conservative majority may have reflected his overriding concern with the Court's public image more than devotion to constitutional principle.

The Chief Justice, however, returned to solid constitutional ground the next year with his majority opinion in *NLRB v. Jones & Laughlin Steel Corp.*, in which he took an expansive view of congressional power that he had endorsed as an associate justice. In *Jones & Laughlin*, he used his formidable analytical skills to draw the broad contours of the Court's modern commerce clause doctrine, which would serve as the constitutional template in reviewing economic legislation for the next sixty years.

Hughes was at his dominant best in leading the Court toward an era of expansive protection of civil rights and liberties. His unwavering commitment to individual rights dated back to his tenure as an associate justice. With Justice Holmes, he had protested the blatant unfairness of Leo Frank's murder trial in a Georgia courtroom. And he invoked the Thirteenth Amendment's prohibition against involuntary servitude to defend the rights of a poor, black farm worker in Alabama who had been convicted under the state's peonage law and sentenced to hard prison labor. Hughe's outrage at unfairness later prompted him, as a private attorney, to challenge the expulsion of five Socialist members of the New York Assembly.

As Chief Justice, he built impressively on his earlier civil liberties record. His majority opinion in *Near v. Minnesota* stands as a seminal document on freedom of the press. He supported the constitutional claims of unpopular defendants, such as the young American Communist Yetta Stromberg, and Dr. Douglas Macintosh, the conscientious objector. He expressed revulsion at the third-degree methods used to intimidate poor black criminal defendants in *Brown v. Mississippi*. And he initiated the

Court's first serious challenge to the separate but equal doctrine, writing
the 1938 majority opinion that supported the equal protection argument
of an African-American, Lloyd Gaines, who had been barred from the all-
white University of Missouri Law School.

By any objective standard, Hughes ranks as one of the most important Chief Justices in constitutional history. He guided the Supreme Court
through a period of judicial turbulence in which the justices gradually
uprooted the old conservative doctrines of the Taft Court. At times, especially in 1936, it appeared that the Chief Justice had lost control. But
despite the powerful centrifugal forces at work on his right and left, he held
the Court together.

He was well qualified to play that pivotal leadership role. Possessing
a brilliant legal mind, he was by judicial temperament a dedicated centrist. His progressive instincts were deep, but tempered by an innate caution. Had he been an ideologue, either on the right or left, his tenure as
Chief Justice would almost certainly have ended badly, further polarizing a
divided Court. Instead, his incremental approach to constitutional transformation enabled him to preserve both the image and reality of a strong
Supreme Court and, in the process, resist the enormous political pressure
exerted by President Roosevelt. Once the threat of FDR's Court-packing
plan had run its course, Hughes led the Court with renewed confidence,
ushering in the modern constitutional era.

Shortly after Hughes's retirement, the nation's highest judicial tribunal
could accurately be called the Roosevelt Court. When they convened for
the October 1941 term, seven of the nine justices owed their appointments
to Roosevelt, the most since George Washington was president. The president had named Democratic senator James Byrnes of South Carolina to
replace Justice McReynolds, and Attorney General Robert Jackson to take
Stone's seat after he was elevated to the chief justiceship. Only Stone and
Roberts remained as holdovers from the pre-1937 Court.

Chief Justice Stone never truly led the Court—as Hughes had done
even after he was joined by five Roosevelt appointees. The new Chief, who
had bridled under the tight control imposed by Hughes at judicial conferences, allowed meandering discussions among the justices. As a result, the
conferences that Hughes had concluded promptly at 4:30 p.m. on Saturday
afternoons sometimes continued into the following week when the justices

were listening to new oral arguments. This discursiveness, encouraged by Stone's insistence on discussing every point with professorial thoroughness, infuriated his brethren.

Stone's inability to lead the Court allowed personal rivalries among the justices to fester. Two years after Frankfurter had written the majority opinion, supported by his fellow Roosevelt appointees, in the 1940 flag salute decision (*Minersville School District v. Gobitis*), Justices Black, Douglas, and Murphy declared their independence from the former Harvard professor. In a second case brought by Jehovah's Witnesses, the three justices announced in a joint dissent that they had been wrong in *Gobitis*. "[O]ur democratic form of government functioning under the historic Bill of Rights has a high responsibility to accommodate itself to the religious views of minorities, however unpopular and unorthodox those views may be," they wrote. A year later, in another challenge to the compulsory flag salute, a new Court majority, which included Black, Douglas, and Murphy, reversed *Gobitis* over Frankfurter's impassioned dissent.

Frankfurter accused Black, Douglas, and Murphy of apostasy in abandoning his constitutional positions. His resentment was due, in part, to the realization that Hugo Black had begun to emerge as the liberal leader of the Roosevelt appointees, championing civil liberties while Frankfurter continued to counsel judicial restraint. But Frankfurter's criticism was also deeply personal. In private correspondence, Frankfurter charged that Black, Douglas, and Murphy were motivated by politics, not constitutional principle. He began to refer to the three justices as "the Axis," the most pejorative term imaginable at the height of the Second World War. Chief Justice Stone appeared to be a helpless bystander, unable to defuse the tension among his brethren.

During the early 1940s, the constitutional separation of powers between the Court and the president, which Chief Justice Hughes had fought so hard to preserve, effectively collapsed. Roosevelt and the justices who had served as his valued advisers before their Court appointments (Frankfurter, Douglas, and Jackson) continued to engage, full tilt, in policy discussions. Frankfurter, particularly, remained a close Roosevelt confidant, writing long, in-depth memoranda on a broad range of issues, including the urgent need for the efficient mobilization of the nation's resources after the United States declared war on the Japanese Empire.

*   *   *

Roosevelt was eating a late lunch in his upstairs study with Harry Hopkins on December 7, 1941, when he received a phone call from Secretary of the Navy Knox that Japanese planes had attacked Pearl Harbor. Admiral Harold Stark, the chief of naval operations, confirmed the attack and informed the president that the Pacific Fleet had been severely damaged. Outwardly calm, Roosevelt was furious that the Japanese would launch an attack while envoys of the two countries were engaged in private discussions on how to avoid war. He was also angered and perplexed by the ease with which Japanese torpedo planes, dive-bombers, and fighters had penetrated U.S. defenses to bombard the U.S. fleet anchored in the harbor. As a former Assistant Secretary of the Navy, he could not understand how the U.S. Navy, *his* navy, could be caught so unprepared and nakedly vulnerable.

That afternoon, Roosevelt personally answered phone calls in the Oval Office, receiving increasingly horrific reports from the Pacific. He also spoke to Winston Churchill, who called from Chequers, his country estate. "Mr. President, what's this about Japan?" he asked.

"It's quite true," Roosevelt replied somberly. "They have attacked us at Pearl Harbor. We are all in the same boat now."

For the remainder of the afternoon, Roosevelt conducted the nation's emergency business with firm resolve. He instructed Secretary of War Stimson and Secretary of the Navy Knox to draft the necessary orders for the nation to go to war. He discussed at length troop deployments with General George Marshall, the army's chief of staff. He told Secretary of State Hull to inform the Latin American nations of the attack at Pearl Harbor and enlist their support.

Shortly before 5 p.m., Roosevelt asked his secretary, Grace Tully, to come into his study. "Sit down, Grace," he said. "I'm going before Congress tomorrow. I'd like to dictate my message. It will be short." He spoke more deliberately than usual: "Yesterday comma December seventh comma 1941 dash a date which will live in infamy dash . . ."

At noon the next day, the president was driven to Capitol Hill under heavy security to deliver his short speech (twenty-five sentences). He entered the House chamber to tumultuous applause. With his shoulders erect and chin jutting defiantly forward, he asked Congress to declare war on Japan for "the unprovoked and dastardly attack" at Pearl Harbor. Thirty-three minutes later, Congress acted on the president's request. The nation was at war.

Three day later, Germany and Italy declared war on the United States. Hitler exulted at the prospect of joining forces with Japan against the United States. "Now it is impossible for us to lose the war," he told his generals. "We have an ally who has never been vanquished in three thousand years."

Churchill was more prescient. "To have the United States on our side was to me the greatest joy," he later wrote. "I thought of a remark [Sir] Edward Grey [the former British foreign secretary] had made to me more than thirty years before—that the United States was like 'a gigantic boiler. Once the fire is lighted under it there is no limit to the power it can generate.' "

In his State of the Union address on January 6, 1942, Roosevelt set astronomical goals for the nation's military effort: 60,000 aircraft, 45,000 tanks, 20,000 antiaircraft guns, 6 million tons of merchant shipping. "These figures will give the Japanese and the Nazis a little idea of just what they accomplished at Pearl Harbor," he said. His words brought cheering congressmen to their feet and instantly boosted morale across America.

Although FDR's goals were inspiring, they did not provide the balanced assessment of the weaponry needed to win the war. In addition to aircraft, tanks, and antiaircraft guns, U.S. forces required machine guns, field artillery, and anti-tank weapons. The president, who had arbitrarily raised the goals the night before his State of the Union address, quietly revised them downward. But he had indelibly set the tone for the nation, and tens of thousands of Americans eagerly went to work to produce war machines in astounding volume.

There was an ugly underside to Roosevelt's wartime zeal. On February 19, 1942, he signed an executive order authorizing the forcible removal from the west coast of persons of Japanese ancestry, including more than 80,000 Japanese-American citizens. They lost their homes, their jobs, and their constitutional rights in the inexorable tide of racial hostility that swept the nation. Four months later, after two small groups of German saboteurs were arrested on the east coast, Roosevelt demanded that they be executed as quickly as possible. In his roughshod treatment of both Japanese-Americans and the German saboteurs, Roosevelt was supported by decisions of the U.S. Supreme Court.

The presumed layer of separation between the president and the Court

proved especially porous after the arrests of eight German saboteurs carrying explosives who had landed in June 1942 on the beaches of Amagan-
sett, Long Island, and Ponte Vedra, Florida. The men had been trained in
Germany to blow up U.S. bridges and manufacturing plants. Roosevelt
was outraged by the brazen plan and shocked by the security lapse. He told
Attorney General Francis Biddle that he wanted the men tried by a special
military tribunal with no opportunity to appeal to the Supreme Court.

A specially convened military panel comprised exclusively of generals
heard the case in July. Defense attorneys, anticipating guilty verdicts for
their clients, sought an expedited hearing before the Supreme Court to
challenge the constitutionality of the ad hoc military tribunal. Rather than
immediately filing the necessary legal papers, however, they met secretly at
the Pennsylvania farm of Justice Roberts, who was joined by Justice Black
and Attorney General Biddle. The case was placed on the Court's calendar
for July 29, while the defense attorneys were making their final arguments
before the miliary tribunal. Two days later, the Court announced a unanimous order endorsing the authority of the special military tribunal to try
the saboteurs.

All eight defendants, including two who were naturalized U.S. citizens, were found guilty and sentenced to death by electrocution. Six of
the eight defendants were executed on August 8; the other two, who had
cooperated with the FBI, were given long prison sentences. Chief Justice
Stone later wrote the opinion for the Court that carefully sidestepped the
most relevant precedent, a decision immediately following the Civil War
holding that a defendant accused of aiding the enemy should not have
been tried by a military commission in the state of Indiana while the civilian courts were open. Stone, moreover, ignored the fact that procedures
followed by the special military tribunal violated rules in the Articles of
War passed by Congress.

The Court also backed the authority of Roosevelt and General John
De Witt, who was charged with the army's defense on the west coast, to
scatter more than 100,000 Japanese-Americans in internment camps from
the California desert to the hills of Arkansas. In the Court's most egre-
gious decision, the justices rejected the constitutional claim brought by
Fred Korematsu, a San Leandro, California, welder, who had refused to
follow military orders excluding him from his home in preparation for his
forced exodus from the west coast. Justice Black's majority opinion concluded that Korematsu had not been deprived of equal protection of the

laws, even though the government had produced no evidence that he or other Japanese-Americans, as a group, were disloyal.*

As wartime commander in chief, Roosevelt asked Americans to join in common purpose as he had done during the depression. "You can't draw a line down the middle . . . and put the war abroad on one side and put the home front on the other," he said. Farmers, miners, and munition workers at home and soldiers at the front were "all part of the picture of trying to win the war."

Seven months after the attack on Pearl Harbor, Roosevelt received the first encouraging news from the Pacific. Japan, after a lightning-quick series of victories (Thailand, Malaya, Burma, Singapore), had planned a surprise attack on Midway Island, a potential launching pad for an invasion of the Hawaiian Islands. But the U.S. Navy broke the Japanese code and was prepared for the assault on Midway. On June 4, 1942, two squadrons of American dive-bombers pounded the unsuspecting Japanese aircraft carriers, sinking three and badly damaging a fourth. The Japanese fleet reversed course and never regained naval superiority.

No comparable good news came from Europe. German troops had already conquered much of the continent and, by the spring of 1942, were driving deep into the interior of the Soviet Union. The retreating Red Army had suffered enormous losses: 700,000 Russian soldiers killed or captured.

In late May, the Soviet foreign minister, Vyacheslav Molotov, arrived in Washington to persuade Roosevelt to commit the United States to a second European front to take pressure off the Red Army. The president was sympathetic. Before Molotov's visit, he had sent a memo to his Joint Chiefs declaring: "Our principal objective is to help Russia. Russian armies are killing more Germans and destroying more Axis material than all 25 United Nations put together." But he was constrained by reservations expressed by General Marshall and Admiral Ernest King, the commander of the Atlantic Fleet. They did not think U.S. troops were ready, and in any case, did not want to be tied down to a specific deadline. The presi-

---

* Scholars have condemned *Korematsu* and other decisions involving Japanese-Americans during the war, viewing them as glaring aberrations from the modern Supreme Court's record of expanding civil rights and liberties.

dent nonetheless sent Molotov home with a positive message to deliver to Joseph Stalin—that the United States was committed to a second front by the end of the year.

No sooner had Molotov left than Churchill arrived in the United States and promptly dissuaded the president from acting on his pledge to a second European front. Rather than committing untested U.S. troops and the depleted British forces to that risky strategy, he proposed that the Allies attack German troops in North Africa. Roosevelt, eager to have U.S. ground forces engaged in fighting the Germans, agreed to the North African invasion.

In the early morning hours of November 8, U.S. and British troops went ashore at Casablanca, Oran, and Algiers, and a week later, they controlled all of Morocco and Algeria. An elated Roosevelt pre-recorded his congratulations to the French people in German-occupied France and in North Africa. "I know your farms, your villages, your cities," he said. "I salute again and reiterate my faith in Liberty, Equality, and Fraternity."

Brushing aside aides' concern for his safety, Roosevelt boarded a Boeing Clipper on January 9, 1943, for a cross-Atlantic, top-secret journey to Casablanca. He was scheduled to meet with Churchill and to inspect Allied soldiers, the first American president since Lincoln to visit troops in an active theater of war. While he and Churchill were meeting at the Anfa Hotel in Casablanca, they received the first widespread reports of Allied victories. British forces had defeated Rommel's Afrika Korps at Egypt's El Alamein and were driving west toward Libya. The Red Army had mounted a ferocious counterattack at Stalingrad. And in the Pacific, U.S. Marines had begun the bloody recapture of Guadalcanal. An upbeat Roosevelt announced that the Allies would be satisfied with nothing less than the unconditional surrender of Germany, Italy, and Japan.

Roosevelt and Churchill again conferred in Washington five months later and agreed to the long-delayed cross-Channel invasion (code-named OVERLORD) in the spring of 1944. At a summer meeting in Quebec City, Canada, the two leaders began to piece together the details of the Normandy invasion. They agreed that an American, yet unnamed, would be the commander of the invasion and discussed the logistics of the complicated Channel crossing—landing craft, fuel pipelines, and the massive amount of equipment to be unloaded. They also discussed progress on the development of an atomic bomb, which Roosevelt had authorized in 1939 after Albert Einstein had warned him that Germany was probably at work on a nuclear weapon.

When Roosevelt first met Stalin in Teheran on November 28, 1943, at the initial conference of the Big Three, the main topic was the cross-Channel invasion. Churchill began to backtrack from the plan, raising logistical concerns about the invasion and suggesting alternative approaches. When Stalin objected, Roosevelt came down firmly on the side of the Soviet leader. "We are all agreed that OVERLORD is the dominating operation," he declared, "and that any operation which might delay OVERLORD cannot be considered by us." Three days after he left Teheran, Roosevelt appointed General Dwight D. Eisenhower to command the OVERLORD operation.

FDR appeared to be in robust good health and brimming with energy at his first press conference upon his return to the United States. Asked if he still identified his administration with the New Deal, he replied that "Old Doctor New Deal" had saved the banks, rescued agriculture, provided Social Security and unemployment insurance, minimum wage and maximum hour legislation, and created the Civilian Conservation Corps. But on December 7, 1941, he continued, after the patient had recovered, he was in "a very bad accident." Although "Old Doctor New Deal knew a great deal about internal medicine," he said, "he knew nothing about surgery." And so his partner, "Dr. Win-the-War," took over. The patient was recuperating, he reported, but would not fully recover "until he wins the war."

Roosevelt's ebullient public persona was deceiving. By the winter of 1944, there were telltale signs that he was not well. His daughter, Anna, noticed that he had lost color in his face and suffered from a persistent cough.* Grace Tully observed that the president was unusually tired during the morning hours and even nodded off occasionally while he was dictating. In late March, Roosevelt confined himself to bed after his temperature reached 104 degrees. Eleanor did not seem concerned, but Anna demanded an explanation from Admiral Ross McIntire, the White House physician. McIntire, who was an ear, nose, and throat specialist, assured

---

* Anna had moved into the White House to take care of her father. Eleanor was often away, visiting troops, attending conferences, and delivering lectures advocating social reform. At her father's request, Anna arranged for Lucy Mercer Rutherford, recently widowed, to visit the president at the White House when Eleanor was out of town.

her that nothing was wrong with the president that a vacation in the sun would not cure. Anna insisted nonetheless that her father be examined at Bethesda Naval Hospital.

The president was met at the hospital by Lieutenant Commander Howard Bruenn, the staff consultant in cardiology, who immediately noticed Roosevelt's pallid complexion and his difficulty in breathing. After a thorough examination, he concluded that the president was suffering from congestive heart failure. Bruenn's diagnosis was rejected by Admiral McIntire, who refused to believe that his patient had become seriously ill overnight. McIntire did not share Bruenn's conclusions with Roosevelt and blithely told reporters that the results of the medical exam, other than detecting an ordinary case of bronchitis, had been excellent.

In the late afternoon of June 6, a happy and confident Roosevelt met with reporters, bolstered by early reports that the Normandy landing appeared to have gone well. That evening, in a radio broadcast to the nation, he offered a prayer for the troops on Normandy's beaches—"our sons, pride of our Nation . . . give strength to their arms, stoutness to their hearts"— and to the people at home for strong hearts "to wait out the travail."

Shortly before the Democratic Convention opened in July, Roosevelt told Democratic chairman Robert Hannegan that he did not want to run for a fourth presidential term, but duty compelled him to do so. "Reluctantly, but as a good soldier, I will accept and serve in this office," he said, "if I am ordered to do so by the Commander in Chief of us all—the sovereign people of the United States." He won renomination easily on the first ballot but did not address the convention. While Democrats were celebrating his renomination, the president was sailing on the USS *Baltimore* to Pearl Harbor for a strategy meeting with Admiral Chester Nimitz, commander of the Pacific Fleet, and General Douglas MacArthur. His mind was on the war, not politics.

Upon his return to the mainland in early August, while making a speech to Navy Yard workers at Bremerton, Washington, Roosevelt experienced severe chest pains. He managed to complete his speech and return to the captain's cabin to recuperate. Less than a week later, he was back at his desk in the White House. After a quick trip to Quebec for another conference with Churchill, he kicked off his reelection campaign in late September with a speech to the Teamsters Union at Washington's Statler Hotel. He delivered the speech sitting down but was nonetheless in peak form. He began by noting that his Republican opponent, New York governor Thomas E. Dewey, had referred to the "tired old men" who ran the government. "You know, I am actually four years older," he mused, "which is a fact that seems to annoy some people." The crowd roared with laughter. The speech ended with one of his most memorable retorts to his Republican critics. "These Republican leaders have not been content with attacks on me, or my wife, or my sons," he said. "No, they now include my little dog, Fala. Well, of course, I don't resent attacks, and my family doesn't resent attacks, but Fala *does* resent them."

Roosevelt defeated the stiff, self-conscious Dewey by more than 3 million votes, winning thirty-six of the forty-eight states.

After the election, Roosevelt's health began to fail at an alarming rate. Some days his lips turned blue, his hands shook uncontrollably, and his mind seemed incapable of focusing. Following a cabinet meeting in January 1945, Frances Perkins said, "He looked like an invalid who had been allowed to see a guest for the first time and the guest had stayed too long."

The president refused to give in. Two days after his inauguration, he boarded the cruiser *Quincy*, heading for a rendezvous with Churchill on the Mediterranean island of Malta. From Malta, they flew seven hours for a meeting at the Soviet resort town of Yalta on the Black Sea, where Stalin awaited them. The three Allied leaders met eight times in eight days. Despite a "Declaration on Liberated Europe," Roosevelt was well aware that nothing could prevent Poland, already occupied by Russian troops, from escaping the Soviet Union's iron grip. At the same time, he was encouraged by Stalin's agreement to enter the Pacific War against Japan.

On March 1, 1945, after returning from his exhausting trip, Roosevelt addressed a joint session of Congress conference from his wheelchair: "I hope you will pardon me for this unusual posture of sitting down during the presentation, but I know that you will realize that it makes it a lot easier for me not to have to carry about ten pounds of steel around on the bottom of my legs." His first public admission of his crippled condition was greeted with prolonged applause. In his hourlong speech, the president said that the Yalta Conference had been a success in which the three leading nations had found "common ground for peace." It was his last major public appearance.

Roosevelt left Washington for Warm Springs at the end of the month and was joined at the Georgia resort by Lucy Rutherford and an artist friend of hers, Elizabeth Shoumatoff, who had been commissioned to paint a portrait of the president. On April 12, 1945, the president, while sitting for his portrait, collapsed in his chair and never regained consciousness. He was dead at the age of sixty-three.

The nation had not mourned the death of a president with such inconsolable grief since Lincoln's assassination. Hundreds of thousands of Americans wept, sang hymns, or stood in silent vigil along the railroad tracks as the dead president's train moved slowly north toward the nation's capital. He had led them through the Great Depression and the darkest days of the Second World War—with grit, imagination, and an indomitable spirit—to become the greatest president of the twentieth century.

Acknowledgments

I began this book with the enthusiastic support of my superb agent, Esther Newberg, and the expert guidance of my inimitable editor at Simon & Schuster, Alice Mayhew. Roger Labrie at Simon & Schuster demonstrated his usual cool efficiency in moving the book through the production process, and Rachel Bergmann tactfully made sure I met deadlines.

The professional staffs at three institutions were essential to the completion of this book. The librarians at New York Law School under the capable leadership of Camille Broussard responded efficiently to my relentless requests. Bill Mills, my longtime library liaison, supervised the project with his usual good humor and competence. The research staff at the Library of Congress, as with my previous books, dealt with my needs with high professionalism. At the Franklin D. Roosevelt Presidential Library at Hyde Park, New York, the archivists served as both guides and experts on that remarkable collection.

Dean Richard A. Matasar at New York Law School was supportive throughout the project. Three colleagues—Professors R. B. Bernstein, William P. LaPiana and Edward A. Purcell read the manuscript and made important suggestions for its improvement. I also was fortunate to receive useful feedback from the NYLS faculty after I presented a chapter of the book at a faculty luncheon. My student research assistants—Adam Jason,

Adam Rich, Alexander Spilberg, and Julie Stein—spent long hours track-ing down my requests. My assistant, Cathy Jenkins, provided excellent clerical and computer support. Theodore Hughes Waddell, the Chief Jus-tice's grandson, generously shared photographs from his extraordinary col-lection of Charles Evans Hughes memorabilia. I also want to thank my sister, Elizabeth Simon, and my brother-in-law, Mike Kennedy, for assis-tance in reviewing Mr. Waddell's collection of photographs.

As with my previous books, my greatest debt is to my family. Sara and Keith More, Lauren and Tom Irwin, David and Lara Simon, and their wonderful children (my grandchildren) provided unwavering love and joy. Special thanks go to my cousin, Dr. N. Paul Rosman, who gave expert advice at a critical time, and to his wife, Syrille, for her generous hospital-ity. I am also grateful for the treatment I received from the superb team of physicians at Tufts Medical Center. Finally, I want to express my love and gratitude to my wife, Marcia, an exacting editor, but, more importantly, my indispensable life partner.

Notes

The bibliography on Roosevelt is immense and too great to reproduce here. I have limited the source notes on Roosevelt to primary source materials and the basic secondary works that I have used. Roosevelt's papers are available in his presidential library at Hyde Park, New York. His personal letters have been published in four volumes, edited by his son Elliott.

The Hughes Papers are at the Library of Congress. The collection includes extensive memoranda, prepared by Henry C. Beerits in 1933 and 1934 at Hughes's request, that cover his family history, his early years, and his career through his term as U.S. Secretary of State. The Hughes collection also includes his autobiographical notes and the papers of his authorized biographer, Merlo J. Pusey. Pusey's biography, *Charles Evans Hughes*, was published by Columbia University Press in two volumes in 1951. *The Autobiographical Notes of Charles Evans Hughes*, edited by David J. Danelski and Joseph S. Tulchin, was published by Harvard University Press in 1973.

The source notes are, for the most part, self-explanatory. I have used acronyms to identify frequently cited sources. Thus, a citation from p. 51 of Vol. 4 of Roosevelt's personal letters becomes FDRL4, p. 51. U.S. Supreme Court decisions follow legal methods of citation: *Schechter Poultry Corporation v. United States*, 295 U.S. 495 (1935), means that the Supreme Court decided the case in 1935 and the decision begins at p. 495 of Vol. 295 of the *U.S. Reports*.

Abbreviations Used

AN—*Autobiographical Notes of Charles Evans Hughes*, ed. David J. Danelski and Joseph S. Tulchin

CEHP—Papers of Charles Evans Hughes, Library of Congress

FDRP—Papers of Franklin D. Roosevelt, Hyde Park, NY

FDRPC—*Complete Presidential Press Conferences of Franklin D. Roosevelt*, 25 vols. (1972)

FDRPP—*Public Papers and Addresses of Franklin D. Roosevelt*, ed. Samuel I. Rosenman, 13 vols. (1933–50)

FDRL—*F.D.R.: His Personal Letters*, ed. Elliott Roosevelt, 4 vols. (1947–50)

HFSP—Papers of Harlan Fiske Stone, Library of Congress

MP—Merlo J. Pusey, *Charles Evans Hughes*, 2 vols.

Prologue

1   On a gray, chilly morning: For background on the Washington Conference, see AN, pp. 238–48; Beerits memoranda, "The Washington Conference" and "Treaty for the Limitation of Naval Armament," CEHP; Charles Evans Hughes, *The Pathway to Peace* (1925), pp. 20–31; *Conference on the Limitation of Armament* (1922); MP2, pp. 453–73; Mark Sullivan, *The Great Adventure at Washington: The Story of the Conference* (1922); and *Foreign Relations, 1921*, Vols. 1 and 2; *1922*, Vol. 1.

2   "Competition—in armament": Sullivan, p. 20.

3   "all the admirals": *Manchester Guardian Weekly*, November 18, 1921.

3   "With the acceptance": Hughes, *The Pathway to Peace*, p. 31.

4   was being fitted: For background on FDR's polio, see FDR, Eleanor Roosevelt (ER) and Louis Howe Papers; FDRP; ER's letters to James Roosevelt Roosevelt during the first month of FDR's illness, FDRL2, pp. 522–26, and the correspondence of Roosevelt's physician, Dr. Robert Lovett, in the Countway Library of Medicine, Boston, as well as ER's recollections in Eleanor Roosevelt, *This Is My Story* (1937), and in Joseph P. Lash, *Eleanor and Franklin* (1971). FDR's polio is central to his life's story and covered by his major biographers: H. W. Brands, *Traitor to His Class: The Privileged Life and Radical Presidency of Franklin Delano Roosevelt* (2008); James MacGregor Burns, *Roosevelt: The Lion and the Fox* (1956); Kenneth S. Davis, *FDR: The Beckoning of Destiny, 1882–1928, A History* (1971); Frank Freidel, *Franklin D. Roosevelt: The Ordeal* (1954) and *A Rendevous with Destiny* (1990); Ernest K. Lindley, *Franklin D. Roosevelt: A Career in Progressive Democracy* (1931); Ted Morgan, *FDR: A Biography* (1985); Jean Edward Smith, *FDR* (2007); and Geoffrey C. Ward, *A First-Class Temperament: The Emergence of Franklin Roosevelt* (1989).

4   *New York Times*'s story front-page: *New York Times*, September 16, 1921.

6   the " 'Happy Warrior' on": FDR speech to Democratic Convention, June 26, 1924, FDRP.

6   "especially prized the opportunity": CEH to FDR, February 28, 1933, CEHP.

6   "direct, vigorous action": FDR inaugural address, March 4, 1933, FDRPP2, p. 11.

6   "a new deal for": FDR speech to Democratic Convention, July 2, 1932, FDRPP1, p. 647.

7   "horse and buggy" era: FDR press conference, May 31, 1935, FDRPC5, p. 309.

7   the best politician: Roosevelt's opinion of CEH as politician, William O. Douglas, *Go East, Young Man* (1974), p. 327.

8   a heartfelt letter of regret: FDR to CEH, June 2, 1941, CEHP.

One: "An Honest, Fearless, Square Man"

9   a "providential call": MP1, p. 2.

9   "I see you": AN, p. 5.

10   "Who was this upstart": Ibid., p. 10.

11   "she would have gone": Ibid.

11   "Mary" . . . "I could not": Ibid.

12   "Charles E. Hughes' Plan": Ibid., p. 14.

13   "I would sit and watch": Ibid., p. 17.

13   "It was the fondest hope": Ibid., p. 26.

13   "sat in silent": Ibid., p. 25.

13   "For in the end": Ibid.

13   "I hope that you": CEH to parents, June 14, 1875, CEHP.

14   "had begun to flutter": AN, p. 27.

14   "I found that": Ibid., p. 23.

14   "who delighted the class": Ibid., p. 24.

14   Charlie's essays: See CEHP.

15   "I thought we might": AN, p. 18.

15   "When I was tired": Ibid., p. 21.

16   "Was not Hamilton": Ibid., p. 27.

17   "party spirit": DCH to CEH, November 6, 1876, CEHP.

17   "there is not even": CEH to parents, December 13, 1876, CEHP.

17   "Returning to Hamilton": AN, p. 32.

17   "Charlie, I fear": MCH to CEH, September 4, 1876, CEHP.

17   "the result might be": MCH to CEH, September 30, 1876, CEHP.

17   "I am so apprehensive": MCH to CEH, December (undated), 1876, CEHP.

17   "NEVER for the sake": DCH to CEH, October 16, 1876, CEHP.

17   "In regard to my": CEH to parents, January 2, 1877, CEHP.

18   "Studies are going swimmingly": CEH to MCH, January 13, 1877, CEHP.

18 "Come on, old Kentucky": AN, p. 33.

18 "earning money": CEH to MCH, February 17, 1880, CEHP.

19 "Well, I might as well": CEH to parents, February 22, 1880, CEHP.

19 "a heavy dose": AN, p. 44.

19 "Despite my new experiences": Ibid., p. 40.

19 "Whatever I do": Ibid., p. xvi.

19 "I want to do": CEH to MCH, December 7, 1880, CEHP.

20 "Of course, you'll be": AN, p. 49.

20 "The more I think": CEH to MCH, March 6, 1881, CEHP.

21 "a new insight into": AN, p. 54.

22 "Who appears": Ibid., p. 70.

22 "suffered keenly": Ibid.

23 "I inherited": MP1, p. 95.

23 "In truth, despite": AN, p. 88.

23 "Now I was tired": Ibid., p. 89.

23 "What a happy home": CEH to parents, January 3, 1892, CEHP.

24 "Far from being": AN, p. 96.

25 "But I needed": Ibid., pp. 114, 115.

25 "that interest now": Ibid., p. 111.

25 "While I maintained": Ibid., p. 113.

25 "I hold what religious": CEH to MCH, November 30, 1893, CEHP.

26 "dear wifie": CEH to AH, August 1894, CEHP.

26 investigating the utilities: For background on the utilities and insurance investigations, see AN, pp. 119–27; Beerits, "Gas and Insurance Investigations," CEHP; press clippings on investigations, CEHP; *Testimony and Report of the Gas and Electric Light Investigation Committee*, 4 vols. (Albany, 1905); *Testimony and Report of the Insurance Investigation*, 7 vols. (Albany, 1906); MP1, pp. 132–68; Mark Sullivan, *Our Times: The United States, 1900–1925*, Vol. 3 (1930), pp. 52–68; and Robert F. Wesser, *Charles Evans Hughes: Politics and Reform in New York, 1905–1910* (1967), pp. 18–48.

26 In December 1904: *New York World*, December 7, 1904.

27 "Take Hughes": *Outlook*, October 20, 1906.

27 "Mr. Stevens, I belong": *New York American*, March 26, 1905.

27 "I told Senator Stevens": *New York Daily Tribune*, March 25, 1905.

28 FRIEND OF ROCKEFELLER: *New York American*, March 26, 1905.

28 "If Hughes gets out": *New York Journal*, March 31, 1905.

28 "I once had an umbrella": *Testimony, Gas and Electric Investigation*, Vol. I, p. 383.

29 "The company is entitled": *Gas and Electric Report*, pp. 17, 18.

29 "and his whiskers": *New York Evening Mail*, April 1, 1905.

29 "The people wanted": *New York World*, April 24, 1905.

29 "a model inquiry": *New York Globe*, April 24, 1905.

30 "My dear, you don't": AN, p. 121.

30 "as unemotionally as": Sullivan, Vol. 3, p. 55.

30 "from a pure spirit": Insurance *Testimony*, Vol. 2, p. 1842.

31 "You are trying to": Ibid., p. 1870.

32 "Large rewards": Ibid., p. 1872.

32 "The witness who": Ibid., Vol. 3, p. 2021.

32 "occasionally at night": AN, pp. 126, 127.

32 The president: CEH-McCall exchange, Insurance *Testimony*, Vol. 1, p. 788.

33 "The sensational disclosures": AN, p. 123.

34 "Mr. Hughes . . . you're handling": Beerits memorandum No. 2, p. 19.

34 "Hughes calls himself": MP1, p. 147.

35 "Most of the evils": Insurance *Report*, p. 356.

36 "has given us Charles": *New York World*, January 1, 1906.

36 "Nobody in New York": *New York American*, December 30, 1905.

36 "To think of one": CEH to AH, August 10, 1906, CEHP.

37 Still, his name continued: For background on CEH's campaign and terms as governor, see AN, pp. 128–58; Beerits memoranda: "Entry into Politics and Election as Governor," "First Term as Governor," and "Second Term as Governor," CEHP; CEH correspondence, speeches, and press clippings, CEHP; *Public Papers of Charles Evans Hughes*, 4 vols. (Albany, 1908–11); MP1, pp. 169–270; Mark Sullivan, *Our Times*, Vol. 3, pp. 281–88; and Wesser, *Charles Evans Hughes*, pp. 49–347.

37 "It gives me": CEH to parents, July 26, 1906, CEHP.

37 "[f]lame feeds flame": *New York Times*, October 6, 1906.

37 "My dear sir": TR to CEH, October 5, 1906, CEHP.

37 "I hope that": *McClure's* (March 1908).

38 "I'm not disheartened": MP1, p. 198.

39 "Charles the Baptist": Ibid., p. 221.

39 "We are under": CEH speech, Elmira, NY, May 3, 1907, CEHP; CEH explanation, AN, pp. 143–45.

41 "We cannot maintain": CEH speech on behalf of Tuskegee Institute, January 17, 1908, CEHP.

41 "In a fight like this": TR to CEH, October 14, 1908, CEHP.

43 "I do not dare to run": Archie Butt, *Taft and Roosevelt: The Intimate Letters of Archie Butt* (1924), Vol. 1, p. 309.

43 "I don't know": Ibid., p. 310.

43 "I believe as strongly": WHT to CEH, April 22, 1910, CEHP.

43 "My training and professional": CEH to WHT, April 24, 1910, CEHP.

44 HUGHES TO HEAD: *Washington Post*, November 11, 1910.

44 "I should bet": OWH to FP, in Mark D. Howe, ed., *Holmes Pollack Letters: The Correspondence of Mr. Justice Holmes and Sir Frederick Pollack, 1874–1932*, Vol. 1, p. 170.

44 "I felt, too, that": AN, p. 168.

44 When he arrived: For background on CEH's nomination to the Court and his

term as associate justice, see AN, pp. 159–77; CEH correspondence, Court files, and press clippings, CEHP; Samuel Hendel, *Charles Evans Hughes and the Supreme Court* (1951), pp. 16–67; MP1, pp. 267–94; Melvin I. Urofsky and Paul Finkelman, *A March to Liberty: A Constitutional History of the United States, From 1877 to the Present*, Vol. 2 (2002); and Charles Warren, *The History of the Supreme Court of the United States* (1926), Vol. 2.

45   "my lion-hearted": AN, p. 168.

45   "Our Constitution is": *Plessy v. Ferguson*, 163 U.S. 537, 559 (1896).

46   "I knew enough": AN, p. 164.

46   the insouciant comments: Ibid., pp. 173, 174.

47   "Without imputing any": *Bailey v. Alabama*, 219 U.S. 219, 244 (1911).

48   "the trial was dominated": *Frank v. Mangum*, 237 U.S. 309, 347, 350 (1915).

48   "If this could be": *Truax v. Raich*, 239 U.S. 33, 41 (1915).

49   "In order to end these evils": *Simpson v. Shepard* (*Minnesota Rate Cases*), 230 U.S. 352, 398 (1913).

49   "[a]dmirably well done": EW to CEH, [undated, June 1913], CEHP.

50   "Whenever the interstate": *Houston & Texas Ry. v. U.S.* [*Shreveport Rate Case*], 234 U.S. 342, 351, 352 (1914).

51   A third case: See *Sturgis v. Beauchamp*, 231 U.S. 320 (1913). The CEH opinions in cases argued by Brandeis are *Miller v. Wilson*, 236 U.S. 373; *Bosley v. McLaughlin*, 236 U.S. 385 (1915).

52   When the case was next: Decision in Oregon minimum wage case, *Stettler v. O'Hara*, 243 U.S. 629 (1917).

Two: "Rising Star"

For background on FDR's ancestry and early life, see Roosevelt Family Papers, Roosevelt Family Papers Donated by the Children, FDR and ER's Papers FDRP and FDRL1. For FDR's childhood, see also Rita Halle Kleeman, *Gracious Lady: The Life of Sara Delano Roosevelt* (1935), and Sara Roosevelt, *My Boy Franklin* (1933). In addition to FDR biographies previously cited, see Frank Freidel, *Franklin D. Roosevelt: The Apprenticeship* (1952), and Geoffrey C. Ward, *Before the Trumpet: Young Franklin Roosevelt, 1882–1905* (1985).

57   "Nonsense": Ward, *Before the Trumpet*, p. 85.

57   "the beautiful Delano sisters": Kleeman, p. 81.

58   "Every mother ought": Sara Roosevelt, pp. 12, 13.

58   "Baby Franklin": Kleeman, p. 137.

59   "If he must go down": Ibid., p. 153.

59   "My little man": Ibid., p. 146.

59   "I shall try always": FDR to SDR, November 1888, FDRL1, p. 13.

60   "London Brige": FDR to SDR, February 26, 1889, FDRL1, p. 11.

61 "The best thing": Ward, *Before the Trumpet*, p. 179.

62 "I have served off": FDR to parents, May 14, 1897, FDRL1, p. 97.

62 "I am getting on": FDR to parents, September 18, 1896, ibid., p. 35.

62 "a quiet, satisfactory": Freidel, *FDR: The Apprenticeship*, p. 51.

63 "killing stories": FDR to parents, June 4, 1897, FDRL1, p. 110.

63 "I am hoarse": FDR to parents, November 5, 1896, ibid., p. 51.

63 "More than forty years": Smith, *FDR*, p. 29.

64 "If a man has courage": Ward, *A First-Class Temperament*, p. 89.

64 "great fun & most": FDR to parents, September 28, 1900, FDRL1, p. 423.

65 "You need the lamp": L. L. Cowperthwaite, "Franklin D. Roosevelt at Harvard," *Quarterly Journal of Speech*, 38 (February 1952), pp. 37–41.

65 "[I]t will be well": FDR to parents, October 23, 1900, FDRL1, p. 430.

65 "I wonder how": Kleeman, p. 209.

66 a four-column headline: FDRL1, p. 457.

66 Franklin later claimed: Ibid., p. 458.

66 another of his scoops: Morgan, *FDR*, p. 76.

67 "many of the qualities": Ibid., pp. 478, 479.

67 "In spite of his": FDR to SDR, October 26, 1902, FDRL1, p. 481.

67 "most glorious fun": FDR to SDR, January 6, 1902, ibid., p. 467.

68 "near enough to the": Sara Roosevelt, pp. 55, 56.

69 "Dearest Mama": FDR to SDR, December 4, 1903, FDRL1, p. 518.

70 "a man who had made": Kleeman, p. 235.

70 "felt like a D . . . F . . .": FDR to SDR, October 26, 1903, FDRL1, p. 510.

70 "frictionless": Freidel, *FDR: The Apprenticeship*, p. 66.

70 "quite indifferent": FDR to SDR, October 7, 1903, FDRL1, p. 507.

71 He cast his first vote: For background on FDR's early political career, see FDR Papers as State Senator, FDR speeches and press clippings, ER and Howe Papers, FDRP, and FDR correspondence in FDRL2.

72 "and a cunning little": FDR to SDR, August 14, 1905, FDRL2, p. 65.

72 "and got covered": FDR to SDR, July 3, 1905, FDRL2, p. 25.

72 "danced with Mme. Menardi": FDR to SDR, July 15, 1905, FDRL2, p. 36.

72 "at the UnChristian": Ibid.

72 "You are always just": ER to SDR, June 7, 1905, FDRL2, p. 4.

72 good-natured teasing: FDR to SDR, June 16, 1905, FDRL2, p. 11.

73 "When my bewildered": ER, *This Is My Story*, p. 162.

73 "You will never be": Horace Coon, *Columbia Colossus on the Hudson* (1947), p. 99.

74 "a real chance to be": Grenville Clark in *Harvard Alumni Bulletin*, April 28, 1945.

74 "I do not recall": Ibid.

76 "You bet I do": *Poughkeepsie News-Press*, October 27, 1910.

76 "I'm not Teddy": Ibid.

76 "Whether it is": Ibid.

78 "There is nothing": *New York Times*, January 22, 1911.

78 "Never in the history": *New York Herald*, January 18, 1911.

78 "with a well set up figure": *New York Globe*, February 6, 1911.

78 "damned fool": Morgan, p. 119.

78 "I know I can't": Lindley, *Franklin D. Roosevelt*, p. 92.

79 "Mr. Sheehan is delightful": *New York American*, February 5, 1911.

79 "Tam-ma-nee": *New York Tribune*, April 1, 1911.

79 "A known fighter": *Cleveland Plain-Dealer*, March 30, 1911.

80 "throwing his head": Frances Perkins, *The Roosevelt I Knew* (1946), pp. 11, 12.

80 "root and branch": FDR speech to Saturn Club, Buffalo, NY, December 23, 1911, FDRP.

80 "Do you remember": FDR to H. Lunger, January 30, 1928, in Freidel, *FDR: The Apprenticeship*, p. 116.

81 "Every new star": *Poughkeepsie News-Press*, March 5, 1912.

82 "I don't want to fight": Ward, *A First-Class Temperament*, p. 183.

82 "succeeded in stirring": FDR to R. S. Baker, March 20, 1935, FDRL3, p. 467.

83 "willing . . . to accept": Davis, p. 276.

83 ALL MY PLANS: FDR to ER, July 2, 1912, FDRL2, p. 192.

84 "Perkins has no spine": Freidel, *FDR: The Apprenticeship*, p. 147.

85 "FARMERS!": Morgan, p. 136.

86 "As I have pledged": LH to FDR (undated), FDRP.

86 "I am having": Lela Stiles, *The Man Behind Roosevelt: Louis McHenry Howe* (1954), p. 37.

87 "How would you like": Josephus Daniels, *The Wilson Era: Years of Peace, 1910–1917* (1944), p. 124.

87 Since childhood: For background on FDR's years as Assistant Secretary of the Navy, see FDR's Papers as Assistant Secretary of the Navy, FDR speeches and press clippings, ER and Howe Papers, FDRP and FDR correspondence in FDRL2.

88 "[W]e are confronted": FDR speech to Navy League, April 10, 1913, FDRP.

88 "My senses have not": FDR to LH, August 13, 1914, FDRP.

89 "I have been offering": FDR to LH, August 22, 1914, FDRP.

89 "You can't fight": *Milwaukee Sentinel*, April 27, 1914.

89 "There's a Roosevelt": *New York Sun*, March 19, 1913.

90 "These are history-making": *New York Times*, July 18, 1914.

90 "feeling chiefly": FDR to ER, August 2, 1914, FDRL2, 238.

90 "on the other side": WW to Josephus Daniels, August 6, 1914, in Freidel, *FDR: The Apprenticeship*, p. 240.

91 "These dear good": FDR to ER, August 2, 1914, FDRL2, p. 238.

91 "The enclosed is": FDR to ER, October 1914, FDRL2, pp. 256, 257.

92 "just plain common sense": FDR speech to National Civic Federation, December 5, 1914, FDRP.

92 "We are at peace": *New York Times*, December 9, 1914.

92   "had exhibited a grasp": *New York Sun*, December 17, 1914.

92   "had made a most": *New York Herald*, December 16, 1914.

93   "tried to quiz me": FDR to SDR, December, 17, 1914, FDRL2, p. 261.

93   "the truth and": *Congressional Record*, December 18, 1914, p. 1059.

93   "There is such a thing": Arthur S. Link, *The Struggle for Neutrality, 1914–1915* (1960), p. 382.

93   "wanton murder": Ibid., p. 498.

93   "strict accountability": Ray Standard Baker, *Woodrow Wilson: Life and Letters* (1927), Vol. 5, p. 354.

93   "I want to tell you": FDR to WW, June 9, 1915, FDRP.

94   "the President does": FDR to ER, August 18, 1915, FDRL2, p. 288.

94   "indulge in a ": FDR speech to Navy League Convention, April 13, 1916, FDRP.

Three: "Common Sense Idealism"

For background on CEH's 1916 presidential campaign, see AN, pp. 178–85; Beerits memorandum, "The Presidential Campaign of 1916," CEH correspondence, speeches, and press clippings, CEHP; MP1, pp. 315–66.

95   "at peace with": *The Nation*, September 30, 1915.

95   "It seems to me": *New York Times*, June 2, 1916.

96   "[N]o man can keep": *Washington Post*, November 19, 1915.

96   "What is the country's": WHT to CEH, April 11, 1916, CEHP.

97   "could not rightly": AN, p. 180.

97   "I was torn": Ibid.

97   "Why, President Wilson": Ibid.

98   "We have seen": *New York Times*, June 10, 1916.

99   "I recognize that": AN, p. 181.

99   "without orphaning": Baker, Vol. 7, p. 253.

100   the "bearded iceberg": MP1, p. 336.

100   "another Wilson with": William Henry Harbaugh, *Power and Responsibility: The Life and Times of Theodore Roosevelt* (1961), p. 491.

100   "America First" speech: July 31, 1916, CEHP.

101   "a campaign speech": Harlan B. Phillips, ed., *Felix Frankfurter Reminisces* (1960), p. 50.

102   "He has protected": AN, p. 184.

102   "I can show him": *Albany Argus*, October 28, 1916.

103   "Wait til the Democrats": *New York Times*, November 8, 1916.

103   "The most extraordinary": FF to ER, November 8, 1916, FDRL2, p. 338.

103   "the misadventure": AN, p. 184.

104   "Darkest Africa": Ward, *A First-Class Temperament*, p. 326.

105 BECAUSE OF: JD to FDR, February 3, 1917, FDRP.

105 "What can political": "Trip to Haiti and Santo Domingo 1917," FDRP.

105 "no lights were showing": Ibid.

106 "no excitement": Ibid.

106 "I want history": Freidel, *FDR: The Apprenticeship*, p. 288.

107 "I backed TR's theory": FDR diary, March 11, 1917, FDRP.

107 "Mr. Daniels has one": *Chicago Post*, March 20, 1917.

107 "Let us not": *New York Times*, March 21, 1917.

107 "I must go": AN, p. 187.

108 "guilty of throwing": *New York Times*, April 3, 1917.

108 "Mr. President, you": Smith, p. 138.

108 "breathlessly" ER, *This Is My story*, p. 245.

108 "Tell the young man": Davis, p. 460.

109 "How much of that": Freidel, *FDR: The Apprenticeship*, p. 312.

109 one of Roosevelt's pet projects: FDR to Josephus Daniels, October 29, 1917, FDR2, pp. 364–66; FDR to Woodrow Wilson, October 29, 1917, FDRL2, pp. 366, 367.

109 the USS *Dyer* voyage and European trip: FDRL2, pp. 375–439.

109 "A German submarine": FDR to ER, July 17, 1918, FDRP.

110 "I knew at once": FDR diary, August, 2, 1917, FDRL2, p. 409.

110 " 'Do not think':" Ibid., p. 410.

111 "We feel sufficiently": Freidel, *FDR: The Apprenticeship*, p. 363.

111 "a naval classic": Ibid., p. 434.

112 "Miss Mercer": FDR to ER (undated, spring 1914), FDRL2, p. 219.

113 "I really can't": FDR to ER, July 16, 1917, FDRL2, p. 347.

113 "I saw you": Ward, *A First-Class Temperament*, p. 366.

113 "He *deserved* a good": Ibid.

115 After his narrow defeat: For background on CEH's legal career and civic activities, 1917–21, see AN, pp. 186–97; Beerits memorandum, "Activities during the years 1916–1921," CEHP; CEH correspondence, speeches, and press clippings, 1916–21, CEHP; MP1, pp. 367–409.

115 a speech to the American Bar Association: September 5, 1917, CEHP.

116 special investigator of the aircraft industry: U.S. Department of Justice, *Aircraft Inquiry*, and Attorney General Gregory's *Supplementary Report* (1918), CEHP.

116 "guilty of censurable": *Supplementary Report*, p. 7.

116 "there has never been": *New York Times*, November 1, 1918.

117 filed a brief as *amicus curiae*: CEHP.

117 Hughes defended . . . five Socialist: CEHP; see also Zéchariah Chafee, Jr., *Free Speech in the United States* (1941), p. 269–82.

118 His expressed interest: CEH speech to Union League Club, March 26, 1919, CEHP; CEH proposals, *New York Times*, July 29 and August 5, 1919; MP1, pp. 395–400.

118 "Now my dear Admiral": FDR to Samuel Robinson, December 30, 1919, FDRP.

119 "Death had to": Smith, p. 166.

120 "The United States must go in": ER, p. 289.

121 "This is a time": FDR speech to New York County Lawyers' Association, March 8, 1919, FDRP.

121 "an old Chinese": FDR speech to Worcester Polytechnic Institute, June 25, 1919, ibid.

121 "the hand of God": Smith, p. 174.

121 "will never stand": MP1, p. 395.

122 "I have read": FDRL2, p. 477.

123 He was devastated: AN, p. 196.

123 "I beg of you": MP1, p. 403.

123 had kept in close touch: For background on FDR's first national campaign, see "Campaign of 1920," FDR, ER, and Howe Papers; FDR speeches, and press clippings, FDRP; FDRL2, pp. 492–522.

124 "pet groups": FDR speech to Democratic National Committee, May 29, 1919, FDRP.

125 "Oh, Franklin!": *Grand Rapids* [Mich.] *Herald*, June 1, 1919.

125 PALMER LOSES: *Chicago Tribune*, May 30, 1919.

125 "just about 100 years": *Rochester Post Express*, December 27, 1919.

125 "talk and talk": FDR speech to Harvard Union, February, 26, 1920, FDRP.

126 "a wonder": FDR to Hugh Gibson, January 2, 1920, FDRP.

127 Cox agreed: James M. Cox, *Journey Through My Years* (1946), p. 232.

128 "I don't like": *San Francisco Chronicle*, July 7, 1920.

128 "The young man": *Proceedings of the Democratic National Convention*, 1920, pp. 420–50.

128 "Today we are": FDRL2, pp. 504, 508.

129 "His [Roosevelt's] nomination": *Poughkeepsie Eagle*, July 21, 1920.

129 burning "up coal enough": Ibid., p. 516.

130 "I do not profess": Ward, *A First-Class Temperament*, p. 530.

130 "Franklin is as": *Chicago Tribune*, August 13, 1920.

130 "He [Franklin] is a maverick": *New York Times*, September 18, 1920.

130 "You know I have had": *New York Times*, August 19, 1920.

131 "I will not empower": *New York Times*, August 29, 1920.

131 "their bread baskets": SE to FDR, August 9, 1920, FDRP.

131 "a pilgrimage to": FDR speech at Centralia, WA, August 21, 1920, FDRP.

131 Eight years later: FDR to Oswald Villard, May 24, 1928, FDRP.

132 "[T]o bring America": *Washington Post*, October 15, 1920.

132 "This is not": Ward, *A First-Class Temperament*, p. 556.

132 "I do not feel": FDR to Mathew Hale, November 6, 1920, FDRP.

132 "the problem we have": WH to CEH, November 13, 1920, CEHP.

Four: Searching for the Next Jefferson

For background on FDR's career as businessman, see Roosevelt Family Papers (Business and Personal), FDRP; for the Navy Department scandal and investigation, see "Newport Matter" in Roosevelt Family Papers, FDRP; Report of U.S. Senate Committee on Naval Affairs (1921); for FDR's polio, see the sources cited for the Prologue.

133   "younger capitalists": FDR to Ralph Hayes, January 7, 1921, FDRP.

135   "after a wild 1904": ER's diary, FDRP.

136   "ill-advised" Ward, *A First-Class Temperament*, p. 568.

136   "libelous": JD to FDR, July 13, 1921, FDRP.

136   his worst fears: "Newport Matter," FDRP.

137   LAY NAVY: *New York Times*, July 20, 1921.

137   "Of the whole number": FDR to HK, July 21, 1921, FDRP.

138   "the glow I'd expected": Earle Looker, *This Man Roosevelt* (1932), p. 111.

138   "too tired even": Ibid.

140   "perfectly clear": Ward, *A First-Class Temperament*, p. 590.

140   ATROPHY INCREASING: EB to RL, August 31, 1921, Lovett Papers.

140   "a severe chill": Ward, *A First-Class Temperament*, p. 595.

141   "Don't worry chicks": Ibid., p. 599.

141   F. D. ROOSEVELT: *New York Times*, September 16, 1921.

141   "[H]e definitely will not": Ibid.

141   "While doctors were": FDR to AO, September 16, 1921, FDRP.

142   "You thought you": Ward, *A First-Class Temperament*, p. 606.

142   "He has such": GD to RL, September 24, 1921, Lovett Papers.

142   NOT IMPROVING: Davis, p. 666.

143   "that dirty, ugly": Ward, *A First-Class Temperament*, p. 620.

144   "below the knee": Ibid., p. 626.

145   "in the name of countless": FDR to AS, August 13, 1922, FDRP.

145   "a grand and glorious": Ward, *A First-Class Temperament*, p. 652.

146   "I have been in": FDR to SDR, March 5, 1923, FDRL2, p. 535.

146   "I know it is": FDR to SDR, February 22, 1924, FDRL2, pp. 543, 544.

146   "I am very much": Ward, *A First-Class Temperament*, p. 675.

147   "I cannot help": FDR to Abram Elkus, August 20, 1923, FDRP.

148   "has a power to": *New York Times*, June 27, 1924.

149   "the bungalow mind": Arthur Schlesinger, Jr., *The Age of Roosevelt: The Crisis of the Old Order, 1919–1933* (1957), p. 50.

149   "the best of the": Dan Rather, ed., *Our Times: America at the Birth of the 20th Century* (1996), p. 609.

149   The Republican power brokers: For background on CEH as Secretary of State, see AN, pp. 199–289; Beerits memoranda, CEH correspondence,

speeches, and press clippings, CEHP; *Foreign Relations, 1921*, Vols. 1 and 2, and *1922*, Vol. 1; Hughes, *Pathway to Peace*; MP2, pp. 411–593; and Sullivan, *The Great Adventure at Washington*.

149 "bloviate": Ernest R. May, *The Life History of the United States: War, Boom and Bust, 1917–1932*, Vol. 10, p. 65.

149 "You'd be in": Schlesinger, p. 50.

150 "a most agreeable Chief": AN, p. 199.

150 "Hughes, this is": Ibid., p. 200.

151 "whiskered": MP2, p. 432.

151 "[T]here will be no betrayal": Ibid.

151 "impractical to suggest": CEH to ALL, March 28, 1923, CEHP.

152 "all rights, privileges": Beerits memorandum, "The Separate Peace with Germany," CEHP.

153 "This gives us": CEH to son, August 27, 1921, CEHP.

153 "I seldom went": MP2, p. 420.

156 "I had not planned": Ibid., p. 465.

157 "every hair": Sullivan, *Great Adventure*, p. 7.

157 "Here in the United States": *Conference on the Limitation of Armament*, p. 48.

158 "We can no longer content": Ibid., p. 52.

158 "turned red and then": MP2, p. 470.

158 "to aid the progress": Hughes, *Pathway to Peace*, p. 25.

159 "intensely dramatic": William Allen White, *Autobiography* (1946), p. 598.

159 "I'm going home": Sullivan, *Great Adventure*, p. 67.

159 "master stroke" . . . "practical idealism": MP2, p. 472.

159 "This is simply": OWH to CEH, November 12, 1921, CEHP.

159 "he could not find": George Harvey to CEH, November 14, 1921, CEHP.

159 "among the fortunate": *Conference on the Limitation of Armament*, p. 96.

159 "a few modifications": MP2, p. 476.

160 "so much naval": AN, p. 244.

160 "How could we possibly": *Foreign Relations, 1922*, Vol. 1, p. 125.

161 "But I think": Ibid.

161 "The Washington Naval Conference": *Foreign Relations, Japan, 1931–1941*, Vol. 1, p. 282.

163 "a sort of quiet bleeding": *Foreign Relations, 1922*, Vol. 2, p. 172.

163 "working toward dictatorship": AH to CEH, November 21, 1922, CEHP.

164 "We cannot dispose": CEH speech to American Historical Association, December 29, 1922, CEHP.

164 "has reestablished": *The Times* (London), August 18, 1924.

165 "If you are treat": CEH speech to American Society of International Law, April 27, 1923, CEHP.

165 "the most compelling": *The Times* (London), March 3, 1925.

165 "you are personally": CC to CEH, January 10, 1925, CEHP.

165 "Much as I wish": MP2, p. 613.

166 "a perfectly good": Donald Day, *Franklin D. Roosevelt's Own Story* (1951), p. 82.

166 "I don't think": Davis, p. 766.

166 "Franklin Roosevelt Will": Freidel, *FDR: The Ordeal*, pp. 193, 194.

166 "I walk around": Looker, *This Man Roosevelt*, pp. 121, 122.

167 "Well, I would take": Freidel, p. 194.

167 "Old Doctor Roosevelt": FDRL2, p. 578.

167 "I sometimes wish": FDR to LD, April 25, 1925, FDRP.

168 "stands for conservatism": FDR to Charles Murphy (not sent), December 5, 1924, FDRP.

168 Later, in an article: *Foreign Affairs, 1927–1928*, Vol. 6, p. 573.

168 "It will always": Ibid., p. 578.

169 "We are approaching": Ibid.

169 "my legs are coming": FDR to Adolphus Ragan, December 9, 1925, FDRP.

169 "the quality of soul": *New York Times*, June 28, 1928.

170 "Frank, I told you": Lindley, pp. 19, 20.

171 "Too bad about": FDRPP1, pp. 53, 54.

171 "I suppose that": Ibid., pp. 38–44.

172 "large, varied": AN, p. 285.

172 to serve as a special master: See Beerits memorandum, "Activities During the Years 1925–1930," CEHP; Court decisions, *Wisconsin v. Illinois*, 278 U.S. 367 (1929) and 281 U.S. 179 (1930).

173 "the intolerant spirit": CEH speech to American Bar Association, September 2, 1925, CEHP.

173 "about the most useful": WL to CEH, August 27, 1925, CEHP. Lippmann was sent an advance copy of the speech.

173 At Princeton and at Yale: CEHP.

173 most significant lectures: Charles Evans Hughes, *The Supreme Court of the United States: Its Foundations, Methods and Achievement, An Interpretation* (1928).

173 "a capacity for": Ibid., p. 46.

173 "self-inflicted": Ibid., p. 50.

173 "I am too old": CEH statement, May 20, 1927, CEHP.

174 "Stone is not": Henry F. Pringle, *The Life and Times of William Howard Taft* (1939), Vol. 2, p. 1044.

175 "to prevent all": MP2, p. 652.

175 "Finally . . . I think": Ibid.

175 "It is your duty": Ibid.; see also CEH's description of meeting with Hoover and later exchange of letters with HH, AN, pp. 291–94.

Five: "An Emergency More Serious Than War"

177   "In no nation": *New York Times*, March 5, 1929.

178   "If you are convinced": MP2, p. 652; see also AN, p. 291.

178   "We have reached": *Congressional Record*, February 10, 1930, p. 3372.

179   struck down a Maryland regulation: *United Railways v. West*, 280 U.S. 234 (1930).

179   "the Supreme Court's": *Congressional Record*, February 10, 1930, p. 3564.

179   "There is a very surprising": HFS to FF, April 4, 1930, HFSP.

180   "[t]he participation of": Carl Brent Swisher, *American Constitutional Development* (1954), p. 777.

181   "Brethren, the time": MP2, p. 664.

181   "pen paralysis": MP1, p. 284.

181   "of a renaissance cardinal": Urofsky and Finkelman, Vol. 2, p. 626.

182   "essentially wicked": Leon Friedman and Fred Israel, eds., *The Justices of the U.S. Supreme Court: Their Lives and Major Opinions*, Vol. 3, p. 2026.

182   "I see the": Ibid.

182   "beset and bedeviled": Ibid., p. 2136.

182   "the methodical habits": Fred Rodell, *Nine Men* (1955), p. 220.

182   "a naked, arbitrary": *Adkins v. Children's Hospital*, 261 U.S. 525, 559 (1923).

183   "The life of the law": Oliver Wendell Holmes, Jr., *The Common Law*, p. 1 (1881).

184   "[A] constitution is not": *Lochner v. New York*, 198 U.S. 45, 75 (1905).

186   When Franklin Roosevelt was pressed: For background on FDR as governor, see Papers as Governor of New York State, 1929–1932; FDR, ER, and Howe Papers, FDRP; FDRL3, pp. 3–316; Davis, *FDR: The New York Years, 1928–1933* (1979); Freidel, *Franklin D. Roosevelt: The Triumph* (1956); and previously cited FDR biographies.

186   "It's Stone": Account in *Baltimore Sun*, June 3, 1941; see also Gerald Gunther, *Learned Hand: The Man and the Judge* (1994), pp. 357–63.

187   "a public servant": FDR inaugural address, January 1, 1929, FDRPP1, p. 75.

188   "one continuous": FDR to Edward McCauley, Jr., March 21, 1929, FDRL3, p. 43.

188   Roosevelt asked Louis Howe: FDR to J. Davis, October 5, 1929, FDRL3, p. 79; LH to FDR, March 11, 1930, FDRL3, pp. 111, 112.

189   "Oh, Franklin": *New York Times*, April 14, 1929.

190   "If Thomas Jefferson": *New York Times*, April 27, 1930.

190   "one of the real": FDR to BW, June 3, 1930, FDRL3, p. 129.

191   "Never let your opponent": Samuel Rosenman, *Working with Roosevelt* (1952), p. 45.

191   "a desperate and futile": FDRPP1, p. 421.

191   "The people did not": Ibid., p. 437.

191   "If there are corrupt": Ibid., p. 443.

192 "I do not see": James A. Farley, *Behind the Ballots* (1938), p. 62.

192 Three years before: For background on CEH's early years as Chief Justice, see AN, pp. 290–303; CEH correspondence and Court files, CEHP; Stone correspondence and Court files, HFSP; Hendel, Charles Evans Hughes and the Supreme Court, pp. 91–245; Alpheus Thomas Mason, *Harlan Fiske Stone: Pillar of the Law* (1956), pp. 293–405; Michael E. Parrish, *The Hughes Court: Justices, Rulings, and Legacy* (2002); MP2, pp. 648–730; William G. Ross, *The Chief Justiceship of Charles Evans Hughes, 1930–1941* (2007), pp. 1–57; William E. Swindler, *Court and Constitution in the Twentieth Century: The New Legality, 1932–1968* (1970); and Urofsky and Finkelman, A *March of Liberty*, Vol. 2.

192 "strength of character": Hughes, *The Supreme Court*, p. 57.

192 "preeminence was due": Ibid., p. 58.

192 "self-inflicted wound": Ibid., p. 50.

193 "all able men": AN, p. 300.

194 "Hughes has real": Parrish, p. 9.

194 "painstaking care": *American Bar Association Journal* (July 1941), p. 407.

194 "was always a matter": Roberts memorial address to New York Bar, December 12, 1948.

194 the Hughes Court heard: See *O'Gorman & Young v. Hartford Fire Insurance Co.*, 282 U.S. 251 (1931); *Stromberg v. California*, 283 U.S. 359 (1931); *U.S. v. Macintosh*, 283 U.S. 605 (1931).

197 *Near v. Minnesota*: 283 U.S. 697 (1931). For background on *Near*, see Fred W. Friendly, *The Dramatic Story of the Landmark Supreme Court Case That Gave New Meaning to the Freedom of Press* (1981), and Paul L. Murphy, "The Case of the Miscreant Purveyor of Scandal," in John A. Garraty, ed., *Quarrels That Have Shaped the Constitution* (1962), p. 209.

199 "weighty and conclusive": *New York Times*, June 2, 1931.

199 "The decision of": *Chicago Tribune*, June 2, 1931.

199 McCormick also wrote: Friendly, p. 161.

199 Justice Stone expressed satisfaction: Mason, p. 316.

199 "The Court is not": *Yale Law Journal* (December 1931), p. 267.

200 "We honor him": Francis Biddle, *Mr. Justice Holmes* (1942), p. 193.

200 "to expose the inconsistency": Friendly, p. 144.

201 "Yes! And a dirtier": Charles Warren, *The Supreme Court of the United States*, Vol. 1, p. 76.

201 "the finest act": *Congressional Record*, January 14, 1932.

201 "I know of no jurist": FDRPP1, p. 580.

201 "delighted": MP2, p. 682.

203 "While I doubt": Mason, p. 322.

203 Chief Justice Hughes: *New State Ice Co. v. Liebmann*, 285 U.S. 262 (1932).

203 "the case was near": MP2, p. 698.

204 In his speech: June 9, 1932, CEHP.

205 "Confidentially": FDR to NT, January 5, 1931, FDRP.

205   "By merely blocking": FDRPP1, p. 127.

206   "the dole": FDR to S. Eben, November 15, 1930, FDRP.

206   he told a Conference of Governors: July 16, 1929, FDRPP1, p. 367.

206   "Modern society": FDRPP1, p. 173.

207   "I am giving no": *New York World*, November 6, 1930.

208   "the name of Roosevelt": Freidel, *FDR: The Triumph*, p. 209.

208   "In so far as": Looker article, *Liberty*, July 25, 1931.

210   Clark Howell . . . wrote Roosevelt: CH to FDR, December 2, 1931, FDRL3, pp. 229–32.

210   "Governor Roosevelt belongs": Walter Lippmann, *Interpretations, 1931–1932* (1932), pp. 257–59.

211   "The country needs": FDR speech at Oglethorpe University, May 22, 1932, FDRPP1, p. 639.

212   "My friends from": Freidel, *FDR: The Triumph*, p. 297.

213   to caucus the Texas delegation: Daniel Roper and Frank Lovette, *Fifty Years of Public Life* (1948), pp. 258–60.

213   California's . . . switch to FDR: *Proceedings of the Democratic National Convention, 1932*, pp. 325–27.

213   "Good old McAdoo": Freidel, *FDR: The Triumph*, p. 311.

214   He spoke movingly: FDR speech to Democratic Convention, July 2, 1932, FDRPP1, p. 647.

215   "a bad looking mob": Herbert Hoover, *Memoirs* (1952), Vol. 3, p. 225.

216   "The fellow out": James Farley, *Behind the Ballots* (1938), p. 159.

216   "Hello, Al, I'm glad": Ibid., p. 176.

217   "He [Hoover] is personally": Freidel, *FDR: The Triumph*, p. 324.

218   "like a chameleon": *New York Times*, November 1, 1932.

218   "the most powerful": David M. Kennedy, *Freedom from Fear: The American People in Depression and War, 1929–1945* (1999), p. 84.

219   "The day of the enlightened": FDR speech in San Francisco, September 23, 1932, FDRPP1, p. 742.

219   "the most reckless": *New York Times*, October 20, 1932.

219   declaring in Baltimore: "Four Horsemen" speech, October 25, 1932, FDRPP1, p. 832.

219   an "atrocious slur": Davis, p. 368.

219   "It'll be a great relief": Freidel, *FDR: The Triumph*, p. 368.

220   "To be the means": Davis, p. 374.

220   "This is the greatest night": *New York Times*, November 9, 1932.

Six: "Black Monday"

For background on FDR and the New Deal, see President's Official, Personal and Secretary Files, ER and Howe Papers, FDRP; FDRL3, pp. 317–738; Jonathan

Alter, *The Defining Moment: FDR's Hundred Days and the Triumph of Hope* (2006); Adam Cohen, *Nothing to Fear: FDR's Inner Circle and the Hundred Days That Created Modern America* (2009); Kenneth S. Davis, *FDR: The New Deal Years, 1933–1937* (1979); Frank Freidel, *Franklin D. Roosevelt: Launching the New Deal* (1973); Harold L. Ickes, *The Secret Diary of Harold L. Ickes: The First Thousand Days, 1933–1936*, Vol. 1 (1953); Kennedy, *Freedom from Fear*; William E. Leuchtenburg, *Franklin D. Roosevelt and the New Deal, 1932–1940* (1963); Raymond Moley, *After Nine Years* (1939); Perkins, *The Roosevelt I Knew*; Arthur M. Schlesinger, Jr., *The Age of Roosevelt: The Coming of the New Deal* (1958) and *The Politics of Upheaval* (1960); and Rexford G. Tugwell, *The Brains Trust* (1968).

221   "my dear Chief": FDR to JD, November 17, 1932, FDRL3, p. 306.
221   "my place in exile": BC to FDR, November 9, 1932, ibid., p. 308.
221   "delightful relations with": FDR to BC, December 9, 1932, ibid., p. 307.
221   a telegram from President Hoover, and FDR drafts in response: President's Personal File, FDRP; see also Moley, p. 67.
222   "There is nothing": Tugwell, p. 357.
222   he told Secretary of State Henry Stimson: Freidel, *FDR: Launching the New Deal*, p. 19.
222   "the grass will grow": *New York Times*, November 1, 1932.
223   "could scarcely have": Moley, p. 68.
223   "as a private citizen": *New York Times*, November 22, 1932.
223   At the White House meeting: See Hoover *Memoirs*, Vol. 3, pp. 179, 180; Moley, pp. 72–77.
224   "educating a very ignorant": Freidel, *FDR: Launching the New Deal*, p. 35.
225   "When I talk to": Alan Brinkley, *Voices of Protest* (1982), p. 58.
225   "I am getting a": FDR to SDR, February 6, 1933, FDRL3, pp. 327, 328.
226   "Tony, keep quiet": *New York Times*, February 17, 1933.
226   "There was nothing": Moley, p. 139.
227   "unselfish courage": *New York Times*, February 20, 1933.
227   "I'm feeling fine": *New York Times*, February 18, 1933.
227   "A most critical": HH to FDR, February 18, 1933, FDRP.
228   "I realize that": Freidel, *FDR: Launching the New Deal*, p. 177.
228   "your fine spirit": FDR to HH, February 28, 1933, FDRP.
228   "cheeky": Alter, p. 179.
229   "very large and heavy": FDR to Charles Cropley, February 25, 1933, FDRL3, p. 331.
230   "our long time friendship": FDR to CEH, February 25, 1933, ibid., p. 332.
230   "the more dignified": CEH to FDR, February 28, 1933, ibid., p. 333.
230   "Mr. Roosevelt": Grace Tully, *F.D.R.: My Boss* (1949), p. 64.
231   the "lovely steel," Freidel, *FDR: Launching the New Deal*, p. 198.
232   his fifteen-minute address: March 4, 1933, FDRPP2, p. 11.
233   "No cabinet has been": Farley, p. 209.

234   "readiness to assume": Smith, p. 306.

234   Roosevelt held his first press conference: March 8, 1933, FDRPC1, p. 1.

235   "And that's exactly": Alter, p. 234.

235   "It won't look like": Moley, p. 152.

235   Roosevelt held the first: March 12, 1933, FDRPP2, p. 61.

236   "Last week marked": *Wall Street Journal*, March 13, 1933.

236   "The President drove": Leuchtenburg, p. 44.

237   "Too often in recent": Freidel, *FDR: Launching the New Deal*, p. 244.

237   "in many ways": FDR to Col. Edward House, April 5, 1933, FDRL3, p. 342.

237   "I think this would": Davis, p. 63.

238   "We are all keeping": FDR to JK, March 29, 1933, FDRL3, p. 340.

238   "Unless something is": Davis, p. 71.

239   "My position toward": FDR press conference, March 15, 1933, FDRPC1, p. 32.

239   "a new means to": Freidel, *FDR: Launching the New Deal*, p. 311.

240   "This is the end": Ibid., p. 334.

240   "the moral and spiritual": FDR message to Congress, March 21, 1933, FDRPP2, p. 81.

241   "He is more than": Schlesinger, *The Coming of the New Deal*, p. 324.

241   Even Norris was stunned: See Kennedy, p. 148.

242   "To the ancient rule": FDRPP2, p. 93.

242   "to the rhythm of": Perkins, p. 194.

242   *Hammer v. Dagenhart*, 247 U.S. 251 (1918).

243   "If that philosophy": Moley, p. 189.

243   "To look upon": Ibid., pp. 369, 370.

244   "Tell the Chief Justice": James F. Simon, *In His Own Image: The Supreme Court in Richard Nixon's America* (1973), p. 53.

245   "I am praying that": WVD to Mrs. J. Lacey, October 26, 1932, Van Devanter Papers, LC.

245   "thinks Roosevelt unfitted": WVD to D. Flynn, October 3, 1932, ibid.

245   "I am with the President": HFS to W. Newton, October 11, 1932, HFSP.

245   "I cannot see in": HFS to S. Carr, December 6, 1932, ibid.

245   "Why people should": FF to HFS, May 10, 1932, ibid.

246   "I can assure you": FF to J. Goldmark, January 6, 1933, Cohen Papers, LC.

246   The *Blaisdell* case: *Home Building & Loan Association v. Blaisdell*, 290 U.S. 398 (1934).

247   "entertained the thought": *New York Herald Tribune*, January 9, 1934.

247   "was exceedingly": Cummings Diary, January 8, 1934, Homer Cummings Papers (HCP), University of Virginia.

247   the *Nebbia* case: *Nebbia v. New York*, 291 U.S. 502 (1934); for an in-depth analysis of the Court opinions of Justice Roberts, see Barry Cushman, *Rethinking the New Deal Court: The Structure of Constitutional Revolution* (1998).

248   "appears to mark": *Washington Post*, March 6, 1934.

248   "The Supreme Court": *New York Times*, March 6, 1934.

248 "a glimmer of hope": FDRPP4, p. 6.

249 "Why are you so": Mason, p. 386.

250 in the "hip pocket of": Ibid., p. 388.

250 "It is a rather": HFS to LS, January 8, 1935, HFSP.

250 "Is there any official": *Washington Post*, December 11, 1934.

250 to strike down the "hot oil" section: *Panama Refining Co. v. Ryan*, 293 U.S. 388 (1935).

251 "Yes, Sir": LB to CEH, December (undated) 1934, CEHP.

251 "distinguished": *Chicago Daily Tribune*, January 8, 1935.

251 "[T]he highest tribunal": *New York Times*, January 9, 1935.

251 "profound anxiety": Robert H. Jackson, *The Struggle for Judicial Supremacy* (1941), p. 94.

251 "[T]he whole American": Ibid., p. 101.

252 "is terrifying in": Urofsky, *Louis D. Brandeis: A Life* (2009), p. 697.

252 "[t]o countenance": HFS to JBM, February 20, 1935, HFSP.

252 "power of self": *New York Times*, January 9, 1935.

253 "Here we have": *New York Times*, January 11, 1935.

253 "the Court is not": *New York Times*, February 3, 1935.

253 dictated his answer: FDRL3, pp. 456–60.

254 "for use if needed": FDR draft remarks, HCP.

255 Whether the federal government: For the gold standard decisions, see *Norman v. B. & O. R.R.*, 294 U.S. 240 (1935); *Perry v. United States*, 294 U.S. 330 (1935).

256 "This is Nero": *New York Times*, February 19, 1935.

256 "swept away the": *Washington Post*, February 19, 1935.

256 a "golden ruling" *New York Times*, February 24, 1935.

256 "The Constitution has": *San Francisco Chronicle*, February 19, 1935.

256 "In history the name": MP2, p. 737.

256 Marshall's famous opinion: *Marbury v. Madison*, 5 U.S. 137 (1803).

256 "The President is": *Chicago Daily Tribune*, February 19, 1935.

256 "As a lawyer": FDR to JK, February 19, 1935, FDRL3, p. 455.

257 "it would have marked": *New York Times*, February 21, 1935.

257 struck down the Railroad Retirement Act: *Retirement Board v. Alton R. Co.*, 295 U.S. 330 (1935).

257 Jackson resented: *Worcester v. Georgia*, 6 Peter 515 (1832).

258 "Rotten": Charles A. Leonard, *A Search for a Judicial Philosophy: Mr. Justice Roberts and the Constitutional Revolution of 1937* (1971), p. 62.

258 "What is the distinction": BC to CEH, April 19, 1935, CEHP.

259 "What about old": Urofsky, p. 705.

259 "the most important day": Alpheus Thomas Mason, *Brandeis: A Free Man's Life* (1946), p. 620.

259 for sacking William Humphrey: *Humphrey's Executor v. United States*, 295 U.S. 602 (1935).

259   "the kind of a country": Mason, *Harlan Fiske Stone*, p. 394.

261   "The case was far from ideal": Jackson, p. 113.

261   "most impolitic and": Schlesinger, *The Politics of Upheaval*, p. 278.

261   "What does unfair": Frank Freidel, "The Sick Chicken Case," in Garrity, ed., p. 246.

262   "in charge of all": *Time*, May 13, 1935.

262   "The NRA law was": Garrity, ed., p. 247.

262   "I feel as though": Ibid.

262   his *Schechter* opinion: *Schechter Poultry Corporation v. United States*, 295 U.S. 495 (1935).

263   "This decision of the": Garrity, ed., p. 248.

263   a morning press conference: FDRPC5, May 31, 1935, p. 309.

Seven: "A Stratosphere of Icy Certainty"

265   "As soon as": *The New Yorker*, June 29, 1935.

265   "the crown of": Ibid.

266   "Hughes has ruled: *The New Yorker*, July 13, 1935.

266   "[t]he President has": Bruce Allen Murphy, *The Brandeis/Frankfurter Connection: The Secret Political Activities of Two Supreme Court Justices* (1982), pp. 155, 156.

266   he received a letter: FDRL3, p. 485.

266   taking exception only: AN, p. 292.

267   In a cordial reply: FDR to HS, June 10, 1935, FDRL3, pp. 484, 485.

267   he listed in caps nine: FDR to legislative leaders, June 4, 1935, ibid., p. 481.

267   "F.D. is making": Urofsky, p. 710.

268   "Manifestly, no one": FDR to SH, July 5, 1935, FDRP.

268   "I was so tired": John Morton Blum, *From the Morgenthau Diaries: Years of Crisis, 1928–1938* (1959), p. 257.

268   the columnist Walter Lippmann: *Los Angeles Times*, July 27, 1935.

269   "If the Court does": Schlesinger, *Politics of Upheaval*, p. 453.

269   "It is the deep": *Collier's*, September 7, 1935.

271   "On the first day": *The New Yorker*, July 13, 1935.

271   At issue in: *Colgate v. Harvey*, 296 U.S. 404 (1935).

271   "in his usual fashion": HFS statement on the *Colgate* case, February 4, 1936, HFSP.

272   "any unnecessary": HFS to FF, December 23, 1935, ibid.

272   "The Court suffered": HFS to FF, December 20, 1935, ibid.

273   "Gosh, it is": FF to HFS, December 18, 1935, ibid.

273   "Constitutional theory": Felix Frankfurter and Henry Hart, Jr., "The Business of the Supreme Court at October Term, 1934," *Harvard Law Review* (November 1935).

274 "I like to think": FDR's Fremont speech, September 28, 1935, FDRPP4, p. 379.

275 a "concerted effort": *New York Times*, December 10, 1935.

277 "to see if they favored": *New York Times*, December 11, 1935.

277 "I believe": *Time*, December 16, 1935.

277 Gridiron Dinner: *New York Times*, December 15, 1935; Jeff Shesol, *Supreme Power: Franklin Roosevelt vs. the Supreme Court* (2010) pp. 179, 180.

278 At the justices' Saturday conference: HFS memorandum, February 4, 1936, HFSP.

278 Hughes assigned the majority opinion: *United States v. Butler*, 297 U.S. 1 (1936).

281 "There was fire there": *Washington Post*, January 7, 1936.

282 "There was a report": Ickes, Vol. 1, p. 536.

282 "the most significant": AN, p. 309.

282 "What bothers me most": FF to HFS, February 14, 1936, HFSP.

282 "[P]erhaps it can be": HFS to FF, February 17, 1936, ibid.

282 "a political stump": *Baltimore Sun*, January 7, 1936.

283 "throwing the alphabet": Leuchtenburg, 178.

283 In a "Memorandum for AAA": January 24, 1936, FDRL3, pp. 548, 549.

283 "packing the Supreme Court": Ibid., p. 495.

283 "What was the": FDR to HC, January 14, 1936, FDRL3, p. 546.

284 "to the Supreme Court": Ickes, Vol. 1, p. 524.

284 "would carry out": Ickes, Vol. 1, p. 530.

284 *Ex parte McCardle*: 74 U.S. 506 (1868).

285 Hughes's opinion: *Ashwander v. Tennessee Valley Authority*, 297 U.S. 288 (1936).

285 "There was gratification": Jackson, p. 146.

285 "Probably the faults": *New York Times Sunday Magazine*, March 20, 1936.

285 "I am glad you found": CEH to AK, March 21, 1936, CEHP.

286 "I am happy": *New York Times*, May 8, 1936.

286 struck down the Guffey Coal Act: *Carter v. Carter Coal Co.*, 298 U.S. 238 (1936).

288 "a form of indecent": HFS to FF, May 30, 1936, HFSP.

289 in *Morehead v. Tipaldo*: 298 U.S. 587 (1936).

290 "a sad business": HFS to FF, June 3, 1936, ibid.

290 "He [Hughes] is deeply": Richard D. Friedman, "Switching Time and Other Thought Experiments: The Hughes Court and Constitutional Transformation," *University of Pennsylvania Law Review*, 142 (June 1994), p. 1962.

290 "The majority decision": *New York Times*, June 2, 1936.

290 "a shocking blow": *Boston Herald*, June 2, 1936.

290 "new *Dred Scott*": *Congressional Record*, June 5, 1936, p. 9040.

290 "It seems to be": HFS to LB, June 20, 1936, HFSP.

291 "Yes, the consternation": LB to HFS, June 22, 1936, ibid.

291 presidential news conference: FDRPC7, p. 280.

291 "We would be less than": BC to HFS, June 9, 1936, HFSP.

291 "the resplendent": FDR's State of the Union address, January 3, 1936, FDRPP5, p. 8.

292 plotted his reelection strategy: FDR to James Farley, March 26, 1936, FDRL3, p. 574.

292 "the rounded picture": Schlesinger, *The Politics of Upheaval*, p. 574.

292 "the frame of mind": FDR to Norman Hapgood, February 24, 1936, FDRL3, p. 561.

292 "Don't tell them": Schlesinger, p. 574.

293 "[N]o section of the": FDR to JF, May 26, 1936, FDRL3, p. 591.

293 "the succeeding stages": Schlesinger, p. 544.

293 "the great betrayer": Leuchtenburg, pp. 181, 182.

293 "Religion and patriotism": Schlesinger, p. 627.

294 "There's one issue": Ibid., p. 578.

294 "Over against the": Ibid., p. 580.

295 "Clean me up": Ibid., p. 584.

295 "I was the damnedest": Ibid.

295 one of the best speeches: June 27, 1936, FDRPP5, p. 230.

296 "He saved my home": Leuchtenburg, p. 193.

296 "Hello, Bill, glad": Schlesinger, p. 632.

297 "the greatest statesman": Ibid., p. 593.

297 "Mr. Roosevelt is the only": Eric Goldman, *Rendevous with Destiny* (1952), p. 345.

297 "among American citizens": Schlesinger, p. 634.

297 crowd in Madison Square Garden: October 31, 1936, FDRPP5, p. 566.

298 "will give me a chance": FDR to JP, November 9, 1936, FDRL3, p. 625.

Eight: The "Most Dangerous, Implacable Enemy"

299 was despondent: MP2, p. 747.

300 they visited Justice Owen Roberts: William E. Leuchtenburg, "Charles Evans Hughes: The Center Holds," *North Carolina Law Review*, 83 (June 2005), pp. 1199, 1200; Shesol, pp. 232, 233; for additional documentation supporting Highes's influence on Roberts, see Steven T. Early, "James Clark McReynolds and the Judicial Process," unpublished Ph.D. dissertation, Department of Political Science, University of Virginia, 1954, p. 101.

300 "got to the end": Leuchtenburg, "Charles Evans Hughes," p. 1199.

301 "rejoicing in your": CEH to HFS, December 20, 1936, CEHP.

301 "the No. 1 high": Drew Pearson and Robert Allen, *The Nine Old Men* (1936), p. 75.

302   upheld the New York unemployment law: *Chamberlin v. Andrews*, 299 U.S.
      515 (1936).

302   voted to preserve Washington State's: AN, p. 312.

303   In *United States v. Curtiss-Wright Export Corp.*: 299 U.S. 304 (1936).

303   "a Christmas present": Jackson, p. 201.

304   The decision in *Kentucky Whip*: 299 U.S. 334 (1937); *Hammer v. Dagenhart*,
      247 U.S. 251 (1918).

305   On the same day that: *De Jonge v. Oregon*, 299 U.S. 353 (1937).

305   "The judges are trying": *The Nation*, January 9, 1937.

305   "this splendid": *New York Times*, January 6, 1937.

306   "Is the Court Shifting?": *Washington Daily News*, January 5, 1937.

306   "Now that the": Marian C. McKenna, *Franklin Roosevelt and the Great Con-
      stitutional War* (2002), p. 243.

306   betrayed a private determination: For background on FDR's Court-packing
      plan, see CEH correspondence and phone transcriptions (conversations with
      Senators King and Wheeler), March–April 1937, CEHP; FDR Official, Per-
      sonal, and Secretary Files, FDRP; Joseph Alsop and Turner Catledge, *The
      168 Days* (1938); AN, pp. 303–13; Leonard Baker, *Back to Back: The Duel
      between FDR and the Supreme Court* (1967); James MacGregor Burns, *Pack-
      ing the Court: The Rise of Judicial Power and the Coming Crisis of the Supreme
      Court* (2009); Cushman, *Rethinking the New Deal Court*; Harold L. Ickes, *The
      Secret Diary of Harold L. Ickes: The Inside Struggle, 1936–1939*, Vol. 2 (1954);
      Jackson, *The Struggle for Judicial Supremacy*; William E. Leuchtenburg, *The
      Supreme Court Reborn: The Constitutional Revolution in the Age of Roosevelt*
      (1995); George McJimsey, ed., *Documentary History of the Franklin D. Roo-
      sevelt Presidency*. Vol. 1: " 'Packing' the Supreme Court and the Judicial Reorga-
      nization Bill, January–July 1937" (2001); MP2, pp. 749–65; Schlesinger, *The
      Politics of Upheaval*; Shesol, *Supreme Power*; Burt Solomon, *FDR v. The Con-
      stitution: The Court-Packing Fight and the Triumph of Democracy* (2009); and
      G. Edward White, *The Constitution and the New Deal* (2000).

307   "Give me ten": Ickes, Vol. 2, p. 65.

307   "never [to] resign": Pearson and Allen, p. 2.

307   "for an appeal to": Ickes, Vol. 1, p. 705 (italics in the original).

307   "possible changes in" (italics added): Cummings diary, November 15, 1936,
      HCP; see generally, Leuchtenburg, *The Supreme Court Reborn*, pp. 114–31;
      Shesol, pp. 250–64.

308   "bursting": HC to FDR, December 22, 1936, FDRP.

309   "the superficial character": Warner Gardener, "Memorandum for the Solici-
      tor General," December 10, 1936, Frankfurter Papers, LC.

309   "who would preside": Report of the Attorney General for the Fiscal Year
      Ending June 30, 1913, p. 5.

309   "Congress can enlarge": George Creel, *Rebel at Large: Recollections of Fifty
      Crowded Years* (1947), pp. 293, 294.

309 "Roosevelt's Plans": *Collier's*, December 26, 1936.

310 "substantial objection": Cummings diary, December 26, 1936, HCP.

310 "constitutional difficulties": Ickes, Vol. 2, p. 26.

310 In the early drafts: See Thomas G. Corcoran Papers, LC.

311 "raised the Supreme Court": Ickes, Vol. 2, p. 31.

311 His State of Union address: January 6, 1937, FDRPP5, p. 634.

311 "I had a little fun": FDR to CB, January 15, 1937, FDRL3, p. 651.

311 "It is possible": *New York Herald Tribune*, January 7, 1937.

312 "Do we . . . dare": *New Republic*, January 23, 1937.

312 Roosevelt delivered: FDR's inaugural address, January 20, 1937, FDRPP6, p. 1.

312 "There was no": Rosenman, p. 144.

312 "When the Chief Justice": Ibid.

313 "Very confidentially": FDR to FF, January 15, 1937, in Max Freedman, ed., *Roosevelt and Frankfurter: Their Correspondence, 1928–1945* (1967), p. 377.

313 "determined to curb": Clapper Diary, January 20, 1937, Clapper Papers, LC.

314 "pack the Court": *New York Times*, January 11, 1937.

315 "the Roman Emperor": Leuchtenburg, *The Supreme Court Reborn*, p. 130.

315 At his press conference: February 5, 1937, FDRPC9, p. 130.

316 "It was the French": *New York Herald Tribune*, February 6, 1937.

316 "Surely, Mr. Roosevelt's": McKenna, p. 308.

316 "We are going down": Ibid., p. 310.

316 "eager to jump": Leuchtenburg, *The Supreme Court Reborn*, p. 140.

316 "Hands off": Herbert Hoover, *Addresses on the American Road, 1933–1938* (1938), p. 236.

317 "The people are": Alsop and Catledge, *The 168 Days*, p. 74.

317 "As a boy I": Leuchtenburg, p. 138.

317 "To all intents": Ibid.

317 "Can you calculate": *Washington Post*, March 10, 1937.

317 "Boys, here's where": Alsop and Catledge, p. 67.

318 On March 4: FDR speech to Democratic Victory Dinner, March 4, 1937, FDRPP6, p. 113.

318 his eighth fireside chat: March 9, 1937, ibid., p. 122.

319 "There has been": Alsop and Catledge, p. 115.

320 "It's going to pass": Ibid., p. 100; Wheeler's account of conversation, Burton K. Wheeler with Paul F. Healy, *Yankee from the West* (1962), p. 322.

320 "I speak to you": Solomon, p. 123.

320 Senate Judiciary Committee, Convened hearings: "Reorganization of the Federal Judiciary," 75th Congress, 1st sess., March 1937.

320 "would be like": Ibid., p. 7.

320 "Suppose after": Ibid., p. 15.

321 "being lost in a": Ibid., p. 38.

321 "I was entirely willing": AN, pp. 304, 305.

321 "the very strong feeling": CEH phone transcripts, March 19, 1937, CEHP.

321 "a powerful exposition": HFS to sons, March 12, 1937, HFSP.

321 Hughes wrote a letter: CEH to OR, April 5, 1937, CEHP.

322 "Tell your father": Wheeler, p. 327.

322 "You call the Chief Justice": Ibid., p. 328.

322 "Did Brandeis tell you": Ibid., p. 329.

323 Press invitations to CEH and replies: CEHP; Baker, p. 36.

323 "The proposal of": Ickes, Vol. 2, pp. 66, 67.

323 differed from Hughes's own account: See AN, p. 304; CEH telephone transcriptions, CEHP.

323 The letter: CEH's letter to committee, March 21, 1937, in Senate Judiciary
Committee Hearings on "Reorganization of the Federal Judiciary," 75th
Congress, 1st sess., I: Part 3, p. 488.

324 But Justice Stone resented: Mason, *Harlan Fiske Stone*, pp. 451, 452; see also,
Friedman, "Chief Justice Hughes' Letter on the Court-Packing Plan," *Journal
of Supreme Court History*, 1, 1997, pp. 76–86.

325 *West Coast Hotel Co. v. Parrish*: 300 U.S. 379 (1937).

326 Roberts later explained: See Frankfurter, "Mr. Justice Roberts," *University of
Pennsylvania Law Review*, 104, pp. 313–16 (December 1955).

327 "[W]ith the shift by Roberts": FF to FDR, March 30, 1937, Freedman, p. 392.

327 "the switch in time": Cushman, pp. 3–5.

327 He not only resented: MP2, p. 753.

327 "If they want me": Ibid.

327 three other opinions: The National Firearms Act decision, *Sonzinsky v. U.S.*
506 (1937); *Wright v. Vinton*, 300 U.S. 440 (1937); and *Virginia Railroad Co.
v. System Federation*, 300 U.S. 515 (1937).

327 and later wrote an article: See Frankfurter, "Mr. Justice Roberts."

328 comprehensive opinion: *NLRB v. Jones & Laughlin Steel Corp.* 301 U.S. 1
(1937).

329 In two other decisions: *NLRB v. Freuhauf Trailer Co.*, 301 U.S. 49 (1937),
and *NLRB v. Friedman-Harry Marks Clothing*, 301 U.S. 58 (1937).

329 "nothing short of a": *The Nation*, April 17, 1937.

329 "Who knows when": *New Republic*, April 21, 1937.

330 "Chief Justice Hughes's Letter": *Christian Science Monitor*, March 23, 1937.

330 "were jittery about": Ickes, Vol. 2, p. 102.

330 "good tactics": Ibid., p. 103.

330 Green asserted: FDL3, pp. 669, 670.

330 Roosevelt thanked: FDR to JG, March 24, 1937, ibid., p. 669 (italics added).

331 "Mr. President, do you": FDR press conference, March 30, 1937, FDRPC9,
p. 225.

331 "From 1922 until a few": *Congressional Record*, March 29, 1937, p. 2832.

331 the Gridiron Club Dinner: *Washington Post*, April 11, 1937; Shesol, pp. 427,
428; Solomon, pp. 177, 178.

332   "It was political": Alsop and Catledge, p. 154.

332   "chortling": FDR press conference, April 13, 1937, FDRPC9, p. 258.

333   "At the White House": Baker, p. 193.

333   "It is quite clear": FDR to FF, April 5, 1937, Freedman, p. 397.

333   "We're all taking": *Washington Post*, May 18, 1937.

333   "unfavorable report would": *New York Times*, April 25, 1937.

334   "would come in": FDR to WVD, May 18, 1937, FDRL3, p. 681.

335   "Mr. Justice": Alsop and Catledge, p. 210.

335   "Do you intend": FDR press conference, May 18, 1937, FDRPC9, p. 370.

335   "Everybody's told me": Alsop and Catledge, pp. 212, 213.

336   In upholding the constitutionality: *Steward Machine Co. v. Davis*, 301 U.S. 548 (1937); second decision, *Helvering v. Davis*, 301 U.S. 619 (1937).

336   "[T]he Court is fully": CEH speech to ALI, May 5, 1937, CEHP.

336   "[T]he New Deal's victory": *Washington Post*, May 25, 1937.

336   "the permanence of": HFS to FF, May 20, 1937, HFSP.

337   "because of the political": FF to HFS, May 25, 1937, ibid.

337   "Father's been": Alsop and Catledge, p. 215.

338   "Tell us about": FDR press conference, June 4, 1937, FDRPC9, p. 407.

339   "Why run for a train": Alsop and Catledge, p. 152.

339   released its final report: Report of the Senate Judiciary Committee on "Reorganization of the Federal Judiciary," 75th Congress, 1st sess., June 1937.

340   Once, a reporter: See *New York Times*, June 16, 1937.

340   On June 19: CEH speech at Amherst, June 19, 1937, CEHP.

340   at Brown University: June 21, 1937, CEHP.

341   "coming out as": Baker, p. 238.

341   "with the bark on": Alsop and Catledge, p. 280.

Nine: "The Great Arsenal of Democracy"

343   "some pretty effective": FDR press conference, July 23, 1937, FDRPC10, p. 57.

344   "He [Roosevelt] doesn't overlook": Ickes, Vol. 2, pp. 173, 174.

346   "Father was very angry": Roger K. Newman, *Hugo Black: A Biography* (1994), p. 236.

347   "Hugo, I'd like to": Alsop and Catledge, p. 307.

347   "deeply interested in": *New York Times*, August 19, 1937.

347   "Hugo Lafayette Black": *Pittsburgh Post-Gazette*, September 13, 1937.

348   he told a crowd: September 17, 1937, FDRP6, p. 359.

349   the most important speech: *New York Times*, October 2, 1937.

349   "It was a grand job": James A. Farley, *Jim Farley's Story: The Roosevelt Years* (1948), p. 108.

350   "Why can't these": Perkins, p. 321.

350 "It ill behooves": Melvin Dubofsky and Warren Van Tine, *John L. Lewis: A Biography* (1977), p. 327.

350 "who insist on": FDR to John McCormack, October 22, 1937, FDR3, p. 722.

351 "who respond to": FDR to Col. Edward House, October 19, 1937, ibid., p. 719.

351 "met with pretty": Ickes, Vol. 2, pp. 222, 223.

351 "a kind of founding": Kennedy, p. 340.

351 "I believe in": Ibid., p. 343.

352 "to lynch the": Smith, p. 398.

352 "the forerunner of": Kennedy, p. 342.

352 "I have not": FDR press conference, January 14, 1938, FDRPC11, p. 88.

352 "I did not choose": Walter White, *A Man Called White: The Autobiography of Walter White* (1948), p. 169, 170.

353 "That's that": Leuchtenburg, *Franklin D. Roosevelt and the New Deal*, p. 262.

353 "a scholar and": Kenneth S. Davis, *FDR: Into the Storm, 1937–1940, A History* (1993), pp. 279–80.

353 "Not as long": Kennedy, p. 348.

354 "When I viewed": Newman, p. 269.

354 "a season of": Mason, p. 467.

354 "the Court is": HFS to HB, August 18, 1937, HFSP.

355 "no warmer admirer": HB to HFS, August 27, 1937, ibid.

355 the Indianapolis Water Company: *McCart v. Indianapolis Water Co.*, 302 U.S. 419 (1938).

355 "a good deal troubled": HFS to CEH, December 30, 1937, HFSP.

355 Stone suspected: Mason, p. 468.

356 In a second dissent: *Connecticut General Life Insurance Co. v. Johnson*, 303 U.S., 77 (1938).

356 "an inside view": *St. Louis Post-Dispatch*, January 22, 1938.

356 "Do you know": HFS to FF, February 8, 1938, HFSP.

356 "I used to say": Frankfurter memorandum to Black, in Mason, p. 470.

356 He believed that dissents: Hughes, *Supreme Court*, pp. 67–70.

357 Besides treating Black: MP2, p. 773.

357 "not disturbed in": Mason, p. 476.

357 "on some rational basis": *U.S. v. Carolene Products Co.*, 304 U.S. 144, 152 (1938).

358 "mathematical or": *Santa Cruz Fruit Packing Co. v. Labor Board*, 303 U.S. 453, 469 (1938).

358 When Dean Charles Houston: For a description of the oral argument in the *Gaines* case, see A. Leon Higginbotham and William C. Smith, "The Hughes Court and the Beginning of the End of the 'Separate But Equal' Doctrine," *Minnesota Law Review* 76, pp. 1099–1131 (1992).

359 "Those racial supremacy": James F. Simon, *In His Own Image*, p. 26.

359 The decision: *Missouri ex rel. Gaines v. Canada*, 305 U.S. 337 (1938).

360 FDR told reporters: November 15, 1938, FDRPP7, p. 597.

360 In his State of the Union address: January 4, 1939, FDRPP6, p. 1.

360 worked quietly behind the scenes: Kennedy, *Freedom From Fear*, p. 416.

361 "conquered chaos": Ibid., p. 424.

361 "Gad, what a chance": Leuchtenburg, *Franklin D. Roosevelt and the New Deal*, p. 287.

361 "put his chin out": Kennedy, *Freedom from Fear*, p. 424.

361 "He asked for": Burns, *Roosevelt: The Lion and the Fox*, pp. 391, 392.

361 "may well affect": Kennedy, p. 423.

361 "There's not going": Burns, *Roosevelt: The Lion and the Fox*, p. 392.

361 "Well, Bill": Ibid., p. 394.

362 "I'm all right": MP2, p. 782.

362 Summoning all of his energy: Hughes's speech to Congress, March 4, 1939, CEHP.

362 "Oh, Chief Justice": MP2, p. 784.

363 "All I can say": Harlan Phillips, *Felix Frankfurter Reminisces*, p. 283.

363 Frankfurter's appointment was applauded: *New York Times*, January 6, 1939.

363 Frankfurter dressed casually: For the alpaca coat story, see Joseph Lash, *From the Diaries of Felix Frankfurter* (1975, cited hereafter as *Diaries*), p. 66.

363 Two months after: For background on Justices Black, Douglas, and Frankfurter, see William O. Douglas, *Go East, Young Man* (1974) and *The Court Years* (1980); Noah Feldman, *Scorpions: The Battles and Triumphs of FDR's Great Supreme Court Justices* (2010); Lash, *Diaries*; Newman, *Hugo Black*; Michael Parrish, *Felix Frankfurter and His Times: The Reform Years* (1982); Phillips, *Felix Frankfurter Reminisces*; James F. Simon, *The Antagonists: Hugo Black, Felix Frankfurter, and Civil Liberties in Modern America* (1989) and *Independent Journey: The Life of William O. Douglas* (1980); and Melvin I. Urofsky, ed., *The Douglas Letters: Selections from the Private Papers of Justice William O. Douglas* (1987).

364 "The fact that": *Currin v. Wallace*, 306 U.S. 1, 11 (1939).

364 The 1938 AAA decision: *Mulford v. Smith*, 307 U.S. 38 (1939).

365 Roosevelt personally called: MP2, p. 786.

365 "Can we stay": FDR press conference, September 1, 1939, FDRPC14, p. 130.

365 "Even a neutral": FDR fireside chat, September 3, 1939, FDRPP8, p. 460.

366 In an address to Congress: September 21, 1939, ibid., p. 512.

366 "This is not": *Vital Speeches*, Vol. 5, p. 751.

366 "I am almost": Burns, *Roosevelt: The Lion and the Fox*, p. 396.

367 "The scene has": WC to FDR, May 15, 1940, in Francis L. Loewenheim, Harold D. Langley, and Manfred Jones, eds., *Roosevelt and Churchill: Their Secret Wartime Correspondence* (1975), pp. 94, 95.

367 spoke to a joint session of Congress: May 16, 1940, FDRPP9, p. 198.

367 the commencement address: June 10, 1940, FDRPP9, p. 259.

367 "the hand that": Leuchtenburg, *Franklin D. Roosevelt and the New Deal*, p. 302.

367 "afire with scorn": William L. Shirer, *The Rise and Fall of the Third Reich* (1959), p. 742.

368 the Gridiron Dinner: Burns, *Roosevelt: The Lion and the Fox,* pp. 408, 409.

368 undecided: Doris Kearns Goodwin, *No Ordinary Time: Franklin and Eleanor Roosevelt: The Home Front in World War II* (1994), pp. 106, 107.

369 "I do not want": Freidel, *A Rendevous with Destiny,* p. 328.

369 Postmaster General Jim Farley: For the FDR-Farley meeting at Hyde Park, see Farley, *Jim Farley's Story,* pp. 246–58; Burns, *Roosevelt: The Lion and the Fox,* p. 425.

370 "with the enthusiasm": *Chicago Daily News,* July 16, 1940.

370 THIS CONVENTION IS: HI to FDR, July 16, 1940, FDRP.

370 WE WANT ROOSEVELT: Davis, p. 597.

370 had sat for hours: Ibid.; Smith, p. 460.

371 He sent word: Rosenman, pp. 210–16.

371 "These plans": FDR acceptance speech, July 18, 1940, FDRPP9, p. 293.

372 In his opinion: Hughes's 1911 dissent, *Bailey v. Alabama,* 219 U.S. 219 (1911).

373 "The rack and torture": *Brown v. Mississippi,* 297 U.S. 278, 285 (1936).

373 asked Justice Black: *Chambers v. Florida,* 309 U.S. 227 (1940).

373 "I think Chief": Newman, p. 281, 282.

374 Jesse Cantwell: See *Cantwell v. Connecticut,* 310 U.S. 296 (1940).

374 The Gobitis children: For background on the *Gobitis* case, see Irving Dilliard, "The Flag-Salute Cases," in Garrity, ed., pp. 285–306; Feldman, pp. 179–186; Simon, *The Antagonists,* pp. 106–14.

375 "I come up to": J. W. Howard, *Mr. Justice Murphy: A Political Biography* (1968), p. 287.

376 the large crowd: *Minersville School District v. Gobitis,* 310 U.S. 586 (1940).

376 "When a liberal judge": Garrity, ed., pp. 298, 299.

376 Eleanor listened: Lash, *Diaries,* p. 70.

376 the Court reversed: *West Virginia State Board of Education v. Barnette,* 319 U.S. 624 (1943).

377 "I shall not": FDR acceptance speech, July 18, 1940, FDRPP9, p. 293.

377 "Hitler knows": Burns, *Roosevelt: The Lion and the Fox,* p. 437.

377 "Mr. President": WC to FDR. July 31, 1940, Winston Churchill, *The Second World War: Their Finest Hour* (1949), p. 401.

377 "the importance of": FDR memorandum, August 2, 1940, FDRL4, p. 1051.

378 "Say, ain't you": FDR to DW, August 22, 1940, ibid., p. 1056.

378 in a carefully argued letter: *New York Times,* August 11, 1940.

379 "If his promise": *New York Times,* October 23, 1940.

379 "On the basis of": *New York Times,* October 31, 1940.

379 "I am an old": FDR's Philadelphia speech, October 23, 1940, FDRPP9, p. 485.

379 In Madison Square Garden: Speech, October 28, 1940, ibid., p. 499.

379   "I have said": FDR's Boston speech, October 30, 1940, ibid., p. 514.

379   "If we're attacked": Rosenman, p. 242.

380   "hold the front": WC to FDR, December 8, 1940, in Warren F. Kimball, ed., *Churchill and Roosevelt: The Complete Correspondence* (1984), Vol. 1, p. 89.

381   a press conference: December 19, 1940, FDRPC16, p. 350.

381   in a fireside chat: December 29, 1940, FDRPP9, p. 633.

382   his State of the Union address: January 6, 1941, ibid., p. 663.

382   "To Hell with": *Time*, January 27, 1941.

382   In his inaugural address: January 20, 1941,

383   "I am about to": HH to CEH, October 17, 1940, CEHP.

383   Arthur Mitchell: *Mitchell v. Interstate Commerce Commission*, 313 U.S. 80 (1941).

383   Hughes also wrote: *Cox v. New Hampshire*, 312 U.S. 569 (1941).

384   sweeping commerce clause decision: *U.S. v. Darby*, 312 U.S. 100 (1941).

384   "I hope you won't": Jackson, p. 67.

384   "affectionate regards": FDR to CEH, April 11, 1941, CEHP.

384   "I had an impish": AN, p. 313.

385   a state-of-the-judiciary speech: *American Bar Association Journal* (June 1941), p. 335.

385   "the New Deal's triple": Freidel, *A Rendevous with Destiny*, p. 362.

385   a brief letter: CEH to FDR, June 2, 1941, CEHP.

386   "This comes to me": FDR to CEH, June 2, 1941, ibid.

Epilogue

387   the luncheon conversation: AN, p. 324; MP2, pp. 787, 788.

387   Frankfurter too recommended: Mason, *Harlan Fiske Stone*, pp. 566, 567.

387   "As you know": FDR to CEH, August 25, 1941, CEHP.

388   "I feel that": CEH to FDR, August 30, 1941, ibid.

388   In 1944: CEH memorandum, May 11, 1944, CEHP.

388   "a beacon in a darkened": MP2, p. 795.

389   "Don't you worry": Ibid., p. 796.

389   "Happy Birthday": CEH to AH, September 14, 1944, CEHP.

389   "Today is our": MP2, p. 797.

389   "Mother is sinking": Ibid.

389   In a prefatory note: AN, p. 2.

390   Hoover's letter of February 19, 1937: Ibid., p. 292.

390   He defended two: Ibid., pp. 307–11.

390   the justices' votes at their conference: Ibid., pp. 311, 312.

393   Stone's inability to lead: Feldman, pp. 204, 205; Simon, *Independent Journey*, p. 11.

393   "[O]ur democratic form": *Jones v. Opelika*, 316 U.S. 584, 623 (1942).

393   "the Axis": Lash, *Diaries*, pp. 76, 197.

393   including the urgent need: See FF's memo on War Production Board, FF to FDR, December 17, 1941, in Freedman, pp. 631, 632.

394   "Mr. President": Winston S. Churchill, *The Grand Alliance* (1951), p. 605.

394   "Sit down": Tully, p. 256.

394   "the unprovoked": FDR speech, December 8, 1941, FDRPP10, p. 514.

395   "Now it is impossible": John Keegan, *The Second World War* (1989), p. 240.

395   "To have the United States": Churchill, *Grand Alliance*, pp. 608, 609.

395   In his State of the Union: January 6, 1942, FDRPP11, p. 32.

395   German saboteurs: See Michael Dobbs, *Saboteurs: The Nazi Raid on America* (2004); David Danelski, "The Saboteurs Case," *Journal of Supreme Court History* 1 (1996), p. 66; and Feldman, pp. 215–25.

396   Two days later: *Ex parte Quirin*, 317 U.S. 1 (1942). Courts, post–Civil War precedent: *Ex parte Milligan*, 71 U.S. 2 (1866).

396   100,000 Japanese-Americans: For background on the Japanese-American cases, see Feldman, pp. 235–53; Peters Irons, *Justice at War* (1983); Greg Robinson, *A Tragedy of Democracy: Japanese Confinement in North America* (2009); and Simon, *The Antagonists*, pp. 147–56.

396   Fred Korematsu: *Korematsu v. U.S.*, 323 U.S. 214 (1944).

397   "You can't draw": *New York Times*, July 28, 1943.

397   "Our principal objective": FDR to Joint Chiefs, May 6, 1942, FDRP.

397   Scholars have condemned: See, e.g., E. Rostow, "The Japanese-American Cases—A Disaster," 54 *Yale Law Journal*, p. 489 (1945).

398   "I know your farms": FDR broadcast, November 7, 1942, FDRPP11, p. 451.

399   "We are all agreed": Smith, p. 592.

399   "Old Doctor New Deal": FDR press conference, December 28, 1943, FDRPC22, p. 246.

399   telltale signs: See Tully, p. 274; Goodwin, pp. 491–97.

400   "our sons": Goodwin, p. 510.

400   "Reluctantly, but": FDR to RH, July 11, 1944, FDRPP13, p. 197.

401   "You know, I am": FDR speech to Teamsters Union, September 23, 1944, ibid., p. 284.

401   "He looked like": Goodwin, p. 570.

401   "I hope you will": FDR address to Congress, March 1, 1945, FDRPP13, p. 570.

401   On April 12, 1945: Elizabeth Shoumatoff, *FDR's Unfinished Portrait* (1990), p. 116.

Index

Illustration Credits

1. Franklin D. Roosevelt Library
2. Courtesy of Theodore Hughes Waddell
3. Franklin D. Roosevelt Library
4. Brown University Archives
5. Franklin D. Roosevelt Library
6. Courtesy of Theodore Hughes Waddell
7. Courtesy of Theodore Hughes Waddell
8. Franklin D. Roosevelt Library
9. Courtesy of Theodore Hughes Waddell
10. Courtesy of Theodore Hughes Waddell
11. Franklin D. Roosevelt Library
12. Franklin D. Roosevelt Library
13. Franklin D. Roosevelt Library
14. Franklin D. Roosevelt Library
15. Franklin D. Roosevelt Library
16. Collection of the Supreme Court of the United States
17. Franklin D. Roosevelt Library
18. Franklin D. Roosevelt Library
19. *Christian Science Monitor*
20. Courtesy of Theodore Hughes Waddell
21. Franklin D. Roosevelt Library
22. Franklin D. Roosevelt Library

About the Author

James F. Simon is the Martin Professor of Law and Dean Emeritus at New York Law School. He is the author of seven previous books on American history, law, and politics, including *What Kind of Nation: Thomas Jefferson, John Marshall, and the Epic Struggle to Create a United States*, and *Lincoln and Chief Justice Taney: Slavery, Secession, and the President's War Powers*. His books have been awarded the American Bar Association's Silver Gavel Award and twice been named *New York Times* Notable Books. He lives with his wife in West Nyack, New York.